History and Theory

History and Theory

Contemporary Readings

Edited by

Brian Fay, Philip Pomper, and Richard T. Vann

BLACKWELL
Publishers

Library of Congress Cataloging-in-Publication Data

History and theory: contemporary readings /
  edited by Brian Fay, Philip Pomper, and Richard T. Vann.
    p. cm.
  Includes bibliographical references and index.
  ISBN 0–631–20952–2 (hbk.: alk. paper). — ISBN 0–631–20953–0
(pbk.: alk. paper)
    1. History—Philosophy. I. Fay, Brian. II. Pomper, Philip.
III. Vann, Richard T.
D16.8.C645 1998
901—dc21   98–21303
                                             CIP

British Library Cataloguing in Publication Data

A CIP catalogue record for this book is available from the British Library

Typeset in 10 on 12 pt Sabon
by Graphicraft Limited, Hong Kong
Printed in Great Britain by MPG Books Ltd, Bodmin, Cornwall

This book is printed on acid-free paper

Contents

Contributors   vii

Acknowledgments   x

Introduction: The Linguistic Turn and Beyond in Contemporary
Theory of History *Brian Fay*   1

Part I   Narrativity   13

1   The Historical Text as Literary Artifact *Hayden White*   15

2   Interpretation, History, and Narrative *Noël Carroll*   34

Part II   Writing and Reading History   57

3   The Rhetoric of History *J. H. Hexter*   59

4   Making Up Lost Time: Writing on the Writing of History
Nancy F. Partner   69

5   History, Language, and Reading: Waiting for Crillon
Dominick LaCapra   90

Part III   Realism, Constructivism, and Beyond   119

6   History and Fiction as Modes of Comprehension
Louis Mink   121

7   Narrative and the Real World: An Argument for
Continuity *David Carr*   137

8   Telling It Like It Was: Historical Narratives On Their
Own Terms *Andrew P. Norman*   153

Part IV   Postmodernism and the Theory of History   173

9   Historiography and Postmodernism *F. R. Ankersmit*   175

10   Historiography and Postmodernism: Reconsiderations
Perez Zagorin   193

11   Reply to Professor Zagorin *F. R. Ankersmit*   206

Part V   Representation and Trauma   223

12   "Never Again" is Now *Hans Kellner*   225

13   Is It Possible to Misrepresent the Holocaust? *Berel Lang*   245

Part VI   Gender, Sexuality, Sex   251

14   Is There a History of Sexuality? *David M. Halperin*   253

15   No Sex, No Gender *Nancy F. Partner*   268

Part VII   Objectivity   297

16   Objectivity Is Not Neutrality: Rhetoric versus Practice
in Peter Novick's *That Noble Dream Thomas Haskell*   299

17   Objectivity and Truth in History *J. L. Gorman*   320

18   Historical Knowledge and Historical Reality: A Plea for
"Internal Realism" *Chris Lorenz*   342

19   Progress in Historical Studies *Raymond Martin*   377

Name Index   404

Contributors

F. R. Ankersmit is Professor of Intellectual History and Historical Theory at the University of Groningen, Netherlands and a member of the Editorial Board of *History and Theory*. He is the author of *History and Tropology: The Rise and Fall of Metaphor* (1994), *The Reality Effect in the Writing of History* (1990), and *Narrative Logic: A Semantic Analysis of the Historian's Language* (1983), as well as numerous works in Dutch.

David Carr received his Ph.D. from Yale University in 1966, and has taught at Yale and the University of Ottawa. Since 1991 he has been Professor and Chair of the Philosophy Department at Emory University. His books include *The Paradox of Subjectivity* (1999), *Interpreting Husserl* (1987), *Time, Narrative and History* (1986), and *Phenomenology and the Problem of History* (1974).

Noël Carroll is the Monroe C. Beardsley Professor of Philosophy at the University of Wisconsin–Madison and the president-elect of the American Society for Aesthetics. His most recent book is *A Philosophy of Mass Art* (1998).

Brian Fay is the William Griffin Professor of Philosophy, Senior Tutor in the College of Social Studies at Wesleyan University, and Executive Editor of *History and Theory*. He is the author of *Contemporary Philosophy of Social Science: A Multicultural Approach* (1996), *Critical Social Science: Liberation and its Limits* (1987), *Social Theory and Political Practice* (1976), and co-editor with Richard T. Vann and Eugene O. Golob of Louis O. Mink's *Historical Understanding* (1987).

J. L. Gorman is Professor of Moral Philosophy at the Queen's University of Belfast. He received his MA from Edinburgh, specializing in philosophy of history under W. H. Walsh and L. Pompa, and his Ph.D. from Cambridge, studying with W. B. Gallie. He has had visiting appointments at Princeton and Queen's University, Kingston, Ontario. He is the author of *Understanding History* (1992) and *The Expression of Historical Knowledge* (1982).

David M. Halperin teaches queer theory in the School of Sociology at the University of New South Wales. He is the author of *Saint Foucault* (1995), *One Hundred Years of Homosexuality* (1990), and *Before Pastoral* (1983), as well as an editor of *The Lesbian and Gay Studies Reader* (1993), *Before Sexuality* (1990), and *GLQ: A Journal of Lesbian and Gay Studies*.

Thomas L. Haskell, McCann Professor of History at Rice University, is the author of *Objectivity is not Neutrality: Explanatory Schemes in History* (1998).

He is also a principal contributor to *The Antislavery Debate: Capitalism and Abolitionism as a Problem in Historical Interpretation* (1992), edited by Thomas Bender.

J. H. Hexter was Emeritus Professor of History at Washington University in St. Louis (where he was founding Director of the Center for the History of Freedom) and at Yale University (where he was Director of the Center for Parliamentary History) at the time of his death in 1996. He was the author of numerous books, including *On Historians* (1979), *The Vision of Politics on the Eve of the Reformation* (1973), *Doing History* (1971), *The History Primer* (1971), and *More's Utopia: The Biography of an Idea* (1952).

Hans Kellner teaches rhetoric and historical discourse in the English Department at the University of Texas, Arlington. He is the author of *Language and Historical Representation: Getting the Story Crooked* (1989) and co-editor with F. R. Ankersmit of *A New Philosophy of History* (1995).

Dominick LaCapra has been teaching at Cornell University since 1969. He is currently Professor of History, Bryce and Edith M. Bowmar Professor of Humanistic Studies, and Director of the Society for the Humanities at Cornell University. He is the author of nine books including *Rethinking Intellectual History: Texts, Contexts, Language* (1983) and *History and Criticism*, as well as editor of two others. His most recent book is *History and Memory after Auschwitz* (1998).

Berel Lang is Professor of Humanities at Trinity College (Hartford). Previously he was Professor of Philosophy at SUNY at Albany and the University of Colorado, and Visiting Professor at Hebrew University and Wesleyan University. He is the author of *Heidegger's Silence* (1996), *Mind's Bodies* (1995), *Writing and the Moral Self* (1991), and *Act and Idea in the Nazi Genocide* (1990).

Chris Lorenz is Professor of Philosophy of History at Leiden University and at the Free University Amsterdam, both in the Netherlands. His published works include "Herausforderungen der Gesellschaftsgeschichte durch die Postmoderne?" in *Geschichte und Gesellschaft* 24 (1998), *Konstruktion der Vergangenheit: Eine Einfuerung in die Geschichtstheorie* (1997), "Beyond Good and Evil? The Second German Empire of 1871 and Modern German Historiography" in *Journal of Contemporary History* 30 (1995), and *De Constructie van het Verleden* (1994).

Raymond Martin is Professor of Philosophy at the University of Maryland, College Park. He writes primarily in the areas of philosophical psychology and philosophy of history. He is the author of *Self-Concern: An Experiential Approach to What Matters in Survival* (1998) and co-author of *Naturalization of the Soul: Theories of Self and Personal Identity in the Eighteenth-Century* (1999). In philosophy of history, he is the author of *The Past Within Us: An Empirical Approach to Philosophy of History* (1989). Martin is currently working on a new book, tentatively titled *Philosophy of History from the Bottom Up: An American Revolution*.

Louis O. Mink was Kenan Professor of Philosophy, Senior Tutor in the College of Social Studies at Wesleyan University, and Associate Editor of *History and Theory* at the time of his death in 1983. He was one of the world's leading theorists in the philosophy of history, and his work in this area, which was mostly published in journals and anthologies, was collected in *Historical Understanding* (1987), edited by Brian Fay, Eugene O. Golob, and Richard T. Vann.

Andrew P. Norman teaches philosophy at Hamilton College in central New York. His interests range from epistemology and informal logic to Heidegger, the philosophy of history, the philosophy of language, and complexity theory. He is the author of several published essays, and is currently at work on a book about the dialogical character of justification.

Nancy F. Partner is Associate Professor of History at McGill University and a member of the Editorial Board of *History and Theory*. She is currently completing a book on psychoanalytic theory and its applications to medieval history and literature, with a working title of *Medieval Minds: Psychoanalysis and the Medieval Self*. Also on this topic is "The Family Romance of Guibert of Nogent: His Story/Her Story," in *Medieval Mothering*, edited by B. Wheeler and J. Parsons (1996). She is also the author of "Historicity in an Age of Reality Fictions," in *A New Philosophy of History*, edited by Hans Kellner and F. R. Ankersmit (1995).

Philip Pomper is the William Armstrong Professor of History at Wesleyan University, and Associate Editor of *History and Theory*. Aside from a general study of the Russian revolutionary intelligentsia, he has written biographies of leading revolutionaries. He has also investigated psychoanalytic theories of history in his book, *The Structure of Mind in History: Five Major Figures in Psychohistory* (1985).

Richard T. Vann is Professor of History and Professor of Letters at Wesleyan University, and Senior Editor of *History and Theory*. He is the co-author, with David Eversley, of *Friends in Life and Death: The British and Irish Quakers in the Demographic Transition, 1650–1900* (1992), author of *The Social Development of English Quakerism, 1655–1755* (1969), and co-editor with Brian Fay and Eugene O. Golob of Louis O. Mink's *Historical Understanding* (1987).

Hayden White is University Professor Emeritus, University of California, (currently) Professor of Comparative Literature at Stanford University, Visiting Professor in Italy (Bologna and Venezia) and Poland (Poznan) during the last two years, and a member of the Editorial Board of *History and Theory*. He has been working on discourse theory as a method for the study of intellectual history – including the history of historical thought – for the last three decades. His principal publications address these topics: *Figural Realism* (1998), *The Content of the Form* (1987), *Tropics of Discourse* (1978), and *Metahistory* (1973).

Perez Zagorin is Joseph C. Wilson Professor of History Emeritus at the University of Rochester, a Fellow of the American Academy of Arts and Sciences, and a Fellow of the Shannon Center for Advanced Studies at the University of Virginia. His most recent book is *Francis Bacon* (1998).

Acknowledgments

The editors and publisher are grateful for permission to reproduce the following copyright material:

Noël Carroll, "Interpretation, History, and Narrative," copyright © 1990 *The Monist*, La Salle, Illinois 61301. Reprinted by permission.

J. L. Gorman, "Objectivity and Truth in History," *Inquiry* 17 (1974), 373–94, permission granted by the author.

David M. Halperin, "Is There a History of Sexuality?" *History and Theory* 28 (1989), permission granted by the author.

Dominick LaCapra, "History, Language, and Reading: Waiting for Crillon," *American Historical Review* (1995), 100, 799–828, permission granted by the author.

Louis Mink, "History and Fiction as Modes of Comprehension," *New Literary History* 1 (1970): 514–58, © 1970 Johns Hopkins University Press.

Nancy F. Partner, "Making Up Lost Time: Writing on the Writing of History," *Speculum* 61 (1986): 90–117, Medieval Academy of America, Cambridge, Mass.

Nancy F. Partner, "No Sex, No Gender," *Speculum* 68 (1993): 419–43, Medieval Academy of America, Cambridge, Mass.

Hayden White, "The Historical Text as Literary Artifact," from *Tropics of Discourse*, pp. 81–100, © 1978 Johns Hopkins University Press.

All other contributions originally appeared in *History and Theory*, Wesleyan Station, Middletown, Connecticut, and are reprinted by permission.

Introduction
The Linguistic Turn and Beyond in Contemporary Theory of History

Brian Fay

Traditionally and by temperament historians have been averse to theoretical speculation. Practicing historians tend to focus on discovering and assessing concrete evidence, and they are suspicious of abstraction. However, beginning in the 1960s (in part as a result of the upheavals of that time) an entire generation of historians was educated to theory and metatheory in a way no previous generation was. This is even more the case for today's students of history. Theory and metatheory have become part and parcel of historical discourse. (One only has to examine the kinds of essays published in the *American Historical Review* since 1985, and compare it to previous volumes, to see this.) Today, teachers find it necessary to teach what empowered them and to respond to those who criticize them; students demand that courses explore the large epistemological and rhetorical issues they have encountered in many courses in the humanities and social sciences. And both students and teachers cannot help being aware of the vehement public debate carried on in the mass media as well as professional journals about the nature of history as a discipline.

This book does not just bring together a number of significant essays which speak to the concerns raised in these different contexts, but it does so with two clear guidelines in mind. First, it is informed by the belief that issues in the philosophy and theory of history are best explored by taking real and substantive bits of historical prose for examination, and working out ideas in and through these examples. Some of the essays in this volume are written by practicing historians, and the editors hope that all of them to an acceptable degree speak to the actual experience of doing history. This is not to say that these issues are not properly philosophical or abstract; indeed they are. But the philosophical reflection here represented arises out of historical practice and the editors hope returns readers to it enlightened and revivified.[1]

Second, the selections in this volume express a particular vision of the meaning of recent work in philosophy and theory of history. The purpose of the rest of this Introduction is to outline this vision.

It seems clear that an important shift in the theory and philosophy of history occurred about twenty-five years ago (a convenient date is 1973, the publication of Hayden White's *Metahistory*): the so-called "linguistic turn."[2] Earlier thought about history had largely been epistemological in nature (asking such questions as, How can we know about the past? What does it mean to explain historical events? Is objective knowledge possible?). But during the last quarter century or so this epistemological focus was displaced by a linguistic one, as questions regarding the form of discourse by means of which historians describe and explain the past became the central concern. With this linguistic turn, the topics of narration and representation replaced law and explanation as burning issues of the theory and philosophy of history. And because what might be called the poetics of history now came to the fore, the question "how is history like and unlike fiction?" replaced "how is history like and unlike science?" as the guiding question of metahistorical reflection.

I examine the nature and consequences of the linguistic turn in historiography on page 3. But before that this turn itself needs to be put into a broader historical perspective. The linguistic turn in history and philosophical reflection about it was part of a larger "discursive turn" which was simultaneously occurring in the humanities as a whole. (This might be dated from 1963, when Thomas Kuhn's *The Structure of Scientific Revolutions* was first published.) For the previous half-century positivism broadly conceived – with its claim that reality is directly knowable by means of a single correct method (that of natural science) – had dominated thought. But in the late 1950s thinkers increasingly criticized a number of the concepts and distinctions central to positivism: the analytic vs. the synthetic; fact vs. theory; description vs. explanation; fact vs. value; the verifiable vs. the non-verifiable; science vs. metaphysics. In so doing they began to emphasize the perspectival character of all knowledge. On this emerging view, knowledge-claims and their assessment always are situated within a framework that provides the conceptual resources in and through which the world is described and explained. Knowers never know reality directly as it is in itself; rather, they approach it from their own perspective, with their own assumptions and preconceptions.

Kuhn's paradigms in science, and Hayden White's tropes in history, are two stellar instances of this approach, but it can also be found in the emergence of interpretivism in the social sciences, in "theory" in literary studies, and generally in hermeneutics, deconstructionism, and postmodernism in all areas of learning. All of these emphasize the rhetorical dimension to knowing, the way that forms of discourse deeply affect what (is claimed to be) known.

But like the linguistic turn, this "discursive turn" itself needs to be put in a wider perspective. Similar shifts have occurred many times in the history of thought in the West. Indeed, Richard Lanham in *Literacy and the Survival of Humanism* describes a recurring pattern in the history of Western literature and art, from approaches which focus on the reality which language can reveal to those approaches which feature the rhetorical devices which language employs.[3] The former prize a "transparent" style exhibiting to an audience *what* is being revealed; the latter prize an "opaque" style promoting stylistic self-consciousness about *how* various effects are achieved through figurative language and other rhetorical devices.

These two approaches invoke two broad attitudes towards language and its relation to reality, which Lanham calls "Through and At." In the former, language is something to be looked *through* to the Real, the given, the found; in the latter, language is something to be looked *at* as something which creates or structures what is called Real. The first attitude sees language as a means for getting to or connecting with what is extralinguistic; the second attitude sees language as the means by which meaningful reality is constituted. The former is referent-oriented; the latter is text-oriented. In Western culture the conflict between these attitudes began more than two thousand years ago in the debates between Socrates and the Sophists, and continues up to the present in debates between logical positivists and perspectivists.[4]

Call these two attitudes "the Scientific Attitude" and "the Rhetorical Attitude." The relevant point here is the seesawing between the Scientific Attitude and the Rhetorical Attitude throughout Western thought. The recent linguistic turn in metahistory, and the discursive turn in philosophy and all areas of thought more generally, are instances of the displacement of the Scientific Attitude (expressed in positivisms of various sorts) by the Rhetorical Attitude.[5]

The Rhetorical Attitude may emerge when reigning ideologies and rhetorical conventions are experienced as exclusionary and/or repressive by people who have gained sufficient power to give voice to their dissatisfactions. In this case the excluded claim: (a) we aren't acknowledged to be part of the way things are, and we want to be; (b) we aren't acknowledged because of the way knowledge is conceived; (c) knowledge is a function of the regnant ideologies and rhetorical devices which are themselves changeable; and (d) here's the way to change the rhetorical conventions, thereby opening up room for us. The excluded see what is called science as itself rhetorical and they call for a change in the rhetorical conventions which govern it, or for the abandonment of science as too rhetorically restrictive and its replacement with something else (in our day, by "hermeneutics," "critical theory," "deconstruction," "genealogy," "theory," and so on).

It is thus no accident that the Rhetorical Attitude arose during the 1960s at which time African-Americans, women, gays, post-colonialists, and others felt not only that their stories were excluded from "legitimate" (read "scientific") history, but that they were so in part because the ascendant rhetorical conventions of science and scientifically inspired grand narrative (including Marxism) necessarily prevented their inclusion. The excluded assumed the Rhetorical Attitude in part as a way of combating oppressors legitimized, so they thought, by science.

However, one should *not* assume that only the Rhetorical Attitude is in the long-run interest of the oppressed, that the Scientific Attitude neatly lines up with conservatism and the Rhetorical with political radicalism. True, the relativism that rhetors both presuppose and foster can be a powerful critical tool which those bent on changing current social arrangements can use to undermine their supposed legitimacy. Claims to legitimacy traditionally appeal to some sort of Absolute Truth whose debunking can undermine those whose authority is buttressed by such appeals. This is especially so when this authority is based on the power to exclude by labeling people as inferior or abnormal. But the features which make rhetoric well suited for burning down edifices make it less obviously well suited for building up alternative structures. Furthermore, one of the chief weapons of the oppressed has often been an appeal to newly discovered truths not recognized in the regnant system of thought as the basis for relief of their situation and a progressive vision of social life. This weapon is something more obviously supplied by the Scientific Attitude than the Rhetorical. Indeed, the Scientific Attitude can rightfully claim the possibility of liberating the oppressed by "unmasking" the true nature of their social relations, showing how an ideology serves those in power, and revealing the potential for development inherent in a particular social situation.

The point here is that, though the Rhetorical Attitude may well gain momentum because of its usefulness to groups which feel excluded from current ways of thinking about and organizing social existence, the ultimate political import of either the Rhetorical or the Scientific Attitude is far from clear. This import may well be determined by a particular historical context, and in any case is certainly more complex than the simple equation Rhetorical = left, Scientific = right so common in contemporary discussions.

The Rhetorical Attitude in the discipline of history has gone through a number of distinct phases. At the outset it concentrated on narrative form as characteristic of history, and on the various rhetorical devices at work in narrative representation. This phase was dominated by such questions as: how do narratives explain events? What is the relation between narrative explanation and causal explanation? What role do narrators have in the construction of narratives?

Many answered these questions by emphasizing the *constructed* character of historical narratives. That is, they highlighted the ways historians select events to figure in a narrative account (indeed, how incidents become historical events only by being brought within a narrative framework); how historians assign significance to events by placing them into a narrative context; and how historians themselves (rather than Reality) decide the basic form which a narrative will take. Historical narratives were seen to be in part the product of the historian's imagination, and to derive their meaning not just from the so-called facts they describe, but from the narrative form into which historians fit the "facts." By adopting a broadly constructivist approach metahistorians focused attention on shared features of historical narratives and fictional narratives: emplotment, story-types, figurative language, and so on.

This focus on the poetic nature of historical narrative provided an opening through which the Rhetorical Attitude entered metahistory in a more full-blown way. According to this extension of the Rhetorical Attitude, historians could no longer be conceived as disinterested inquirers representing the past as it actually happened. Historians necessarily ask questions and construct accounts which derive from their own historical position as they best understand it. This has a number of repercussions for metahistorical reflection. First, it raises in a new and more powerful way problems about objectivity as an ideal. If the Rhetorical Attitude is correct, historians cannot be neutral observers who uncover the basic structures of historical reality by eliminating their own presuppositions and transcending their narrow interests; indeed, without these presuppositions (in the form of the questions historians ask, principles of selection and significance they employ, language they use – including metaphors and plot-types, and the values these embody) no history is possible. So if history is necessarily perspectival, how can it claim to be objective? This is a question metahistorians have debated persistently throughout the last twenty-five years.

Second, under the sway of the Rhetorical Attitude history cannot be conceived as Ranke hoped – as recovering the past "as it actually was" – but only as the past shows itself to the present of the historian. But this introduces a deep tension into the entire enterprise of history: isn't history about the past, and doesn't the emphasis on the present of the historian reduce the past to an aspect of the present? Or, to put this another way: doesn't the presentist conception of history seemingly decreed by the Rhetorical Attitude make the past an extension or reflection of the present rather than something different? The question metahistorians have felt compelled to address in this connection is: is the presentist conception of history a subtle form of temporocentrism?

The focus on the rhetorical aspects of history not only raised questions about the poetics of historical narration, objectivity, and the sameness and difference of the past and the present, but also about the truth-value of historical narration. How can the form of a narrative be assessed in terms of truth? Or, if it is the historian who emplots historical events, in what sense can historical narratives represent or mirror historical reality? Does reality come already packaged, so to speak, as a tragedy or a comedy? It would seem that the features of stories are not to be found in the lived experience of historical agents but are imposed on them after the fact – that, in Louis Mink's words, "stories are told but not lived." And if this is true, doesn't this mean that narratives are in some deep sense *misleading*: don't they force reality into a mold in which reality itself is not cast? At this point, metahistorical reflection must address questions deriving from a clash between some versions of realism (historical experience itself is already emplotted) and constructivism (narrative plots are imposed on essentially plotless experience).

But inquiry must be pressed further; for if narratives are in some fundamental way deceptive, the question naturally arises as to their very usefulness and appropriateness. With this question postmodernism boldly enters the field. For narratives connote a kind of continuity of a central subject, coherence of events through which this subject passes, and an intelligibility which an entire story about this subject possesses which may deeply belie the shifting, transitory, and fluid nature of reality itself. Postmodernists have vigorously attacked the idea of a "metanarrative" such as provided by Marxism or Christianity in which a subject such as "humanity" progresses through a series of coherent stages along the way to some final end of self-fulfillment. They attack the very idea of humanity as a central subject, and they emphasize the accidental and constructed character of any form of human identity.

Postmodernists have also attacked the ability of narrative form to capture lesser historical agents than "humanity"; indeed, they argue that *every* historical occurrence or agent is marked by discontinuity, accident, and variability. There is no central subject present over time in any event, nor is there an inherently intelligible process which a putative subject undergoes. Everything is marked by a merely momentary "identity," by contingency, and by a plethora of meanings. For historians to speak of "the Middle Ages" or "homosexuality" or "democratization" or "the United States" – or even single historical agents like Jesus Christ or George Washington – is to falsify the polysemous, conditional, and shifting character of everything in the human world.

In light of this sort of reflection some postmodernists have called for non-narrative forms of historical expression (such as "genealogy"). Others have declared that history itself must be abandoned as a form of knowledge, that it is necessarily tainted by a metaphysics which is "logocentric." Still others have sought some "middle way" between abandoning history as an enterprise and returning to the scientific attitudes of the nineteenth century. Metahistorical reflection here centers on the question, is there a way to re-conceive representation, objectivity, the past's relation to the present, and historical meaning which can acknowledge the insights of the Rhetorical Attitude and even some of its postmodern variants without abandoning history or reducing it to propaganda or mere ideology?

This rather quick survey of the terrain of metahistorical reflection over the past twenty-five years shows the way the Rhetorical Attitude once introduced carries with it a kind of inner logic which calls ever more deeply into question the nature of history as a discipline. Thus, those who began by drawing attention to the rhetorical features of history which distinguish it from the natural sciences and establish it as an autonomous discipline were ultimately compelled to question its capacity to illuminate the past. Of course, these difficulties were not lost on defenders of the Scientific Attitude, who continued to be heard (for reasons to be examined below). These defenders offered vigorous justifications of history as a legitimate cognitive enterprise, often offering new insights into its workings as a way of revealing the power of its conceptual resources. However, the development of the Rhetorical Attitude set the terms of metahistorical reflection. The probing questions posed by rhetors in history have provided the impetus for the rich and illuminating exploration of the nature of history which has marked the last quarter-century.

In light of this, the categories in terms of which the selections in this volume are organized attempt to capture the various implications of the development of the Rhetorical Attitude. To recapitulate, the topics to which the following essays are addressed include: narrative as the form of history, the poetics of narrative, objectivity as an ideal, constructivism versus realism, history's relation to the past, and the postmodernist questioning of history itself.

As Lanham's, Fish's, and Kimball's work shows, the current ascendancy of the Rhetorical Attitude is no reason to think that the insights of the Scientific Attitude should or will disappear, or already have done so. All three of these authors show that periods in which one Attitude dominates are followed by periods in which the other Attitude is in the ascendant. There is no reason to assume that the Rhetorical will prevail indefinitely.[6]

But there is a more important point than the temporal oscillation of the Attitudes, one which is not made by the three authors mentioned above. The point is this: *the Rhetorical Attitude and the Scientific Attitude need one another for their continued viability.* It is crucial to see why this is so.

That it must be so can be seen within the discipline of history itself. Historians want to tell their audience about something other than themselves. But if the "looking at" of the rhetorical is insisted upon to the exclusion of the "looking through" of the scientific, history simply loses contact with that which it aims to illuminate and therefore its *raison d'être*. But if the scientific is insisted upon to the exclusion of the rhetorical, history is converted into a mere recording device in which the historian has no real role to play in assessing the meaning of events – again sub-verting its *raison d'être*.[7] To be true to itself, the discipline of history must invoke both its scientific dimension and its rhetorical dimension.

That these two Attitudes require each other to remain viable is a fact not just about history but obtains more generally. Consider the Rhetorical Attitude first. When one insists on the creative and constructive use of language to the exclusion of its ability to connect to a world outside itself (when one, that is, ignores referentiality), the connection between the language-user and the world is broken. But if nothing external anchors one's utterances, then the result is solipsism, and solipsism renders one's utterances uninformative and thus useless. The Rhetorical Attitude taken to the extreme of denying the relevance of insights of the Scientific Attitude ends in the "infinite play of signifiers" in which nothing is or can be said.

(This may seem to be too quick a claim: mightn't the coherence of the Rhetorical Attitude be saved if one supposed a group of language-users who spoke according to shared communicative rules and conventions? Then it might appear that significant communication could still pro-ceed. But this is a mistake: other language-users are themselves part of the world, are themselves referents. How, if the Rhetorical account captured the entire story, could any language-user know that he or she was using the same conventions and meanings as any other language-user? Each would be isolated in an island of rhetoric, which is to say, each would no longer be speaking.)[8]

When the Rhetorical Attitude excludes the Scientific Attitude it ulti-mately ends in the breakdown of the communication which the Rhetorical Attitude was meant to highlight. The result is Babel – that is, something about which rhetoric has nothing to say. The Rhetorical Attitude needs the Scientific Attitude to prevent it from undermining itself.

The opposite is also the case: the domination of the Scientific Attitude to such an extent that the insights of the Rhetorical Attitude are ignored or silenced can obscure the representational dimensions of science and thereby misrepresent the scientific enterprise. Of course, the Scientific Attitude calls for an *exact* representation of reality, and in this way might appear to be reducing the importance of representation to nil: the goal on this account would be to show reality directly. But no matter how veridical a representation is, it is still a representation: a facsimile of reality is not reality itself; an equation describing a process, or a map of a territory, or a model of a machine are not ontologically identical with what they represent. (One might put this in a homely manner by saying that a menu is not a meal.)

Science is representational and not a simulacrum of reality. Its the-ories aspire to pick out and explain basic structures and patterns from the buzzing confusion of the world. Science seeks the melody of reality by filtering out its noise. But this requires criteria of significance and con-cepts by virtue of which these criteria are expressed. (In the language of cartography, this requires methods of projection.) Such criteria, concepts, and methods are rhetorical tools which scientists must employ in their quest to ascertain what is important and revelatory. In this way science necessarily has a rhetorical dimension. To pretend that science is not rhetorical is to ignore its essential representational conventions and therefore to ignore a fundamental aspect of the scientific enterprise. (Also, by ignoring the nature and role of its representations, the Scientific Attitude often ends up canonizing one historically contingent way of apprehending reality as Reality-As-It-Is-In-Itself, and thus as the *only* way which is cognitively legitimate.)

The Scientific Attitude emphasized to the point that it excludes any recognition of the rhetorical dimension of its representations undermines the idea of representation and therefore the whole point of science. The Scientific Attitude thus needs the Rhetorical Attitude to prevent it from undermining itself.

That the Rhetorical and the Scientific Attitudes need one another for each to remain coherent helps to explain why the history of thought has so often been marked by a swing from one pole to the other. The very success of one calls forth its opposite, which in turn becomes dominant and thereby elicits the other, and so forth. (This dialectical movement back and forth is not a mere repetition: the terms and what might be called the problematic by which each attitude is expressed differ over time, in part as a result of their previous clashes.) Thus, one may reasonably expect the current success of the Rhetorical Attitude to be followed by the re-emergence of the Scientific Attitude.

But even though one anticipates a turn away from the linguistic turn (and a turn away from *this* turn), it is important to affirm as essential to any adequate view of history an ongoing dialectical tension between the Rhetorical and the Scientific Attitudes. Put another way: *no expression of either the Rhetorical or the Scientific Attitude which is of lasting interest will fail to take account of the insights of its opponent.* It is for this reason that this book includes essays which recognize the pull of the Attitude which they oppose, or links essays which express one Attitude with those which express the other. That is, the book aspires to *maintain the tension between the Scientific and the Rhetorical Attitudes* by exhibiting it in the essays chosen and the way they are grouped.

In his lucid and useful essay "Rhetoric," Stanley Fish claims that "the quarrel between rhetorical and foundational thought is itself foundational; its content is a disagreement about the basic constituents of human activity, about the nature of human nature itself" (p. 208).[9] Moreover, he avers that, because the question, which of these views of human nature is the correct one? "can be answered only from within one or the other, and the evidence of one party will be regarded by the other as illusory or as grist for its own mill" (p. 208) that there is "no prospect of ever reaching accord," and that all one can expect is an "endless round of accusation and counteraccusation in which truth, honesty, and linguistic

responsibility are claimed by everyone" (p. 209). On this basis he therefore concludes that in the end it is "the difference that remains" (p. 222)
between what we have been calling the Rhetorical Attitude and the Scientific Attitude.

This suggests that no possibility exists for some dialectical middle
ground which preserves the insights of each Attitude and prunes each of
its excesses. But this suggestion is historically inaccurate. A number of
thinkers have tried to carve out a position which attempts to do justice
to both sides of the divide. Aristotle, for instance, wrote not only the
Metaphysics but also the *Rhetoric*. Taken together these offer a view
which claims that there is a knowable reality but also that rhetoric is
a means to ascertaining truth about this reality: "We must be able to
employ persuasion . . . on opposite sides of a question, not in order that
we may in practice employ it in both ways (for we must not make people
believe what is wrong), but in order that we may see clearly what the
facts are" (*Rhetoric* 1355a, 29–33). Kant, too, may be interpreted as
attempting to preserve the possibility of scientific knowledge but doing
so by recognizing the contribution which categories of thought and expression play in the construction of this knowledge. In our own century,
Dewey can also be seen as attempting to steer a middle course between
the Rhetorical and the Scientific Attitude.

Notice that I used the word "attempt" to describe these putative
middle grounds. Not everyone will agree that these – or, indeed, *any*
thinkers – have actually succeeded in doing what they intended. (Thus,
for instance, Fish himself thinks that Aristotle, in defending the legitimate role of rhetoric, actually "reinforces the very assumptions in relation
to which rhetoric will always be suspect, assumptions of an independent reality whose outlines can be perceived by a sufficiently clear-eyed
observer" ("Rhetoric," p. 206).) But the point here is not that any position has succeeded in establishing a convincing middle, but that historically this has been a way to move out of the endless oscillation of
thought between ends of the spectrum. (Of course, even if a compelling
middle way were discovered it cannot be the "solution" forever: the
terms of the debate between the Scientific and the Rhetorical continually shift so that new formulations of a dialectical middle will always be
required. Here as everywhere there are no fixed answers.)

Indeed, an attempt at synthesis seems to be a legitimate philosophical
aspiration. (This Introduction is itself a move to open up the possibility
of such a "dialectical middle," by placing the dispute in a larger context
and by showing that each side needs the other.) Fish depicts rhetors and
scientists as locked into self-enclosed, incommensurable worlds unable to
convince each other because no independent evidence exists. But this picture is surely overdrawn. If the incommensurability were this complete,
neither opponent would be able to address the other; indeed, neither
would be able to recognize its opponent's position as a competitor. Fish's
depiction is incoherent because a condition necessary for it to work –

that the rhetorical and the scientific confront each other as genuine alternatives – requires that its central assertion (that each is self-enclosed in its own world) be false. The problems with Fish's picture are the problems which beset caricatures of Kuhn's depiction of science (problems which Kuhn himself was quick to point out): no genuine debate between alternative paradigms can occur unless they share a great deal.

Thus, recognizing that both camps can (indeed, must) speak to each other for them to be contending camps suggests a possible philosophical response: to listen to the various points and counterpoints of the argument in an attempt to develop a position which does justice to the deepest insights of both sides. Some may find the result incoherent; others may find merely a "boring middle." But one should not rule out *a priori* the possibility of a position which genuinely captures the truths of both sides. (In the selections which follow, the essays by Carroll, Partner, Norman, Lang, Haskell, Lorenz, and Martin can be seen as attempts at a dialectical middle ground.)

The editors realize that the focus of this collection has meant that a number of especially illuminating and important essays in the theory of history have been excluded. The terrain of contemporary historiography is richer and more varied than any single volume can encompass, so much good work is absent from this volume. We hope the gain in focus and comprehension which a thematic selection such as ours brings outweighs the loss incurred by the omissions we have been forced to make. In addition, note that some of the essays have been cut (though not substantially) for reasons of greater focus and bearing on the themes discussed in this Introduction. Three-point ellipses have been inserted to indicate where text has been cut.[10]

Notes

1 This approach is sometimes called a "bottom up" approach in philosophy. It obviously owes a great deal to Pragmatism. For a particularly well-expressed account of this approach in the philosophy of history, see Raymond Martin, *The Past Within Us: An Empirical Approach to Philosophy of History* (Princeton, 1989).

2 Hayden White, *Metahistory* (Baltimore, 1973). The year 1973 is a convenient date to announce the full-bodied linguistic turn, but there were many precursors to it, including: Arthur Danto's *Analytic Philosophy of History* (Cambridge, 1965); Roland Barthes's "Le Discours de l'histoire," *Social Sciences Information*, VI, 1967, 65–75 (English translation by Stephan Bann in *Comparative Criticism*, III, 1981, 3–20); J. H. Hexter's "The Rhetoric of History" (reprinted in this volume); W. B. Gallie's "The Historical Understanding" in *History and Theory*, 3, 1964, 149–202, and *Philosophy and Historical Understanding* (London, 1964); A. R. Louch's "History and Narration" in *History and Theory*, 8, 1969, 54–70; and behind these, of course, Droysen and Nietzsche in the nineteenth century.

3 Richard Lanham, *Literacy and the Survival of Humanism* (New Haven, 1983).

4 Lanham and Stanley Fish (in "Rhetoric" in Frank Lentricchia and Thomas McLaughlin, *Critical Terms for Literary Study*, Chicago, 1995) both provide excellent historical overviews of the long-standing debate between rhetoric and philosophy/science.

5 Bruce Kimball in *Orators and Philosophers* (New York, 1986) and in *The Condition of American Liberal Education* (New York, 1995) traces pendulum swings in the idea of liberal education between the poles of what he dubs "the orators" and "the philosophers." This typology isn't exactly the same as Lanham's, but is clearly related to it (Kimball asserts as much in *Condition*, p. 8). Philosophers conceive liberal education as the search for truth and training in this search; orators conceive of liberal education as training in the skills of "composing, delivering, and analyzing a speech" (ibid., p. 4), the art of persuasion and being a good citizen. Plato, the Scholastics, Thomas Huxley, and those responsible for the modern research university are Philosophers; the Sophists, Cicero, the Renaissance Humanists, Matthew Arnold, Nietzsche, and Catholic educators are Orators. Kimball sees these as a fundamental split between reason and speech (both present in the term *logos*).

6 Lanham calls the opaque style and the rhetorical attitude it embodies the "'breathing out' which complements an equally necessary 'breathing in'" of the transparent style and the scientific attitude it embodies (*Literacy*, p. 86). This may be somewhat overstated, at least with respect to the history of modern historiography or philosophy – though it seems quite plausible when applied to literature, its intended home. The Scientific Attitude in philosophy (at least since Descartes) and in historiography (at least since Ranke) has so dominated that those who do not subscribe to it have often been written off as amateurs. Perhaps a better way to put the point would be to describe the Rhetorical Attitude in these areas as recessive, underground, or oppositional schools which have occasionally (as in the present) come to prominence.

7 As a way of deepening this point, consider Arthur Danto's concept of the Ideal Chronicler as described in *Narration and Knowledge* (New York, 1985, chapter 8). The Ideal Chronicler (IC) gives an exact iconic representation of every event as it happens. But the IC, trapped as he or she is in the present, cannot employ what Danto calls "narrative sentences," sentences which are distinctive of history. (Narrative sentences are those which refer to at least two time-separated events in such a way that the earlier event is described by means of reference to a later event; examples are: "The invasion of Poland was the start of World War II"; "*Lyrical Ballads* initiated the Romantic movement in English poetry.") Moreover, the IC, because he or she is committed to recording *everything* that happens, cannot distinguish between what is significant and what is not – and so cannot write an account of some important event by picking out its causes and outlining its meaningful effects. Present-centered and indiscriminate, the IC is the Scientific Attitude taken to such an extreme that history becomes impossible. The point here is that because histories necessarily single out some events for their (later) significance, such histories have an irreducibly rhetorical character.

8 This is a version of Wittgenstein's so-called Private Language Argument. See Ludwig Wittgenstein, *Philosophical Investigations* (Oxford, 1968), sections 243–80.

9 Page references in the text are to the essay cited in note 4

10 My fellow editors Philip Pomper and Richard Vann discussed the ideas in this Introduction with me at great length (indeed, some of the ideas are theirs); they also read drafts of the essay and helped to improve it greatly.

Part I
Narrativity

1
The Historical Text as Literary Artifact

Hayden White

One of the ways that a scholarly field takes stock of itself is by considering its history. Yet it is difficult to get an objective history of a scholarly discipline, because if the historian is himself a practitioner of it, he is likely to be a devotee of one or another of its sects and hence biased; and if he is not a practitioner, he is unlikely to have the expertise necessary to distinguish between the significant and the insignificant events of the field's development. One might think that these difficulties would not arise in the field of history itself, but they do and not only for the reasons mentioned above. In order to write the history of any given scholarly discipline or even of a science, one must be prepared to ask questions *about* it of a sort that do not have to be asked in the practice *of* it. One must try to get behind or beneath the presuppositions which sustain a given type of inquiry and ask the questions that can be begged in its practice in the interest of determining why this type of inquiry has been designed to solve the problems it characteristically tries to solve. This is what metahistory seeks to do. It addresses itself to such questions as, What is the structure of a peculiarly *historical* consciousness? What is the epistemological status of historical *explanations*, as compared with other kinds of explanations that might be offered to account for the materials with which historians ordinarily deal? What are the possible *forms* of historical representation and what are their bases? What authority can historical accounts claim as contributions to a secured knowledge of reality in general and to the human sciences in particular?

Now, many of these questions have been dealt with quite competently over the last quarter-century by philosophers concerned to define history's relationships to other disciplines, especially the physical and social sciences, and by historians interested in assessing the success of their discipline in mapping the past and determining the relationship of that past to the present. But there is one problem that neither philosophers nor historians have looked at very seriously and to which literary theorists have given only passing attention. This question has to do with the status of the historical narrative, considered purely as a verbal artifact purporting to be a model of structures and processes long past and therefore not subject to either experimental or observational controls. This is not to say that historians and philosophers of history have failed to take notice of the essentially provisional and contingent nature of historical representations and of their susceptibility to infinite revision in the light of new evidence or more sophisticated conceptualization of problems. One of the marks of a good professional historian is the consistency with which he reminds his readers of the purely provisional nature of his characterizations of events, agents, and agencies found in the always incomplete historical record. Nor is it to say that literary theorists have *never* studied the structure of historical narratives. But in general there has been a reluctance to consider historical narratives as what they most manifestly are: verbal fictions, the contents of which are as much *invented* as *found* and the forms of which have more in common with their counterparts in literature than they have with those in the sciences.

Now, it is obvious that this conflation of mythic and historical consciousness will offend some historians and disturb those literary theorists whose conception of literature presupposes a radical opposition of history to fiction or of fact to fancy. As Northrop Frye has remarked, "In a sense the historical is the opposite of the mythical, and to tell the historian that what gives shape to his book is a myth would sound to him vaguely insulting." Yet Frye himself grants that "when a historian's scheme gets to a certain point of comprehensiveness it becomes mythical in shape, and so approaches the poetic in its structure." He even speaks of different kinds of historical myths: Romantic myths "based on a quest or pilgrimage to a City of God or classless society"; Comic "myths of progress through evolution or revolution"; Tragic myths of "decline and fall, like the works of Gibbon and Spengler"; and Ironic "myths of recurrence or casual catastrophe." But Frye appears to believe that these myths are operative only in such victims of what might be called the "poetic fallacy" as Hegel, Marx, Nietzsche, Spengler, Toynbee, and Sartre – historians whose fascination with the "constructive" capacity of human thought has deadened their responsibility to the "found" data. "The historian works inductively," he says, "collecting his facts and trying to avoid any informing patterns except those he sees, or is honestly convinced he sees, in the facts themselves." He does not work "from" a "unifying form," as the poet does, but "toward" it; and it therefore follows that the historian, like any writer of discursive prose, is to be judged "by the truth of what he says, or by the adequacy of his verbal reproduction of his external model," whether that external model be the actions of past men or the historian's own thought about such actions.

What Frye says is true enough as a statement of the *ideal* that has inspired historical writing since the time of the Greeks, but that ideal presupposes an opposition between myth and history that is as problematical as it is venerable. It serves Frye's purposes very well, since it permits him to locate the specifically "fictive" in the space between the two concepts of the "mythic" and the "historical." As readers of Frye's *Anatomy of Criticism* will remember, Frye conceives fictions to consist in part of sublimates of archetypal myth-structures. These structures have been displaced to the interior of verbal artifacts in such a way as to serve as their latent meanings. The fundamental meanings of all fictions, their thematic content, consist, in Frye's view, of the "pre-generic plot-structures" or *mythoi* derived from the corpora of Classical and Judaeo-Christian religious literature. According to this theory, we understand *why* a particular story has "turned out" as it has when we have identified the archetypal myth, or pregeneric plot structure, of which the story is an exemplification. And we see the "point" of a story when we have identified its theme (Frye's translation of *dianoia*), which makes of it a "parable or illustrative fable." "Every work of literature," Frye insists, "has both a fictional and a thematic aspect," but as we move from "fictional projection" toward the overt articulation of theme, the writing tends to take on the aspect of "direct address, or straight discursive writing and cease[s] to be literature." And in Frye's view, as we have seen, history (or at least "proper history") belongs to the category of "discursive writing," so that when the fictional element – or mythic plot structure – is *obviously* present in it, it ceases to be history altogether and becomes a bastard genre, product of an unholy, though not unnatural, union between history and poetry.

Yet, I would argue, histories gain part of their explanatory effect by their success in making stories out of *mere* chronicles; and stories in turn are made out of chronicles by an operation which I have elsewhere called "emplotment." And by emplotment I mean simply the encodation of the facts contained in the chronicle as components of specific *kinds* of plot structures, in precisely the way that Frye has suggested is the case with "fictions" in general.

The late R. G. Collingwood insisted that the historian was above all a story teller and suggested that historical sensibility was manifested in the capacity to make a plausible story out of a congeries of "facts" which, in their unprocessed form, made no sense at all. In their efforts to make sense of the historical record, which is fragmentary and always incomplete, historians have to make use of what Collingwood called "the constructive imagination," which told the historian – as it tells the competent detective – what "must have been the case" given the available evidence and the formal properties it displayed to the consciousness capable of putting the right question to it. This constructive imagination functions in much the same way that Kant supposed the *a priori* imagination functions when it tells us that even though we cannot perceive both sides of a tabletop simultaneously, we can be certain it has *two* sides if it has one, because the very concept of *one side* entails at least *one other*. Collingwood suggested that historians come to their evidence endowed with a sense of the *possible* forms that different kinds of recognizably human situations *can* take. He called this sense the nose for the "story" contained in the evidence or for the "true" story that was buried in or hidden behind the "apparent" story. And he concluded that historians provide plausible explanations for bodies of historical evidence when they succeed in discovering the story or complex of stories implicitly contained within them.

What Collingwood failed to see was that no given set of casually recorded historical events can in itself constitute a story; the most it might offer to the historian are story *elements*. The events are *made* into a story by the suppression or subordination of certain of them and the highlighting of others, by characterization, motific repetition, variation of tone and point of view, alternative descriptive strategies, and the like – in short, all of the techniques that we would normally expect to find in the emplotment of a novel or a play. For example, no historical event is *intrinsically tragic*; it can only be conceived as such from a particular point of view or from within the context of a structured set of events of which it is an element enjoying a privileged place. For in history what is tragic from one perspective is comic from another, just as in society what appears to be tragic from the standpoint of one class may be, as Marx purported to show of the 18th Brumaire of Louis Bonaparte, only a farce from that of another class. Considered as potential elements of a story, historical events are value-neutral. Whether they find their place finally in a story that is tragic, comic, romantic, or ironic – to use Frye's categories – depends upon the historian's decision to *con*figure them according to the imperatives of one plot structure or mythos rather than another. The same set of events can serve as components of a story that is tragic *or* comic, as the case may be, depending on the historian's choice of the plot structure that he considers most appropriate for ordering events of that kind so as to make them into a comprehensible story.

This suggests that what the historian brings to his consideration of the historical record is a notion of the *types* of configurations of events that can be recognized as stories by the audience for which he is writing. True, he can misfire. I do not suppose that anyone would accept the emplotment of the life of President Kennedy as comedy, but whether it ought to be emplotted romantically, tragically, or satirically is an open question. The important point is that most historical sequences can be emplotted in a number of different ways, so as to provide different interpretations of those events and to endow them with different meanings.

Thus, for example, what Michelet in his great history of the French Revolution construed as a drama of Romantic transcendence, his contemporary Tocqueville emplotted as an ironic Tragedy. Neither can be said to have had more knowledge of the "facts" contained in the record; they simply had different notions of the kind of story that best fitted the facts they knew. Nor should it be thought that they told different stories of the Revolution because they had discovered different *kinds* of facts, political on the one hand, social on the other. They sought out different kinds of facts because they had different kinds of stories to tell. But why did these alternative, not to say mutually exclusive, representations of what was substantially the same set of events appear equally plausible to their respective audiences? Simply because the historians shared with their audiences certain preconceptions about how the Revolution might be emplotted, in response to imperatives that were generally extrahistorical, ideological, aesthetic, or mythical.

Collingwood once remarked that you could never explicate a tragedy to anyone who was not already acquainted with the kinds of situations that are regarded as "tragic" in our culture. Anyone who has taught or taken one of those omnibus courses usually entitled Western Civilization or Introduction to the Classics of Western Literature will know what Collingwood had in mind. Unless you have some idea of the generic attributes of tragic, comic, romantic, or ironic situations, you will be unable to recognize them as such when you come upon them in a literary text. But historical situations do not have built into them intrinsic meanings in the way that literary texts do. Historical situations are not *inherently* tragic, comic, or romantic. They may all be inherently ironic, but they need not be emplotted that way. All the historian needs to do to transform a tragic into a comic situation is to shift his point of view or change the scope of his perceptions. Anyway, we only think of situations as tragic or comic because these concepts are part of our generally cultural and specifically literary heritage. *How* a given historical situation is to be configured depends on the historian's subtlety in matching up a specific plot structure with the set of historical events that he wishes to endow with a meaning of a particular kind. This is essentially a literary, that is to say fiction-making, operation. And to call it that in no way detracts from the status of historical narratives as providing a kind of knowledge. For not only are the pregeneric plot structures by which sets of events can be constituted as stories of a particular kind limited in number, as Frye and other archetypal critics suggest; but the encodation of events in terms of such plot structures is one of the ways that a culture has of making sense of both personal and public pasts.

We can make sense of sets of events in a number of different ways. One of the ways is to subsume the events under the causal laws which may have governed their concatenation in order to produce the particular configuration that the events appear to assume when considered as "effects" of mechanical forces. This is the way of scientific explanation. Another way we make sense of a set of events which appears strange, enigmatic, or mysterious in its immediate manifestations is to encode the set in terms of culturally provided categories, such as metaphysical concepts, religious beliefs, or story forms. The effect of such encodations is to familiarize the unfamiliar; and in general this is the way of historiography, whose "data" are always immediately strange, not to say exotic, simply by virtue of their distance from us in time and their origin in a way of life different from our own.

The historian shares with his audience *general notions* of the *forms* that significant human situations *must* take by virtue of his participation in the specific processes of sense-making which identify him as a member of one cultural endowment rather than another. In the process of studying a given complex of events, he begins to perceive the *possible* story form that such events *may* figure. In his narrative account of how this set of events took on the shape which he perceives to inhere within it, he emplots his account as a story of a particular kind. The reader, in the process of following the historian's account of those events, gradually comes to realize that the story he is reading is of one kind rather than another: romance, tragedy, comedy, satire, epic, or what have you. And when he has perceived the class or type to which the story that he is reading belongs, he experiences the effect of having the events in the story explained to him. He has at this point not only successfully *followed* the story; he has grasped the point of it, *understood* it, as well. The original strangeness, mystery, or exoticism of the events is dispelled, and they take on a familiar aspect, not in their details, but in their functions as elements of a familiar kind of configuration. They are rendered comprehensible by being subsumed under the categories of the plot structure in which they are encoded as a story of a particular kind. They are familiarized, not only because the reader now has more *information* about the events, but also because he has been shown how the data conform to an *icon* of a comprehensible finished process, a plot structure with which he is familiar as a part of his cultural endowment.

This is not unlike what happens, or is supposed to happen, in psychotherapy. The sets of events in the patient's past which are the presumed cause of his distress, manifested in the neurotic syndrome, have been defamiliarized, rendered strange, mysterious, and threatening and have assumed a meaning that he can neither accept nor effectively reject. It is not that the patient does not *know* what those events were, does not know the facts; for if he did not in some sense know the facts, he would be unable to recognize them and repress them whenever they arise in his consciousness. On the contrary, he knows them all too well. He knows them so well, in fact, that he lives with them constantly and in such a way as to make it impossible for him to see any other facts except through the coloration that the set of events in question gives to his perception of the world. We might say that, according to the theory of psychoanalysis, the patient has overemplotted these events, has charged them with a meaning so intense that, whether real or merely imagined, they continue to shape both his perceptions and his responses to the world long after they should have become "past history." The therapist's problem, then, is not to hold up before the patient the "real facts" of the matter, the "truth" as against the "fantasy" that obsesses him. Nor is it to give him a short course in psychoanalytical theory by which to enlighten him as to the true nature of his distress by cataloging it as a manifestation of some "complex." This is what the analyst might do in relating the patient's case to a third party, and especially to another analyst. But psychoanalytic theory recognizes that the patient will resist both of these tactics in the same way that he resists the intrusion into consciousness of the traumatized memory traces in the *form* that he obsessively remembers them. The problem is to get the patient to "re-emplot" his whole life history in such a way as to change the *meaning* of those events for him and their *significance* for the economy of the whole set of events that make up his life. As thus envisaged, the thera-peutic process is an exercise in the refamiliarization of events that have been defamiliarized, rendered alienated from the patient's life-history, by virtue of their overdetermination as causal forces. And we might say that the events are detraumatized by being removed from the plot struc-ture in which they have a dominant place and inserted in another in which they have a subordinate or simply ordinary function as elements of a life shared with all other men.

Now, I am not interested in forcing the analogy between psychother-apy and historiography; I use the example merely to illustrate a point about the fictive component in historical narratives. Historians seek to refamiliarize us with events which have been forgotten through either accident, neglect, or repression. Moreover, the greatest historians have always dealt with those events in the histories of their cultures which are "traumatic" in nature and the meaning of which is either prob-lematical or overdetermined in the significance that they still have for current life, events such as revolutions, civil wars, large-scale processes such as industrialization and urbanization, or institutions which have lost their original function in a society but continue to play an impor-tant role on the current social scene. In looking at the ways in which such structures took shape or evolved, historians *re*familiarize them, not only by providing more information about them, but also by showing how their developments conformed to one or another of the story-types that we conventionally invoke to make sense of our own life-histories.

Now, if any of this is plausible as a characterization of the explana-tory effect of historical narrative, it tells us something important about the *mimetic* aspect of historical narratives. It is generally maintained – as Frye said – that a history is a verbal model of a set of events external to the mind of the historian. But it is wrong to think of a history as a model similar to a scale model of an airplane or ship, a map, or a photograph. For we can check the adequacy of this latter kind of model by going and looking at the original and, by applying the necessary rules of translation, seeing in what respect the model has actually succeeded in reproducing aspects of the original. But historical structures and processes are not like these originals; we cannot go and look at them in order to see if the historian has adequately reproduced them in his narrative. Nor should we want to, even if we could; for after all it was the very strangeness of the original as it appeared in the documents that inspired the historian's efforts to make a model of it in the first place. If the historian only did that for us, we should be in the same situation as the patient whose analyst merely told him, on the basis of interviews with his parents, siblings, and childhood friends, what the "true facts" of the patient's early life were. We would have no reason to think that anything at all had been *explained* to us.

This is what leads me to think that historical narratives are not only models of past events and processes, but also metaphorical statements which suggest a relation of similitude between such events and processes and the story-types that we conventionally use to endow the events of our lives with culturally sanctioned meanings. Viewed in a purely formal way, a historical narrative is not only a *reproduction* of the events reported in it, but also a *complex of symbols* which gives us directions for finding an *icon* of the structure of those events in our literary tradition.

I am here, of course, invoking the distinctions between sign, symbol, and icon which C. S. Peirce developed in his philosophy of language. I think that these distinctions will help us to understand what is fictive in all putatively realistic representations of the world and what is realistic in all manifestly fictive ones. They help us, in short, to answer the question. What are historical representations *representations of*? It seems to me that we must say of histories what Frye seems to think is true only of poetry or philosophies of history, namely that, considered as a system of signs, the historical narrative points in two directions simultaneously: *toward* the events described in the narrative and *toward* the story-type or mythos which the historian has chosen to serve as the icon of the structure of the events. The narrative itself is not the icon; what it does is *describe* events in the historical record in such a way as to inform the reader *what to take as an icon* of the events so as to render them "familiar" to him. The historical narrative thus mediates between the events reported in it on the one side and pregeneric plot structures conventionally used in our culture to endow unfamiliar events and situations with meanings, on the other.

The evasion of the implications of the fictive nature of historical narrative is in part a consequence of the utility of the concept "history" for the definition of other types of discourse. "History" can be set over against "science" by virture of its want of conceptual rigor and failure to produce the kinds of universal laws that the sciences characteristically seek to produce. Similarly, "history" can be set over against "literature" by virtue of its interest in the "actual" rather than the "possible," which is supposedly the object of representation of "literary" works. Thus, within a long and distinguished critical tradition that has sought to determine what is "real" and what is "imagined" in the novel, history has served as a kind of archetype of the "realistic" pole of representation. I am thinking of Frye, Auerbach, Booth, Scholes and Kellogg, and others. Nor is it unusual for literary theorists, when they are speaking about the "context" of a literary work, to suppose that this context – the "historical milieu" – has a concreteness and an accessibility that the work itself can never have, as if it were easier to perceive the reality of a past world put together from a thousand historical documents than it is to probe the depths of a single literary work that is present to the critic studying it. But the presumed concreteness and accessibility of historical milieux, these contexts of the texts that literary scholars study, are themselves products of the fictive capability of the historians who have studied those contexts. The historical documents are not less opaque than the texts studied by the literary critic. Nor is the world those documents figure more accessible. The one is no more "given" than the other. In fact, the opaqueness of the world figured in historical documents is, if anything, increased by the production of historical narratives. Each new historical work only adds to the number of possible texts that have to be interpreted if a full and accurate picture of a given historical milieu is to be faithfully drawn. The relationship between the past to be analyzed and historical works produced by analysis of the documents is paradoxical; the *more* we know about the past, the more difficult it is to generalize about it.

But if the increase in our knowledge of the past makes it more difficult to generalize about it, it should make it easier for us to generalize about the forms in which that knowledge is transmitted to us. Our knowledge of the past may increase incrementally, but our understanding of it does not. Nor does our understanding of the past progress by the kind of revolutionary breakthroughs that we associate with the development of the physical sciences. Like literature, history progresses by the production of classics, the nature of which is such that they cannot be disconfirmed or negated, in the way that the principal conceptual schemata of the sciences are. And it is their nondisconfirmability that testifies to the essentially *literary* nature of historical classics. There is something in a historical masterpiece that cannot be negated, and this nonnegatable element is its form, the form which is its fiction.

It is frequently forgotten or, when remembered, denied that no given set of events attested by the historical record comprises a *story* manifestly finished and complete. This is as true as the events that comprise the life of an individual as it is of an institution, a nation, or a whole people. We do not *live* stories, even if we give our lives meaning by retrospectively casting them in the form of stories. And so too with nations or whole cultures. In an essay on the "mythical" nature of historiography, Lévi-Strauss remarks on the astonishment that a visitor from another planet would feel if confronted by the thousands of histories written about the French Revolution. For in those works, the "authors do not always make use of the same incidents; when they do, the incidents are revealed in different lights. And yet these are variations which have to do with the same country, the same period, and the same events – events whose reality is scattered across every level of a multilayered structure." He goes on to suggest that the criterion of validity by which historical accounts might be assessed cannot depend on their elements" – that is to say – their putative factual content. On the contrary, he notes, "pursued in isolation, each element shows itself to be beyond grasp. But certain of them derive consistency from the fact that they can be integrated into a system whose terms are more or less credible when set against the overall coherence of the series." But his "coherence of the series" cannot be the coherence of the *chronological* series, that sequence of "facts" organized into the temporal order of their original occurrence. For the "chronicle" of events, out of which the historian fashions his story of "what really happened," already comes pre-encoded. There are "hot" and "cold" chronologies, chronologies in which more or fewer dates appear to demand inclusion in a full chronicle of what happened. Moreover, the dates themselves come to us already grouped into classes of dates, classes which are constitutive of putative domains of the historical field, domains which appear as problems for the historian to solve if he is to give a full and culturally responsible account of the past.

All this suggests to Lévi-Strauss that, when it is a matter of working up a comprehensive account of the various domains of the historical record in the form of a story, the "alleged historical continuities" that the historian purports to find in the record are "secured only by dint of fraudulent outlines" imposed by the historian on the record. These "fraudulent outlines" are, in his view, a product of "abstraction" and a means of escape from the "threat of an infinite regress" that always lurks at the interior of every complex set of historical "facts." We can construct a comprehensible story of the past, Lévi-Strauss insists, only by a decision to "give up" one or more of the domains of facts offering themselves for inclusion in our accounts. Our *explanations* of historical structures and processes are thus determined more by what we leave out of our representations than by what we put in. For it is in this brutal capacity to exclude certain facts in the interest of constituting the very constitution of a set of events in such a way as to make a comprehensible story out of them, the historian charges those events with the symbolic significance of a comprehensible plot structure. Historians may not like to think of their works as translations of fact into fictions; but this is one of the effects of their works. By suggesting alternative emplotments of a given sequence of historical events, historians provide historical events with all of the possible meanings with which the literary art of their culture is capable of endowing them. The real dispute between the proper historian and the philosopher of history has to do with the latter's insistence that events can be emplotted in one and only one story form. History-writing thrives on the discovery of all the possible plot structures that might be invoked to endow sets of events with different meanings. And our understanding of the past increases precisely in the degree to which we succeed in determining how far that past conforms to the strategies of sense-making that are contained in their purest forms in literary art.

Conceiving historical narratives in this way may give us some insight into the crisis in historical thinking which has been under way since the beginning of our century. Let us imagine that the problem of the historian is to make sense of a hypothetical *set* of events by arranging them in a *series* that is at once chronologically *and* syntactically structured, in the way that any discourse from a sentence all the way up to a novel is structured. We can see immediately that the imperatives of chronological arrangement of the events constituting the set must exist in tension with the imperatives of the syntactical strategies alluded to, whether the latter are conceived as those of logic (the syllogism) or those of narrative (the plot structure).

Thus, we have a set of events

$$(1) \qquad a, b, c, d, e, \ldots, n,$$

ordered chronologically but requiring description and characterization as elements of plot or argument by which to give them meaning. Now, the series can be emplotted in a number of different ways and thereby endowed with different meanings without violating the imperatives of the chronological arrangement at all. We may briefly characterize some of these emplotments in the following ways:

$$(2) \qquad A, b, c, d, e, \ldots, n$$
$$(3) \qquad a, B, c, d, e, \ldots, n$$
$$(4) \qquad a, b, C, d, e, \ldots, n$$
$$(5) \qquad a, b, c, D, e, \ldots, n$$

And so on.

The capitalized letters indicate the privileged status given to certain events or sets of events in the series by which they are endowed with explanatory force, either as causes explaining the structure of the whole series or as symbols of the plot structure of the series considered as a story of a specific kind. We might say that any history which endows any putatively original event (*a*) with the status of a decisive factor (*A*) in the structuration of the whole series of events following after it is "deterministic." The emplotments of the history of "society" by Rousseau in his *Second Discourse*, Marx in the *Manifesto*, and Freud in *Totem and Taboo* would fall into this category. So too, any history which endows the last event in the series (*e*), whether real or only speculatively projected, with the force of full explanatory power (*E*) is of the type of all eschatological or apocalyptical histories. St Augustine's *City of God* and the various versions of the Joachite notion of the advent of a millennium, Hegel's *Philosophy of History*, and, in general, all Idealist histories are of this sort. In between we would have the various forms of historiography which appeal to plot structures of a distinctively "fictional" sort (Romance, Comedy, Tragedy, and Satire) by which to endow the series with a perceivable form and a conceivable "meaning."

If the series were simply recorded in the order in which the events originally occurred, under the assumption that the ordering of the events in their temporal sequence itself provided a kind of explanation of why they occurred when and where they did, we would have the pure form of the *chronicle*. This would be a "naive" form of chronicle, however, inasmuch as the categories of time and space alone served as the informing interpretative principles. Over against the naive form of chronicle we could postulate as a logical possibility its "sentimental" counterpart, the ironic denial that historical series have any kind of larger significance or describe any imaginable plot structure or indeed can even be construed as a story with a discernible beginning, middle, and end. We could conceive such accounts of history as intending to serve as antidotes to their false or overemplotted counterparts (nos 2, 3, 4, and 5 above) and could represent them as an ironic return to mere chronicle as constituting the only sense which any cognitively responsible history could take. We could characterize such histories thus:

(6)   "*a, b, c, d, e . . . , n*"

with the quotation marks indicating the conscious interpretation of the events as having nothing other than seriality as their meaning.

This schema is of course highly abstract and does not do justice to the possible mixtures of and variations within the types that it is meant to distinguish. But it helps us, I think, to conceive how events might be emplotted in different ways without violating the imperatives of the chronological order of the events (however they are construed) so as to yield alternative, mutually exclusive, and yet, equally plausible interpretations of the set. I have tried to show in *Metahistory* how such mixtures and variations occur in the writings of the master historians of the nineteenth century; and I have suggested in that book that classic historical accounts always represent attempts both to emplot the historical series adequately and implicitly to come to terms with other plausible emplotments. It is this dialectical tension between two or more possible emplotments that signals the element of critical self-consciousness present in any historian of recognizably classical stature.

Histories, then, are not only about events but also about the possible sets of relationships that those events can be demonstrated to figure. These sets of relationships are not, however, immanent in the events themselves; they exist only in the mind of the historian reflecting on them. Here they are present as the modes of relationships conceptualized in the myth, fable, and folklore, scientific knowledge, religion, and literary art, of the historian's own culture. But more importantly, they are, I suggest, immanent in the very language which the historian must use to *describe* events prior to a scientific analysis of them or a fictional emplotment of them. For if the historian's aim is to familiarize us with the unfamiliar, he must use figurative, rather than technical, language. Technical languages are familiarizing only *to* those who have been indoctrinated in their uses and only *of* those sets of events which the practitioners of a discipline have agreed to describe in a uniform terminology. History possesses no such generally accepted technical terminology and in fact no agreement on what kind of events make up its specific subject matter. The historian's characteristic instrument of encodation, communication, and exchange is ordinary educated speech. This implies that the only instruments that he has for endowing his data with meaning, of rendering the strange familiar, and of rendering the mysterious past comprehensible, are the techniques of *figurative* language. All historical narratives presuppose figurative characterizations of the events they purport to represent and explain. And this means that historical narratives, considered purely as verbal artifacts, can be characterized by the mode of figurative discourse in which they are cast.

If this is the case, then it may well be that the kind of emplotment that the historian decides to use to give meaning to a set of historical events is dictated by the dominant figurative mode of the language he has used to *describe* the elements of his account *prior* to his composition of a narrative. Geoffrey Hartman once remarked in my hearing, at a conference on literary history, that he was not sure that he knew what historians of literature might want to do, but he did know that to write a history meant to place an event within a context, by relating it as a part to some conceivable whole. He went on to suggest that as far as he knew, there were only two ways of relating parts to wholes, by metonymy and by synecdoche. Having been engaged for some time in the study of the thought of Giambattista Vico, I was much taken with this thought, because it conformed to Vico's notion that the "logic" of all "poetic wisdom" was contained in the relationships which language itself provided in the four principal modes of figurative representation:

metaphor, metonymy, synecdoche, and irony. My own hunch – and it is
a hunch which I find confirmed in Hegel's reflections on the nature of
nonscientific discourse – is that in any field of study which, like history,
has not yet become disciplinized to the point of constructing a formal
terminological system for describing its objects, in the way that physics
and chemistry have, it is the types of figurative discourse that dictate the
fundamental forms of the data to be studied. This means that the *shape*
of the *relationships* which will appear to be inherent in the objects
inhabiting the field will in reality have been imposed on the field by the
investigator in the very *act of identifying and describing* the objects that
he finds there. The implication is that historians *constitute* their subjects
as possible objects of narrative representation by the very language they
use to *describe* them. And if this is the case, it means that the different
kinds of historical interpretations that we have of the same set of events,
such as the French Revolution as interpreted by Michelet, Tocqueville,
Taine, and others, are little more than projections of the linguistic protocols that these historians used to *pre*-figure that set of events prior to
writing their narratives of it. It is only a hypothesis, but it seems possible that the conviction of the historian that he has "found" the form
of his narrative in the events themselves, rather than imposed it upon
them, in the way the poet does, is a result of a certain lack of linguistic
self-consciousness which obscures the extent to which descriptions of
events *already* constitute interpretations of their nature. As thus envisaged, the difference between Michelet's and Tocqueville's accounts of
the Revolution does not reside only in the fact that the former emplotted
his story in the modality of a Romance and the latter his in the modality
of Tragedy; it resides as well in the tropological mode – metaphorical
and metonymic, respectively – which each brought to his apprehension
of the facts as they appeared in the documents.

I do not have the space to try to demonstrate the plausibility of this
hypothesis, which is the informing principle of my book *Metahistory*.
But I hope that this essay may serve to suggest an approach to the study
of such discursive prose forms as historiography, an approach that is as
old as the study of rhetoric and as new as modern linguistics. Such a
study would proceed along the lines laid out by Roman Jakobson in a
paper entitled "Linguistics and Poetics," in which he characterized the difference between Romantic poetry and the various forms of nineteenth-
century Realistic prose as residing in the essentially metaphorical nature
of the former and the essentially metonymical nature of the latter. I think
that this characterization of the difference between poetry and prose is
too narrow, because it presupposes that complex macrostructural narratives such as the novel are little more than projections of the "selective"
(i.e. phonemic) axis of all speech acts. Poetry, and especially Romantic
poetry, is then characterized by Jakobson as a projection of the "combin-
atory" (i.e. morphemic) axis of language. Such a binary theory pushes

the analyst toward a dualistic opposition between poetry and prose which appears to rule out the possibility of a metonymical poetry and a metaphorical prose. But the fruitfulness of Jakobson's theory lies in its suggestion that the various forms of both poetry and prose, all of which have their counterparts in narrative in general and therefore in historiography too, can be characterized in terms of the dominant trope which serves as the paradigm, provided by language itself, of all significant relationships conceived to exist in the world by anyone wishing to represent those relationships in language.

Narrative, or the syntagmatic dispersion of events across a temporal series presented as a prose discourse, in such a way as to display their progressive elaboration as a comprehensible form, would represent the "inward turn" that discourse takes when it tries to *show* the reader the true form of things existing behind a merely apparent formlessness. Narrative *style*, in history as well as in the novel, would then be construed as the modality of the movement from a representation of some original state of affairs to some subsequent state. The primary *meaning* of a narrative would then consist of the destructuration of a set of events (real or imagined) originally encoded in one tropological mode and the progressive restructuration of the set in another tropological mode. As thus envisaged, narrative would be a process of decodation and recodation in which an original perception is clarified by being cast in a figurative mode different from that in which it has come encoded by convention, authority, or custom. And the explanatory force of the narrative would then depend on the contrast between the original encodation and the later one.

For example, let us suppose that a set of experiences comes to us as a grotesque, i.e. as unclassified and unclassifiable. Our problem is to identify the modality of the relationships that bind the discernible elements of the formless totality together in such a way as to make of it a whole of some sort. If we stress the similarities among the elements, we are working in the mode of metaphor; if we stress the differences among them, we are working in the mode of metonymy. Of course, in order to make sense of any set of experiences, we must obviously identify both the parts of a thing that appear to make it up and the nature of the shared aspects of the parts that make them identifiable as a totality. This implies that all original characterizations of anything must utilize *both* metaphor and metonymy in order to "fix" it as something about which we can meaningfully discourse.

In the case of historiography, the attempts of commentators to make sense of the French Revolution are instructive. Burke decodes the events of the Revolution which his contemporaries experience as a grotesque by recoding it in the mode of irony; Michelet recodes these events in the mode of synecdoche; Tocqueville recodes them in the mode of metonymy. In each case, however, the movement from code to recode is narratively described, i.e. laid out on a time-line in such a way as to

make the interpretation of the events that made up the "Revolution" a
kind of drama that we can recognize as Satirical, Romantic, and Tragic,
respectively. This drama can be followed by the reader of the narrative
in such a way as to be experienced as a progressive revelation of what the
true nature of the events consists of. The revelation is not experienced,
however, as a restructuring of perception so much as an illumination of
a field of occurrence. But actually what has happened is that a set of
events originally encoded in one way is simply being decoded by being
recoded in another. The events themselves are not substantially changed
from one account to another. That is to say, the data that are to be analyzed are not significantly different in the different accounts. What is
different are the modalities of their relationships. These modalities, in
turn, although they *may* appear to the reader to be based on different
theories of the nature of society, politics, and history, ultimately have
their origin in the figurative characterizations of the whole set of events
as representing wholes of fundamentally different sorts. It is for this
reason that, when it is a matter of setting different interpretations of the
same set of historical phenomena over against one another in an attempt
to decide which is the best or most convincing, we are often driven to
confusion or ambiguity. This is not to say that we cannot distinguish
between good and bad historiography, since we can always fall back on
such criteria as responsibility to the rules of evidence, the relative fullness of narrative detail, logical consistency, and the like to determine
this issue. But it is to say that the effort to distinguish between good and
bad interpretations of a historical event such as the Revolution is not as
easy as it might at first appear when it is a matter of dealing with alternative interpretations produced by historians of relatively equal learning
and conceptual sophistication. After all, a great historical classic cannot
be disconfirmed or nullified either by the discovery of some new datum
that might call a specific explanation of some element of the whole
account into question or by the generation of new methods of analysis
which permit us to deal with questions that earlier historians might not
have taken under consideration. And it is precisely because great historical
classics, such as works by Gibbon, Michelet, Thucydides, Mommsen,
Ranke, Burckhardt, Bancroft, and so on, cannot be definitely disconfirmed
that we must look to the specifically literary aspects of their work as
crucial, and not merely subsidiary, elements in their historiographical
technique.

  What all this points to is the necessity of revising the distinction conventionally drawn between poetic and prose discourse in discussion of
such narrative forms as historiography and recognizing that the distinction, as old as Aristotle, between history and poetry obscures as much
as it illuminates about both. If there is an element of the historical in all
poetry, there is an element of poetry in every historical account of the
world. And this because in our account of the historical world we are

dependent, in ways perhaps that we are not in the natural sciences, on the techniques of *figurative language* both for our *characterization* of the objects of our narrative representations and for the *strategies* by which to constitute narrative accounts of the transformations of those objects in time. And this because history has no stipulatable subject matter uniquely its own; it is always written as part of a contest between contending poetic figurations of what the past *might* consist of.

The older distinction between fiction and history, in which fiction is conceived as the representation of the imaginable and history as the representation of the actual, must give place to the recognition that we can only know the *actual* by contrasting it with or likening it to the *imaginable*. As thus conceived, historical narratives are complex structures in which a world of experience is imagined to exist under at least two modes, one of which is encoded as "real," the other of which is "revealed" to have been illusory in the course of the narrative. Of course, it is a fiction of the historian that the various states of affairs which he constitutes as the beginning, the middle, and the end of a course of development are all "actual" or "real" and that he has merely recorded "what happened" in the transition from the inaugural to the terminal phase. But both the beginning state of affairs and the ending one are inevitably poetic constructions, and as such, dependent upon the modality of the figurative language used to give them the aspect of coherence. This implies that all narrative is not simply a recording of "what happened" in the transition from one state of affairs to another, but a progressive *redescription* of sets of events in such a way as to dismantle a structure encoded in one verbal mode in the beginning so as to justify a recoding of it in another mode at the end. This is what the "middle" of all narratives consist of.

All of this is highly schematic, and I know that this insistence on the fictive element in all historical narratives is certain to arouse the ire of historians who believe that they are doing something fundamentally different from the novelist, by virtue of the fact that they deal with "real," while the novelist deals with "imagined," events. But neither the form nor the explanatory power of narrative derives from the different contents it is presumed to be able to accommodate. In point of fact, history – the real world as it evolves in time – is made sense of in the same way that the poet or novelist tries to make sense of it, i.e. by endowing what originally appears to be problematical and mysterious with the aspect of a recognizable, because it is a familiar, form. It does not matter whether the world is conceived to be real or only imagined; the manner of making sense of it is the same.

So too, to say that we make sense of the real world by imposing upon it the formal coherency that we customarily associate with the products of writers of fiction in no way detracts from the status as knowledge which we ascribe to historiography. It would only detract from it if we were to believe that literature did not teach us anything about reality, but was a product of an imagination which was not of this world but of some other, inhuman one. In my view, we experience the "fictionalization" of history as an "explanation" for the same reason that we experience great fiction as an illumination of a world that we inhabit along with the author. In both we recognize the forms by which consciousness both constitutes and colonizes the world it seeks to inhabit comfortably.

Finally, it may be observed that if historians were to recognize the fictive element in their narratives, this would not mean the degradation of historiography to the status of ideology or propaganda. In fact, this recognition would serve as a potent antidote to the tendency of historians to become captive of ideological preconceptions which they do not recognize as such but honor as the "correct" perception of "the way things *really* are." By drawing historiography nearer to its origins in literary sensibility, we should be able to identify the ideological, because it is the fictive, element in our own discourse. We are always able to see the fictive element in those historians with whose interpretations of a given set of events we disagree; we seldom perceive that element in our own prose. So, too, if we recognized the literary or fictive element in every historical account, we would be able to move the teaching of historiography onto a higher level of self-consciousness than it currently occupies.

What teacher has not lamented his inability to give instruction to apprentices in the *writing* of history? What graduate student of history has not despaired at trying to comprehend and imitate the model which his instructors *appear* to honor but the principles of which remain uncharted? If we recognize that there is a fictive element in all historical narrative, we would find in the theory of language and narrative itself the basis for a more subtle presentation of what historiography consists of than that which simply tells the student to go and "find out the facts" and write them up in such a way as to tell "what really happened."

In my view, history as a discipline is in bad shape today because it has lost sight of its origins in the literary imagination. In the interest of *appearing* scientific and objective, it has repressed and denied to itself its own greatest source of strength and renewal. By drawing historiography back once more to an intimate connection with its literary basis, we should not only be putting ourselves on guard against *merely* ideological distortions; we should be by way of arriving at that "theory" of history without which it cannot pass for a "discipline" at all.

Note

This essay is a revised version of a lecture given before the Comparative Literature Colloquium of Yale University on 24 January, 1974. In it I have tried to elaborate some of the themes that I originally discussed in an article, "The

Structure of Historical Narrative," *Clio* I (1972): 5–20. I have also drawn upon the materials of my book *Metahistory: The Historical Imagination in Nineteenth-Century Europe* (Baltimore, 1973), especially the introduction, entitled "The Poetics of History." The essay profited from conversations with Michael Holquist and Geoffrey Hartman, both of Yale University and both experts in the theory of narrative. The quotations from Claude Lévi-Strauss are taken from his *Savage Mind* (London, 1966) and "Overture to *Le Cru et le cuit*," in *Structuralism*, ed. Jacques Ehrmann (New York, 1966). The remarks on the iconic nature of metaphor draw upon Paul Henle, *Language, Thought, and Culture* (Ann Arbor, 1966). Jakobson's notions of the tropological nature of style are in "Linguistics and Poetics," in *Style and Language*, ed. Thomas A. Sebeok (New York and London, 1960). In addition to Northrop Frye's *Anatomy of Criticism* (Princeton, 1957), see also his essay on philosophy of history, "New Directions from Old," in *Fables of Identity* (New York, 1963). On story and plot in historical narrative in R. G. Collingwood's thought, see, of course, *The Idea of History* (Oxford, 1956).

2

Interpretation, History, and Narrative

Noël Carroll

1 Introduction: Historical Narratives as Fictions and as Metaphors

At present, one of the most recurrent views in the philosophy of history claims that historical writing is interpretive and that a primary form that this interpretation takes is narration. Furthermore, narration, according to this approach, is thought to possess an inevitably fictional element, viz., a plot, and, in this regard, the work of the narrative historian is said to be more like that of the imaginative writer than has been admitted heretofore. The upshot of this philosophically, moreover, is the assertion that historical narrations, *qua* narrative interpretations, are to be assessed, in large measure, in terms of the kind of criterion of truth that is appropriate to literary works. And a subsidiary, though far less tendentious, consequence is that our understanding of historical interpretation can profit from literary or "discourse" analysis.

This position, which was perhaps anticipated by Nietzsche,[1] is suggested in varying degrees by Roland Barthes[2] and Louis Mink;[3] it has been developed most extensively by Hayden White;[4] and it commands a following among historians, literary critics, and philosophers of history.[5]

For White, historical writing is interpretive in several separable, though interrelated, registers. Historical argumentation in the dissertative mode involves a paradigm choice; second, in a broad sense, a historical tract requires the choice of an ideological perspective; and, also, a historical narrative itself enjoins a choice of a plot structure, which, in turn, is related to the discursive tropes that "figure" the writing of the text.[6] For the purposes of this essay, it is White's conclusions about the specific status that he assigns to narrative interpretation which preoccupy us.[7]

Stated roughly, White identifies historical discourse with interpretation and historical interpretation with narrativization. A historical narrative is not a *transparent* representation or copy of a sequence of past events. Narration irreducibly entails selecting the events to be included in its exposition as well as filling in links that are not available in the evidential record. The historian does not find or discover her narrative; she constructs it. This process of construction involves distortion[8] and the imposition of generic plot structures (such as Romance, Tragedy, Comedy, and Satire) on the sequence of past events. The plot structures that are culturally available to the narrative historian are inherently fictional; they are not merely neutral, formal armatures on which events are displayed; they have a content – hence, White's emphasis on the notion of the *content of form*. Moreover, that content is fictional.

This conclusion, however, does not lead White to argue that historical interpretations cannot be truthful. Rather they are truthful, but in the way that White takes fictions to be truthful. That is, historical narratives, like fictional narratives, are, by virtue of their plot structures, true in the ways that metaphors are true.

Marx's characterization of the Eighteenth Brumaire of Louis Bonaparte as a farce is assessable in the same way that the sentence "our last faculty meeting was a farce" is assessable. Here, the presiding idea is that there is a variety of metaphorical truth, in contradistinction to literal truth, and that fictions and that historical narratives (with plot structures derived ultimately from myths) are a subspecies thereof.

In according historical narrative this means, albeit fictional in nature, of characterizing reality, White stands at odds with various Continental theorists, such as Lévi-Strauss[9] and the *Annales* school,[10] who disparage narrative history as regressively unscientific, alternatively mythic and fantastic. White, in contrast, grants historical narration cognitive purchase, specifically in terms of metaphor (though sometimes he also uses the notion of allegory to make this point).

White summarizes his position succinctly by saying:

> To emplot real events as a story of a specific kind (or as a mixture of stories of a specific kind) is to trope these events. This is because stories are not lived; there is no such thing as a "real" story. Stories are told or written, not found. And as for the notion of a "true" *story*, this is virtually a contradiction in terms. *All* stories are fictions which means, of course, that they can be "true" in a metaphorical sense and in the sense in which any figure of speech can be true. Is this true enough?[11]

Though as a slogan this is quite pointed, it does require some care in order to understand what White is asserting. Contra Paul Ricoeur's analysis of White,[12] White is not entirely erasing the distinction between fiction and historical writing. Historical writing does refer to past events and those references must be supportable on the basis of the evidential record. In virtue of this evidential requirement, historical writing can be assessed in terms of a literal criterion for truth in a way that fictional exercises should not be. However, in addition to this standard of truth, the historical narrative – i.e. the selection, combination, and arrangement of events attested to by the record – is to be evaluated by another criterion, one shared with fictional narratives – to wit: metaphorical aptness.

In this regard, there is a superficial resemblance between the structure of White's account of historical interpretation and Joseph Margolis's notion of robust relativism. For Margolis, the descriptions that ground interpretations are susceptible to evaluation in terms of truth and falsity, whereas the overall interpretation requires some other sort of assessment, say in terms of plausibility.[13] For White, the notation of the events by the historian is responsible to literal canons of evidence, whereas the narrative constructions themselves are metaphorically true. The historian promotes understanding in her reader by casting a sequence of historical events in the form of a culturally shared and familiar narrative pattern (e.g. tragedy), and we assimilate the past under a common myth. This pattern of meaning – embodied in the plot structure, which itself has a kind of mythic content – illuminates insofar as it is a serviceable analog for the past.

So far, I have merely offered a sketch of historical constructivism *à la* White. In the next section, I will try to refine the various arguments that he uses to advance this position, and, in the concluding section, I will review the problems that confront White at almost every turn, along with offering a diagnosis of certain of the deep presuppositions that I believe lead White astray.

2 White's Arguments

White characterizes his approach as concerned with a *specifically* historical kind of writing[14] and he explicitly aligns himself with the narrativist, as opposed to a *scientific*, conception of historiography.[15] This seems extravagant to me, for clearly science can be narrative in form – e.g. the geological account of the disposition of the continents – without ceasing to be scientific, and, therefore, narrative cannot be the quiddity of history as differentiated from science.[16] However, even if White's commitment to narrativism is sometimes overzealous, his position is still a challenging one. For, obviously, history is often (most often?) presented in narrative form – even if narration is not the essence of historical exposition – and, thus, the finding (if it is that) that historical narrative is always in fundamental ways fictional remains a significant epistemological thesis.[17]

White's leading idea is that historical interpretation is a construction or an imposition on a sequence of past events insofar as it involves narration. The coherence that narration supplies to a sequence of events is an imaginative invention. The historical series of events is not coherent – despite the claims of speculative philosophers of history like Hegel; rather, historical events begin to take coherent shape only through the historian's narrative efforts.

In this respect, White is not thoroughly anti-realist; he does not deny that the past existed. He is only opposed to the notion that there are "real stories," that is, that narratives of the past reflect the structure of ongoing, successive, past events. The past, in other words, is not storied, and representing sequences of events in story form is, strictly speaking, adding something to them.

Furthermore, even if the references to past events in the historical account are assessable in terms of truth or falsity, that added "something" – the narrative configuration or pattern (which is more than the conjunction of all the truth-functional references in a historical account) – is not. It must be evaluated as metaphor or allegory. That is, narrative histories must be thought of in terms of something called *narrative truth* which involves more than establishing the truth-values of the conjunction of the atomic sentences that comprise them and which is spoken of as a different kind of truth.[18]

On White's account, typical historiographic practice proceeds under the assumption that narrative historians are discovering the structure of past processes – that is to say, "real stories." But for White stories are invented, not found, and their invention by historians is structurally continuous with the efforts of authors of fiction. Thus, historical narratives are on a par with fictional narratives in this respect, and their cognitive value, *qua* narration, is of a piece with things like novels – viz., they are sources of metaphorical insight.

White attempts to support his view with a wide range of considerations, involving slogans, contrasts, and analyses of the nature of narrative. These different forms of argumentation build on and segue with each other in various ways. Their effect, one supposes, is meant to be cumulative, though one also suspects that White thinks that each has force independently of the others. So for purposes of this presentation, I will introduce them as separate considerations, while also taking note of the ways in which later analyses and arguments build on and flesh out earlier ones.

White's often repeated[19] core slogan, which he shares with Louis Mink,[20] is that lives are lived and stories are told. Our lives do not come packaged as stories; we invent stories about them retrospectively through imaginative effort. Thus, the historians' narrative cannot be taken as a reflection of the lives lived by historical agents. If historians think this way – as White believes they do, despite what they may say – then narrative historians are woefully mistaken.

Though the invocation of "lives" here, as we shall see, is too restrictive as well as infelicitous in other ways, what is intended can be put more rigorously and comprehensively: "Histories, then, are not only about events but also about the possible sets of relationships that those events can be demonstrated to figure. These sets of relationships are not, however, immanent in the events themselves; they exist only in the mind of the historian reflecting on them."[21]

This slogan is fleshed out in terms of various, further contrasts. Since the past is not storied, historical narratives are not *found* or *discovered*; rather they are *invented*.[22] In this sense, historical narratives are con-structions[23] – constructions that give a sequence of events, such as one might find notated in a historical chronicle or annal, a *meaning*.[24] Historical narratives, in this regard, are also said to *constitute* meaning.[25]

But events, as lived, do not have meanings. They only get meanings by being invested with a function in a narrative. That the Battle of Stalingrad was the *turning point* of World War II, for example, acquires this significance by being a complication in a narrative plot about World War II. The Battle of Stalingrad, *qua* event, had no meaning; and, indeed, it could figure in other stories in which it would have a different meaning. (In an architectual history, for example, the significance of the battle might be that it occasioned the destruction of important buildings.)

Related to the meaning/real event contrast is a contrast between meaning and a copy of an event. Putatively, practicing historians have the naive view that their narratives could be *copies* of events past – by which I understand White to mean something like a perfect replica or mirror-image.[26] But historical writing cannot afford a perfect simulacrum of the past. It involves selection and filling in; so it is actually a deviation from an exact copy or representation of the succession of events. In fact, White does not hesitate to call it a *distortion*,[27] presumably a distortion in contrast to whatever would count as a perfect replica or mirror-image of a succession of past events.

Narration has its own conditions of intelligibility. Narrative coherence requires features like beginnings, middles, and ends – ends, particularly in the technical sense of closure. But, on what must be ontological grounds, White thinks it is obvious that events do not emerge from the flux of history closured. Closure is a product of narrative coherence. It is the aim of achieving narrative coherence that leads to the selection and hierarchical ordering that imbues the relevant events with meaning, while also *distorting* them in the sense at play in the preceding paragraph.

Narrative coherence, then, is an *imposition*[28] on the historical past. Moreover, the patterns of narrative coherence thus imposed upon (or constructed out of) a collection of historical events are *conventional* (rather than, say, realistically motivated).[29] This inventing, distorting, constructing, imposing, constituting, meaning-making (signifying), and convention-applying activity are all acts of the imagination (in contrast, one supposes, to some more literal information-assimilating process). Moreover, this imaginative activity on the part of narrative historians is not different in kind from the activity of the literary fabulist and should be treated as telling us about the world in the same way.

White runs his various foils to actual sequences of events (and perfect replicas thereof) together rather indiscriminately. That is, imagining, constructing, distorting, signifying, constituting, and so on are never scrupulously and differentially defined, and they are all used to serve roughly the same purpose: to underpin the animating distinction between living (the succession of real events) and telling (narrating). One would think that signifying, imagining, distorting, conventionalizing, and so on – not to mention selecting – (though potentially interrelated in interesting ways) should not be lumped together so cavalierly. However, in White's brief they serve as "intuition pumps"[30] directed at consolidating the reigning slogan that distinguishes between living (history as process) and telling (history as narrative *artifact*). Each contrast, that is, is meant to convince us of a disjunction between a sequence of real events or a perfect replica thereof (whatever that might be) and a narrative structure which introduces fictional elements into the flow of events.

White expands upon and concretizes his slogans and intuition pumps by exploiting analyses of narrative by literary theorists – both those of the recent structuralist/poststructuralist dispensation, and that of Northrop Frye.

From Continental literary theory, White derives the idea of what he calls "narrativizing discourse."[31] This is putatively discourse that gives the impression that there is no narrator. It is the discourse that in contemporary literary circles is often called "transparent," that is, writing which presents itself to the reader as unmediated and full – a transcription of reality without gaps: "the whole unvarnished truth and nothing but," so to speak. Such discourse, ostensibly appearing without a narrator, presents itself as if "the events seem to tell themselves."[32] The property of "events telling themselves" is called narrativity, and discourse that imbues the events it recounts with this property is narrativizing.

The transparency or narrativizing effect is the hallmark of what many literary theorists call the realist text, such as is supposedly found in the form of the nineteenth-century novel. In adopting the narrating strategies of the realist text, the historian, likewise, presents events as if they were "telling themselves." For White, this implies that naive, narrative historians really have a deep, though unacknowledged and even disavowed, affinity with substantive philosophers of history, like Marx and Hegel, who see the historical process as a single unfolding story – history speaking through the acts of humankind. Thus, if substantive philosophers of history are open to criticism, then less grandiose but nevertheless still narrativizing historians should be vulnerable to the same kind of criticisms.

So, both ordinary narrativizing historians and philosophers of history can be charged with distortion and with masking their highly selective procedures with an imaginary aura of coherence, integrity, and fullness that exploits our desires (for coherence, etc.), but which misrepresents reality.[33] White writes, "Does the world really present itself to perception in the form of well-made stories, with central subjects, proper beginnings, middles and ends, and a coherence that permits us to see 'the end' in every beginning?"[34] Any form of narrativity – which is the presupposition that narrative structure literally corresponds to something in the historical past – amounts to the belief that "events tell themselves." But "real events should not speak, should not tell themselves. Real events should simply be."[35] Or, to return to White's earlier slogan: stories can't be found because *real stories* aren't out there in the world of the past to be found. . . .

3 Resisting White's Constructivism

. . . According to White, lives are lived and stories are told. The putative consequence of this is that insofar as historical narratives represent the lives of the past in story form, they do not correspond to what existed in the past and are, therefore, fictional. This is not compelling comprehensively. For it is often the case that we plan – if not our entire lives, at least important episodes therein – by means of telling or visualizing stories to ourselves, and, then, we go about enacting them. That is, lives can be storied; indeed there is a branch of psychology that uses this idea as a research hypothesis.[36] Consequently, with certain life episodes – and, in some cases, perhaps with some monomaniacal lives – there are stories, hatched by historical agents, that had causal efficacy in the past and which could be discovered and written up by historians. Thus, to the extent that the contrast between lives and stories is not thoroughly exclusive, the conclusion that any historical narrative must be fictional is not without exception; there could be historical narratives of storied lives, or, at least, of storied episodes in the lives of historical agents.

Of course, this is not the real issue that the lives/stories dichotomy is meant to broach. For historians are not merely biographers in search of life stories. The contrast between lives and stories is meant to call to mind colorfully the idea that historical narratives are not found or discovered in the past, but are constructions or inventions. The notion of *invention* here is a bit tricky and open to equivocation. In one sense, historical narratives are inventions, viz., in the sense that they are made by historians; but it is not clear that it follows from this that they are *made-up* (and are, therefore, fictional).

Narratives are a form of representation, and it is true that historians do not go about finding their representations as one might find a lost picture, a lost photo, or a lost piece of film footage. Photos and film strips are made (invented) and they are not found. We could say that lives are lived, and home movies are invented. But this doesn't entail that a stretch of film footage cannot record the past or yield accurate information about it. Similarly, narratives are a form of representation, and, in that sense, they are invented, but that does not preclude their capacity to provide accurate information. Narratives can provide accurate knowledge about the past in terms of the kinds of features they track, namely, the ingredients of *courses of events*,[37] which include: background conditions, causes and effects, as well as social context, the logic of situations, practical deliberations, and ensuing actions.

Recently, for example, on July 3, 1989, the United States Supreme Court announced a decision that delegated responsibility for regulating the availability of abortions to the discretion of individual states. This decision was the result, in significant respects, of the success of the Reagan regime in appointing a series of like-minded, conservative judges to the Supreme Court. The appointment of those judges, including O'Connor and Scalia, in the context of a background project of contesting the perceived past liberalism of the Supreme Court, was part of a real historical process, a course of events, that culminated on July 3, 1989.

This is not to say that there will not be further consequences to the court's decision nor that this is the *final* culmination of Reagan's successful efforts to reorient the court. But the fact that there is more to come does not vitiate the fact that the Reagan administration's decisions and appointments were significant ingredients in a real historical process which had as one result – *one*, for there will be more – the decision on July 3, 1989. The historian who tracks these decisions and appointments, situating them in their social contexts, will make something – something that may take imagination to accomplish – namely, a historical representation. But there is no reason to suppose that such historical representations are necessarily *made-up* or invented unless, for some as yet undemonstrated reason, courses of events must be excluded from our ontology. Moreover, if courses of events are admissable ontologically, then they are there to be discovered and represented.

That my counterexamples so far often rely on the idea of deliberations and decisions implemented in ensuing actions may appear open to the objection that they presuppose a commitment on the part of historians to recreating the internal perspective of historical agents. This, in turn, would be criticized as problematic for two related reasons. First, that historians are not simply concerned with narrating events in terms of how the agents saw them *and* that, even if historians were so disposed, they should not be so exclusively preoccupied since it is often (most often?) the unintended consequences of people's deliberations and decisions about which we most care.

These objections, however, require two remarks. First, if there are courses of events that did issue as planned from the agent's perhaps storied deliberation, this would be enough to show that there is a sense in which the thesis that stories are never found fails to be fully comprehensive. But a second and more important point is that in speaking of courses of events, we are not committed to rendering them solely in terms of the original intentions of the agents involved in them. A course of events may involve failed attempts, like Reagan's nomination of Bork to the Supreme Court, which will result in more deliberative activity which may have further unintended consequences. Or, the agent's deliberative activity may involve miscalculations that call for the historian to illuminate the prevailing conditions that made the attempt misfire. That practical reasoning and its implementation in action provide some of the ingredients that make a course of events cohere in no way implies that the representation of a course of events will be a string of successful practical syllogisms. That practical, deliberative activity will supply some measure of cohesiveness to the narratives of human events does not restrict us to a form of historical intentionalism nor does it preclude discussion of corporate entities like states or classes.[38]

Of course, in speaking of courses of events, I do not mean to imply that any given event is only a member of one course of events. The appointment of Sandra Day O'Connor to the Supreme Court is part of the course of events that led to the decision alluded to above. But that event also undoubtedly figured in various other courses of events – some in the history of the O'Connor family and some concerning the social advancement of women in the United States. And, equally, the event of O'Connor's appointment will also figure in courses of events still in the making. The same event can be part of different courses of events, and, therefore, can be represented in different stories. But the fact that different events can figure in different stories in no way indicates that the stories are fictional. For this suspicion to counterfeit plausibility, we would have to assume that in order to be nonfictional, there would have to be only one relevant story, perhaps of the sort proposed by speculative philosophers of history, and that each event in it would be significant in one and only one way. That is, if there is more than one story, then stories are invented, and, therefore, fictional. But the presumed disjunction that either there is one real story or a multiplicity of fictional ones fails to accommodate the fact that courses of action intersect and branch off from shared events, which intersections and branches can be found or discovered.

In White's way of speaking, when a given event is situated in different narratives it can acquire a different meaning. That events have these differential meanings indicates that they are imposed and, therefore, fictional. But talk of meanings here may be a little misleading. Events have different significances in different courses of events.[39] Antonin Scalia's appointment to the Supreme Court has one significance in terms of the great abortion debate and another, though perhaps not completely unrelated, significance in the history of Italian-Americans. In these examples, the idea of significance can be cashed in causally. If *meaning* here amounts to playing a role in a network of socially significant causation, then there should be no problems in admitting that Scalia's appointment may have a different meaning in different courses of events. This simply allows that a single event can play a different role in different causal chains. This does not indicate that a meaning has been imposed on the event. Again, the event may occur in different stories because the different stories track different courses of overlapping events.[40]

White's use of the notion of meaning in his arguments gives his thesis a semantic flavor, which perhaps suggests a level of arbitrariness that would warrant talk of imposition. However, it is important to stress that the kind of *meaning* that an event has in a narrative is a matter of its significance with respect to subsequent events, often in terms of causation and/or practical reasoning. And whether significance in this sense obtains is not arbitrary or imposed. That the historian wants to know what caused the American entry into WWII does not make her citation of the attack on Pearl Harbor an imposition on the historical train of events nor is her imputation of causal efficacy to the attack arbitrary in any way. This is not to deny that events in historical narratives will be events under a description; but within the context of a given research project, the description of a pertinent event is not arbitrary in the way that on some views of language the relation between a signifier and a signified is arbitrary. Similarly, it is not helpful to think of the historian's description of an action in terms of its significance in a course of events as constitutive of the event in any strong sense; whether Pearl Harbor, for example, was a cause of WWII is a fact even if it were not asserted in historical accounts.

White contrasts historical narratives replete with meanings to copies of the past. The historical narrative, involving selection and abduction, is not a copy of the past, and, therefore, is fictional. The contrast here seems forced; the visual references to copies and mirrors is particularly strained though revelatory of an empiricist residue in White's thinking. Obviously, historical narratives are not mirror images of the past; in general (save things like cinematic documentaries) they are not even pictorial, let alone perfect pictorial replicas of anything. But why should the fact that they are not pictures imply they are fictions?

However, the preceding worry misses the point. The idea of a copy of the past should probably be understood metaphorically. A copy of the past would be a perfect reflection of everything that transpired in the relevant time span with nothing added or subtracted. It would bear an exact correspondence to all and only what came about, or even more strictly, to what could have been perceived as past events unfolded. Anything that falls short of this is said to be fictional.

Of course, it is difficult to imagine that practicing historians pursue the production of such copies in their work, or that, informed as they are of the historical evidence, they construe their narratives as perfect replicas of the past. But White, it seems, wants to confront them with a dilemma. Either historical narratives are copies in the relevant sense or they are fictional. The way to deal with this dilemma is to reject it – to maintain that historical narratives are not and, in fact, should not be copies in the mirror sense while also maintaining that this does not make them fictional.

The notion that only copies in the mirror sense would not be fictional presupposes something like a narrowly empiricist, correspondence criterion of truth. White explicitly denies the viability of this approach in one sense – he denies that historical narratives could meet it. However, this does not seem to lead him to reject the criterion entirely. That is, he appears to continue to regard it as the ideal criterion for nonfictional historical exposition, even if it is an unrealizable ideal. And, to the extent that it is unrealizable, he consigns historical narration to the realm of fiction. But what is strange here is that White doesn't take the inapplicability of this ideal of truth as a grounds for advancing alternative criteria of nonfictional truth for historical narratives.

Confronted by the inapplicability of the copy ideal of an empiricist view of correspondence truth, it seems to me that the line one should take is to search for some other grounds for accommodating the truth of historical narratives construed as nonfictional. That is, we should hold onto the intuition that historical narratives can be truthful in the way that nonfictional discourse is true, drop the expectation that this is explicable in terms of a naive view of correspondence to the past as a whole, and explore alternative models. White, in effect, maintains the criteria of empiricist correspondence, which leads him to reassigning historical narration to the realm of fiction. In this respect, oddly enough, he turns out to be a closet empiricist – presupposing that anything that falls short of the correspondence standard is fictional.[41]

Undoubtedly, there is a parallel between White's strategy here and that of many deconstructionists. When they note the failure of certain theories of language on the grounds that no language is an absolute mirror of the world, they conclude that meaning is an arbitrary, infinitely fluctuating construct rather than surmising that the expectation that a language might absolutely mirror the world was a theoretical error to begin with, and that a better view of the way in which a language is objectively constrained should be sought. That is, they remain in the thrall of a bad theory of language, employing it to motivate their skepticism, at the same time that they agree that no language squares with the idealization. This is akin to reasoning that either existence has an absolute meaning ordained by God or it has no meaning; since there is no God, there is no meaning. This way of thinking shares the theistic assumption that only something like God could serve as a source of meaning. An alternative would be to search for other sources of meaning once the hypothesis that there is no God is endorsed. Similarly, in consigning historical narration to the realm of fiction on the grounds that it is not a perfect replica of the past, White remains implicitly in the very empiricist camp from which he explicitly wishes to part company.

Armed with the copy ideal of nonfictionality, White recycles the issue of selectivity, which must be the most perennial pretext for suspecting the objectivity of historical narration. Obviously, a narrative selects a subset of events and event relationships from the historical flow; thus, if candidacy for nonfictionality depends on correspondence to the whole past, or the whole past within certain stipulated time parameters, a historical narrative will be discounted. But, again, this should lead us to drop the copy ideal of nonfictionality and not to jettison the idea that historical narratives are nonfictional. This is not the place to review all the arguments that are designed to show that the selectivity of historical narratives need not be epistemologically problematic in any way that warrants special attention. Some historians may select the events they highlight in dubitable ways, but there are procedures for ascertaining whether the processes of selection a given historian employs are questionable. That is, historians may produce distortive representations of the past because of biased procedures, but this only goes to show that the selective attention of a given narrative may be distorting, and not that selectivity, in and of itself, is problematic. If it were, then scientific findings, which are also selective, would also, by parity of reasoning, be fictional.

White, himself, may remain unmoved by our last argument. For he is apparently convinced of the constructivist/conventionalist view of science. Thus, he seems to gain confidence by analogizing historical narratives with scientific theories, as construed by constructivists. Surmising that scientific theories are constructed on the basis of observational data that underdetermine theory choice, which data themselves are theory-laden, White thinks of narratives as similarly constructed, in contexts where the data would support alternative stories, and he thinks of narrative events as, so to speak, story-laden. Thus, if the adoption of a scientific theory is conventional, given the putative fact that it is one construction of the data within a range of equally acceptable ones, then historical narratives, assuming the analogy to scientific theories, are equally conventional. Their selective organization of the data does not correspond to reality, but is an invention developed within conventional choice procedures. Thus, one dispels the argument of the preceding paragraph by maintaining that scientific selectivity forces us to concede that scientific theories are imaginative constructions – and in that sense fictions – and, therefore, no incongruity is engendered by maintaining that comparable processes of selection with respect to historical narratives render them fictional as well.[42]

A major problem with this invocation of the philosophy of science is that it presumes that the facts of scientific theorizing pointed to by constructivists entail anti-realism. But a solid case for the compatibility of scientific realism with the facts of the history of science, upon which constructivists rely, is available,[43] thereby blocking any facile attempt to derive historical anti-realism with respect to narrative from scientific anti-realism with respect to theories. That is, the selective procedures and inferred nature of theoretical entities does not commit us to anti-realism; it does not force us to deny that scientific theories are approximately true. Therefore, even if suitable analogies could be drawn between constructivism in science and constructivism in historiography,[44] we would not have to regard historical narratives as fictional.

A course of events transpiring between t1 and t5 need not comprise every event or state of affairs in its temporal neighborhood. Therefore, a narrative representation that tracks that course of events need not refer to every occurrence in the stipulated time span. Narratives are selective but this is appropriate given the nature of courses of events. Nor is it useful to call the reconstruction of a course of events distortive just because it involves selection. Indeed, from the perspective of attempting cognitively to assimilate a representation of the past, the portrayal of a course of events that chronicled all of the events in the temporal neighborhood would distort insofar as it would muddy the links between the pertinent elements in the sequence.

Likewise, our narrative accounts may have to be revised in the light of subsequent events; this does not show that historical narratives are fictional, but only that there are always more stories to tell. Moreover, that some historical narratives may be superseded by ones that are more fine-grained no more shows that the earlier ones were fictional than the adjustment of one approximately true scientific theory with further details (atomic theory amplified by the characterization of subatomic particles) shows that the earlier viewpoint must now be evaluated according to a different standard of truth.

No historical narrative says everything there is to say, not even about all of the events within the time frame that it discusses. The historian exercises choice in the sense that the linkage between some events and not others will be given salience in order to illuminate a given course of events. It is true, as White repeatedly emphasizes, that in charting these linkages and in making the relevant selections, the historian uses her imagination. But, *pace* White, it is quite a long throw from the historian's use of her imagination in discerning said linkages to the inference that the historian's narrative is on a par with that of the imaginative writer (i.e. the writer of fiction). White appears to presume that there is a correlation between the use of the imagination and fiction. But this is illicit. On many views of the imagination, such as Kant's, the imagination plays a role in perception, but my perception of my house is in no way fictional.

Many of White's arguments for the fictionality of historical narrative hinge on contrasting said narratives with copies of the past. Any addition (imaginative construction) or subtraction of detail (selection) from such a copy, conceived of on the model of a mirror, is evidence of fictionality. But the foil is inadmissible. Not only is the visual metaphor inapplicable – it is not the case that not being an exact copy of x entails being a fictional representation of x; but it indicates a residual commitment to a very radical version of an empiricist expectation of exact "perceptual" correspondence between a representation and its referent, which is not only philosophically bogus but is at odds with White's own suspicion of empiricism. Like the skeptic who arrives at her position by accepting a phenomenalist account of perception and who, therefore, remains effectively an empiricist, White regards historical narration as fictional, because he continues to employ something as implausible as perceptual correspondence as the standard of nonfictionality.

White's emphasis on the verbal dimension of historical narration sends him to contemporary discourse theory for insight. There he encounters the idea that narration in what is called the realist text gives the reader the impression that the text is transparent – that it is unmediated, for example, by a narrator exercising selectivity – indeed, that it is as if the text were reality narrating itself. This corresponds to White's own view that historians write as if they were discovering real stories, stories immanent in the historical process, whereas they are really fitting pre-existing story templates onto past events. The ideas that "events narrate themselves" and that the historian, so to speak, records them as a dictaphone might, ostensibly shows acceptance of the disreputable assumption of speculative philosophers of history to the effect that the historical process is storied – i.e. that historical events have a single significance in some overarching historical narrative.

This is a very perplexing argument. It begins by attributing transparency – or narrativity, as White calls it – to realist texts. But to whom does the text appear transparent? Presumably, to naive readers and to the naive historians who write under the supposedly misguided faith that they could track a historical course of events. These naive readers and writers are somehow possessed by the idea that reality is narrating itself. Stated this way, the belief attributed to them is at least obscure and, on a number of readings, absurd.

It is absurd to think of events as telling or narrating their own story in any literal sense, as White notes. But, in fact, it is so absurd on a literal reading that it is hard to believe that any readers or writers, no matter how naive, can be taken in by it. No one could believe that reality literally narrates itself, so it is an inadequate starting point from which to field a dialectically alternative account. It is, so to say, an argumentative red herring, rather than a genuine competing theory whose defeat gives way to White's alternative, fictional account of historical narration. That is, faced with a transparency account of historical narration and White's account, we are not moved to White's theory by the all-too-easy defeat of the attributed transparency view, but rather suspect that we have not started with a viable field of competing accounts.

Stated nonabsurdly, but still obscurely, the transparency effect might be thought of as the impression on the part of naive readers and naive historians that the text is unmediated, that it is without gaps, that it renders a full account of the past. However, this too seems to be such a bizarre conviction to attribute to anyone that it is a non-starter. Historians obviously know that they are selecting a series of events from a larger sequence, and readers have only to look at the title page of the book to learn the identity of the narrator/mediator. No one, in short, believes that historical texts are unmediated; or, to put it positively, any informed reader or writer is aware that a text involves selection. In this, everyone agrees with White, and the view that some do not is a straw man. Where there is undoubtedly disagreement is in the assumption that selection implies fictionality. But the burden of proof is on White to show this, and, in my opinion, the only means at his disposal is the dubious, implicit assumption that nonfiction requires exact correspondence.[45]

Associated with White's implicit presumption of a standard of exact correspondence is his apparent view that if one assumes that there are "real stories," then said stories would have to be of the nature of what we can call absolute stories. For any series of events, an event emplotted in a narrative structure that is immanent in the historical process will have one and only one fixed significance. Something like this view is what leads him to believe that the narrative exploits of practicing historians correspond to those of substantive philosophers of history. I suppose that White is prompted to this intuition on the grounds that if one actually composed a nonfictional narrative in accordance with the exact correspondence standard, one would have a unitary picture of the past in which every event had a determinate place. Of course, White, and perhaps everyone else, thinks that this is impracticable. But White goes on to argue from the infeasibility of absolute stories to the fictionality of all historical narratives.

That is, given an event or a series of events, we can develop a number of stories. No event or event series has one final, i.e. *single*, fixed significance for reasons rehearsed above. Events and event series can, through narration, be connected with alternative events and event series. A collection of events, in a manner of speaking, underdetermines the stories in which they can play a role. From this, White infers that there can be no "real stories"; if there were "real stories," immanent in the historical process, events would fall into one and only one train of events, said train inscribed in events like the evolution of Hegel's world spirit. Historical narrative presumes that the historical process is narrativized and if the historical process is narrativized and there are real stories, the significance of each event fits into one and only one story. So, since there is always more than one derivable story, there are no real stories.

But once again, the argument proceeds on the basis of a straw man. The requirement that "real stories" be absolute stories is exorbitant from the outset. Stories will be nonfictionally accurate insofar as they track courses of events. But courses of events overlap and branch, and there is no need to presume – as perhaps Hegel did – that there is only one course of events. Thus, events and series of events may play different roles in different stories. But that events and series of events figure in different stories is no obstacle to those stories being nonfictional. There are different stories because there are discrete courses of events whose interest is relative to the questions the historian asks of the evidence. This relativity, which precludes the possibility of an absolute story, however, does not make the historical narrative fictional. Rather it makes the accuracy of the nonfictional account assessable in terms of what questions are being directed to the relevant courses of events.[46]

Like innumerable poststructuralist commentators, White appears to believe that agreement that there is no absolute interpretation, no final word, so to say, with respect to x, should impel us to avoid the imputation of truth to an interpretation of x. That is, if there is a multiplicity of interpretations available for x, then the question of literal truth goes by the boards. A true interpretation would have to be an absolute interpretation; an absolute interpretation would have to be the final word on its subject; but since there are no such absolute interpretations – here with respect to historical narratives – there is no question of literal truth.

Needless to say, this is a bad argument with respect to literary criticism. To say a literary interpretation is true if and only if it is the only acceptable account of a text is absurd; one does not deny the truth of a literary interpretation by showing that another interpretation is possible. For the other interpretation may be compatible with the interpretation under scrutiny. That a text supports a multiplicity of interpretations does not disallow the possibility that all of them are literally true; the epistemological issue with respect to a collection of interpretations of texts only becomes live when they are inconsistent.

But here it is important to keep two very different arguments separate: one says that truth is inapplicable to interpretations because there is always a multiplicity of acceptable interpretations of x available; the other says that truth is inapplicable to interpretations because there is always, at least in principle, a multiplicity of equally acceptable but inconsistent interpretations of x available. The former view is based on the truism that there may be no absolute interpretation of x, but from that truism it does not follow that several different interpretations of x cannot be conjointly true, for example, that *1984* is about totalitarianism *and* that it is about Stalinism. The pressure to abandon the question of truth with respect to interpretations only impinges when it can be argued that we are always confronted by a multiplicity of incompatible interpretations.

Turning from literary interpretation to historical narration, the pressing question is which of the preceding arguments can be sustained.

Here, it seems to me that it is obvious that there are multiple stories that can be derived from a given set of events, but, without buying into White's confidence in generic emplotment, there is no reason to presume that these different stories must conflict, and, therefore, no reason to believe that they cannot be assessed in terms of literal truth.[47] Sandra Day O'Connor's appointment to the Supreme Court is part of the narrative of recent abortion decisions and part of the narrative of women's social empowerment. These stories need not conflict and both could be true. Insofar as White's arguments about historical narration, unlike Joseph Margolis's arguments about literary interpretation, do not show that different historical narratives can always in principle be nonconverging and inconsistent, historical narrations remain assessable in terms of literal standards of truth.

Again, the recognition that an event or an event series affords an ingredient for more than one story is a truism. It does not force us to concede that historical narratives cannot be assessed in terms of literal truth. Nor does it seem compelling to suppose that ordinary historians must buy into the presuppositions of substantive philosophers of history in order to regard their narratives in terms of truth. For there is no logical requirement that true narratives be absolutely true. Historians can trace alternative courses of events without presupposing that some one course of event is privileged because history is *the* story of human emancipation or class struggle. . . .

Underlying White's overall view, it seems to me, is a picture of the following sort: a narrative, specifically a nonfiction narrative, is a collection of sentences ordered in a certain way. Narratives, however, are not simply evaluated in terms of the truth or falsity of their constituent sentences. The way in which the sentences are ordered is also epistemically crucial. But this dimension of epistemic evaluation would not be assessed if the narrative were evaluated solely in terms of the conjunction of the truth-values of its individual, fact-asserting sentences. Moreover, it seems to be presumed that saying a narrative's epistemic adequacy for White would have to be reducible to the assessment of the truth-value of the conjunction of the constituent atomic sentences in the narrative. But since the adequacy of the narrative – with respect to its structure of ordering relations – involves something beyond the truth of the sum of the truth-values of its atomic sentences, the narrative as a whole must, at least in part, be assessable in terms of some other standard.

Furthermore, White also appears to presuppose that the sole epistemic category relevant to the assessment of historical narratives is truth – either literal truth construed on the model of some picture theory in which each atomic sentence corresponds to some past fact (or facts), or to some kind of truth construed in other terms. White then worries that whatever governs the selective structure of a narrative may not correspond to anything in the past. Thus the truth of that structure must be assessable in other terms, such as metaphorical accuracy.

Now if this diagnosis of White's presuppositions is correct, it is easy to avoid his conclusions. First of all, too much is being made of the idea of atomic sentences.[48] Narratives are typically written in sentences. But nothing of great importance should hinge on this. For where the relevant narrative linkages are of the nature of relations between background conditions, causes, effects, reasons, choices, actions, and the like, the text can be reconstructed perspicuously in terms of propositions which can, in turn, be straightforwardly evaluated with respect to truth. In some cases, these reconstructions will be a matter of paraphrasing the individual sentences in such a way as to make the relevant narrative relations obtaining between them evident. In other cases, the sentences found in the text will have to be expanded so as to make narrative linkages that are presupposed or conversationally implied explicit. But paraphrases and expansions of this sort in nowise mandate some special criteria of truth.

Undoubtedly, White might concede the preceding point, but still maintain that it does not get at the heart of his misgivings. For even allowing the paraphrases and expansions adverted to above, he will argue that narratives still add something and that this added something – the principles that guide the narrator's selections – is not to be literally found in the past. To the extent that that something is a matter of linkages like causes and reasons, White's argument is not compelling. However, he is right to point out that we will assess a given narrative as a good narrative in terms of criteria over and above the truthfulness of all of its propositions even when suitably expanded and/or paraphrased. Should this drive us toward regarding narration as fictional and as assessable as metaphor?

I think not. To be an adequate narrative, indeed to be an adequate historical account of any sort, a candidate needs to do more than merely state the truth (indeed, a historical account could contain only true statements and yet be adjudged unacceptable[49]). It must also meet various standards of objectivity. For example, a historical narrative should be comprehensive; it should incorporate all those events which previous research has identified to be germane to the subject that the historian is seeking to illuminate.[50] A narrative of the outbreak of the American Revolution that failed to recount the debates over taxation could include only true, chronologically intelligible statements, and still be regarded as an inadequate standard. Like any other cognitive enterprise, historical narration will be assessed in terms of rational standards which, though they are endorsed because they appear to be reliable guides to the truth, are not reducible to the standard of truth.

Obviously, the selective procedures that historians respect in composing their narratives will be evaluated in terms of all sorts of rational standards, like comprehensiveness, that do not correspond to anything found in the past. However, this does not mean that the selections and deletions in a historical narrative are divorced from literal questions of truth or falsity. For the selections and deletions are assessed in terms of those sorts of standards that experience indicates reliably track the truth.

White's deepest problem seems to be that he believes that truth is the only relevant grounds for the epistemic assessment of historical narratives. And, since narrative selectivity cannot be epistemically assessed without remainder in terms of truth on his correspondence model, it must be assessed in terms of some other standard of truth, such as metaphorical truth. But we can dodge this dilemma by noting that the selections and deletions of a historical narrative are subject to objective standards, which though not unrelated to ascertaining truth, are not reducible to truth. Such standards may be considered our best means for discovering the truth. Desiderata like comprehensiveness are, so to speak, truth-tracking. Thus, in evaluating the selections and deletions the narrative historian makes, we need not feel that we must embrace some special standard of truth, like metaphorical truth. Rather, our concern with historical narratives is that they be true in the ordinary sense of truth and that our assessments of their adequacy in terms of standards like comprehensiveness are keyed to determining truth. That principles governing the inclusion of an event in a narrative, like comprehensiveness, are not reducible to the standard of truth in no way implies that the narrative is fictional, nor that it should be understood as some kind of metaphor. This alternative only presents itself if one mistakenly circumscribes the options for epistemically evaluating nonfiction narratives in the way White does.[51]

White believes that the selections and deletions in a historical narrative are to be explained in terms of literary exigencies. Events are included or excluded with respect to whether they can function as beginnings, middles, and ends in comedies, tragedies, romances, and satires. I doubt that every historical narrative falls or must fall into one of White's generic types, and I even doubt that historical narratives require middles, and ends, in the technical sense of closure. A historical course of affairs may have a turning point and it may have results, but these need not be taken to be mere literary artifacts. Similarly, White writes as though the coherence of a historical narrative is solely a function of a literary imposition. But events in human life very often appear coherent, unfolding in terms of causes, reasons, complications, and consequences, and elucidating these relations between actions and their background conditions need not be exercises in fiction.

White and his followers regard historical interpretation as fictional insofar as it relies on narrative. This follows from their conviction that narrative, as such, is fictional. However, neither the philosophical considerations nor the empirical theses advanced in behalf of these views seem persuasive. At the very least, the reduction of all narrative to the status of fiction seems a desperate and inevitably self-defeating way in which to grant the literary dimension of historiography its due.

Notes

1 See Friedrich Nietzsche, *On the Advantage and Disadvantage of History for Life*, translated by Peter Preuss (Indianapolis, IN: Hackett Publishing Company, 1980). Speaking of "monumental history," for example, Nietzsche claims that this venture risks distorting the past by reinterpreting it according to aesthetic criteria and, thereby, brings it closer to fiction (p. 17). Nietzsche's specific reason for this belief is that insofar as monumental history functions to provide models for emulation, it will occlude attention to sufficient causes in order to produce representations available for imitation.

2 Roland Barthes, "The Discourse of History," in *Comparative Criticism: A Yearbook*, edited by E. S. Shaffer; translated by Stephen Bann (Cambridge: Cambridge University Press, 1981), pp. 7–20.

3 Louis Mink, "Narrative Form as a Cognitive Instrument," in his *Historical Understanding*, edited by Brian Fay, Eugene Golob, and Richard Vann (Ithaca, NY: Cornell University Press, 1987), pp. 183–203.

4 See Hayden White, *Metahistory: The Historical Imagination in Nineteenth-Century Europe* (Baltimore, MD: Johns Hopkins University Press, 1973); White, *Tropics of Discourse: Essays in Cultural Criticism* (Baltimore, MD: Johns Hopkins University Press, 1978); White, *The Content of Form* (Baltimore, MD: Johns Hopkins University Press, 1987); "White," in *Future Literary Theory*, edited by Ralph Cohen (New York: Routledge, 1989), pp. 19–43.

5 For its impact on literary critics and historians see the essays by K. Egan, L. Gossman, and R. Reinitz in *The Writing of History: Literary Form and Historical Understanding*, edited by Robert H. Canary and Henry Kozicki (Madison, WI: University of Wisconsin Press, 1978). For an example of a philosopher of history influenced by this view, see F. R. Ankersmit, "The Dilemma of Contemporary Anglo-Saxon Philosophy of History," in the journal *History and Theory*, Beiheft 25 (1986), 1–27. The view is also endorsed in Stephen Bann, "Toward a Critical Historiography: Recent Work in Philosophy of History," *Philosophy*, 56 (1981), 365–85.

6 See White, "Interpretation in History," in *Tropics*, pp. 51–80. The interrelation between these different interpretive registers is also discussed in the "Introduction" to *Metahistory* (pp. 1–42), among other places. That White continues to regard historical narrative as interpretive is evident in his recent "'Figuring the Nature of Times Deceased'; Literary Theory and Historical Writing"; see, for example, p. 21.

7 Here it is important to note that our reservations about White have less to do with his view that historical narratives are interpretive and more to do with his claims that such interpretive narratives are, in decisive respects, fictional.

8 See White, "Historicism, History and the Figurative Imagination," in *Tropics*, for example, pp. 111–12.

9 Claude Lévi-Strauss, *The Savage Mind* (Chicago: University of Chicago Press, 1966).

10 See, for example, Fernand Braudel, "The Situation of History in 1950," in his *On History* (Chicago: University of Chicago Press, 1980), and François Furet, "From Narrative History to History as a Problem," *Diogenes*, spring 1975. W. H. Dray criticizes the latter article in his "Narrative Versus Analysis in History," in *Rationality, Relativism and the Human Sciences*, edited

by Joseph Margolis, Michael Krausz, and R. M. Burian (Dordrecht, Nether-lands: Martinus Nijhoff, 1986).

11 White, "'Figuring the Nature of Times Deceased,'" p. 27. I take the gnomic, rhetorical question at the end of this quotation to signify that narratives as metaphors (in virtue of their generic plot structures) are true in the way analogies are true – do they provide an insightful fit; are they true *enough*?

12 Paul Ricoeur, *The Reality of the Historical Past* (Milwaukee, WI: Marquette University Press, 1984), pp. 33–4.

13 Joseph Margolis, *Art and Philosophy* (Atlantic Highlands, NJ: Humanities Press, 1980), p. 158.

14 White, "'Figuring the Nature of Times Deceased,'" p. 18.

15 White, "'Figuring the Nature of Times Deceased,'" p. 21.

16 For a discussion of the failure of both the narrative and the covering-law models to pith the essence of history, see Gordon Graham, *Historical Explana-tion Reconsidered* (Aberdeen: Aberdeen University Press, 1983).

17 This is the case even if we accept Maurice Mandelbaum's distinction between inquiry and narrative for it would remain a question as to what kind of knowl-edge (if any) readers could derive from historical narratives. See Maurice Mandelbaum, "A Note on History as Narrative," in *History and Theory*, VI, 1967; and Mandelbaum, *The Anatomy of Historical Knowledge* (Baltimore, MD: Johns Hopkins University Press, 1977).

18 White, "The Question of Narrative in Contemporary Historical Theory," in *Content*, p. 46. White derives this argument from Louis Mink, "Narrative Form as a Cognitive Instrument," pp. 197–8.

19 See, for example: White, "The Historical Text as Literary Artifact," in *Tropics*, p. 90; "Historicism, History and The Figurative Imagination," in *Tropics*, p. 111; "Preface," in *Content*, pp. ix–x; "'Figuring the Nature of Times Deceased,'" p. 27; among others.

20 See Louis Mink, "History and Fiction as Modes of Comprehension," and "Narrative Form as a Cognitive Instrument" in his *Historical Understanding*.

21 White, "The Historical Text as Literary Artifact," in *Tropics*, p. 4.

22 For example, White, "The Historical Text as Literary Artifact," in *Tropics*, p. 82. Here, *invention* seems to follow from the verbal nature of the historical text.

23 For example, White, "The Burden of History," in *Tropics*, pp. 28–9.

24 For example, White, "The Question of Narrative in Contemporary Historical Theory," in *Content*, p. 42.

25 For example, White, "The Burden of History," in *Tropics*, p. 47.

26 For example, in "Interpretation in History," White uses the metaphor of the mirror of a whole for what narrative *passes* as (*Tropics*, p. 51). Also note the analogies to replicas like model airplanes in "The Historical Text as Literary Artifact" in *Tropics*, p. 88.

27 See White, "Historicism, History and the Figurative Imagination," in *Tropics*, pp. 111–12.

28 See, for example, White, "The Question of Narrative in Contemporary Historical Theory," in *Content*, p. 42.

29 That is, for White, narrative forms are the culture's patterns of story-telling and a given event can be plotted in accordance with more than one such structure (which White sometimes refers to as *codes* [*Content*, p. 43]). And in his "The Value of Narrativity in the Representation of Reality," White says that the relation between historiography and narrative is conventional (*Content*, p. 6).

30 For an account of the argumentative function of intuition pumps, see Daniel Dennett, *Elbow Room* (Cambridge, MA: MIT Press, 1984).

31 See especially, White, "The Value of Narrativity in the Representation of Reality," in *Content*, pp. 1–25.

32 Gerard Genette as quoted by White in *Content*, p. 3.

33 Though White flirts with the notion of the *imaginary* as that figures in Lacanian literary theory, he does not accept it whole cloth. He does apparently agree that narrative seduces us through our desire for the kind of coherence and completeness that it counterfeits. However, narratives are also imaginary for him in the sense of being products of the imagination. And, as we have already noted, White does not regard the imagination as discredited epistemically; it has its own realms of veracity, such as the metaphorical. Thus, unlike many contemporary literary theorists, White is not committed to the view that the imaginary structures of narrative necessarily coerce us into misrecognizing reality. They can, rather, reveal reality if they are construed metaphorically.

34 White, "The Value of Narrativity in the Representation of Reality," in *Content*, p. 24.

35 White, "The Value of Narrativity in the Representation of Reality," p. 3.

36 See Roger Schank and R. P. Abelson, *Scripts, Plans, Goals and Understanding* (Hillsdale, NJ: Lawrence Erlbaum Associates, 1977).

37 I've derived this term from John Passmore, "Narratives and Events," in *History and Theory*, Beiheft 26 (1987), 73.

38 For an expansion of these points, see Frederick A. Olafson, *The Dialectic of Action: A Philosophical Interpretation of History and the Humanities* (Chicago: University of Chicago Press, 1979). In his *Time, Narrative, and History* (Bloomington, IN: Indiana University Press, 1986), David Carr attempts to defend the notion of "real stories" with reference to corporate entities like nations in terms of the shared myths that serve in practical deliberations. For my objections to this way of confronting historical constructivism, see my article-review of Carr's book in *History and Theory*, vol. XXVII, no. 3, 1988.

39 The idea of significance here is derived from Arthur Danto, *Knowledge and Narration* (New York: Columbia University Press, 1985).

40 Of course, if the meaning of events is to be conceptualized at the level of comedy or tragedy, then the issue of fiction cannot be dealt with in the above fashion. But remobilizing the argument in this way depends on the viability of White's theory of generic emplotment which we will take up shortly.

41 In his reliance on the "copy" standard of truth, one suspects that White is endorsing the myth of the Ideal Chronicler which Danto attacked so persuasively in *Narration and Knowledge*, pp. 142–82.

42 White's analogies to science, as comprehended by the constructivist dispensation, sit uncomfortably with his claims to be concerned with the specificity of history.

43 See, for example, Richard N. Boyd, "The Current Status of Scientific Realism," in *Scientific Realism*, edited by Jarrett Leplin (Berkeley, CA: University of California Press, 1984), pp. 41–82.

44 This may be a big *if* since the "unobservables" the historian deals with are categorically disanalogous to the "unobservables" of scientific theories.

45 For further criticism of the notion of transparency as it is used in contemporary literary theory see Noël Carroll, "Conspiracy Theories of Representation," *Philosophy of the Social Sciences*, vol. 17, 1987.

46 Moreover, the fact that in one story, told for one reason, a causal relation between events A and B is cited while in another story, undertaken for other purposes, that causal relation is not cited does not imply that the causal/narrative linkage in the first story is an "imposition."

47 A related point is made against Louis Mink by William Dray in his review of *Historical Understanding* in *Clio*, vol. 17, no. 4 (summer, 1988), 397.

48 Leon Goldstein attacks the atomic sentences model for other reasons in his "Impediments to Epistemology in the Philosophy of History," in *History and Theory*, Beiheft 25 (1986), 82–100.

49 See J. L. Gorman, *The Expression of Historical Knowledge* (Edinburgh: Edinburgh University Press, 1982), ch. 3. See also, J. L. Gorman, "Objectivity and Truth in History," in *Inquiry*, 17 (1974), 373–97.

50 See C. Behan McCullagh, "The Truth of Historical Narratives," *History and Theory*, Beiheft 26 (1987), 33–40.

51 It seems to me that Paul Ricoeur makes a similar error in his *Time and Narrative* (Chicago: University of Chicago Press, 1984), vol. I. Pressed to account for historical narrative, he opts for a correspondence theory of truth and maintains that narrative corresponds to temporality. White justifiably rejects this view for its obscurity, but stays with the commitment to truth, modifying it in terms of metaphorical truth. Both White and Ricoeur on my view would do better to recognize that truth is not the only relevant epistemic standard for evaluating narratives. Granting that, they could avoid commitments to strange correspondents (temporality) and special standards of truth.

Part II

Writing and Reading History

3
The Rhetoric of History

J. H. Hexter

If I had entitled this essay "Footnotes, Quotations, and Name-lists," readers would, I fear, pass rapidly to the next contribution. But since I am going to discuss footnotes, quotations, and name-lists, I owe some explanation as to why I chose so odd and apparently incoherent a set of subjects, linked only by the fact that historians – but not only historians – use them.

I have long been interested in what goes on between the time an historian says to himself: "Well, I guess I understand this matter about as well as I ever will, so I may as well start writing," and the time he lays down his pen ruefully beside a stack of scrawled pages and says: "Well, it's a damned bad job, but it's about as good as I can do, so that's that." In the intervening time the historian has been trying to find suitable ways to impart to others what he believes he understood; he has been writing history. This activity once had a name; it was called historiography. In recent years that name has been ruthlessly misappropriated, and its meaning drastically altered. Historiography has been used to designate the *history* of what at one time or another historians have written about the past. Thus understood, it is a special kind of intellectual history or a branch – or perhaps a twig – of the sociology of knowledge. I am simply reappropriating the term to its original use, since there is no other single term to describe the process of writing history.

On the face of it, the outcome of writing history, the rhetoric of history, is unmistakably different from the rhetoric of, say, physics or lyric poetry. Whatever an historian may profess that he is up to when he writes history, the result of his activity, an article, say, in the *American Historical Review*, does not look at all like an article in the *Physical Review* or an epic poem or a sonnet. Indeed if it does look like either a physicist's paper or a poet's sonnet, its chance of publication in the *American Historical Review* is fairly slim. And since the serious commitment of craftsmen is better revealed by their common activity than by their often idiosyncratic individual professions of intent, from the look of what they write it appears that historians are committed to writing in a different way, committed to a different rhetoric, from what science as exemplified by the physicists, or *belles lettres* as exemplified by the poets, is committed to. By carefully examining and analyzing the differences can we discover anything about the infrastructure, the bone and gristle, of the trade we historians follow? What do the manifest gross differences between historiography and the rhetoric of the natural sciences on the one hand and of *belles lettres* on the other tell us about the historian's often inarticulate conception of his vocation? Are the differences casual and trivial, or do the peculiarities of its rhetoric mark history as a unique and separate domain of human knowing, in important respects incommensurate with the other two? In this essay I shall focus on the relations between historiography and the rhetoric of the natural sciences. One difference becomes manifest in the divergent attitude of the historian and, say, the physicist to the lowly item in their common repertoire – the footnote. It is so lowly, indeed, that it may seem unworthy of notice; but we must remember that the lowly and humble things of the earth may be more instructive than the great and mighty – after all, geneticists learned a good deal more about genetics by considering the fruit fly than they could have learned in an equal span of time from a contemplation of the somewhat more impressive elephant.

Suppose both physicists and historians were prohibited from using footnotes for any purpose except citation to the so-called literature of their subjects. The physicists, I suspect, would regard such a prohibition as a minor nuisance. But because it would bar them from citation to the records of the past, most historians would regard it as a major calamity. Citation to those records is the way an historian makes his professional commitment clear in action, as the report on the experiment is the way a physicist makes his commitment clear. In both instances it is a commitment to maximum verisimilitude. For the physicist it is a maximum verisimilitude to the operations of nature as glimpsed through consideration of the experimental cluster; for the historian, verisimilitude to the happenings of the past as glimpsed through consideration of the surviving record. Experiment and citation to the record, then, are activities which more significantly than any theoretical pronouncements indicate the actual common commitment of physicists and historians to exploration, understanding, and rendering the best possible account of reality: for the physicist, the reality of the operations of nature; for the historian, the reality of what happened in the past.

As noted above, men's actual commitments are much more accurately revealed by what they do in the practice of their calling than by their quasi-philosophical excursions into methodology. The well-nigh universal use of footnotes to the records by historians indicates that no matter what form of intricate epistemological fancy work they fiddle around with in their spare time, when they actually get down to writing history they all still commit themselves to trying to write about the past, as Ranke put it so very long ago, "*Wie es eigentlich gewesen,*" as it really happened. Today we might put that old and much derided aphorism in a somewhat more sophisticated language. We might say that historians are concerned and committed to tell about the past the best and most likely story that can be sustained by the relevant extrinsic evidence. Still we would only be saying what Ranke intended in a form hopefully more satisfactory to a generation acutely conscious of linguistic niceties. Abandoning such niceties in the interest of brevity, let us call this statement about the historian's commitment the Reality Rule.

Historians employ the footnote for a host of residual matters other than citations to the record – lists of names, minor qualifications of assertions made in the text, polemical criticisms of other historians, short statistical tables, suggestions for future historical investigation. And these are but a beginning of the tasks to which historians have turned that versatile tool of their trade; even if one allowed them the footnote for citation to the records, they would be loath to forego its use for these many other jobs. And this confronts us with two questions: (1) Amid the apparent chaos of "residual" footnotes can we find any rule at all regulating their use? (2) What is the relation of any rule we find to the first rule that emerged from our examination of the peculiarities of the footnote as a device of historiographic rhetoric – the Reality Rule?

As to the first question, the application of any rule about footnotes requires an act of judgment in each case, and among historians judgment about the uses of residual footnotes differs. It might seem that in matters of judgment, as in those of taste, there is no disputing. But is this so? Let us consider an example:

> At Shilbottle, in the case of three separate parcels of meadow, 31, 20 and 14 acres respectively, the first rendered 42s. in 1415–16 and 30s. in 1435–6, the second 28s. in 1420–1 and 23s. in 1435–6, and the third 24s. in 1422–3 and 14s. in 1435–6. At Guyzance 61/2 husbandlands each rendered 13s. 4d. in 1406–7, but 10s. in 1435–6. At Chatton and Rennington, on the other hand, the situation was more stable. At Rennington the clear revenues were £17. 8s. 3d. in 1435–6 and £17 in 1471–2 and at Chatton £40. 18s. 7d. in 1434–5 and £36. 18s. 7d. in 1472–3. At Chatton the decline was due to a fall in the value of the farm of the park, from £6. 13s. 4d. to £2. 13s. 4d. . . .

This dashing passage is embedded in the *text* of a study of the wealth of a magnate family in the fifteenth and early sixteenth centuries and of the effect on it of concurrent changes in the economy, the military apparatus, and the political situation in England. Can it be suggested that the young man who inserted it in the text instead of quarantining it in a footnote did *not* commit an error of judgment? But to say he did commit one is to imply a *rule* from which his erroneous judgment made him deviate. Can such a rule – a "law" of historical rhetoric or historiography, if you will – to cover this case be stated? I think so. As a rough approximation, the rule might go: "Place in footnotes evidence and information which, if inserted in the text, diminishes the impact on the reader of what you, as an historian, aim to convey to him."

So although in the matter of the use of residual footnotes judgment is inescapable, we are not at all confronted with chaos or anarchy, but with a reasonably precise rule or law. We may name it the Maximum Impact Rule. Inevitably there are marginal situations on which there will be divergent views among historians as to how to achieve maximum impact or whether a particular rhetorical presentation has in fact achieved it. The existence of such marginal situations, however, does not mean that all situations are marginal, and that therefore there is no rule, or that any rule is as good as any other. Lawyers have a saying that hard cases make bad law, but they do not feel impelled thereupon to take a deep dive into a *non sequitur* and argue that there are no easy cases and no good law. Because there are some matters both substantive and procedural concerning which they are very uncertain, historians somehow have permitted themselves to be nudged into accepting the notion that everything about the past and about writing about it is infected with a total uncertainty. This is not so. Specifically, as we have just seen, it is not so in the case of the residual footnote. There without difficulty we found a rule not heavily infected with uncertainty.

But this turns our attention to the second question we foresaw earlier, that of the relation of the two rules – the Reality Rule and the Maximum Impact Rule – to each other. Note, first, that in our example the data that ought to be withdrawn from the text and consigned to a residual footnote, are informative and relevant with respect to the substantive historical argument the historian in the case is presenting, and that they are as complete, as accurate, and as exact as possible. Note, second, that what the historian, applying the second rule, is committed to seek to convey to the reader with maximum impact is his conception and understanding of the past as it actually happened, the "Reality" of the first rule. And thereupon we run head on into a paradox, for the clear implication of the two points we have just made is that *in the interest of conveying historical reality to the reader with maximum impact, the rules of historiography may sometimes require an historian to subordinate completeness and exactness to other considerations.* If this is so, it indeed differentiates historiography from the rhetoric of the sciences as currently conceived. A look at our next rhetorical device of historiography may help not to resolve our paradox but perhaps to transcend it. The device is the quotation in the text. Let us again note a difference between the historians and the physicists. Suppose the editor were to issue an edict that in the text of the *Physical Review* neither quotation marks nor their equivalents would henceforth be permitted. Contributors would probably be annoyed, but with respect to the advancement of knowledge of the natural world they would not feel that much was at stake. Suppose the editor of *American Historical Review* were to issue such an edict. At the very least he would promptly be fired. A luxury for physicists, quotation is a necessity for historians, indispensable to historiography.

The kind of quotation that historians deem indispensable is quotation from the record. And again we may ask two questions: (1) Is there any rule governing quotation from the record? (2) How does the rule relate to the Reality Rule?

Let us start with a purely imaginary case of inept quotation. Suppose in writing the history of the Civil Rights Act of 1964, a historian were to quote verbatim from the *Congressional Record* the entire debate on the Act in both the House and the Senate. The result would be undeniably relevant and exact – and the historian who perpetrated it would find his sanity under grave suspicion. Again our paradox: maximum completeness and exactness are not always essential, and they are not even always desirable in the historian's work of trying to tell the reader what really happened. Perhaps we can escape the paradox by way of an adept quotation. It comes from the late Professor Harbison's *The Christian Scholar in the Age of the Reformation.* He says:

> Erasmus had absorbed [Lorenzo] Valla's historical perspective, his sense of the historical discontinuity between pagan antiquity and the Christian era . . . a sensitivity to anachronism. On one occasion he ridiculed the absurdity of the practice . . . of using Ciceronian words to describe an utterly different modern world: "Wherever I turn my eyes I see all things changed, I stand before another stage and I behold a different play, nay, even a different world." The world of Cicero (or of Paul) can be understood and even in a sense relived – but only if we recognize that it had its unique existence, once, in a past now dead.

What is the function of Harbison's brief but apt quotation from Erasmus? Not mere validation or proof of his assertions; he could as well have effected that by citation or quotation in a footnote. By using Erasmus' own words in the text, he seeks and wins a response not merely of assent but of *conviction*, not just a "yes," but "yes, indeed!" Nothing Harbison could have said about Erasmus' sense of history could produce the conviction about it that Erasmus' own assertion of his intense feeling of distance from antiquity produces.

The quotation aims at something in addition to conviction, however. The quotation communicates the historian's own view of what happened in the past by the particular means of *confrontation*. It says in effect, "In my judgment the most economical way at this point to tell you what I believe Erasmus meant and to convince you that he meant it is to confront you directly with what Erasmus said." This provides us with a third general rule of historiography – an Economy-of-Quotation Rule: "Quote from the record of the past only when and to the extent that confrontation with that record is the best way to help the reader to an understanding of the past *wie es eigentlich gewesen.*"

We saw, however, in the instance of our hypothetical case of the *Congressional Record* that mere confrontation with the *record* of the past is not necessarily the best way to achieve this understanding or even to achieve confrontation. Indeed, far from being a clear glass window through which the reader may capture an image of the past, quotations from the record injudiciously used can be a thick opaque wall that cuts him off from it. Once we recognize that confrontation is one of the means by which the historian seeks to convey to the reader an understanding of what actually happened, we may be on our way to transcending the paradox which up to now has perplexed us. For it opens up the possibility that the microscopic means of historiography have to be adapted to its macroscopic ends and that it is part of the task of the writer of history to mediate understanding and confrontation by devices of the rhetoric of history less direct but more compelling, and more to the purpose than any simple maximizing of completeness and exactness. And this brings us to the word list. It is a device of both the rhetoric of history and the rhetoric of the sciences, and neither would willingly forego it. Consider the following:

> An inert element will not react or enter into chemical combination with any other element. In order of increasing atomic weight the inert elements are helium (4), neon (20), argon (39), krypton (84), xenon (131), and radon (222).

These two sentences exemplify the rhetoric of the scientist. In intent the words composing them are totally denotative. They cast no shadow; they evoke nothing; and their arrangement is wholly dictated by the mandates of rational order and utility. The list of the names of the elements is intended to suggest nothing more than it overtly states, that by agreed convention among chemists the word helium designates the inert element whose atomic weight is 4, neon the one whose atomic weight is 20, and so on. The arrangement of the name cluster is dictated by the simple quantitative principle of increasing weight. What the scientist wants and gets from the list is a method of labeling. He wants each entity and process he has to deal with labeled in such a way that the label denotes unambiguously and unequivocally that entity or process only. Although language can be evocative, suggestive, packed with overtones, massively and unpredictably connotative, such language is barred from the rhetoric of the sciences. For the scientist's purposes when he is communicating what he knows, words should be as free of connotative contamination, as sterile, as the apparatus in an operating room.

In contrast consider an example of a historiographical list to illustrate the rhetoric of history.

> A vast stratum of events, the Christian Revival, lies on both sides of that conspicuous historical watershed, the year 1517. We offer the name Christian Revival for this historical structure because hitherto historians have had no single covering phrase to describe this intensification of religious sentiment and concern that began long before 1517 and extended long beyond, that in its full span had room for Luther and Loyola, the Reformed Churches and the Jesuits, John of Leiden and Paul IV, Thomas Cranmer and Edmund Campion and Michael Servetus.

The names in the paragraph above constitute a historiographical list, intended to serve the particular purposes of the rhetoric of history. It emits a signal, and what the signal says to all who hear it is: "Draw on the reservoir of your knowledge of the times in which these men named lived to give meaning to this list." If that reservoir is altogether empty, then inevitably the list will itself be historiographically empty, meaningless, a mere collection of sounds, just as the sentences about the inert gases must have been empty of meaning to anyone who had no notion of what a chemical element or a chemical reaction or atomic weight were. The reason for this similarity is that in the present case both the historiographic rhetoric and the scientific rhetoric presuppose that the reader already possesses a body of precise and exact knowledge of the particular universes to which they refer. The scientific and the historiographical statements conform to the Reality Rule; they are meaningless unless there are such elements as helium and neon, and unless there were such men as Loyola, Cranmer, and Paul IV. Yet the historiographical list serves a rhetorical function quite different from that served by the scientific list. First, consider the order of the two lists. Given the common trait of inertness the order of the scientific list indicates the scientists' normal preoccupation with establishing scalable differences of homogeneous traits – in this case, weight. In the historiographical list, on the other hand, no such preoccupation is discernible, yet the arrangement of the names lies at the very heart of the matter.

Note that there are three alternative ways of writing the historiographical list, all of which maintain the essential arrangement, to convey whatever information it contains.

1 Luther and Loyola, the Reformed Churches and the Jesuits, John of Leiden and Paul IV, Thomas Cranmer and Edmund Campion and Michael Servetus.

2 The first great figure of the Reformation and the first great figure of
  the Counter Reformation; the cutting edge of the Protestant attack
  and the cutting edge of the Catholic counter attack; the most fanatical prophet of the radical Reformation and the most fanatical pope of
  the era of religious strife; the Protestant martyr burned by the Catholics,
  the Catholic martyr beheaded by the Protestants, and the martyr who
  escaped burning by the Catholics only to be burned by the Protestants.
3 Luther, the first great figure of the Reformation, and Loyola, the first
  great figure of the Counter Reformation; the Reformed Churches, the
  cutting edge of the Protestant attack, and the Jesuits, the cutting edge
  of the Catholic counter attack – and so on through the list.

The persons balanced in tension with one another are the same for each
version, and the arraying is identical in all three. On mathematical principles a member of any of the lists should be freely substitutable for the
corresponding member of either of the other two, but in writing history
this is not so. Each list must retain its integrity. On what grounds can
an historian choose among the three? One might argue that the second
list is preferable to the first since it explicates the rationale upon which
the persons in the first list were arrayed; and that, in point of information about the past, the third is best of all, since it both names the persons and explicates the rationale of their array. Then why in the world
would a reasonably experienced historian committed to communicate what he understands about the past choose the *first* option – the
bare list of names with no indication as to his grounds for choosing
them, or for ordering them as he did? Remember what we said earlier
about the signal emitted by the list: "Draw on the reservoir of your
knowledge of the times in which these men lived to give meaning to the
list." The writer assumed that most of his readers could and would in
fact draw from their particular reservoirs the items of general information in the second and the third list. The effect of giving that information in greater detail, however, is to send another kind of rhetorical
signal, a stop signal: "Stop drawing on the reservoir of your knowledge.
I have already told you how I want you to think about these men." And
this stop signal is just what the writer did *not* want the list to emit. The
third version of the list is more exact, more overtly informative, than the
bare names in the first list and just for that reason it is more empty, less
ample. It dams up the informed reader's imagination instead of letting
it flow freely, bringing with it the mass of connotation and association that those names have for him. Therefore to prevent such a block-
age the writer chose the first list. In doing so, he made a judgment. He
judged – or gambled – that the connotative evocative list would communicate a fuller meaning than the exact one, that it would more effectively confront the reader with the reality of the Christian Revival, and
that therefore it was the more appropriate device for advancing the
reader's understanding of it. Whether he was correct in his judgment is

immaterial. But in setting forth his findings, a scientist never needs to make such a judgment at all. Scientific rhetoric is purposefully constructed to free him of that need by barring connotative terms and evocative devices. To a scientist the idea that he had to choose between a rhetoric of clarity and precision on the one hand and one of evocative force on the other would be shocking. The idea that the writer of history has to select between *mutually exclusive ways of setting forth the same data* and that the knowledge of history that he conveys in some measure depends on his judgment in selecting among alternative rhetorical devices is perhaps as disturbing and perplexing. But to the latter conclusion our investigation of footnotes, quotations, and word-lists has driven us. What is the yield of our examination of these minor devices of historical rhetoric – the footnote, the quotation, the name-list?

First, that historiography is a rule-bound discipline by means of which historians seek to communicate their knowledge of the past.

Second, that the relation of writing history, of its rhetoric, to history itself is quite other than it has traditionally been conceived. That rhetoric is ordinarily deemed icing on the cake of history; but our recent investigation indicates that it is mixed right into the batter. It affects not merely the outward appearance of history, its delight and seemliness, but its inward character, its essential function – its capacity to convey knowledge of the past as it actually was. And if this is indeed the case, historians need to subject historiography, the way they write history, to an investigation far broader and far more intense than any that they have hitherto conducted.

Third, that there is an irreducible divergence between the rhetoric of history and the rhetoric of science, that the vocabulary and syntax that constitute the appropriate response of the historian to his data are neither identical with nor identifiable with the vocabulary and syntax that constitute the appropriate response of the scientist to his data. But the historian's goal in his response to the data is to render the best account he can of the past as it really was. Therefore by his resort to the rhetoric of history, regardless of its divergence from that of the sciences, the historian affirms in practice and action his belief that it is more adequate than the latter as a vehicle to convey the kind of knowledge, understanding, truth, and meaning that history achieves. Indeed, we discovered instances in which, in order to transmit an increment of knowledge and meaning, the very rules of historiography demanded a rhetoric which sacrificed generality, precision, control, and exactness to evocative force and scope – a choice entirely out of bounds according to the rules of scientific statement. And this implies that in the rhetoric of history itself there are embedded assumptions about the nature of knowing, understanding, meaning, and truth and about the means of augmenting them that are not completely congruent with the corresponding assumptions in the sciences, at least insofar as the philosophy of science has succeeded in identifying them. . . .

Perhaps what we have learned about the rhetoric of history suggests the possible character of an imminent paradigm shift. It might start by asking why anyone should take seriously the attempt to confine the activity of historians to offering explanations structured according to the pattern of the sciences, to subject historiography solely to the standard of knowing, understanding, meaning, and truth acceptable for – presumably because efficacious in – the pursuit of those ends in the sciences. The attempt has never gotten further anyhow than hacking bits and pieces out of the actual flow of historical discourse and arguing about the extent to which those bits can or cannot be made to fit the scientific model or alternately how the scientific model can be modified and redefined to encompass the selected bits. The trouble is that those bits are just that – mere disjointed fragments of the flow of historical discourse. The success or failure of the attempt to incorporate them into the scientific model therefore remains a matter of only trivial concern, since, regardless of its outcome, it leaves untouched the larger part of historical discourse, of the rhetoric of history, and of the activities of the historians who produce it.

Why should we not then simply regard those activities and the flow of historical discourse, the historiography, in which they take form, as by and large an acceptable response to the demand for an account of what went on in the past? At first sight this seems like a modest enough proposal. Indeed it is no more than we do in actual fact. Few men after all can seriously doubt that in skillful hands historical investigations which are formulated and communicated in the sometimes inexact and evocative rhetoric of history provide viable explanations of the past, increase our knowledge of it, enhance our understanding of it. On the face of it such a suggestion seems less outrageous than its contrary. Yet the suggestion is radical; it involves a drastic paradigm shift, and we have seen why. It assumes that in their writing at its best historians make an appropriate response to the demand for knowledge, understanding, and truth about what happened in the past. But according to our science-oriented notions they make their response in a rhetoric that is *inappropriate* to the attainment of knowledge, understanding, and truth. And so we have a choice. We can say that by and large history is bunk; but I really do not think that this will wash. Or we can say that our science-oriented notions of meaning, knowing, understanding, and truth and especially of the lines of access to them need a thorough overhauling. This would indeed be a revolution, and one in which I think I would enjoy taking a place at the barricades.

4
Making Up Lost Time: Writing on the Writing of History

Nancy F. Partner

One could only suppose that the apparently forgotten beginning of any story was unforgettable; perpetually one was subject to the sense of there having had to be a beginning *somewhere*. Like the lost first sheet of a letter or missing first pages of a book, the beginning kept on suggesting what must have been its nature. One never was out of reach of the power of what had been written first. Call it what you liked, call it a miscarried love, it imparted, or was always ready and liable to impart, the nature of an alternative, attempted recovery or enforced second start to whatever followed. The beginning, in which was conceived the end, could not but continue to shape the middle part of the story, so that none of the realisations along that course were what had been expected, quite whole, quite final.[1]

An acute sense of history, the feeling of being in the middle of a story fraught with meaning, which must have had a beginning *somewhere* and will somewhere have an ending, in which the pattern will be completed and revealed, is characteristic of a highly self-conscious culture. The sense of history and the sense of story are in this way identical, and identically human.

Thee I have heard relating what was done
Ere my remembrance: now hear me relate
My story, which perhaps thou hast not heard.

The speaker is Adam; the listener to whom he proposes to tell his story is the Archangel Gabriel. Here, in book eight of Milton's *Paradise Lost*, Gabriel has just concluded Adam's first lesson in history – an account of the constitutional arrangements of the polity of heaven and

the civil war between God and Lucifer, rendered in rigorous conformity
to the conventions of classical historiography from Thucydides to Tacitus:
high style and public affairs. Adam quickly takes in the idea of history,
being human, endowed with memory, and underemployed in gardening,
and immediately insists on telling Gabriel "my story" – the history of
his consciousness of life, which comprehended, after all, the whole of
secular history to date. This, Milton's compressed insertion of the idea
of history into his epic story, is the literary illustration to the first definition of the word "story" in Samuel Johnson's *Dictionary*:

> Story: History; account of things past.

Thus, in a few words, with a brief quotation from Milton as illustration, Dr Johnson, who cannot be conceived as being put to any difficulty
over the distinction between fiction and nonfiction, effortlessly assigned
story/history/things past/remembrance/narrative/and poetry – the entire
traditional configuration.

The impulse to tell his story was perhaps Adam's first intimation of
mortality: he admitted that "for Man to tell how human life began is
hard; for who himself beginning knew?" And harder yet, he would soon
learn that in beginnings are conceived ends. Milton was clearly reluctant to portray human life in protracted silence and so he improved on
Genesis and gave Adam an early opportunity for narrative. In Genesis,
Adam and Eve did not do much talking until they had sinned, and they
celebrated entry into the human condition by telling their shifty, shame-
faced stories to God. But Milton knew that creatures who would suffer
pain and death had to learn story or they could not bear it. It is simply
the nature of our kind that whenever we are not wholly concentrated on
something emphatically "else," we remember that we are mortal. And
we console ourselves with a story.

Our first and last consolation, our primal defiance of the endless point-
lessness of successive time, is the secret insistence on seeing our own life
as a story, our own birth and death imposing a beginning and an end
on the formless flow of time, charging the middle with meaning, with
plot and tension, "none of the realisations along that course" bearing
the full significance of the whole, for the beginning held implicit the
end, and the full meaningfulness of the story. We live attentive to every
detail of experience, sorting out the merely contingent from the "real"
events, correspondences, connections, and minor fulfillments, determined
to read the story into conscious significance before consciousness fails.
Fully and humanly against reason, we are determined to work out the
pattern of our plot, even after we realize that no one dies at the end, but
in the middle of everything, and is born into the middle as well.

Knowing that time is resistless, amorphous, the universal solvent
of meaning, we yet demand, lately with a doubled and redoubled self-
consciousness, *form*, and in this quintessentially human act of imposing

form on formless time are coiled the high tensions of art, religion, and philosophy. This triumphant human failing, our persistent sense of "there having had to be a beginning *somewhere* . . . in which was conceived the end," is discussed tellingly and profoundly by Frank Kermode in his book on apocalyptic tendencies in ancient and modern literature, *The Sense of an Ending*.[2] Time is the central fiction for human culture, and even at its most naive and rudimentary level of expression, it is a fiction of great force: Kermode notes that time has even been made to speak its name in the "tick-tock" of clocks, and in that single spondee, whose "tock" confers structure, middleness, on the interval it ends and defines, is a "model of what we call a plot, an organization that humanizes time by giving it form. . . ."[3] Kermode's discussion of the tick-tock plot also made me understand the marginal anxious depression I associate with watching digital clocks – emblems of pure succession and the engulfing gray of undifferentiated chronicity. Through plot we escape chronicity, because we cannot live without meaning however coldly we acknowledge that reality is not plotted, and time does not say "tick-tock."

> "Your son had a happy life," said Susan.
> "You see that a reason for his losing it? People state it as if it were."
> "We have to think of reasons," said Priscilla. "It is too shocking that there shouldn't be any. When people have had a sad life, we say that death is a release. It is to prevent things from being without any plan."[4]

Irony is acceptable, and all degrees of self-consciousness and disillusion, but we will persist in telling our stories.

The concepts of beginning and end, including forgotten beginnings and unreached ends, of measurable time, of our simultaneous awareness of impenetrable reality and intelligible story, all are essential to all forms of writing in prose, and it is at this conceptual level that the discussion of written history has to begin if it is to proceed interestingly. (I forgo any reference to ends, middle seeming to me the interesting place.)

There is a certain superficiality to the discussion of writing history as carried on in "the profession." It stops at the stylistic surface of language; our usual vocabulary runs from praise: "beautifully written," to damn: "mere rhetoric!" Some of this can be charged to the fact that the privileged makers of language about language, literary critics and linguistic philosophers, so often write in a language available only to initiates of "the profession" – theirs. (Browsing through an issue of *Diacritics* can be an astonishing experience.) But prose and how it works is not someone else's "field," regardless of how the journals divide up the intellectual turf. Making prose of a certain sort is what historians do.

The very concept of narrative has to be re-examined and not separated so sharply from analysis; so too the ideas of story and plot, as well as all the formal elements of prose styles we call realism. Historians tend to pay conscious attention to some prior sequence of events, those assumed to have had actual existence in past time (and about whose priority to language they do not like too many questions), and many of them adopt models of explanation from the social sciences as their formal structure of analysis, but there is less attention paid to the very structure of discourse (that useful if, alas, trendy word), the subtle, powerful ways in which the telling of something makes its own demands and forms expectation and significance. This is the province of the fairly recent field of narrative analysis and it concerns all prose, including history, and *not* excluding history organized in other than chronological sequence.[5]

It is very confusing and misleading that the crucial terms "narrative" and "story" are used in casually disparaging ways. The general idea among professional historians is that there is such a thing as "non-narrative" history which exhibits more sophisticated intellectual activity than narrative, a lower mode practiced chiefly by "popular" historians whose books betray a strong family likeness to novels. This scheme, an institutional myth taken very seriously by graduate students who like to feel they are being initiated into a higher and scientific state of mind, ignores the question of what non-narrative prose might be, and whether such a form of language (if it, in fact, exists) could convey anything at all about the past. All past events, persons, and phenomena, however abstractly defined, emerge into identity only as part of a formal pattern which controls time. "Tick" = origins, causes, predisposing factors, fundamental premises. "Tock" = results, effects, achievements, recovered meanings. In the "middle," our plot enables us to identify manifestations, symptoms, developments, characteristics. The most rigorously eventless, characterless, "non-narrative" history has to tell something, has to begin somewhere and proceed and conclude. The necessity of choosing a beginning, crucial to plotting a story, including stories of argument, induction, and interpretation, unites historians of civil war battles with historians of demographic change or the symbolism of coronation ceremonies. Historians are the professional custodians of pattern, and our writing expresses more single-mindedly than any other use of prose the relentless human demand, in the face of all contrary evidence including our strongest fears, that time have form so that life might have meaning. Story is our essential mode of explanation because it turns the unmeaning "and next, and next, and next . . ." of reality into significant sequence; any series of events (including events of the mind, of large populations, or economic events) which can be described in a single intelligible and significant pattern is a story, and the verbal arrangement that describes the pattern is narrative.

A narrative that starts in the middle and stays there is no less a narrative for telling its plot by indirection and implication. In fact, the best stories seem to start in the middle; good art acknowledges the candid fictionality of all beginnings. We are never confused by literary entrance into the middle. Curiosity looks forward; memory, experience, and a quick sense of order reach back for the beginning; the more complexly our faculties are engaged, the more satisfying and convincing the experience. Something happens when it all works, something connects and makes us happily connive at our own illusions about black marks on white surfaces, and happily share the conviction of truth and reality between the world and a book. The conceptual données of prose narrative – the sense of story, of intelligibility, of meaningful sequence, of the continuous self, of development and connection – are the essence of all historical writing.

Historians characteristically interpret evidence (itself a metaphor of visual perception) into some special version of what Elizabeth Bowen meant by the "realisations along that course," which are never "quite whole, quite final." Evidence is that which can be metaphorically read as a manifestation, or "realization" of something (event, process, thought) whose meaning cannot be grasped without reference to a beginning, however elusive and remote, and an end, even one not yet reached. The non-narrative historian usually conceives of what he has marked out for study as a realization of something in past process whose significance, inexorably linked to fictions of time, is to be uncovered and described. He, almost more than any other writer, is "subject to the sense of there having had to be a beginning *somewhere*."[6] All non-narrative history has this quality of "middleness" – a quality which unites all forms of history in common search for a story subtle enough to satisfy modern minds.

Henry James urged novelists to "speak with assurance, with the tone of the historian."[7] History depends, for its special "tone," on a concept of language which unhesitatingly asserts the external reality of the world, its intelligibility in the form of ideas, concepts, phenomena, or other mental things, and a direct connection between mental things and verbal signs. Without denying all of that or some version of it, all students of linguistic philosophy admit that the connection between the verbal signifier and the mental thing signified is more understandable and easier to describe than the connection of either with a world we revealingly qualify as "out there." Language-model epistemology (smuggled out of linguistics and philosophy departments by literary critics and free-ranging or metacritics, and lobbed like grenades into unsuspecting history departments) threatens to sever the tie between language and any reality external to language on the ground that language (here the generic *langage* as distinct from *langue*) *is* the very structure of mental life, and no metalanguage can ever stand outside itself to observe a reality external to itself. These are issues of venerable ancestry in philosophic discourse, but the more recent version has aggressively worked out some peculiarly upsetting conclusions about the ability of language to refer to anything outside itself (the death of mimesis) and threatens, or at least mocks, the premises of historical knowledge.

Historians tend to get nervous rapidly at any threat, however subtle, to the "out-thereness" of the ultimate term of reference, because their world is no longer there at all. The Past is like memorably maligned Oakland: when you're there, there is no there there. Thinking about these matters for more than a few minutes produces angry, impatient reactions, and we secretly applaud Dr Johnson when he kicked Berkeley's philosophy out of his path. But even visionaries inhabit a world of words. Dante and Bunyan had to narrate moments of direct enlightenment rapt beyond language, in language, which made of them, as we say, a likely story. In any case, no sooner was Christian admitted to the Celestial City where, he was promised, "*You shall see him as he is*," than, "I awoke, and behold it was all a dream." So much for unmediated reality.

The fact is that there is no need for anyone to play Dr Johnson over the issue of external reality and the language of reference. No one really believes we are sealed in a linguistic house of mirrors, even if we are. The black-hole epistemology can be ignored with the same little lurch of faith that takes us out of bed each morning rashly confident that the floor will be where we left it. The "problem" posed by the distinct possibility that we cannot know anything outside language (using a modestly strict definition of "know") folds up in a moment since no one who passes for sane is willing to accept any of the consequences of such a position, and everyone eventually resorts to some version of "we have to assume . . . ," from which follow Other Minds, an External World, and soon after, Descriptive Language or something that passes for it, and the whole show carries on as usual. Except that we feel more sophisticated doing it.

But the real issue for historians is still language. Even Johnson tacitly admitted it: "Story: History; *account of* things past [my emphasis]." All accounts tell things and what is told is contained in the telling. Further, all accounts of things are of "things past." In an important and primary, not secondary, sense, history is contained in the category of all "accounts of," all stories, and cannot exempt itself because of claims made about the actuality of things outside the text. Those claims simply make history a special class of accounts. The central conventions which govern all narrative – the organization of time, the distinction between contingent and significant sequence, alias story – unite history and fiction profoundly and permanently.[8]

Most definitions of history begin with some term like inquiry, mode of thought, or knowledge, which asserts the primacy of something prelinguistic, apart from language entirely. The fact that the only history we know anything about is an artifact of words is ignored, sunk beneath serious discussion as though that fact were too obvious and insignificant to deserve attention. The notion that making books and talking about them is what they do is an uncomfortable one for historians. A characteristic example is Herbert Butterfield's last book, *The Origins of History*,

an unfinished, posthumously edited work which nonetheless happily preserves the personal robust tone, full of learning and good sense. The
author draws a firm line between literature and history in its essence:
"What concerns us, therefore, is not just 'the History of Historiography,'
the mere story of the development of a branch of literature, but the unfolding of a whole great aspect of human experience. We need to know
how man came to acquire a concept of 'the past.' . . ."[9] This "concept of
the past," also described in self-consciously nonliterary terms as "man's
consciousness of history," "a feeling for history and a sense of the past,"[10]
has to be traced through texts, of course, but throughout the book writing is kept at a skeptical remove from the true sources of time-conscious,
truth-seeking history.

> Like other peoples, the Greeks would cling to fabulous explanations or
> create a legend out of a crude piece of etymological interpretation; but
> there is an appointed way of explaining these matters – it has to be done
> by telling a story. The results of these first attempts at historical enquiry
> or conjecture, therefore, are liable to be highly questionable. . . .[11]

With these premises, the Greek achievement in history has to be ascribed
to something vaguely mental – "the development of a scientific way of
treating the historical data" – and of course *scientific*, which turned the
making of historical prose into something different and more – "investigation."[12] This strenuous attempt to strain out the prose contamination
from history makes turning back to Herodotus and Thucydides something
of a surprise.

It is not that we don't know that history is the definitive human audac-
ity imposed on formless time and meaningless event with the human
meaning-maker: language; but the silent shared conspiracy of all historians (who otherwise agree on nothing these days) is to talk about the
past as though it were really "there." The whole of historical discourse
is calculated to induce a sense of referential reality in a conceptual field
with no external reference at all.

⸀History is meaning imposed on time by means of language: history
imposes syntax on time. As the form of writing whose central purpose
is to affirm our consciousness of a shared experience over generations
of one external and real world, history has a great investment in mimesis
– the ability of language to imitate reality. Here, of course, is where
historians balk, for, alas, the mimetic abilities of prose are common
to fiction and history without distinction. Fiction's persuasive force, its
"sense of reality," results from an author's ability to offer the reader a
suggestive array of fictional elements that satisfy the requirements of
possible reality in the shared world of writer and reader. The historian,
using techniques that differ only a little from those of a novelist, has to
persuade the reader not only of the *possible* reality of his array of verbal

elements, but that those on display in the text are "guaranteed" by their relation (reference, logical inference) to things outside the text, and thus the result is a real mimesis. (This discussion should be modified by the idea of probability; historians generally do not claim more than some high degree of probability for their constructs, as measured against a standard of absolute correspondence with external reality.) Fiction too has to persuade, not refer in any immediate or literal way; it satisfies the ancient rhetorical standards of plausibility and coherence, while history aspires to the equally ancient philosophical demand for pure reference and correspondence with reality, although its ambition is hopelessly compromised from the start because the past, being what it is, incorrigibly slips into fiction. Even our willing acquiescence in the illusion of the printed page as a symbolic representation of reality is itself a complex and vital fiction of our ability to grasp and control some of the intractable "out there." And, being endlessly resourceful makers of fictions, we can believe and disbelieve at the same time, according to the fictional occasions of our own invention.

By the rules of fiction, with which life to be credible must comply . . .[13]

. . . The creation of character is not taught in departments of history; if anything, it is assumed that students bring the sense of character as part of their basic mental equipment and can enlarge it metaphorically from persons to institutions, communities, cultures. The rule, rather more reliable in fiction than in life, that character consists of an array of intelligibly related, integrated characteristics of one subject, continuous over time, prevails.[14] Consider the passage in the life of Duke William of Normandy while he waited for a favorable wind to enable his fleet to sail to England in 1066. As his most eminent biographer describes it:

> The uncertain factor was the channel wind. Duke William was himself fully conscious of this, and contemporary writers describe his supplications for a change in the weather, and picture him during these fateful days as constantly gazing towards the vane on the church of Saint-Valéry.[15]

Should one want to fill out that, perfectly good, description, some choices might be as follows:
While waiting for a favorable channel wind, Duke William:

(a) felt secretly anxious because he did not know how to swim;
(b) began to embroider a nice tablecloth with scenes depicting his connection with the English monarchy;
(c) felt frustration and impatience.

Normal professional logic can countenance only "(c)," and "(c)" is so pointlessly obvious that David Douglas quite rightly chose to suggest

William's state of mind by indirection and depicted action. "(b)" is too interesting even to consider, and we are quite fortunate the "contemporary writers" did not offer us "(a)" because we could not fit it into the character who calmly ate his dinner when lost at sea, and loved the deer as if he were their father. This all seems reductive but it is generally how we proceed with respect to persons. When a historical person "steps out of character," as Thomas Becket did, we are at a loss because he broke the rule of fiction and broke into two. No one has quite put him together again.

> By the rules of fiction, with which life to be credible must comply, he was as a character "impossible" – each time they met, for instance, he showed no shred or trace of having been continuous since they last met.

Historians will already have noted that there is no opening in Douglas's passage for a Duke William sewing while thinking nervously about water, because his actions and feelings were reported by "contemporary writers," identified in the footnotes. Correct modern historical style draws attention away from the verbal symbols chosen by the author and directs it to the words of others (or artifacts or natural objects), thus creating by literary convention the illusion of transparency, through the text into time. The style conveys a symbolic anti-aesthetic gesture of good faith by exposing the evidence/text structure – a symbolic equivalent of candor. Stylistic features that "tend to reduce transparency, that tend to require concentration upon the symbol to determine what it is and what it refers to,"[16] signal writing which is aesthetic in its function and effects. Writing with noticeable aesthetic features tends to attract the ancient suspicions of artful words as reliable conveyors of truth. Elsewhere, in an essay on history, Douglas quotes Thomas Huxley's condemnation of writers guilty of "plastering the fair face of truth with that pestilent cosmetic rhetoric,"[17] aptly noting that Huxley was laying it on a bit thick. Modern historians endorse the traditional view by staying well within the boundaries of the transparent style.

These clichés about makeup and making up the truth are too naive a view of how words work. The features often associated with literary art, repleteness of meaning, syntactic and semantic density, multiple and complex reference, reduction of transparency, do not have any invariable connection to fiction;[18] indeed, a good case can be made for the superior honesty of ornate or assertive style. The classic contrast of the novelists Samuel Richardson and Henry Fielding exemplifies this point about language itself. Richardson's central fiction was that he was merely the collector and editor of Clarissa's letters, of Pamela's letters and diaries, that he was merely offering these artless, spontaneous documents to his readers so that they too might enter directly into the hearts of the women who wrote them. The fiction is a fiction about reading, not a

deception about authorship; it manipulates the conditions of our reading so that we are placed in a relation to the fictional Pamela which is
seamless, uninterrupted, and direct – a complete illusion of reality. The
interesting thing is how powerful such a contrived illusion is. The books
are interminably long, the letters are produced under wildly incongruous conditions; we may scoff and put down the book, but so long as we
read, the illusion of nearly unmediated messages from Pamela or Clarissa
holds, just as Richardson intended. The page insists on dissolving into a
reality not itself. If an unrelieved sense of reality is the moral danger of
fiction, then *Clarissa* and *Pamela* are deeply immoral.

Fielding insistently presented his stories as the *author's* story, and he
used every device to prevent the reader from sinking into a naive relation with the text. The author interrupts the action, walks onto the stage
to address the reader directly, does comic turns on exaggerated styles
(the mock epic early in *Tom Jones*). The effect is to keep the reader
consciously aware of artifice, of the conventions of language, aware
that realistic scenes and mock epic are, at heart, the same bag of tricks.
There is a certain moral stance taken by such prose, an austere refusal
by the author to allow the reader even the illusions he *wants* to enjoy.
The voice of Gibbon's *Decline and Fall of the Roman Empire* also tells
us, with its stylized cadences, expressive rhythms, and Tacitean echoes,
that this is a story *told*.[19] In a culture which has highly developed conventions for producing and receiving realistic works of art, extreme
artifice can be a kind of moral austerity.

But just as many contemporary novelists write a prose in which
noticeable stylistic features are almost entirely absent, the artistry of
historical writings does not have to reside at that level of the text. It
consists of selection and pattern. Many historians consciously work to
perfect "documentary" effects. An adroit selection and display of facts
and quoted evidence in the text woven together with nicely modulated
comment by the author can make a firm pattern or generalization seem
to "emerge" from the materials with only modestly unobtrusive coaching
from the historian. The technique is not entirely unlike the one employed
to produce a recording on which a group of dogs unmistakably barks
Jingle Bells. I am emphatically *not* suggesting that what I call the documentary technique is a poor or fraudulent technique; it is a neutral
technique, and "letting the evidence speak for itself" is the historian's
equivalent of Richardson allowing Pamela to speak for herself.

If anything reliably separates history from novels, it is that histories
are relentlessly overplotted. In historical writing (modern, not medieval)
everything presented is significant to the major themes of the work, since
intelligible coherence was the principle of selection which determined
what would be presented in the book. This makes history, by definition,
an overplotted genre, even outrageously so for one claiming a higher
degree of verisimilitude than fiction. History's reality has no room for

contingency, although we acknowledge that reality untouched by interpretation is nothing but. No amount of pontificating about facts and evidence, research, archives, or scientific methods can get around the central fictionality of history, which is its unrelenting meaningfulness. Nothing could be more unreal, more flagrantly fictional, or more necessary. In a novel, if two characters meet "by chance," we raise an eyebrow (or register some mental analogue) at the puppeteer's hands showing on the strings, but in history that is the only kind of thing that happens.

Why, after all, did people accept histories *as* histories before professionalism loaded the text with the icons and artifacts of scholarship? It was chiefly the author's assurance that it *was* a history, made out of other histories, and the components of them. As in antiquity and in the Middle Ages, the *author* was accepted for general moral reliability, and that assurance gave credit to his work. This standard always allowed fiction writers to play games with the "found" story, the "retold" tale, the "true history," the fictional memoir, none of which would have worked if there had been no presumption of a difference between history and fiction (even allowing for occasional works of fiction that played the game too well, like Geoffrey of Monmouth's history). Even as history was becoming professional the assumption lingered that it was perfectly acceptable for an honest historian to write a positive, omniscient prose so long as his readers could know in ways external to the text that he was submitting to the constraints of evidence and reasonable inference. It is only as the traditional mode of narrative has come under suspicion as an inadequate or misleading form of historical explanation that historians have had to give up their unequivocal assertion of past reality....

Since the Renaissance the elements of an acceptable history which the author is allowed, in good conscience, to invent have progressively shrunk, and the degree of explanatory candor demanded of him has grown until now the mere omission of those formal and symbolic explanations automatically relegates a history, however scrupulous, to the secondary level of "popular" history. A history without its system of signals pointing outside itself (its "apparatus," in our revealing mechanical metaphor) demands of its readers a trust we no longer are willing to give. None of the mysteries of the toilet table are supposed to be concealed when a history approaches in published hardcover finery. To change metaphors, the visual relation of notes to text suggests just how long a distance the author thinks he can bridge between supports. And it is exactly that relation of text to notes and all that it implies which historians look to for our essential difference from fiction, our anchor to external reality, to verification and shared standards of truth.

Evidence is the heart of the whole semiotic structure of history – regarded as text, discipline, inquiry, according to taste. Many historians, not always sorting out clearly enough what they fear, seem to regard attention to the writing of history as an affront to evidence, a displacement of apparently finite historical energy from truth to text, from things to signs. Within the professoriate, the word "evidence" (enunciated with a certain special *gravitas*) serves so many purposes, so many of them censorious, that it is best regarded as a minor sign-system in itself.

In the ordinary historian's acceptance, "evidence" indicates a great range of presently existing but previously produced stuff which is the surviving remnant of the past. Most of it is writing, both words and numbers, covering the entire spectrum of denotative and narrative intelligibility (ranging, say, from previous histories to fragmented records of commercial transactions involving archaic and unexplained measures and procedures); some is nonverbal artifact and remains of purposeful activity (buildings, graves, plow furrows); and a portion is natural or not purposely produced phenomena (tree rings, bones of certain chemical composition). All of this and more is included in the category of "evidence," which is a metaphor based on visual perception. The Latinate "evidence," meaning that which is manifest or in plain sight, metaphorically indicates that historical evidence brings the vanished past back into sight. Everything regarded as "evidence" is, of course, evident, present and visible, simply by virtue of its existence, but it is not thereby "evidence." It is only through its metaphorical transformation into the present pieces of a past whole, the partial *visibilia* of an entire invisible world, that it becomes "evidence." In this fundamental sense all of historical evidence is a major trope, a figure of speech and thought which organizes and extends the visible present world to induce the invisible past into intelligible form. Hayden White has described the macrocosmic forms of history in rhetorical terms; I think that the interior mechanism of history, reasoning about evidence, is also rhetorical in structure.

If the dominant trope of history is metaphor, the favorite trope of historians is metonymy. Whether or not historians use the language of rhetoric themselves (and they don't!), they perforce think in it. For the language of evidence is a sign language and even in its apparently simplest forms (a memoir written by a truthful and accurate observer) involves elaborate strategies of interpretive reading. No assemblage of "evidence," however large, can reproduce the past point for point and so the trope of metonymy, which extrapolates a whole thing from its contiguous part, is the organizing concept and argument of even the dryest and most cautious historical construct. Historians like metonymy (with or without its name) for its no-nonsense physicality and straightforward logic: "three head of cattle" informs us of the equally real existence of three tails, six ears, twelve legs. . . . The strategy is reassuringly like archeology, the metonymic discipline *par excellence*: a section of wall implies an entire past building; fragments of pottery imply a vessel. And in a related metonymic argument, artifacts present now in the same stratum are taken to be similarly related in past time. Archeologists, bold-faced masters of the "tone of the historian," present us with the whole Sutton Hoo burial ship treasure: the lute and the helmet (now in its second authoritative version) projected around a few scraps of wood and metal. As bits of metal and wood, regarded by themselves and in the present tense, the corroded and decayed scraps from Sutton Hoo are nothing so much as pathetic; but transformed metaphorically into "evidence" they seem to struggle into intelligibility, and the lute and the helmet in their assertive "thingness" are quite irresistible. Historians like to see themselves as doing something like that.

Sometimes they do, or seem to. But metonymy (alternatively: positivism, the jigsaw-puzzle technique, or following the dots) is not a flexible enough trope for many purposes: it always produces more of the same. A great deal of what we use as evidence has to be "read" (quotation marks to acknowledge the great metaphoric capacities of that verb) in complicated ways approximating synecdoche (as when we discern that something is characteristic or tellingly significant); metaphor (as when we discover a hidden cause or structure underlying apparent or professed meanings); or even irony (as when we notice that conscious human effort in one direction contributes to an opposite result). Metonymy remains the privileged strategy whose presence is often signaled by the term "data," used instead of "evidence" – suggesting scientific, or at least social scientific, accumulations of facts whose engulfing presence seems to leave no room for anything very different in the past – history's equivalent of a proof. As the trope of contiguity (à la Kenneth Burke), metonymy asserts consubstantiality and coexistence between present part and past whole; as the trope of prose (à la Roman Jakobson), of linear connection and rational argument, it asserts the truth-value of present texts as representations of past reality. And if consubstantiality and coexistence have a suspiciously theological ring, then it might as well be admitted that the distance between present text and past reality can only be bridged by a leap of faith.

In professional code, as used in seminar rooms, the subtler tropes are engaged by "asking the right questions of the evidence." The cleverest questions are those that make the evidence give answers about things it did not profess to know. Thus the clever historian asks sermons about economic power; and the sermons obligingly answer in metaphor a great many things about religious enforcement of class stratification. Or the clever historian asks a shrine what it has to say about secular society; and the shrine synecdochically replies that, in fact, it does exhibit in striking miniature a whole network of typical social structures. The historical constructs resulting from these tropes are more interesting and more debatable than metonymic constructs. . . .

This sketch of the rhetorical structure of historical evidence might remind us that rhetoric in its longest tradition is not merely the collection of commonplaces and platitudes (the maligned "cosmetics") but offers a vocabulary to describe the interlinked poetic and logical structures of language and inference. Historians must believe that "evidence" is, in fact, *evidence* (a link to a previously existing reality), understand its rhetorical structures, and write with scrupulous attention to their own special poetics.

> Life being all inclusion and confusion, and art being all discrimination and selection. . . .[20]

All transactions with evidence, from the first creative decision to regard some present thing under the poetic trope of "evidence," through the various and subtle manipulations of textual criticism, diplomatics, statistical correlation, to architectonic decisions about part/whole relations, are acts of interpretation. History is perhaps the most thoroughly hermeneutic creation of all culture: from the "inside" because historians begin by creating a text, the Past, through the interpretive creation of and with evidence; and from the "outside" because they then proceed to explain it. I obviously mean interpretation in the inclusive sense associated most recently with Hans-Georg Gadamer; acts of interpretation do not only attempt to assimilate difficult or unfamiliar objects to our familiar world of meanings, but constitute our understanding of that familiar world and its commonplaces.[21] Our sense of the past, the sense of distance, difference, and silence, which underlies all modern historical study is, in Gadamer's terms, one of the two major "experiences of alienation" which mark off a modern sensibility: aesthetic consciousness, which judges a work of art on aesthetic grounds distinct from religious or other truth claims proceeding from the work; and historical consciousness, "the noble and slowly perfected art of holding ourselves at a critical distance in dealing with witnesses to past life."[22] The processes by which we both stand away from the past in conscious removal and strive to bridge and overcome that critical alienation are those of language, conceived as more than the metaphoric mirror of reality, fully as "the realm of common understanding, of ever-replenished common agreement. . . ."[23] Language is the ability to "make what is not present manifest"[24] – and first among those objects for which we hermeneutically reach is the past.

From Gadamer's standpoint, or from any hermeneutically conditioned standpoint, historical interpretation must always move backward from the finally understood meaning (which can also and appropriately be expressed as a question) back through the connections of men and events which developed and constituted that meaning. This is very like Kermode's paradigm tick-tock plot, which by announcing an end (the recognition of a meaning which is linguistic and has closure) then enables us to see the middleness of what preceded it. Fixing an anchor in the onwardness of time allows certain things (persons, groups, thoughts, actions) to take on intelligible meaning because they can be described as evolving, tending, causing, contributing to, exhibiting, exemplifying, resisting, denying, or irrelevant to the closure that anchors time and meaning. This indispensable pattern is not unlike the formal structure of biblical exegesis as developed by Christian exegetes, for whom the closure of Incarnation and Passion revealed the truth so long hidden in the open-ended narrative struggle of Jewish Scripture.

> Thus, history, with all its concrete force, remains forever a figure, cloaked and needful of interpretation.[25]

The intellectual process of turning the Jewish Scripture into the Old Testament was one of declaring an end and then discovering the "middle-ness" of all that had come before. Gadamer's hermeneutic demands a far more open or conversational sense of meaning, but the basic human demand for meaning in time seems to require some version of these formal patterns of interpretation.

I do want it to be quite clear that this analysis is not intended as a deconstruction. History *is* exegesis and to explain it as such is not to make it deny itself or its truth, but to explain the kind of truth it is. History is a hermeneutic of fragmentary present texts which makes them yield something intelligible and larger than themselves. The hermeneutic necessarily involves layers of figurative interpretation, creating of present odds and ends a metaphoric world called "evidence," and then working out within its confines intricate patterns which force silence and time to take on form. If that sounds disconcertingly far from a simple truthful representation of the past, it is because we are just that distance from the past, the same distance from simple truth. The rules of the game, in such circumstances, are necessarily strict. Words *are* amoral, not immoral, and only too obliging, and history is vulnerable to overdetermination, to crass and clever fraud.

In its professionalized form, among the academic disciplines, history is, I think, specially and peculiarly open to immorality: simple dishonesty, subtle dishonesty, distortions of self-interest, the rationalized spite of ideology, thefts from the living, from the dead, impertinence, disrespect, tendentiousness, and every variety of bad faith. It is certainly possible to misbehave badly in every other art and science, but not in such depth and offensive variety. Scientists can fiddle their data, steal from one another, and defraud the public; only historians can betray all the generations of the dead. It is precisely this capacity for depravity that attests to the essential moral center of history. If the idea of history-as-writing is taken seriously, eradicating or at least blurring most of the traditional distinctions between fiction and nonfiction, then the central and deeply troubling question must be confronted all over again: that of anchoring the integrity of written history. Many historians, including

one who is on the happiest terms with prose style himself, would seem
to have history tie itself to the archival mast and stop its ears against the
siren call of textuality: "history is too pragmatically respectful of archival source materials to be one of those free-floating humanities that are
adrift in an uncharted sea of 'discourse,' verbal ambiguities and fiction.
Historians are still old-fashioned enough to have a regard for truth. . . ."[26]
Archives contain many interesting things, but Truth is not included
among them.

Ideological manipulation and bad-faith tendentiousness cannot always
be counted on to "show themselves up" by being crudely intrusive, internally illogical, obviously selective. Once we relinquish ideas of pure objectivity, and dispassion grounded in a language of reference, in favor of
the standards of interior coherence and culture-bound acceptability which
are the only ones available to us, then we must reconsider what objection
can be legitimately brought against subtle, clever, coherent historical narratives designed to support and forward some ideological program. In
fact, once we loosen our grip, however desperate, on an objective past
and mimetic truth (those amoebic objects shrinking from our grasp),
how can we distinguish between interest and disinterest, between interpretation and ideology?

The standards invoked in the past to ground history in truth were
moral: the moral witness was the man supplied by experience with direct observation of the historical event, and willing (in an exacting sense)
to tell it truthfully. The rhetorical tradition was exemplified by the honest
witness in court – the man of moral integrity and moral independence
whose stance was summed up by the classical, and neoclassical, tag:
"having nothing to hope and nothing to fear." Slaves, we recall, were
systematically tortured in antiquity for judicial purposes, in order to
substitute an immediate motive of self-preservation for the moral weak-
ness of their dependent state. The historian, in the long-lived classical
tradition, was the moral witness.

Acknowledging the confusions and mistakes this approach introduces
into history, historians, ancient and modern, have tried to collect and
collate testimonies to correct for the partial vision of the individual subject. This mode of correction, in its fully elaborated and refined guise,
is more or less what is meant by "critical history" or the "historical
method." The historian remains the moral center and dispassionately
asks "cui bono" and more adroit versions of that question, and then
gives his deposition – in writing. Even sophisticated critics like Hayden
White tend to detour around the question of what goes on between the
historian and his evidence, assuming that careful and good-faith transactions take place which underlie and support whatever veracity the
written history lays claim to, and the written thing is the object of his
interest. And even in history which is precisely about the radical relativity of all intelligible meanings, and regards them as the superstructures

of self-interested classes, energetically "covering" themselves with self-justifying culture, the historian is still at the moral center, exposing past culture for the clever fraud it always was. After all solemn invocations of critical method, evidence, archives, we are just left to hope for the best: hope, namely, that persuasion will necessarily involve the traditional values of honesty, restraint, respect for sources, and that their absence will result in some fairly obvious flaw.

We no longer possess, in Art or Science, a simple unified framework – a world and its verifiable expression in descriptive language – to be taken as existing, without opposition or alternative.[27] This is true for present experience of the presently existing world (by which I primarily mean its meaning and values); the case of history is merely the most exaggerated, endlessly problematic form of it. If there is a genre distinction to be made between fiction and history (and there still is), it is going to rest heavily on the highly specialized, rigorously evolved methods for discerning, selecting, and interpreting the materials from which a narrative claiming nonfictional status may be constructed, and on the narrative point of view – the implied relation between the teller and the told. These are distinctions of degree, not kind, and they underlie claims to acceptable knowledge, not certainty. The truth for history must be something close to integrity of method, and its philosophical allegiance is with pragmatism, not relativism.[28] The truth of an art true to its rules is human, provisional, self-critical, and self-disciplining, and it will have to do.

History is a hermeneutic expressed in narrative prose constructed under special, severe constraints such as an architect might accept when designing a building to be stable, safe, and suitable for its proposed use, harmonious and continuous with existing buildings and the traditional character of its neighborhood, but also distinctive and original in its satisfaction of these requirements.[29] The special constraints governing the finding and handling of evidence, previous scholarship, argumentation, provisional and declarative statements, constitute the epistemological (and artistic) foundation of history, which is one of common agreements and standards in an intellectual community. We still "have a regard for truth"; the very aesthetic of history is inseparable from it.[30]

The first historians, the redactors of the Hebrew Bible, preserved the truth of Moses, chosen by God to lead his people out of slavery in Egypt, convey to them the Torah, and direct them to the land promised them.

The Christians of antiquity said that the Moses of the Hebrew Scripture was indeed those things, but Truth was the Moses of the Old Testament who prefigured the Christ who came to lead his people from bondage under the law to salvation through belief in the new dispensation.

Tacitus said that the Jews were a vile people who had been expelled from Egypt because they were diseased; the Christians were a disgusting lot as well; and all of them were bad for Rome.

Nancy F. Partner

Augustine said that the Jews were trapped in a literal reading of their own history; the Christians were not bad for Rome, and the whole question was cosmically beside the point.

Gibbon, offering more elevated reasons, tended, on the whole, to agree with Tacitus.

Modern scholars say that the Hebrew redactors scrupulously compiled the historical traditions of their people in the light of their belief in revealed truth; that the Christians strenuously reinterpreted those writings in the light of their new conception of truth; that Tacitus was tendentious and wrong but had his reasons; Augustine tendentious and right by his lights; and Gibbon doesn't count.

I mention these issues simply because they are the paradigm cases of historical consciousness and the struggle with truth in the Western tradition. I may have made the modern historical approach sound like relativism, which was not my intention. Attempting to arrive at certainty or a description of the past actuality of any of the events suggested by my sketch has to involve framing and reframing questions of such intricacy and so flexibly aligned to points of view that the whole enterprise may as well be called hermeneutic from the start, but a hermeneutic striving for truth. In the Western tradition, history occupies an uncomfortable dividing stage between epistemology and hermeneutics, between logic and interpretation, because, in its bluntest reduction, the ancient Hebrews *wrote* their experience, wrote it as books, as story, as history, and thereby locked history crucially to truth and to reality, while committing it to the narration of the half-known. For Butterfield the Hebrew consciousness of the past, their greater obsession with history than possibly any other nation, is "the greatest surprise in the whole story"; and the creation of their own history stands as the epitome, the microcosm, "a pocket-sized example of the very rise of historiography."[31]

Near the same time that Herodotus was recording the valiant stand of the Spartan three hundred at Thermopylae, securing with his record that final necessary completion of glory and memory for an action which fulfilled entirely the demands that the Greek conception of life could make on men, Hebrew scribes whose names we do not know were recording the struggling failures of generations of Jews to meet the endless requirements which life in the knowledge of the one God opened to human history. There could be no Hebrew Thermopylae – an action complete in the classical unities, and morally complete. The God of history made neatness no longer count, and no action would ever again be morally complete. History in the created world is open-ended and cannot evade ambiguity. The Hebraic God of history rules the ethos of history in our culture – an ethos which subjects history to the withering attentions of logical inquiry while demanding continual renewal in acts of creative imagination. History asserts truths which are unprovable, undemonstrable by any rigorous standard, and which shift around in shameless publicity (whatever happened to King Arthur, the Donation of Constantine, the idea of progress?) and yet it carries the burden of human identity and moral dignity. . . .

All historians know that history is no longer the discipline busily fulfilling its positivistic promise to tell it all as it really happened. And, in fact, that cultural moment, of naive assertions about splicing together an entire, indubitable, objectively once-existing Past, was a very brief digression in history's longer, more richly compromised life as the expressive artifact of tradition, culture, human defiance of time – the whole cultural baggage carried variously and jointly by religion, literature, art, and history. Somewhere in that baggage are truth, objectivity, and dispassionate reason, but as part of the culture, not outside in some preverbal higher reality. In an important way, epistemology and fiction threaten only to restore history to its ancient place among the creators of culture, of meaning and continuity.

Perhaps historians must learn to reconsider representation, as an *act*, the verb of conscious intention, not the placid noun, target of philosophic bombs. Mimesis as the continuing assertion of the existence of the centered world can continue, but *as* an assertion, an action which creates exteriority, and sustains it. By rendering a world whose attributes are "pastness" and "reality," we lay claim to it as fully as we can to anything. And if this more desolate version, this post-lapsarian version, of Auerbach's classic search for the literature of reality seems hopelessly entangled in self-consciousness – so be it. Some worlds are just more difficult than others.

Notes

1 Elizabeth Bowen, *The Heat of the Day* (New York, 1949), p. 146.
2 Frank Kermode, *The Sense of an Ending: Studies in the Theory of Fiction* (New York, 1967). This widely read and deservedly influential book holds many suggestions and provocations for writers and readers of history.
3 Kermode, *Sense of an Ending*, p. 45.
4 Ivy Compton-Burnett, *Parents and Children* (London, 1941; reprinted 1960), p. 209.
5 Among the most interesting books which are not about history specifically but which seem to speak to its special concerns are: Frank Kermode, *The Genesis of Secrecy: On the Interpretation of Narrative* (Cambridge, Mass., 1979); Robert Alter, *The Art of Biblical Narrative* (New York, 1981); Richard Lanham, *Style: An Anti-Textbook* (New Haven, 1974), and *The Motives of Eloquence* (New Haven, 1976).
6 The fragment of quotation is from the Bowen epigraph; an exceptionally subtle awareness of the determining power of beginnings for historical interpretation can be seen in John Gager's discussion of how traditional choices of textual starting points have determined centuries of understanding of

Paul's letters: *The Origins of Anti-Semitism* (New York and Oxford, 1983), pp. 204–5.

7 Henry James, "The Art of Fiction," in *Henry James: Representative Selections*, ed. L. N. Richardson (Urbana, 1966), p. 77: ". . . to insist on the fact that as the picture is reality, so the novel is history. That is the only general description (which does it justice) that we may give of the novel. . . . It must speak with assurance, with the tone of the historian."

8 A note on consoling stories: one of the sources of the power of the Genesis creation story is that it affirms that the world is external and independent of us, that reality is real. In this respect, the Genesis story is the primal true fiction: it asserts what we have to believe before we can reason to anything else. Further, the candid fictionality of the story, its conflated alternative versions, acknowledges our inability to confront reality unmediated by language and the necessary fictionality of all "beginnings."

9 Herbert Butterfield, *The Origins of History* (New York, 1981), p. 14. A recent, more specialized book, John Van Seters, *In Search of History: Historiography in the Ancient World and the Origins of Biblical History* (New Haven, 1983), starts from entirely different assumptions. The author notes his divergence from Butterfield and the reasons for it on p. 5.

10 Butterfield, *Origins*, pp. 14, 15.

11 Ibid., p. 129.

12 Ibid., p. 134.

13 Bowen, *Heat of the Day*, p. 155.

14 A subtle discussion of the multifaceted elements, supplied by artist and viewer, which combine to produce the effect of portraiture, the perception of "what is constant behind the changing appearance," is Ernst Gombrich's "The Mask and the Face: The Perception of Physiognomic Likeness in Life and in Art," in Ernst Gombrich, Julian Hachberg, and Max Black, *Art, Perception, and Reality* (Baltimore, 1972), pp. 1–46, esp. the passage on pp. 42–6.

15 David Douglas, *William the Conqueror* (Berkeley, 1964), p. 194.

16 Nelson Goodman, "On Symptoms of the Aesthetic," in *Of Mind and Other Matters* (Cambridge, Mass., 1984), p. 137.

17 Douglas, "The Seamless Robe: An Historian's Apology," in *Time and the Hour* (London, 1977), p. 16. Douglas defends the view that history is a branch of literature and an art of a special kind on pp. 18–19.

18 Goodman, "Symptoms," pp. 135–8. Among other provocative comments and reflections in this book of replies to critics and questions, see: "About Truth About," pp. 99–107; "Fiction for Five Fingers," pp. 123–6.

19 Peter Gay's chapter on Gibbon in *Style in History* (New York, 1974) is the best exposition of the implications of Gibbon's imitation of Tacitus.

20 Henry James, *The Notebooks of Henry James* (New York, 1955), p. xiv.

21 Hans-Georg Gadamer, "The Universality of the Hermeneutical Problem," in *Philosophical Hermeneutics*, ed. and trans. David E. Linge (Berkeley, 1976), pp. 3–17, esp. 7–8 and 15: "There is always a world already interpreted, already organized in its basic relations, into which experience steps as something new, upsetting what has led our expectations and undergoing reorganization itself in the upheaval."

22 Ibid., p. 5.

23 Gadamer, "Man and Language," in *Hermeneutics*, p. 68: "Hence language is the real medium of human being, if we only see it in the realm that it

alone fills out, the realm of human being-together, the realm of common understanding, of ever-replenished common agreement – a realm as indispensable to human life as the air we breathe. As Aristotle said, man is truly the being who has language. For we should let everything human be spoken to us."

24 Ibid., p. 60.
25 Erich Auerbach, "Figura," in *Scenes from the Drama of European Literature* (New York, 1959), p. 58.
26 Stone, review of John Kenyon, *The History Men*, in *New York Times Book Review*, March 18, 1984.
27 Again, I like thinking about the succinct and wittily drawn formulations of Nelson Goodman, who does not hedge his bets: see "The Telling and the Told," in *Of Mind and Other Matters*, pp. 122–3. For Goodman, who is *not* a relativist, there is no "absolute order of events independent of all versions" (p. 122). All stories, including true ones, are versions.
28 Richard Rorty defends pragmatism against the spurious charge of relativism in "Pragmatism, Relativism, and Irrationalism," presidential address in *Proceedings and Addresses of the American Philosophical Association* 53 (Aug. 1980), 719–38. His radical criticism of standard academic epistemologically centered philosophy and its desire to ground all culture, belief, religion, politics, and morality on philosophic bases of certain knowledge offers, incidentally, the strongest argument against ideas that history is intrinsically weak because it lacks scientific proofs.
29 In a recent lecture, Nelson Goodman proposed a fundamental revision of the philosophical enterprise, along lines consonant with Rorty's proposed revival of pragmatism. Goodman suggests that the central philosophical concepts of truth, certainty, and knowledge (all posited on an epistemology of exact correspondence) be replaced by "rightness" (whose test is whether something "fits" into a construct in such a way that the created whole "works"); "adoption" (a provisional acceptance based on fitting and working); "understanding" (intellectual accomplishment with respect to the process of adoption and fitting). The "work" he refers to is not that of practical usefulness but aesthetic or cognitive, chiefly conceived as the intellectual work toward new understandings within and extending the traditional culture. History could make a good case in point, and I think that the metaphor of architecture works fairly well both for history and for Goodman's version of pragmatism. Goodman, lecture: "A Reconception of Philosophy," University of California, Berkeley, February 4, 1985.
30 David Couzens Hoy, whose book on Gadamer, his critics, and the implications of hermeneutics for historical inquiry and literary criticism has been widely read, specifically protests any suggestion that Gadamer's ideas lead to "a position that history is purely literary. . . ." *The Critical Circle: Literature, History, and Philosophical Hermeneutics* (Berkeley, 1978), p. 148, and generally part five: "Hermes and Clio," pp. 131–68.
31 Butterfield, *Origins*, pp. 81, 95. He is significantly kinder to the creation of historical narrative here: "They may have needed to learn nothing [from other peoples] except the fact that the past could be marshalled into a story and history could be a form of literature and also the fact that the story could be so constructed as to show the judgment of heaven on human sin" (pp. 95ff.).

5
History, Language, and Reading: Waiting for Crillon

Dominick LaCapra

A comparison of the first number of the first volume of the *American Historical Review* (October 1895) with recent issues of the journal might expectably reveal both continuities and discontinuities. Immediately evident is the basic format of substantive, monographic articles followed by book reviews. No longer retained is the special section on "documents." Still prominent, however, are the articles that contribute to research on specific topics. And the continued role of book reviews attests to their crucial function in establishing in practice the criteria of the discipline through quality control and policing procedures in which the selection of aspects of the work under review for special mention and the allocation of praise or blame affirm, reinforce, or attempt to revise disciplinary norms. An obvious yet important difference between "then" and "now" is indicated by the overwhelmingly Eurocentric nature of the early issues, in which the bulk of attention is lavished on the United States and England.

More striking, or at least less expected, a juxtaposition of the articles by William M. Sloane ("History and Democracy") and Henry Adams ("Count Edward de Crillon") might prepare one for recent controversies, notably debates bearing on the relation between history and deconstruction.[1] When one reads these inaugural articles together, it seems that Sloane takes the high road and almost appears as the "straight man" in sharp contrast to Adams as the doubting *eiron*. The very titles of their articles sound a significant difference, for in contrast to a "sit-up-and-take-notice" response to the weighty issues of "history and democracy," one is tempted to ask: Who was Edward de Crillon? And who cares?

For Sloane, history is a science, and his advocacy of objectivity may seem to imply the existence of an invariant characteristic of the discipline over time. . . . The linkage of science and democracy also prompts "the final question" – "whether [history] will continue to be literary in the old or in any sense." Here, Sloane once again invokes the principle of unity, for science may readily be reconciled with art in the interest of truth, notably because "the highest form of literacy, as it is of historical, criticism is to separate the permanent from the transitory in its own age." . . .[2]

By marked contrast with Sloane's harmonizing and idealizing dedication to unity, Henry Adams introduces chasms into the very core of historiography itself, and he emphasizes its erring nature with an insistence that might bring to the mind of today's reader the theories of Paul de Man. Adams's topic seems less than transitory, and his vision of disconcerting and uncannily proliferating error in the work of the historian eventuates in an idea of the historian's craft as threatened by melt-down into "an inextricable mess." For him, "the historian is properly responsible only for his own personal error, but this he can never calculate, since it is hopelessly confused with the conditions of his education, his society, and his age . . . Some historians are more, some less, inaccurate; but the best must always stand in terror of the blunders which no precaution and no anxiety can save him from committing." Indeed, such is the historian's plight that, "conscious of the pitfalls that surround him, the writer of history can only wait in silent hope that no one will read him, – at least with too much attention."[3]

After these hyperbolic words of caution, which are difficult to distinguish from ironic counsels of despair, Adams goes on to interweave "documents" with his own commentary in a rather bizarre and seemingly pointless effort to determine just who Count Edward de Crillon – mistakenly identified by James Madison as one of Napoleon's secret agents – really was. . . .

Adams asserts that the "blunder" involved in the identification of Crillon as an official French secret agent, which can be "found in Volume II, page 186, of the *History of the First Administration of Madison*," is "fortunately of so little consequence as to allow of attaching a story to it."[4] If it is not taken as a warning signal concerning the role of "literary" techniques in Adams's own account that are less easily harmonized with "science" than Sloane believed, this statement is suspiciously paradoxical, for it acknowledges the relative unimportance of Crillon's identity yet asserts that this very status allows "attaching a story to it." In history, one would expect a "story" to be warranted in relation to real matters of some importance.

Adams's style is strongly reminiscent of that in *The Education of Henry Adams* (1907). Its ironic nature, along with the fantastic tale it unfolds, almost leads one to expect that Adams will follow novelistic convention by informing the reader that he found the documents relating to Crillon in a trunk or a bottle washed up on shore. In fact, he informs us that "a volume of the archives of the French Foreign Office, overlooked in the original search for documents relating to the United States, contains some papers relating to this matter, which seems at the time to have perplexed the French government almost as much as it annoyed Mr. Madison." The suspect "identity" that the hitherto-undiscovered archival stash reveals for Crillon is that of a chameleon-like confidence man who was originally named Soubiron and acquired the name of Crillon (as well as his benefactor's fortune) from a M. de Crillon Partorias, one of the many who confided in him.[5] Adams himself tells the reader that "Soubiron was a lineal descendant from that society which the Spaniards called *picaresque*, and which had a literature of its own . . . Soubiron was a Gascon, and must have been a more or less plausible rogue." Adams even concludes that the man was "merely a common swindler."[6] Indeed, aspects of Soubiron-Crillon's story are so implausible that they would not pass muster in serious fiction. While Adams was not a "common swindler," he had more than a touch of the picaro; and the sustained ironic style, hyperbolic skepticism, disorienting stress on blunders, ludic melancholy, and intertextual resonances (both with reference to *The Education* and to picaresque novels of adventure) may leave the reader somewhat perplexed, if not annoyed, about what precisely to make of his contribution to the inaugural volume of the *AHR*. In any case, its features may lead one to question a reliance on a golden-age mythology that nostalgically invokes the glories of a more "objective," less "deconstructive" past and bemoans a putative recent descent of the profession into epistemological and methodological disarray.

My introductory comments in certain ways confirm the narrative (but not the apparently gloomy import of the "no-king-in-Israel" conclusion) of Peter Novick's *That Noble Dream: The "Objectivity Question" and the American Historical Profession*.[7] They indicate that it is deceptive to rely on any simple "from/to" scenario in relating the past to the present of the discipline. The model Novick's treatment suggests is one of repetition with more or less significant – at times, seemingly traumatic – change. Disciplinary consensus on the ideal of objectivity has not only varied with changing or tensely interacting conceptions of science. It has been disturbed in the past by skepticism and doubt often seen as implying relativism, not only in Henry Adams but most notably at the time of Charles Beard, Carl Becker, and the New History. In certain ways, recent controversies about various "new historicisms" recall these earlier debates. But Novick himself sees the recent period not simply as bringing a heightened intensity of questioning but as involving a more specific focus on the problems of language and signification. This emphasis on language also typifies the influential review essay by John Toews on the "linguistic turn," which I shall discuss later in this article.[8] This turn, which of course has many and at times incompatible variants, is most fruitfully understood as involving a recognition of the problematic nature of language or any signifying practice (ritual or dance, for example).

Language in this sense is not a purely transparent medium that may simply be looked through (or bracketed) in the interest of (re)presenting the object or findings of research. It poses problems for the historian (or other analyst) and signals the manner in which the observer is constitutively implicated in the object of research. With reference to psychoanalysis, Freud framed this problem in terms of transference, and transference involves both the tendency of the analyst–analysand relation to repeat typically inappropriate parent–child relations and the more general tendency of an analytic discourse to repeat the problems at issue in its object of analysis. . . . The goal for Freud was to pass from a perhaps inevitable and necessary tendency to "act out" (or compulsively relive) these problems – a tendency particularly insistent with respect to traumatic events – to the attempt to recall them in memory and critically work through them.[9]

The linguistic turn brings with it an openness to literary and critical theory, including aspects of (Continental) philosophy, in the effort to rethink the nature and acceptable boundaries of historiography. It also mitigates the stark dichotomy between history and metahistory, if by the latter one means critical and self-critical theory bearing on the practice of history itself. Insofar as the professionalization of the discipline was experienced as requiring boundary setting, and literature, literary theory, and philosophy were either positioned as largely negative identities or effortlessly harmonized with science in a deceptively ideal unity, then the recent turn to theory and the controversies it stimulates may be interpreted as a return of the repressed. Moreover, the varying fortunes of narrative in historiography indicate the role of a variable proximity to a certain dimension of literature and literary theory, but this proximity – both in those who cultivate and in those who excoriate it – has until recently been typically enacted or acted out rather than lucidly theorized. And the recent emphasis on narrativity has not brought consensus among historians either about the role of narrative in historiography or about the precise nature and status of narrative procedures in history and literature.[10] The possibility that the turn to narrative theory (and the "literary" more generally) may be a sign of a returning repressed also helps to explain the excesses in the gesture, including the tendency at times to cannibalize literary theory and to make an unmediated and uncritical application of it to historiography. Moreover, it induces opponents of the turn to run together those who have shown an interest in it and to castigate them in an indiscriminate manner as herdlike creatures in a night in which all cows are gray.[11]

There is a sense in which placing language or, more generally, signification in the foreground of attention and having it apply self-reflexively to the practice of the historian creates a crisis or at least a minor trauma in historiography. For this turn means that one cannot stay fixated on the object of research, construe this object in a purely objectified manner, and provide unproblematic, "sun-clear" reports about its nature. Moreover, one cannot situate language or signification in a merely instrumental and subordinate position, and it cannot be confined to the status of simply one more object of investigation. Indeed, with the turn to language, an entire research paradigm may be placed in question.

A relatively self-sufficient research paradigm was in certain ways important for the professionalization of history as a discipline, and attacks on tendencies that question it may be taken as one indication of the extent to which it is still understood (perhaps misleadingly) as essential to the discipline even today. This paradigm enjoins gathering and analyzing (preferably archival) information about an object of study in contrast to reading and interpreting texts or textualized phenomena. (In this exclusionary sense, reading a text, especially a published text, is *not* doing research.) In its self-sufficient form, which may be common to conceptions of history as science and as narrative art, the research paradigm is at least loosely modeled on a certain objectifying idea of science (or narrative) in which there is a definitive separation and relation of cognitive mastery between the observer and the observed. The observer puts forth certain theses or hypotheses about the observed that are subject to confirmation or disconfirmation through empirical investigation.

Obviously, important elements of this paradigm, such as the gathering and analysis of information or the testing of propositions, may be defended and distinguished from their role in what I am terming a relatively self-sufficient research paradigm, and the very concept of what counts as research may change (initiatives I deem desirable). Moreover, this paradigm or model should be seen as objectivist or one-sidedly objectifying rather than as simply objective, for it is possible to have a conception of objectivity that does not depend on it, and criticisms of it should not be seen as entailing an indiscriminate skepticism or a theory of history (or historiography) as endless erring in abyssal chasms.

An alternative conception of objectivity would stress the importance of thorough research and accuracy, while nonetheless recognizing that language helps to constitute its object, historical statements depend on inferences from textualized traces, and the position of the historian cannot be taken for granted. There would be an active awareness that such issues as the subject-position(s) and voice(s) of the historian are an integral component of historiography complicating research and that the elucidation of one's implication in a contemporary network of research and methodological–theoretical–ideological controversy is not simply a dispensable matter of "metahistory" or a specialized activity to be relegated to the "think-piece." Moreover, one could not rely on the idea that objectivity is a normal given of historiography assured by established procedures or that bias is a deviation from normality for which one may simply "correct." Rather, one's perspective would be transformed insofar as one recognized the constitutive place of the historian in the research project and saw objectivity not as the simple opposite of subjectivity but as a tenuous yet valuable goal of a process of elaborating a range of subject-positions (for example, those of researcher, reader, and theorist or intellectual) by negotiating "transferential" relations in a critical and self-critical manner. Research would be combined with reading and interpretation in a larger, more problematic conception of historiography in which the work of different historians would justifiably show different weightings and articulations and the decisive opposition between texts and documents would be questioned. Documents would be read textually, and the manner in which they construct their object in an institutional and ideological field would be a matter of critical scrutiny, while the documentary dimensions of texts would be posed as an explicit problem and elucidated.

Reading in both its literal and metaphoric senses is a crucial constituent of the problem of language. And it is reciprocally related to writing. A mode of reading implies a mode of writing (and vice versa). In this sense, a different mode of reading would imply that the writing of history would also undergo significant variations and that historical works might take different forms. I do not think there is any simple choice between research and practices of reading and writing, although there is a tense and at times agonistic relation between them. But the problem in historiography is to conjoin them and to attempt to determine what range of practices combines in an acceptable manner a revised understanding of research and modes of reading and writing (or, more generally, practices of signification). I am here assuming that historiography as a professional discipline need not be – and in fact has not been – predicated on one monological disciplinary practice but that it requires a certain coherence that can be satisfied by a range of practices evincing different emphases (for example, between research and reading or interpretation). What this range of practices is, however, should be seen as contestable and not subject to decision in an *a priori* manner. It should be a matter of informed argument and debate. In this sense, one should not be able to rule someone out of the profession in an apodictic manner because one disagrees with his or her practice.

Moreover, one should be open to the possibility that, in the event a certain practice is not "properly" historical, a given individual may combine it with historical practices in hybridized roles or subject-positions. The question of what modes of hybridization are acceptable would raise debates about historiography to another level and would reinforce the argument that the definition of historiography is contestable, perhaps essentially contestable. Such hybridized or cross-disciplinary positions could be seen as blurred only from within secure, decisive disciplinary enclosures, and such a view of them might well obscure newer articulations that are being formulated in and through them – articulations that may be most suitable for addressing problems that themselves cut across disciplines (such as the relation between text and context or between the present and the past). In practice, of course, decisions have to – and would be – made, and such material matters as whether new departments or programs should be instituted or who should be hired for a given position would provide a pragmatic court of appeal – but one whose determinations might well change over time with changing conceptions of the acceptable range of disciplinary practices. For example, one might decide that the hybridization of historian with critical theorist or public intellectual was acceptable, indeed, desirable if the latter role did not involve direct propagandizing in the classroom or the use of professional arenas, such as conventions or the pages of the *AHR*, for narrow partisan–political activities.

I would propose that there are at present at least five important approaches to reading that are relevant to the practice of history. . . . Any given historian may employ or even combine two or more approaches, although it is often the case that one approach is most prominent in a historian's work; it shapes the character of inquiry and is used to determine what aspects of the other four are particularly useful or open to appropriation. In any event, there are more or less pronounced tensions involved in the combination of at least certain types with one another in discursive practice. . . . The goal of the typology is to locate important protocols of reading that cut across both thematic emphases on issues such as race, gender, class, and sexual orientation (prominent in Marxism, feminism, ethnic studies, and gay and lesbian studies) and disciplines (notably history, philosophy, social theory, and literary criticism), although certain protocols may be much more prominent in certain emphases or disciplines than in others. Problems of race, gender, class, and sexual orientation are of crucial importance, and they should be addressed. The question for further inquiry is whether they are best addressed through one or more of the protocols of reading I shall discuss – or whether another approach I do not envision would be better still.

1 The Denial or Repression of Reading

Here, the dominance of a seemingly self-sufficient research paradigm leads to an inability to recognize reading as a problem. All texts and documents are assimilated to a homogeneous status as sources or evidence that enable the determination of certain findings. Research findings are often "written up" rather than written in a stronger sense, and an unadorned plain style is favored. Typically, literary or philosophical texts are reduced to the status of unreliable sources because they do not yield solid evidence or clear-cut facts about empirical states of affairs. They tend to be excluded from the record or at most referred to in brief, allusive ways as possibly suggestive for research. In any event, whatever they yield must be checked against more reliable documents, thus rendering their status redundant.[12]

In this approach, a priority has often been placed on archival sources and extensive archival research in which the critique of sources is limited to validating the authenticity of documents.[13] But this priority is in no sense necessary, and texts of both high and popular culture may be treated in accordance with a research paradigm for which reading is not a problem. Motives and ideological "bias" in those one investigates may of course be suspected, but such bias refers primarily to conscious intentions or well-defined strategies that may be established with the same certainty as the meaning of a text through straightforward reading of its context. Ideally, other texts (such as letters) give grounds for the ascription of ideological intentions that may be compared with what the manifest content of documents reveals. The goal is to elaborate either a particularistic or a more panoptic, panoramic account of a context in relation to which texts are strictly subordinate if not merely symptomatic documents. Instruction at the graduate level tends to take the form of devising research projects that emulate valued exemplars of successful research, thus avoiding the lures of approaches to history that do not conform to a self-sufficient research paradigm. Research itself is successful if it revises a hypothesis or retells a story in a manner that adds to, revises, or, in rare cases, overturns earlier respected examples of successful research on the basis of extensive (ideally, exhaustive), solidly grounded empirical inquiry.

At present, the above description may seem like a caricature, but the question is the extent to which the caricature still captures crucial aspects of actual practice and graduate training. To refer briefly to a "then" of which I still have a vivid memory, my own graduate training in the 1960s by and large conformed to this model. . . .

Whenever I am inclined to believe that at present the preceding caricature no longer applies, I encounter a historian who arises to enact or act it out even while he or she may want to dismiss it as inapplicable. To the extent my experience is representative, it bears witness to inner division and anxiety in the profession provoked by recent critical–theoretical initiatives. Still, certain procedures have been modified and in certain places (such as my own university) drastically overhauled, at least in some areas of history. These procedures embodied virtues that many (myself included) would like to retain in a different conception of research, reading, and graduate education – virtues such as the insistence on extensive (ideally, exhaustive) research concerning a topic; a thorough knowledge of literature relevant to one's object of inquiry; an ability to conduct independent research; a concern for meticulous care in making statements or assertions and in validating their more empirical or constative aspects; and the judgment necessary to make significant distinctions and to frame explicitly (but not simply to exclude) as speculative or hyperbolic certain dimensions of an account or argument. But the limitations of a narrowly construed, exclusionary research paradigm need not be belabored, notably confinement of historical understanding to a restricted, constative, empirical–analytic model and unconcern (if not disdain) for critical and self-critical theory.[14] It is no doubt true that a lack of concern for theoretical problems, including the complexities of reading texts and documents, facilitates both a mellifluous, accessible writing style and the acquisition of large amounts of empirical information, while problematizing certain procedures can have an inhibiting effect or at least subject certain procedures to time-consuming and possibly doubt-creating critical processes. But the issue is not simply whether the gains of problematization outweigh the losses but whether certain procedures of exclusion are acceptable or even cognitively responsible once questions about them do arise and seem cogent.

2 Synoptic Reading

The synoptic approach to reading, typically with a focus on content or theme, in a sense makes explicit the practice of reading that is operative when reading is not taken as problematic in a research paradigm. It thus may help open certain practices to inspection and debate, enabling a more precise idea of their virtues and limitations. Furthermore, literary or philosophical texts may now be objects of extended study or even focal points of research. But the synoptic or paraphrastic approach remains geared to reporting the "findings" of reading or summarizing the meaning of large runs of texts or documents in a concise, lucid manner. Moreover, it downplays nuances and is geared to the reconstruction of the object, often to the exclusion (or occlusion) of a more dialogic, critical exchange with the past and its artifacts.

Synopsis may, of course, be the primary method of reading in intellectual and cultural history as well as in other subdisciplines. Typically, the goal of such reading is to derive reliable information, to state the manifest meaning of a text or document, and to develop some overarching thesis about a period, phenomenon, or development to which specific texts contribute primarily as symptom, illustration, or evidence. One may at times grant priority to texts and documents from which facts can be extracted to reinforce or supplement one's reconstruction of a phenomenon or period. Texts (such as those of James Joyce, Virginia Woolf, Samuel Beckett, or even Jacques Derrida) that render precious little for this method may be declared to be unreadable, unintelligible, or obscurantist, and their authors deemed hermetic or nihilistic. The difficulty in some periods, including the modern one, is that so many texts and writers tend to fall into this category that the historian is inclined to develop reductive theses about their disastrous effects or their status as mere symptoms of the worst modernity has to offer. They by and large bear witness to a destruction of reason, a misguided departure from cherished Enlightenment ideals, a death-dance of principles, a past imperfect, or an "after-everything" phantasmagoria.[15]

The synoptic approach shares with the denial of reading a focus on the signified (or meaning) and the referents of texts to the virtual exclusion of a concern for the work and play of the signifier or, more generally, for the way a text does what it does. It is in good part for this reason that reading (and writing) remain relatively unproblematic in this approach. But one should recognize that synopsis and its attendant procedures remain a basic and important level of all reading concerned with meaning, reference, and the reconstruction of the object of study.[16] Moreover, certain procedures that typically attend it are desirable, for example, the insistence on thorough research, the importance of substantiating empirical statements, and the careful distinction between empirical and more speculative assertions – procedures that are ingrained as common sense in professional historiography. This insistence may at times be misplaced insofar as it inhibits or invalidates more insistently interpretive or speculative ventures even when they are clearly framed as such. But it is nonetheless valuable as a characteristic of research and a check on more extravagant tendencies in reading and interpretation.

It is arguable that the synoptic approach and procedures related to it have become hegemonic or conventional in the historical discipline. But what is taken to be conventional changes over time and with different disciplines or discursive–institutional areas of society, and the attempt to determine what is or is not hegemonic in a complex field, especially at a time of intense controversy and change, is tentative at best. For example, New Criticism may now be conventional, even old-fashioned in literary criticism, and it did pay attention to the signifier, if only in a restricted, formalistic manner geared to the discovery of formal principles and the integrating role of irony and paradox. In historiography, by contrast, New Critical formalism is not conventional, and certain theorists who, from a literary-critical point of view, might be seen as in good measure New Critical (such as Hayden White in *Metahistory*) may be taken as radical or revolutionary within the historiographical field. Indeed, the goal of a counter-hegemonic practice (in contrast to an endlessly transgressive or anarchistic one) is to establish new conventions and norms in a discursive practice, although the norms deemed more desirable may be more open and self-questioning, notably with respect to the role of hybridization and the need for contestation or periodic transgression.

3 Deconstructive Reading

Deconstruction is of course a complex, heterogeneous movement that has been more prominent in literary criticism and certain branches of

Continental philosophy than in history. But historians have shown interest in it, if only to learn enough about it in order to criticize it and its "lures," often, if not typically, understanding it in rather reductive or truncated terms.[17] But, given the complexity of deconstruction and the variety of ways in which it is construed or employed, it is difficult not to be reductive in making generalizations about it or its more prominent practitioners, and I cannot claim to have escaped this difficulty in my own discussion.

In deconstructive reading, there is a pronounced suspicion of synoptic or contextual reductionism, and virtually everything is to be found in nuance and the close reader's response to it. This approach to reading often brings extremely dismissive reactions to synoptic, content-oriented, and constative (or representational) reading practices – reactions espe- cially evident in radical forms of deconstruction. Paul de Man and those modeling themselves on him tend to be radically deconstructive in the sense I am invoking. The writings of Derrida are more divided and at times involve countervailing forces, although they have a strong pull in a radically deconstructive direction that has perhaps been exacerbated with de Man's death and Derrida's inclination at times to identify with his theoretical views and reading practices.[18] In any case, the problem of the relationship between de Man and Derrida over time has received inadequate analysis because of the prevalent tendency of American decon- structionists to amalgamate the writings of de Man and Derrida into an insufficiently differentiated deconstructive reading practice or mode of criticism.[19]

By radical deconstruction, I mean the tendency to take the impor- tant resistances to meaning and the internal contestations or tensions in texts and to become fixated on them by reading all texts in terms of an almost compulsively repeated process of locating an aporia, *mise en abîme*, uncanny nodal point, or process of internal undoing. The resis- tance to meaning thus threatens to become an externally predictable but internally compelling evacuation of meaning, and all roads in reading seem to lead to the aporia. Indeed, meaning (or the signified) tends to be eliminated or at least bracketed, and attention is riveted on the enig- matic play of the signifier that becomes arbitrary, mechanical, inhuman, "free" play. Moreover, the valuable emphasis on the conditions of pos- sibility of a phenomenon or a historical process may be absolutized such that these conditions displace rather than inform history and lead to an abstract, meta-metaphysical mode of analysis in which specificity is lost or obscured.

In de Man, there is a marked contrast or unstable binary opposition between hermeneutics and poetics. Hermeneutics is interpretation that seeks the meaning of texts, while poetics focuses on the play of the mate- rial signifier that is both the condition of meaning and the force that prevents meaning from being satisfying or even at times from constitut- ing itself in any intelligible manner.[20] De Man sees an inevitable "fall" into hermeneutics even in the most "rigorous" critical practice, but this movement to meaning is evidently a "fall" in the strong sense, bringing with it displaced religious connotations. The ideal is an ascetic practice of criticism in which rigor entails resistance to meaning – particularly unearned meaning – and its seemingly all-consuming ideological lures. . . .

In Derrida, one may distinguish between two related processes that have different weights in Derrida's various writings: deconstruction and dissemination. Deconstruction involves the analysis of the tensely related, internally "dialogized" forces in a text that place its author's explicit goals or intentions in more or less extreme jeopardy. Most prominently, an author's reliance on traditional binary oppositions (inside/outside, identity/difference, male/female) and an attendant desire for totalization may be upset, undercut, or disoriented by less readily classifiable, more disconcerting movements in a text that leave undecidable residues, re-mainders, or hybridized elements. Since binaries are typically arranged in a "violent" hierarchy, deconstruction involves interrelated movements or phases: reversal (wherein the subordinate term is given priority) and generalized displacement. The latter movement requires an attempt to counteract the simple inversion of hierarchy that remains within a given frame of reference and establishes a new form of dominance, but where it leads is less clear. It often involves generalizing the residue or remainder and refiguring the subordinate term until one has a less stable field of meaning that may suggest (while never quite seeming to work out) newer articulations. It may also lead in the direction of dissemination where wordplay is pronounced and articulations are at best elusive and extremely labile. In any case, deconstruction does not simply exclude or bracket meaning and reference; it places them within a general text or interplay of textualized traces that they do not simply transcend or master. The notorious statement that "there is no outside-the-text [*il n'y a pas de hors-texte*]"[21] certainly questions any idea of full, unmediated pres-ence (for example, of an experience, meaning, or divinity), but it does not eliminate all meaning or reference. Rather, it situates meaning and reference within a network of instituted traces or a generalized trace-structure, and it makes their situation a matter of a function within, or an inference from, such a "structure."

For Derrida, moreover, a text never simply conforms to its author's intentions, and its language is never fully transparent. More specifically, a text puts into play longstanding assumptions of the metaphysical tradi-tion – assumptions that are not themselves fully homogeneous and that receive more or less critical and explicit formulation in the texts of signifi-cant philosophers. In his early "Structure, Sign, and Play in the Discourse of the Human Sciences," Derrida provided this principle for distinguish-ing between the relative critical and self-critical strengths of texts: "But if nobody can escape this necessity [of being within traditions and, in the West, within the tradition of inherited metaphysical concepts], and if no one is therefore responsible for giving in to it, however little, this does not mean that all the ways of giving in to it are of equal pertinence. The quality and fecundity of a discourse are perhaps measured by the critical rigor with which this relationship to the history of metaphysics and to inherited concepts is thought."[22] . . .

Dissemination in general supplements deconstruction through an active intervention in which a text is indeed rewritten in terms of possibilities that were underexploited or even unexplored by its author and perhaps remain submerged in the text. At its most extreme, this rewriting is a ludic improvisation that follows associative processes of a waking dream, making more or less regulated and lucid use of the processes Freud disclosed in dream-work (condensation, displacement, secondary revision, and suitability for staging or *mise en scène* [*Darstellbarkeit*]). Disseminatory writing thus enacts or acts out "free" association and dream-work, especially in response to a trauma that disrupts a text (in the broad sense that may include a life).

In Freud, of course, "free" association is not simply arbitrary; it brings out significant relations that may be repressed or denied by consciousness. The most effective associations are "free" in this disclosive sense. Reading that follows associative processes is thus a procedure that emulates psychoanalytic mechanisms. Its performative quality indicates that it does not simply copy or imitate the manifest content of the text being read but actually makes something happen (or makes history in its own way) through its associations and improvisations. Oneiric improvisation accounts for the "through-the-looking-glass" quality of certain deconstructive readings where what is made of a text departs drastically from anything a more conventional reading might reveal. Moreover, disseminatory writing and strong misreading may put into play a practice of radical decontextualization or diremption whereby textual segments are severed from their own time or place and made to take on new, unheard-of significations in their rewritten form.[23]

In literary criticism that emulates creative writing, a reading may be praised to the extent that it is a strong misreading and engages its object in an unpredictable, even strangely disconcerting or uncanny, performative manner. Indeed, the stronger the misreading the better insofar as the strength of a misreading is indicative of the extent to which it appears performative, creative, or even original and brings out what is not evident in the text that becomes its pretext. The process is most remarkable when the resultant reading is as ingeniously creative as the text being read, for example, in many of Derrida's texts (notably *Glas*) or in Roland Barthes's *S/Z*, where Honoré de Balzac's *Sarrasine* is decomposed and put together again in a fashion that would have astounded Humpty-Dumpty. Disseminatory writing as well as strong misreading is somewhat comparable to the "riff" in jazz wherein one musician improvises on a tune or on the style of an earlier musician. As in jazz, the more traumatic or disjunctive variations (or changes within repetition) may from a certain point of view be the most impressive. In this respect, Derrida may perhaps be seen as the John Coltrane of philosophy or of some hybridized genre it remains difficult to name.

It is, of course, difficult to determine whether a style emulating dream-work generates associations that are genuinely disclosive about both the text being read and a contemporary relation to it. Moreover, the improvisational procedure may border on the questionable, even in literary criticism or philosophy, when it becomes overwhelmingly pro-jective reprocessing, in which the "voice" or perspective of the other is not attended to but is assimilated into a participatory discourse or generalized "free indirect style" that amounts to a monologic approach, however internally dialogized or self-contestatory it may be. This is, for example, the style in which Michel Foucault's *Folie et déraison: Histoire de la folie à l'âge classique*[24] is often written, and it is one reason why the book is "exciting" as a mode of writing but questionable as history. In it, the "voices" of those classified as "mad" or radically "other" are not directly quoted or even commented on but are made to agitate Foucault's own tortured, flamboyant prose and his internally divided, self-questioning style – a style that is internally dialogized but may still in an important sense be monologic (or narcissistic) insofar as it assimilates or incorporates the voices of others without respecting their resistances to assimilation. An internally dialogized, indeed, radically fragmented style that projectively reprocesses the voices of others may be lucidly theorized and defended as "schizophrenic" writing that attempts to break up the "paranoid" rigidities of classical or conventional writ-ing. But the dangers are obvious in the view that a desirable alternative to paranoia is a strategic, willed release of "schizo" flows of energy and desire.[25]

The preceding discussion may enable a delimitation of the point at which deconstruction and its disseminatory supplement – and, more gen-erally, certain poststructural tendencies – have the most dubious relation to historical reading and interpretation. One may argue that historical reading should pay close attention to the "voices" of the other and try to reconstruct these "voices" or perspectives as closely and carefully as possible, however problematic the undertaking may be. This is one reason why contextualization is important even in approaches stressing the signif-icance of reading and interpretation, although one may certainly debate the precise form and limits of contextualization in historiography.[26] One may also argue that the historian should elicit the possibilities and the repressed or denied dimensions of texts or documents. But the attempt to specify these dimensions of a text or phenomenon is always tentative, problematic, and even speculative. At the minimum, one would demand in historical reading and interpretation a specification of a configuration (or an articulation of the repeated and the changed) that would help to delimit better what may be ascribed to the past and what is being added in the present. Moreover, in history, the principle cannot be that the stronger the misreading the better, for here history does not emulate creative writing and is constrained by different norms of inquiry. At the very least, there is in history a basic distinction between the attempt to reconstruct the object of inquiry, including its meaning or possibilities at its own time or over time, and the entry into a dialogic exchange with it that tries to bring out its potential in the present and for the future. The question is whether deconstruction, disseminatory writing, and related poststructural tendencies tend to conflate or collapse the distinction between reconstruction and dialogic exchange through a kind of generalized free indirect style or middle voice that may neutralize or collapse not only binary oppositions but all distinctions.

It may, however, be the case that the historian may take up another role and engage in freer variations or speculations insofar as they are explicitly framed as such and not placed on the same level or indiscriminately intertwined with other readings and interpretations that are more explicitly controlled and subject to ordinary processes of validation. Here, one would have a hybridized role or genre of writing that is more or less close to Derrida's own. But how justifiable the specific instances of this genre might be is a subsequent question requiring further investigation and argument. . . . Such a hybridized genre involving clearly framed speculations would seem most justifiable or acceptable to the extent that it is indeed difficult to determine what belongs to the past and what to the present, notably with respect to deep-seated philosophical assumptions and the repressed dimensions of a culture or tradition, for example, those related to a quest for origins, full presence, and purity that may be conjoined with displaced sacrificial and scapegoating mechanisms. But even here it should not lead to the loss or elimination of all historical specificity in treating phenomena.

I would make further mention of one important tendency in contemporary criticism that is evident in many writers sympathetic to deconstruction and at times in Derrida himself.[27] This is an ethos of renunciation combined with a propensity for a generalized aesthetics of the sublime.[28] Renunciation appears in methodological humility or modesty that avoids direct, "aggressive" criticism of the other as well as in the quest for an undecidable "position" that neutralizes or disempowers opposites such as activity and passivity. It also arises in the tendency to abandon not only mastery but seemingly all control in the more disseminatory extreme where language in its most hyperbolic forms takes over and, in a self-sacrificial or immolating gesture, distributes the decentered self in the flow of discourse. (This stance may be most appealing to men who are striving for sensitivity, especially in the face of feminist critiques of "phallocentrism" and patriarchy. In the case of women or minorities, it may have the tendency to reinforce unfortunate stereotypes of abjection.) The *mise en abîme* of the text may even coincide with the much-heralded (and greatly exaggerated) death of the author: language is presumably left to write itself in unpredictable, aleatory movements reminiscent of automatic writing in surrealism and open to the possibility (or necessity) of misreading. Yet the movement toward the abyss, in which all meaning and reference threaten to be lost, brings with it the possibility of reading infinite heights – or at least infinite deferral of meaning – as the self confronts symbolic excess (or dire lack) that simulates death and transfiguration. Trauma (including the induced trauma of the *mise en abîme* of the text) is transvalued in an aesthetics of the sublime into an occasion for ecstasy and exhilaration.[29] And the very ability to confront death, however symbolically, empowers the self and brings an intimation of the sublime as one steps away from the near annihilation threatened by the "abyss" of a radical excess or lack of meaning.

The fascination with excess that gestures toward death and a secular sacred – indeed, toward a secularized, symbolic sacrificial process that may paradoxically undo itself by playing itself out – is a powerful force in poststructural thought in general, and it harks back to the work of Georges Bataille, Maurice Blanchot, and Martin Heidegger. The problem is that its fascination is often so great that it induces a quasi-transcendental mode of thinking in which the deconstruction of metaphysics – including the very important deconstruction of the binary logic that subtends scapegoating and victimization – continues to gravitate in a meta-metaphysical orbit. To the extent that the inverted or parodic tracking of metaphysics prevails, the role of history and politics loses its specificity and becomes at best allusive, and any sense of limits or guardrails (whose importance Derrida himself at times invokes) easily becomes only a faint memory. The actual victims of history may be lost in an indiscriminate generalization of victimage (or abjection), a leveling identification of all history with trauma, and an abstract, tortuous conception of witnessing, all of which tend to have apologetic functions and to incapacitate all knowledge, judgment, and practice. The attendant difficulty is a near fixation on trauma, as well as its transvaluation in the sublime, that induces a compulsively repetitive acting out of traumatic crisis and disorientation. . . .

4 Redemptive Reading

The more extreme form of deconstruction or its disseminatory supplement may, as in de Man, lead one repeatedly to the abyss, with any redemptive gesture adamantly refused. Or it may hint, however obliquely or paradoxically, at redemption through a secularized sacrificial process and an aesthetics of the sublime. Another variant of reading, often in opposition or reaction to deconstruction, is more prevalent in historiography; it takes a rather sober if not placid approach to the redemption of meaning in and through interpretation. Close reading or attention to nuance is not the forte of this tendency. Indeed, reading becomes integrated into harmonizing interpretation, especially when a neo-Hegelian frame of reference explicitly encourages a model of speculative, dialectical transcendence that is often combined with a phenomenological notion of experience as the foundation of meaning. And interpretation is easily reconciled with the most conventional use of contextualization as the full meaning of a text or experience is presumed to be available to the interpreter through an attempt to capture the meaning-in-context of a past text or phenomenon – even of an entire series of events or sweep of a tradition. But redemptive reading often leads to a projective reprocessing of the past that is more secure and self-satisfying in its results than that operative in deconstruction, for the meaning redeemed is typically that which one desires in the present, and figures in the past tend to become vehicles or mouthpieces for contemporary values. This possibility is perhaps most available in its extreme form for historians and theorists who employ a neo-Hegelian frame of reference that applies to history the model of the speculative dialectic, in which a past phenomenon is "transcended" or "sublated" (*aufgehoben*) in time with only minor and essentially recuperable losses. Thus, where radical forms of deconstruction tend to evacuate meaning even where it seems to be significant, hermeneutic approaches may find ultimately satisfying or full meaning by filling in or covering over traumas and gaps that would seem to mark its limit.

The more moderate advocates of this approach to history as the story of "symbolic" meaning may look to Clifford Geertz and a delimited "anthropological" understanding of the nature of historical inquiry. Geertz's work is especially appealing because of its remarkable insights and relative accessibility as well as its stylistic charms, which often are quite distant from the more difficult or even "rebarbative" nature of deconstructive and, more generally, poststructural approaches. Moreover, it provides a stimulating alternative to cut-and-dried approaches, especially those relying on "number-crunching." It also allows for a measure of fictionalization not as pronounced or blatant as that evoked by strong misreadings – one that supports a turn to narrative in historical writing. The beautifully orchestrated, finely crafted, arrestingly dramatized narrative of the Balinese cockfight may here be seen as a *locus classicus* for a certain kind of history, and Geertz himself often seems to be the *genius loci* in the work of a significant number of historians.[30]

More recently, the influence of Charles Taylor has brought into renewed prominence a neo-Hegelian model that is insistent and comprehensive in its construction of history as the story of meaning. This hermeneutic approach may be combined with a phenomenological notion of experience, as it was in earlier theorists and historians such as Wilhelm Dilthey. But I think that the redemptive model of reading is quite prevalent,

often on a nontheoretical, conventional level in which there is a determined striving to seek out the meaning of past experience, frequently in
terms that put into play or even help to validate contemporary desires
and values.[31] . . .

In the present context, I would like to turn briefly to John Toews'
substantial, justly influential review essay, "Intellectual History after
the Linguistic Turn: The Autonomy of Meaning and the Irreducibility
of Experience. . . ." Toews' contribution appeared at a crucial juncture
in the recent history of the profession. Variants of the "linguistic turn"
had captured the interest of historians. Some historians even seemed to
be appropriating aspects of contemporary critical theory in their own
work, and others were looking for a way to understand and respond to
these newer, or "new-fangled," initiatives. Toews' essay quickly became
the avenue through which many historians came to understand – and
react to – the so-called linguistic turn in historiography and especially
the use in the profession of deconstructive and more generally poststructural thought. Moreover, Toews' essay helped to inaugurate a significant turn in the *American Historical Review* itself in the direction of
questions of theory and method as at least a necessary and valuable
supplement to monographic research. The level of Toews' discussion is
consistently high, and, whether or not one agrees with all of his arguments, one must appreciate the serious thought – what Hegel in the
preface to *The Phenomenology of Mind* called the *Ernst des Begriffs*
(the seriousness of the concept) – that lies behind them and the critical
inquiry they are able to prompt.

Toews' basic argument is summarized in his subtitle: the autonomy of
meaning and the irreducibility of experience. In accordance with his neo-
Hegelian view, culture is a medium (or mediation) to make experience
meaningful, and language is its primary means of accomplishing this
(redemptive) feat. The engaging movement of the review essay, similar
to Hegel's *Phenomenology of Mind*, involves bringing each work under
discussion to the cliff-hanging juncture of some internal difficulty, which
then motivates the move to the next work, until one arrives at a penul-
timate point of dialectical reversal and at least a hint of the ultimate hope
of speculative synthesis. The dialectical reversal indicates that not only
must meaning be redeemed from experience but experience itself must
be saved from meaning in a two-way repudiation of reductionism that
is not completely terminal insofar as there is the hope of some form of
reconciliation or integration.

Meaning, experience, and language triangulate Toews' argument as
its threefold conceptual foundation, but their definition, relations, and
history may be more problematic that Toews allows. It is, for example,
significant that contemporary linguistic theories of meaning stem in
good part from Ferdinand de Saussure. Saussure's narrowly linguistic
orientation is explicitly criticized by Mikhail Bakhtin and his school,

who argue against its abstract, ahistorical formalism and by contrast defend a theory of language in historical use involving the problem of contextualization. Foucault takes the latter understanding of language-in-use in the direction of power and institutions, while Derrida elaborates a notion of a generalized text or a network of institutionalized traces that does not exclude reference, reality, or "experience" but attempts (however debatably at times) to situate them in a critical manner and to explore their limits. Moreover, meaning is contested internally and limited by forces that relate language to other phenomena in complex ways (for example, phonemes, drives, and bodily processes – including psychosomatic ones – that have complex relations to signification but cannot be reduced to it).

The most problematic term in Toews' discussion may well be "experience," for in other quarters it has become something of a scare word that intimidates opponents (those who do not share or at least empathetically understand the "experience" in question – those who have not been through it). It is also a means of authenticating one's own position or argument. Indeed, it often functions as the blackest of black boxes in general usage and perhaps to some extent in Toews' own sophisticated, well-developed argument. If one means by it the common-sense notion of having lived through something, for example, with reference to the experience of the Holocaust or of rape victims, it retains an important role. But one should specify the nature of this role and inquire into its implications. For example, one may argue that experience provides a basis for a subject-position that, especially in certain cases (such as that of victims), should be respected and attended to, and it may even give a *prima facie* claim to knowledge. But experience in and of itself neither authenticates nor invalidates an argument or point of view, and it cannot be invoked to silence others – either those having or those not having it.[32] Moreover, there are many types of experience, including that of reading or writing texts, and the latter may in certain cases be quite significant. They may even be crucial components in working through other experiences or even traumas.

One should not peremptorily dismiss the concept of experience or the need to come to terms with it, and Toews' article is extremely helpful in prompting significant questions about it. One of the merits of his complicated account is to introduce unexpected intricacies into one's conception of "experience" and to indicate how a contemporary development of Hegel's thought – or even a fair appreciation of it – would resist a facile tendency to reject all constructive, substantively rational activity as redemptive or totalizing. But three further points may be made concerning the way this concept may function to exclude crucial possibilities. One concerns the role of trauma that escapes experience in the ordinary sense and upsets the movement of a harmonizing or synthesizing speculative dialectic. The "significance" of trauma is that it disrupts experience and cannot be integrated into it. For Freud, trauma cannot be located punctually but takes place belatedly (*nachträglich*) as a later, seemingly insignificant "experience" somehow recalls an earlier one, charged but unassimilated. The trauma in the technical, psychoanalytic sense is marked by an interval between experiences, and it involves a period of latency between the initial and triggering "experiences." More generally, trauma does not conform to either a phenomenological or a common-sense model of experience, and it is typically repressed or denied in a manner that induces its compulsive re-enactment and the need to work through it. Rather than repressing or excessively mitigating its role (as in Taylor's *Sources of the Self*), a critical historiography would allow trauma to register in the (perhaps never fully successful) attempt to work it through. Moreover, it may, paradoxically, be the case that the only "full," pre-possessing experience is phantasmatic, and its relation to meaning is problematic: the experience of compulsively acting out a (real and/or imagined) traumatic past that is relived as if it were entirely present (rather than remembered with the risk of gaps and other difficulties that memory brings). One may also insist that working through trauma does not deliver full meaning or speculative synthesis but instead permits a significant measure of critical control that may never entirely – at least in cases of severe trauma – dispense with at least the possibility (and in all probability the reality) of acting out.

A second point is that one of the main purposes of history is to inquire into the significance of what one did *not* experience and what one reconstructs on the basis of multiple remains, including at best the traces of others' experiences and traumas. In this sense, one cannot simply ground history in experience, and the problem is not to guard against the reduction of experience to meaning but to enable oneself and others to understand and remember what may be distant from one's own experience or that of one's community (or what one takes that experience to be). How understanding and memory should work is debatable, for example, in terms of the role and relative importance of empathy, the interpretation of meaning, and the active recognition of the limits of both empathy and meaning. But that history extends beyond (or falls short of) experience, without simply providing either full meaning or deceptively vicarious experience, should be evident.

A third consideration is that a prevalent characteristic of "postmodern" culture is the commodification of experience, and the invasiveness of this process may raise doubts about the uncritical invocation of the term. We now buy and sell experiences and not simply goods and services – the experience of visiting an Indian reservation, of getting to know Santa Fe, of living for a while in a monastery, of attending a university such as Harvard or Yale, or even of spending an afternoon in a Holocaust museum participating in certain "experiences" of victims. With the advent of virtual reality, we now can market simulated experiences

detached from their "real" referents. Indeed, we try to escape from commodification through a phenomenon that is readily fed back into the
commodity loop through soap operas and popular literature: the meaningful experience itself. The meaningful experience does not reduce experience to meaning (the move Toews fears); it joins the two in a blissful
Aufhebung, which shows how Hegel, too, can be conventionalized, can
provide one facile way to shoot the gap between high and mass culture,
and can be made to render good service for contemporary life. ("His
pain, our gain," as one postmodern, Christological T-shirt has it.)

5 Dialogic Reading

Since I have attempted in my own work to develop and apply a dialogic
approach to reading and interpretation, I shall tend in this section to
speak more fully in my own voice. Yet here, a strong caveat is in order.
"Dialogue" is itself a contemporary "buzz word" that is like "experience" in that it, too, has been thoroughly commodified if not banalized.
And it is difficult in discussing an approach one has advocated to avoid
an upbeat Hollywood ending that strikes a redemptive note. For these
reasons, it is important to distinguish dialogism from dialogue in the
ordinary, banalized sense. Dialogism refers in a dual fashion both to the
mutually challenging or contestatory interplay of forces in language and
to the comparable interaction between social agents in various specific
historical contexts. (Especially in the former sense, its concerns parallel
those of a certain mode of deconstruction.) Basic to it is a power of
provocation or an exchange that has the effect of testing assumptions,
legitimating those that stand its critical test and preparing others for
change. (This is, I think, the crucial sense of dialogism in Bakhtin that
involves the role of the carnivalesque.) Moreover, in my understanding of
it, a dialogic approach is based on a distinction that may be problematic
in certain cases but is nonetheless important to formulate and explore.
This is the distinction between accurate reconstruction of an object of
study and exchange with that object as well as with other inquirers into
it. This distinction itself indicates that there are limits to dialogism that
prevent it from achieving the status of a redemptive or totalizing perspective. It is both necessarily supplemented by other perspectives, such
as reconstruction, and questioned by forces it does not entirely master
(such as differences in power, the effects of trauma, or the workings of
the unconscious).

History in accordance with a self-sufficient research paradigm gives
priority if not exclusive status to accurate reconstruction, restricts exchange with other inquirers to a subordinate, instrumental status (signaled
textually by a relegation to footnotes or a bibliography), and is forced
to disguise dialogic exchange as reconstruction, often in a manner that

infiltrates values into a seemingly objective or value-neutral account. It is less deceptive to argue that one may make a problematic yet significant distinction between reconstruction and exchange and that exchange is permissible – indeed, both unavoidable and desirable – for the historian, with respect both to the object of inquiry and to other inquirers.

The distinction between reconstruction and exchange does not imply the feasibility of a binary opposition or separation of the two into autonomous activities or spheres. Exchange with other inquirers is constitutive of research, for it helps to shape the very questions one poses to the past and establishes a contemporary context (typically involving ideological issues) that should be critically elucidated rather than occluded, repressed, or relegated to a secondary position. In this sense, there is a mutually reciprocal relation between research and dialogic exchange, for the object of research is constructed in and through exchange with past and present inquirers. In addition, exchange with the object of inquiry (which is always mediated by exchange with other inquirers) is necessary, notably with respect to intensely "cathected" or traumatizing objects, such as the Holocaust, or texts that themselves raise problems of continuing concern and demand a response from the reader not restricted to purely empirical–analytic inquiry or contextualization.

A dialogic approach involves the recognition that projection is to some extent unavoidable insofar as objects of inquiry are of intense concern to us because they pose questions that address significant values or assumptions. At times, they may pose such questions precisely because they differ drastically from what we hold, or would like to believe we hold, our basic values or assumptions to be. This point applies both to the beliefs and practices of very different cultures or time periods and to more recent phenomena that upset cherished convictions about the nature of our civilization. The difficulty in coming to terms with the Nazi period and the desire to normalize it in one way or another, if only by showing the prevalence of genocide or, on the contrary, the manner in which it was presumably anomalous or marginal in German or Western history, attest to the manner in which we tend to refuse to see that it was indeed a real possibility for an important part of "our" civilization and thus for "us" under certain conditions. An obvious but basic point is that something would not shock us if it were not already in us, in however potential, subdominant, or repressed a form. If it were not already in us, it would not provoke anxiety but simply leave us indifferent as an object of idle curiosity. The very incredulity evinced by the fact that the Shoah could have happened in the land of Goethe and Kant is remarkable both because of its naïveté and because of the manner in which it signals the occurrence of a shock or trauma we find difficult to assimilate.

A combination of accurate reconstruction and dialogic exchange is necessary in that it accords an important place to the "voices" and specific situations of others at the same time as it creates a place for our "voices" in an attempt to come to terms with the past in a manner that has implications for the present and future. It is in this sense that it remains important to provide quotations from a text being interpreted or from agents in the period being discussed. The principle here is that such quotations should be extensive enough to provide the reader with a basis for a possible counter-reading or interpretation in the event that the latter is indeed called for. In reading a text, one may formulate the combination of reconstruction and dialogic exchange most simply in terms of two related questions: What is the other saying? How do I – or we – respond to it?

This formulation is simplistic in that it does not address the complexity of determining what the other is saying or explicate the divergent possibilities of response. To arrive at what the other is saying requires some determination of literal and figurative meaning, the role of irony, parody, and "voice" or positionality in general, the possible intervention of unconscious forces such as repression and denial, and the articulation of undeveloped potentials of the text or utterance. It also requires sensitivity to the projective dimensions of our attempts at reconstruction that become more insistent to the extent that the object of inquiry is still highly charged for us. Here, there is the possibility of a postdeconstructive notion of objectivity that supplements rather than obviates the role of dialogic exchange: a notion of objectivity in which we attempt to check projection and prevent it from becoming a unilateral if not narcissistic reprocessing or monologic rewriting of the phenomenon or text. Instead, we employ contextualizing techniques, requiring meticulous research and the attempt to substantiate statements, precisely as checks on projection. Deconstruction may signal points at which the attempt at dialogic exchange is blocked because the traumatic aspect of the text or phenomenon is so great that it makes exchange and perhaps language in general break down in a more or less telling way – a possibility that entails not the futility of all dialogue but the recognition of its limits. Moreover, radical deconstruction tends to stay within trauma and to act it out or perform it; and this procedure, while to some extent necessary in the face of traumatic crises or limit-cases, is especially misleading when it is autonomized and does not broach the question of how to work through problems. Still, deconstruction can be of value in bringing out the internal tensions, contradictions, and aporias of texts or phenomena, and such inner contestations may well indicate problems that were not – and may still not be – acceptably thought and worked through. In certain of its forms (notably in Derrida's writings), it may also bring out the significance of play and laughter as well as their possible role in working through problems. But a dialogic approach does not postulate an antinomy between reading and interpretation, hermeneutics and poetics, work and play. Rather, it takes those relations to be problematic as it investigates the possibility and limits of meaning in the past in its bearing on the present and future. Here, the attempt at reconstruction itself broaches the question of how to engage in dialogic exchange.

Dialogic exchange indicates how the basic problems in reading and interpretation may ultimately be normative and require a direct engagement with normative issues that are often concealed or allusively embedded in a seemingly "objective" account. It also brings out the problem of the relations among historiography, ethics, and politics. For the dialogic dimension of inquiry complicates the research paradigm and confronts one with the problem of the voice and subject-position(s) in which one responds to the past in a manner that always has implications for the present and future. The use of the "I" is relatively uncommon in historiography and is often restricted to a preface or coda. It is becoming more common, perhaps too common, in literary criticism and anthropology. Its use is, in any case, ambivalent or even equivocal. It disrupts a value-neutral façade and raises questions about the possibilities and limits of objectivity. It foregrounds the problem of subjectivity. But it easily reinforces an individualistic ideology, obscures the problem of subject-positions, and may foreclose other possible responses, such as collective and more politically germane ones. The notion of subject-position signals the intimate relation of subject and subjectivity to social positionality and the manner in which "voice" is not a purely individual or subjective issue. It also brings "voice" in contact with ethical and political issues that are not confined to the individual psyche or biography. It thus forces the issue of the nature of a desirable dialogic response to the past.

The dialogic dimension of research in which a response is required of the investigator has been acknowledged in a restricted manner in the notion of observer-participation. This dimension heightens awareness of, even anxieties about, the historian's interactions with the object of inquiry. It is thus worth returning to the proposal that one consider these transactions in psychoanalytic terms – as involving a transferential relation to the object of study (as well as to other inquirers). Transference in Freud rested on the tendency to repeat, either in a compulsive form of acting out (in which one relived a typically traumatic past as if it were fully present) or in a more critically controlled "working-through" that allowed for significant change and a reinvestment in life. The transferential repetition in the clinical context of the relationship between parent and child was seen by Freud as occurring in less controlled or safe environments such as the adult romantic or even the work relationship. Even in its restricted, orthodox Freudian sense, transference may have a bearing on the relation among scholars (notably the teacher–graduate student relationship) that has yet to be sufficiently acknowledged and accounted for.[33] But the more general and basic sense of transference as a tendency to repeat applies as well to the way in which processes active in the object of study tend to be replicated in our accounts of them. This transferential relation in the broad sense requires that we come to terms with it in one way or another – through denial (as in positivism or notions of pure objectivity), repression (in research that brackets or marginalizes values, only to see them return in encrypted or covert form), acting out (as in certain views of performativity or active rewriting), or working-through (the goal of a critically controlled dialogic exchange with the past). Indeed, insofar as the fundamental concepts of psychoanalysis (such as transference, repression, denial, resistance, acting out, and working-through) are not restricted to the individual psyche or the one-on-one clinical situation but recognized as undercutting the opposition between the individual and society and linked with the notion of subject-position, they provide a way of rethinking the problem of reading and interpretation in history. They may even furnish the basis for developing an ethics of reading that is not insensitive to the role of play, laughter, and carnivalesque forces in general.

In concluding, I would reiterate the basic point that different historians may justifiably embody in their work a different combination of reconstruction of the object, involving contextualization in terms of the past, and dialogic exchange with it that itself calls for self-contextualization in a present network of discussion and debate. Indeed, different works or portions of a work by the same historian may show differing stresses and strains. This view considerably broadens the field of history without depriving it of all coherence. Rather, it introduces into it the need for informed argument about boundaries and the recognition of how certain forms of testing – or even periodic transgressing – of those boundaries may be fruitful for the very self-understanding of historians and the reconsideration of disciplinary definitions. Finally, it also raises the question of what combinations of subject-positions should be deemed allowable or desirable even when they involve the passage beyond a delimited disciplinary conception of the historical profession.

Notes

1 William M. Sloane, "History and Democracy," *American Historical Review*, 1 (1895–6): 1–23; Henry Adams, "Count Edward de Crillon," *AHR*, 1 (1895–6): 51–69.
2 Sloane, "History and Democracy," 16, 17, 3–4.
3 Adams, "Count Edward de Crillon," 52, 51.
4 Adams, "Count Edward de Crillon," 52.
5 Adams, "Count Edward de Crillon," 53. For more on Edward (or Edouard) de Crillon, see Samuel Eliot Morison, *By Land and by Sea* (New York, 1953), 269–73; and Clifford L. Egan, *Neither Peace nor War: Franco-American Relations, 1803–1812* (Baton Rough, La., 1983), 171–2.

6 Adams, "Count Edward de Crillon," 60. It is also curious that Adams ends his article abruptly with a letter from Soubiron to Henry (John Henry, not Henry Adams) on which Adams provides no further commentary.

7 Cambridge, 1988.

8 John E. Toews, "Intellectual History after the Linguistic Turn: The Autonomy of Meaning and the Irreducibility of Experience," *AHR*, 92 (October 1987): 879–907. See also John H. Zammito, "Are We Being Theoretical Yet? The New Historicism, the New Philosophy of History, and 'Practicing' Historians," *Journal of Modern History*, 65 (1993): 783–814. Zammito's basic argument draws much from Toews' article.

9 See especially Sigmund Freud, "Remembering, Repeating and Working Through" (1914), in *The Standard Edition of the Complete Psychological Works of Sigmund Freud*, vol. 12, James Strachey, trans. (London, 1958), 145–56; and "Mourning and Melancholia" (1917), in *The Standard Edition*, vol. 14 (1957), 237–60.

10 See, for example, Philippe Carrard, *Poetics of the New History: French Historical Discourse from Braudel to Chartier* (Baltimore, Md., 1992); Lionel Gossman, *Between History and Literature* (Cambridge, Mass., 1990); Hans Kellner, *Language and Historical Representation: Getting the Story Crooked* (Madison, Wis., 1989); Louis O. Mink, *Historical Understanding*, Brian Fay, Eugene O. Golob, and Richard T. Vann, eds (Ithaca, NY, 1987); and Hayden White, *Metahistory: The Historical Imagination in Nineteenth-Century Europe* (Baltimore, 1973); *Tropics of Discourse: Essays in Cultural Criticism* (Baltimore, 1978); *The Content of the Form: Narrative Discourse and Historical Representation* (Baltimore, 1987).

11 Indiscriminate polemic based on excessively homogenizing reading is pronounced in Bryan D. Palmer, *Descent into Discourse: The Reification of Language and the Writing of Social History* (Philadelphia Pa., 1990); and Gertrude Himmelfarb, "Post-modernist History and the Flight from Fact," *Times Literary Supplement* (October 16, 1992): 12–15.

12 In Louis Chevalier, *Classes laborieuses et classes dangereuses* (Paris, 1958), documents such as police reports are used to check the "findings" derived from novels, as if both police reports and novels did not require more complex protocols of reading. . . .

13 I would note that the problem of reading in the archives has increasingly become a concern of those doing archival research, thus leading historians who do extensive archival work to become interested in problems raised later in this article. See, for example, Robert Darnton, *The Great Cat Massacre and Other Episodes in French Cultural History* (New York, 1984); Natalie Zemon Davis, *Fiction in the Archives: Pardon Tales and Their Tellers in Sixteenth-Century France* (Stanford, Calif., 1987); Steven L. Kaplan, *Adieu 89* (Paris, 1993); and Emmanuel Le Roy-Ladurie, *La Sorcière de Jasmin* (Paris, 1983).

14 Even so important and sophisticated a historian as J. G. A. Pocock resorts to the invidious binary opposition between the "working" historian and his or her "other," the metahistorian, thereby reducing an interest in critical theory to what might facetiously be called an "attitude problem." Hence Pocock writes: "It is possible to define 'intellectual history' as the pursuit by the 'intellectual' of an attitude towards 'history,' and to write it as a series of dialogues between the historian himself, as intellectual, and his probably French or German predecessors, in the attempt to arrive at a 'philosophy of

history' or something to take the place of one. Such 'intellectual history' will be metahistory, meaning that it will be reflection about 'history' itself. But it is also possible to imagine a 'working historian' who desires to be a historian but not (in this sense) an intellectual, who desires to practise the writing of history but not to arrive at an attitude towards it, and who does not look beyond the construction of those narrative histories of various kinds of intellectual activity which she or he knows how to write . . . It is such a working historian of this kind whom I have presupposed in this article." *Intellectual History Newsletter* (1986): 8.

15 For a range of perspectives on these problems, see Georg Lukács, *Die Zerstörung der Vernunft* (Berlin, 1954); Jürgen Habermas, *The Philosophical Discourse of Modernity*, Frederick G. Lawrence, trans. (Cambridge, Mass., 1987); Carl E. Schorske, *Fin-de-Siècle Vienna: Politics and Culture* (New York, 1980); Tony Judt, *Past Imperfect: French Intellectuals, 1944–1956* (Berkeley, Calif., 1992); John Lukács, *The Passing of the Modern Age* (New York, 1970); and Roland N. Stromberg, *After Everything: Western Intellectual History since 1945* (New York, 1975). A. J. P. Taylor writes: "Literature tells us little when we deal, as we must in the twentieth century, with the people of England. The novels of Virginia Woolf, for example, were greatly esteemed by a small intellectual group, and their destruction of the tight narrative frame has influenced later writers. They are irrelevant for the historian." Taylor, *English History, 1914–1945* (New York, 1965), 311. (I thank Jonathan Sadowsky for calling my attention to this reference.) "A small intellectual group" is apparently not part of "the people" for Taylor, and the irrelevance of Woolf's novels is so obvious that an apodictic non sequitur is sufficient to establish it.

16 For a cogent defense of synopsis that is also sensitive to certain of its limitations, see Martin Jay, "Two Cheers for Paraphrase: The Confessions of a Synoptic Intellectual Historian," in *Fin-de-Siècle Socialism and Other Essays* (New York, 1988), 52–63.

17 See, for example, James T. Kloppenberg, "Objectivity and Historicism: A Century of American Historical Writing," *AHR*, 94 (October 1989): 1011–30. . . .

18 See Jacques Derrida, *Mémoires for Paul de Man*, Cecile Lindsay, Jonathan Culler, and Eduardo Cadava, trans. (New York, 1986); and "Like the Sound of the Sea Deep within a Shell: Paul de Man's War," Peggy Kamuf, trans., in *Critical Inquiry*, 14 (1988): 590–652 (reprinted in a slightly revised form in *Responses: On Paul de Man's Wartime Journalism*, Werner Hamacher, Neil Hertz, and Thomas Keenan, eds (Lincoln, Neb., 1989). See also my critique of the latter essay in *Representing the Holocaust*, 125–33.

19 For a lucid discussion of this problem, see Jeffrey T. Nealon, "The Discipline of Deconstruction," *Publications of the Modern Language Association*, 107 (1992): 1266–79.

20 See de Man, *Resistance to Theory*, esp. 55–6.

21 Jacques Derrida, *Of Grammatology*, Gayatri Chakravorty Spivak, trans. (Baltimore, Md., 1976), 158.

22 Jacques Derrida, *The Structuralist Controversy: The Languages of Criticism and the Sciences of Man*, Richard Macksey and Eugenio Donato, eds (Baltimore, Md., 1970), 252.

23 See Jacques Derrida, "Signature, Event, Context," in *Margins of Philosophy*, Alan Bass, trans. (Chicago, 1982), 307–30.

24 Paris, 1961.
25 See, for example, Gilles Deleuze and Félix Guattari, *Anti-Oedipus: Capitalism and Schizophrenia*, Robert Hurley, Mark Seem, and Helen R. Lane, trans. (New York, 1977); and *A Thousand Plateaus*, Brian Massumi, trans. (Minneapolis, Minn., 1987). These books seem to take as their premise a naïve, utopian conception of desire opposed to all forms of limiting norms that are indiscriminately identified with repression and paranoia or even with fascism.
26 On this problem, see my *Rethinking Intellectual History: Texts, Contexts, Language* (Ithaca, 1983), esp. ch. 1; *History and Criticism* (Ithaca, 1985); and *Representing the Holocaust: History, Theory, Trauma* (Ithaca, 1994), esp. ch. 1.
27 See especially Leo Bersani, *The Culture of Redemption* (Cambridge, Mass., 1990). In opposing both conventionality and totalizing tyranny, Bersani elaborates a theory of presumably nonviolent masochistic desire in which the explosively narcissistic self seeks "the ecstatic suffering of a pure ébranlement" (p. 38) or self-shattering, thus averting frustration that, for Bersani, causes violence and aggression against others. Here, one may ask whether Bersani's intricate, probing, and demanding analyses, which provide arresting insight into the problematic nature of modern writing, seem at times to be based on a utopian anarchism close to the viewpoint of Deleuze and Guattari.
28 See the independently developed but convergent analyses in my *Representing the Holocaust*; and Steven Connor, *Postmodernist Culture: An Introduction to Theories of the Contemporary* (Oxford, 1990), esp. ch. 8.
29 For this transvaluation, the works of Jean-François Lyotard and Slavoj Žižek are especially significant. See especially Lyotard, *The Postmodern Condition: A Report on Knowledge*, Geoff Bennington and Brian Massumi, trans. (Minneapolis, Minn., 1984); *The Different: Phrases in Dispute*, George Van Den Abbeele, trans. (Minneapolis, 1988); and *Heidegger and "The Jews"*, Andreas Michel and Mark S. Roberts, trans. (Minneapolis, 1990); Žižek, *The Sublime Object of Ideology* (London, 1990); *Looking Awry: An Introduction to Jacques Lacan through Popular Culture* (Cambridge, Mass., 1991); and *Enjoy Your Symptom! Jacques Lacan in Hollywood and Out* (New York, 1992).
30 See, for example, *New Directions in American Intellectual History*, John Higham and Paul K. Conkin, eds (Baltimore, Md., 1979). Among European historians, Robert Darnton acknowledges the influence of Geertz; see *Great Cat Massacre*; and "The Symbolic Element in History," *Journal of Modern History*, 58 (1986): 218–34. For Geertz's treatment of the Balinese cockfight, see "Deep Play: Notes on a Balinese Cockfight," in *The Interpretation of Cultures* (New York, 1972). For a critique of it, see Vincent Crapanzano, "Hermes' Dilemma: The Masking of Subversion in Ethnographic Description," in *Writing Culture: The Poetics and Politics of Ethnography*, James Clifford and George E. Marcus, eds (Berkeley, Calif., 1986), esp. 68–76. . . .
31 For a truly masterful instance of the redemptive model, see M. H. Abrams, *Natural Supernaturalism: Tradition and Revolution in Romantic Literature* (1971; New York, 1973). For a different approach to history as the story of meaning, which is less concerned with contemporary values and more attuned to ideological conflict in the past, see Keith Michael Baker, "On the Problem of the Ideological Origins of the French Revolution," in Dominick LaCapra and Steven L. Kaplan, eds, *Modern European Intellectual History: Reappraisals and New Perspectives* (Ithaca, NY, 1982), 197–219.

32 Those with extreme experience, such as rape victims, may be placed in the
double bind of being authenticated as witnesses but invalidated as knowledgeable commentators concerning that experience. Thus, on talk shows, one
typically has the victim as witness but the expert (for example, the psychiatrist)
as the one who knows the meaning of the experience. (I thank Linda Alcoff
for this insight.) This double bind is more generally at play with respect to
those in subordinate or "abject-ified" and objectified positions, for example,
"native informants."
33 On this issue, see Peter Loewenberg, *Decoding the Past: The Psychohistorical
Approach* (New York, 1983), 45–80.

Part III

Realism, Constructivism, and Beyond

6
History and Fiction as Modes of Comprehension

Louis Mink

I

Philosophers have always betrayed a certain scorn for both history and romance. "I knew that the delicacy of fiction enlivens the mind," said Descartes, explaining how he had liberated himself from the errors of the schools, and "that famous deeds of history ennoble it." But in the end, he concluded, these are negligible merits, because "fiction makes us imagine a number of events as possible which are really impossible, and even the most faithful histories, if they do not alter or embroider things to make them more worth reading, almost always omit the meanest and least illustrious circumstances, so that the remainder is distorted."[1] This was Descartes's first and final word on all the tales and stories of human life, and until very recently it could have served to sum up the consensus of Western philosophy. Even when Hegel discovered that history is more philosophical than poetry, he gave no more comfort to the practitioners of historical inquiry than Aristotle had given to wise poets; for in both cases it was for relative proximity to the first principles of philosophy itself that the marks were passed out. It was the universals bodied forth rather than the vivid and particular details of the stories which bore them that commanded the attention of philosophers.

In recent years, however, there has come into being a new and still developing interest among philosophers in what is called (rather misleadingly) the logic of narration. This has not been a product of aesthetics, as one might think, and it has as yet made no connection with the sort of analysis of narrative fiction represented in such studies as Scholes and Kellogg's *The Nature of Narrative*. Rather it belongs to the analytical philosophy of history – the theory of historical knowledge, that is, rather than the speculative metaphysics of the historical process. The philosophical problems whose coastlines are being explored were discovered in the following way. Since the seventeenth century, philosophy has been dominated by the problems of the cognitive status of perception on the one hand and the interpretation of natural science on the other. The great controversies of rationalism and empiricism now appear to have been complementary phases of the enterprise, extending over three centuries, to construct a comprehensive account of the relation between our direct perception of the world and our inferential knowledge of that world through the discoveries of natural science. In this epistemological enterprise there was no room for either imaginative worlds or the inaccessible world of the past. The latter, in particular, appeared significant only as something not perceptible, not as something *past*. In the riot of epistemological theories – new realism, critical realism, subjective idealism, pragmatism, objective relativism, phenomenalism, etc., etc. – in which the modern epoch of philosophy came to an end within recent memory, not one took seriously the problem of how it is possible that the past should be knowable, although each constructed a more or less embarrassed appendix which restored some sort of cognitive status to history, some possibility of meaning to "statements about the past." Meanwhile, historians were laying successful siege to the records of the past, but while they could point to notable achievements of inquiry there was no theory of historical knowledge to compare with the increasingly sophisticated philosophy of science. The "theory of knowledge" in fact was, by the implicit consensus of philosophers, the theory of *scientific* knowledge, and its very vocabulary – the language of induction and classification, of hypothesis and verification, of dependent and independent variables, general laws and probability coefficients, quantification and calculation – had its primary referents in astronomy, physics, chemistry, and biology.

The clearest and most influential systematization of the view that philosophy is the logical analysis of scientific procedure has been that self-designated as logical empiricism, *né* "positivism." A major principle of logical empiricism is the so-called methodological unity of science, that is, the view that there is no formal or logical difference among the various bodies of practice and consolidated inquiry which can count as scientific. With respect to explanation and the criteria for adequate explanation, for example, there is a single although complex formal model of explanation, which consists in showing that the statement asserting the occurrence of an event or other phenomenon to be explained follows by strict formal deduction (including mathematical deduction) from one or more statements about initial conditions of the system to which the laws apply and in which the phenomenon to be explained occurs. This is also the model of prediction; one can think of, say, either the prediction or the explanation of an eclipse as a clear example in which this model is realized. Now to apply such a model of explanation to human action or social change raises grave problems; few if any explanations in psychology or social science can be shown to have this form, not least because the general laws formally required have not been empirically discovered. Nevertheless, the claim was not that the deductive or "covering-law" model of explanation can be discerned in every putative explanation but that it represents a rational demand by comparison with which most "explanations" reveal themselves as defective. The methodological preoccupations of psychology, sociology, and other social sciences in recent years have in effect resulted from the adoption of positivist prescriptions as imperatives for the organization of research. In history, however, these prescriptions have seemed least applicable and also least able to account for the fact that some historical accounts *seem* to explain and illuminate although they cannot by any Procrustean efforts be restated in such a way as to exhibit the required form. Yet the case for positivism is strong. "Do you claim to have explained why this event occurred?" it asks. "Well, then, you are claiming more than *that* it happened; you are claiming that given whatever you refer to as bringing it about or causing it to occur, it *must* have happened as it did, in fact that it could not have *not* happened. The force of explanation lies in the recognition of necessity, and necessity can be shown only by showing that the event is connected with its antecedents by a general and well-confirmed law. Until that is done, there is no explanation but only a sketch of what an explanation would be like if there were one."[2]

At this point historians have been known to say something about history being an art rather than a science. Some philosophers, however, agreeing with the positivists that the task of philosophy is to make explicit the patterns of rational inference which inform complex thinking of all sorts, but unlike the positivists willing to entertain the hypothesis that there are different patterns of rationality not reducible to a single and fundamental pattern, have taken history to be a possibly autonomous and in any case rich and logically unanalyzed mode of inquiry and knowledge. As Arthur Danto has said, not casually but prefatory to a detailed analysis of historical language and explanation, "The difference between history and science is not that history does and science does not employ organizing schemes which go beyond what is given. Both do. The difference has to do with the *kind* of organizing schemes employed by each. *History* tells stories."[3]

So here there is a beginning of an attempt to carry out the program originally signaled by Collingwood: that while "the chief business of seventeenth-century philosophy was to reckon with seventeenth-century natural science . . . the chief business of twentieth-century philosophy is to reckon with twentieth-century history."[4] By "history," of course, Collingwood did not mean the course of public events (as in history vs. nature) but rather the inquiry, practiced by professional historians but not limited to them, into institutional change and purposive human action (as in history vs. natural science). The change is from a preoccupation with theory to an interest in narrative: "narrative explanation" is no longer a contradiction in terms. But there is also a shift from the concept of explanation, defined in terms of a formal model, to the concept of understanding, perhaps indefinable but clarified by reflection on the experiences in which it has been achieved.

No one has gone further in this direction than W. B. Gallie, in his book *Philosophy and the Historical Understanding*. I shall review his argument briefly, at the expense of doing scant justice to its intrinsic interest, for the sake of calling attention to what I think to be an unusually interesting and suggestive mistake. Gallie observes, quite correctly, that no critical (that is, post-Kantian) philosopher has worked out a clear account of "what it is to follow or construct an historical narrative."[5] History, he eventually is to conclude, is "a species of the genus Story."[6] But to understand what a story is, is to know what it is to *follow* a story, that is, not merely to have done so (as everyone has) but to know what in general are the features of a story which make it followable. And this in turn is not significantly different from following a game in progress, such as a cricket match, and understanding the features which make it followable. In following a story, as in being a spectator at a match, there must be a quickly established sense of a promised although unpredictable outcome: the county team will win, lose, or draw, the separated lovers will be reunited or will not. Surprises and contingencies are the stuff of stories, as of games, yet by virtue of the promised yet open outcome we are enabled to follow a series of events across their contingent relations and to understand them as leading to an as yet unrevealed conclusion without however necessitating that conclusion. We may follow understandingly what we could not predict or infer. At the same time, following requires the enlistment of our sympathies and antipathies, the "basic directing feelings" which account for one's being pulled along by a story; in fact, "what discontinuities we are willing to accept or able to follow depends partly upon the set or orientation of our sympathy . . . and partly upon the intrinsic nature of the kind of sympathy that has been established."[7] Stories may be followed more or less completely, as a wise old hand at cricket may notice nice details which escape the spectator of average keenness, and there can be no criteria for following *completely*.[8] But the minimal conditions are the same for all. The features which enable a story to flow and us to follow, then, are the clues to the nature of historical understanding. An historical narrative does not demonstrate the necessity of events but makes them intelligible by unfolding the story which connects their significance.[9] History does not as such differ from fiction, therefore, insofar as it essentially depends on and develops our skill and subtlety in following stories. History *does* of course differ from fiction insofar as it is obligated to rest upon evidence of the occurrence in real space and time of what it describes and insofar as it must grow out of a critical assessment of the received materials of history, including the analyses and interpretations of other historians.[10] But the researches of historians, however arduous and technical, only increase the amount and precision of knowledge of facts which remain contingent and discontinuous. It is by being assigned to stories that they become intelligible and increase understanding by going beyond "What?" and "When?" to "How?" and "Why?"

The difficulty in Gallie's adventurous account is not, I believe, in his emphasis on narrative but in his assumption that its essential features are revealed by a phenomenology of "following." What he has provided is a description of the naive reader, that is, the reader *who does not know how the story ends*, and who is "pulled along" by interest, sympathy, and curiosity. It is not incidental but essential to Gallie's view that contingent events are made acceptable and intelligible insofar as the story so far directs them toward a promised but open conclusion. Yet of course this is an experience which no *historian* and no moderately knowledgeable reader of historical narrative can have. Nor can a critic reading *King Lear* for the twentieth time nor any reader for the second find himself carried along by sympathetic curiosity about the fate of Lear and Cordelia. It may be that narrative historians more or less artfully construct their stories in order to lead readers through "possible routes towards the required but as yet undisclosed conclusion," but of the many historians who regard Garrett Mattingly's *The Defeat of the Spanish Armada* as the unsurpassed recent example of narrative history, I have never heard one complain that his reading of it was marred by knowing how it all came out. Among both historians and critics, on the contrary, familiarity sometimes breeds respect.

What I mean to suggest is that the difference between following a story and *having followed* a story is more than the incidental difference between present experience and past experience. Anticipation and retrospection are not simply different attitudes or vantage points which may be taken (or must be taken) toward the same event or course of events. We know that the difference between past and future is crucial in the case of moral and affective attitudes; we do not fear something that is over and done with, nor feel regret for something not yet undertaken. My thesis is that the difference is crucial as well for cognition: at least in the case of human actions and changes, to know an event by retrospection is categorically, not incidentally, different from knowing it by prediction or anticipation. It cannot even, in any strict sense, be called the "same" event, for in the former case the descriptions under which it is known are governed by a story to which it belongs, and there is no story of the future. But to give this thesis plausibility requires a consideration of what the "logic of narration" neglects: not what the structure or generic features of narratives are nor what it means to "follow," but what it means *to have followed* a story.

II

As we have known since Kant, one of the most difficult of all tasks is to discern and describe correctly those generic features of experience which we do not attend to and which we have no appropriate vocabulary to describe, precisely because their ubiquity leaves them unnoticed; their presence is not signaled by contrast with the absence or with competing features. It is only by the most intense conceptual effort that the structure of all experience can be distinguished from the vivid details of particular experience which commonly command our attention. It is perhaps for this reason that theories of knowledge have unaccountably neglected the significance of the simple fact that experiences come to us *seriatim* in a stream of transience and yet must be capable of being held together in a single image of the manifold of events in order for us to be aware of transience at all. It is a contingent fact of empirical psychology that the "specious present" – that duration in which we seem to be simultaneously aware of actually successive events such as the series of sounds that make up a spoken word – is of the order of between half a second and a second. But it is a necessary truth that we could not even form the concept of the specious present were we not able to hold in mind, through *this* sequence of presents, right *now*, the thought of past and future, of past futures and future pasts. Memory, imagination, and conceptualization all serve this function, whatever else they do: they are ways of grasping together in a single mental act things which are not experienced together, or even capable of being so experienced, because they are separated by time, space, or logical kind. And the ability to do this is a necessary (although not a sufficient) condition of *understanding*.

A few random examples may help to bring out the way in which the act of "grasping together" can be found in every variety of experience. For one case: in hearing the first movement of an unfamiliar Haydn symphony, one may "understand" the development in the sense that melodic motion and harmonic modulations are familiar and anticipatable. But of course this would be the case even if we had entered the hall or set down the needle in the middle of the movement. There is a different and more appropriately named kind of "understanding" when we hear and assimilate the exposition of the themes from the beginning, and then hear the development together with the retained memory of the themes. Without the ability to hold in mind the sequence already passed through, one would simply not understand, in *any* sense of "understand," musical passages such as the minuet of Beethoven's seventh symphony, in which the trio returns for a third appearance but is cut off abruptly after a few bars. Or again: Faulkner's *The Sound and the Fury* begins with the first-person impressions and recollections of the cretin Benjy. No one "understands" these pages on a first reading; no one is expected to. It is not until later in the book that these opaque pages become intelligible in retrospect; one must read the later pages with the earlier in mind, and in fact reread the earlier pages with the later in mind. But of course this is merely an especially vivid illustration of a character which every narrative has in some degree. Aristotle's observation that a play must have a beginning, a middle, and an end is not a trivially formal description but a corollary of his principle that a drama is an imitation of a *single* action, that is, that both action and mimesis must be capable of being understood as a single complex whole. It is also the sense in which Weigand said of *The Magic Mountain* that "the whole novel is present on every page."

But the phenomenon of grasping things together is not limited, as these examples might suggest, to the temporal arts. Consider logical inference, as represented in the following simple argument: All creatures are mortal; all men are creatures; all Athenian citizens are men; Socrates is an Athenian citizen; hence Socrates is mortal. Now suppose that we infer from the first two premises that all men are mortal, and then destroy our notes and forget the premises; and similarly with the premises which yield intermediate conclusions and again with these when the final conclusion has been drawn. This is analogous to the addition of a column of figures, forgetting the earlier figures with each subtotal, and also to every more complex instance of mathematical inference. In such hypothetical cases it is clear that we have lost the special quality of understanding the conclusion *as following from* the premises. We could in such a circumstance still *test* the validity of an argument, but could not *see* it. That grasping together a complex sequence of inference is possible is attested to by mathematicians, who commonly are able to see a demonstration as a whole rather than as merely a sequence of rule-governed transformations; and most probably the ascription of "elegance" to a proof acknowledges the especial neatness of its presentation in such a way as to facilitate one's seeing it as a whole.

In all of these instances, and in indefinitely many more, there thus seems to be a characteristic kind of understanding which consists in thinking together in a single act, or in a cumulative series of acts, the complicated relationships of parts which can be experienced only *seriatim*. I propose to call this act (for obvious etymological reasons) "comprehension." It is operative, I believe, at every level of consciousness, reflection, and inquiry. At the lowest level, it is the grasping together of data of sensation, memory, and imagination, and issues in perception and recognition of objects. At an intermediate level, it is the grasping together of a set of objects, and issues in classification and generalization. At the highest level, it is the attempt to order together our knowledge into a single system – to comprehend the world as a totality. Of course this is an unattainable goal, but it is significant as an ideal aim against which partial comprehension can be judged. To put it differently, it is unattainable because such comprehension would be divine, but significant because the human project is to take God's place. Naturally enough, attempts to describe the aim of ideal comprehension have always been put into theological terms. Boethius, explaining why human freedom does not limit God's knowledge, described God's knowledge of the world as a *totum simul*, in which the successive moments of all time are copresent in a single perception, as of a landscape of events. The omniscient scientist envisioned by LaPlace, knowing the laws of nature and the position and velocity of every particle of the universe at a single instant, could predict and retrodict the detailed character of the world at any moment of time. (So, in the classic story, when Napoleon remarked to LaPlace that he had found no mention of God in the *System of the World*, LaPlace replied, "Sire, I have had no need of that hypothesis.") And Plato, who thought divine knowledge not unattainable, regarded it as the contemplative vision of a set of essences grasped as a single intelligible system – a "comprehensive view," he calls it in discussing the education of the Rulers in Book VI of the *Republic*, "of the mutual relations and affinities which bind all the sciences together."

These different descriptions of the ideal aim of comprehension are not merely visionary. Rather they are extrapolations of several different and mutually exclusive modes of comprehension which run through our more mundane and partial understanding. There are, I suggest, three such fundamental modes, irreducible to each other or to any more general mode. I shall call these the *theoretical* mode, the *categoreal* mode, and the *configurational* mode. They are roughly associated with types of understanding characteristic of natural science, philosophy, and history; but they are not by any means identical with these, and in fact their real differences expose the artificial and misleading nature of academic classifications. It is the configurational mode alone which is relevant to the concepts of a story, but the issues which it may illuminate cannot be clearly stated except by contrasting it with the alternative modes.

What are the different ways in which a number of objects can be comprehended in a single mental act?

First, they may be comprehended as instances of the same generalization. This way is powerful but thin. It is powerful because the generalization refers to things as members of a class or as instances of a formula, and thereby embraces both the experienced and the unexperienced, the actual and the possible. It is thin because it refers to them only in virtue of their possession of certain common characteristics, omitting everything else in the concrete particularity of each. I discover, let us say, that a piece of paper ignites easily, and repeat the experiment with an old letter, a page from a calendar, a sheet of music, and an unpaid bill. Thus I quickly reach the generalization "Paper burns," by which I comprehend an indefinite number of similar observations. By analogous experience of needles, fenders, boathooks, and washing machines, I can

comprehend an equally great number of instances under the generalization, "Steel rusts." But then it occurs to me that both processes may be
the result of chemical combination, and I am on the way toward explaining both combustion and rusting as instances of oxidation. And in this
way I can comprehend both classes of phenomena, superficially very
unlike each other, as instances of a single law. This *theoretical* mode of
comprehension is also often called "hypothetico-deductive," and its ideal
type is that expressed by LaPlace.

A second and quite different way of comprehending a number of
objects is as examples of the same category. Thus both a painting and a
geometry are examples of complex form, and Edna St. Vincent Millay's
famous line, "Euclid alone hath looked on beauty bare," issues from
categoreal comprehension in which the category of the aesthetic is linked
with the category of form, and both subsume not merely works of art
but all formal complexes in a scale of degrees. Categoreal comprehension superficially resembles theoretical comprehension and is often confused with it, but such confusion is virtually the defining property of
philosophical obtuseness. The relation of theory to its objects is that it
enables us to infer and coordinate a body of true statements about that
kind of object; the relation of categories to their objects is that they
determine of what kind those objects may be. Thus a set of categories is
what is now often called a conceptual framework: a system of concepts
functioning *a priori* in giving form to otherwise inchoate experience.
Perhaps the simplest examples of categoreal comprehension are those
cases in which a concept belonging to a developed theory – e.g. evolution,
equilibrium, repression – is extended to cover a range of instances for
which the theory itself has no validity in principle. Thus we come, for
example, to think of the "evolution" of ideas, as a way of conceiving
what counts as an idea rather than as a theory about natural variation
and selection. It is categoreal comprehension, of course, which Plato –
and, in fact, most systematic philosophers – envisioned as an ideal aim.

Yet a third way in which a number of things may be comprehended
is as elements in a single and concrete complex of relationships. Thus a
letter I burn may be understood not only as an oxidizable substance but
as a link with an old friend. It may have relieved a misunderstanding,
raised a question, or changed my plans at a crucial moment. As a letter,
it belongs to a kind of story, a narrative of events which would be
unintelligible without reference to it. But to explain this, I would not
construct a theory of letters or of friendships but would, rather, show
how it belongs to a particular configuration of events like a part to a
jigsaw puzzle. It is in this *configurational* mode that we see together the
complex of imagery in a poem, or the combination of motives, pressures, promises, and principles which explain a senator's vote, or the
pattern of words, gestures, and actions which constitute our understanding of the personality of a friend. As the theoretical mode corresponds

to what Pascal called *l'esprit de géométrie*, so the configurational mode corresponds to what he called *l'esprit de finesse* – the ability to hold together a number of elements in just balance. The *totum simul* which Boethius regarded as God's knowledge of the world would of course be the highest degree of configurational comprehension.

Now it may seem that what I have tried to call attention to is merely an array of techniques or "approaches" from which one may select now one, now another as is appropriate to the subject matter at hand and its particular problems. It is true that one *may* do this, and also that each mode may enter into a process of inquiry – which, however, must culminate in a single mode. But they cannot be combined in a single act. One reason for such a conclusion is simply the observation that notable intellectual achievements and the style of undeniably powerful minds are characterized by a kind of single-mindedness: the attempt to extend to every possible subject of interest a single one of the modes. One notes that eminently theoretical minds attempt to apply to political problems or even to personal relationships the techniques of abstraction and generalization which enable messy particularities to be stripped away from the formulary type. Configurational minds on the other hand organize whatever they know of biology into a sense of place. As ecologists, they use their theoretical knowledge to illuminate their grasp of the concrete interactions of individual plants and animals in a specific environment; for a population biologist, on the other hand, the foxglove and the hare are countable units of their species. A more general reason for concluding that the modes are incompatible is that each has ultimately the totality of human experience, or if one prefers, the "world of fact," as its subject matter. There is nothing which cannot in principle be brought within each mode, although of course it will be modified by being comprehended in one mode rather than another. Of course it would be a mistake to try to understand subatomic particles in the mode of configurational comprehension; but this is because subatomic particles are not objects of direct experience but hypothetical constructs whose very meaning is given within the mode of theoretical comprehension. Moreover, the *practice* of each mode is an object for the others; hence there can be a psychology of philosophy and a philosophy of psychology, a biography of Freud and a psychoanalysis of the biographer. Each mode tends to represent the others as special cases or imperfect approximations of itself. And those to whom a single mode has become a second nature tend to regard the others like Gulliver's Houyhnhnm master, who thought Gulliver's forelegs impractical because his forehooves were too tender to bear his weight.

One of the more convincing reasons for acknowledging the intellectual function of comprehension and distinguishing its modes, I have come to think, is that it provides a way of understanding and explaining *rationally* the disputes of the schools and the misunderstandings in which intellectual controversy abounds. One can see, in this light, that what are called "disciplines" are actually arenas in which the partisans of each mode contend for dominance, each with its own aim of understanding, identification of problems, and privileged language. Behaviorism, for example, is essentially the claim that human action and social reality can be understood only in the mode of theoretical comprehension, as against the more traditional historical and institutional schools, whose aim was to grasp configurations or organization and stages of change. Or again there are the differences among psychoanalytic critics who seek to understand a poem by psychoanalyzing the poet or the reader (seeking theoretical comprehension), the New Criticism, whose aim is to achieve configurational comprehension of the poem alone in all its internal complexity, and archetypal critics, who apply everywhere a cat-egoreal system – which unfortunately, unlike the categoreal systems of philosophy, fails to include concepts of logic. If it is true that the three modes are incompatible as ultimate aims, we must abandon hope of achieving an eclectic or panperspectival outcome, but we might hope for an increase in intellectual charity, and be grateful for a rational defense against the imperialism of methodologies.

Everything I have said in the attempt to distinguish modes of compre-hension, of course, is in the categoreal mode.

III

It is not a theory of knowledge which is at issue. Comprehension is not knowledge, nor even a condition of knowledge: we know many things as unrelated facts – Voltaire's full name, the population of Romania in 1930, the binomial theorem, the longitude of Vancouver. On the other hand, a pseudo-scientific theory such as "hollow-earth" astronomy is as much an instance of theoretical comprehension as is astrophysics. It is by reference to standards other than comprehension that we must decide what is true and what is false. Knowledge is essentially public and may even be distributed through a community; we know collectively what no one individually could possess. But comprehension is an indi-vidual act of seeing-things-together, and only that. It can be neither an input nor an output of data-retrieval systems, nor can it be symbolically transformed for convenient reference. As the human activity by which ele-ments of knowledge are converted into *understanding*, it is the synoptic vision without which (even though transiently and partially attained) we might forever pass in review our shards of knowledge as in some night-mare quiz show where nothing relates "fact" to "fact" except the frag-mented identities of the participants and the mounting total of the score. Some physicists speculate in conversation that the physics of the future may be entirely unlike the physics of the past, since computation at electronic speeds permits the development of theories too complex for any mind to grasp as a whole. In the past, of course, the achievements of physics have been distinguished by the construction of elegant models, whether visual or just sets of equations, which were intellectually satisfying because they could be so grasped and seen to comprehend a vast range of otherwise unorganized data. So it may be that the possibility and even the desire for comprehension may disappear from some kinds of theoretical inquiry, as problem-solving and techniques of control and manipulation become dissociated from the satisfactions of understanding.

It is in the light of such a possibility that it seems not unimportant to make a just estimate of the nature and autonomy of other modes of comprehension than the theoretical mode. And it is the configurational mode which seems most often to be confused with the others or regarded, so to speak, as one of the shadows where their light has failed to reach. Implicit in the classical positivist account of explanation as it was summarized above is the theoretical principle that it is only as an instance of a law-governed type that an event or action can be truly understood. From this standpoint, a narrative may enliven sensibility (if it is fiction) or recount facts (if it is history), but it answers no questions except "And then what happened?" and affords no understanding beyond such answers. In reply to this, "narrativists" like Gallie have had a firm sense that stories produce a different and sometimes indispensable kind of understanding. But they have, I believe, failed to identify the genus to which narrative belongs, and therefore have tried to find it in the sequential form of stories, in the techniques of telling and the capacity for following, in the experience of interest, expectation, surprise, acceptability, and resolution. But as we saw, this cannot be an illuminating account of the *historian's* understanding of his own narrative. One must set against it the testimony of an eminent historian, in whose considered judgment Lord Acton was an amateur, even though a prince of amateurs, because "he was for ever expressing distress or surprise at some turn in the story." The professional historian, Geoffrey Elton goes on to say, must do more than just immerse himself in his period until he hears its people speak; one must "read them, study their creations and think about them until one knows *what they are going to say next.*"[11] It is worth reflecting, too, on those stories which we want to hear over and over again, and those which shape the common consciousness of a community, whether they end with the funeral rites of Hector or before the empty tomb.

Why do stories bear repeating? In some cases, no doubt, because of the pleasure they give, in others because of the meaning they bear. But in any case, if the theory of comprehension is right, because they aim at producing and strengthening the act of understanding in which actions and events, although represented as occurring in the order of time, can be surveyed as it were in a single glance as bound together in an order of significance, a representation of the *totum simul* which we can never more than partially achieve. This outcome must seem either a truism or a paradox: in the understanding of a narrative the thought of temporal succession as such vanishes – or perhaps, one might say, remains like the smile of the Cheshire Cat. It is a paradox, of course, if like Gallie one fixes one's attention on following the development of a story or the course of a game. But in the configurational comprehension of a story which one *has followed*, the end is connected with the promise of the beginning as well as the beginning with the promise of the end, and the necessity of the backward references cancels out, so to speak, the contingency of the forward references. To comprehend temporal succession means to think of it in both directions at once, and then time is no longer the river which bears us along but the river in aerial view, upstream and downstream seen in a single survey.

The thesis that time is not of the essence of narratives also loses its paradoxical air if one considers that historians commonly say (if they are asked) that they think less and less of chronology as they learn more and more of their fields. The date of an event is functionally an artificial mnemonic by which one can maintain the minimum sense of its *possible* relation to other events. The more one comes to understand the actual relations among a number of events, as expressed in the story or stories to which they all belong, the less one needs to remember dates. Before comprehension of events is achieved, one reasons *from* dates; having achieved comprehension, one understands, say, a certain action as a response to an event, and understands this directly. So one could reason *to* the conclusion that the event preceded the action, but from the standpoint of comprehension this would be trivial, except as information for someone else who did not already understand what the action was – who, that is, did not know its story. Even to describe the action correctly would mean describing it as a response and therefore *as* an element in a story. Otherwise it would not even be represented as an action (that is, as intentional and having a meaning for the agent), but as an opaque bit of behavior waiting for its story to be told.

It is implied by this account that the *techniques* by which narratives are shaped – from "Meanwhile, back at the ranch . . ." to the ironies of the fictive narrator who fails to see in his own tale a significance which author and reader share – can be regarded as, in part, instruments for facilitating the comprehension of the story as a whole. But one should ask at this point: what *are* the connections of the events arrayed in a single configuration? According to Gallie, the fundamental connection between the events of a story is their mutual orientation toward the promised end. According to Morton White's well-known account of historical narration, the fundamental connection is causal: antecedent events are presented as contributory or decisive causes of subsequent events.[12] There is also the unreflective view that the connection is simply that of temporal succession, but our whole argument has been that the significance of this connection evanesces between the activity of following a story and the act of comprehending it.

The example given above of an action in response to an event suggests an entirely different understanding of the internal organization of a comprehended story. For we do not describe the action and then add the statement that it was a response ("Next morning he sent off a telegram. I forgot to say that he had received an offer the day before for his interest in the company, and the telegram was his reply to the offer, actually . . ."). Rather we describe it correctly *as* a response ("He considered the offer overnight, and next morning accepted it by telegram . . ."). There are two points here. The first is that the correct description of the significant action is "accepting the offer," and "sending the telegram" is not a different action but part of the first. The second is that "accepting the offer" is already what might be called a story-statement. It refers to the story of which it is a part and overlaps conceptually with earlier statements about receiving the offer, and the like. "Sending a telegram" is not a story-statement. It suggests that there *is* a story to which it belongs, but it does not refer to that story and tells us nothing about what sort of earlier statements if any it may be linked to.

Not all parts of a story are about actions correctly describable only by story-statements, of course. But if we generalize from this paradigm we can say that the actions and events of a story comprehended as a whole are *connected by a network of overlapping descriptions*. And the overlap of descriptions may not be part of the story itself (as one thing after another) but only of the comprehension of it as a whole. For consider the narrative function of "discovery": we follow Oedipus on the road from Delphi to the crossroads where he is insulted by a stranger and in anger kills him. And then we follow him along the road to Thebes and across the years to his dreadful discovery. With Jocasta, we know the truth before Oedipus does, but not much before. All this occurs in following the story. But since we already know the story, we can only play at following it. In the comprehension of the story as a whole, there are no discoveries, and descriptions have no tense. For comprehension, the incident at the crossroads is *fully* describable only by a set of descriptions which jointly refer to all the rest of the story. The doomed man is a noble stranger to Oedipus, but he is also king of Thebes, the father of Oedipus, the husband of Jocasta, the predecessor of Oedipus as husband of Jocasta, the man whose house is cursed, the man who sent Oedipus to be bound and exposed as an infant, the man whose wife is a suicide, the man whose son blinds himself, and above all the man whose identity is discovered after his death by his slayer. He is alive and he is dead, and he could not be elsewhere than at the crossroads in the sunshine.

For comprehension, of course, there is a similar array of descriptions for every incident and character. The blinded Oedipus is the son of the king of Thebes, the man who brought the plague to the city, and the one who killed the stranger at the crossroads. Thus in the array of descriptions grasped together in the understanding of any incident or character, each overlaps with at least one in another array, and at least one overlaps with a description in every other array.[13] But this is only a formal account of a complex act of mind which directly apprehends its tableau of objects in their concrete particularity as well as in their manifold of relations.

IV

"Narrative," Barbara Hardy has said, "like lyric or dance, is not to be regarded as an aesthetic invention used by artists to control, manipulate and order experience, but as a primary act of mind transferred to art from life." More important than the artifices of fiction are the qualities which narrative shares with the storytelling of lived experience: "For we dream in narrative, daydream in narrative, remember, anticipate, hope, despair, believe, doubt, plan, revise, criticize, construct, gossip, learn, hate, and love by narrative."[14] It is true, I have argued, that narratives are in an important sense primary and irreducible. They are not imperfect substitutes for more sophisticated forms of explanation and understanding, nor are they the unreflective first steps along the road which leads toward the goal of scientific or philosophical knowledge. The comprehension at which narratives aim is a primary act of mind, although it is a capacity which can be indefinitely developed in range, clarity, and subtlety. But to say that the qualities of narrative are transferred to art from life seems a *hysteron proteron*. Stories are not lived but told. Life has no beginnings, middles, or ends; there are meetings, but the start of an affair belongs to the story we tell ourselves later, and there are partings, but final partings only in the story. There are hopes, plans, battles, and ideas, but only in retrospective stories are hopes unfulfilled, plans miscarried, battles decisive, and ideas seminal. Only in the story is it America which Columbus discovers, and only in the story is the kingdom lost for want of a nail. We do not dream or remember in narrative, I think, but tell stories which weave together the separate images of recollection. (One recounts a dream: "And then suddenly I was in the Piazza Navona – now how did I get *there*?") So it seems truer to say that narrative qualities are transferred from art to life. We could learn to tell stories of our lives from nursery rhymes, or from culture-myths if we had any, but it is from history and fiction that we learn how to tell and to understand *complex* stories, and how it is that stories answer questions.

Notes

From *New Literary History* 1 (1970): 541–58. Reprinted by permission of the Johns Hopkins University Press.

1 *Discourse on Method*, trans. Laurence J. Lafleur (New York, 1950), 4–5.

2 The classic statement is by C. G. Hempel, in "The Function of General Laws in History," *Journal of Philosophy* (1942), later weakened to accommodate probability laws in "Deductive–Nomological vs. Statistical Explanation," *Minnesota Studies in the Philosophy of Science*, vol. III, ed. Herbert Feigl and Grover Maxwell (Minneapolis, 1962), and in "Reasons and Covering Laws in Historical Explanation," *Philosophy and History*, ed. Sidney Hook (New York, 1963). There are also characteristic statements in Karl Popper's *The Logic of Scientific Discovery* (London, 1959) and Ernest Nagel's *The Structure of Science* (New York, 1961).

3 Other discussions of historical narrative are by Morton White, *The Foundations of Historical Knowledge* (New York, 1965), ch. 6; A. R. Louch, "History as Narrative," *History and Theory*, 8 (1969); Maurice Mandelbaum, "A Note on History as Narrative," *History and Theory* (1967); replies to Mandelbaum by Richard C. Ely, Rolf Gruner, and William H. Dray, *History and Theory* (1969); and W. B. Gallie, *Philosophy and the Historical Understanding* (London, 1964), which is discussed below. For the reflections of a working historian: G. R. Elton, *The Practice of History* (Sydney and New York, 1967), ch. 3.

4 R. G. Collingwood, *An Autobiography* (Oxford, 1939), 78–9.

5 *Philosophy and the Historical Understanding*, 12–13.

6 Ibid., 66.

7 Ibid., 44–7.

8 Ibid., 33.

9 "What is contingent . . . is of course, *per se* unintelligible. But in relation to a man's life, or to a particular theme in a man's life, it can be understood as having contributed to a particular, acceptable and accepted conclusion" (ibid., 41). While this sums up a notion of intelligibility with which I would quite agree, it does not support what Gallie thinks it supports, namely, the "intellectual indispensability of the act of following." As I try to argue below, it is not following but *having followed* which carries the force of understanding.

10 Ibid., 56–64, 71.

11 *The Practice of History*, 17; italics added.

12 *The Foundations of Historical Knowledge*, 223–5, and ch. 4.

13 Descriptions of course must belong to the narrative and not to our interpretation of it. It is not a description of Creon in *this* story that he is the man who condemns Antigone to death, nor a description of Oedipus that his downfall comes about as a result of a flaw in his nature. But we could not very well discuss the latter claim unless we already had the whole story in mind; and I even suspect that many interpretations or "readings" have very little point except as an aid to achieving or maintaining comprehension. In any case, comprehension is a necessary condition of interpretation but not vice versa.

14 Barbara Hardy, "Towards a Poetics of Fiction: An Approach through Narrative," *Novel* 2 (1968): 5.

7
Narrative and the Real World: An Argument for Continuity

David Carr

What is the relation between a narrative and the events it depicts? This is one of the questions that has been debated by many contributors to the lively interdisciplinary discussion of narrative in recent years.

The debate concerns the truthfulness, in a very broad sense of that term, of narrative accounts. Traditional narrative histories claim to tell us what really happened. Fictional narratives portray events that of course by definition never happened, but they are often said to be true-to-life; that is, to tell us how certain events might have occurred if they had really happened. Some histories may be inaccurate and some stories *invraisemblable*, but nothing in principle prevents such narratives from succeeding at their aim. Indeed, we take certain exemplary cases to have succeeded brilliantly.

But against this common-sense view a strong coalition of philosophers, literary theorists, and historians has risen up of late, declaring it mistaken and naive. Real events simply do not hang together in a narrative way, and if we treat them as if they did we are being *un*true to life. Thus not merely for lack of evidence or of verisimilitude, but in virtue of its very form, any narrative account will present us with a distorted picture of the events it relates. One result for literary theory is a view of narrative fiction which stresses its autonomy and separateness from the real world. One result for the theory of history is skepticism about narrative historical accounts.

I want to argue against this coalition, not so much for the common-sense view as for the deeper and more interesting truth which I think underlies it. Narrative is not merely a possibly successful way of describing events; its structure inheres in the events themselves. Far from being a formal distortion of the events it relates, a narrative account is an extension of one of their primary features. While others argue for the radical discontinuity between narrative and reality, I shall maintain not only their continuity but also their community of form.

Let us look briefly at the discontinuity view before going on to argue against it.

I

In the theory of history one might expect such a view from those, from the positivists to the *Annales* historians, who believe narrative history has always contained elements of fiction that must now be exorcised by a new scientific history. The irony is that skepticism about narrative history should have grown up among those who lavish on it the kind of attention reserved for an object of admiration and affection. Consider the work of Louis Mink. Though he speaks of narrative as a "mode of comprehension" and a "cognitive instrument," and seems at first to defend narrative history against reductionists like Hempel, in the end he comes to a similar conclusion, namely that traditional history is prevented by its very form from realizing its epistemic pretentions. Narrative structure, particularly the closure and configuration given to the sequence of events by a story's beginning, middle, and end, is a structure derived from the act of telling the story, not from the events themselves. In the end the term "narrative history" is an oxymoron: "As historical it claims to represent, through its form, part of the real complexity of the past, but as narrative it is a product of imaginative construction which cannot defend its claim to truth by any accepted procedure of argument or authentication."[1] "Stories are not lived but told," he says. "Life has no beginnings, middles, or ends. . . . Narrative qualities are transferred from art to life."[2]

If Mink arrives only reluctantly at such skeptical conclusions, Hayden White embraces them boldly. Like Mink he raises the question of narrative's capacity to *represent*. Inquiring after "The Value of Narrativity in the Representation of Reality" he seems clearly to conclude that in this respect its value is nil. "What wish is enacted, what desire is gratified," he asks, "by the fantasy that *real* events are properly represented when they can be shown to display the formal coherence of a story?"[3] "Does the world really present itself to perception in the form of well-made stories . . . ? Or does it present itself more in the way that the annals and chronicles suggest, either as a mere sequence without beginning or end or as sequences of beginnings that only terminate and never conclude?" For White the answer is clear: "The notion that sequences of real events possess the formal attributes of the stories we tell about imaginary events could only have its origin in wishes, daydreams, reveries." It is precisely annals and chronicles that offer us the "paradigms of ways that reality offers itself to perception."[4]

Mink and White are led in this skeptical direction in part by their shared belief in the close relation between historical and fictional narratives; and if we look at some of the most influential studies of literary narrative in recent years, we find a similar view of the relation between narrative and the real. It is shared by structuralists and non-structuralists alike. Frank Kermode, in his influential study *The Sense of An Ending*, puts it this way: "In 'making sense' of the world we . . . feel a need . . . to experience that concordance of beginning, middle and end which is the essence of our explanatory fictions. . . ."[5] But such fictions "degenerate," he says, into "myths" whenever we actually believe them or ascribe their narrative properties to the real, that is, "whenever they are not consciously held to be fictive."[6] In his useful recent presentation of structuralist theories of narrative, Seymour Chatman, also speaking of the beginning-middle-end structure, insists that it applies "to the narrative, to story-events as narrated, rather than to . . . actions themselves, simply because such terms are meaningless in the real world."[7] In this he echoes his mentor Roland Barthes. In his famous introduction to the structural analysis of narrative, Barthes says that "art knows no static." In other words, in a story everything has its place in a structure while the extraneous has been eliminated; and that in this it differs from "life," in which everything is "scrambled messages" (*communications brouillées*).[8] Thus, like Mink, Barthes raises the old question about the relation between "art" and "life," and arrives at the same conclusion: the one is constitutionally incapable of *representing* the other.

Paul Ricoeur draws together the theory of history and of literature in his recent *Time and Narrative* to form a complex account of narrative which is supposed to be neutral with respect to the distinction between history and fiction. For Ricoeur, as for White, the problem of representation is of central importance: the key concept in his account is that of *mimesis*, derived from Aristotle's *Poetics*.

By retaining rather than rejecting this concept Ricoeur's theory seems at first to run counter to the emphasis we have found in others on the *discontinuity* between narrative and the "real world." But in elaborating his complete theory of the mimetic relation he reveals himself to be much closer to Mink, White, and the structuralists than he at first appears. He does not go so far as to say with them that the real world is merely sequential, maintaining instead that it has a "pre-narrative structure" of elements that lend themselves to narrative configuration.[9]

But this prefiguration is not itself narrative structure, and it does not save us from what Ricoeur seems to regard as a sort of constitutional disarray attached to the experience of time, which in itself is "confused, unformed and, at the limit, mute."[10] From a study of Augustine's *Confessions* he concludes that the experience of time is characterized essentially by "discordance." Literature, in narrative form, brings concord to this "aporia" by means of the invention of a plot. Narrative is a "synthesis

of the heterogenous" in which disparate elements of the human world –
"agents, goals, means, interactions, circumstances, unexpected results,
etc."[11] – are brought together and harmonized. Like metaphor, to which
Ricoeur has also devoted an important study, narrative is a "semantic
innovation" in which something new is brought into the world by means
of language.[12] Instead of describing the world it *redescribes* it. Metaphor,
he says, is the capacity of "seeing-as."[13] Narrative opens us to "the realm
of the 'as if'."[14]

So in the end for Ricoeur narrative structure is as separate from the
"real world" as it is for the other authors we quoted. Ricoeur echoes
Mink, White, et al. when he says, "The ideas of beginning, middle, and
end are not taken from experience: they are not traits of real action but
effects of poetic ordering."[15] If the role of narrative is to introduce something new into the world, and what it introduces is the synthesis of the
heterogeneous, then presumably it attaches to the events of the world a
form they do not otherwise have. A story *redescribes* the world; in other
words, in describes it *as if* it were what presumably, in fact, it is not.[16]

This brief survey of important recent views of narrative shows not
only that narrative structure is being considered strictly as a feature of
literary and historical *texts*, but also that that structure is regarded as
belonging *only* to such texts. The various approaches to the problem of
representation place stories or histories on a radically different plane
from the real world they profess to depict. Ricoeur's is a fairly benign
and approving view. He believes that fictional and historical narratives
enlarge reality, expanding our notion of ourselves and of what is possible. Their mimesis is not imitative but creative of reality. Hayden White
seems by contrast to hold a darker, more suspicious view – one which he
shares with Barthes and poststructuralists such as Foucault and Deleuze.
Narrative not only constitutes an escape, consolation, or diversion from
reality; at worst it is an opiate – a distortion imposed from without as
an instrument of power and manipulation. In either case narrative is a
cultural, literary artifact at odds with the real.[17]

There have been some dissenters, such as the literary critic Barbara
Hardy, the historian Peter Munz, and the philosopher Frederick Olafson.[18]
Alasdair MacIntyre presents a very different view in *After Virtue*, and I
shall have more to say about him later. It is clear, however, that what I
have called the discontinuity theory is held by some of the most important people writing about narrative in history and fiction. I would now
like to show why I think this view mistaken.

II

My first criticism is that it rests on a serious equivocation. What is it
that narrative, on the discontinuity view, is supposed to distort? "Reality" is one of the terms used. But what reality is meant? Sometimes it

seems that the "real" world must be the physical world, which is supposed to be random and haphazard, or, alternatively and contradictorily, to be rigorously ordered along causal lines; but in any case it is supposed to be totally indifferent to human concerns. Things just happen in meaningless sequence, like the ticking clock mentioned by Frank Kermode. When asked what it says "we agree that it says *tick-tock*. By this fiction we humanize it. . . . Of course, it is we who provide the fictional difference between the two sounds; *tick* is our word for a physical beginning, *tock* our word for an end."[19]

This ingenious example merely confused the issue, nonetheless, since it is not primarily physical reality but human reality, including the very activity of "humanizing" physical events, which is portrayed in stories and histories and against which narrative must be measured if we are to judge the validity of the discontinuity view. Can we say of human reality that it is mere sequence, one thing after the other, as White seems to suggest? Here we would do well to recall what some philosophers have shown about our experience of the passage of time. According to Husserl even the most passive experience involves not only the retention of the just past but also the tacit anticipation, or what he calls protention, of the future. His point is not simply that we have the psychological capacity to project and to remember. His claim is the conceptual one that we cannot even experience anything as happening, as present, except against the background of what it succeeds and what we anticipate will succeed it.[20] Our very capacity to experience, to be aware of what *is* – "reality as it presents itself to experience," in Hayden White's words – spans future and past.

Husserl's analysis of time-experience is in this respect the counterpart of Merleau-Ponty's critique of the notion of sensation in classical empiricism and his claim that the figure-background scheme is basic in spatial perception.[21] He draws on the Gestalt psychologists, who were in turn indebted to Husserl. The supposedly punctual and distinct units of sensation must be grasped as a configuration to be experienced at all. Merleau-Ponty concludes that, far from being basic units of experience, sensations are highly abstract products of analysis. On the basis of Husserl's analysis of time-experience, one would have to say the same of the idea of a "mere" or "pure" sequence of isolated events. It is this that proves to be a fiction, in this case a theoretical fiction: perhaps we can conceive of it, but it is not real for our experience. As we encounter them, even at our most passive, events are charged with the significance they derive from our retentions and protentions.

If this is true of our most passive experience, it is all the more true of our active lives, in which we quite explicitly consult past experience, envisage the future, and view the present as a passage between the two. Whatever we encounter within our experience functions as instrument or obstacle to our plans, expectations, and hopes. Whatever else "life" may be, it is hardly a structureless sequence of isolated events.

It might be objected that structure is not necessarily narrative structure. But is there not a kinship between the means-end structure of action
and the beginning-middle-end structure of narrative? In action we are
always in the midst of something, caught in the suspense of contingency
which is supposed to find its resolution in the completion of our project.
To be sure, a narrative unites many actions to form a plot. The resulting
whole is often still designated, however, to be an action of larger scale:
coming of age, conducting a love affair, or solving a murder. The structure of action, small-scale and large, is common to art and to life.

What can the proponents of the discontinuity view possibly mean,
then, when they say that life has no beginnings, middles, and ends? It is
not merely that they are forgetting death, as MacIntyre points out,[22]
and birth for that matter. They are forgetting all the other less definitive but still important forms of closure and structure to be found along
the path from the one to the other. Are they saying that a moment in
which, say, an action is inaugurated is no real beginning simply because
it has other moments before it, and that after the action is accomplished
time (or life) goes on and other things happen? Perhaps they are contrasting this with the absoluteness of the beginning and end of a novel,
which begins on page one and ends on the last page with "the end." But
surely it is the interrelation of the events portrayed, not the story as a
sequence of sentences or utterances, that is relevant here. What I am
saying is that the means-end structure of action displays some of the
features of the beginning-middle-end structure which the discontinuity
view says is absent in real life.

Thus the events of life are anything but a mere sequence; they constitute rather a complex structure of temporal configurations that inter-
lock and receive their definition and their meaning from within action
itself. To be sure, the structure of action may not be tidy. Things do not
always work out as planned, but this only adds an element of the same
contingency and suspense to life that we find in stories. It hardly justifies claiming that ordinary action is a chaos of unrelated items.

There may, however, be a different way of stating the discontinuity
view which does not involve the implausible claim that human events
have no temporal structure. A story is not just a temporally organized
sequence of events – even one whose structure is that of beginning,
middle, and end. To our concept of story belongs not only a progression of events but also a story-teller and an audience to whom the story
is told. Perhaps it may be thought that this imparts to the events related
in a story a kind of organization that is in principle denied to the events
of ordinary action.

Three features of narrative might seem to justify this claim. First, in
a good story, to use Barthes's image, all the extraneous noise or static is
cut out. That is, we the audience are told by the story-teller just what is
necessary to "further the plot." A selection is made of all the events and

actions the characters may engage in, and only a small minority finds its way into the story. In life, by contrast, everything is left in; all the static is there.

This first point leads to a second. The selection is possible because the story-teller knows the plot in a way both audience and characters do not (or may not). This knowledge provides the principle for excluding the extraneous. The narrative voice, as Hayden White says,[23] is the voice of authority, especially in relation to the reader or listener. The latter is in a position of voluntary servitude regarding what will be revealed and when. Equally importantly, the narrative voice is an *ironic* voice, at least potentially, since the story-teller knows the real as well as the intended consequences of the characters' actions. This irony is thus embodied primarily in the relation between story-teller and character; but it is related to the audience as well, since their expectations, like the characters', can be rudely disappointed.

The ironic stance of the story-teller can be seen as a function (and this is the third point) of his or her temporal position in relation to the events of the story. Conventionally this is the *ex post* position, the advantage of hindsight shared by the historian and (usually) the teller of fictional stories. As Danto points out, this position permits descriptions of events derived from their relation to later events and thus often closed to participants in the events themselves.[24] This standpoint after the story-events can just as well be seen, in Mink's preferred fashion, as a standpoint *outside* or *above* the events which takes them all in at a glance and sees their interrelation.[25] This apparent freedom from the constraints of time, or at least of following the events, sometimes expresses itself in the disparity between the order of events and the order of their telling. Flashbacks and flashforwards exhibit in no uncertain terms the authority of the narrative voice over both characters and audience.

In sum, the concept of story, as Scholes and Kellogg said, involves not just a sequence of unfolding events but the existence of three distinguishable points of view on those events: those of story-teller, audience, and characters.[26] To be sure, these may seem to coincide in some cases: a story may be told from the viewpoint of a character, or in a character's voice. Here even the audience knows no more or less than the character and all points of view seem identical; but even a first-person account is usually narrated after the fact, and the selection process still depends on the difference in point of view between participant and teller. In any case the very possibility of the disparity between the three points of view is enough to establish this point – that the events, experiences, and actions of a story may have a sense, and thus a principle of organization, which is excluded from the purview of the characters in the story.

As participants and agents in our own lives, according to this view, we are forced to swim with events and take things as they come. We are constrained by the present and denied the authoritative, retrospective point of view of the story-teller. Thus the real difference between "art" and "life" is not organization vs. chaos, but rather the absence in life of that point of view which transforms events into a story by *telling* them. Telling is not just a verbal activity and not just a recounting of events but one informed by a certain kind of superior knowledge.

There is, no doubt, much truth in this analysis, and as an argument for the discontinuity view it is certainly superior to the claim that human events form a meaningless sequence. Nonetheless this argument, like its predecessor, neglects some important features of "real life."

The key to this neglect is a mistaken sense of our being "confined to the present." The present is precisely a point of view or vantage point which opens onto or gives access to future and past. This I take to be the sense of the Husserlian analysis. Even in the relatively passive experience of hearing a melody, to use his example, we do not simply sit and wait for stimuli to hit us. We grasp a configuration extending into the future which gives to each of the sounding notes their sense. Thus present and past figure in our experience as a function of what will be.

The teleological nature of action, of course, lends it the same future-oriented character. Not only do our acts and our movements, present and past, derive their sense from the projected end they serve; our surroundings function as sphere of operations and the objects we encounter figure in our experience in furtherance of (or hindrance to) our purposes. Indeed, in our active lives it could be said that the focus of our attention is not the present but the future – as Heidegger says, not on the tools but on the work to be done.[27] It has been noted by Alfred Schutz that action has, temporally speaking, the quasi-retrospective character which corresponds to the future perfect tense: the elements and phases of an action, though they unfold in time, are viewed from the perspective of their having been completed.[28]

If this is true when we are absorbed in action, it is all the more true of the reflective or deliberative detachment involved – not only in the formulating of projects and plans but also in the constant revision and reassessment required as we go along and are forced to deal with changing circumstances. The essence of deliberative activity is to anticipate the future and lay out the whole action as a unified sequence of steps and stages, interlocking means and ends. In all this it can hardly be said that our concern is limited to the present. Nor can it be said that no selection takes place. To be sure, the noise or static is not eliminated, but it is recognized as static and pushed into the background.

The obvious rejoinder here, of course, is that the future involved in all these cases is only the envisaged or projected future, and that the agent has only a quasi-hindsight, an as-if retrospection at his or her disposal. What is essential to the story-teller's position is the advantage of real hindsight, a real freedom from the constraint of the present assured by occupying a position after, above, or outside the events narrated. The story-teller is situated in that enviable position beyond all the unforeseen circumstances that intrude, all the unintended consequences of our action that plague our days and plans.

Of course this is true; the agent does not occupy a real future with respect to current action. My point is simply that action seems to involve, indeed quite essentially, the adoption of an anticipated future-retrospective point of view on the present. We know we are in the present and that the unforeseen can happen; but the very essence of action is to strive to overcome that limitation by foreseeing as much as possible. It is not only novelists and historians who view events in terms of their relation to later events, to use Danto's formulation of the narrative point of view; we all do it all the time, in everyday life. Action is thus a kind of oscillation between two points of view on the events we are living through and the things we are doing. Not only do we not simply sit back and let things happen to us; for the most part, or at least in large measure, our negotiation with the future is successful. We are, after all, able to act.

What I am saying, then, is that we are constantly striving, with more or less success, to occupy the story-tellers' position with respect to our own lives. Lest this be thought merely a far-fetched metaphor, consider how important, in the reflective and deliberative process, is the activity of literally telling, to others and to ourselves, what we are doing. When asked, "What are you doing?" we may be expected to come up with a story, complete with beginning, middle, and end, an accounting or recounting which is description and justification all at once.

The fact that we often need to tell such a story even to ourselves in order to become clear on what we are about brings to light two important things. The first is that such narrative activity, even apart from its social role, is a constitutive part of action, and not just an embellishment, commentary, or other incidental accompaniment. The second is that we sometimes assume, in a sense, the point of view of audience to whom the story is told, even with regard to our own action, as well as the two points of view already mentioned – those of agent or character and of story-teller.

Louis Mink was thus operating with a totally false distinction when he said that stories are not lived but told. They are told in being lived and lived in being told. The actions and sufferings of life can be viewed as a process of telling ourselves stories, listening to those stories, acting them out, or living them through. I am thinking here only of living one's own life, quite apart from both the cooperative and antagonistical social dimension of our action which is even more obviously intertwined with narrative. Sometimes we must change the story to accommodate the events; sometimes we change the events, by acting, to accommodate the story. It is not the case, as Mink seems to suggest, that we first live and act and then afterward, seated around the fire as it were, tell about what we have done, thereby creating something entirely new thanks to a new perspective. The retrospective view of the narrator, with its capacity for seeing the whole in all its irony, is not in irreconcilable opposition to the agent's view but is an extension and refinement of a viewpoint inherent in action itself. Mink and the others are right, of course, to believe that narration constitutes something, creates meaning rather than just reflecting or imitating something that exists independently of it. Narration, nevertheless intertwined as it is with action, does this in the course of life itself – not merely after the fact, at the hands of authors, in the pages of books.

In this sense the narrative activity I am referring to is practical before it becomes cognitive or aesthetic in history and fiction. We can also call it ethical or moral in the broad sense used by Alasdair MacIntyre and derived ultimately from Aristotle. This is to say that narration in our sense is constitutive not only of action and experience but also of the self which acts and experiences. Rather than a merely temporally persisting substance which underlies and supports the changing effects of time, like a thing in relation to its properties, I am the subject of a life-story which is constantly being told and retold in the process of being lived. I am also the principal teller of this tale, and belong as well to the audience to which it is told. The ethical–practical problem of self-identity and self-coherence may be seen as the problem of unifying these three roles. MacIntyre is probably right to attack the ideal of self-*authorship* or authenticity as an idol of modern individualism and self-centeredness.[29] But the problem of coherence cannot always be settled, as he seems to think, by the security of a story laid out in advance by society and its roles. My identity as a self may depend on which story I choose and whether I can make it hang together in the manner of its narrator, if not its author. The idea of life as a meaningless sequence, which we denounced earlier as an inaccurate description, may have significance if regarded as the constant possibility of fragmentation, disintegration, and dissolution which haunts and threatens the self.

III

But what has all this to do with history? We have reproached the discontinuity theory for misunderstanding "human reality," but our sense of this latter term seems tailored, as the conclusion of the previous section indicates, to *individual* experience, action, and existence. Indeed, our recourse to certain phenomenological themes may suggest that what we have said is methodologically tied to a first-person point of view. History, by contrast, deals primarily with social units, and with individuals only to the extent that their lives and actions are important for the society to which they belong. Is the narrative conception of experience, action, and existence developed in the previous section at all relevant to "human reality" in its specifically social forms?

I think it is, and in this section I shall present a brief sketch of how this is so. There is an obvious sense, of course, in which our conception of narrative is social right from the start. The story-telling function, whether metaphorical or literal, is a social activity, and though we spoke of the self as audience to its own narration, the story of one's life and activity is told as much to others as to oneself. On our view the self is itself an interplay of roles, but clearly the individual is constituted in inter-personal transaction as well as intrapersonal reflection. It is one thing to speak of the social construction of the self, however, and another to inquire into the make-up of social entities as such.

To consider this question it is not necessary to take up the attitude of the social scientist or historian observing something from the outside. We are also participants in groups, and our best understanding of their nature may come from a reflection on what it means to participate. What strikes me about social life is the extent to which an individual takes part in experiences and engages in actions whose proper subject is not the individual himself or herself but that of the group. To inhabit a territory, to organize politically and economically for its cultivation and civilization, to experience a natural or human threat and rise to meet it – these are experiences and actions usually not properly attributable to me alone, or to me, you, and the others individually. They belong rather to us: it is not my experience but *ours*, not *I* who act but *we* who act in concert. To say that *we* build a house is not equivalent to saying that I build a house, and you build a house, and he builds a house, and so on. To be sure, not all linguistic uses of *we* carry this sense of concerted action, division of labor, distributed tasks, and a shared end. In some cases the *we* is just shorthand for a collection of individual actions. But social life does involve certain very important cases in which individuals, by participation, attribute their experiences and acts to a larger subject or agent of which they are a part.

If this is so, it may not be necessary to give up the first-person approach, but only to explore its plural rather than its singular form in order to move from the individual to the social. If we make this move, we find many parallels to our analysis of the individual's experience and action. *We* have an experience in common when *we* grasp a sequence of events as a temporal configuration such that its present phase derives its significance from its relation to a common past and future. To engage in a common action is likewise to constitute a succession of phases articu-lated as steps and stages, subprojects, means and ends. Social human time, like individual human time, is constructed into configured sequences which make up the events and projects of our common action and experience.

As before, I think the structure of social time can be called a narrative structure, not only because it has the same sort of closure and configura-tion we found at the individual level, but also because this very structure is again made possible by a kind of reflexivity which is comparable to that of a narrative voice. The temporal sequence must be brought under a prospective–retrospective grasp which gives it its configuration, and lends to its phases their sense of presenting a commonly experienced event or of realizing a common goal. In the case of groups, however, the division of labor, necessary for carrying out common projects, may be characteristic of the narrative structure itself. That is, the interplay of roles – narrator, audience, and character – may here be literally divided among participants in the group. Certain individuals may speak on behalf of, or in the name of, the group, and articulate for the others what "we" are experiencing or doing. The resulting "story" must of course be believed or accepted by the audience to whom it is addressed if its members are to act out or live through as "characters" the story that is told.

In the last section I spoke of the temporal–narrative organization not only of experiences and actions but also of the self who experiences and acts. As the unity of many experiences and actions, the self is constituted as the subject of a life-story. So too with the constitution of certain kinds of groups which outlive particular common experiences and actions to acquire a stable existence over time. Not all groups are of this sort: collections of individuals make up groups simply by sharing objective traits such as location, race, sex, or economic class. But groups of a very special and socially and historically important sort are constituted when individuals regard each other in just such a way that they use the *we* in describing what is happening to them, what they are doing, and who they are. This is, of course, the sort of group for which the word "community" is reserved. In some of the most interesting cases, merely objective traits like sex, race, or class become the basis for the transformation of the one sort of group into the other: individuals recognize that it is *as* a race, sex, or class that they are oppressed or disadvantaged. What is grasped as common experience can be met by common action.

A community in this sense exists by virtue of a story which is articulated and accepted, which typically concerns the group's origins and its destiny, and which interprets what is happening now in the light of these two temporal poles. Nor is the prospect of death irrelevant in such cases, since the group must deal not only with possible external threats of destruction but also with its own centrifugal tendency to fragment. Again we can say that the narrative function is practical before it is cognitive or aesthetic; it renders concerted action possible and also works toward the self-preservation of the subject which acts. Indeed, we must go even further and say that it is literally *constitutive* of the group. As before, narrative is not a description or account of something that already exists independently of it and which it merely helps along. Rather, narration, as the unity of story, story-teller, audience, and protagonist, is what constitutes the community, its activities, and its coherence in the first place.

In this essay I have begun with a discussion of the individual's action, experience, and identity and have proceeded from there to the community, treating the latter as an analogue of the former. Since the story-telling and story-hearing metaphor, as already remarked, is more directly appropriate to the group than to the individual, it could be said that our order might better have been reversed. We might have presented the individual self as a kind of community of tellers, listeners, and characters, fused in their comprehension and execution of a common story. I find this interesting, but it could prove misleading; it is a special kind of story that is relevant here – the autobiographical one in which the issue is the unity and coherence of a subject who is identical with both the teller and the hearer of the story. The unity and coherence of one's own self, with all its attendant problems, is a matter closest to all of us. For this reason it serves as the best point of departure for a comparison designed to cast light on social existence.

Some may feel uncomfortable with this revival of the notion of the collective subject. While the idea that the community is a person "writ large" has strong historical precedents, notably in Plato and Hegel, it is regarded with great suspicion today. Everyone recognizes that in ordinary speech we often attribute personal qualities and activities to groups, but few are willing to grant this more than the status of a *façon de parler*. Even those who favor holism over individualism in debates about the methodology of the social sciences generally give a wide berth to any notion of social subjectivity.[30] It is the individualists who insist on the purposeful, rational, and conscious subject as the key to what goes on in society, but they reserve this conception strictly for the individual person; holists stress the degree to which the individual's behavior is embedded in non-intentional contexts of a structural and causal sort.

There are no doubt many and very interesting sorts of reasons why the idea of social subjectivity is not taken seriously, especially by the Anglo-Saxon mind, but one reason is doubtless the way this idea has been presented, or is thought to have been presented, by some of its advocates. The well-known caricature of Hegel's philosophy of history has the world spirit single-mindedly pursuing its own career by cunningly exploiting individuals for purposes unknown to them and usually opposed to the ones they themselves pursue. More recently, Sartre envisages the transcendence of the "seriality" of individual existence in the "group-in-fusion," for which the storming of the Bastille serves as the paradigm.[31] Confronted with these cases, Anglo-Saxon individualists cry alarm, since individuals are either unwitting and manipulated dupes or they are swept up in an unruly mob which obliterates their individuality altogether. Viewed with a combination of disapproval and disbelief, these notions are denied any importance or usefulness for the understanding of society and history.

But what I am talking about is really very different from either of those notions, which I agree must be rejected as paradigms. In abandoning and subverting individual subjectivity, these views do not take us from the I to a *we* but merely to a larger-scale I. What I have in mind here fits not the caricature but the genuine insight behind Hegel's notion of *Geist*, which he describes, when he first introduces it in the *Phenomenology*, as "an I that is We, a We that is I."[32] In describing the community of mutual recognition, Hegel insists as much on the plurality as on the subjectivity and agency of the social unit, and the community is not opposed to the individuals who make it up but exists precisely by virtue of their conscious acknowledgment of each other and consequently of it. Hegel also has a very healthy sense of the fragility and riskiness of this sort of community: it is born as a resolution of the conflict among its independent-minded members, and it never really overcomes the internal threat to its cohesion which is posed by their sense of independence. The *Phenomenology* is the account of the resulting drama in many of its possible social and historical variations. This account has a *narrative* structure: a community exists not only as a development, but also through the reflexive grasp of that development, when its members assume the common *we* of mutual recognition.

For all the objections that may be raised against the idea of a plural subject, the fact is that in the sorts of cases I have described, we do say *we* to each other, and we mean something real by it. Moreover, much of our lives and much of what we do is predicated on its reality for us. By stressing our use of language and our sense of participation I hope to make it clear that I am advancing not a straightforward ontological claim about the real existence of such social entities, but rather a reflexive account based on the individuals that compose and constitute them. Furthermore the term "community" as I am using it has a variable application, from the nation-states of modern history to the many economic, linguistic, and ethnic groups that often stand in conflict with them. I do not maintain, as Hegel may have thought or hoped, that such communities fit inside each other in some hierarchical order. Conflict may be inevitable, there may be no *us* without a *them*. As for individuals, obviously many of their personal conflicts may arise from conflicting loyalties to the different communities they may belong to.

To sum up: a community exists where a narrative account exists of a *we* which persists through its experiences and actions. Such an account exists when it gets articulated or formulated – perhaps by only one or a few of the group's members – by reference to the *we* and is accepted or subscribed to by others.

It may be thought that in saying this I have so watered down the idea of a plural subject that it loses its interest. It seems now to exist only as a projection in the minds of individuals, who are the real entities after all in my account. If I have said that the *we* is constituted as the subject of a story in and through the telling of that story, remember that I have said exactly the same thing about the I. If the narrative that constitutes the individual self is at least partly social in origin, then the I owes its narrative existence as much to the We as the We does to the I. Neither the We nor the I is a *physical* reality; but they are not *fictions* either. In their own peculiar senses they are as real as anything we know.

IV

To return to narrative texts as literary artifacts, whether fictional or historical, I have tried to make good on my claim that such narratives must be regarded not as a departure from the structure of the events they depict, much less a distortion or radical transformation of them, but as an extension of their primary features. The *practical* first-order narrative process that constitutes a person or a community can become a second-order narrative whose subject is unchanged but whose interest is primarily cognitive or aesthetic. This change in interest may also bring about a change in content – for example, an historian may tell a story about a community which is very different from the story the community (through its leaders, journalists, and others) tells about itself. The form, nonetheless, remains the same.

Thus I am not claiming that second-order narratives, particularly in history, simply mirror or reproduce the first-order narratives that constitute their subject-matter. Not only can they change and improve on the story; they can also affect the reality they depict – and here I agree with Ricoeur – by enlarging its view of its possibilities. While histories can do this for communities, fictions can do it for individuals. But I disagree that the narrative *form* is what is produced in these literary genres in order to be imposed on a non-narrative reality – it is in envisaging new content, new ways of telling and living stories, and new kinds of stories, that history and fiction can be both truthful and creative in the best sense.[33]

Notes

1 Louis O. Mink, "Narrative Form as a Cognitive Instrument" in *The Writing of History*, ed. R. H. Canary and H. Kozicki (Madison, 1978), 145.
2 Mink, "History and Fiction as Modes of Comprehension," *New Literary History* 1 (1970), 557ff. [ch. 6, this volume].
3 Hayden White, "The Value of Narrativity in the Representation of Reality," in *On Narrative*, ed. W. J. T. Mitchell (Chicago, 1981), 4.
4 Ibid., 23.
5 Frank Kermode, *The Sense of An Ending: Studies in the Theory of Fiction* (London, 1966), 35ff.
6 Ibid., 39.
7 Seymour Chatman, *Story and Discourse: Narrative Structure in Fiction and Film* (Ithaca, 1978), 47.
8 Roland Barthes, "Introduction à l'analyse structurale des récits," *Communication* 8 (1966), 7.

9 Paul Ricoeur, *Temps et récit* (Paris, 1983), I, 113.
10 Ibid., 14.
11 Ibid., 102.
12 Ibid., 11.
13 Ibid., 13. See Ricoeur's *La Métaphore vive* (Paris, 1975), 305ff.
14 *Temps et récit*, 101.
15 Ibid., 67.
16 For a more detailed critical account of Ricoeur's book see my review-essay in *History and Theory* 23 (1984), 357–70.
17 In a recent article, "The Question of Narrative in Contemporary Historical Theory," *History and Theory* 23 (1984), 1–33, White himself gives a much more thorough account of these developments than I have given here. Concerning his presentation, which is otherwise a model of scholarship and synthesis, I have three reservations: modesty apparently prevents the author from documenting his own important role in the developments he describes; he generally approves of the trends I shall be criticizing; and he has not, I believe, properly assessed the position of Ricoeur, perhaps because *Temps et récit* was not available to him.
18 Barbara Hardy, "Towards a Poetics of Fiction: An Approach Through Narrative" in *Novel* (1968), 5ff; and *Tellers and Listeners: The Narrative Imagination* (London, 1975); Peter Munz, *The Shapes of Time* (Middletown, 1977); Frederick Olafson, *The Dialectic of Action* (Chicago, 1979). Several German theorists have stressed the continuity of experience and narrative. See Wilhelm Schapp, *In Geschichten Verstrickt* (Wiesbaden, 2nd edn, 1979); Hermann Lübbe, *Bewusstsein in Geschichten* (Freiburg, 1972); Karlheinz Stierle, "Erfahrung und narrative Form" in *Theorie und Erzählung in der Geschichte*, ed. J. Kocka and T. Nipperdey (Munich, 1979), 85ff.
19 Kermode, *The Sense of an Ending*, 44ff.
20 Edmund Husserl, *The Phenomenology of Internal Time-Consciousness*, trans. J. S. Churchill (Bloomington, 1964), 40ff.
21 Maurice Merleau-Ponty, *The Phenomenology of Perception*, trans. C. Smith (New York, 1962), 3ff.
22 Alasdair MacIntyre, *After Virtue* (Notre Dame, 1981), 197.
23 Hayden White, "The Structure of Historical Narrative," *Clio* 1 (1972), 12ff.
24 Arthur Danto, *Analytical Philosophy of History* (Cambridge, 1965), 143ff.
25 Mink, "History and Fiction as Modes of Comprehension," 557ff.
26 Robert Scholes and Robert Kellogg, *The Nature of Narrative* (New York, 1966), 240ff.
27 Martin Heidegger, *Being and Time*, trans. J. Macquarrie and E. Robinson (New York, 1962), 99.
28 Alfred Schutz, *The Phenomenology of the Social World*, trans. G. Walsh and F. Lehnert (Evanston, 1967), 61.
29 MacIntyre, *After Virtue*, 191.
30 See Ernst Gellner, "Explanation in History," in *Modes of Individualism and Collectivism*, ed. J. O'Neill (London, 1973), 251; and Anthony Quinton, "Social Objects" in *Proceedings of the Aristotelian Society* 76 (1975–6), 17.
31 Jean-Paul Sartre, *Critique de la raison dialectique* (Paris, 1960), I, 391ff.
32 G. W. F. Hegel, *Phenomenology of Spirit*, trans. A. V. Miller (Oxford, 1977), 110.
33 The themes in this essay are developed at greater length in my *Time, Narrative, and History* (Bloomington, 1986).

8

Telling It Like It Was: Historical Narratives On Their Own Terms

Andrew P. Norman

I

Something is rotten in state-of-the-art narrative theory. Time has done nothing to correct it, and philosophers have managed even less. At issue is the epistemic legitimacy of the historical narrative, and the debates it generates are as protracted as they are confounding. What epistemic status does the kind of stories historians tell claim, and what have they any right to claim, in virtue of their narrative form? – that is the question. Both positive and negative answers have been backed by arguments that can seem quite compelling, at least for a time. Stepping back a bit, however, can make both positions appear strange and unnatural. Sweeping denials of the story's capacity to reflect the past accurately are ever catalyzing equally misleading global affirmations, which in turn and again make the more skeptical stance appear quite attractive. The contortions that both critics and defenders of narrative go through, and the instability of the convictions they generate, should in the end, I believe, make us suspicious of the question. Narrative histories should be taken on their own terms, and their epistemic adequacy assessed on a case-by-case basis.

The issue arises because the constructive activity of the narrator is seen to be in tension with history's professed aim to tell truths about the past. Louis Mink put the problem well: "So we have a . . . dilemma about the historical narrative: as historical it claims to represent, through its form, part of the real complexity of the past, but as narrative it is a product of imaginative construction, which cannot defend its claim to truth by any accepted procedure of argument or authentication."[1] Mink's doubts about the possibility of such a defense have of course not deterred philosophers from trying to provide them. Recent years have seen some rather sophisticated dialectical defenses of the narrative mode. I intend to examine these arguments in some detail, and try to make both their virtues and their shortcomings stand out clearly. More importantly, however, I aim to question the skepticism that inspires such attempts.

Thus recent efforts to defend the epistemic honor of the story should be understood as a response to pervasive worries about its representational adequacy. Such worries are by no means new to our day and age. For Descartes, for example, "even the most faithful histories, if they do not alter or embroider things to make them more worth reading, almost always omit the meanest and least illustrious circumstances, so that the remainder is distorted."[2] Alasdair MacIntyre sees Sartre's *La Nausée* as advancing this idea in its most radical form. For its character Roquentin, "to present human life in the form of a narrative is always to falsify it."[3]

The revival of such sentiments in recent years is owing in part, no doubt, to the fact that philosophers have assailed narrative repeatedly over the last quarter century. Hempel's influential theory of explanation as deduction from physical "covering laws" entailed, as he pointed out, that history practiced as narrative is not genuinely explanatory.[4] History's "narrativist" defenders have struggled to counter this charge, and for the most part seem to have forgotten that the best defense is often a good offense. For one can simply reverse the entailment here: since stories evidently *do* explain, so much the worse for Hempel's theory of explanation.

Narrative historiography was also impugned for being improperly scientific. Maurice Mandelbaum, for instance, argued that historical narratives "ensure explanatory incompleteness," and inevitably constitute a "gross distortion of the subject matter."[5] Even Mink, who was in many ways narrative's most ardent and able defender, seems to David Carr to conclude that "the very form of historical discourse undermines its epistemic pretensions."[6] The same conclusions were being reached on the continent, where narrative was caught between the "social-scientific" historians, like those of the French *Annales* school, and theorists like Roland Barthes, who claimed that "we can see, simply by looking at its structure, and without having to invoke the substance of its content, that historical discourse is in its essence a form of ideological elaboration."[7]

And although the question of narrative's cognitive legitimacy is not new, the recent controversy has given the issue its own peculiar formulation. The concern these days is whether "narrative structure" is "imposed" by the historian upon a "pre-narrativized" past. What I will call "impositionalism" is the idea, raised (or lowered) to the level of a philosophical position, that telling a story about the past necessarily involves a certain kind of interpretative violence. The contemporary theorist who has pushed the impositionalist line hardest is Hayden White:

> Since no given set or sequence of real events is intrinsically tragic, comic, farcical, and so on, but can be constructed as such only by the imposition

of the structure of a given story type on the events, it is the choice of the story type and its imposition upon the events that endow them with meaning.[8]

Constructing a narrative, for White, always involves the "projection onto the facts of the plot structure of one or another of the genres of literary figuration." The "real" past is devoid of meaning and order, on this view, for "in the historical narrative, the systems of meaning production peculiar to a culture or society are tested *against* the capacity of any set of 'real' events to yield to such systems."[9] Positivist attacks on the narrative mode, it seems, have left scars on its epistemic reputation that have never fully healed.

Several forms of interpretative violence, or "imposition of structure," are commonly pointed to as endemic to story-construction. To begin with, an historian must always *select* the facts he or she will use, often on the basis of some identifiable criterion, interest, or bias. This is commonly held to insure a story's radical incompleteness, if not guarantee its falsehood. Artificial *closure* is created by the choice of beginning and end. The facts must then be integrated or configured in a way that creates a unity and coherence that are, strictly speaking, foreign to the past itself. "Imposition," then, signifies the activity wherein criteria of relevance are applied, closure is attained, and coherence and unity are created – a process, in short, that generates an *emplotted* account of the past.

Entering the 1980s, the issue of narrative's epistemic legitimacy had assumed the contours of the realism–constructivism controversies that philosophers of science and ethical ontologists, for example, know all too well. Do we, in constructing a narrative history, impose a narrative order on the past, or do we simply read off an order that is already there? What I will call "historical realism" is the idea that history exists as a determinate, untold story until discovered and told by the historian. Such a position naturally inclines in the direction of a high regard for narrative's epistemic legitimacy. Although seldom explicitly defended, it or something like it is often inveighed against.[10]

The important point for our purposes is that those arrayed against this realism have included narrative's supporters as well as its detractors. Narrativist affirmations of storytelling as a selective, creative activity have understandably done little to further its epistemic standing, for such affirmations give rise immediately to suspicions of misrepresentation. Without intending to impugn the epistemic status of the story, narrativist contributions to the recent debate have in fact had that effect. In short, with the battle-lines thus drawn, the blatantly constructed character of the historical narrative has put narrativists on the defensive, and given impositionalists the upper hand.

A number of philosophers have come to the defense of narrative, however, offering innovative arguments for its cognitive validity. There are at least two quite distinct approaches that can be discerned in the literature. One grows out of a phenomenological understanding of the world as "already" structured in certain definite ways. It argues that narratives do not impose order or intelligibility where there is none, but instead merely give voice to a past that is already narratively structured. The second has its roots in the speech-act theory that is trying to situate and delimit truth-seeking discourse within a wider and more diverse set of language-games. The idea here is that historical narratives have wrongly been assumed to be making *truth* claims, and consequently judged by the wrong standard.

The first approach, in defending narrative's representational adequacy, amounts to a kind of moderated realism. The second, in challenging the very ideal of representational adequacy, tacitly admits narrative's representational *in*adequacy, and thus falls out as a sort of radicalized impositionalism. Although both develop important insights that must be retained, it will be shown that they misdescribe the way we construct and treat historical narratives and remain inadequate answers to the problem of their epistemic status.

II

The work of Alasdair MacIntyre, David Carr, and Frederick Olafson suggests a way of defending historical narrative against the charges brought against it by the impositionalists.[11] The impositionalist claim was that recounting the past in the form of a story inevitably imposes a false narrative structure upon it. By exploiting the phenomenological insight that the lived world of everyday experience is "already" structured in a number of ways, the response is made that that about which we tell stories is already *narratively* structured. The argument is that, because life, experience, and the past as lived are coherent and intelligible *before* we begin telling stories about them, the skeptical worries about imposing false coherence are ill-founded.

This line differs significantly from that of the (naive) "historical realism" mentioned earlier, in that both story and past are now taken to be thoroughly and inescapably interpreted: the "objectivity" of neither is presupposed. More precisely, neither the naive metaphysical posit of a past-in-itself, nor the problematic claim of epistemological access to such a past is taken for granted or defended. Rather than worry about our lack of access to a "real" past, independent of human acts of interpretation and cognition, the defenders of this line get on with the task of describing and thinking about the lived world: a world that is for them already narratively structured.

MacIntyre's account of the "narrative structure of a human life" is a small but important part of the argument of his book *After Virtue*.

"Narrative," he claims, "is not the work of poets, dramatists and novelists reflecting upon the events which had no narrative order before one was imposed by the singer or the writer; narrative form is neither disguise nor decoration." He goes on to say,

> It is because we all live out narratives in our lives and because we understand our own lives in terms of the narratives we live out that the form of narrative is appropriate for understanding the actions of others. Stories are lived before they are told – except in the case of fiction. . . . What I have called a history is an enacted dramatic narrative in which the characters are also the authors.[12]

MacIntyre, then, would have us believe that our lives, and human history more broadly, are "enacted narratives." Both *our* pasts, and *the* past have a "narrative structure," for MacIntyre, prior to and independently of any explicit act of storytelling. Now this is not just the claim that we constantly and ordinarily understand ourselves and our past in the narrative mode; that is, with the aid of stories told with greater or lesser degrees of explicitness. MacIntyre wants to be taken quite literally when he says that our lives actually *are* enacted narratives, that human history actually *is* a dramatic enactment of some story or set of stories. He needs to make this stronger claim in order to give his account of the moral life the determinacy, continuity, and rootedness it needs in the face of the fact that disparate practices give rise to conflicting virtues.[13]

In any case, it is only because this stronger claim is made that the position articulated here represents an answer to impositionalism – a defense of the epistemic status of narrative. Because narrative structure actually inheres in that about which we write narrative histories, telling the story of the past is not a matter of imposing such a structure upon it. As Carr puts it:

> For if I am right in thinking that narrative structure pervades our very experience of time and social existence, independently of our contemplating the past as historians, then we shall have a way of answering the charge that narrative is nothing but window-dressing or packaging, something incidental to our knowledge of the past.[14]

The idea of the narrative structure of human experience (MacIntyre uses "life" where Carr speaks of "experience")

> permits us to correct the view that structure in general and narrative structure in particular is imposed upon a human experience intrinsically devoid of it, so that such structure is an artifice, something not natural but forced, something that distorts or does violence to the true nature of human reality.[15]

This view has several virtues atop its simple, homely appeal. To begin with, it goes a long ways towards correcting a certain "atomistic prejudice" that has long been part of the analytic approach to the philosophy of history. The argument here is that, contrary to what many analytic philosophers (especially the impositionalists) have assumed, the past is not initially or primarily given to us in the form of separate, isolated incidents that are then given a false narrative coherence by an historian. Doing history is as much the breaking up of an initially seamless whole as it is the bringing together of initially unrelated events. World War II was no less real, no more a fiction, than was D-Day. And the D-Day of the historian is not just the events that happened during a certain twenty-four hour period. We understand the battle in terms of its being a pivotal episode of the war, and its boundaries and significance are set accordingly. The individuation of constitutive events is seldom unproblematic, and is usually guided by concerns informed by a prior understanding of the larger historical context.

Now I think that this objection cuts pretty deep. There does not seem to be any reason why the individuated "event" should enjoy epistemic priority over broader or more extended historical structures. In history, the parts are no more unproblematically "given" than is the whole. Impositionalism, it seems, has given unreflective priority to the "atomic" event (a questionable notion at best), and based its critique of narrative in large part upon this misleading supposition. Unity, coherence, and structure cannot be viewed as mere artifacts of the historian's work. The appearance of coherence should not by itself arouse skeptical suspicions, any more than should disjointed incoherence. Either can be an imposition of a false order (or lack thereof), but neither need be.

A second virtue of the plot-reifier's account is that it seems to explain how historical narratives can be true. A story about the past is true, on such an account, when it accurately maps the real narrative structure of the lived past. This is not an insignificant result, given that we *do* speak of histories as claiming and attaining truth, and that it is difficult to see how else we might explain the capacity of a history to be true, in light of the impositionalist charge that stories contain structures that do not appear in the past itself.

In an earlier work, MacIntyre had expressed an interest in defending the truth-claims of narratives. "To raise the question of truth," he wrote, "need not entail rejecting myth or story as the appropriate and perhaps the only appropriate form in which certain truths can be told."[16] The conclusion he reaches in *After Virtue* seems to have been forced by a need to explain how this can be so. The apparent reasoning is not difficult to trace. If stories about the past have a certain narrative structure, and some of them at least are true, then the past itself (on a correspondentist view of truth, it seems) must have that structure also. The thought that our lives are already narratively structured, then, represents a solution to what has been a long-standing problem for MacIntyre, and indeed, narrative theorists more generally.

I do not think we need to go to such extremes to affirm the epistemic status of the narrative history. Histories can be true without their being isomorphic structures in the past. Nor need we invoke or presuppose "correspondence" theories of truth to make sense of such claims. To call a story true is just to say that what it tells us about the past did happen – that what it says once was, was. It is when we go beyond this homely understanding that we run into problems. For accounts of truth in terms of correspondence (or some other sort of structural isomorphism) seem to require that "narrative structure" belong to both true stories and that which they are about. What history tells stories about is the past, and quite frankly, I do not think we can make sense of the notion of a past that is "already" narratively structured. To focus this critique, let us ask first what "narrative structures" are supposed to be, and then inquire into whether they are the kind of thing that even *can* belong to the past.

How are we to understand this crucial notion of "narrative structure"? I have not been able to find a clear account of it anywhere in the literature.[17] I think that it is crucial to MacIntyre and Carr that this central notion remain unexplicated, for as soon as we begin to spell it out, we run into difficulties. I should note, initially, that I do not think the same is true of other "structures" that serve as a model for this type of claim. To say that the past has a *temporal* structure, for example, strikes me as relatively unproblematic. I think we can also grant that the lived past is at least for the most part meaningfully arranged.[18] We might even say that the past as we know it is crisscrossed by the kind of intelligibility and significance structures that story-lines must trace out in portraying that past.

My point here is that, whatever it is a *narrative* structure is supposed to be, it must be more than just these things. To deserve the modifier "narrative," a structure must have the characteristics that are peculiar to and definitive of stories. And stories are discursive entities that display at least the traces of a plot. I can think of no account of narrative structure that does not come back, in the end, to the idea of plot. Even a discursive entity without a plot has an extremely tenuous claim to be called a story. Something that is neither discursive nor emplotted, it seems to me, has even less. But suppose we go along with the metaphorical extension of "narrative" to nondiscursive things. Such entities would still have to have something resembling a plot even to begin to count as "narratively structured." Thus something's not having a narrative structure would seem to follow pretty directly from its not having a plot.

But can the past have a plot? The notion of an already emplotted past is not an idea I think we can understand. For to speak of something as having a plot is to raise questions of its emplotment: of who authored it, how, when, and for whom. The notion entails not just that the past has an author, but implies also the occurrence of a prior storytelling. The "already," of course (on MacIntyre's own admission), means: prior to its story ever being told.[19] Putting aside questions of authorship and audience, we can ask: how and when did the past come to be emplotted? Either the storytelling that emplots the past never occurred, in which case the claim that it is actually emplotted is dubious or metaphorical at best, or it occurred prior to its story ever being told, which seems like a conceptual impossibility. The point, of course, is neither more nor less than this: that talk of a narratively structured past is, *strictly speaking*, nonsense.

It will be objected that this rebuttal relies upon a relatively straightforward denial of what MacIntyre and Carr assert. For MacIntyre's claim was that "stories are lived before they are told," and the suppressed premise of the above argument is clearly that, in order to *be*, a story must first be told. If one bare assertion is as good as another, what reason do we have for preferring either?

The bare implausibility of an emplotted past, I contend, places the burden of proof squarely on MacIntyre and Carr. This is a burden they tacitly accept by providing arguments for their central claim. Unfortunately, these arguments do not work. Carr's argument takes the form of a chapter-long excursus that never addresses the primary objection, which I have given above. That Carr's argument begs the central question at issue is made clear by his own formulation of his argumentative strategy: "Unless we can find some *semblance* of this complex relationship (that of story, story-teller, and audience) in the ordinary *experience* of time, it may be thought that the concept of narrative is badly miscast."[20] One reply, of course, is that it is not enough to show, as Carr proceeds to do, a *semblance* in this respect, and that, because of this, the concept *is* badly miscast.

But more to the point, it is not enough to show that our ordinary *experience* has this form. For noting a structural similarity between narrative histories and our experience of the past does not allow us to explain how those histories can be true. On the concept of truth that motivates this line, it is what histories are *about* that must be shown to have narrative structure, and the fact is, such stories purport to be about the past, not just our experience of it. If an historical narrative recounts our ordinary experience of the past, but does not report what actually happened, we rightly do not call it true. Hence it does not suffice to defend this far weaker claim.

The only gesture MacIntyre makes by way of argument here is quite clever, but it relies on a trick. The inference to the past's narrative structure is carried by the idea that it is "historical."[21] But this move only gets MacIntyre where he needs to go by exploiting the double sense of the term "history." If we spell out the argument, we find that its major premise is a falsehood disguised as a tautology: since history (in the sense of "our stories") has a narrative structure, history (in the sense of "the past") has a narrative structure. But when we recognize this ploy for what it is, the plot-reifiers are left without an argument for their central claim.

Quite simply, our concept of narrative is not as radically separable from that of discourse as this approach to defending narrative hopes and/or presupposes. Plot or narrative structure appears for the first time, if not exclusively, in the realm of discourse. The fact that a true historical account has a plot structure does not imply that the past it articulates has a plot structure, any more than the fact that "the sky is blue" has a grammatical structure implies that the sky has a grammatical structure.[22] The past need not have a narrative structure for a story about it to be true. To deny this is to confuse discursive form with semantic content: the presentation of a story with what it tells us. A plot, like grammar, is a structure that belongs to discursive entities. The past, like the sky, is not a discursive entity.

We have found no warrant, then, for the claim that the past is narratively structured. Taken literally, it is a flat out contradiction in terms – a simple category mistake. Of course it could quite properly be objected here that this rebuttal relies upon an uncharitably literal construal of the plot-reifier's central premise. The account fares better if simply accepted as the metaphor it is. Now this reply is well, true, and good as far as it goes. The plot-reifier's line *does* build on an instructive and worthwhile metaphor. But unless it is taken literally, the plot-reifier's thesis simply does not explain how stories can be true. Nor does it constitute a solution to the problem of narrative history's epistemic status. To eliminate the worry that narrative construction involves an interpretative violence, this defense of narrative must reify the structures that properly belong to stories, and project them onto the past. For then they can be "found" there, thus making narrative true. But, as we have seen, at least one of those structures – that of plot – is to be found only in stories.

And it seems to me that the plot-reifier's account suffers in another respect as well. It does not adequately acknowledge the truly constructive nature of the historian's work. If narrative structure is already there, prior to the historian's arrival, it begins to look as if the historian's task is simply a matter of finding and more or less passively (and literally!) *reading* narrative structures off of the past. What is already emplotted requires no emplotment, and the historian's creative skills never even come into play. On such an account, the past has its own story to tell, and the historian becomes a mere stenographer! This is misleading, however, for (except in rare cases) narrative histories must be hunted out and pieced together, arranged and articulated, worked and reworked in a constructive and often painstaking process. The plot-reifier's account does not do justice to the creative, actively configuring character of narrative construction.

I think, then, that we can follow the plot-reifiers in their attempt to affirm the truth-claims of (some) narratives, and still reject the strategy of reifying narrative structures in order to validate narratological representation. No matter how integrated, coherent, and structured our experience of the past "already" is, one cannot deny that the historian must piece together, interpret, articulate, and configure remnants of the past in constructing a narrative about it. And this will always leave room for suspicions of misrepresentation. There is no global defense of the narrative form that will insulate it, once and for all, from skeptical doubts.

III

The second approach to defending narrative as a respectable discursive tool is not as concerned that its representational adequacy be vindicated. It involves throwing into radical question the assumption that narrative histories even *purport* to be true, and amounts to the demand that we look at narrative histories as seeking something other than referential legitimacy. Histories must be seen, not as simple representations of what once was, but as practically oriented attempts to reshape our effective collective understanding of the past.[23] The rallying-cry of this movement has been that truth-claims belong to one language game, and historical narratives to another.

I will take J. F. Lyotard and Roland Barthes as the main proponents of this view, although there are suggestions of it in the works of Louis Mink and John McCumber, among others. Although all of these thinkers suggest that a defense of narrative can be constructed by denying that they even *claim* truth, none of them holds this line consistently. Nonetheless, that is what they would have to do for such a defense to work. What I will call *anti-referentialism*, then, is a distillation of suggestive attempts to exempt narrative histories from the "criterion of truth." After discussing the arguments that motivate this line, I will show why I think they fail.

Lyotard argues that narrative knowledge and scientific knowledge belong to different language games. "Scientific knowledge requires that one language game, denotation, be retained and all others excluded. A statement's truth-value is the criterion determining its acceptability." Such knowledge, however, is "in this way set apart from the language games that combine to form the social bond. Unlike narrative knowledge it [science] is no longer a direct and shared component of that bond." Scientific and "non-scientific" narrative knowledge belong to "parallel" frameworks of rules. Denotative knowledge requires evidence, argument, and proof, but "narrative knowledge does not give priority to the question of its own legitimation. [It rather] certifies itself in the pragmatics of its own transmission, without having recourse to argumentation and truth." Thus it is "impossible to judge the existence or validity of narrative knowledge on the basis of scientific knowledge and vice versa: the relevant criteria are different."[24]

Lyotard thinks that denotative statements "easily slip in" to narratives, but insists that narratives constitute a kind of knowledge that must be insulated from the "criterion of truth."[25] Lyotard does not spell out very carefully what he means by this last point, but presumably he means that stories – including our histories – are not answerable to the requirement that they be true. Mink sometimes spoke in a similar fashion. In trying to construct a "rational defense against the imperialism of methodologies," he went so far as to assert that historical narratives are "not subject to confirmation or disconfirmation."[26]

Barthes critically notes that "the narration of past events" has, in our culture, been "subject to the sanction of historical 'science,'" and historically "bound to the underlying standard of the 'real.'"[27] He thinks this is unfortunate, and concludes:

> Claims concerning the "realism" of narrative are therefore to be discounted. ... The function of narrative is not to "represent," it is to constitute a spectacle.... Narrative does not show, does not imitate.... "What takes place" in a narrative is from the referential point of view literally nothing; "what happens" is language alone.[28]

Anti-referentialism, then, may be seen as part of the movement – running from Wittgenstein through Austin to contemporary speech-act theory – to correct for the oversights and misperceptions that come from a view of language as a purely representational medium. It aims to bring to light the often obscured normative, performative, and practical dimensions of narrative language use.

The placing of narrative and the "criterion of truth" into separate realms also creates a fissure between the natural and human sciences that is intended to block the methodological imperialism of positivism. Habermas conceives this move in even broader terms. It is for him part of the attempt to halt the steady encroachment of instrumental rationality upon the symbolic–interactive realm that includes the historical–hermeneutical sciences.[29] On the anti-referentialist view, the criterion of truth as accurate representation has been wrongly imported across a fundamental divide, and used to dismiss historical narratives as epistemologically inadequate.

Narrative, on this account, should not be regarded as a mimetic mode. Rather than looking at historical narratives as referential, or candidates for truth, anti-referentialists would have us see them as striving to attain other discursive virtues such as coherence, comprehensiveness, and followability. If the function they serve is to foster comprehension, for example, then they must be evaluated according to whether or not (or to what degree) they achieve this end, not according to whether or not they correspond to what was once reality.[30]

Of course, in order to count as history rather than fiction, narratives must attend to the facts, but by and large this is reconceived to be a side issue. John McCumber, for example, defines narrative for his own purposes as the "reconstruction of a progress" that "aims at coherence" as opposed to "accuracy." "The 're-' in 'reconstruct,' to be sure, means that [one is] not engaged in fiction . . . but this does not mean that narrative aims at historical truth."[31]

Now I would like to applaud the motives of this attempt to protect history from the imposition of foreign standards, and I think that the need to correct an imbalance caused by a disproportionate attention to the representational function of language indeed calls for strong measures. My concern, however, is that the anti-referentialists have gone too far, and introduced arbitrary and pernicious distinctions in order to further these worthy ends. To point out the dimensions of storytelling that accounts of them as purely representational leave out is surely worthwhile, but to deny the referential function of narrative is likewise to miss something important. To argue that narratives ought not to be evaluated on their truth-content *alone* is one thing, but to develop a dichotomy that places narratives in a language game wholly apart from truth is another thing again.

The fact is, historical narratives for the most part *do* purport to tell us what the past was like. They consist of assertions *about* the past, and they attempt to tell us what actually occurred. This means precisely that narrative histories purport to refer – that they claim truth. Furthermore, they are generally offered for critical scrutiny on the understanding that entitlement to assert them can be revoked for inability to defend them successfully against significant challenges. Histories do belong – and properly – to language games wherein evidence must be given for novel claims, challenges to the truth of a given account are often appropriate, and confirmation and disconfirmation do in fact occur. It is highly artificial, not to mention outright dangerous, to claim that the question of whether or not an historical narrative is true is not a good question, or a category mistake of some kind. This is often a perfectly appropriate question, and at times it is of the utmost importance that it be answered. The recent revisionist histories that claim that the Holocaust never occurred, for example, challenge the truth of received accounts, and themselves call for immediate disconfirmation. It just would not do to exempt such stories from "the criterion of truth." As MacIntyre puts it: "It matters enormously that our histories be true."[32]

IV

The breakdown of both the plot-reifier's and the anti-referentialist's defenses of narrative casts us back upon the question of the epistemic legitimacy of the story. How can the impositionalist charge be answered short of reifying plot-structures or pulling narratives out of the truth-game entirely? The charge, again, was that casting the past into the form of a narrative inevitably falsifies that past by imposing a foreign structure upon it. I do not think that a knock-down argument against the skeptic is possible. But I do think we can indicate, in a preliminary manner, a way in which the impositionalist's skeptical conclusion can be reasonably avoided.

The first thing to note is that an argument advanced earlier (to block the inference to real narrative structures) can be used again here against the impositionalist charge. The fact that a discursive representation has a structure that that which it represents does not, does not itself entail that a falsifying imposition has taken place. To make this inference reflex-ively is again to confuse discursive form and semantic content. Discursive structure is not inherently falsifying, for it constitutes the positive condition of the possibility of language having *any* semantic content – of its being able to represent or be true at all. (This is as true of simple descriptive claims as it is of narratives. Without the grammatical structures that are a necessary part of any language, there would not even be any candidates for truth or falsity, and "true" would be meaningless. It follows from this that we must accept such structure as non-falsifying if the idea of truth is to remain meaningful.) A narrative certainly *may* impose a false coherence, or simply get the past wrong, but it *need* not.

The second argument against impositionalism, quite briefly, is that it does not adequately characterize the process of doing history. It is undeniable that historians must select, piece together, interpret, arrange, and so on, but to say that this constitutes an *imposition* on the past is to imply a violence that "misses the properly dialectical character" of histor-ical inquiry.[33] A good historian will interact dialogically with the his-torical record, recognizing the limits it places on possible construals of the past. Although the traces of the past *underdetermine* the stories that can be told about that past, it is simply not the case that an historian must invent and impose to achieve a concrete determination. Historians are accountable for their choice of facts, wording, arrangement, and cast, and generally make these choices with an eye towards what the histor-ical record will support. Characterizing what a good historian does as imposition – that is, in terms that suggest violence – is on a par with attempts to portray the process as simple transcription – a description that misleadingly implies passivity.

And those specific skeptical worries that were mentioned above can be answered, briefly, in turn. *Of course* historians select their facts, and obviously the stories they tell are incomplete. But by itself this does not mean that the result is distorted or false. To say so is to posit implicitly an evaluative ideal of a history that is complete and non-perspectival. But this very idea is incoherent. I have never read a history that claimed perfect objectivity or completeness, nor do I expect to. We learn to read such histories as situated and discriminating; and eventually learn, too, that such general skeptical objections count for nothing.

Nor need the charge of artificial closure worry us unduly. It is certainly true that, as MacIntyre acknowledges, "in taking an event as a beginning or an ending we bestow a significance upon it which may be debatable."[34] That is why historians usually go out of their way to situate the stories they tell in the larger context of what came before and after. But the fact that a story must begin somewhere and end somewhere else does not necessarily mislead. It might, of course, but the critic must shoulder the burden of showing that it does in any given case. In some cases, it will be possible to make the case for a falsifying imposition, and in others the attempt to do so will seem like a trivial academic excercise.

Nor does the appearance of coherence, unity, or intelligibility in a told story about the past indicate that distorting forces were at work in its creation. To make this argument, one must assume that the past is initially without order, coherence, or intelligibility. But we have no evidence for this. What we do know is that the past as we experience it in memory often does have unity, coherence, and intelligibility. Even where our initial, inarticulate experience of the past does not exhibit this coherence, the process of constructing a coherent story about it need not, and often does not, have the violent character of an imposition. Quite simply, it often has the unobjectionable character of a disclosure.

V

I have argued that there is something strained and artificial in each of three major positions in the philosophy of history. Some theorists insist, in spite of numerous counterexamples, that historical narratives cannot be true. In opposition, there are those who are driven to make bizarre ontological claims in order to defend the epistemic honor of the story. Finally, yet another group of theorists have embraced the conclusion that narrative histories do not even *claim* truth.

Each of these claims grows out of what can be formulated as a paradox. If you accept that narrative histories *purport to be* true, and believe that some of them *are* true, then you must explain how they *can be* true, given that story-construction brings new narrative figures into existence. Common sense will acknowledge the constructive, configuring activity of narrativizing, and simultaneously want to affirm the truth of some narratives. With a little philosophical coaching, however, this view can be made to seem incoherent, or at least paradoxical: for how can a process that imposes a foreign structure on the past produce true stories? The task is then to decide which of the three premises that generate the paradox one is going to throw out.

Impositionalists, as I have described them, accept that historical narratives purport to refer. They also believe that telling a story inevitably imposes a falsifying narrative structure on the past, and come to the unhappy (and contrary to experience) skeptical conclusion that narratives cannot be true.

Anti-referentialists opt out of the problem by denying that narrative histories even claim truth. This position, of course, is motivated largely by the desire to foreground the other, non-referential functions of narrative discourse. But to the extent that it constitutes a solution to this problem, it must deny the seemingly evident fact that historical narratives ask to be taken as true.

Plot-reifiers agree with the impositionalists that history aims at truth, but differ with them in thinking that it sometimes succeeds. This puts pressure on the central premise that narratives inevitably falsify the past by imposing a narrative structure upon it. By pretending to have discovered that the past is already narratively structured, these theorists can claim unique epistemic merits for the story. In brief, they reify plots in order for there to be something in the world to which narrative structures can correspond in being true.

In conclusion I would like to sketch the outlines of a stance towards narrative that escapes this trilemma. I have argued that it is important to preserve an understanding of histories as claiming, and sometimes attaining, truth. This means getting used to the idea that constructing an historical narrative need not falsify the past. Now some will argue that there is an unresolved or unresolvable tension between historical narrative's constructed and its (purportedly) referential character. In response to such a view, I would like to point out that some narrative histories simply *are* true constructs. I am urging that we take this fact seriously, and come to grips with what it means for narrative theory. Quite simply, *construction does not entail falsification*. Narrative history may be *figural* in the sense of generating new discursive figures, and at the same time *literal* in the sense of asking (and deserving) to be understood literally, and *there is nothing contradictory in this*.

So far this line does not differ in any significant respect from that of the plot-reifiers. Both accounts assert that historical narratives claim and sometimes attain truth, and are confronted with the task of explaining how this can be so. Plot-reifiers met this demand with assertions of the past's narrative structure, an "explanation" that suggests a pronounced tendency to think of truth in correspondence-like terms.

The dialectical option I am trying to articulate here distinguishes itself, first off, by distancing itself from the correspondence theory of truth and all of its attendant problems.[35] Correspondence accounts are built on the paradigm of simple descriptive (observation-) statements, and above and beyond difficulties in this, their stronghold, they grow increasingly inadequate the further one gets from that paradigm. For example, it is difficult to see or say in what respect, if any, a scientific theory that posits unobservables "corresponds" to the world. Some say that, for this or like reasons, we must cease speaking of such theories as being true.[36] Such recommendations draw upon arbitrary-seeming distinctions, however, and distort ordinary usage to no apparent end.[37] How a true ethical judgment or a moral theory can correspond to the world is perhaps even more puzzling. But that does not mean that it is not true to say: "Murder is wrong." The same, I think, goes for narrative histories: they can be true without our being able to make any sense of the claim that they correspond.

Closer to the heart of what separates this common-sense line from more traditional accounts, however, is the issue of whether we need or want *any* theory of truth. Realisms and anti-realisms alike are often inclined to accept the burden of explaining what it is that truth consists in. There is a reasoned alternative to shouldering this burden, however. It is based on a denial that we need any such thing. The felt need for such a theory may itself be questioned, and in fact has been the target of rather telling critique.[38] No doubt those who push theories of truth will use familiar marketing techniques to preserve the illusion that we need what they have. Without such an account, they will say, we do not really understand what truth-claims are saying. But this simply is not true. We do not typically experience a problem understanding such claims. Nor is this any less true in cases where truth is predicated of stories. Even philosophers, who cultivate an ability to have their under-standing of such things lapse, show definite performative signs that they understand well enough what they profess to be mystified by.

Thus scientific attempts to *describe* an eternal present, ethical attempts to *prescribe* a better future, and historical attempts to *reinscribe* the past can each be true in their own way. For those with a hankering for gen-eralities, perhaps we can say (colloquially and in lieu of any proper theory of truth) that the first can be true for *telling it like it is*, the second for *telling it like it ought to be*, and the third for *telling it like it was*. What this amounts to in specific cases will of course vary widely. We must not expect more precision at this level of generality than the subject-matter allows.

Of course much more than this is required to carve out this dialectical niche and show that it is viable. My purpose has merely been to moti-vate a closer look at an alternative that avoids some of the recurrent difficulties of traditional accounts. A more adequate treatment would include a thorough explanation of why a relatively simple alternative to such problematic positions has been so seldom taken up. I will not attempt such an explanation here. It is worth noting, however, that it is extremely easy to generate a sense that a narrative's being true requires some sort of explanation. (How is it that each narrative history can articulate the past uniquely, yet somehow entirely different stories can disclose one and the same past? How is it that it can be at the same time figural and literal?) It may seem difficult to understand how this can be so, but we are in a position now to see our very puzzlement here as questionable. Might not this perceived lack of comprehension be the artifact of a deep-rooted "descriptivist" prejudice – the mistaken idea that we don't really understand how language works until we can see it as "standing in" for something?

The fact that a narrative is the product of a creative process, a construct that articulates the past anew, does not by itself compromise its truth. It might do so badly or wrongly, of course, in which case that would have to be pointed out. But such critique must be carried out on a case-specific basis. Global judgments require some external measure, and narratives do not need to be treated as an approximation to some foreign ideal. Instead, we might try simply understanding narratives on their own terms. What more is there to such understanding, after all, than our respective abilities to construct, recount, enact, embellish, share, and enjoy them?

Notes

1 Louis O. Mink, "Narrative Form as a Cognitive Instrument," in *The Writing of History*, ed. Robert H. Canary and Henry Kozicki (Madison, Wisc. 1978), 145.

2 René Descartes, *Discourse on Method* [1635], trans. Donald A. Cress (Indianapolis, 1980).

3 Alasdair MacIntyre, *After Virtue* (South Bend, Ind., 1984), 214.

4 Carl Hempel, "The Function of General Laws in History," *Journal of Philosophy* 39 (1942), 35–48, and "Explanation in Science and History" in *Frontiers of Science and Philosophy*, ed. R. Colodny (Pittsburgh, 1962).

5 Maurice Mandelbaum, "A Note on History as Narrative," *History and Theory* 6 (1967), 414–15.

6 David Carr, *Time, Narrative and History* (Bloomington, 1986), 11.

7 Roland Barthes, "Introduction à l'analyse structurale des récits," *Communications* 8 (1966).

8 Hayden White, "The Question of Narrative in Contemporary Historical Theory," *History and Theory* 23 (1984), 20, reprinted in *The Content of the Form* (Baltimore, 1987), 44.

9 Ibid., 47 (my italics).

10 Leon Goldstein is perhaps the notable exception. See his *Historical Knowing* (Austin, 1976). What I am calling "historical realism" Mink referred to as "universal history" – an idea, he says, with deep roots in the moral project

of the Enlightenment, and perhaps even deeper roots in common sense. Although "seldom explicitly held," he argues, this view is "almost universally presupposed," as is evidenced by the intelligibility to us of the idea of an objective chronicle of history. Mink, "Narrative Form," 137–41.

11 MacIntyre, n. 3; Carr, n. 6; and Olafson's *The Dialectic of Action* (Chicago, 1979).

12 MacIntyre, *After Virtue*, 212, 215.

13 For a convincing account of the contortions MacIntyre goes through to find determinacy for the ethical life, see Pablo DeGreiff's "MacIntyre: Narrativa y tradicion," *Sistema* 92 (Madrid, 1989), 99–116.

14 Carr, *Time, Narrative and History*, 9.

15 Ibid., 43.

16 Alasdair MacIntyre, "Epistemological Crises, Dramatic Narrative, and the Philosophy of Science," *The Monist* 60 (1978), 457.

17 Earlier attempts by M. White, A. Danto, and W. B. Gallie to cash out this notion in terms of causal chains, temporal sequence, and followability are unlikely to be of any use here, for White's and Danto's attempts to develop causal models of narrative – that is, accounts in which the ordering principle of a story is that later events are caused by earlier ones – were undermined by Gallie's argument that antecedent events in an historical narrative seldom if ever amount to sufficient causal conditions for the occurrence of later events. Gallie's own account in terms of followability faces what seem to be insurmountable difficulties. In addition to being too vague to be of any real use, the notion of an unfollowable narrative does not seem to be a contradiction in terms. See Morton White, *Foundations of Historical Knowledge* (New York, 1965); Arthur Danto, *Analytical Philosophy of History* (Cambridge, 1965); W. B. Gallie, *Philosophy and Historical Understanding* (London, 1964).

18 "For the most part" because the past is not *always* already meaningfully arranged. As Paul Roth pointed out to me, patients in psychoanalysis often suffer precisely from an inability to find any meaningful arrangement to the past.

19 "Stories are lived before they are told . . ." MacIntyre, *After Virtue*, 212.

20 Carr, *Time, Narrative and History*, 46, and the rest of chapter two (my italics).

21 MacIntyre, *After Virtue*, 212: "We render the actions of others intelligible in this way (with narrative histories) because action itself has a basically historical character." For the argument here to go, what MacIntyre claims explicitly about "action" must go, too, for the past.

22 For Aristotle, of course, the grammatical structure of subject–predicate mirrored the ontological structure of substance–property. We need not deny the similarity that supports this analogy, of course, to deny that the sky has a grammatical structure.

23 Gadamer's notion of effective historical consciousness, or *Wirkungsgeschichtsbewusstsein*, is useful for conceptualizing the ethico-political import of history. The idea seems to be that there is a "field" of overlapping narratives that shape a society's awareness of its historical situation. This consciousness is "effective" because it orients us practically. The historian, through research and storytelling, can help to reshape this field, and in so doing alter the field of possibilities we confront, both individually and as a society.

24 Jean-François Lyotard, *The Postmodern Condition: A Report on Knowledge* (Minneapolis, 1984), 25–7.

25 Ibid., 20, 26.
26 Mink, "Narrative Form," 145.
27 As cited in White, *The Content*, 35.
28 Ibid., 37.
29 Jürgen Habermas, *Knowledge and Human Interests*, trans. Jeremy J. Shapiro (Boston, 1971), esp. the Appendix. I do not wish to include Habermas among the anti-referentialists, for he does not to my knowledge deny that truth is a standard appropriate for the evaluation of narratives.
30 Mink argued in the late 1960s that there were three irreducible modes of comprehension – the theoretical, the categoreal, and the configurational. Configurational comprehension, he argued, was the end for which storytelling was the proper means. Mink, "History and Fiction as Modes of Comprehension," *New Literary History* (1969), 549ff. [ch. 6, this volume].
31 John McCumber, *Poetic Interaction: Freedom, Language, and the Situation of Reason* (Chicago, 1989), xv.
32 MacIntyre, "Epistemological Crises," 469.
33 Paul Ricoeur, *Time and Narrative* (Chicago, 1984), 70–3. Ricouer arrives at many of the same conclusions I reach here, though his argument seems a good bit more roundabout. What it lacks in directness, however, it more than makes up for in richness and suggestion.
34 MacIntyre, *After Virtue*, 212.
35 The basic problem is that of making sense of correspondence, of spelling out what it means in a nontrivial way.
36 I have in mind Bas van Fraasen, *The Scientific Image* (Oxford, 1980), 11ff. Van Fraasen urges that we stop speaking of theories that posit unobservables as being true, arguing that we have no warrant for asserting anything more than their empirical adequacy, or usefulness for explaining and predicting. The similarity here between the move made by van Fraasen to escape the scientific realism dilemma, and that made by the anti-referentialists to escape what is essentially the same dilemma in the philosophy of history is striking, and of course no accident. The major positions in the two fields correspond almost exactly, due to a common set of argumentative pressures. The solution offered here is self-consciously modeled on Arthur Fine's "overcoming" of the realism–anti-realism debate. *The Shaky Game* (Chicago, 1986), chs 7 and 8.
37 Fine pokes fun at van Fraasen's distinctions, calling them "arbitrary" and "obnoxious." Fine, *The Shaky Game*, 142–4.
38 Ibid., 139–42, but see all of chapters 7 and 8.

Part IV

Postmodernism and the Theory of History

9
Historiography and Postmodernism

F. R. Ankersmit

My point of departure in this article is the present-day overproduction in our discipline. We are all familiar with the fact that in any imaginable area of historiography, within any specialty, an overwhelming number of books and articles is produced annually, making a comprehensive view of them all impossible. This is true even of the separate topics within one and the same specialty. Let me illustrate this with an example from political theory, a field with which I am fairly familiar. Anyone who some twenty years ago wanted to go into Hobbes's political philosophy needed only two important commentaries on Hobbes: the studies written by Watkins and Warrender. Of course, there were more even then but after reading these two books one was pretty well "in the picture." However, anyone who in 1989 has the courage to try to say anything significant about Hobbes will first have to read his way through a pile of twenty to twenty-five studies which are as carefully written as they are extensive; I will spare you an enumeration of them. Moreover, these studies are usually of such high quality that one certainly cannot afford to leave them unread.

There are two aspects to the unintended result of this overproduction. In the first place, the discussion of Hobbes tends to take on the nature of a discussion of the *interpretation* of Hobbes, rather than of his work *itself*. The work itself sometimes seems to be little more than the almost forgotten reason for the war of interpretations going on today. In the second place, because of its evident multi-interpretability, Hobbes's original text gradually lost its capacity to function as arbiter in the historical debate. Owing to all the interpretations, the text *itself* became vague, a watercolor in which the lines flow into one another. This meant that the naive faith in the text itself being able to offer a solution to our interpretation problems became just as absurd as the faith in a signpost attached to a weathervane. The paradoxical result of all this is that the text itself no longer has any authority in an interpretation and that we even feel compelled to advise our students not to read *Leviathan* independently; they are better off first trying to hack a path through the jungle of interpretation. To put it in a nutshell, we no longer have any texts, any past, but just interpretations of them.

When I read the reviews and notices announcing new books in the *Times Literary Supplement*, the *New York Review of Books*, or in the professional journals which are increasing in number at an alarming rate, I do not doubt that things are very much the same in other areas of historiography. The situation which Nietzsche feared more than a hundred years ago, the situation in which historiography itself impedes our view of the past, seems to have become reality. Not only does this flood of historical literature give us all a feeling of intense despondency, but this overproduction undeniably has something uncivilized about it. We associate civilization with, among other things, a feeling for moderation, for a happy medium between excess and shortage. Any feeling for moderation, however, seems to have been lost in our present-day intellectual alcoholism. This comparison with alcoholism is also very apt because the most recent book or article on a particular topic always pretends to be the very last intellectual drink.

Of course, this situation is not new and there has therefore been no lack of attempts to retain some reassuring prospects for the future for disheartened historians. The Dutch historian Romein saw in this overproduction a tendency towards specialization; he therefore called for a theoretical history which would undo the pulverization of our grasp of the past which had been caused by specialization. Theoretical history would be able to lift us to a more elevated viewpoint from which we would again be able to survey and to bring order to the chaos caused by specialization and overproduction.[1] But Romein's book on the watershed of two ages is proof that this is easier said than done. Above all, the problem seems to be that on this higher level postulated by Romein a real interaction among the various specialties remains difficult to realize. Integral historiography leads to enumeration rather than to integration.

Another way out of the dilemma is the strategy adopted by the *Annales* school. They have devoted their attention chiefly to the discovery of new objects of inquiry in the past; with this strategy they do indeed allow themselves the chance of once again finding history in an unspoiled state. Of course, this offers only temporary solace: before too long, countless other historians, French or not, will pounce upon these new topics and soon they too will be covered by a thick and opaque crust of interpretations. There is, however, more to be said about how resourceful the *Annales* school is in finding new and exciting topics. In the course of this article I shall return to this matter.

The crucial question now is what attitude we should take with regard to this overproduction of historical literature which is spreading like a cancer in all fields. A reactionary longing for the neat historical world of fifty years ago is just as pointless as despondent resignation. We have to realize that there is no way back. It has been calculated that at this moment there are more historians occupied with the past than the total number of historians from Herodotus up until 1960. It goes without saying that it is impossible to forbid the production of new books and articles by all these scholars presently writing. Complaining about the loss of a direct link with the past does not get us any further. However, what *does* help and *does* have a point is the defining of a new and different link with the past based on a complete and honest recognition of the position in which we now see ourselves placed as historians.

There is, moreover, another reason to make an attempt in that direction. The present-day overproduction of historical literature can indeed be called monstrous if our point of departure is *traditional* ideas about the task and the meaning of historiography. Historiography today has burst out of its traditional, self-legitimating, theoretical jacket and is therefore in need of new clothes. This is not in order to teach the historian how he should set about his work as an historian, nor to develop a theory *Vom Nutzen und Nachteil der Historie für das Leben*. With regard to the first half of this statement, there is no point outside historiography itself from which rules for the historian's method of work can be drawn up: if historians consider something to be meaningful, then it is meaningful and that is all there is to it. As for the second half of the statement, I do not believe that historiography is useful or has a recognizable disadvantage. By this I do not mean that historiography is useless, but that the question concerning the usefulness and disadvantage of historiography is an unsuitable question – a "category mistake," to use Ryle's expression. Along with poetry, literature, painting, and the like, history and historical consciousness belong to culture, and no questions can meaningfully be asked about the usefulness of culture. Culture, of which historiography is a part, is rather the background *from which* or *against which* we can form our opinion concerning the usefulness of, for example, certain kinds of scientific research or certain political objectives. For that reason science and politics do not belong to culture; if something can have a use or a disadvantage or enables us to manipulate the world it is not a part of civilization. Culture and history define use, but cannot themselves be defined in terms of usefulness. They belong to the domain of the "absolute presuppositions,"[2] to use Collingwood's terminology. This is also the reason that politics should not interfere with culture.

That is why, if we were to try to find a new jacket for historiography, as was considered necessary above, the most important problem would be to situate historiography within present-day civilization as a whole. This problem is of a cultural–historical or an interpretative nature, and could be compared with the sort of problem which we sometimes pose ourselves when we are considering the place and the meaning of a particular event within the totality of our life-history. In general, it is strange that historians and philosophers of history have paid so little attention over the last forty years to parallels between the development of present-day historiography on the one hand and that of literature, literary criticism, printing – in short, civilization – on the other. Apparently, the historian did not see any more reason to suspect the existence of such parallels than did the chemist or the astronomer.

It is not my goal to determine here the place of historiography in this way. Instead, I will move further away to ascertain whether the overproduction in historiography has its counterpart in a considerable part of present-day civilization and society. Who does not know the cliché that we are living in an age of an information surplus? In the course of all this theorizing about information – which is more profound at some times than at others – two things stand out which are of importance for the rest of my essay. In the first place, it is strange that one often talks about information as if it is something almost physical. Information "flows," "moves," "spreads," "is traded," "is stored," or "is organized." Lyotard speaks of the State as a body which restrains or disperses information flows.[3] Information appears to be a sort of liquid with a low viscosity; we are flooded by it and are in imminent danger of drowning in it. Second, when we talk about information, information as such has assumed a conspicuously prominent place with respect to the actual subject matter of that information. This relationship was usually the other way around. Take a statement giving information such as "In 1984 Ronald Reagan was elected President of the US." This informative statement itself is hidden by the state of affairs described by it. However, within our present-day way of speaking about information, the reality which that information concerns tends to be relegated to the background. The reality is the information itself and no longer the reality behind that information. This gives information an autonomy of its own, a substantiality of its own. Just as there are laws describing the behavior of things in reality, there would also seem to be a scientific system possible to describe the behavior of that remarkable liquid we call information. Incidentally, I would like to add at this point that, from the perspective of Austin's speech act theory, information could just as well be said to be purely performative as not at all performative. This is certainly one of the fascinating aspects of the phenomenon of information.[4]

In recent years, many people have observed our changed attitude towards the phenomenon of information. Theories have been formed about it and the theoreticians concerned have, as usually happens, given themselves a name. In this context we often talk about postmodernists or poststructuralists and they are, understandably, contrasted with the

modernists or structuralists from the recent past. In 1984, a very interesting conference in Utrecht was devoted to postmodernism, and anyone who heard the lectures read at the conference will agree that it is
not easy to define the concepts postmodernism or poststructuralism satisfactorily.[5] Nevertheless, it is possible to discern a general line, as did
Jonathan Culler in a recent book.[6] Science was the alpha and omega of
the modernists and the structuralists; they saw science as not only the
most important given but at the same time the ultimate given of modernity. Scientific rationality as such does not pose a problem for postmodernists and poststructuralists; they look at it, as it were, from outside or
from above. They neither criticize nor reject science; they are not irration-
alists, but they show the same aloofness with respect to science as we
observed above in our present attitude towards information. This is not
a question of metacriticism of scientific research or scientific method as
we are used to in philosophy of science. Philosophy of science remains
inherent in the scientism of the modernists; philosophers of science
follow the line of thought of scientists and study the path they have
covered between the discovery of empirical data and theory. For postmodernists, both the philosophy of science and science itself form the
given, the point of departure for their reflections. And postmodernists
are just as little interested in the sociological question of how research
scientists react to one another or what the relation is between science and
society. The postmodernist's attention is focused neither on scientific
research nor on the way in which society digests the results of scientific
research, but only on the functioning of science and of scientific information itself.

For postmodernism, science and information are independent objects
of study which obey their own laws. The first principal law of postmodernist information theory is the law that information multiplies.
One of the most fundamental characteristics of information is that really
important information is never the end of an information genealogy,
but that its importance is in fact assessed by the intellectual posterity
it gives rise to. Historiography itself forms an excellent illustration of
this. The great works from the history of historiography, those of a
de Tocqueville, Marx, Burckhardt, Weber, Huizinga, or Braudel, proved
repeatedly to be the most powerful stimulants for a new wave of publications, instead of concluding an information genealogy as if a particular problem had then been solved once and for all: "Paradoxically, the
more powerful and authoritative an interpretation, the more writing it
generates."[7] In the modernist view, the way in which precisely interesting
information generates more information is, of course, incomprehensible.
For modernists, meaningful information is information which does put
an end to writing; they cannot explain why precisely what is debatable
is fundamental to the progress of science, why, as Bachelard said, it is
the *debatable* facts which are the *true* facts.

It is important within the framework of this essay to look in greater detail at this postmodernism which is ascientistic rather than antiscientistic. In the first place, it can teach us what we should understand by a postmodernist historiography and, in the second place, that historiography, remarkably enough, has always had already something postmodernist about it. A good example of a postmodernist criterion of science is Nietzsche's "deconstruction" – to use the right term – of causality, which many consider to be one of the most important pillars of scientific thought. In causalistic terminology, the cause is the source and the effect the secondary given. Nietzsche then points out that only on the basis of our observation of the effect are we led to look for the causes and that therefore the effect is *in fact* the primary given and the cause the secondary given. "If the effect is what causes the cause to become a cause, then the effect, not the cause, should be treated as the origin."[8] Anyone who puts forward the objection that Nietzsche has confused the order of things in research and reality respectively is missing the point of Nietzsche's line of thought; for the point is precisely the artificiality of the traditional hierarchy of cause and effect. Our scientific training has, so to speak, "stabilized" us to adhere to this traditional hierarchy, but beyond this intellectual training there is nothing that forces us to continue to do so. Just as much, albeit not *more*, can be said in favor of reversing this hierarchy.

This is the way things always are in postmodernism. Science is "destabilized," is placed outside its own center, the reversibility of patterns of thought and categories of thought is emphasized, without suggesting any definite alternative. It is a sort of disloyal criticism of science, a blow below the belt which is perhaps not fair, but which for that very reason does hit science where it hurts most. Scientific rationality is not *aufgehoben* in an Hegelian way to something else, nor is it true to say that every view automatically evokes its antithesis; it is rather the recognition that every view has, besides its scientifically approved inside, an outside not noticed by science. In his *Tractatus*, Wittgenstein had already suggested something similar with respect to every valid line of reasoning. It is in fact the valid line of reasoning which aims at making itself superfluous, which therefore is always a journey over the territory of the untrue – that is, the journey from initial misconception to correct insight. Consequently, what is true always remains tainted by what is untrue.

Both a logical and an ontological conclusion can be attached to this insight; together they give an idea of the revolutionary nature of postmodernism. Let us first look at logic. For the postmodernist, the scientific certainties on which the modernists have always built are all as many variants on the paradox of the liar. That is, the paradox of the Cretan who says that all Cretans lie; or, to put it more compactly, the paradox of the statement "this statement is untrue," where this statement is a statement about itself. Of course, all the drama of postmodernism is contained in the insight that these paradoxes should be seen as unsolvable. And here we should bear in mind that the solution to the paradox of the liar which Russell, with his theory of types and his distinction between predicates and predicates of predicates, proposed in the *Principia Mathematica*, is still recognized today as one of the most important foundations of contemporary logic.[9] The postmodernist's aim, therefore, is to pull the carpet out from under the feet of science and modernism. Here, too, the best illustration of the postmodernist thesis is actually provided by historiography. Historical interpretations of the past first become recognizable, they first acquire their identity, through the contrast with *other* interpretations; they are what they are only on the basis of what they are *not*. Anyone who knows only one interpretation of, for example, the Cold War, does not know any interpretation at all of that phenomenon. Every historical insight, therefore, intrinsically has a paradoxical nature.[10] No doubt Hayden White in his *Metahistory* – the most revolutionary book in philosophy of history over the past twenty-five years – was thinking along the same lines when he characterized all historiography as fundamentally ironic.[11]

Let us now turn to ontology. In his deconstruction of the traditional hierarchy of cause and effect, Nietzsche was playing off our way of speaking about reality against processes in reality itself. The current distinction between language and reality thus loses its *raison d'être*. In particular, scientific language is no longer a "mirror of nature" but just as much a part of the inventory of reality as the objects in reality which science studies. Language as used in science is a thing,[12] and as Hans Bertens argued at the Utrecht Conference on postmodernism,[13] things in reality acquire a "language-like" nature. Once again, historiography provides the best illustration for all this. As we will see presently, it is historical language which has the same opacity as we associate with things in reality. Furthermore, both Hayden White and Ricoeur (whom I certainly do not mean to call a postmodernist) like to say that past reality should be seen as a text formulated in a foreign language with the same lexical, grammatical, syntactical, and semantic dimensions as any other text.[14] It is equally characteristic that historians in their theoretical reflections often show a marked tendency to speak about historical language as if it were part of reality itself and vice versa. Thus, Marx spoke of the *contradiction* between the production forces and production relations as if he were discussing *statements* about reality instead of *aspects* of this reality. Similarly, historians very often would like to see the same uniqueness realized for historical language as is characteristic of historical phenomena.[15] In short, the latent and often subconscious resistance to the language/reality dichotomy which historians have always displayed in fact had its origin in the unconsidered but nevertheless correct insight of historians into the fundamentally postmodernist nature of their discipline.

When the dichotomy between language and reality is under attack we are not far from aestheticism. Does not both the language of the novelist and of the historian give us the illusion of a reality, either fictitious or genuine? More important still, Gombrich has in various works taught us that the work of art, that is to say, the language of the artist, is not a *mimetic reproduction* of reality but a *replacement* or *substitute* for it.[16] Language and art are not situated *opposite* reality but are themselves a pseudo-reality and are therefore situated *within* reality. As a matter of fact, Megill in his brilliant genealogy of postmodernism has shown to what extent postmodernists from Nietzsche up to and including Derrida want to extend aestheticism over the entire domain of the representation of reality.[17]

This aestheticism is also in harmony with recently acquired insights into the nature of historiography – that is, the recognition of the stylistic dimension of historical writing. To the modernists, style was anathema or, at best, irrelevant. I quote from a recent lecture by C. P. Bertels: "fine writing, the display of literary style, does not add an iota of truth to historical research nor to any other scientific research."[18] What is important is the content; the way, the style in which it is expressed, is irrelevant. However, since Quine and Goodman, this pleasant distinction between form or style and content can no longer be taken for granted. Their argument can be summarized as follows. If various historians are occupied with various aspects of the same research subject, the resulting difference in *content* can just as well be described as a different *style* in the treatment of that research subject. "*What* is said . . . may be a way of talking about something else; for example, writing about Renaissance battles and writing about Renaissance arts, are different ways of writing about the Renaissance."[19] Or, in the words of Gay, "manner," style, implies at the same time a decision with regard to "matter," to content.[20] And where style and content might be distinguished from one another, we can even attribute to style priority over content; for because of the incommensurability of historiographical views – that is to say, the fact that the nature of historical differences of opinion cannot be satisfactorily defined in terms of research subjects – there remains nothing for us but to concentrate on the style embodied in every historical view or way of looking at the past, if we are to guarantee the meaningful progress of historical debate. Style, not content, is the issue in such debates. Content is a derivative of style.

The postmodernist recognition of the aesthetic nature of historiography can be described more precisely as follows. In analytical philosophy, there is the phenomenon of the so-called "intensional context." An example is the statement "John believes that p" or "John hopes that p" (where p stands for a particular statement). The point is that in an intensional context like this, p can never be replaced by another statement even if this other statement is equivalent to p, or results directly from it. After all, we do not know whether John is in fact aware of the consequences of his belief or hope that p. It is possible that John believes that the water is boiling, to give an example, without his believing that the temperature of the water is a hundred degrees centigrade. In other words, the exact form in which a statement in an intensional context was formulated is one of the prerequisites for the truth of this statement. The sentence attracts, so to speak, attention to itself. Thus, the *form* of the statement is certainly just as important here as the *content*. In a particularly interesting book, Danto has pointed out that this intensional nature of statements and texts (or at least some of them) is nowhere clearer than in literature: "we may see this [this intensional element] perhaps nowhere more clearly than in those literary texts, where in addition to whatever facts the author means to state, he or she *chooses the words* with which they are stated" and the literary intention of the writer "would fail if other words were used instead."[21] Because of its intensional nature, the literary text has a certain opacity, a capacity to attract attention to itself, instead of drawing attention to a fictitious or historical reality behind the text. And this is a feature which the literary text shares with historiography; for the nature of the view of the past presented in an historical work is defined exactly by the language used by the historian in his or her historical work. Because of the relation between the historiographical view and the language used by the historian in order to express this view – a relation which nowhere intersects the domain of the past – historiography possesses the same opacity and intensional dimension as art.

Art and historiography can therefore be contrasted with science. Scientific language at least has the pretension of being transparent; if it impedes our view of reality, it will have to be refined or elucidated. It is true that some philosophers of science, such as Mary Hesse, want to attribute even to science the above-mentioned aesthetic and literary dimensions. That would, of course, lend some extra plausibility to my claim regarding historiography, but I see the differences between the exact sciences and historiography as *more* than a question of nuances. Where the insight provided in a discipline is far more of a syntactical than of a semantic nature – as is the case in the exact sciences – there is comparatively less room for intensional contexts. After all, only from the perspective of semantics is it meaningful to ask the question whether there is synonymy or not (and that is the most important issue in intensional contexts).

If we are in agreement with the above, that is to say, with the applicability of postmodernist insight to historiography, I would like to draw a number of conclusions before rounding off this essay. For the modernist, within the scientific world-picture, within the view of history we all initially accept, evidence is in essence the evidence that something happened in the past. The modernist historian follows a line of reasoning from his sources and evidence to an historical reality hidden behind the sources. On the other hand, in the postmodernist view, evidence does not point towards the *past* but to other *interpretations* of the past; for that is what we in fact use evidence for. To express this by means of imagery: for the modernist, the evidence is a tile which he picks up to see what is underneath it; for the postmodernist, on the other hand, it is a tile which he steps on in order to move on to other tiles: horizontality instead of verticality.

This is not only an insight into what actually happens but just as much an insight into what historians should concentrate on in the future. The suggestion could best be described as the contemporization of the historical source. Evidence is not a magnifying glass through which we can study the past, but bears more resemblance to the brushstrokes used by the painter to achieve a certain effect. Evidence does not send us back to the past, but gives rise to the question what an historian here and now can or cannot do with it. Georges Duby illustrates this new attitude towards evidence. When his intelligent interviewer Guy Lardreau asks him what constitutes for him, Duby, the most interesting evidence, he says that this can be found in what is not said, in what a period has *not* said about itself, and he therefore compares his historical work with the developing of a negative.[22] Just as the fish does not know that it is swimming in the water, what is most characteristic of a period, most omnipresent in a period, is unknown to the period itself. It is not revealed until a period has come to an end. The fragrance of a period can only be inhaled in a subsequent period. Of course, Hegel and Foucault have already made many interesting comments about this. However, the point here is Duby's observation that the essence of a period is determined by the *destinataire*, to use the term of the French postmodernists, by the historian who has to develop here and now his negative of a period from that which was not said or was only whispered, or was expressed only in insignificant details. The historian is like the connoisseur who recognizes the artist not by that which is characteristic of him (and consequently imitable) but by that which, so to speak, spontaneously "escaped" him. "Le style, c'est l'homme" and our style is where we are ourselves without having thought about ourselves. That is why so few people still have style in our narcissistic era. In short, the way of dealing with the evidence as suggested by Duby is special because it points not so much to something that was concealed behind it in the past, but because it acquires its point and meaning only through the confrontation with the mentality of the later period in which the historian lives and writes. The mentality of a period is revealed only in the difference between it and that of a later period; the direction in which the evidence points thus undergoes a shift of ninety degrees. As has so often been the case, this, too, had been anticipated by Huizinga. Writing about the historical sensation, he says: "this contact with the past, which is accompanied by the complete conviction of genuineness, truth, can be evoked by a line from a charter or a chronicle, by a print, a few notes from an old song. It is not an element introduced into his work by the writer [in the past] by means of certain words. . . . *The reader brings it to meet the writer*, it is his response to the latter's call."[23]

It is not surprising that Duby and Lardreau point out in this connection the relation between historiography and psychoanalysis.[24] In both historiography and psychoanalysis, we are concerned with interpretation in the most fundamental sense of the word. In historiography, this way of dealing with traces of the past as suggested by Duby compels us to refrain from searching for some initially invisible machine in the past itself which has caused these traces discernible on the surface. In the same way, psychoanalysis, in spite of the positivist notes struck by Freud himself, is in fact a repertory of interpretation strategies. Psychoanalysis teaches us to understand what the neurotic *says* and does not draw our attention to the causal effects of a number of elementary and undivided homunculi in his mind.[25] Both the psychoanalyst and the historian try to project a pattern *onto* the traces and do not search for something *behind* the traces. In both cases, the activity of interpretation is understood strictly nominalistically: there is nothing in historical reality or in the mind of the neurotic that corresponds with the content of interpretations.

However, there is a still more interesting parallel to psychoanalytic interpretation. Of course, Duby's thesis that the historian should pay attention to what is not said and to what is suppressed – madness, untruth, and taboo, to use Foucault's criteria – is obviously related to the analyst's method of work. Just as we are what we are not, or do not want to be, in a certain sense the past is also what it was not. In both psychoanalysis and history, what is suppressed manifests itself only in minor and seemingly irrelevant details. In psychoanalysis, this results in the insight that man does not have an easily observable being or essence on the basis of which he can be understood, but that the secret of personality lies in what only rarely and fleetingly becomes visible behind the usual presentation. Our personality is, as Rorty put it, a collage rather than a substance: "the ability to think of ourselves as idiosyncratically formed collages rather than as substances has been an important factor in our ability to slough off the idea that we have a true self, one shared with all other humans. . . . Freud made the paradigm of self-knowledge the discovery of little idiosyncratic accidents rather than of an essence."[26]

This is also the case in historiography, at least in what I would like to call postmodernist history (of mentalities). To formulate this in the paradoxical manner so popular among postmodernists: the essence of the past is not, or does not lie in, the essence of the past. It is the scraps, the slips of the tongue, the *Fehlleistungen* of the past, the rare moments when the past "let itself go," where we discover what is really of importance for us. I suspect that at least a partial explanation can be found here for what Jörn Rüsen referred to as the "paradigm change" in present-day historiography, a paradigm change which in his opinion consists mainly of exchanging *makrohistorische Strukturen* for *mikrohistorische Situationen und Lebensverhältnisse* as the object of the historian's attention.[27] What we are witnessing could perhaps be nothing less than the definitive farewell for the time being to all the essentialist aspirations which have actually dominated historiography as long as it has existed. Historians have always been searching for something they could label as the essence of the past – the principle that held everything together in the past (or in a part of it) and on the basis of which, consequently, everything could be understood. In the course of the centuries, this essentialism in historiography has manifested itself in countless different ways. Of course, essentialism was conspicuously present in the various speculative systems which have directed the thinking of Western man about his past. The Augustinian theological concept of history and its secularized variants,[28] the idea of progress, with its blind faith in the progress of science and the social blessings it was expected to bring, were always the "meta-narratives," to use Lyotard's term, by means of which not only historiography but also other fundamental aspects of civilization and society were legitimated.[29]

Then came historism which, with a strange naiveté,[30] saw the essence of the past as embodied in a curious mixture of fact and idea. The epistemological naiveté of the historist doctrine of historical ideas was only possible in a time when the belief and faith in the perceptibility of the essence of the past were so easily taken for granted that nobody had an inkling of his own ontological arrogance. The social history discussed by Rüsen was the last link in this chain of essentialist views of history. The triumphant note with which social history made its entry, particularly in Germany, is the most striking proof of the optimistic self-overestimation on the part of these historians, who feel they have now found the long sought-after key which will open all historical doors. Anyone who is aware of the essentialist nature of this social history and of the traditional enmity between essentialism and science cannot fail to notice the ludicrous nature of the pretensions of the social historians. But the worst modernists are still to be found among philosophers of history – which, incidentally, is not so surprising; they cheer any pseudoscientific ostentation even more readily than do historians, as soon as they think they see in it the confirmation of their worn-out positivist ideas.

I would like to clarify the movement in historical consciousness indicated above by means of the following image. Compare history to a tree. The essentialist tradition within Western historiography focused the attention of historians on the trunk of the tree. This was, of course, the case with the speculative systems; they defined, so to speak, the nature and form of this trunk. Historism and modernist scientific historiography, with their basically praiseworthy attention to what in fact happened in the past and their lack of receptiveness towards apriorist schemes, were situated on the branches of the tree. However, from that position their attention did remain focused on the trunk. Just like their speculative predecessors, both the historists and the protagonists of a so-called scientific historiography still had the hope and the pretension of ultimately being able to say something about that trunk after all. The close ties between this so-called scientific social history and Marxism are significant in this context. Whether it was formulated in ontological, epistemological, or methodological terminology, historiography since historism has always aimed at the reconstruction of the essentialist line running through the past or parts of it.

With the postmodernist historiography found in particular in the history of mentalities, a break is made for the first time with this centuries-old essentialist tradition – to which I immediately add, to avoid any pathos and exaggeration, that I am referring here to trends and not to radical breaks. The choice no longer falls on the trunk or on the branches, but on the leaves of the tree. Within the postmodernist view of history, the goal is no longer integration, synthesis, and totality, but it is those historical scraps which are the center of attention. Take, for example, *Montaillou* and other books written subsequently by Le Roy Ladurie, Ginzburg's *Microstorie*, Duby's *Sunday of Bouvines* or Natalie Zemon Davis's *Return of Martin Guerre*. Fifteen to twenty years ago we would have asked ourselves in amazement whatever the point could be of this kind of historical writing, what it is trying to prove. And this very obvious question would have been prompted then, as it always is, by our modernist desire to get to know how the machine of history works. However, in the anti-essentialist, nominalistic view of postmodernism, this question has lost its meaning. If we want to adhere to essentialism anyway, we can say that the essence is not situated in the branches, nor in the trunk, but in the leaves of the historical tree.

This brings me to the main point of this article. It is characteristic of leaves that they are relatively loosely attached to the tree and when autumn or winter comes, they are blown away by the wind. For various reasons, we can presume that autumn has come to Western historiography. In the first place, there is of course the postmodernist nature of our own time. Our anti-essentialism, or, as it is popularly called these days, "anti-foundationalism," has lessened our commitment to science and traditional historiography. The changed position of Europe in the world since 1945 is a second important indication. The history of this appendage to the Eurasian continent is no longer world history.[31] What we would like to see as the trunk of the tree of Western history has become part of a whole forest. The *meta-récits* we would like to tell ourselves about our history, the triumph of Reason, the glorious struggle for emancipation of the nineteenth-century workers' proletariat, are only of local importance and for that reason can no longer be suitable meta-narratives. The chilly wind which, according to Romein, rose around 1900 simultaneously in both the West and the East,[32] finally blew the leaves off our historical tree as well in the second half of this century.

What remains now for Western historiography is to gather the leaves that have been blown away and to study them independently of their origins. This means that our historical consciousness has, so to speak, been turned inside out. When we collect the leaves of the past in the same way as Le Roy Ladurie or Ginzburg, what is important is no longer the place they had on the tree, but the pattern we can form from them *now*, the way in which this pattern can be adapted to other forms of civilization existing now. "Beginning in the days of Goethe and Macaulay and Carlyle and Emerson," wrote Rorty, "a kind of writing has developed which is neither the evaluation of the relative merits of literary productions, nor intellectual history, nor moral philosophy, nor epistemology, nor social prophecy, but all of these mingled together in a new genre."[33] In his commentary on this statement of Rorty's, Culler points out the remarkable indifference with regard to origin and context, historical or otherwise, which is so characteristic of "this new kind of writing":

> the practitioners of particular disciplines complain that works claimed by the genre are studied outside the proper disciplinary matrix: students of theory read Freud without enquiring whether later psychological research may have disputed his formulations; they read Derrida without having mastered the philosophical tradition; they read Marx without studying alternative descriptions of political and economic situations.[34]

The right historical context has lost its traditional importance, function, and naturalness as background, not because one is so eager to take up an ahistorical position or lacks the desire to do justice to the course of history, but because one has "let go of" the historical context. Everything now announces itself unannounced and in this lies the only hope we still have of being able to keep our heads above water in the future. Just as the leaves of the tree are not attached to one another and their interrelation was only guaranteed by the branch or the trunk, it was the above-mentioned essentialist assumptions which used to ensure the very prominent role played by this reassuring "historical context."

Don't misunderstand me. I am not talking about the candidacy of a new form of subjectivity, the legitimation of imposing contemporary patterns on the past. Legitimating anything at all can best be left to the modernists. The essence of postmodernism is precisely that we should avoid pointing out essentialist patterns in the past. We can consequently have our doubts about the meaningfulness of recent attempts to breathe new life into the old German ideal of *Bildung* for the sake of the position and the reputation of historiography. . . . The resuscitation of the ideal of *Bildung*, on the other hand, is indeed a meaningful reaction to the map-like nature of our present-day civilization. Whereas civilization in the past showed more resemblance to a direction-indicator which provided relatively unambiguous directions for social and moral behavior, present-day civilization does not teach us where we have to go any more than a map does; nor, if we have already made our choice, does it teach us whether we should travel by way of the shortest route or by way of a picturesque detour. Realization of the ideal of *Bildung* would at most give us a good picture of the road we have traveled up until now. The ideal of *Bildung* is the cultural counterpart of Ernst Haeckel's famous thesis that the development of the separate individual is a shortened version of that of the species. *Bildung* is the shortened version of the history of civilization on the scale of the separate individual, through which he can become a valuable and decent member of our society.

However, within the postmodernist historical consciousness, this shortened ontogenetic repeat of our cultural phylogenesis is no longer meaningful. The links in the evolution of this series of historical contexts of which our cultural phylogenesis consists have after all been broken apart. Everything has become contemporary, with the remarkable correlate, to use Duby's expression, that everything has also become history. When history is reassembled in the present, this means that the present has taken on the stigma of the past. *Bildung* consequently requires the orientation on a compass that is rejected by postmodernism. We must not shape ourselves according to or in conformity with the past, but learn to play our cultural game with it. What this statement means *in concrete terms* was described by Rousseau for the separate individual in the following way in his *Les Rêveries du promeneur solitaire*: there is an

> état où l'âme trouve une assiette assez solide pour s'y reposer tout entière et rassemble là tout son être, sans avoir besoin de rappeler le passé ni d'enjamber sur l'avenir; où le temps ne soit rien pour elle, où le présent dure toujours sans néanmoins marquer sa durée et sans aucune trace de succession.[35]

And Rousseau subsequently points out that such a way of dealing with time awakes a feeling of complete happiness in our lives – "un bonheur suffisant, parfait et plein, qui ne laisse dans l'âme aucun vide qu'elle sente le besoin de remplir."[36]

History here is no longer the reconstruction of what has happened to us in the various phases of our lives, but a continuous playing with the memory of this. The memory has priority over what is remembered. Something similar is true for historiography. The wild, greedy, and uncontrolled digging into the past, inspired by the desire to discover a past reality and reconstruct it scientifically, is no longer the historian's unquestioned task. We would do better to examine the result of a hundred and fifty years' digging more attentively and ask ourselves more often what all this adds up to. The time has come that we should *think* about the past, rather than *investigate* it.

However, a phase in historiography has perhaps now begun in which meaning is more important than reconstruction and genesis; a phase in which the goal historians set themselves is to discover the meaning of a number of fundamental conflicts in our past by demonstrating their contemporaneity. Let us look at a few examples. An insight such as Hegel's into the conflict between Socrates and the Athenian State may conflict in a thousand places with what we now know about the Athens of about 400 BC, but it will nevertheless not lose its force. A second example: what Foucault wrote about the close link between power and discourse aiming at truth or about the very curious relation between language and reality in the sixteenth century was attacked on factual grounds by many critics, but this does not mean that his conceptions have lost their fascination. I am not saying that historical truth and reliability are of no importance or are even obstacles on the road to a more meaningful historiography. On the contrary: examples like Hegel or Foucault show us, however – and that is why I chose them – that the metaphorical dimension in historiography is more powerful than the literal or factual dimensions. The philological Wilamowitz, who tries to refute Nietzsche's *Die Geburt der Tragödie*, is like someone who tries to overturn a train carriage singlehanded; criticizing metaphors on factual grounds is indeed an activity which is just as pointless as it is tasteless. Only metaphors "refute" metaphors.

And that brings me to my final remarks. As I have suggested, there is reason to assume that our relation to the past and our insight into it will in future be of a metaphorical nature rather than a literal one. What I mean is this. The literal statement "this table is two meters long" directs our attention to a particular state of affairs outside language itself which is expressed by it. A metaphorical utterance such as "history is a tree without a trunk" – to use an apt example – shifts the accent to what is happening between the mere *words* "history" and "tree without a trunk." In the postmodernist view, the focus is no longer on the past itself, but on the incongruity between present and past, between the language we presently use for speaking about the past and the past itself. There is no longer "one line running through history" to neutralize this incongruity. This explains the attention to the seemingly incongruous but surprising and hopefully even disturbing detail which Freud in his essay on the *Unheimliche* defined as "was im Verborgenen hatte bleiben sollen und hervorgetreten ist";[37] in short, attention to everything which is meaningless and irrelevant precisely from the point of view of scientific historiography. For these incongruous, *Unheimliche* events do justice to the incongruity of the historian's language in its relation to the past.

Just as postmodernism since Nietzsche and Heidegger has criticized the whole so-called logocentric tradition in philosophy since Socrates and Plato, that is, the rationalistic faith that Reason will enable us to solve the secrets of reality, postmodernist historiography also has a natural nostalgia for a pre-Socratic early history. The earliest historiography of the Greeks was epic; the Greeks told one another about the deeds of their ancestors in the past in narrative epics. The stories they told one another were not mutually exclusive, despite their contradicting each other, because they inspired above all ethical and aesthetic contemplation. Because war and political conflict stimulated a more profound social and political awareness and because the written word has much less tolerance for divergent traditions than the spoken word, the "logocentric" uniformization of the past was introduced after and by Hecataeus, Herodotus, and Thucydides.[38] With this, the young trunk of the tree of the past appeared above ground. I certainly do not mean to suggest that we should return to the days before Hecataeus. Here, too, it is a question of a metaphorical truth rather than a literal one. Postmodernism does not reject scientific historiography, but only draws our attention to the modernists' vicious circle which would have us believe that nothing exists outside it. However, outside it is the whole domain of historical purpose and meaning.

Notes

1 J. Romein, "Het vergruisde beeld," and "Theoretische geschiedenis," in *Historische Lijnen en Patronen* (Amsterdam, 1971).
2 R. G. Collingwood, *An Essay on Metaphysics* (Oxford, 1940).
3 J. F. Lyotard, *La Condition postmoderne* (Paris, 1979), 15.
4 Information is performative, has purely "illocutionary" and "perlocutionary" force, because the constatory element has been lost; information is not performative, because it is subject to its own laws and not to those of interhuman communication – communication is only a part of the life of information.
5 W. van Reijen, "Postscriptum," in *Modernen versus Postmodernen*, ed. W. Hudson and W. van Reijen (Utrecht, 1986), 9–51; W. Hudson, "The Question of Postmodern Philosophy?," ibid., 51–91.
6 J. Culler, *On Deconstruction: Theory and Criticism after Structuralism* (London, 1985), 18ff.
7 Ibid., 90.
8 Ibid., 88.
9 J. van Heijenoort, "Logical Paradoxes," in *The Encyclopedia of Philosophy*, ed. P. Edwards (London, 1967), 45–51.
10 F. R. Ankersmit, *Narrative Logic: A Semantic Analysis of the Historian's Language* (The Hague, 1983), 239, 240.
11 H. White, *Metahistory: The Historical Imagination in Nineteenth Century Europe* (Baltimore, 1973), 37.
12 F. R. Ankersmit, "The Use of Language in the Writing of History," in *Working with Language*, ed. H. Coleman (Berlin, 1989).

13 H. Bertens, "Het 'Talige' Karakter van de Postmoderne Werkelijkheid," in *Modernen versus postmodernen*, 135–53. Bertens's position is actually still modernist: his thesis that language can never represent the fullness of reality makes him choose a position *within* the polarity of language and reality, instead of outside it as would be required by the postmodernists.

14 White, *Metahistory*, 30; P. Ricoeur, "The Model of the Text: Meaningful Action Considered as a Text," in *Interpretative Social Science*, ed. P. Rabinow and W. M. Sullivan (London, 1979), 73.

15 Von der Dunk, *De Organisatie van het Verleden* (Bussum, 1982); see for example 169, 170, 344, 362, 369.

16 E. H. Gombrich, "Meditations on a Hobby Horse, or the Roots of Artistic Form," in *Aesthetics Today*, ed. P. J. Gudel (New York, 1980).

17 A. Megill, *Prophets of Extremity: Nietzsche, Heidegger, Foucault, Derrida* (Berkeley, 1985); see in particular 2–20.

18 C. P. Bertels, "Stijl: Een Verkeerde Categorie in de Geschiedwetenschap," in *Groniek* 89/90 (1984), 150.

19 N. Goodman, "The Status of Style," in N. Goodman, *Ways of Worldmaking* (Hassocks, 1978), 26.

20 P. Gay, *Style in History* (London, 1974), 3.

21 A. C. Danto, *The Transfiguration of the Commonplace: A Philosophy of Art* (Cambridge, Mass., 1983), 188.

22 G. Duby and G. Lardreau, *Geschichte und Geschichtswissenschaft: Dialoge* (Frankfurt am Main, 1982), 97, 98.

23 J. Huizinga, "De Taak der Cultuurgeschiedenis," in *J. Huizinga: Verzamelde Werken* 7 (Haarlem, 1950), 71, 72; italics mine.

24 Duby and Lardreau, *Geschichte*, 98ff.

25 This is the *Leitmotif* in D. P. Spence, *Narrative Truth and Historical Truth: Meaning and Interpretation in Psychoanalysis* (New York, 1982).

26 R. Rorty, "Freud and Moral Reflection," 17. (I was given a photocopy of this article by the author; unfortunately, I have no further information on it.)

27 *Programmaboek Congres "Balans en Perspectief"* (Utrecht, 1986), 50.

28 This, of course, refers to K. Löwith's thesis in his *Meaning in History* (Chicago, 1970).

29 Lyotard, *La Condition postmoderne*, 49–63.

30 F. R. Ankersmit, "De Chiastische Verhouding Tussen Literatuur en Geschiedenis," in *Spektator* (October, 1986), 101–20.

31 Striking proof of the sharply decreased significance of the European past is offered by M. Ferro, *Hoe de Geschiedenis aan Kinderen Wordt Verteld* (Weesp, 1985).

32 J. Romein, *Op het Breukvlak van Twee Eeuwen* (Amsterdam, 1967), I, 35.

33 Culler, *On Deconstruction*, 8.

34 Ibid.

35 J.-J. Rousseau, *Les Rêveries du promeneur solitaire* (Paris, 1972), 101.

36 Ibid.

37 S. Freud, "Das Unheimliche," in *Sigmund Freud: Studienausgabe IV. Psychologische Schriften* (Frankfurt, 1982), 264.

38 For these remarks on the origins of Greek historical consciousness I am greatly indebted to Mrs J. Krul-Blok.

10
Historiography and Postmodernism: Reconsiderations

Perez Zagorin

Historiography today has become so pluralistic and subject to the play of fashion that it need come as no surprise to find F. R. Ankersmit recommending in a recent essay in *History and Theory* that historians should now adopt the perspective of postmodernism as the new, superior form of understanding of their discipline.[1] Such a move was only to be expected, considering the current influence of postmodernism in some of the arts as well as in literary theory and other fields through its affiliation with deconstructionism. Ankersmit may not even be the first to have extended an embrace to postmodernism on behalf of historiography, though he is perhaps the first to do so explicitly. The same tendency is evident among the disciples of Foucault. Some of the essays collected in a lately published volume arguing for the predominantly rhetorical character of history and the human sciences may also be taken as implying a similar position.[2]

Until now Ankersmit has been best known to readers of *History and Theory* as a contributor to a recent collection of essays dealing with current issues in Anglo-American discussions of the philosophy of history.[3] In his own article in this collection he appeared as an ardent advocate of the narrativist–rhetorical conception of historiography which Hayden White put forward in his *Metahistory* (1973) and subsequent writings. He has stressed the revolutionary import of White's ideas ascribing primacy in historical thinking to literary tropes and verbal structures, and has hailed his work as the wave of the future. It is therefore noteworthy that in contrast to literary theorists, who have provided the majority of supporters of White's view, most philosophers and philosophically inclined historians have been decidedly critical of it, when they have not simply ignored it. Many historians in particular seem as resistant to it as they were previously to the Hempelian positivist covering-law doctrine of historical explanation. Just as they opposed Hempel's scientism as a damaging misconception of the character of historical knowledge, so they have likewise tended to reject White's linguistic turn and its rhetorical approach for its disregard and distortion of certain essential characteristics of historical inquiry and writing.[4]

In his espousal of postmodernism, Ankersmit acts as a philosophic trend-spotter who has his eye out for the latest thing. No doubt some merit may be granted to an author who strives to discern the newest fashion in his discipline and bring out its implications. Ankersmit, however, is not only intent on recognizing what is new, but also identifies with it. He does not want to resist it as fallacious or harmful. Rather, like other historicists (although I know he would reject this designation, I believe it is justifiable in this context), he greets its novelty as an inevitable development and makes its cause his own.

Ankersmit's postmodernism may be regarded as an extension of his earlier commitment to White's narrativist principles. It represents a further step in the attempt to aestheticize history and sever it from its formerly accepted grounding in conditions of truth and reality. Although he offers no definition of postmodernism, he relates the latter to certain new situations and necessities that he believes leave us no choice but to accept it. In the following remarks I want to examine the validity of some of the claims and reasons he advances in behalf of his position.

At the outset, however, it is important for the sake of clarity to stress several features generally associated with the theory or idea of postmodernism. First it must be recognized as an essentially historicist conception. Those who announce the advent of postmodernism regard it as an inevitable stage of present-day culture and a break with the past that, owing to the conditions of contemporary society, cannot be withstood. Thus, a strong sense of fatality and the irresistible hovers over the notion.

Second, the basic impulse of postmodernism lies in its repudiation of the values and assumptions of the preceding high modernist movement which revolutionized the arts of the twentieth century, along with an equal repudiation of the philosophy it calls logocentrism – the belief in the referentiality of language, in the determinacy of textual meaning, and in the presence of a meaningful world to which language and knowledge are related. Yet it is striking that these postmodernist themes are unsustained by any feeling of *élan* or conviction of advance or progress. On the contrary, postmodernism, as its name implies, carries with it strong connotations of decline, exhaustion, and of being at the end rather than the commencement of an era.

Finally, a central element in postmodernism is its hostility to humanism. Foretelling, as Foucault wishfully predicted, the end of man, it rejects humanism as an outmoded relic and illusion of bourgeois ideology: the illusion of individuals creating their history though their free activity, which it sees as merely a cover for bourgeois society's oppression of women, the working class, non-whites, sexual deviants, and colonized natives. As a corollary, it also criticizes as elitist and oppressive the idea of a canon, which both modernism and humanism hold strongly in common, with its necessary discrimination and hierarchization among the creations of culture. The consequence is that postmodernism lends itself to a marked relaxation of cultural standards and sanctions an extreme eclecticism and heterogeneity without any critical or ordering principle. In the cultural domain as a whole it implies a total erasure of the distinction between high or elite culture and mass popular culture largely shaped and dominated by advertising and the commercial media, a distinction that both modernism and humanism accepted as axiomatic.

Some of the features I have just noted are touched upon, albeit in a much more favorable way, by Fredric Jameson, a Marxian literary theorist, in a wide-ranging survey entitled "Postmodernism, or the Cultural Logic of Late Capitalism." In considering the bearings of postmodernism upon historiography, it will be useful to look briefly at his account in order to enlarge our understanding of the concept of the postmodern. . . .

The most striking part of Jameson's treatment . . . is its analysis of the postmodern as exemplified in a variety of contemporary cultural products drawn from a spectrum of the arts. The fact that he ascribes to some of these, like Andy Warhol's paintings or the architecture of John Portman's Bonaventure Hotel in downtown Los Angeles, not only a representative and symptomatic importance, but also an artistic value which is highly debatable need not concern us. What is significant, rather, is the constellation of generic traits his scrutiny of these works leads him to identify as synonymous with postmodernism. They include the following: a new depthlessness and superficiality; a culture fixated upon the image; the waning of affect and disappearance of or liberation from emotion; abandonment of the concept of truth as useless metaphysical baggage; disappearance of the autonomous individual and the death of the subject; loss of historicity and the past; disintegration of the time sense into a series of pure, unrelated presents; the prevalence of pastiche and imitation and cannibalization of past styles. Such, according to Jameson's perceptive observation, are among the leading characteristics and thematics of the postmodern as the inevitably ascendant style of the culture of late capitalism.[5]

Ankersmit would no doubt be unwilling to accept every one of these features as indicative of what he advocates as postmodernism. Nevertheless, the affinity between them and his own point of view is unmistakable. The historicist fatalism implicit in the theory of the postmodern is reflected in his belief that "autumn has come to Western historiography," which no longer has a theme or metanarrative, now that Europe since the end of World War II has ceased to be identical with world history and declined to an appendage of the Eurasian continent. The turning away from the past is apparent in his rejection of the importance of historical origin and context and in his conviction that evidence has nothing to do with a past reality but points only to the interpretations given by historians. The similarity between the two is further manifest in the conception of historiography Ankersmit proposes. According to his postmodernist philosophy, the historian would renounce the task of explanation and principle of causality, along with the idea of truth, all of which are dismissed as part of a superseded "essentialism." Instead, he would recognize historiography as an aesthetic pursuit in which style is all-important.

What stands out in Ankersmit's postmodernist concept of historiography is its superficiality and remoteness from historical practice and the way historians usually think about their work. It trivializes history and renders it void of any intellectual responsibility. The logic and factual judgments which bring him to this conclusion, moreover, are far from convincing.

His point of departure is the present overproduction of historical writings, which he tells us is spreading like a cancer and fills him with intense despondency. Perhaps it is not very important that he fails to mention the reasons for this condition, which are largely sociological in nature. They lie, as we all know, in the great postwar expansion of higher education and university faculties, plus the necessity of publication imposed on academics as a prerequisite of career advancement. In any case, however, taking the literature on the philosopher Hobbes as an example, he notes that it has become so voluminous that Hobbes's text no longer possesses any authority and vanishes before its many interpretations. From this instance he infers that "we no longer have any texts, any past, but just interpretations of them."

Many things might be said about the troubling problem of the ever-growing quantity of historical publication without succumbing to the pessimistic opinion to which Ankersmit's spectacular illogic has led him. For one thing, the situation as J. H. Hexter pictured it in 1967 is even more the case today:

> 1. Never in the past has the writing of history been so fatuous as it is today; never has it yielded so enormous and suffocating a mass of stultifying trivia, the product of small minds engaged in the congenial occupation of writing badly about insignificant matters to which they have given little or no thought and for which they feel small concern.
> 2. Never in the past have historians written history so competently, vigorously, and thoughtfully as they do today, penetrating into domains hitherto neglected or in an obscurantist way shunned, bringing effectively to bear on the record of the past disciplines wholly inaccessible to their predecessors, treating the problems they confront with both a catholicity and a rigor and sophistication of method hitherto without precedent among practitioners of the historical craft.[6]

I am sure most historians would agree with this appraisal. What it means is that despite the burden of an increasing amount of mediocre and ephemeral historical work, there likewise exists in contrast a considerable body of work of exceptional originality, learning, and insight which has not only widened our intellectual horizons but deepened and even transformed our knowledge of many areas of the past.

For another thing, while the phenomenon of historical overproduction may sometimes depress us and seem unmanageable, we may also take some comfort from the fact that its effect is usually counteracted over time by a selective process which relegates trivial publications to obscurity and insures that the more significant contributions will in due course become known to specialists and, if they merit it, to a large part of the historical profession.

But how, in any event, can the condition of historical overproduction deprive us both of the text and the past, leaving us only with interpretations? As it happens, like Ankersmit, I too have had Hobbes as one of my special interests on which I have occasionally written. In a recent essay I have attempted to survey the literature concerning Hobbes which has appeared in the last several years.[7] Contrary to Ankersmit's assertion, even twenty years ago it would not have been sufficient for someone desiring to orient himself in the discussion of Hobbes's political philosophy to have read only Warrender and Watkins. At the least he would also have had to know the classic work by Leo Strauss, Oakeshott's introduction to his edition of *Leviathan*, and MacPhersons's *The Political Theory of Possessive Individualism*. For any claim to expertise, he would have needed to be familiar as well with other important contributions such as A. E. Taylor's article on Hobbes's ethical doctrine, and David Gauthier's study of *Leviathan*, not to mention still other works that would be pertinent.

By now, of course, the literature on Hobbes has indeed become very large. Yet, as is almost too obvious to state, in both previous and more recent writings, the relationship between the text of Hobbes's political theory and its interpretations remains extremely close. Far from being displaced or lost, the text is always scrutinized and discussed as the foundation for any proffered interpretative conclusion. Among the students of Hobbes, moreover, some, like Quentin Skinner, in their aim of recovering Hobbes's meaning and intention, insist on a reading fully grounded in the historical context, by which is meant an understanding of the intellectual tradition, ideological and political situation, and conventions of political language within which Hobbes wrote. For those in particular who see the study of political philosophy as an essentially historical discipline, interpretation does not eclipse the past; rather, the latter, comprehended as history, serves as a crucial test of the former's validity.

It is also plain that interpretations may stand or fall on textual and historical grounds. Two of the most widely discussed interpretations of

Hobbes in the past generation have been Warrender's and Macpherson's. The first sought to explain Hobbes's theory of moral and political obligation as ultimately founded on the command of God; the second argued that Hobbes's conception of both the state of nature and the political order was a reflection of the nascent capitalist market society of competitive possessive individualism. Neither of these interpretations, it is fair to say, has commended itself to the majority of Hobbes scholars, who have judged them incompatible either with the meaning of Hobbes's text and the character of his beliefs or with a proper understanding of his society.

What I have said about Hobbes is no less true of the other areas of early modern British and European history with which I am familiar as part of my principal field of study. Wherever in any of these a revisionary interpretation has been offered, textual evidence (in which I include not only literary sources and philosophical texts, but archival documents of all kinds) and contextual considerations are invariably central to the discussion. It would be superfluous to emphasize this point were it not for Ankersmit's curious discovery that in our postmodern age interpretation has abolished the text and the past.

Although the work of Gadamer, Ricoeur, and other thinkers has helped to reinstate the problem of interpretation and hermeneutic understanding as a major issue in the philosophy of history, Ankersmit's essay throws no light on this subject. Instead, he concentrates some of his remarks on the claim that interpretation has acquired a new status in postmodern historiography. Observing that in contemporary society information and interpretations continually increase as if by a law of their being, he stresses what he calls the paradox that powerful new interpretations do not put an end to writing but only generate more of it. This allegedly paradoxical fact is supposed to be explicable only from a postmodernist perspective. But why should it be considered a paradox? Historical interpretations are similar in some respects to scientific theories and hypotheses. Like them, any original new interpretation will have both adherents and opponents. The former will attempt to apply, strengthen, and extend it so as to demonstrate its superiority over its competitors. The latter will seek out its weaknesses and try to refute it. If an historical interpretation comes to be widely accepted, it may even cease to be the subject of debate and take its place as an established part of our understanding of the past. Of course, this may not last. The subsequent emergence of another interpretation may force it to undergo renewed challenges which throw it into question and perhaps displace it. There is nothing paradoxical, however, or unique to the present, in the fact that significant new interpretations stimulate rather than close off discussion.

The lack of substance in Ankersmit's position is further illustrated in his comments on postmodernist historiography's attitude to science, which he describes as one of apartness and detachment but not opposition, hence "ascientistic" rather than "antiscientistic." This is scarcely consistent, though, with his claim that postmodernism has succeeded in destabilizing science and hitting it where it hurts most by deconstructing the concept of causality, one of the main pillars of scientific thought. How does it accomplish this remarkable feat? The ensuing demonstration is the same as the one given in Jonathan Culler's *On Deconstruction* and derives from the latter's inspirer, Nietzsche. It runs as follows. When we consider an effect, it makes us look for the cause; the effect thus precedes or becomes the cause of the cause; hence the effect is the origin of the cause. This accordingly reverses the traditional hierarchy of cause and effect and proves its artificiality.

This verbal juggling is a transparent confusion, as John Searle has already pointed out in his critical review of Culler's book.[8] While an effect may be the epistemic source of an inquiry into its cause, this cannot mean that it is temporally prior or that it produces or originates the cause. If my car stops running for want of gas, I look for the cause. It is the empty tank, however, not my curiosity about why it will not run, that caused it to stop. The effect, in short, is the origin of my interest, but not of the cause. There is no question here, moreover, of conceiving cause and effect as a hierarchy, a point that is entirely irrelevant. The two are simply correlatives, each entailing the other.

In making these criticisms, I have not committed myself to any particular meaning which the historian should attach to the notion of causality as he uses it. Whether "cause" in the historian's language always signifies a reason or motive on the part of historical agents, or the subsumption of an event, action, or phenomenon under a general causal law, or perhaps neither, depending on the subject under consideration, continues to be a disputed question in the philosophy of history. It is an illusion, nevertheless, to assume that historiography can dispense with the concept of causality. As long as it includes explanation as one of its objectives, causal attribution will remain a necessary ingredient of historical thinking. Postmodernism's revelation to the contrary is not only mistaken, but futile.

One of the principal aims of Ankersmit's discussion is to bring out "the revolutionary nature of postmodernism" which enables it to perform its subversive function. As a manifestation of the latter he adduces not only its alleged deconstruction of the principle of causality, but its view that all our scientific certainties are logically implicated in the liar's paradox. As a succinct version of this paradox, he instances the statement, "this statement is false." By means of this logical weapon, he imagines, postmodernism pulls the carpet out from under science and modernism. Historiography is supposed to provide an illustration of this operation in the intrinsically paradoxical character of interpretation.

The looseness and absence of clarity in these assertions make it hard to deal with them seriously as argument. One could say the following, however, about their proposed conclusion. The liar's paradox poses a problem of reflexivity in which a statement is logically included in its own verdict of falsity on a class of statements of which it is itself a member. But how does such reflexivity apply to historiography or the theories of science? Ankersmit presents no reason for his contention that the interpretations or factual statements of historians are paradoxical in this way. Apart from this failure, it is also doubtful whether the paradox he has chosen as an example is really a paradox. This is because the sentence does not actually state anything and is thus not a proposition. To be a proposition, it would need to entail a truth-value or particular truth-conditions, and this it is unable to do. It can hardly yield, therefore, the subversive result Ankersmit would like to assign to it.

The most important insight Ankersmit credits to postmodernism is its recognition of the aesthetic nature of historiography. He relates this insight to the new understanding in contemporary thought that the distinction between language and reality has lost its *raison d'être*. With the disappearance of this distinction, he points out, aestheticism extends its sway over all forms of representation. Historiography is thereby finally perceived to be a literary product in which the historian does not produce a representation of reality (or we may also say, of the past), but a replacement or substitute for it. Style is seen as prior to content and content as a derivative of style. Historical differences likewise prove to be due to differences of style.

One of the characteristic moves of postmodernist and deconstructionist theory has been to try to obliterate the boundaries between literature and other disciplines by reducing all modes of thought to the common condition of writing. So it maintains that philosophy, like historiography, is merely another kind of writing and subject to its laws, rather than a separate species of reflection concerned with distinctively philosophical questions.[9] Putting aside, however, the identification of language and reality, a thesis construable in different ways (which in any case is well beyond the subject of my discussion), I venture to say that few historians would agree with Ankersmit's consignment of historiography to the category of the aesthetic. Nor would they be likely to approve a characterization that gives preeminence to its literariness. As the Russian formalists and Roman Jakobson have told us, the quality of literariness consists in the way it thrusts language and expression into the foreground and grants them an independent value and importance. Although Ankersmit holds that literary and historical works are similar in this respect, this is surely not the case. In historiography, the attempt by language to draw attention to itself would commonly be regarded as highly inappropriate and an obtrusive breach of the rules of historical writing. In history language is very largely subservient to the historian's effort to convey in the fullest, clearest, and most sensitive way an understanding or knowledge of something in the past.

To sustain the opinion that style is the predominant factor in historiography, Ankersmit emphasizes the intensional character and context of the words and statements in historical works, which entail that they cannot be replaced by other equivalent statements. This opinion seems to me to be equally mistaken. If it were true, it would be impossible to paraphrase or summarize a work of history without altering its substance or meaning. But such summaries are possible; we can very well give a description of something as distinctive in style as Gibbon's narration of the origin and triumph of Christianity in the Roman Empire which effectively conveys not only his understanding of how and why this development occurred but also the irony that pervades his account of it.

Generally it must be said that Ankersmit fails to provide any explanation of how style can determine or engender the content of historical works. Like the notion that interpretation has eliminated the text and the past, this is another of those extreme claims which, despite its inherent implausibility, postmodernists like to put forward as proof of the revolutionary import of their ideas. Certainly it runs counter to some of the strongest convictions and intuitions historians feel about their discipline. Their comment on it would most likely be that content derives from the critical study of sources and evidence, from the critical consideration of other writings dealing with their subject, and from their perception of the interrelationships that exist among the indefinite multiplicity of facts pertaining to the object of their inquiry.

Ankersmit's postmodernist attempt to absorb historiography into the literary and aesthetic domain ignores features that are central to the very concept of history. One of these is the difference history presumes between fact or truth and fictionality, for which the aesthetic perspective makes no provision. Unlike the work of literature, the historical work does not contain an invented or imaginary world. It presents itself as consisting, to a great degree, of facts and true or probable statements about the past. Many of its sentences are propositions with truth-conditions attached to them. If this were not so, the reader would take no interest in it. The distinctive significance that history asserts for itself, therefore, is entirely dependent on its claim to veridicality. Even though historical writing may contain many false or erroneous statements and propound debatable interpretations resting on very complex evidential considerations, veridicality in the widest sense is generally taken to be among its basic regulatory principles.

Another feature, for which the aesthetic domain contains no place, is the role occupied by evidence. Historians operate within definite constraints, of which they are fully conscious, arising from the nature and limitations of their evidence. While it is for them to determine that something is evidence and what it is evidence for, when they have done so the evidence exerts a continuous force upon them. They are not free to ignore it or make of it whatever they please. Its pressure acts as a major determinant in giving shape to the historical work.

Connected with the preceding is yet another intrinsic feature of historiography, the necessity for justification of its specific knowledge-claims, a requirement it shares with other types of inquiry. Historians know that they may be called upon to justify the veridicality, adequacy, and reliability of particular statements, interpretations, and even of their entire account. Their form of writing is apt to incorporate many justifications for the judgments they make, the opinions they express, and the descriptions and analyses they present in their treatment of the past. Even the purest narrative history is unable to dispense with the necessity of justification if it is to be acceptable to critical readers and students.

The aestheticizing of historiography which Ankersmit conceives as a major postmodernist insight inevitably results in the trivialization of history through its failure to acknowledge features that both define history as a form of thought and give it its significance. The same effect is apparent in the prescriptions for historiography which form the conclusion of his article. One of them is that historians should concentrate, as psychoanalysis does, on the unconscious aspects of the past that have been repressed and come to light only involuntarily through "slips of the tongue." Although I do not deny that this aim may possess a certain value, it is of much less consequence than the attempt to discover and understand the values, beliefs, assumptions, conventions, rules, and social practices that constitute a large part of the conscious life of past societies. The study of these is not only a task of extreme difficulty, requiring exceptional insight and imagination, but one of fundamental importance of which the priorities of postmodernism take no account.

Another of Ankersmit's prescriptions tells historians that they can no longer deal with big problems or seek to reconstruct or discover patterns in the past, as modern scientific historiography once aspired and pretended to do. All that now remains for them to be concerned with are micro-subjects and "historical scraps," as exemplified in the work of some contemporary social historians, despite the fact that writings such as the latter produce may seem to have little point. In the postmodernist view, he states, "the goal is no longer integration, synthesis, and totality," and small topics now come to occupy the center of attention.

Needless to say, few historians would look with favor on this formula for a new antiquarianism which springs from a trivialized, tired, and defeatist conception of historical inquiry. Contrary to Ankersmit's belief, the expansion and fragmentation of historiography in our time through the simultaneous growth of specialization and extension of our historical horizons has made the need for integration and synthesis greater and more important than ever before. It is a need, moreover, that is widely recognized. The point is not whether it is possible to attain a total conception of world history or the historical process, for it almost certainly is not. This does not preclude the feasibility, nevertheless, of focusing on large-scale subjects at a quite general level and on questions that transcend specialist and disciplinary boundaries in order to provide an understanding of whole societies and civilizations and of broad areas and aspects of the past. Not only does modern historical literature contain numerous examples of works of this kind, but there will always be historians with the intellectual ambition to tackle subjects of exceptional breadth and significance.

In the course of his article Ankersmit touches on the question of the usefulness of historiography, only to dismiss it as impertinent and a category mistake. As historiography is a part of culture, he explains, the question of its usefulness cannot meaningfully arise any more than it can about culture itself. While we may concede this point, we can nevertheless ask what the function of history is and what purpose it serves or should serve in culture and society. Although Western society is sometimes said to be fast losing its connection to its past, that it still values history and believes it important is apparent from the considerable resources it provides to support historical research and teaching. Why does it or should it do so?

An indirect answer to this question was once given by Ankersmit's compatriot, Huizinga, a scholar humanist of distinctive mind and sensibility, who defined history as "the intellectual form in which a civilization renders account to itself of its past." This definition also implies a description of history's function. Huizinga went on to say that "our civilization is the first to have for its past the past of the world, our history is the first to be world-history." To this observation he added that

> a history adequate to our civilization can only be a scientific history. The instrument of modern Western civilization for the intellectual understanding of the world is critical science. We cannot sacrifice the demand for scientific certainty without injury to the conscience of our civilization. Mythical and fictitious representations of the past may have a literary value as forms of play, but for us they are not history.[10]

In this statement Huizinga was not speaking of science as a positivist. By scientific history he understood precisely what Collingwood did by the term, namely, the rigorous cognitive standards, exigent critical methods, and global sense of the past that became characteristic of Western historiography in the course of its development during the nineteenth and twentieth centuries.

Of course, historiography serves a number of functions, including several practical ones, but Huizinga was looking at the question from the general standpoint of society as a whole. Whether we agree entirely with him or not, his vision of historiography is probably not far different from the way many Western historians today would conceive their craft. Ankersmit disparages this vision as modernist, but his alternative postmodernist view seems woefully impoverished by comparison. If it were to prevail – though there is little likelihood of this happening – history would no longer have a real function. It could no longer perform its principal intellectual obligation in education and culture, which must be to give to each living generation the broadest and best possible knowledge of the past of its own society and civilization as well as of the larger human past of which it is part. Postmodernism represents the abnegation of this obligation which is the ultimate cultural responsibility of historiography and one that remains indispensable as the rapidly changing world moves faster into the future than ever before.

Notes

1 F. R. Ankersmit, "Historiography and Postmodernism," *History and Theory* 28 (1989), 137–53 [ch. 9, this volume].
2 John S. Nelson, Allan Megill, and Donald N. McCloskey, *The Rhetoric of the Human Sciences* (Madison, Wisc., 1987).
3 F. R. Ankersmit, "The Dilemma of Contemporary Anglo-American Philosophy of History," *Knowing & Telling History: The Anglo-Saxon Debate, History and Theory, Beiheft* 25 (1986).
4 See some of the papers in *Metahistory: Six Critiques, History and Theory, Beiheft* 19 (1980), particularly Maurice Mandelbaum's "The Presuppositions of *Metahistory*," as well as Frederick A. Olafson's comments in his "Hermeneutics: 'Analytical' and 'Dialectical,'" in *Knowing & Telling History*, 40–1. See, too, the critical observations and cautions regarding White's views in Paul Ricoeur, *The Reality of the Historical Past* (Milwaukee, Wisc., 1984), 33–4, and William H. Dray, "Narrative and Historical Realism," in *On History and Philosophy of History* (Leiden, 1989), ch. 7. I have also observed from conversations with historians and discussions with doctoral students in seminars on the philosophy of history that their response to White's *Metahistory* and *Tropics of Discourse* is generally unfavorable.
5 Fredric Jameson, "Postmodernism, or the Cultural Logic of Late Capitalism," *New Left Review*, no. 146 (1984), 53–92. The literature on postmodernism is by now considerable; for further discussion of what it stands for and its relationship to deconstructionism, see Terry Eagleton, *Literary Theory* (Minneapolis, 1983), and the essays in *Postmodernism*, ed. Lisa Appignanesi (London, 1986).
6 J. H. Hexter, "Some American Observations," *Journal of Contemporary History* 2 (1967), 5–6, cited in Peter Novick, *That Noble Dream: The "Objectivity Question" and the American Historical Profession* (Cambridge and New York, 1988), 377.
7 Perez Zagorin, *A History of Political Thought in the English Revolution* (London, 1954), ch. 13; "Thomas Hobbes," *International Encyclopedia of the Social Sciences*; "Clarendon and Hobbes," *Journal of Modern History* 57 (1985), 593–616; "Cudworth and Hobbes on Is and Ought," in *Philosophy, Science and Religion in England 1640–1700*, ed. Richard Ashcraft, Richard Kroll, and Perez Zagorin (Cambridge University Press, 1991); "Hobbes on Our Mind," *Journal of the History of Ideas* 51 (1990), 317–35.

8 See Searle's review of Jonathan Culler, *On Deconstruction: Theory and Criticism after Structuralism* (Ithaca, NY, 1983), in *New York Review of Books* 27 (October, 1983), 74–9.

9 For a discussion, see Christopher Norris, *Deconstruction, Theory and Practice* (London, 1982), and *The Deconstructive Turn: Essays in the Rhetoric of Philosophy* (London, 1983).

10 J. Huizinga, "A Definition of the Concept of History," in *Philosophy and History*, ed. Raymond Klibansky and H. J. Paton [1936] (New York, 1963), 8–9.

11
Reply to Professor Zagorin

F. R. Ankersmit

As with every discipline, philosophy of history has a history of its own. If we wish, we can trace that history as far back as that of the writing of history itself. Classical authors from Hesiod onwards pronounced on the nature and the uses of the writing of history.[1] If, then, we consider this long history of philosophy of history, one feature of that history immediately catches the eye. I have in mind philosophy of history's lack of autonomy. That is, the development and, especially, the most conspicuous metamorphoses that philosophy of history underwent during its long life have always depended on what happened outside philosophy of history itself. Philosophy of history never had much momentum of its own and ordinarily limited itself to the application to the domain of historical thought of insights that had already been gained elsewhere.

Thus, for most of its life philosophy of history has been an appendage of Christian theology. At a later stage, when the theological interpretation of the past was secularized, philosophy of history presented itself in the form of theories of historical progress. And once again these philosophies of history were founded not upon history or historical thought, but upon doctrines about (dialectical) reason (Hegel), scientific reason (Condorcet, Comte), or about the rational nature of man (Kant). Next, if we take a look at our own time, we find that philosophy of science determined philosophy of history for the first decades after World War II. It is ironic that the so-called "critical philosophy of history" that was born from this orientation had a shorter life than any of its predecessors, in spite of its belief in having finally provided philosophy of history with the right kind of questions after so many centuries of useless speculation. For, less than thirty years after its genesis, this critical philosophy of history had to abandon the field to a philosophy of history that uses the tools of literary theory and literary criticism. We find the only exception to the general rule that philosophy of history possesses no momentum or autonomy of its own in German historism as developed by Ranke, Humboldt, Droysen, or Meinecke. It is quite characteristic, then, of philosophy of history's disinclination to stand on its own feet that philosophers of history have ordinarily turned up their noses at historism. And it is no less characteristic that historism was dealt its death-blow by ethics (in "the crisis of historism") and by philosophy of science (in post-World War II critical philosophy of history), hence by two philosophical sub-disciplines that have always been notoriously hostile to historical thought.[2]

One can thus discern a number of phases in the history of philosophy of history, where each of these phases is governed by the alliance between philosophy of history and some other discipline. For convenience's sake I shall speak here of the "paradigms" of philosophy of history. But it must immediately be added that the term "paradigm" is misleading. For in the history of science, paradigm changes find their origin and explanation in the autonomous development of a science, whereas such changes in philosophy of history are effected by the idealization of a new and different "master-discipline" by the most influential philosophers of history. And one starts completely afresh in such cases. If, then, the debate between the adherents of different scientific paradigms is already handicapped by the absence of a common ground, it is not difficult to imagine the obstacles that must thwart a meaningful debate across the frontiers between two different paradigms in philosophy of history. In such situations impotent accusations of intellectual conservatism and radicalism are all too easily bandied to and fro; similarly, we may expect that the adherents of different paradigms will consider one another's intellectual preoccupations shallow and futile. The speculative philosopher of history in search of the meaning of history will feel nothing but contempt for the critical philosopher of history wrestling with the technicalities of the "covering-law model" or of the "logical connection argument." And it is therefore only natural that Professor Zagorin should consider postmodernism "superficial," "lacking in substance," and indifferent to the real problems of the writing of history.

Indeed, this is the state of affairs that obtains in the disagreement between Zagorin and me. Zagorin's interest in problems of historical truth, evidence, and causality; his repeated insistence on the essentially unproblematic borderline between historical fact and fiction; the style of his reasoning; all make clear that he argues within the "modernist" paradigm, more specifically within that of critical philosophy of history. Moreover, Zagorin has obligingly described his position as "modernist." How then to conduct this discussion, I asked myself, after having read Zagorin's eloquent, perspicacious, and persuasive attack on my post-modernist views? I could have pointed out to him that the modernist paradigm has become worn out and that in such a situation we are well advised to change the discussion (as Rorty would have put it) because intellectual activity in the old paradigm, fruitful in its own time, has finally fallen victim to the law of diminishing returns. I could have enumerated for Zagorin a series of postmodernist insights into the nature of the text and I could then have shown him how theorists like Hayden White, Dominick LaCapra, and Hans Kellner[3] did use these insights in order to make us aware of hitherto unsuspected aspects of the writing of history. But I am afraid that such a strategy would have been of no avail in my debate with Zagorin. He would, not unreasonably, riposte that such an answer begs the question. Besides, by implicating the authors just mentioned in Zagorin's attack on me I would make them suffer by guilt of association: not a polite way of repaying them for the services they would have rendered me. I shall therefore adopt another strategy. I shall start from "modernist" assumptions – assumptions that are at least not necessarily incompatible with the modernist outlook – and I shall proceed from there with the help of a "modernist" way of reasoning to *post*modernist conclusions. I derive some confidence in this strategy from the fact that in adopting it I retrace the same route that has led me in recent years from modernist (that is, historist)[4] convictions to a postmodernist position.[5]

At the start of our line of march from modernism to postmodernism we find the (historical) text. We can say about the text the following two things. First, the historical text consists of (many) individual statements. These statements may have many different functions to perform in the historical text, but it seems unobjectionable to say that most of these statements claim to give an accurate description of some state of affairs in the past. Historians formulate these statements on the basis of the evidence they discover in the archives or elsewhere and it is this evidence, available either now or in the future, that will decide about the truth or falsity of the statements in question. Second, with the exception of fields like archeology or ancient history, the evidence available to historians would have permitted them to write many more true statements about the past than we actually find in their texts. Nor are the way the statements are formulated and the emphasis they get in the text matters of chance or arbitrariness. Out of all the statements historians could possibly have made about the relevant part of the past, they carefully select *qua* descriptive content and *qua* formulation the statements they will ultimately decide to mention in their books or articles – one might say that the writing of the historical text requires of historians a *politics* with regard to the statement, and the text is the result of this politics. The reason for historians' carefulness in this selection-procedure is that these statements, when considered together, determine "the picture" of part of the past they wish to present to their readers and for historians this "picture" is no less important than the statements that make it up.

One may thus say the following two things about the text's statements: (1) they refer to and describe part of the past and can be either true or false; (2) they define (I shall use in this connection the technical term "to individuate," not to be confused with the term "to identify") the "picture of the past" historians wish to convey to their readers. Different statements, different "pictures of the past." Two comments must be added. First, it is in practice hard to tell what actually is the set of statements to individuate the identity of a "picture of the past." Historians (including the author of the text) may disagree about how the set is constituted, and if there is consensus in one age this may change in the course of time, as the history of historical writing demonstrates. I shall discuss later this problem of the identification (as opposed to individuation) of what "picture of the past" has been proposed and what is the set of statements involved in this process of identification. But whatever difficulties we may have in identifying the set in question, there can be no doubt that there is *some* set that individuates the "picture of the past" in question. Second, all that is essential and interesting in the writing of history (both in theory and practice) is not to be found at the level of the individual statements, but at that of the politics adopted by historians when they select the statements that individuate their "picture of the past." There we find what most stimulates historical debate and what most determines our sense of the past. Saying *true* things about the past is easy – anybody can do that – but saying the *right* things about the past is difficult. That truly requires historical insight and originality. So if we want to say something worthwhile about the writing of history we must focus our theoretical reflection on these "pictures of the past" and not on individual (subsets of) statements and on what they say about the past.

The latter comment brings me to the most crucial phase in my whole argument. For reasons unnecessary to repeat here I have elsewhere called these "pictures of the past" "narrative substances."[6] The question everything turns on, then, is whether or not we are prepared to recognize these narrative substances as logical entities *next* to the logical entities like subject, predicate, theoretical concept, statement, and so on, we already know from philosophical logic. If we are, as I will show later, all the postmodernist extravagances that have provoked Zagorin's ire follow as a matter of course. If we are not, we will remain enclosed within the compass of modernist conceptions and within the modernist matrix of argument. If we take seriously the text and its narrative substances we will become postmodernists; if we see only the statement we will remain modernist. Or, to put it in a slogan, the statement is modernist, the (historical) text is postmodernist.[7]

I recognize that it is not at all easy to demonstrate the necessity of postulating this new logical entity and that much more ought to be said about it than I could possibly do here.[8] I restrict myself to answering what is intuitively the most obvious objection against the introduction of the notion. It will be argued that the narrative substance is a superfluous entity since everything one might wish to say about texts in terms of narrative substances can *also* be expressed in terms of statements. My initial reply would be that what statements do tell us about texts and the way they differ from one another can be seen as merely the marks of another difference, namely a difference in narrative substances. Of course the disagreement ends here in a stalemate as long as no additional argument is adduced in favor of the latter view that a difference lying more deeply is involved as well. This additional argument is found in the consideration that without the notion of the narrative substance, it is impossible to state what is at stake in debates between historians about historical interpretations and why the effort of the historian goes beyond merely writing down true statements – as is the case in the writing of history.

Once again, a few comments are in order. First, it should be noted that since any (subset of) statement(s) we might use to individuate a narrative substance can be part of another narrative substance, the conclusion must follow that the thing I have called a narrative substance can only be individuated by an enumeration of *all* its properties (this is why the metaphysical constitution of the universe of narrative substances differs from that of our own).[9] (I repeat that I shall explain below how to find out about the statements concerned.) Second, it follows that statements about narrative substances are always analytically and never contingently true. Every statement of the form "N_1 is p" (where N_1 is the name of a narrative substance referring to that specific narrative substance and p is a statement contained by that narrative substance) is analytically true since the statement could not be true if it were false of N_1 – whereas the statements about the objects in our universe are only contingently true if they are true. This implies that Leibniz's so-called "predicate in notion principle," according to which all predicates can be derived from the subject-terms in propositions, is correct for statements like "N_1 is p" that express the narrative meaning of the text's statements.[10]

To individuate the narrative substance proposed in an historical text, we must read the relevant statements of the text each as "N_1 is $p_1 \ldots _n$" (where N_1 names the narrative substance in question and $p_1 \ldots p_n$ is the relevant set of statements). Statements like "N_1 is p" express what I would like to call the narrative meaning of the text's individual statements as contrasted with their descriptive meaning (that is, their capacity to describe the past). The necessity to read $p_1 \ldots p_n$ as "N_1 is p_1" $\ldots$ "N_1 is p_n" if we want to grasp the narrative meaning of the text explains the self-referential character of the historical text that Zagorin objects to as "highly inappropriate and an obtrusive breach of historical writing." However, without this self-reference of the text (as a set of statements)

to the text (as proposing a narrative substance), we would have no interpretations of the past. Without this self-referentiality the text would
immediately disintegrate into meaningless incoherence: self-reference truly
is the "transcendental condition" for the possibility of historical insight.[11]
We also find here the explanation of the opacity of the historical text:
from the point of view of its narrative meaning the text is not transparent with regard to the past but it draws the reader's attention to
itself and in doing so obscures from view the past itself – a tendency
that is reinforced by the historical text's "disciplinary goal" of effectively replacing the past by the text (for an elaboration of this claim, see
my account below of historical representation). And this may dispel
Zagorin's worries about the intensional character of the historical text.
The intensionality of the text must be related to the object the text refers
to when we consider its dimension of self-referentiality. And this object
is far from accidental: changing it would change the nature of the account
of the past given by the historian. Thus, without intensionality no pictures
or interpretations of the past are possible at all.

Let us take a closer look at these narrative substances. We may ask
what the relation is between the narrative substance and the part of
the past represented by it. It may be illuminating to give the question
a context. Narrative substances do not often get a name of their own,
but sometimes they are accorded one in the history of historical writing.
Here we can think of terms or notions like "the Industrial Revolution"
or "the Cold War." Obviously, with such notions we have to do with
interpretations or representations of the past, that is, with narrative substances. What, then, is the relation between such notions and the actual
past? The modernist will undoubtedly look here for some kind of correspondence between the notion in question and some part of the past, or
credit the notion with a capacity to describe that part of the past. This
is, I suppose, how Walsh or Mink (to whom we owe many valuable
contributions to the analysis of the kind of notions discussed here)[12]
would look at the matter. Within my view, however, these notions
should be seen as the *names* of narrative substances and, therefore, as
far as reference or correspondence is concerned, these names must be
denied the capacity to refer to anything outside the text: they refer to
narrative substances (that is, a set of statements contained by and within
the text). But this certainly does not mean that these notions are completely unrelated to the past itself: in the set of statements the name of
the narrative substance refers to, reference is made to the past. Let us
investigate, next, the reference of narrative substances themselves, that
is, not of their names. The narrative substance must be identified with
the set of statements expressing the narrative meaning (as contrasted
with the descriptive meaning) of the relevant statements in the historical
text, hence with the set "N_1 is p_1" ... "N_1 is p_n." It follows from this
that the referent of the narrative substance must be the narrative substance

itself since it is the referent of the name N_1 – a conclusion that will not astonish us after what was said a moment ago about the self-referentiality of narrative language. So the narrative substance is a linguistic object we can refer to, either in statements using its name, in case it happens to have one, or in statements expressing the narrative meaning of the historical text, but that never refers to anything other than or outside itself. Narrative substances are truly semantic "black holes" in the universe of the language we use.

We can approach the problem from another perspective. Suppose we have two or more historical texts on roughly the same historical topic and we wish to decide between them. As constructivists like Oakeshott, Goldstein, or Stanford[13] have successfully shown, there is no past that is given to us and to which we could compare these two or more texts in order to find out which of them does correspond to the past and which does not. One may conclude from their constructivist argumentation that the past as the complex referent of the historical text as a whole has no role to play in historical debate. From the point of view of historical practice this referential past is epistemically a useless notion – something like Wittgenstein's wheel in the machine that is turned but does not drive anything else. Texts are all we have and we can only compare texts with texts. If we are looking for the best account of the past, we ought to ask ourselves in which of these texts the available historical evidence has been most successfully used. But we can never test our conclusions by comparing the elected text with "the past" itself. So narrative substances do not refer to the past, nor is such reference required from the point of view of historical debate.

One might put it as follows. When we speak about reality in simple constative statements like "the cat lies on the mat" there are a number of semantic conventions that decide about the meaning, the truth, and the reference of such statements. How these conventions – meaning, truth, and reference – hang together is an immensely complicated problem that has inspired a major part of twentieth-century philosophy. But such semantic conventions are conspicuously absent when we use the kind of historical notions we are now investigating; hence, at this stage we cannot properly speak of truth, falsity, reference, or of a failure to refer. What we can say, however, is that these historical notions or narrative substances are very complex linguistic signs that have been carefully constructed by historians to *stipulate* such a semantic convention for a very specific purpose (that is, for relating words to things in the case of *this* specific part of the past). And, indeed, if a narrative substance with exactly the meaning an historian has given to it were to become universally accepted by all historians and even by non-historians we could say that a new convention has been introduced in language for relating words to things. But as long as such a universal agreement has not been reached (and a word has not yet made its transition from historical to ordinary discourse), we can only say that a semantic convention was *proposed* by the historian. This may, therefore, induce us to see narrative substances as essentially *proposals* for connecting things with words.[14] The implication is – and I answer herewith another of Zagorin's objections – that at the level of the historical text and of historical interpretation, we cannot appropriately use the words truth and falsity. For we can say a lot of things about proposals, for example, that they are fruitful, well-considered, intelligent, to the point (or not), and so on, but not that they are true or false. As my examples of how we can characterize proposals may show, the fact that proposals cannot be either true or false does not imply that no good reasons can be given for or against a certain proposal. The mere fact that we cannot label narrative interpretations or narrative substances as either true or false does not in the least leave us empty-handed in historical debate.[15] It is a fallacy as silly as it is dangerous to believe that we can or ought to restrict historical interpretation and historical argument to what can truthfully be said about the past on the basis of available evidence. . . .

Since the identity of narrative substances is determined by other narrative substances that have been proposed by historians in the course of time, it follows that the identity of narrative substances is something we can never have very clear and definite ideas about. Their identity will depend on the available set of narrative substances considered of central importance by historians, and opinions may differ here; moreover, when at a later time new narrative substances are proposed, the identity of the existing set will change accordingly. But always the identity of narrative substances will remain caught between two "extremes of description": the extreme when only one narrative substance is present, and the other extreme of an infinity of narrative substances whose overlap is complete, with the exception of at least one statement for each narrative substance (and in such an extreme case the narrative substance would be reduced to that statement). I note in passing the similarity of this argument to that of Saussure about the meaning of signs being determined by its differences from that of other signs. "A language is a system," writes Saussure, "in which all the elements fit together, and in which the value of any one element depends on the simultaneous coexistence of all the others."[16] French postmodernism – whether as linguistic theory, as literary criticism, or as sociological theory (Bourdieu) – is essentially an endless variation on this Saussurian melody. I shall not pronounce upon the fruitfulness, let alone the validity, of these Saussurian claims in these fields, but restrict myself to repeating the assertion that the identity of narrative substances is determined by the system of differences that obtain in the set of narrative substances of which a narrative substance is part. And this enables me to answer Zagorin's complaint that I did not make clear how and why the liar's paradox is applicable to the writing of history. The answer goes as follows. First, we must note that in the context of historical debate, narrative substances are polarized in a position of mutual exclusion: if we accept *this* narrative substance we must *eo ipso* reject the other(s). Second, these other narrative substances are required for the identification of the narrative substance we accept. Views of the past we *reject* are, therefore, an integral part of the identity of the view of the past, of the narrative substance we *accept*. Thus one can justifiably say that a view of the past, or narrative substance, is what it is not. The parallelism with the liar's paradox is obvious.

Now I come to Zagorin's discussion of causality. He criticized me for having substituted heuristics (what makes us look for causes?) for the actual course of events in reality where the cause always precedes the effect. And with an example that has the ring of being decisive he wishes to demonstrate that effects can never precede their causes (as I had suggested). Yet even at the level of relatively straightforward examples, like the one proposed by Zagorin, the issue is not so simple as he believes. In theories of causality it is customary to distinguish between sufficient and necessary conditions. A is a sufficient condition for B if each A is accompanied by a B; A is a necessary condition for B if each B is accompanied by an A. Hence there is a relation of symmetry between sufficient and necessary causes and this means that if A is a sufficient condition for B, then B must be a necessary condition for A and vice versa. So if there exists a causal relation between two events A and B and if A is a necessary condition for B, we can agree with Danto when he concludes that "a sufficient condition for an event may thus occur later in time than the event."[17]

Another consideration which leads to similar results is that we can describe events in such a way that, thanks to the redescription, the arrow of causality is turned in a direction opposite to the one Zagorin thinks it always ought to point. Danto gives the following example. One can say that Copernicus's discovery of heliocentrism in 1543 was the cause of the event we can correctly describe with the statement "in 270 BC Aristarchos anticipated Copernicus by discovering heliocentrism."[18] Without the discovery, at a later time, of heliocentrism Aristarchos could not have anticipated that discovery. Once again, the cause is later than the effect.

Remarks like these, that can routinely be made even within the modernist paradigm, are already a decisive reply to Zagorin's queries. But I will not leave the matter there and will look a bit more closely at his argument that I confuse heuristics with the actual course of events. Suppose we ask for the cause of, for example, "the Industrial Revolution" or of "the Cold War." We now ought to remember that these terms do not refer to an historical reality outside the text but to narrative substances. This means such questions are not questions about the cause of a complex state of affairs at the end of the eighteenth century or after

World War II, but a question about the cause of a notion or narrative substance. I suppose we could not interpret such an admittedly odd question differently from the question why some historian decided to propose this particular narrative substance. And, obviously, that is precisely the heuristic question Zagorin says I should not ask.

Undoubtedly it will now be objected that something must have gone wrong here: no sensible person would interpret the question of what is the cause of the Industrial Revolution as a question about why an historian came to defend a specific interpretation of the past. I quite agree. But if something went wrong it is because causalistic language was used here outside the range of its proper application. Causal language must be restricted to the level of the statement: only at *that* level can causal relations be established between the states of affairs individual statements describe.[19] Causalistic language can only lead to confusion and unsubstantiated claims if introduced at the level of the text and of the narrative substance. Someone who asks for the causes of the Industrial Revolution asks, in fact, for a convincing narrative interpretation covering both the period of the beginning of that revolution and the period immediately preceding it and not for the isolation of two (complex) historical events that can be related by some causal mechanism.[20] The latter strategy can, at most, result in suggesting a *conceptual* relation between two different narrative substances (one for the former, and another for the other period) and such conceptual relations only provide us with truths *de dicto* and not *de re* (whereas it is only the latter we are interested in in the case of causal explanation).[21] And, indeed, if one carefully reads books like those written by Immanuel Wallerstein or Theda Skocpol, one will see that what is presented there as *causal* relations is already implicit in the principal notions used by those authors.

I now arrive at a number of issues that can be dispatched more easily. Zagorin wonders how "style can engender content." Think of a painting by Van Eyck as different from a painting by Fragonard. It will be observed that whereas Van Eyck always likes to depict a great number of tiny details with the utmost accuracy, Fragonard never strives for such "reality effects," to borrow Barthes's terminology. Of course this is an important difference in style between the two artists, but, equally obviously, it is also a matter of content.[22] The painter adopting Van Eyck's style will paint different things (content) from Fragonard. Thus style engenders content. It requires little effort to translate this insight to the writing of history. A moment ago I discussed the difficulty of identifying the narrative substances proposed in historical writing because of their intrinsic vagueness and dependence on the presence of other narrative substances. I am convinced that style is a helpful instrument if we wish to overcome these difficulties. Stylistic categories are like a web that enables us to catch the interpretations and narrative substances proposed by historians – Hayden White's essay on Foucault and Hans Kellner's on Braudel are the best illustrations of what I have in mind.[23]

Zagorin attacks my views on the intensional character of historical writing with the argument that it is possible "to paraphrase or summarize a work of history without altering its substance or meaning" – a possibility my thesis about intensionality effectively rules out. Now I find it hard to believe that Zagorin really holds that for example Gay's or Gossman's "summary" of Gibbon's *Decline and Fall* has exactly the same meaning as the original work by Gibbon. If so, we could spare ourselves valuable time by reading only "summaries" instead of the original works. So I suppose Zagorin will allow for *some* differences. But if there will always be differences between the meaning of the original work and its "summaries," which differences in meaning exceed our criteria for the identity of meaning and which do not (so that we are sufficiently justified to speak of an identity of meaning)? Obviously, this problem is precisely what the writing of history (or, in this case, the writing of the history of historical writing) is all about. For example, when Zagorin writes about Hobbes, he gives us a "paraphrase" or "summary" of Hobbes's work he thinks to have roughly the same meaning as the original. Other students of Hobbes provide us with different "paraphrases" also pretending to reproduce "the meaning" of that great man's work. Identity of meaning is not a *given* here, but a *problem*. So I am afraid that when Zagorin colloquially speaks about "paraphrases" that summarize "a work of history without altering its substance or meaning" he begs the question precisely at the point where vague speculation ends and history (or the history of historical writing) takes off.

I object, moreover, to this idea of the identity of "the meaning" of Gibbon's *Decline and Fall* and that of, for example, Gossman's brilliant study of that work. All we have are strings of words and sentences in books like Gibbon's on the one hand and interpretations of these strings of words and sentences (including the one of the author himself) on the other. If we speak about "the meaning" of Gibbon's *Decline and Fall* we do, in fact, refer to one of these interpretations (in most cases proudly announced to be identical with the one of Gibbon himself), but not to some hidden essence in Gibbon's work. This hidden essence, which one often has in mind when speaking of "the meaning of Gibbon's work," is epistemologically just as useless a notion as the notion of "the" past we discussed a moment ago – it is another Wittgensteinian wheel in the machine that drives nothing itself. I am not being unduly relativistic or cynical about the historical profession here; I merely state how things are and that meaningful debate in the historical profession can both be conducted and analyzed philosophically without having recourse to this kind of epistemological sop.

Elsewhere Zagorin stresses that "the need for integration and synthesis [is] greater and more important than ever before." I entirely agree: I am as ardent an advocate of historical synthesis and integration as is Zagorin.

But it is not our dreams for a happy future that are the issue here. The issue is whether contemporary historiography moves in the direction of fragmentation rather than synthesis. I see that Zagorin's diagnosis accords with mine when I said that at present fragmentation prevails over synthesis. Since Zagorin is silent about my explanation for this tendency in contemporary historiography (although it happened to be the main thesis of my essay), I suppose we have no argument here.[24]

At the end of his polemic against my essay Zagorin contrasts my views unfavorably with those of Huizinga when the latter urges the historian to conform to all the relevant standards of scientificity. But neither in this essay nor in the one criticized by Zagorin have I recommended that the historian "abandon vigorous cognitive standards, exigent critical methods," and so forth. It was, and still is, my point, however, that when we reach the level of historical interpretation, such standards will be of little help to us. Here we move "beyond," although not "against" such standards of scientificity – a fact I have characterized by speaking of the a-scientificity rather than anti-scientificity of historical writing. . . .

Against Zagorin's well-contrived insinuation that I regard history with contempt I venture to say that my argument that to ask about the use of history is to commit a category mistake testifies to more respect for history than one can attribute to the person, like Zagorin, who believes the question of the utility of history to be a meaningful one. Debates about utility always require a more comprehensive background against which such debates can be settled. But for me history is part of that background and therefore a measuring-staff in questions of utility rather than what is measured.[25]

At the beginning of his argument Zagorin enumerated three characteristics of postmodernism. I wonder whether most postmodernists will recognize themselves in Zagorin's portrait. They will perhaps have their reservations about Zagorin's association of postmodernism with historicism and the belief in historical inevitability. But since the term is vague – a good example of a narrative substance, I would say – and everybody can therefore be his or her own postmodernist, I shall not dispute Zagorin's portrait of postmodernism. However, if I am permitted a similar liberty I would say that for me postmodernism is above all a theory of writing. That is, not so much a theory of interpretation like hermeneutics but a theory of the (unintended) *effects* of interpretative writing as we find these effects in literary theory and, of course, in the writing of history.

Zagorin rejects my claim that in historiography interpretative writing generates ever more writing with the unintended result that all this writing increases rather than diminishes our distance from what the writing is about (a claim I formulated with the statement that historical writing tends to take the place of the past or the text itself). Zagorin also recognizes the phenomenon of historical overproduction, but he prefers to take a more sanguine view of it. He compares the recent explosion in historical writing to the sciences, where the same has happened in the last few decades without causing the kind of unintended side-effects I had observed in the writing of history. However, Zagorin's own account demonstrates that his comparison to the sciences is unwarranted.

My point of departure here is Zagorin's confident assertion that history knows historical interpretations which have "come to be widely accepted" and that finally are universally recognized by historians as "an established part of our understanding of the past." And, innocently, Zagorin adds when referring to this happy consensus: "of course, this may not last." The addition must be an understatement, I suppose, for when Zagorin offers an exposition of the recent history of the debate on Hobbes's political philosophy he presents us with a picture that contradicts his optimistic confidence in the parallelism between history and science. I would like to ask Zagorin to point out to me the science where – as in the debate about Hobbes as depicted by him – for several decades, two, three, or even more mutually incompatible theories coexist more or less peacefully (that is, no scientist has the impression that something unusual or dramatic is taking place), finally all disappearing from the scene in order to make way for a plurality of newer theories, but perhaps only to reappear at some future time when an intelligent revisionist decides to take one of them up again. Apart from a number of resemblances I have no wish to deny, there exist a number of conspicuous differences between the sciences and history that we cannot afford to disregard if we strive for a realistic and unbiased appraisal of the latter. And the fact that Zagorin's scenario of the debate about Hobbes would be utterly inconceivable in one of the sciences is one of those differences.

The difference between history and the sciences that is most relevant in the context of this discussion can be identified if we make use of Bruno Latour's convenient concept of the "black box."[26] In science a black box is a theory that is so universally accepted that no scientist bothers "to open up" the box any more in order to test what the box contains (only on the rare occasion when science gets caught in a complete impasse is one prepared to reconsider the black boxes). Science progresses by the production of black boxes. History, on the other hand, in contrast to what I suppose would be Zagorin's view, knows no black boxes. As his own account of the debate about Hobbes's political philosophy sufficiently shows, discussion did not result there in the production of a black box. That is the explanation of my claim, attacked by Zagorin, that the writing of history generates ever new interpretations without coming to a conclusion (a black box).

But this notion of the black box can be of further use for us. Zagorin says that historical debate (like the one about Hobbes) always develops in close relation with the original text and that historical debate always sends us back to the text (of Hobbes) itself. This is undoubtedly correct: in case of disagreement about interpretations the text *itself* will be the point of departure both for the purpose of the debate itself and for the development of new interpretations. But this fact undermines rather than justifies Zagorin's assertion that historians can test "the validity" (his term) of their interpretations as this is done in the sciences. For scientists settle their disputes by translating them in terms of the black boxes that are accepted by them all; it is to these black boxes that they retrace their disagreement in order to find out who is right and who is wrong (of course, further disagreement may arise about what should be considered the relevant set of black boxes). Physical reality is certainly *no* such black box; black boxes are theories and it is they that are instrumental for scientific progress. In many, though not all, cases an appeal to physical reality will simply beg the question. Consequently, when Zagorin (correctly) points out that historical debate sends us back to the *text* – the historian's counterpart of the physical reality of the scientist – and not to some historical black box, he could not have stated more clearly where to look for the essential difference between history and the sciences.

If, then, there is this difference between the conduct of debate in history and the sciences, we may ask how historians settle their disputes. What is rational argument like in historiography? Once again I appeal to the notion of the narrative substance – and naturally so, since the narrative substance is the embodiment of the kind of insight (I deliberately avoid the word knowledge, because of its affinity with notions like truth, falsity, and so on) characteristic of the writing of history. We can say, then, that in the text the historian aims at the constitution of a linguistic object, the narrative substance, in terms of which he wishes us to understand the past. . . .

I expect that most readers of Zagorin's always fair and pertinent critique of my essay will have concluded that I had maneuvered myself into a pretty hopeless position and that there would be left to me little more than an idle attempt to rescue some debris from the wreckage. I hope that this reply will have convinced those readers that my case is not quite so hopeless as they initially had thought. To the extent that I have been successful in this, it is proof of the necessity to postulate the logical entity I have called the narrative substance. That narrative language has the ontological status of being an object; that it is opaque; that it is self-referential; that it is intensional and, hence, intrinsically aestheticist; that the narrative meaning of an (historical) text is undecidable in an important sense of that word and even bears the marks of self-contradiction; that narrative meaning can only be identified in the presence of *other* meaning (intertextuality); that as far as narrative meaning is concerned the text refers but not to a reality outside itself; that criteria of truth and falsity do not apply to historical representations of the past; that we can only properly speak of causes and effects at the level of the statement; that narrative language is metaphorical (tropological) and as such embodies a proposal for how we should see the past; that the historical text is a substitute for the absent past; that narrative representations of the past have a tendency to disintegrate (especially when many rival representations of the past are present);[27] all these postmodernist claims so amazing and even repulsive to the modernist can be given a formal or even "modernist" justification if we are prepared to develop a philosophical logic suitable for dealing with the narrative substance. And "justification" does not have here the connotation of recommendation; it is not my wish to applaud or condemn anything. Narrative logic serves no other purpose than merely to understand.

If, however, the modernist and Zagorin object to the argumentative style of many postmodernists, I shall not disagree with them. It is true that one often finds in postmodernist writings poor and unconvincing argument, superfluous technicalities, and obscure jargon. Moreover, the argumentative nucleus and the length of postmodernist writings are often inversely proportional to each other. In a metaphorical way, the story that in each fat man there is a thin man who wants to get out, is almost paradigmatically true of postmodernism. But I am convinced that underneath the postmodernist fat the thin man really is there and that we ought to listen to him since he can tell us a lot about the (historical) text that we do not yet know and that the modernist never bothered to tell us.

Notes

1 For a catalogue of theoretical statements by classical authors, see F. Wagner, *Geschichtswissenschaft* (Munich, 1966), 8–41.
2 For a development of this theme, see F. R. Ankersmit, *De navel van de geschiedenis* (Groningen, 1990), introduction.
3 H. White, *Metahistory: The Historical Imagination in Nineteenth Century Europe* (Baltimore, 1973), *Tropics of Discourse* (Baltimore, 1978), and *The Content of the Form* (Baltimore, 1978); D. LaCapra, *History and Criticism* (Ithaca and London, 1985); H. Kellner, *Language and Historical Representation* (Madison, 1989); in the last book chapters 1, 3, 7, 8, and 9 are specifically representative of the kind of insights I have in mind here.
4 The surprising thesis that historism was not an attack on, but, on the contrary, a new culminating point in the history of the Enlightened "modernistic" program was defended by Gadamer; see H. G. Gadamer, *Wahrheit und Methode* (Tübingen, 1973), 185–205.
5 If historism is transformed from a theory about historical things like nations, peoples, or individuals into a theory about the linguistic things we use for speaking about these historical things, postmodernism is the result. Postmodernism is the nominalist version of historism.

6 F. R. Ankersmit, *Narrative Logic: A Semantic Analysis of the Historian's Language* (The Hague, 1983), 96–104.

7 I therefore condemn a "postmodernist" approach to the *statement* as can sometimes be found in postmodernist writings. I completely agree with Louch when he criticizes Barthes for the supposed ambiguities that the latter wishes to discover in the greetings: "Monday. Returning tomorrow. Jean Louis." See A. Louch, "Does Deconstruction Make Any Difference?," *Philosophy and Literature* 10 (1986), 330, 331.

8 Ankersmit, *Narrative Logic*, 104–40.

9 Ibid., 116–18.

10 For an exposition of Leibniz's logic as the heart of narrative logic, see Ankersmit, *Narrative Logic*, 140–55.

11 The way the narrative substance organizes knowledge of the past as expressed in individual statements about the past is reminiscent of Cassirer's notion of the symbol. Cassirer attributed to the symbol the transcendental capacity to organize the manifold of experience into the unity of perception that Kant had always attributed to the transcendental self. See S. W. Itzkoff, *Ernst Cassirer: Philosopher of Culture* (Boston, 1977), ch. 4.

12 W. H. Walsh, "Colligatory Concepts in History," in *Studies in the Nature and Teaching of History*, ed. W. H. Burston and D. Thompson (London, 1967); L. O. Mink, *Historical Understanding*, ed. Brian Fay, Eugene O. Golob, and Richard T. Vann (Ithaca and London, 1987); see especially chs 2, 3, 6, and 9.

13 M. Oakeshott, *Experience and Its Modes* (Cambridge, 1978), ch. 3; L. Goldstein, *Historical Knowing* (Austin and London, 1976); and *The Constitution of the Historical Past, History and Theory, Beiheft* 16 (1977); M. Stanford, *The Nature of Historical Knowledge* (New York, 1987), 114–15.

14 F. R. Ankersmit, "The Use of Language in the Writing of History," in *Working with Language*, ed. H. Coleman (Berlin, 1989), 57–83.

15 Speaking generally, one could say that we should use the words true and false only with regard to the narrative's statements. From this general rule should be excluded, however, statements containing the names of narrative substances. On the other hand, it would be pedantic to forbid the use of the words true and false in the case of very simple narratives. See Ankersmit, *Narrative Logic*, 178, 179.

16 F. de Saussure, *Course in General Linguistics*, translated and annotated by Roy Harris (London, 1983), 113.

17 A. C. Danto, *Analytical Philosophy of History* (Cambridge, 1968), 155; F. R. Ankersmit, *Denken over geschiedenis* (Groningen, 1986), 160–3.

18 Danto, *Analytical Philosophy*, 156.

19 A brilliant synthesis of the latest developments in theoretical thought about causal explanation with the latest developments in socioeconomic history is C. L. Lorenz, *De constructie van het verleden* (Amsterdam, 1987).

20 Ankersmit, *Narrative Logic*, 154–5. See also M. Mandelbaum, *The Anatomy of Historical Knowledge* (London, 1977), 49–53 for a similar argument.

21 Ankersmit, *Narrative Logic*, 144.

22 N. Goodman, *Ways of Worldmaking* (Hassocks, 1978), 26. Needless to say, it does not follow that *all* differences in style are differences in content and vice versa: "only *some* features of what is said count as aspects of style; only certain characteristic differences in what is said constitute differences in style." See Goodman, *Worldmaking*, 26, 27.

23 H. White, "Michel Foucault," in *Structuralism and Since*, ed. J. Sturrock (Oxford, 1979), 81–116; N. Kellner, "Disorderly Conduct: Braudel's Mediterranean Satire," *History and Theory* 18 (1979), 187–222, reprinted in *Language and Historical Representation* (Madison, 1989), 153–89.

24 For another approach to this fragmentation of the historical discipline, see F. R. Ankersmit, *The Reality Effect in the Writing of History* (Amsterdam, 1989).

25 For an interesting attempt to link the problem of the use of history to that of the role of values in the writing of history, see C. Lorenz, "Het gewicht van de geschiedenis: Over het waardeprobleem in de geschiedwetenschap," *Kennis en methode* 14 (1990), 129–63.

26 B. Latour, *Science in Action* (Stony Stratford, 1987), especially the introduction.

27 For an explanation of this tendency of narrative representations to disintegrate, see F. R. Ankersmit, "Het verhaal in de filosofie," in *Op verhaal komen*, ed. F. R. Ankersmit, M. C. Doeser, and A. Kibédi Varga (Kampen, 1990).

Part V

Representation and Trauma

12

"Never Again" is Now

Hans Kellner

Approaching the Beth Emet synagogue in Evanston, Illinois in the fall of 1993 on the occasion of my niece's Bat Mitzvah, I saw on a large sign in front of the building the words, "'Never Again' is Now." These words offer a compact expression of the contradictions and disruptions, paradoxes and aporias of representation and the Holocaust. Put simply, the notion of non-repetition ("Never Again") filling an eternal present ("is Now"), which is, in part, what I take the words to mean, poses questions about time that are hard to answer.

Obviously, no formal linguistic understanding of "'Never Again' is Now" can do more than hint at their sense as discourse. Unpacking the semantic contents of "Never Again" would be an enormous task. Suffice it to say that this phrase, despite its non-imperative form as a speech act, orders someone to resolve that something shall not happen for a second time. The someone, in the first instance, is a Jew; the something is usually called the Holocaust. Involved in these words is the biblical imperative of memory, *Zakhor*, derived from the crucial order in Deuteronomy 5:15, "And remember that thou wast a servant in the land of Egypt, and that the Lord thy God brought thee out thence through a mighty hand and by a stretched out arm." This command to remember a past event is cited as justification for remembering to observe the Sabbath, a ritual present as a figure of eternity. The previous injunction to remember the Sabbath, in the earlier rendition of the commandments in Exodus, contains no such imperative of *historical* remembrance. The command to repeat thus appears at a point of repetition ("remember the Sabbath," again). And this repeated historical remembrance (a repetition by definition), retold each Passover, has a specific function: to remind Jews of God's past and future intervention on their behalf. The tension between this originary call to commemorate and the memory invoked by the words "Never Again" is the source of the problem explored in these essays on historical representation and the Holocaust. The words "Never Again" do not cause us much difficulty. In any community of discourse that I know, they are self-evident. The "is Now," however, creates a problem. It makes present over and over the event that must not happen again. Why do this? Why do this especially if the resultant representations are so problematic, so likely to fail and to be condemned as failures? Both fictional and historical representations are dreamlike in that they express some sort of desire, in all the complexity of that term. The pressing need to represent the Holocaust in poetry, novels, films, drama, music, and history must come from a desire to repeat in the imagination happenings and events that horrify and fascinate. We only represent what we desire. The desire to represent the Holocaust, however, is not the desire to repeat it as an event, nor necessarily the desire to repeat the form-giving pleasure of representation itself; rather, it is a desire to repeat the Holocaust in a suitably altered form to meet complex, often contradictory, sets of present needs. It is the power of these needs, often unrecognized and elusive, that drives the process, and, in my opinion, creates the problem. Once we acknowledge the reality of need and desire in representations of the past, we are open to the tacit contrast of the weight of the event represented and the weight of present desires. It is the overwhelming sense of imbalance between the Holocaust and any interest in it that leads to the quest for limits to representation, which is actually a reproach to the consuming power of discursive desire. The limits of representation are the limits of desire and of the present. These are very hard to limit.

The Holocaust puts constraints upon the libidinal aspect of representation. Guilt arises at every turn, whether turned upon a missing enemy or upon the audience or upon representation. Somehow, all the elements of the representation are inadequate to what is represented. The enemy is too banal, the audience too forgetful, the genre too aesthetic. Because we are a historical society, the Holocaust must become historical for its memory to survive. The changeless repetitions of ritual will not suffice. Memorialization must ultimately be in language. Even when the memorials take the form of photographs or museum objects, their sense will depend upon a discourse that articulates them. Language, however, or rather the discourse language prompts, destroys the memorializing function it makes possible. The risks of putting something into discourse, into free discussion and representation, however governed, are palpable. It is as much the fear of these risks as the desire for the benefits of historical representation that motivates historical culture. According to Jacques Le Goff: "To make themselves the master of memory and forgetfulness is one of the great preoccupations of the classes, groups, and individuals who have dominated and continue to dominate historical societies."[1]

It is the nature of an active historical culture to revise. Each new contribution to the discourse (and this means each new career, each new publishing venture) must acquire its own identity by foregrounding those features which deform and challenge the sense of the material. What had before been keenly felt recedes to the status of the background, effaced and unnoticed. Its familiarity has made it difficult to see. To be brought to life, or at least to the simulacrum of life that makes possible academic or even popular publication, the material will have to be reshaped, and this, in turn, means revision. The alternative is ritual, and even ritual is always open to the demands of the present. After all, did not Armistice Day, in honor of a specific historical memory, become Veteran's Day, in honor of an interest group? In time, the event is generalized, ritualized, and lost.

According to this pattern, Decoration Day gave way to Memorial Day as the last old men in gray or blue vanished from the parades to decorate the Confederate or Union graves. As the survivors pass, the dangers of representation become most intense. The highest ethical/rhetorical position in Holocaust representations belongs to the survivor.[2] The intense listening to the words of the survivor parallels the interest Roland Barthes ascribed to the photograph – "that, there it is, lo!"[3] Like Barthes looking at a photograph of Jerome Bonaparte and thinking that these eyes saw the Emperor, one listens to a Holocaust survivor. The text is written on the body there, and not on the page. How can one say that one has *read* about the Holocaust after watching Claude Lanzmann's *Shoah*?[4] Yet here is another example of the paradoxical, self-consuming nature of representations of the Holocaust. The rhetorical role of the Holocaust survivor is to quiet talk. The literary critic and Holocaust survivor Ruth Klüger notes her reluctance to enter conversations on the subject because no one will talk once she speaks: "At that time I always thought I would have something interesting and important to tell after the war. But people don't want to hear it, or only in a certain pose or attitude – not as a conversational partner but rather as those who must submit to an unpleasant task with a kind of reverence that easily turns into disgust, two feelings that complement each other. For objects of reverence as with objects of disgust, we keep at arm's length."[5] By seeming to shift the center of discussion from the inescapable moment of its happening (the telling) to the absent moment of the event (what is told), the survivor bears witness to the imbalance between the two and the relative triviality of any present need to speak. The witness feels that the audience will certainly not understand.[6] Raul Hilberg puts the matter this way at the beginning of an article entitled, "I Was Not There": " 'If you were not there, you cannot imagine what it was like.' These words were said to me in Dusseldorf some years ago by a one-legged veteran of the German army who had been trapped in the Demyansk pocket on the Russian front at the end of 1941. The man had been wounded six times. One cannot deny that he had a valid point."[7] Hilberg, the distinguished historian of the destruction of the European Jews, uses this tale to begin his reflections on the ethics of writing about the Holocaust. He mentions the risk involved in taking any license with the "crude reality"; the rules of representation as they have evolved in forty years entail a generous use of silence, and an aesthetic of minimalism.[8] Saying less apparently says more. Or does it merely lessen risk and responsibility?

The tacit presumption by writers and readers of history is that the magnitude of an event is dependent upon the magnitude of its cause. Great events have great causes, and chance is unacceptable on moral grounds.[9] Battle history is held in low esteem because it so often seems to hinge upon the courage or ineptness of small groups of soldiers, or of one. "All for the want of a horseshoe nail," goes the old rhyme, and few are willing to believe that kingdoms may be lost so trivially.[10] To believe that would remove one from the realm of linear understanding, the linear equations that describe its operation, and the linear narrative force of its explanations. Yet, as Donald McCloskey has recently suggested in this journal, the mathematics of nonlinearity reinforces the possibility of an absurd disproportion, an unpredictability of cause and effect: "As students of chaos theory since Poincaré have pointed out, simple models can generate astonishingly complicated patterns. The slightest perturbation can yield an entirely different history. (And in catastrophe theories, quickly.)"[11] McCloskey may jibe that "one does not avoid nonlinearities by not knowing what they are called," but I think that this is precisely what is avoided.[12] It is the diction, the speech register, the decorum of mathematics that rules it out of historical consideration for matters outside the griminess of economics. Humans are presumed to live stories, not equations.

This problem is called to mind by the exchange of letters between Hannah Arendt and Karl Jaspers shortly after World War II. Arendt: "The Nazi crimes, it seems to me, explode the limits of the law, and that is precisely what constitutes their monstrousness. For these crimes, no punishment is severe enough. It may be essential to hang Goering, but it is totally inadequate. That is, the guilt, in contrast to all criminal guilt, oversteps and shatters any and all legal systems. That is the reason why the Nazis in Nuremberg are so smug."[13] What is the law that Arendt believed was exploded, overstepped, and shattered by the actions of the defendants at Nuremberg? Why did she feel that hanging Goering was inadequate? Surely she did not have a more theatrical treatment, like public torture, in mind. Her expressed frustration, I think, was that no available conclusion to the drama was adequate to the events. The stage of representation offered by the Nuremberg courtroom and its noose was absurdly disproportionate to the acts represented. In wishing to emplot the events of the Holocaust as beyond emplotment, she dreamed of an imaginary mode of representation that would place the characters and their deeds in a proper relation to reality.

But no such mode of representation existed, as Jaspers knew, and prudent wisdom must see things within the bounds and psychological necessities of audience expectations. So Jaspers replied, "a guilt that goes beyond all criminal guilt inevitably takes on a streak of 'greatness' – of satanic greatness – which is, for me, as inappropriate for the Nazis as all the talk about the 'demonic' element in Hitler and so forth." Jaspers saw immediately that the situation was literary. The cast of characters at Nuremberg would be seen in a context of culturally available models; above all, he wanted to deny them the grandeur of the Miltonic Satan or of Goethe's "demon." The great revenge he proposed would be that of the critic, to deny any stature at all to the actors. "It seems to me that we have to see these things in their total banality, in their prosaic triviality, because that's what truly characterizes them. Bacteria can cause epidemics that wipe out nations, but they remain merely bacteria. I regard any hint of myth and legend with horror, and everything unspecific is just such a hint." And, to be sure, Arendt took his point. Evil in her Eichmann book would be banal. The furor over the "banality of evil" that dominated Holocaust discussions in the 1960s derived from the point McCloskey makes, that we take as a historical given that great events have great causes. But horseshoe nails or brave junior officers at key places on a battlefield at crucial moments may decisively change the course of things, assuming that things have a course.

Hilberg stresses that the most important fact about the Holocaust was its unexpectedness. This is an essential part of history, which I have described elsewhere as its "terror."[14] What is particular about the Holocaust, as opposed to the Terror of the French Revolution, is not that it was unforeseen (almost everything is), but that it cannot be made to seem inevitable through narrativization. It is hard to make any story that accounts for this event; perhaps it is misleading to try.[15] Challenging the rhetoric of "large causes – large effects," even the logic of cause and effect itself, the Holocaust is a scandal for rational representation. A writer about the Holocaust will either be seen as adding what does not belong, or omitting something that does. The unprocessed oral reports of witnesses will tell us many things, but not about the Holocaust, because no one witnessed the Holocaust.

So the question arises whether a special kind of representation may be found, suitable for coping with the special nature of this event. Berel Lang and Hayden White have separately posed this question. Implicitly acknowledging the "rules" cited by Hilberg, they see the key to preserving the "responsible," "proper" representations of the Holocaust in maintaining a restricted discourse before it. This is what Lang and White call for in their advocacies of a literalism and a writerly intransitivity, respectively.[16] Something must be silenced, and each of them conceives of that something as a form of language use.

White finds in the ancient Greek grammatical form of the "middle voice" a possible way of avoiding the unwanted intrusion of the subject into the action it wants to represent. In this form, "the subject is presumed to be interior to the action."[17] As he works it out, the rhetorical stance of the middle voice asserts the disappearance of the writer, dissolution of any point of view outside the work, the questioning of epistemological assumptions, and the use of chance characteristic of modernist writing. In short, it seems to be the sort of modernist historiography that he has called for since *History and Theory* published "The Burden of History" in 1966.

White's suggestion that a certain sort of language found under the heading of modernism is available which might prove suitable for putatively *special sorts of events* is challenging. The essence of intransitive writing seems to be that it erases the separation of subject and object that dominates the terminology of linguistic "voice" in normal usage. Active voice ("I kick you") and passive voice ("I am being kicked" [by you]) both separate the world from the position of the speaker as he or she speaks. There are, however, ways of seeing the world that efface the distinction and create a more fluid sense of things. To use an analogy, Barry Manilow sings "I write the songs" actively; a passive phrasing (and reversal of perspective) of this would be "I am written by the songs" or perhaps "The songs write (me?)"; a middle-voiced phrasing would be "I am the song and it (I) is (am) writing me (it)." This last example, which is not so absurd as it seems when seen in a Heideggerian context in which "language speaks," throws attention on the being of the agents (subject, object) and their mutual involvement in the historical moment of writing.

The middle voice of ancient Greek is far older than the passive, a latecomer in Indo-European languages. It corresponds somewhat to modern reflexive sentences ("I am washing myself") or it may be transitive in a certain way (as in the Greek *loúomai khitôna*, "I am washing [my] shirt," or the French *Je me lave une chemise*, "I am washing [myself] a shirt"). Thus, there are two forms of middle voice.

> From the glosses that have been attached to some of the examples it will be clear that the subject of the "middle" can be interpreted as "non-agentive" or "agentive" according to the context or the meaning of the verb; and, if the subject is taken as "non-agentive," it can also be identified in certain instances with the object of a corresponding transitive sentence in the active voice. Under these conditions, the distinction between the middle and the passive is neutralized.[18]

White seems to want a poststructuralist version of the middle voice, which will not give way to the passive under the pressure of context. (The linguist Lyons's example of this is the middling "I am getting [myself] shaved" becoming the passive "I am being shaved.") White's version suggests rather that the intransitivity of the middle voice is the answer to Yeats's question "How can we tell the dancer from the dance?" by denoting that the ambiguity derives from a poor fit between reality and language. There is an undecidability here which can be glossed only by changing the terms. (This middle voice would almost be the voice of the Zen Buddhist who told the hot dog vendor, "Make me one with everything.")

When Roland Barthes put the concept of the middle voice into circulation among literary theorists at the fabled Johns Hopkins structuralism conference in 1966, he was immediately interrogated by members of his audience. Jean-Pierre Vernant posed (and answered) the question why the middle voice had in effect died out in most Western languages. Vernant's answer had to do with responsibility and the developing Greek sense of self (or subjecthood, as one says today):

> The psychological conclusion that Benveniste doesn't draw, because he is not a psychologist, is that in thought as expressed in Greek or ancient Indo-European there is no idea of the agent being the *source* of his action. Or, if I may translate that, as a historian of Greek civilization, there is no category of the *will* in Greece. But what we see in the Western world, through language, the evolution of law, the creation of a vocabulary of the will, is precisely the idea of the human subject as agent, the source of actions, creating them, assuming them, carrying responsibility for them.[19]

So I conclude that the middle voice, once a relic from before the birth of the subject, is what may be spoken again after the death of the subject, the death of the author, and so forth, these "deaths" being understood as the figural signs of an awareness of the historicity of discourse and the situated nature of any speech act.[20] In fact, if one acknowledges the social construction of the self and reality, or at least their effective linguistic construction as we can know them, all utterances may be understood as middle-voiced, even when they are not explicitly so. For example, Caesar's "all Gaul is divided into three parts" might be read as "Gaul is having its tripartite being hailed here, now." (Is this the same Hayden White who wrote, "But the moral implications of the human sciences will never be perceived until the faculty of the will is reinstated in theory"?)[21] The will finds its expression in rhetoric, which is entailed in any use of language which involves free choice among socially sanctioned alternatives. The will and the restricted middle voice find themselves in tension.

White cites Art Spiegelman's *Maus: A Survivor's Tale*, a comic strip account of a man's confrontation with his father and his father's experience of the Holocaust and Auschwitz. Although White does not associate *Maus* with the middle voice he is promoting, I suggest that it is an instructive example of the middle-voiced *stance* White advocates. Spiegelman is both the author of his work and a character in it. The subject is both the Holocaust and the process of writing about it; within the text, there is no distinguishing between the two because each intrudes upon the other constantly. Spiegelman, one might say, is neither active nor passive. He does not create his tale (and yet he does), but it does not happen to him (and yet it does). He is part of the event of its creation, which changes him. His evidence, his father, is difficult; their relationship is not at all objective or stable. Memory and its vagaries plays a role at every turn. The story is Spiegelman's and it is not. It is his father's, and it is not. The willful authority of these figures is present in the narrative, but it is always questioned and undermined. Finally, as I read it, the story of *Maus* and its sequel becomes no one's story, but without asserting a falsifiable claim to objective realism.

Writing the kind of self-reflexive history that places the historian in the moment – or better, process – of creating the historical text, enacting the work of research, has its current exemplars and theoreticians. Robert Rosenstone's *Mirror in the Shrine: American Encounters with Meiji Japan* (Cambridge, Mass., 1988) begins with his encounter with Japan, and contrasts his feelings and experiences confronting the foreignness of Japan with those of his chosen texts. Linda Orr describes her emotional and sensual responses to the mildewed, crumbling books she discusses in *Headless History: Nineteenth-Century French Historiography of the Revolution*. This work is a full-length account of the reflexivity of romantic French historiography, and a thoughtful presentation of the paradoxes and ironies of authority.

> Seen from the "mimetic" perspective by which the representation of the real gets its legitimacy from a possible coincidence (word with object, word with signification), the author assumes a position of authority second only to reality, which occupies the sovereign position. In the beginning a simple mediator of the real, the author eventually seizes all power, since the real in question appears only by his or her doing. But let us invert this mimetic view of representation. Without looking any different on the outside, the once established hierarchy of power is turned inside out. (Roland Barthes's short essay "Historical Discourse" is a good example of this exercise.) If the hypothetical center is now the text, no matter how unstable, upon which the characters, both narrator and narratee, depend, then author and reader also assume an identity by the effect of the text. They occupy a position whose insignificance is exceeded only by the real itself, a projection both phantasmatic and material, that derives its legitimacy from rhetoric and language. The figure of the author, after the exercise of inversion, refers

then to a space opened up by the narrative. It is a metaphorical space that this narrative, however, cannot grasp – but that gives the author ostensible authority, parental authenticity.[22]

Although few historians since Michelet have participated in the hypothetical extremes of textual inversion that Orr describes, there has been a noticeable change in authorial practice. Philippe Carrard notes in his recent *Poetics of the New History* that there has been a general relaxation of the classic positivist rules restricting the presence of the scholar in the historical enunciation. "They [the changes] point to a questioning of the possibility of objective knowledge, and, since this questioning started in the early twentieth century, to the lag between rhetoric and epistemology: the now commonplace argument that all knowledge is grounded in a subject keeps being made in the human sciences (and in this very sentence) through a rhetoric which signals the researcher's reluctance to leave marks of his involvement, or even his hope of dispensing with them altogether."[23] What we have here is a willed choice on the part of those who are calling the will into question, a rhetorical stance assumed in order to annul the privilege of the rhetorical subject. The moment represented must be the moment of representation. The distance between the knower and what is known dissolves somewhat through refocusing. Representing the Holocaust becomes representing "coming to know the Holocaust." At least, this is the illusion offered by the new rhetoric that enacts the grammatical function of the old middle voice.

White, I suspect, understands the voracious dynamism of professional history, its need to recreate the past as a set of ever-varied commodities, and its absolute inadequacy as a memorializing force of any kind. It would be then his genuine wish to protect a certain image of the Holocaust that impels him to suggest the enormous self-restraints of middle-voiced writing as suitable to that event. This is not, however, his stated reason – namely, that some social and institutional changes in modernity have made this mode of writing appropriate to certain kinds of subjects. To pursue this notion, borrowed from Erich Auerbach, would harken back to sixty-year-old visions of correspondences between social structures, events, and aesthetic forms. Lukács *redivivus*! It would imply that there is a language of translation (in every era?) by which events may be made into discourse responsibly. *Metahistory*, however, effectively denies this possibility, noting "elective affinities" only among discursive options, but not between those options and something outside discourse, not even "events, such as the Holocaust, which are themselves 'modernist' in nature."[24] Furthermore, while one might call an event "modernist," following the postmodern trend of aestheticizing history, it is surely wrong to call an event " 'modernist' in nature."[25]

The philosopher Berel Lang also proposes a special status for the Holocaust, as an event that virtually speaks for itself, at least in the

sense that its *literal* presentation will constitute an adequate account
of the event, an account that does not lessen its moral weight by the
intrusion of rhetorical decisions.

> Whatever else it does, figurative discourse and the elaboration of figur-
> ative space obtrudes the author's voice and a range of imaginative turns
> and decisions on the literary subject, irrespective of that subject's char-
> acter and irrespective of – indeed defying – the "facts" of that subject
> which might otherwise have spoken for themselves and which at the very
> least, do not depend on the author's voice for their existence. The claim
> is entailed in imaginative representation that the facts *do not* speak for
> themselves, that figurative condensation and displacement and the author-
> ial presence these articulate will turn or supplement the historical subject
> (whatever it is) in a way that represents the subject more compellingly
> or effectively – in the end, more truly – than would be the case without
> them.[26]

Lang claims that the "Final Solution" is one instance (he suggests no
others) of an event that challenges the premise that all representation is
a figural work of the imagination. He justifies this conclusion by asserting that figural language and emplotment contradict the "denial of individuality and personhood" and the "abstract bureaucracy" of evil that
characterize the event. A literal "chronicle" lessens the risks entailed in
any historical representation.

Lang's suggestion – that in some cases the facts speak for themselves
– runs so drastically against the stream of current opinion on historical
representation that one hesitates to restate the case against it, a case
with which he is certainly familiar. Lang understands chronicle to be
"foundational" for historiography, and believes that an emphasis on
chronicle rather than the fully figured narrative emplotment, which
he takes to be logically subsequent to chronicle, will provide the sort
of representation that will avoid the risks and disruptions inherent in
discourse. But this is mistaken. A chronicle is the result of a pre-existing
narrative; it is not the origin of such a narrative. For example, Andreas
Hillgruber's notorious *Zweierlei Untergang*, which parallels somewhat
the respective plights of the Jews and the displaced Eastern Germans,
contains a very different chronicle of facts from Hilberg's *Destruction of
the European Jews*.[27] Hilberg wanted to tell a different story. To object
that one might sort out a proper chronicle from even Hilberg's work is
simply to reiterate that chronicles depend on pre-existing narratives that
tell us which facts are proper and which are not.

The troubles even of naming the events point to the issue at hand:
Holocaust, Greek for a sacrificial burnt offering with Homeric overtones; "Final Solution," a bitterly ironic assumption of the Nazi's language; Shoah, with the defamiliarization of a word from a language
that was the vernacular of virtually none of the participants in the event,

and generalized by a work of cinematic art. All of these terms are figural, imaginative, literary. "The destruction of the European Jews," Raul Hilberg's title, is the simplest, most literal of all, and perhaps the most effective in its minimal descriptiveness. That effectiveness, however, is aesthetic. It indeed possesses the sparse, modernist decorum now deemed suited to the event, reminding us that decorum is a fluid social convention. Even literality is the handmaiden of rhetoric. When Hayden White notes, "In point of fact I do not think that the Holocaust, Final Solution, Shoah, Churban, or German genocide of the Jews is any more unrepresentable than any other event in human history," his list of names tells us the problem.[28] There are too many possible and competing representations of these events. This new literalism seems today not so much a return to "the positivist paradigm" Carrard describes at the beginning of *The Poetics of the New History*.[29] It seems instead a sort of postmodern literalism, a self-critical (or self-deconstructing, if you will) literalism that points querulously to its own impossibility.

Ironically, in one example the literality that Lang has in mind is of a special, mimetic sort. He writes of the Holocaust literature that does not exist, the works from Vilna, Prague, Warsaw, or Vienna that might have existed had the Holocaust not taken place. "Their absence," he comments, "remains in fact the most closely literal representation of the Holocaust."[30] Since representation requires a presence, we would ordinarily say that the presence of an absence represents the absence of a presence. We do not know the titles of the works we do not have, but we know that those works would have existed. It was Isaac Babel who described this as a "genre of silence," but historians know it as the *argumentum ex silentio*. John Lange, in his essay "The Argument from Silence," emphasized the risks of this traditional strategy of historical logic, concluding that historians must still rely on their hunches, skill, and good sense, but surely his reasoning would be misapplied to Lang's statement.[31] There is an intuitive certainty that the "genre of silence" exists that overrides any of the probabilities suggested by analysis.

Of course, it is possible that there is a certain form of discourse that is appropriate for a certain kind of event, and one should not rule this out. Freud suggested that, at times, the subject of writing takes command of the writing subject, but his description of this does not bode well for any hope to control the process: "But one cannot always carry out one's reasonable intentions. There is often something in the material itself which takes charge of one and diverts one from one's first intentions. Even such a trivial achievement as the arrangement of a familiar piece of material is not entirely subject to an author's own choice; it takes what line it likes and all one can do is to ask oneself after the event why it has happened in this way and no other."[32] It is hard to imagine a topic more likely than the Holocaust to tap some unconscious source, with unpredictable results. Things do not turn out as planned.

If the Holocaust requires a certain form of discourse, however, there is no way of proving it, one way or the other. Such an idea also runs counter to White's project of the last twenty years, as I understand it. For this reason, I attribute his advocacy of a subject-effacing middle voice and Lang's call for an unfigured chronicle to an act of will, and a revealing one. These attempts to silence a certain aspect of the full narrative voice bespeak a fear, but I think a different one from the fears expressed by Lang and White. The threat to a "responsible" representation of the Holocaust, this ostensibly modern event, is modern, responsible historical scholarship.

Martin Jay correctly identifies the missing ingredient in most of the discussions of historical representations, namely, the reader. By reader here I mean, although Jay does not, anyone who has experienced a representation of some part of the past, whether a scholar who has studied, say, the Holocaust, or a student being taught about it in school or the mass media, or even someone who has the vaguest sense (what "everybody knows") that "Hitler" did something "bad" to the Jews. Any intended representation of the Holocaust will have an intended audience. That audience, which is always an imaginary and often unconscious construction of the author, will be expected to make sense and grasp the intended force of the representation that is aimed at it.[33]

Creating a reader for the Holocaust has been the work of writers, artists, filmmakers, poets, and historians since the end of the war. As Jay notes, there was no Holocaust for anyone to experience or witness; it was an imaginative creation, like all historical events.[34] The witness to a massacre is a witness to a massacre, a participant in a meeting may tell what he saw and heard. The events we have named Babi Yar or Wannsee, however, are not the Holocaust, nor even part of it until it has been imaginatively constituted. Creating the event means creating the reader who will recognize the event as an event when it is presented, and who can then follow its course according to the prevailing conventions of readability.[35] No writer can be sure of his audience, however. Genre, *topoi*, emplotment are the traditional formal devices of rhetoric that are supposed to secure the adherence of a reader to a vision of the subject. We expect a different protocol from what announces itself as a novel than from a film, or an academic history. We expect to see perpetrators and victims differentiated, atrocities linked together, concepts defined and exemplified. We expect that certain events will not be made comic or absurd; we object when certain events are made tragic. Use of the old, the expected, secures the creation of the new by making its novelty nevertheless recognizable as meaning.

This rhetorical constitution of events depends for its existence on the social codes that prevail in a group, a time, a place. The signs of gravity, clarity, and sense that are appropriate to a subject are given in advance, and the creation of meaning in discourse is indeed, as Jay puts it, a negotiation among a number of forces. Among these, I suggest, are the

factual material itself (which has already been constituted by a negotiation with other forces); the intention of the author (never to be ignored,
but far from dominant); the resources of discourse that govern authorial
choices; and the reading expectations of the audience (which is constituted ideally in the text long before the unpredictable appearance of any
actual reader). Formal possibilities and the social institutions that guide
them create the verisimilitude of real events, especially of such real events
that seem as untrue to real – that is, imaginable – life as the Holocaust.
Jay, however, follows Carlo Ginzburg in expressing an unwillingness to
accept that the meaningfulness of our truth is a product of an enormously complex and diffuse cultural process. Or, to put it another way,
Jay admits that this is indeed the case, but places his faith in *one of the
social institutions* that creates the standard of verisimilitude. He asserts
that the historical profession, with all its faults and limitations, raises
knowledge above the merely conventional, at least in terms of the verification of facts, by relentless institutional criticism.

Let us suppose that the profession of history in a non-totalitarian
world functions more or less as it represents itself. It certifies the skills
and standards of its members through granting degrees; it informally
designates the hierarchy of prestige and reputations that determines professional credibility; it culls published material for errors of documentation or false inferences. It is able to maintain its control of justified
belief: what the consensus of professional historians believe to be the best
information and judgment is taken to be the best information and judgment. Most importantly, this process is dynamic; the work of criticism
is ongoing. This is how the system is supposed to work, and I believe
that it does, for the most part. The critical dynamism of the profession
is driven by professionalism itself, the need to make careers. Proximate
truth results from constant historical revision. Rewards exist to keep the
structure moving.

It is the dynamism of the structure, however, that should undermine
any confidence one might place in it of maintaining the memory of
any event whatever. In practice, the profession eats up historical events
through normal professional behavior. Professional historical accounts
do not appear to serve a great or continuous image of what truly, responsibly, properly happened in the past. They are rather sent into a marketplace or exchange of texts where, once they have been admitted by meeting
certain standards, they will be valued precisely to the extent that they
differ from or challenge existing accounts. Every ambitious historian, even
in the bureaucratized and team-oriented feudalism of old world historical
institutions, knows that a name and career are advanced by novelty. At
the most basic level, the doctoral degree is attained by producing something new, and thus different.

Now the most elementary fact about the modern historical profession
is that it produces an enormous amount of discourse. This avalanche
of solid historical work relates less to the past than to other historical

accounts; it must be so because of the vast quantity of material that has to be taken note of to gain entry to the marketplace. The historical work that does not change our view of a given topic by adding information that alters our picture, or by reframing the conventional questions in such a way as to produce a different topic entirely, will not get more than a grudging 750-word notice in the *American Historical Review*. With each successful work things must *change*, if the profession is working as it should. It may be argued that this process must bring us more comprehensive, better documented, and more finely argued representations of past events. There is no question but that this is often the short-term result, especially in regard to events with no immediate impact. For events, however, that have a special pressure within them (and the Holocaust is surely such an event, as was in the 1960s and 1970s the question of the black family in slavery and reconstruction), the research will yield too much, will inevitably stray from any centrality of the event into areas that relate to other aspects of life, will produce nuances and exceptions to any pertinent generalizations, will bring forth schools of interpretation that cannot be reconciled by any possible appeal to evidence because at the heart of the dispute is the question of what shall *be* the appropriate evidence. At a certain point, the question will no longer bear professional reward. The things that are interesting to say will have been said, the possible encodings exhausted for the moment, at least until newer forms of representation are offered (as the large-scale, novelistic narrative offered Gibbon opportunities for considering Roman history that Montesquieu did not use). The centrality of the political will give way to intellectual history which will give way to social history which will give way to group histories, histories of the everyday, or the intimate, of the body, of death. On this process, F. R. Ankersmit has written:

> The logic in this development is that in each phase, with each new set of historical topics, meaning is given to what seemed historically irrelevant, meaningless, static, or belonging to an a-historical domain during a previous phase in the development of historiography. One might say that history always moves *backwards* instead of *forwards*: it does not penetrate deeper into what at a certain phase is seen as the essence of historical reality, but tends to turn away from that essence. Historiography is, to use another metaphor, centrifugal instead of centripetal. What were mere details under a previous dispensation becomes the center or the essence under a later one.[36]

The narrative plots of the Western tradition may pass, along with a focused interest in the history of Europe, of which the Holocaust is unmistakably a part. Certainly, the account given by Peter Novick in *That Noble Dream* (Cambridge, 1988) of the decentering of American historical practice should warn anyone who places his or her faith in professionalism to safeguard any historical subject. It is not that the system of modern research and institutional verification does not work. It works all too well, producing an endless supply of competing verifiable accounts, the significance of which is always in question. The institution in which Martin Jay believes will do its task; it will swallow the event.[37] Raul Hilberg, however, senses the danger of successful historical practice to the desire to memorialize. Echoing Adorno's judgment that it is barbaric to write poetry after Auschwitz, Hilberg suggests that it may be equally barbaric to write footnotes, for historians "usurp history" precisely when they succeed.[38]

If the modern historical profession cannot well serve any memorializing function, nor sustain a stable referent, and if there is no particular form of writing that naturally suits the sort of event exemplified by the Holocaust, then what conclusion must be drawn by someone who sees the ethical truth of the matter in the vow "Never Again?," and who believes that no responsible historical imagination may disregard it? However strong our belief in the transcendent truth of the evil, uniqueness, and centrality of the Holocaust in history, we must confront the fact that this is *our* belief; any efforts to maintain this for the future will be an essentially conservative task to preserve a certain sort of moral community, as Lang calls it, or interpretive community, as a literary critic might.

In a passionate rejection of White's assertion that the truth of an account of an event like the Holocaust would be its political effectiveness, Ginzburg writes: "We must conclude that if [the Holocaust denier Robert] Faurisson's narrative were ever to prove *effective*, it would be regarded by White as true as well."[39] Ginzburg appeals to the authority of just one witness to establish the truth of "things in themselves." But the philosopher of things in themselves gives us no confidence that we can know them other than through faith.

Although I do not care to contradict Ginzburg's moving invocation to the authority of one witness, nor Lyotard's description of the authority of no witnesses at all in *The Differend* (Manchester, 1988), I would cite against them a tale from the Talmud (Baba Metzia 59a–b). Rabbi Eliezer was debating a point of law with the other rabbis, who would not agree with his interpretation. He called upon a carob tree to move a great distance if he were correct. The tree moved, but the rabbis said no proof can come from a carob tree. Rabbi Eliezer then called upon the stream outside to flow backward if he was correct. The stream flowed backward, but the rabbis said no proof can come from a stream. Eliezer then said that if he were correct, the walls of the academy should testify to it. They began to shake, but did not collapse from respect for Rabbi Joshua, an important sage who said to the walls that these disputes were no business of theirs. They leaned, however, from respect for Rabbi Eliezer.

Rabbi Eliezer appealed to heaven, and a heavenly voice replied that he was indeed correct, and that the rabbis should argue no further. But the rabbis did not accept this sign, saying that the Torah is not in heaven, and it proclaims that decisions about its meaning are to be decided by a majority. Eliezer was in a minority, and so did not prevail. Later, one of the rabbis met the prophet Elijah, and asked him how God had reacted to this. Elijah told him that God had laughed, saying, "My children have defeated me."

This tale, as I interpret it, would seem to reinforce the irredeemably earthly and immanent status of interpretation. Even if there were an Elijah to interrogate about divine opinion, the issue is meant to be *our* issue. There is no escape from the risks of representation, no limit that will guarantee any witness. The work must be recommenced within a changing discourse, always differently. And so, with all its paradoxes, "'Never Again' is Now."

Notes

1 Jacques Le Goff, *History and Memory*, trans. Steven Rendall and Elizabeth Claman (New York, 1992), 54.

2 The use of the term "survivor" in popular psychology to describe a person who has not been somehow destroyed by individual difficulties is an index of how worn down from use the term has become. Indeed, the expression "I'm a survivor" may well describe no particular experience at all, being simply an index of toughness with a touch of paranoia.

3 Roland Barthes, *Camera Lucida: Reflections on Photography*, trans. Richard Howard (New York, 1981), 5.

4 In *Holocaust Testimonies: The Ruins of Memory* (New Haven, 1991), Lawrence Langer contrasts Filip Müller's autobiographical *Eyewitness Auschwitz: Three Years in the Gas Chambers* [1979] (New York, 1984) with his oral testimony in Lanzmann's documentary. The written word contains reflections that have no unmediated oral spontaneity. Langer writes: "Beyond dispute in oral testimony is that every word falls directly from the lips of the witness. Not as much can be said for written survivor testimony that is openly or silently edited. Whether this seriously limits the value of some written memoirs is a question that still needs to be investigated" (Langer, *Holocaust Testimonies*, 210). Yet aside from the philosophical (Derrida) and linguistic (Bakhtin) objections to Langer's faith in the immediacy of the words falling from the lips of the witnesses, he promptly adds that Lanzmann had painstakingly edited away Müller's stammer "with a technological dexterity that must have been nothing short of Herculean" (ibid.)

5 Ruth Klüger, *Weiter leben: Eine Jugend* (Göttingen, 1992), 110.

6 Langer, *Holocaust Testimonies*, xiii.

7 Raul Hilberg, "I Was Not There," in *Writing and the Holocaust*, ed. Berel Lang (New York, 1988), 17.

8 Ibid., 23.

9 Kant expresses this idea, believing that chance or chaos in history essentially devalues the status of humanity: "It is a vain affair to have good so alternate

with evil that the whole traffic of our species with itself on this globe would have to be considered as a mere farcical comedy, for this can endow our species with no greater values in the eyes of reason than that which other animal species possess, species which carry on this game with fewer costs and without expenditure of thought." Immanuel Kant, "An Old Question Raised Again: Is the Human Race Constantly Progressing?" in *On History*, ed. L. W. Beck (Indianapolis, 1963), 141.

10 Donald N. McCloskey, "History, Differential Equations, and the Problem of Narration," *History and Theory* 30 (1991), 25–6.

11 Ibid., 28.

12 Ibid., 36.

13 *Arendt-Jaspers Correspondence*, cited in Gordon A. Craig, "Letters on Dark Times," *New York Review of Books* (May 13, 1993), 12.

14 Hans Kellner, "Beautifying the Nightmare: The Aesthetics of Postmodern History," *Strategies: A Journal of Theory, Culture, and Politics* 4–5 (1991), 289–313.

15 Klüger: "Already at that time, a thought struck me and is unfortunately still deeply impressed upon me more than the indignation about the great atrocity, namely the consciousness of the absurdity of the whole thing, the nonsensical about it, the complete senselessness of those murders and deportations, which we call the Final Solution, Holocaust, Jewish catastrophe, and recently Shoah – always new names because the words for it very quickly rot in our mouths. The absurdity, unreasonableness of it, how easily it could have been avoided, how nobody profited from my carrying tracks [and] railroad ties instead of sitting at a school bench, and the role that coincidence had in it. I don't mean that I don't understand how it came about. At least I know as much as others about the backgrounds. But this knowledge doesn't explain anything. We recount on our fingers what went on before and rely upon the fact that the radical Other occurred out of those events. Everyone before our time who drew attention to himself in Germany must be accountable. Then it was Bismarck and Nietzsche and the Romantics and even Luther, who supposedly created the preliminary conditions for the great genocide of our century. But why? Because every child has a great grandmother, so every thing must have its cause. And the poor grandmother suddenly holds the responsibility for the wrongs that her progeny perpetrate. If this were so, one would have to be able to state: if Calvin rather than Luther or realistic novels rather than Hoffmann's tales, then no horrors in the 1940s. That doesn't compute. One could not predict because everything was possible, because no idea is so absurd that it can't be carried out in highly civilized societies." (Klüger, *Weiter leben*, 147–8).

16 Berel Lang, "The Representation of Limits," and Hayden White, "Historical Emplotment and the Problem of Truth," in *Probing the Limits of Representation: Nazism and the "Final Solution,"* ed. Saul Friedlander (Cambridge, Mass., 1992), 300–17 and 37–53 respectively.

17 White, "Historical Emplotment," 48.

18 John Lyons, *Introduction to Theoretical Linguistics* (Cambridge, 1968), 374.

19 Vernant, "Discussion: Barthes–Todorov," in *The Structuralist Controversy: The Languages of Criticism and the Sciences of Man*, ed. Richard Macksey and Eugenio Donato (Baltimore, 1972), 152.

20 Langer, in *Holocaust Testimonies*, tells of the narration of Edith P., who yearns for someone who knows her *really*, having found a "permanent estrangement" (Langer's words) in her life after Auschwitz. Langer draws

a connection with White's discussion in *The Content of the Form* of the annalistic genre of reflection on the past. In medieval annals, White tells us, things happen to people, rather than people doing things. Disorder and fear characterize that world, and the form that represents it. "Up to a point, this is the experience of which the surviving victim speaks" (Langer, *Holocaust Testimonies*, 108).

The disrupted narrative selfhood that Edith P. experiences corresponds to the absence of any central authority, an absence which White associates with the drift of annalistic presentation, and which is perhaps not terribly far from his decentered middle-voiced writing. Langer, however, takes the traditional humanistic view: "The key factor is a responsive and transforming consciousness. At this point, annals become narrative, and narrative makes possible the birth of history for succeeding generations." It is interesting to note that Langer's study of the "raw" data of survivor videotapes leads him to yearn for the processing voice of narrative that White and Lang distrust.

21 Hayden White, *Tropics of Discourse: Essays in Cultural Criticism* (Baltimore, 1978), 23.
22 Linda Orr, *Headless History: Nineteenth-Century French Historiography of the Revolution* (Ithaca, NY, 1990), 74–5.
23 Philippe Carrard, *The Poetics of the New History: French Historical Discourse from Braudel to Chartier* (Baltimore, 1992), 104.
24 White, "Historical Emplotment and the Problem of Truth," 50. From *Metahistory*: "In my view, a historiographical style represents a particular *combination* of modes of emplotment, argument, and ideological implication. But the various modes of modes of emplotment, argument, and ideological implication cannot be indiscriminately combined in a given work. For example, a Comic emplotment is not compatible with a Mechanistic argument, just as a Radical ideology is not compatible with a Satirical emplotment. There are, as it were, elective affinities among the various modes that might be used to gain an explanatory effect on the different levels of composition. And these elective affinities are based on the structural homologies which can be discerned among the possible modes of modes of emplotment, argument, and ideological implication. . . . These affinities are not to be taken as *necessary* combinations of the modes in a given historian. On the contrary, the dialectical tension which characterizes the work of every master historian usually arises from an effort to wed a mode of emplotment with a mode of argument or of ideological implication which is inconsonant with it." (White, *Metahistory: The Historical Imagination in Nineteenth-Century Europe* [Baltimore, 1973], 29).

F. R. Ankersmit puts the matter somewhat differently in *Narrative Logic: A Semantic Analysis of the Historian's Language* (The Hague, 1983): "The idea that the historian should offer a narrative 'translation' of what the past really is like is the misunderstanding that this and similar proposals have in common. For there are no translation-rules which, when carefully applied, can guarantee the objectivity of a narratio" (236).

25 Allan Megill discusses the postmodern aestheticization of "the whole of reality" in *Prophets of Extremity: Nietzsche, Heidegger, Foucault, Derrida* (Berkeley, 1985), *passim*. Stephen Kern has described how modernism changed the experience of time and space, creating a parallel between the arts and historical events; see *The Culture of Time and Space: 1880–1918* (Cambridge,

Mass., 1983), esp. chapter 11: "The Cubist War." He does not, however, suggest that World War I was cubist "in nature."

26 Lang, "The Representation of Limits," 316.

27 Martin Jay points this out in "Of Plots, Witnesses, and Judgments," in *Probing the Limits of Representation*, 103.

28 White, "Historical Emplotment," 52.

29 "Finally, the *Introduction* [by Langlois and Seignobos] proposes a stylistics: a set of rules about selecting the proper word, phrase, and sentence pattern. This stylistics advocates what Anglo-Saxon composition teachers call the 'plain style': a language that would be 'unadorned by figures, unmoved by emotions, unclouded by images, and universalistic in its conceptual or mathematical scope,' as LaCapra (1985, 42) defines it with obvious irony. Langlois and Seignobos again proscribe 'literary effects,' in this instance the 'rhetoric' whose ornaments are incompatible with the sobriety that must characterize historical writing (267, 273). The main culprit is of course metaphor, since this trope combines the drive to 'do literature' with a wrong view of what the world is 'really like.'" Carrard, *Poetics*, 8.

30 Lang, "Introduction," in *Writing and the Holocaust*, 15.

31 John Lange, "The Argument from Silence," *History and Theory* 5 (1966), 300–1.

32 *The Standard Edition of the Complete Psychological Works of Sigmund Freud*, trans. James Strachey (London, 1953), XVI, 379.

33 "If the writer succeeds in writing, it is generally because he can fictionalize in his imagination an audience he has learned to know not from daily life but from earlier writers who were fictionalizing in their imaginations, audiences they had learned to know in still earlier writers, and so on back to the dawn of written narrative." Walter J. Ong, "The Writer's Audience Is a Fiction," in *Interfaces of the Word* (Ithaca, NY, 1977), 60.

34 The notion that events are narratively constructed from an undifferentiated "advent" is put forth in Hans Kellner, "Naive and Sentimental Realism: From Advent to Event," *Storia della storiografia* 22 (1992), 117–23.

35 It may be objected that some events are named at once, and thus experienced in their historical identity. World War II, for example, was experienced as such, at least after the entry of the United States. Yet World War II was seen and named immediately as the counterpart of World War I, although World War I had not existed before World War II caused it to be so named. It was transformed from the vaguely named Great War by the happenings that were its completion and repetition, and which changed its nature entirely, from a unique and self-consuming tale (the war to end war) into an example of a modern form of activity, world war. It is also instructive to note that the subsequent conflict in Korea became the Korean War despite the efforts of American leaders to represent it as a police action. The Vietnam War became that without the formal congressional speech act declaring legal hostilities. One may say that "readers" constituted these events against the official actions and intentions of the principal participants. They knew the plot that constructed a certain kind of event when they saw it, and refused to believe that anything else could occur under that description.

36 F. R. Ankersmit, "On Historiographical Progress," *Storia della storiografia* 22 (1992), 107.

37 As a literary critic, Ruth Klüger is particularly sensitive to the automatization of reader response. Her observation, cited above, that the "Final Solution,

Holocaust, Jewish catastrophe, and recently Shoah" need "always new names because the words for it very quickly rot in our mouths" (Klüger, *Weiter Ieben*, 147) is an immediate allusion to Hugo von Hofmannsthal's Lord Chandos letter of 1902 on the crisis of language, but her example also calls to mind the Russian formalist Viktor Shklovsky's dictum that habituation devours everything. ("Art as Technique," in *Russian Formalist Criticism: Four Essays*, trans. L. T. Lemon and M. J. Reis [Lincoln, Nebr., 1965], 12.)

38 Hilberg, "I Was Not There," 25.

39 Carlo Ginzburg, "Just One Witness," in *Probing the Limits of Representation*, 93.

13

Is It Possible to Misrepresent the Holocaust?

Berel Lang

Metaphysics may be a mug's game, but those who think they can avoid it by burying their heads in the sand are likely to wind up playing the game anyway but from the other end (reviving the "Posterior Analytics"?). This is, it seems to me, a lesson taught by the three essays in the *History and Theory* Forum on "Representing the Holocaust" (May, 1994) by Hans Kellner, Wulf Kansteiner, and Robert Braun respectively. Those essays differ tactically and rhetorically, but a common enemy – realism in all its guises – motivates them and then serves as the alien "other" against which their conclusions stand in solidarity. This oppositional stance may explain why the essays do not bother to consider – let alone to defend – the implications of their own views of historical representation, but obviously it does not justify that avoidance which has the effect of undercutting their initial criticism. As it is unlikely, for any two conceptual alternatives, that the choice of either will come without certain costs, the reluctance of the three authors to weigh the price of their own proposal is proportionate to the strength of the one they reject.

The topic of the Forum has, of course, been much discussed; indeed the history of this discussion is what concerns the three contributors. The principal question at issue in that history can be simply formulated: what special limitations or demands (if any) does, or should, the character of the Holocaust impose on its historical representation? This question evidently assumes a "normal" – that is, "*non*-special" – form of historical representation as a background against which specific representations (including those of the Holocaust) will be assessed. The question cited thus asks whether changes in the normal form are required by the (allegedly) unusual character of the Holocaust – either on a "one-off" basis or in the normal form as such. Although the three authors differ on certain aspects of the normal form of historical representation, there is no disagreement among them either on what they consider the most essential element of that form (that is, its contextualist and anti-realistic drive) or on their negative answer to the historiographical question concerning the Holocaust's special representational status. There are, in their common view, *no* special limitations or requirements in the historical representation of the Holocaust – certainly none that would alter the normal and thus generally applicable form of historical representation.

The last part of this response is controversial only in its rejection of accounts of the Holocaust which assert its historical uniqueness and/or its historical "unrepresentability." *Those* two claims are by no means equivalent or mutually entailed (as Kansteiner assumes), but this objection is a small matter in the larger context. At least it would be a small matter if the rejection of the two claims were itself based on historical grounds. Admittedly, some advocates of the Holocaust's uniqueness or unrepresentability have argued from theological or other transhistorical premises, and such claims can hardly be contested in historical terms. But there *is also* a historical claim about the failure of precedents for the Holocaust (and/or the phenomenon of genocide), as is demonstrated in Steven Katz's broadly based thesis that the convergence of causal factors in the Holocaust is historically unprecedented.[1] Whatever one infers from Katz's thesis – and indeed even if one rejects it – he surely demonstrates that the historical question of Holocaust-precedents is not intrinsically mystifying or ideologically tendentious – which is how Kellner, Kansteiner, and Braun finally "represent" it.[2] This non-historical dismissal of claims of the Holocaust's historical distinctiveness is symptomatic of their more basic and also *a priori* premise concerning the normal form of historical representation: on the one hand, a rejection of any such representation as even possibly referential or factual; on the other hand – in its positive version – the assertion that historical representation (with all history *as* representational) is uniformly contextual and interpretive. They assume that historical accounts are frozen between brackets all the way down.

Their other differences aside, the agreement among the three authors on these two contentions is firm and unquestioned. From these premises they then conclude that no exceptions need be made for representing the Holocaust. At this poststructuralist stage on the mind's way, we are to understand, only the naif would credit historical discourse with a "stable referent" (Kellner) or the possibility of "factual singularity" (Kansteiner) or the "'reality' of the past as an object of study" (Braun). Their common oppositional stance is epitomized by Braun's use of quotation marks wherever he finds himself compelled even to mention the terms "fact" or "truth" (or "reality"). Like the skeptic's raised eyebrows, those marks surround and presumably defeat any use of language hinting at an extra-linguistic or extra-interpretive historical referent. Since there is no extra-interpretive fulcrum, any historical claim of uniqueness must also allow for another representation in which the object at issue is not exceptional but commonplace – a possibility that by itself defeats the original claim.

The point at issue here, again, is not the substantive question of the Holocaust's uniqueness, but the normal form prescribed by the symposiasts for historical analysis. In both their practice as well as in principle they assert that historical representations are not permitted the reactionary invocation of nineteenth-century realism or positivism, such as Ranke's tropological and thus self-refuting view of history as the search for the "eigentlich." Insofar as this proscription applies to the normal form of historical discourse in general, it holds also for historical representations of the Holocaust: harder justice in that case, perhaps, but justice nonetheless. (Even if Kellner allows that some forms of discourse may be more "appropriate" than others for "some" events, this does not entail a point-zero at which the structure of discourse is not itself part of the subject of discourse.) The Hayden White of *Metahistory* is thus recalled nostalgically by all three authors. (Their erstwhile forebear, groundbreaker in the discovery of history as narrative form, has recently regressed, honorably but mistakenly troubled by the phenomenon of the Holocaust in relation to his own earlier historiographical tour de force. Now he looks to the middle-voice or, in any event, to *some* voice that will speak for non-interpreted facts.)

What arguments are made for this dismissal of historical realism? One might dispute this question itself on the grounds that where the status of facts or truth is at issue, it begs the question to require arguments in their traditional form. To be sure, the latter consideration doesn't prevent certain voluntary inconsistencies (so, Kellner: "The most elementary fact about the modern historical profession is that it produces an enormous amount of discourse" [141]: what silent miracle keeps the subject of this sentence afloat?). In general, however, the oppositional point of departure in the three essays carries over into their positive moment, shaping their respective versions of an adequate (or at least *more* adequate) view of historical representation, although still without adducing proof or evidence. (Kansteiner claims only to be identifying the "limits and blind spots" in each of the two major paradigms; but he leaves no doubt about which, in his view, is the blinder of the two which he associates, perhaps more than metaphorically, with their respective ages.) Again, like the negative critique in the three essays' origins, the refrain here is constant:

> *Kellner*: The rhetorical constitution of events depends for its existence on the social codes that prevail in a group, a time, a place. (140)
> *Kansteiner*: Only *Alltagsgeschichte*... offers the kind of consistent, intuitively [!] convincing image of Nazism which furthers historicization proper, that is the routinization of the representation of Nazism compatible with the parameters of historiography and of more popular forms of historical culture. (171)

> *Braun*: In our perception of past social reality vis-à-vis documents and
> other "facts," there is no difference between the politically possible, the
> socially plausible, and the morally imaginary – nor do we know with
> which we are dealing. (196)

To be sure, some room remains at the edges of these assertions. Kellner's
reference to "the rhetorical constitution of events" may leave open the
possibility of another means of constituting them; Kansteiner elsewhere
cites a "problem inherent in structuralist poetics" (as in James Young's
Writing and Rewriting the Holocaust),[3] in that it provides no grounds
for dismissing "certain appropriations of the Holocaust" as compared
to others (159); Braun, in claiming the legitimization of the past "by the
authority of the present" acknowledges the latter as at least a provisional terminus. But what is thus given offhandedly is invariably taken
back directly. The locus of history is always and only a point at the
convergence of vectors of social custom or political power or linguistic
figuration or moral tendency. Not only do facts never speak for themselves, but post-Kantians all, have we not suffered enough from political
and literary and historical mystification to recognize in the ontology of
facts a second world of "things-in-themselves" still more inaccessible than
anything we might hope for (also in vain) from "facts-in-themselves"?
We should rather be confident and glad of the "irredeemably earthly and
immanent status of interpretation" (Kellner, 144); that "after Auschwitz
poetry can be written, but history, as the 'realistic' interpretation of the
past, cannot" (Braun, 196).

Here occurs the metaphysical failure of nerve that disables at once the
symposiasts' criticism of one normal form of historical representation
and the form by which they mean to replace it. This failure is evident
from a critique of ordinary usage: if representation or interpretation is
representation or interpretation *of* some "thing," what is the ontological
status of whatever the representation or interpretation is of? Or more
bluntly, in reconceiving the Forum's title: "Representing the *What*?" No
one would deny that the term "Holocaust" is a matter of (disputed) convention; but are we to suppose that the ontology of conventions (itself
neither simple nor conventional) applies also and directly to whatever
the convention incorporates or cites? If "factual material itself . . . [is] constituted by a negotiation with other forms" (Kellner, 140), does not this
imply that some *non*-negotiated material is part of the negotiation with
the "other forces"? But what then would be the status of this material?

Kellner objects to the proposal in one of my own essays that at least
chronicles are non-interpretive: "But this," he announces, "is mistaken.
A chronicle is the result of a pre-existing narrative; it is not the origin of
such a narrative" (138). There are two alternative positions that Kellner
might be disputing with this objection. The first would construe a chronicle as a corporate structure of selected, albeit elementary, data. To call
such a chronicle mimetic or directly referential would, *of course*, be

"mistaken": the act of selection precludes such claims. Who, one might ask, would deny that chronicle in this sense is narrative-dependent (although why one of them should "precede" the other or even why they should be distinguished at all are questions Kellner – who makes both these claims – ignores)?

There *is* an issue, however, in the question of whether the items constituting a chronicle (that is, its atomic elements or, more prosaically, the facts: who did what to whom, when or where) are individually dependent – ontologically and epistemically – on a "pre-existing" narrative. This indeed is the issue I reiterate here against the three contextualist views of historical representation in the Forum as they would place the Holocaust or any other historical event (that is, "event") always and entirely within the circle of interpretation. If the narrative-dependence of facts holds in general, then for any particular narrative (and its derivative "facts") an alternate "pre-existing" narrative might produce other, even contradictory, "facts." In other words, narrative and interpretation first, facts, second. The implication here is – or should be – clear: not only is history accessible only in variant, sometimes conflicting narratives, but nothing that the narratives tell or talk *about* is exempt. We must distrust the tale as well as the teller – with no place else to turn.

That the Holocaust has at times been proposed as a test case for historical representation is due, of course, to its moral enormity. So far as concerns the normal form of historical representation *in general*, the judgment about this test case by the authors of "Representing the Holocaust" – to the effect that the Holocaust changes nothing in this normal form – may well hold. But one could accept *this* claim and still maintain that the Holocaust is a test case of the normal form itself. So indeed I would argue – not for its uniqueness as a test but because the consequences that hinge on the status of alternate Holocaust-narratives (consequences which the contributors to the Forum consistently ignore) demonstrate graphically what is at stake in the issue of historical representation more generally.

Consider this item of chronicle: "On January 20, 1942, Nazi officials at Wannsee formulated a protocol for the 'Final Solution of the Jewish Question'." There are, to be sure, matters that might require specification in this statement – for example, the status of the officials or whether the formulation of the "Final Solution" originated then or before. But with or without such additional clauses, the crucial question remains whether what the statement asserts (and so its truth or falsity) is *essentially* a matter of interpretation. Is the statement's truth or falsity a function only of a larger narrative – and thus open to contradiction in each or even every point when transposed to another narrative?

A large and obvious difference exists between answering "Yes" or "No" to these two questions. In everything they affirm and nothing they deny, Kellner, Kansteiner, and Braun seem committed to answering "Yes" to both questions – and then to accepting the consequence that an alternate narrative to the one they presumably accept (which affirms the occurrence of the Wannsee Conference) could equally legitimately find the Conference *not* to have occurred. Moreover, these two claims are not even contradictory since there is no metanarrative by which to judge the two. Is this what the authors and the several versions of contextualism they propose, mean to affirm? If not, on what grounds do they deny it?

The issue here is perilously Either/Or. *Either* there is, at the ground of historical writing (whatever subsequent appropriations make of it), an element of reference: facts.

Or history is as you like it, not only in the stratosphere where historians and readers might on any account enjoy free flight, but in the trenches, with the masses of names, dates, and numbers elbowing each other for place. Can any possible narrative appear as superstructure for any sub- or infra-structure of fact, undoing or redoing any or all of the latter's elements? The Holocaust can be described as one event or many, and as soon as narrative connectives are imposed on individual items of chronicle, alternate paths open up for alternate narratives. But to say that historical narratives when they thus move beyond the items of chronicle are unfettered by anything more than the historian's imagination or will is to imply that the items of chronicle also are functions of imagination or will – thus (for example) that it is the *historian's* responsibility whether or not Nazi officialdom met at Wannsee. Most people (including, I would guess, the symposiasts themselves) would be reluctant to concede that whether or not they existed five minutes ago depends entirely on what historians (singly or collectively) say about them. The basis for this reluctance is not a matter of psychology or physics or linguistic tropology. But this is how, in various combinations reflecting *their* imaginations and will, Kellner, Kansteiner, and Braun represent history. And the Holocaust.

Notes

1 Steven Katz, *The Holocaust in Historical Context* (New York, 1994).
2 I would instance here – symptomatically – their misreading of my own work as maintaining the "uniqueness" *and* the "unrepresentable" or incomprehensible nature of the Holocaust – all of which views I have opposed in *Act and Idea in the Nazi Genocide* (Chicago, 1990), and elsewhere (cf., e.g., "The History of Evil and the Future of the Holocaust," in *Lessons and Legacies*, ed. Peter Hayes [Evanston, Ill., 1991], 90–105; "The Interpretation of Limits," in *Probing the Limits of Representation*, ed. Saul Friedlander [Cambridge, Mass., 1992], 300–17; "Genocide," in *Encyclopedia of Ethics*, ed. Lawrence Becker [New York, 1992], 760–1).
3 James E. Young, *Writing and Rewriting the Holocaust: Narrative and the Consequences of Interpretation* (Bloomington, Ind., 1988).

Part VI

Gender, Sexuality, Sex

14

Is There a History of Sexuality?

David M. Halperin

Sex has no history.[1] It is a natural fact, grounded in the functioning of the body, and, as such, it lies outside of history and culture. Sexuality, by contrast, does not properly refer to some aspect or attribute of bodies. Unlike sex, sexuality is a cultural production: it represents the *appropriation* of the human body and of its physiological capacities by an ideological discourse.[2] Sexuality is not a somatic fact; it is a cultural effect. Sexuality, then, does have a history – though (as I shall argue) not a very long one.

To say that, of course, is not to state the obvious – despite the tone of assurance with which I just said it – but to advance a controversial, suspiciously fashionable, and, perhaps, a strongly counter-intuitive claim. The plausibility of such a claim might seem to rest on nothing more substantial than the prestige of the brilliant, pioneering, but largely theoretical work of the late French philosopher Michel Foucault.[3] According to Foucault, sexuality is not a thing, a natural fact, a fixed and immovable element in the eternal grammar of human subjectivity, but that "set of effects produced in bodies, behaviors, and social relations by a certain deployment" of "a complex political technology."[4] "Sexuality," Foucault insists in another passage,

> must not be thought of as a kind of natural given which power tries to hold in check, or as an obscure domain which knowledge tries gradually to uncover. It is the name that can be given to a historical construct [*dispositif*]: not a furtive reality that is difficult to grasp, but a great surface network in which the stimulation of bodies, the intensification of pleasures, the incitement to discourse, the formation of special knowledges, the strengthening of controls and resistances, are linked to one another, in accordance with a few major strategies of knowledge and power.[5]

Is Foucault right? I believe he is, but I also believe that more is required to establish the historicity of sexuality than the mere weight of Foucault's authority. To be sure, a great deal of work, both conceptual and empirical, has already been done to sustain Foucault's central insights and to carry forward the historicist project that he did so much to advance.[6] But much more needs to be accomplished if we are to fill in the outlines of the picture that Foucault had time only to sketch – hastily and inadequately, as he was the first to admit[7] – and if we are to demonstrate that sexuality is indeed, as he claimed, a uniquely modern production.

The study of classical antiquity has a special role to play in this historical enterprise. The sheer interval of time separating the ancient from the modern world spans cultural changes of such magnitude that the contrasts to which they give rise cannot fail to strike anyone who is on the lookout for them. The student of classical antiquity is inevitably confronted in the ancient record by a radically unfamiliar set of values, behaviors, and social practices, by ways of organizing and articulating experience that challenge modern notions about what life is like, and that call into question the supposed universality of "human nature" as we currently understand it. Not only does this historical distance permit us to view ancient social and sexual conventions with particular sharpness; it also enables us to bring more clearly into focus the ideological dimension – the purely conventional and arbitrary character – of our own social and sexual experiences.[8] One of the currently unquestioned assumptions about sexual experience which the study of antiquity calls into question is the assumption that sexual behavior reflects or expresses an individual's "sexuality."

Now that would seem to be a relatively harmless and unproblematic assumption to make, empty of all ideological content, but what exactly do we have in mind when we make it? What, in particular, do we understand by our concept of "sexuality"? I think we understand "sexuality" to refer to a positive, distinct, and constitutive feature of the human personality, to the characterological seat within the individual of sexual acts, desires, and pleasures – the determinate source from which all sexual expression proceeds. "Sexuality" in this sense is not a purely descriptive term, a neutral representation of some objective state of affairs or a simple recognition of some familiar facts about us; rather, it is a distinctive way of constructing, organizing, and interpreting those "facts," and it performs quite a lot of conceptual work.

First of all, sexuality defines itself as a separate, sexual domain within the larger field of human psychophysical nature. Second, sexuality effects the conceptual demarcation and isolation of that domain from other areas of personal and social life that have traditionally cut across it, such as carnality, venery, libertinism, virility, passion, amorousness, eroticism, intimacy, love, affection, appetite, and desire – to name but a few of the older claimants to territories more recently staked out by sexuality.

Finally, sexuality generates sexual identity: it endows each of us with an individual sexual nature, with a personal essence defined (at least in part) in specifically sexual terms; it implies that human beings are individuated at the level of their sexuality, that they differ from one another in their sexuality and, indeed, belong to different types or kinds of being by virtue of their sexuality.

These, at least, appear to me to be some of the significant ramifications of "sexuality," as it is currently conceptualized. I shall argue that the outlook it represents is alien to the recorded experience of the ancients. Two themes, in particular, that seem intrinsic to the modern conceptualization of sexuality but that hardly find an echo in ancient sources will provide the focus of my investigation: the autonomy of sexuality as a separate sphere of existence (deeply implicated in other areas of life, to be sure, but distinct from them and capable of acting on them at least as much as it is acted on by them), and the function of sexuality as a principle of individuation in human natures. In what follows, I shall take up each theme in turn, attempting to document in this fashion the extent of the divergence between ancient and modern varieties of sexual experience.

First, the autonomy of sexuality as a separate sphere of existence. The basic point I should like to make has already been made for me by Robert Padgug in a now-classic essay on conceptualizing sexuality in history. Padgug argues that

> what we consider "sexuality" was, in the pre-bourgeois world, a group of acts and institutions not necessarily linked to one another, or, if they were linked, combined in ways very different from our own. Intercourse, kinship, and the family, and gender, did not form anything like a "field" of sexuality. Rather, each group of sexual acts was connected directly or indirectly – that is, formed part of – institutions and thought patterns which we tend to view as political, economic, or social in nature, and the connections cut across our idea of sexuality as a thing, detachable from other things, and as a separate sphere of private existence.[9]

The ancient evidence amply supports Padgug's claim. In classical Athens, for example, sex did not express inward dispositions or inclinations so much as it served to position social actors in the places assigned to them, by virtue of their political standing, in the hierarchical structure of the Athenian polity. Let me expand this formulation.

In classical Athens a relatively small group made up of the adult male citizens held a virtual monopoly of social power and constituted a clearly defined élite within the political and social life of the city-state. The predominant feature of the social landscape of classical Athens was the great divide in status between this superordinate group, composed of citizens, and a subordinate group, composed of women, children, foreigners, and slaves – all of whom lacked full civil rights (though they were not all equally subordinate). Sexual relations not only respected that divide but were strictly polarized in conformity with it.

Sex is portrayed in Athenian documents not as a mutual enterprise in which two or more persons jointly engage but as an action performed by a social superior upon a social inferior. Consisting as it was held to do in an asymmetrical gesture – the penetration of the body of one person by the body (and, specifically, by the phallus)[10] of another – sex effectively divided and distributed its participants into radically distinct and incommensurable categories ("penetrator" versus "penetrated"), categories which in turn were wholly congruent with superordinate and subordinate social categories. For sexual penetration was thematized as domination: the relation between the insertive and the receptive sexual partner was taken to be the same kind of relation as that obtaining between social superior and social inferior.[11] Insertive and receptive sexual roles were therefore necessarily isomorphic with superordinate and subordinate social status; an adult, male citizen of Athens could have legitimate sexual relations *only* with statutory minors (his inferiors not in age but in social and political status): the proper targets of his sexual desire included, specifically, women of any age, free males past the age of puberty who were not yet old enough to be citizens (I'll call them "boys," for short), as well as foreigners and slaves of either sex.[12]

Moreover, the physical act of sex between a citizen and a statutory minor was stylized in such a way as to mirror in the minute details of its hierarchical arrangement the relation of structured inequality that governed the wider social interaction of the two lovers. What an Athenian did in bed was determined by the differential in status that distinguished him or her from his or her sexual partner; the (male) citizen's superior prestige and authority expressed themselves in his sexual precedence – in his power to initiate a sexual act, his right to obtain pleasure from it, and his assumption of an insertive rather than a receptive sexual role. Different social actors had different sexual roles: to assimilate both the superordinate and the subordinate member of a sexual relationship to the same "sexuality" would have been as bizarre, in Athenian eyes, as classifying a burglar as an "active criminal," his victim as a "passive criminal," and the two of them alike as partners in crime – it would have been to confuse what, in reality, were supposedly separate and distinct identities.[13] Each act of sex was no doubt an expression of real, personal desire on the part of the sexual actors involved, but their very desires had already been shaped by the shared cultural definition of sex as an activity that generally occurred only between a citizen and a non-citizen, between a person invested with full civil status and a statutory minor.

The "sexuality" of the classical Athenians, then, far from being independent of "politics" (each construed as an autonomous sphere) *was constituted by the very principles* on which Athenian public life was organized. In fact, the correspondences in classical Athens between sexual norms and social practices were so strict that an inquiry into Athenian "sexuality" *per se* would be nonsensical: such an inquiry could only obscure the phenomenon it was intended to elucidate, for it would conceal the sole context in which the sexual protocols of the classical Athenians make any sense – namely, the structure of the Athenian polity. The social articulation of sexual desire in classical Athens thus furnishes a telling illustration of the interdependence in culture of social practices and subjective experiences. Indeed, the classical Greek record strongly supports the conclusion drawn (from a quite different body of evidence) by the French anthropologist Maurice Godelier: "it is not sexuality which haunts society, but society which haunts the body's sexuality."[14]

For those inhabitants of the ancient world about whom it is possible to generalize, sexuality did not hold the key to the secrets of the human personality. (In fact, the very concept of and set of practices centering on "the human personality" – the physical and social sciences of the blank individual – belong to a much later era and bespeak the modern social and economic conditions that accompanied their rise.) In the Hellenic world, by contrast, the measure of a free male was most often taken by observing how he fared when tested in public competition against other free males, not by scrutinizing his sexual constitution. War (and other agonistic contests), not love, served to reveal the inner man, the stuff a free Greek male was made of.[15] A striking instance of this emphasis on public life as the primary locus of signification can be found in the work of Artemidorus, a master dream-interpreter who lived and wrote in the second century of our era and whose testimony, there is good reason to believe, accurately represents the sexual norms of ancient Mediterranean culture.[16] Artemidorus saw public life, not erotic life, as the principal tenor of dreams. Even sexual dreams, in Artemidorus's system, are seldom *really* about sex: rather, they are about the rise and fall of the dreamer's public fortunes, the vicissitudes of his domestic economy.[17] If a man dreams of having sex with his mother, for example, his dream signifies to Artemidorus nothing in particular about the dreamer's own sexual psychology, his fantasy life, or the history of his relations with his parents; it's a very common dream, and so it's a bit tricky to interpret precisely, but basically it's a lucky dream: it may signify – depending on the family's circumstances at the time, the postures of the partners in the dream, and the mode of penetration – that the dreamer will be successful in politics ("success" meaning, evidently, the power to screw one's country), that he will go into exile or return from exile, that he will win his lawsuit, obtain a rich harvest from his lands, or change professions, among many other things (1.79). Artemidorus's system of dream interpretation resembles the indigenous dream-lore of certain Amazonian tribes who, despite their quite different sociosexual systems, share with the ancient Greeks a belief in the predictive value of dreams. Like Artemidorus, these Amazonian peoples reverse what modern bourgeois Westerners take to be the natural flow of signification in dreams (from images of public and social events to private and sexual meanings): in both Kagwahiv and Mehinaku culture, for example, dreaming about the female genitalia portends a wound (and so a man who has such a dream is especially careful when he handles axes or other sharp instruments the next day); dreamt wounds do not symbolize the female genitalia.[18] Both these ancient and modern dream-interpreters, then, are innocent of "sexuality": what is fundamental to their experience of sex is not anything *we* would regard as essentially sexual;[19] it is instead something essentially outward, public, and social. "Sexuality," for cultures not shaped by some very recent European and American bourgeois developments, is not a cause but an effect. The social body precedes the sexual body.

I now come to the second of my two themes – namely, the individuating function of sexuality, its role in generating individual sexual identities. The connection between the modern interpretation of sexuality as an autonomous domain and the modern construction of individual sexual identities has been well analyzed, once again, by Robert Padgug:

> the most commonly held twentieth-century assumptions about sexuality imply that it is a separate category of existence (like "the economy," or "the state," other supposedly independent spheres of reality), almost identical with the sphere of private life. Such a view necessitates the location of sexuality within the individual as a fixed essence, leading to a classic division of individual and society and to a variety of psychological determinisms, and, often enough, to a full-blown biological determinism as well. These in turn involve the enshrinement of contemporary sexual categories as universal, static, and permanent, suitable for the analysis of all human beings and all societies.[20]

The study of ancient Mediterranean societies clearly exposes the defects in any such essentialist conceptualization of sexuality. Because, as we have seen in the case of classical Athens, erotic desires and sexual object-choices in antiquity were generally not determined by a typology of anatomical sexes (male versus female), but rather by the social articulation of power (superordinate versus subordinate), the currently fashionable distinction between homosexuality and heterosexuality (and, similarly, between "homosexuals" and "heterosexuals" as individual types) had no meaning for the classical Athenians: there were not, so far as they knew, two different kinds of "sexuality," two differently structured psychosexual states or modes of affective orientation, but a single form of sexual experience which all free adult males shared – making due allowance for variations in individual tastes, as one might make for individual palates.[21] . . .

... Before the scientific construction of "sexuality" as a positive, distinct, and constitutive feature of individual human beings – an autonomous system within the physiological and psychological economy of the human organism – certain kinds of sexual *acts* could be individually evaluated and categorized, and so could certain sexual tastes or inclinations, but there was no conceptual apparatus available for identifying a person's fixed and determinate sexual *orientation*, much less for assessing and classifying it.[22] That human beings differ, often markedly, from one another in their sexual tastes in a great variety of ways (including sexual object-choice), is an unexceptionable and, indeed, an ancient observation[23]: Plato's Aristophanes invents a myth to explain why some men like women, why some men like boys, why some women like men, and why some women like women (*Symposium* 189c–193d). But it is not immediately evident that patterns of sexual object-choice are by their very nature more revealing about the temperament of individual human beings, more significant determinants of personal *identity*, than, for example, patterns of dietary object-choice.[24] And yet, it would never occur to us to refer a person's dietary preference to some innate, characterological disposition,[25] to see in his or her strongly expressed and even unvarying preference for the white meat of chicken the symptom of a profound psychophysical orientation, leading us to identify him or her in contexts quite removed from that of the eating of food as, say, a "pectoriphage" or a "stethovore"; nor would we be likely to inquire further, making nicer discriminations according to whether an individual's predilection for chicken breasts expressed itself in a tendency to eat them quickly or slowly, seldom or often, alone or in company, under normal circumstances or only in periods of great stress, with a clear or a guilty conscience ("ego-dystonic pectoriphagia"), beginning in earliest childhood or originating with a gastronomic trauma suffered in adolescence. If such questions did occur to us, moreover, I very much doubt whether we would turn to the academic disciplines of anatomy, neurology, clinical psychology, genetics, or sociobiology in the hope of obtaining a clear causal solution to them. That is because (1) we regard the liking for certain foods as a matter of taste; (2) we currently lack a theory of taste; and (3) in the absence of a theory we do not normally subject our behavior to intense, scientific or aetiological, scrutiny.

In the same way, it never occurred to the ancients to ascribe a person's sexual tastes to some positive, structural, or constitutive sexual feature of his or her personality. Just as we tend to assume that human beings are not individuated at the level of dietary preference and that we all, despite many pronounced and frankly acknowledged differences from one another in dietary habits, share the same fundamental set of alimentary appetites, and hence the same "dieticity" or "edility," so most premodern and non-Western cultures, despite an awareness of the range of possible variations in human sexual behavior, refuse to individuate human beings at the level of sexual preference and assume, instead, that we all share the same fundamental set of sexual appetites, the same "sexuality." For most of the world's inhabitants, in other words, "sexuality" is no more a "fact of life" than "dieticity." Far from being a necessary or intrinsic constituent of human life, "sexuality" seems indeed to be a uniquely modern, Western, even bourgeois production – one of those cultural fictions which in every society give human beings access to themselves as meaningful actors in their world, and which are thereby objectivated.

If there is a lesson that we should draw from this picture of ancient sexual attitudes and behaviors, it is that we need to de-center *sexuality* from the focus of the cultural interpretation of sexual experience – and not only ancient varieties of sexual experience. Just because modern bourgeois Westerners are so obsessed with sexuality, so convinced that it holds the key to the hermeneutics of the self (and hence to social psychology as an object of historical study), we ought not therefore to conclude that everyone has always considered sexuality a basic and irreducible element in, or a central feature of, human life. Indeed, there are even sectors of our own societies to which the ideology of "sexuality" has failed to penetrate. A sociosexual system that coincides with the Greek system, insofar as it features a rigid hierarchy of sexual roles based on a set of socially articulated power-relations, has been documented in contemporary America by Jack Abbott, in one of his infamous letters written to Norman Mailer from a federal penitentiary; because the text is now quite inaccessible (it was not reprinted in Abbott's book), and stunningly apropos, I have decided to quote it here at length.

> It really was years, many years, before I began to actually realize that the women in my life – the prostitutes as well as the soft, pretty girls who giggled and teased me so much, my several wives and those of my friends – it was years before I realized that they were not women, but men; years before I assimilated the notion that this was unnatural. I still only know this intellectually, for the most part – but for the small part that remains to my ken, I know it is like a hammer blow to my temple and the shame I feel is profound. Not because of the thing itself, the sexual love I have enjoyed with these women (some so devoted it aches to recall it), but because of shame – and anger – that the world could so intimately betray me; so profoundly touch and move me – and then laugh at me and accuse my soul of a sickness, when that sickness has rescued me from mental derangement and despairs so black as to cast this night that surrounds us in prison into day. I do not mean to say I never knew the physical difference – no one but an imbecile could make such a claim. I took it, without reflection or the slightest doubt, that this was a natural sex that emerged within the society of men, with attributes that naturally complemented masculine attributes. I thought it was a natural phenomenon in the society of women as well. The attributes were feminine and so there seemed no gross misrepresentation of facts to call them (among us men) "women."

... Many of my "women" had merely the appearance of handsome, extremely neat, and polite young men. I have learned, analyzing my feelings today, that those attributes I called feminine a moment ago were not feminine in any way as it appears in the real female sex. These attributes seem now merely a tendency to need, to depend on another man; to need never to become a rival or to compete with other men in the pursuits men, among themselves, engage in. It was, it occurs to me now, almost boyish – not really feminine at all.

This is the way it always was, even in the State Industrial School for Boys – a penal institution for juvenile delinquents – where I served five years, from age twelve to age seventeen. They were the possession and sign of manhood and it never occurred to any of us that this was strange and unnatural. It is how I grew up – a natural part of my life in prison.

It was difficult for me to grasp the definition of the clinical term "homosexual" – and when I finally did it devastated me, as I said.[26]

Abbott's society surpasses classical Athenian society in the extent to which power relations are gendered. Instead of the Greek system which preserves the distinction between males and females but overrides it when articulating categories of the desirable and undesirable in favor of a distinction between dominant and submissive persons, the system described by Abbott wholly assimilates categories of sociosexual identity to categories of gender identity – in order, no doubt, to preserve the association in Abbott's world between "masculinity" and the love of "women." What determines gender, for Abbott, is not anatomical sex but social status and personal style. "Men" are defined as those who "compete with other men in the pursuits men, among themselves, engage in," whereas "women" are characterized by the possession of "attributes that naturally complement masculine attributes" – namely, a "tendency to need, to depend on another man" for the various benefits won by the victors in "male" competition. In this way "a natural sex emerges within the society of men" and qualifies, by virtue of its exclusion from the domain of "male" precedence and autonomy, as a legitimate target of "male" desire.

The salient features of Abbott's society are uncannily reminiscent of those features of classical Athenian society with which we are already familiar. Most notable is the division of the society into superordinate and subordinate groups and *the production of desire* for members of the subordinate group in members of the superordinate one. Desire is sparked in this system, as in classical Athens, only when it arcs across the political divide, only when it traverses the boundary that marks out the limits of intramural competition among the élite and that thereby distinguishes subjects from objects of sexual desire. Sex between "men" – and, therefore, "homosexuality" – remains unthinkable in Abbott's society (even though sex between anatomical males is an accepted and intrinsic part of the system), just as sex between citizens, between members of the empowered social caste, is practically inconceivable in classical Athenian society. Similarly, sex between "men" and "women" in Abbott's world is not a private experience in which social identities are lost or submerged; rather, in Abbott's society as in classical Athens, the act of sex – instead of implicating both sexual partners in a common "sexuality" – helps to articulate, to define, and to actualize the differences in status between them.

To discover and to write the history of sexuality has long seemed to many a sufficiently radical undertaking in itself, inasmuch as its effect (if not always the intention behind it) is to call into question the very naturalness of what we currently take to be essential to our individual natures. But in the course of implementing that ostensibly radical project many historians of sexuality seem to have reversed – perhaps unwittingly – its radical design: by preserving "sexuality" as a stable category of historical analysis not only have they not denaturalized it but, on the contrary, they have newly idealized it.[27] To the extent, in fact, that histories of "sexuality" succeed in concerning themselves with *sexuality*, to just that extent are they doomed to fail as *histories* (Foucault himself taught us that much), unless they also include as an essential part of their proper enterprise the task of demonstrating the historicity, conditions of emergence, modes of construction, and ideological contingencies of the very categories of analysis that undergird their own practice.[28] Instead of concentrating our attention specifically on the history of sexuality, then, we need to define and refine a new, and radical, historical sociology of psychology, an intellectual discipline designed to analyze the cultural poetics of desire, by which I mean the processes whereby sexual desires are constructed, mass-produced, and distributed among the various members of human living-groups.[29] We must train ourselves to recognize conventions of feeling as well as conventions of behavior and to interpret the intricate texture of personal life as an artifact, as the determinate outcome, of a complex and arbitrary constellation of cultural processes. We must, in short, be willing to admit that what seem to be our most inward, authentic, and private experiences are actually, in Adrienne Rich's admirable phrase, "shared, unnecessary/ and political."[30]

A little less than fifty years ago W. H. Auden asked, in the opening lines of a canzone, "When shall we learn, what should be clear as day, We cannot choose what we are free to love?"[31] It is a characteristically judicious formulation: love, if it is to be love, must be a free act, but it is also inscribed within a larger circle of constraint, within conditions that make possible the exercise of that "freedom." The task of distinguishing freedom from constraint in love, of learning to trace the shifting and uncertain boundaries between the self and the world, is a dizzying and, indeed, an endless undertaking. If I have not significantly advanced this project here, I hope at least to have encouraged others not to abandon it.

Notes

Most of the material contained in this article appears, in slightly different form, in the title essay of my collection, *One Hundred Years of Homosexuality and Other Essays on Greek Love* (New York: Routledge, 1989), or in the Editors' Introduction to *Before Sexuality: The Construction of Erotic Experience in the Ancient Greek World*, ed. David M. Halperin, John J. Winkler, and Froma I. Zeitlin (Princeton, 1990).

1 Or, if it does, that history is a matter for the evolutionary biologist, not for the historian; see Lynn Margulis and Dorion Sagan, *The Origins of Sex* (New Haven, 1985).

2 I adapt this formulation from a passage in Louis Adrian Montrose, "'Shaping Fantasies': Figurations of Gender and Power in Elizabethan Culture," *Representations* 2 (1983), 61–94 (passage on p. 62), which describes in turn the concept of the "sex/gender system" introduced by Gayle Rubin, "The Traffic in Women: Notes on the 'Political Economy' of Sex," in *Toward an Anthropology of Women*, ed. Rayna R. Reiter (New York, 1975), 157–210.

3 Volumes Two and Three of Foucault's *History of Sexuality*, published shortly before his death, depart significantly from the theoretical orientation of his earlier work in favor of a more concrete interpretative practice; see my remarks in "Two Views of Greek Love: Harald Patzer and Michel Foucault," *One Hundred Years of Homosexuality*, 62–71, esp. 64.

4 Michel Foucault, *The History of Sexuality, Volume I: An Introduction*, trans. Robert Hurley (New York, 1978), 127. See Teresa de Lauretis, *Technologies of Gender: Essays on Theory, Film, and Fiction* (Bloomington, 1987), 1–30, esp. 3, who extends Foucault's critique of sexuality to gender.

5 Foucault, *The History of Sexuality*, 105–6.

6 Of special relevance are: Robert A. Padgug, "Sexual Matters: On Conceptualizing Sexuality in History," *Radical History Review* 20 (1979), 3–23; George Chauncey, Jr, "From Sexual Inversion to Homosexuality: Medicine and the Changing Conceptualization of Female Deviance," in *Homosexuality: Sacrilege, Vision, Politics*, ed. Robert Boyers and George Steiner = *Salmagundi* 58–9 (1982–3), 114–46; Arnold I. Davidson, "Sex and the Emergence of Sexuality," *Critical Inquiry* 14 (1987–8), 16–48. See also *The Cultural Construction of Sexuality*, ed. Pat Caplan (London, 1987); T. Dunbar Moodie, "Migrancy and Male Sexuality on the South African Gold Mines," *Journal of Southern African Studies* 14 (1987–8), 228–56; George Chauncey, Jr, "Christian Brotherhood or Sexual Perversion? Homosexual Identities and the Construction of Sexual Boundaries in the World War One Era," *Journal of Social History* 19 (1985–6), 189–211.

7 E.g. Michel Foucault, *The Use of Pleasure, The History of Sexuality, Volume Two*, trans. Robert Hurley (New York, 1985), 92, 253.

8 In applying the term "ideological" to sexual experience, I have been influenced by the formulation of Stuart Hall, "Culture, the Media, and the 'Ideological Effect,'" in *Mass Communication and Society*, ed. James Curran, Michael Gurevitch, Janet Woolacott, et al. (London, 1977), 315–48, esp. 330: "ideology as a *social practice* consists of the 'subject' positioning himself in the specific complex, the objectivated field of discourses and codes which are available to him in language and culture at a particular historical conjuncture" (quoted by Ken Tucker and Andrew Treno, "The Culture of Narcissism and the Critical Tradition: An Interpretative Essay," *Berkeley Journal*

of Sociology 25 [1980], 341–55 [quotation on p. 351]); see also Hall's trenchant discussion of the constitutive role of ideology in "Deviance, Politics, and the Media," in *Deviance and Social Control*, ed. Paul Rock and Mary McIntosh, *Explorations in Sociology* 3 (London, 1974), 261–305.

9 Padgug, "Sexual Matters," 16.

10 I say "phallus" rather than "penis" because (1) what qualifies as a phallus in this discursive system does not always turn out to be a penis (see note 29, below) and (2) even when phallus and penis have the same extension, or reference, they still do not have the same intension, or meaning: "phallus" betokens not a specific item of the male anatomy *simpliciter* but that same item *taken under the description* of a cultural signifier; (3) hence, the meaning of "phallus" is ultimately determined by its function in the larger socio-sexual discourse; i.e. it is that which penetrates, that which enables its possessor to play an "active" sexual role, and so forth: see Rubin, "The Traffic in Women," 190–2.

11 Foucault, *The Use of Pleasure*, 215, puts it very well: "sexual relations – always conceived in terms of the model act of penetration, assuming a polarity that opposed activity and passivity – were seen as being of the same type as the relationship between a superior and a subordinate, an individual who dominates and one who is dominated, one who commands and one who complies, one who vanquishes and one who is vanquished."

12 In order to avoid misunderstanding, I should emphasize that by calling all persons belonging to these four groups "statutory minors," I do not wish either to suggest that they enjoyed the *same* status as one another or to obscure the many differences in status that could obtain between members of a single group – e.g. between a wife and a courtesan – differences that may not have been perfectly isomorphic with the legitimate modes of their sexual use. Nonetheless, what is striking about Athenian social usage is the tendency to collapse such distinctions as did indeed obtain between different categories of social subordinates and to create a single opposition between them all, *en masse*, and the class of adult male citizens: on this point, see Mark Golden, "*Pais*, 'Child' and 'Slave,'" *L'Antiquité classique* 54 (1985), 91–104, esp. 101 and 102, n. 38.

13 I have borrowed this analogy from Arno Schmitt, who uses it to convey what the modern sexual categories would look like from a traditional Islamic perspective: see Gianni De Martino and Arno Schmitt, *Kleine Schriften zu zwischenmännlicher Sexualität und Erotik in der muslimischen Gesellschaft* (Berlin, 1985), 19. Note that even the category of anatomical sex, defined in such a way as to include both men and women, seems to be absent from Greek thought for similar reasons: the complementarity of men and women as sexual partners implies to the Greeks a polarity, a difference in species, too extreme to be bridged by a single sexual concept equally applicable to each. In Greek medical writings, therefore, "the notion of sex never gets formalized as a functional identity of male and female, but is expressed solely through the representation of asymmetry and of complementarity between male and female, indicated constantly by abstract adjectives (*to thêly* ['the feminine'], *to arren* ['the masculine'])," according to Paola Manuli, "Donne mascoline, femmine sterili, vergini perpetue: La ginecologia greca tra Ippocrate e Sorano," in Silvia Campese, Paola Manuli, and Giulia Sissa, *Madre materia: Sociologia e biologia della donna greca* (Turin, 1983), 147–92, esp. 151 and 201n.

14 Maurice Godelier, "The Origins of Male Domination," *New Left Review* 127 (May–June, 1981), 3–17 (quotation on p. 17); cf. Maurice Godelier, "Le Sexe comme fondement ultime de l'ordre social et cosmique chez les Baruya de Nouvelle-Guinée. Mythe et réalité," in *Sexualité et pouvoir*, ed. Armando Verdiglione (Paris, 1976), 268–306, esp. 295–6.

15 I am indebted for this observation to Professor Peter M. Smith of the University of North Carolina at Chapel Hill, who notes that Sappho and Plato are the chief exceptions to this general rule.

16 See John J. Winkler, "Unnatural Acts: Erotic Protocols in Artemidoros' *Dream Analysis*," *Constraints of Desire: The Anthropology of Sex and Gender in Ancient Greece* (New York, 1989), 17–44, 221–4.

17 S. R. F. Price, "The Future of Dreams: From Freud to Artemidorus," *Past and Present* 113 (November, 1986), 3–37, abridged in *Before Sexuality: The Construction of Erotic Experience in the Ancient Greek World*, ed. David M. Halperin, John J. Winkler, and Froma I. Zeitlin (Princeton, 1990), 365–87; see also Michel Foucault, *The Care of the Self, The History of Sexuality, Volume Three*, trans. Robert Hurley (New York, 1986), 3–36, esp. 26–34.

18 See Waud H. Kracke, "Dreaming in Kagwahiv: Dream Beliefs and Their Psychic Uses in an Amazonian Indian Culture," *The Psychoanalytic Study of Society* 8 (1979), 119–71, esp. 130–2, 163 (on the predictive value of dreams) and 130–1, 142–5, 163–4, 168 (on the reversal of the Freudian direction of signification – which Kracke takes to be a culturally constituted defense mechanism and which he accordingly undervalues); Thomas Gregor, " 'Far, Far Away My Shadow Wandered . . .': The Dream Symbolism and Dream Theories of the Mehinaku Indians of Brazil," *American Ethnologist* 8 (1981), 709–20, esp. 712–13 (on predictive value) and 714 (on the reversal of signification), largely recapitulated in Thomas Gregor, *Anxious Pleasures: The Sexual Lives of an Amazonian People* (Chicago, 1985), 152–61, esp. 153. Foucault's comments on Artemidorus, in *The Care of the Self*, 35–6, are relevant here: "The movement of analysis and the procedures of valuation do not go from the act to a domain such as sexuality or the flesh, a domain whose divine, civil, or natural laws would delineate the permitted forms; they go from the subject as a sexual actor to the other areas of life in which he pursues his [familial, social, and economic] activity. And it is in the relationship between these different forms of activity that the principles of evaluation of a sexual behavior are essentially, but not exclusively, situated."

19 Note that even the human genitals themselves do not necessarily figure as sexual signifiers in all cultural or representational contexts: for example, Caroline Walker Bynum, "The Body of Christ in the Later Middle Ages: A Reply to Leo Steinberg," *Renaissance Quarterly* 39 (1986), 399–439, argues in considerable detail that there is "reason to think that medieval people saw Christ's penis not primarily as a sexual organ but as the object of circumcision and therefore as the wounded, bleeding flesh with which it was associated in painting and in text" (p. 407).

20 Padgug, "Sexual Matters," 8.

21 Paul Veyne, in "La Famille et l'amour sous le Haut-Empire romain," *Annales* (*E. S. C.*) 33 (1978), 35–63, remarks (p. 50) that Seneca's *Phaedra* is the earliest text to associate homosexual inclinations with a distinct type of subjectivity. The question is more complex than that, however, and a thorough exploration of it would require scrutinizing more closely the ancient figure of the *kinaidos*, a now-defunct sexual life-form: for details, see Maud

W. Gleason, "The Semiotics of Gender: Physiognomy and Self-Fashioning in the Second Century C.E.," in *Before Sexuality*, 389–415; John J. Winkler, "Laying Down the Law: The Oversight of Men's Sexual Behavior in Classical Athens," *Constraints of Desire*, 45–70, 224–6.

22 See Foucault, *The History of Sexuality*, 43: "As defined by the ancient civil or canonical codes, sodomy was a category of forbidden acts; their perpetrator was nothing more than the juridical subject of them. The nineteenth-century homosexual became a personage, a past, a case history, and a childhood, in addition to being a type of life, a life form, and a morphology, with an indiscreet anatomy and possibly a mysterious physiology. Nothing that went into his total composition was unaffected by his sexuality. It was everywhere present in him: at the root of all his actions because it was their insidious and indefinitely active principle; written immodestly on his face and body because it was a secret that always gave itself away. It was consubstantial with him, less as a habitual sin than as a singular nature." See also Randolph Trumbach, "London's Sodomites: Homosexual Behavior and Western Culture in the 18th Century," *Journal of Social History* 11 (1977), 1–33, esp. 9; Richard Sennett, *The Fall of Public Man* (New York, 1977), 6–8; Padgug, "Sexual Matters," 13–14; Jean-Claude Féray, "Une Histoire critique du mot homosexualité, [IV]," *Arcadie* 28, no. 328 (1981), 246–58, esp. 246–7; Alain Schnapp, "Une autre image de l'homosexualité en Grèce ancienne", *Le Débat*' 10 (1981), 116 (speaking of Attic vase-paintings): "One does not paint acts that characterize persons so much as behaviors that distinguish groups"; Pierre J. Payer, *Sex and the Penitentials: The Development of a Sexual Code 550–1150* (Toronto, 1984), 40–4, esp. 40–1: "there is no word in general usage in the penitentials for homosexuality as a category.... Furthermore, the distinction between homosexual acts and people who might be called homosexuals does not seem to be operative in these manuals" (also, pp. 14–15, 140–53); Bynum, "The Body of Christ," 406.

23 For attestations to the strength of individual preferences (even to the point of exclusivity) on the part of Greek males for a sexual partner of one sex rather than another, see Theognis, 1367–1368; Euripides, *Cyclops* 583–584; Xenophon, *Anabasis* 7.4.7–8; Aeschines, 1.41, 195; the *Life of Zeno* by Antigonus of Carystus, cited by Athenaeus, 13.563e; the fragment of Seleucus quoted by Athenaeus, 15.697de (= *Collectanea Alexandrina*, ed. J. U. Powell [Oxford, 1925], 176); an anonymous dramatic fragment cited by Plutarch, *Moralia* 766f–767a (= *Tragicorum Graecorum Fragmenta*, ed. August Nauck, 2nd edn [Leipzig, 1926], 906, #355; also in Theodor Kock, *Comicorum Atticorum Fragmenta* [Leipzig, 1880–1888], III, 467, #360); Athenaeus, 12.540e, 13.601e and ff.; Achilles Tatius, 2.35.2–3; pseudo-Lucian, *Erôtes* 9–10; Firmicus Maternus, *Mathesis* 7.15.1–2; and a number of epigrams by various hands contained in the *Palatine Anthology*: 5.19, 65, 116, 208, 277, 278; 11.216; 12.7, 17, 41, 87, 145, 192, 198, and *passim* (cf. P. G. Maxwell-Stuart, "Strato and the Musa Puerilis," *Hermes* 100 [1972], 215–40). See, generally, Dover, *Greek Homosexuality* (London, 1978), 62–3; John Boswell, "Revolutions, Universals and Sexual Categories," in *Homosexuality: Sacrilege, Vision, Politics* (note 6, above), 89–113, esp. 98–101; Winkler, "Laying Down the Law"; and, for a list of passages, Claude Courouve, *Tableau synoptique de références à l'amour masculin: Auteurs grecs et latins* (Paris, 1986).

24 Hilary Putnam, in *Reason, Truth and History* (Cambridge, 1981), 150–5, in the course of analyzing the various criteria by which we judge matters of

taste to be "subjective," implies that we are right to consider sexual preferences more thoroughly constitutive of the human personality than dietary preferences, but his argument remains circumscribed, as Putnam himself points out, by highly culture-specific assumptions about sex, food, and personhood.

25 Foucault, *The Use of Pleasure*, 51–2, remarks that it would be interesting to determine exactly when in the evolving course of Western cultural history sex became more morally problematic than eating; he seems to think that sex won out only at the turn of the eighteenth century, after a long period of relative equilibrium during the middle ages: see also *The Use of Pleasure*, 10; *The Care of the Self*, 143; "On the Genealogy of Ethics: An Overview of Work in Progress," in Hubert L. Dreyfus and Paul Rabinow, *Michel Foucault: Beyond Structuralism and Hermeneutics*, 2nd edn (Chicago, 1983), 229–52, esp. 229. The evidence lately assembled by Stephen Nissenbaum, *Sex, Diet, and Debility in Jacksonian America: Sylvester Graham and Health Reform*, Contributions in Medical History, 4 (Westport, Conn., 1980), and by Caroline Walker Bynum, *Holy Feast and Holy Fast: The Religious Significance of Food to Medieval Women* (Berkeley, 1987), suggests that moral evolution may not have been quite such a continuously linear affair as Foucault appears to imagine.

26 Jack H. Abbott, "On 'Women,'" *New York Review of Books* 28: 10 (June 11, 1981), 17. It should perhaps be pointed out that this lyrical confession is somewhat at odds with the more gritty account contained in the edited excerpts from Abbott's letters that were published a year earlier in the *New York Review of Books* 27: 11 (June 26, 1980), 34–7. (One might compare Abbott's statement with some remarks uttered by Bernard Boursicot in a similarly apologetic context and quoted by Richard Bernstein, "France Jails Two in a Bizarre Case of Espionage," New York Times [May 11, 1986]: "I was shattered to learn that he [Boursicot's lover of twenty years] is a man, but my conviction remains unshakable that for me at that time he was really a woman and was the first love of my life.")

27 See Davidson (note 6, above), 16.

28 I wish to thank Kostas Demelis for helping me with this formulation. Compare Padgug, "Sexual Matters," 5: "In any approach that takes as predetermined and universal the categories of sexuality, real history disappears."

29 Stephen Greenblatt, "Fiction and Friction," in *Reconstructing Individualism: Autonomy, Individuality, and the Self in Western Thought*, ed. Thomas C. Heller, Morton Sosna, and David E. Wellbery, with Arnold I. Davidson, Ann Swidler, and Ian Watt (Stanford, 1986), 30–52, 329–32, esp. 34, makes a similar point; arguing that "a culture's sexual discourse plays a critical role in shaping individuality," he goes on to say, "It does so by helping to implant in each person an internalized set of dispositions and orientations that governs individual improvisations." See also Padgug, "Sexual Matters," generally, Julian Henriques, Wendy Holloway, Cathy Urwin, Venn Couze, and Valerie Walkerdine, *Changing the Subject: Psychology, Social Regulation and Subjectivity* (London, 1984).

30 "Translations" (1972), lines 32–3, in Adrienne Rich, *Diving into the Wreck: Poems 1971–1972* (New York, 1973), 40–1 (quotation on p. 41).

31 "Canzone" (1942), lines 1–2, in W. H. Auden, *Collected Poems*, ed. Edward Mendelson (New York, 1976), 256–7 (quotation on p. 256).

15
No Sex, No Gender

Nancy F. Partner

1 Man or Woman? And How Do We Know What We Think We Mean By What We Mean By This Question?

Then we Bishops appeared and took our seats on the tribunal of the cathedral. Clotild was called before us. She showered abuse on her Abbess and
made a number of accusations against her. She maintained that the Abbess
kept a man in the nunnery, dressed in woman's clothing and looking like
a woman, although in effect there was no doubt that he was a man. His
job was to sleep with the Abbess whenever she wanted it. "Why! There's the
fellow!" cried Clotild, pointing with her finger. Thereupon a man stepped
forward, dressed in woman's clothing as I have told you. Everyone stared
at him. He said that he was impotent and that that was the reason why he
dressed himself up in this way. He maintained that he had never set eyes
on the Abbess, although, of course, he knew her by name. He had never
spoken to her in his life, and, in any case, he lived more than forty miles
out of Poitiers. Clotild failed to prove her Abbess guilty on this count.[1]

Like a little mass of compacted ambiguity dropped into one's attention, this episode from Gregory of Tours's detailed account of the rebellion in St Radegund's nunnery at Poitiers in 590 CE starts circle after
circle of questions, doubts, puzzles, simple and complex inquiry – and
all the possible answers open out to more questions. Some of the more
obvious matters an ideologically uncommitted pre-postmodern curiosity
might like to know about are:

– If the man allegedly living in the nunnery *looked* like a woman,
as Clotild claimed ("dressed . . . and looking like a woman"; "indutus

vestimenta muliebria pro femina haberetur"), why should there have been no doubt in her mind that he was a man ("vir manifestissime")?
– Bishop Gregory, here reporting as an eyewitness, at once saw and described the person who stepped forward as a *man*, "a man . . . dressed in woman's clothing" ("Qui cum in veste . . . muliebri"). This person apparently was not looking very much like a woman, nor, in his own terse reported comments, did he deny that he was a man. So why would this man cross-dress if he couldn't pass even cursory inspection?
– Did he, for instance, have a beard? Had he tried to alter his appearance at all beyond changing his clothes?[2]
– And what exactly did he mean by "impotent" ("dixit, se nihil opus posse virile agere")? Was this specifically a chronic failure to achieve erection, or was some wider area of powerless behavior involved in his inability at the *opus virile*?
– Why would he signal a private sexual failure in such a public way? Or had this impotence been made public: involving a marriage perhaps, divorce, exposure before kin and neighbors?
– Even on the premise of great public shame, what sort of logic led from male sexual inadequacy to public adoption of the dress of the other sex in a village in sub-Roman, Christian Gaul?

A different tangent of thought leads one to wonder just what he was doing so conveniently in the cathedral at Poitiers on the day of the trial, when he lived a long country distance away. The entertainment value of the trial was compelling, obviously, but could even the ruthless Clotild have suborned and bribed some ordinary man into playing this part? If so, he certainly panicked and went to pieces at the crucial moment. But even on the hypothesis of Clotild's attempting wild dirty tricks in her vendetta against her abbess, that does not clarify the personal and social meaning of the man in the dress. We are still left contemplating a person who seems to agree that he is a man, standing in the cathedral before at least six startled bishops and many interested strangers (and possibly neighbors) and offering his "impotence" as "the reason" ("ideoque") for going about dressed as a woman. A world of mystery is condensed into the banal logic of that connective: "ideoque" – "therefore, and so. . . ." Really?

The sangfroid of Gregory's account is breathtaking, and even more breathtaking is the implication one might begin to draw about the sexual sophistication of Merovingian village society, presented as too imperturbably blasé to do more than blink at a man solving his sexual problems by changing his sex role, or at least his clothing. As is the case with so many of Gregory's episodes, he tells us just enough to let us know how much more he is not telling. With respect to Gregory as historian, this can be read plausibly enough, following Walter Goffart's interpretation, as another instance of his stern disregard of all the trivial concerns of the temporal world, his deep indifference to the meaningless miscellany of carnal life, over too soon and too pointless while it lasts to be worth the effort of narrative satisfactions.[3] For Gregory, the only point worth making (or at least the only one he makes) is that Abbess Leubovera, custodian of the convent St Radegund personally founded, is innocent and worthy of her office.[4]

But profound *contemptus mundi* is a rare and uncommon thing. The unspecified "everyone" gathered in the cathedral were there for the vulgar pleasures of hearing the scandals of St Radegund's nuns rehearsed in all their dreadful detail, and I strongly suspect that Gregory's celebrated narrative deadpan covers an uproar of crude double takes with the laconic "Everyone stared at him." Indeed. Even for Gregory of Tours this is heroic understatement. And for the modern scholarly reader, the sum reaction comes down in the end to a better-articulated version of much the same thing – inwardly, we all do stare.

Yet the questions I posed are inevitable and commonsensical; that is, they request answers that will fit what we know of late Roman/early-medieval social institutions and sexual attitudes. The man in the cathedral offering an aspect (however inadequate) of his genital maleness as the logic for appearing in public as a woman does force us, however reluctantly, toward questions about what we mean by being a man, and being a woman, in private and in public. This reticent little mystery presses us to ask ourselves exactly what we are half-consciously including as necessary and sufficient conditions for male or female human identity, and where we assume this identity is founded – in the self or in society?

We might be thinking about some ineradicable core identity, the namelessly named "Him" in this case, a man who has suffered such massive affront to his sexual and social integrity that he resorted to a mimetic behavioral self-punishment, or had it imposed on him: a sexually powerless man = (i.e. might as well be) a woman. He altered his outer appearance to conform to the nonvirile reality underneath. This approach requires some acceptance of the idea that biological sexual identity (male or female) can stand in very troubled and problematic relation to gender identity (living as man or woman in one's society), and that these aspects require different kinds of understanding. Thinking about "Him" as an essentially male person whom we glimpse for a moment in a painful and distorted way of life means recognizing the need of a depth psychology, because we need a systematic way of discussing core identity, the self, and the centrality of sexual drives and sexual identity to the formation of character. Otherwise, we have no way of discussing what "He" is doing to *himself* by dressing as a woman.

On the other hand, it is possible to weight the discussion almost entirely on the side of exterior social forces. We might consider the possibility that, hidden in the social repertory of sub-Roman Gaulic life, there was an intergendered social role to accommodate males who could not or would not satisfy masculine standards. Perhaps this cross-dressed man went quietly home to his "woman's work" in the village, to a few crude insults but no violence or ostracism, to occupy some understood place at the social margin of kin and neighbors: a social facsimile of a woman. At the very least, we have to concede him or "her" some sort of life before and after that day at the cathedral in Poitiers. Anthropology can offer us some examples of socially condoned transvestism in tribal societies with a strong warrior ethos.[5] Perhaps there was something about the Germans that Tacitus forgot to tell us.

Readers of Gregory's *History* know that there is more to add to the discussion, namely, the next paragraph. Clotild had no sooner "failed to prove her Abbess guilty on this count" of keeping a disguised lover in the convent when, apparently caught up in an association of ideas, she proceeded to accuse the abbess of keeping yet another impotent man about her, this one purposely castrated so that the abbess might imitate the customs of the imperial court at Constantinople. Clotild gave the name of one of the servants "who was a eunuch."[6] This person was not present, but his physician, Reovalis, was:

> "When this servant was a young lad" (lit.: "Puer iste, parvolus cum esset"), he said, "he had terrible pains in the groin. Nobody could do anything for him. His mother went to Saint Radegund and asked her to have the case looked into. I was called in and she told me to do what I could. I cut out the lad's testicles, an operation I had once seen performed by a surgeon in the town of Constantinople. Then I handed him back to his mother."

Reovalis's testimony cleared the abbess of the second charge, and it offers a little more information about sexual identity and social roles among the Merovingians. A boy who was surgically castrated while he was very young ("parvolus"), before puberty, would have grown up looking much more feminine than any recognizable male who classifies himself as "unable to perform the virile act," which suggests that, being anatomically normal, he had expected or hoped to be normally potent. If impotence were a customary Merovingian reason for cross-dressing, then it would surely obtain here. And yet we have no reason to think that the castrated youth was dressed as a woman, and his work, as one of the servants of the convent quite unknown to the abbess, was an ordinary male occupation.[7] He is known as a "eunuch," which is a male category,[8] referred to with masculine grammatical gender, and allowed to live a man's life in his society, at least with regard to livelihood and dress. This allows one to argue that male identity based on anatomical identification at birth and reinforced throughout infancy by a mother who knew she had a son could establish a gender identity strong enough to persist through disabling alteration of the genitals, permanent impotence, and absence of masculine characteristics such as beard, lowered voice, and so forth. Alternatively, it might still be argued that "eunuch" is itself an alternative social/sexual role, specific only to certain times and places, intergendered, defined, and reinforced by forces exterior to the self which, following this logic, might not exist at all in our sense.

This may seem an odd beginning to an essay about studying medieval women, but I wanted to open some fundamental questions about sexual identity, the conventions of gender, and the continuity of human psychology in ways that are historically specific and inevitable-feeling, relatively free of ideological commitments. These are issues that cannot, in the politically and intellectually overwrought climate that prevails, remain long innocent, but it is worth reminding ourselves that unhinging gender identity from sexual identity is not a frivolous abstraction recently invented by oversubtle feminists but the appropriate and inevitable way of discussing central and sometimes overwhelming aspects of the lives of human beings at all times and places.

It is the historical study of women that has opened and defined these curious questions about sexual identity, sexuality, and the sex-linked protocols of social life, matters that never seemed to be questions at all so long as history was chiefly a matter of men studying men. Only the most temperate of feminist criticism was necessary to recognize that biological femaleness did not automatically or "naturally" entail femininity when the "Feminine" turned out to be every society's catchall category for transparent male fears, biological fantasies, and crude excuses for systematic domination. Separation of sexual identity from social identity has been and continues to be a central premise of women's history as well as the related field of the history of sexuality. In theory at least, sexuality as an interiorized defining structure of the integral self, and sexual belief and behavior as semiotic expressions of a culture's preoccupations are now radically separate and incommensurate ways of thinking.

In far too many ways the women whom medieval historians have to study are the imaginative constructions of men: the theoretical women of medical, philosophic, legal, and religious literature; the women seen as the property of masters, fathers, husbands; the women fantasized by poets, romancers, preachers, hagiographers. And yet, historians, men and women alike, have no choice but to do that same sort of work: imagine the women of the past. For this reason, for the sake of a heightened sense of the incorrigibleness of the human mind, and to remind us that the sexes are fated to struggle together, I chose the man in a dress as the emblem for the problems this essay addresses.

2 Sexuality and Social Construction

Fundamental notions of sexuality, identity, and our estimate of how deeply the cultural conventions of gender impinge on individual character not only affect the *way* we think about medieval women but unavoidably determine whether the "women" we think about are human beings or cultural ideograms.

Our intellectual allegiances concerning such matters are being actively courted these days by enthusiastic adherents of a social constructionist theory of human formation and behavior which flatly denies all concepts of the mind and sexuality which proceed from psychoanalytic theory. In its most consistent and dogmatic versions, this view denies any innate endowment of mind universal to human beings, ignores or denies the psychosexual dynamics which culminate in individual character, and concedes only some minimal biologic substratum as shared among all of our species over time. Psychoanalysis assumes that manifest patterns of behavior, speech, and conscious desire all variously reflect the organization of an individual mind, both conscious and unconscious, which must continually adjust its wishes to the demands of a real exterior world. In the constructivist vision, "mind," in this sense, disappears, and the body and its behaviors are a metaphor map shaped solely by the unavoidable and ubiquitous pressures of social processes determined by power relations: social teleology crushes out human ontology.

The topic of homosexuality in the setting of the ancient world has been the major focus of constructivist scholarship, with studies concerned with feminine gender (as conceived by men) a second favorite topic. One of the most active and adamant proponents of this project[9] is David Halperin, whose *One Hundred Years of Homosexuality* is the best introduction to the subject because it combines Halperin's detailed arguments for the constructivist position, a candid transcribed interview with a challenging questioner, and three essays on scholarly subjects, including his clever and searching "Why Is Diotima a Woman?"[10] Diotima, the name of the learned woman who purportedly taught Socrates the lessons on erotic love he expounds to the company in Plato's *Symposium*, turns out to be not merely the female-gendered fiction she seems ("she," after all, is only a name mentioned by Socrates), but, more complicatedly, she is not even a *feminine* fiction at all. "She" is so wholly appropriated by the male discourse of Plato's philosophy as to be a "reinscribed male identity"; "she is an alternate male identity," a metaphor of masculine discourse: " 'Woman' and 'man' are figures of male speech. Gender – no less than sexuality – is an irreducible fiction."[11]

The social constructivist view goes much further than this radical separation of the "fiction" of gender from biological sex. Sexuality in the complexly extended modern sense, the kernel of individual personality which leaves its signature on other, nonsexual behavior, is also a fiction. In this view there is no psychologically organized individual sexuality at all, and an infant's anatomical status (male or female) does not seem to entail anything about its sexual development aside from being the site for the lessons its society imposes. Directly and heavily derived from Michel Foucault's work in general and his *History of Sexuality* in particular, the constructivist view asserts, with Foucault, that the humanist concept of "the subject," the coherently individuated human being which we also indicate by the concept of the "self," is a myth perpetuated within modern discourses of power to impose and conceal the imprisoning designs of social authority. The complex notions of sexuality as a central and universal expression of the self, offered by psychoanalysis, are regarded by Foucault as a specifically modern invention (as opposed to a discovery or an explanation of human reality), another of the malign and subtle modern instruments for imposing an intimate and totalitarian discipline over all of society by means of knowledge, or perhaps "knowledge."

The leading ideas which have been largely accepted by scholars who wish to work out the detailed history of sexual life along lines suggested by Foucault are (1) that history is characterized by disjuncture, discontinuity, rupture; (2) that the self, a self-existent, coherent being persisting through all change until death, is a naive illusion dating only from the eighteenth century; (3) that sexuality as the interior organization of libidinal drives into wishes, repressions, and sublimations is also an illusion, of yet more modern date (related vaguely and variously to capitalism, science, industrialization, the bourgeoisie, etc., the usual suspects). It does seem to be assumed that humans have some general urge to genital pleasure but that only systems of discourse derived from specific patterns of social authority give this urge any special meaning or form. Ideas that were needling, provocative, and brilliantly wrongheaded as interesting aspects of an interesting mind when offered by their originator are now leadenly reduced to the dogmas of a new orthodoxy. The body and its pleasures, Foucault's program for a true history of sexuality, invariably turn out to be metaphors for society and power.[12]

Scholarship collected under this rubric tends to focus on the sexual behaviors, erotic art and language of premodern societies that most sharply differ from modern practice; a well-chosen selection can be found in the anthology edited by Halperin with John Winkler and Froma Zeitlin, *Before Sexuality: The Construction of Erotic Experience in the Ancient Greek World*, a companion volume to his *One Hundred Years*.[13] The tendency of sexual behavior to incorporate and reinforce social hierarchies, class distinctions, masculine competitions, purity and contamination anxieties is subtly and fascinatingly anatomized by scholars attuned to these frequencies, but for all the luxuriant documentation of erotic cum political and social detail that makes these essays enthralling, there is a certain predictability here. "Surfaces" of behavior, language, and image invariably dissolve away to reveal all of hierarchical society pressing its commands and protocols onto human actors – and nothing else. Constructionist scholarship informed by Foucault's sensibilities adopts his signature correlation of sex with power, and attempts his virtuoso ability to parse all eroticism into elements of (disbursed and displaced) sadism.[14] Power *is* pleasure in this vision, and thus all attention is directed to the configurations of social authority which then serve to "explain" human sexuality: that is the formula underlying the surface variety of constructionist work. As in one of John Winkler's essays: ". . . the energy of sex is conceived [in *Daphnis and Chloe*] not as something that relates friend to friend or equal to equal but more as a dynamic that clarifies a relation between enemies, opposites, unequals."[15] "The social body precedes the sexual body": a circular premise and self-proof.[16]

The best work in this mode produces detailed cultural portraits in which sexual players (interchangeably human and literary) re-enact in stylized erotic mime the class, gender, and economic hierarchies of the larger society.[17] The often-startling sexual mores of long-distant societies, when read in this way, as condensed tropes of the structured society, become intelligible and meaningful. The opaque and mysterious quality that clings to human sexuality is exorcised and replaced by the simpler cruelties of privilege and domination. "It begins to look as if the entire procedure [public scrutiny of sexual behavior of Athenian citizens] had very little to do with sex and everything to do with political ambitions and alliances . . ."[18] – this, from John Winkler's essay on the sexual protocol demanded of Athenian men, is a typical sort of interpretation, and typically convincing within its frame of reference. The fixed concentration on social hierarchy and the analogue patterns of sex/status domination which are typical of all traditional societies obscures both individual and cultural variation. Using the constructionist optic, Athens and Sparta are indistinguishable.

Work that conveys the feeling of a genuine "historical anthropology" is the signal achievement of constructionist scholarship, but the philosophic or meta-historical claims made on the basis of these social readings of sexual life are stretched and exaggerated far beyond what the evidence can support. There is something intellectually stifled and rigid underlying the modishly sophisticated language that characterizes this approach: social meaning exhausts all meaning. Once some fragment of a specific cultural pattern (invariably an aspect of dominance: males over females, free over slave, citizens over noncitizens, etc.) can be shown to make a plausible fit with some form of sexual behavior (who can be a penetrator, who a submissive receptor, etc.), the meaning of that behavior is considered complete and nothing more is to be sought. This one-way interpretive move, from experience *outward only* to the group or collective culture, denies by ignoring the other, complementary move from the surface to the personal interior, from public to private, from the historically local to the universal, to the psyche. The interpretive move *outward only* is what Halperin calls a "cultural poetics":

> Cultural poetics refers to the process whereby a society and its subgroups
> construct widely shared meanings. . . . These meanings are jointly produced,
> distributed, enforced, and subverted by human communities. . . . We assume
> the interdependence in culture of social practices and subjective experi-
> ences. The erotic experiences of individual human beings are thus, in our
> view, artifacts that reflect, in part, the larger cultural poetics of the soci-
> eties in which those individuals live.[19]

This "constructionist thesis," in Halperin's term,[20] here given its most
flexible and generous statement, turns out to offer no concept or premise
that could plausibly explain how anyone could possibly begin to "sub-
vert" any of the "widely shared meanings" whose production, distribution, and enforcement have constructed the human thing which has no
self and no personal sexuality. In fact, the "subjective experiences" glan-
cingly conceded by Halperin are never really acknowledged or explored
by him or any of the constructionist scholars, and quite rightly – there are
no individuals with subjectivity in any profound sense in their conceptual
world to have experiences. "Subjective experiences" are, by definition,
miniature replicas of "social practices." There is nothing else they can
be. He is certainly right in noting that, in modern thought, "sexuality is
intrinsic to the concept and set of practices focused on 'the self,'" but is
oddly disengenuous when he goes on to define the self as "the blank
individual who is the subject of the modern social sciences."[21] There is
nothing "blank" about the modern concept of the self – that dense locus
of conscious and unconscious mental processes in continual negotiation
with the social world. If experience is something more than the passive
registration of sensory impact, then only the self can have experience.

Halperin's candid attempts to explain how a constructionist being comes
to be constructed lead nowhere, and his discussion of how (or why) the
modern social processes, which according to him are monomaniacally
intent on creating exclusive heterosexuals, should have carelessly produced
so many homosexuals is convoluted beyond comprehension. The constructionist thesis holds that "our intuitions about the world and about
ourselves are no doubt constituted at the same time as our sexuality
itself," that is, very early in life, and the process of social construction is
therefore beyond the reach of intuition or observation.[22] Aside from the
slight paranoid style of this theory, it offers no clue as to why there
should exist any individual deviation at all (much less, subversion!) after
helpless infants are subjected to a social processing so relentlessly immanent and enveloping as to resemble processing in a waffle iron.

The problem here is that constructionists insist on being at war
with what they call "essentialism" (briefly, any theory that seeks "culture-
independent, objective and intrinsic properties" in human experience),[23]
although, as one anticonstructionist, John Boswell, ironically points out,
nobody will admit to being an "essentialist" in the constructionists' version.[24] It seems to be assumed that the ground being fought over, human

sexuality, has to be taken and wholly occupied by one explanatory force only. This is a reductive and polemical approach to a deeply complex matter. All explanations are instances of some mode of comprehension (in philosopher Louis Mink's phrase) operating with its own concepts and aims, which do implicitly assert epistemological primacy. However, there is no single, all-encompassing mode which satisfies all the aims of understanding:

> But one cannot argue for the primacy of any of the modes except by reference to criteria which themselves are derivative from that mode's aim of comprehension. Hence each mode is self-justifying; critical analysis and intellectual advance are possible within but only within each mode.[25]

This general principle of the nature of explanation, quoted here from Mink's austerely compressed essay, "Modes of Comprehension and the Unity of Knowledge," may seem rather abstract for the subjects under discussion in this essay, but since I am arguing for what is considered an "essentialist" theory as a *contributing* interpretation of complex human behavior in the distant past, I feel I ought to expose the grounds of my position as clearly as I am capable of understanding them.

Rigorous guidance through the intellectual vanity fair of academic theorizing about self and society is offered by George Devereux in some forty years of work as both psychoanalyst and cultural anthropologist. Like Louis Mink, Devereux saw clearly that modes of comprehension appropriate to human behavior proceed from their particular premises toward their intellectual aims; different modes cannot be forced into a single slurred-together unity, nor are they in conflict for ideological dominion over the totality of experience. In "The Argument," introduction to *Ethnopsychoanalysis: Psychoanalysis and Anthropology as Complementary Frames of Reference*, Devereux sets out the principle of "complementarity" as his methodological principle of explanation, which he also calls the "double discourse" – the explanation of human behavior by (at least) two discourses, one addressed outward to society, and one inward to the psycho-dynamics of the individual:

> In the study of Man (but not only in the study of Man) it is not only possible but mandatory to explain a behavior, already explained in one way, also in another way – i.e., within another frame of reference.[26]

We may forgive Devereux his use of the out-of-favor collective noun, for the sake of the breadth of mind and logical clarity which see that "a given human act can be made to seem inevitable in terms of either sociocultural or psychological psychoanalytic explanations of it."[27]

The constructionist argument is too multifaceted and shifts its ground too often for more detailed analysis here,[28] but what is very clear is that in a world in which the sexuality, self-consciousness, intuitions, and desires of young, psycheless humans are simultaneously "constituted," subject to "acculturation [which] consists precisely in learning to accept as natural, normal, and inevitable what is in fact conventional and arbitrary,"[29] incidents such as the following could not, by definition, happen:

> A young girl at Oxford, the daughter of one of the burgesses, and already wedded to a certain youth of the same town, was inflamed by a stronger love for another youth, and deserting her husband, actually lived with him as his wife. Her husband accused her and proved the charge, and the bishop [Hugh of Lincoln] earnestly admonished her to return without delay to him. She, however, was dissuaded by her mother . . . and declared defiantly that she would rather die than live with him. The man of God [Bishop Hugh] then took her husband by his right hand, and combining persuasion with threats said, "If you desire to be my daughter, obey me and give your husband the kiss of peace with God's blessing. If you do not, I shall not spare you and your evil counsellors." He also ordered her husband to give her the kiss of peace, which he would willingly have done, but the wretched girl impudently spat in his face, although he was near the altar and the bishop himself was present in the church. . . . Everyone was deeply shocked. . . .[30]

And everyone should have been shocked! Nothing in the ruling systems of twelfth-century English gender, morality, marital and religious authority would seem to have constructed that willful young woman, who had apparently slipped loose from whole epistemes of discursive processing. But there she *and* her mother are – rejecting husbands, choosing lovers, shrugging off the bishop, and spitting in church. The "run but you can't hide" constructionist thesis has nothing to tell us about this incident, while cultural history with a depth psychology at its heart welcomes and recognizes a self-willed bourgeoise who plainly understood that social disciplines emanate from sources exterior to *herself*, and that, with a little luck (and the support of a strong-willed mother), even women can have erotic projects of their own.

The constructionists of ancient history simply ignore the work of E. R. Dodds with its deftly incorporated psychological insights, but their contemporary Peter Brown, who enters into intricate conversation with ancient and medieval sources with a deep and assured command (and who is around to defend his work), is not so easily ignored. Although he is one of the contributors to the *Before Sexuality* anthology, Brown's essay, "Bodies and Minds: Sexuality and Renunciation in Early Christianity," a summary of the major themes of his brilliant book, *The Body and Society*, so contradicts and disproves central constructionist dogmas as to require some response from the editor:[31]

> To be sure, a certain degree of identification of the self with the sexual self can be noticed in late antiquity and was strengthened by the Christian

confessional; however, it did not become complete, explicit, and authoritative until the eighteenth- and nineteenth-century scientific construction of sexuality as a separate field of positivistic study.[32]

This slighting acknowledgment ("To be sure, a certain degree . . .") precedes a weak and evasive dismissal, which is nothing more than a reassertion of Foucaultian dogma. In any case, I have not noticed constructionists limiting themselves to "complete, explicit, and authoritative" evidence to support their own arguments, and since when has Christianity not been culturally "authoritative"? Brown assembles and analyzes complex masses of difficult materials before arriving at his well-grounded and powerful interpretations:

> As on an X-ray photograph, therefore, a patch of disquieting opacity lay at the center of the human heart. What is distinctive is the speed and the tenacity with which that dark spot came to be identified, in Christian circles, with specifically sexual desires, with unavowed sexual stratagems, and, as we shall see, with the lingering power of sexual fantasy. . . .

> Body and mind, now sensed as mysteriously interconnected through sexuality, had sunk together since the time of Galen, receding into the depths of the half-charted and, from now onward, ever-fascinating unity of the self.[33]

Attentive readers of *The Body and Society* know that the persuasive power of Brown's readings lies in the open secret that he greets all the historical dead as once-complete persons, fully interiorized men and women with, implicitly, the same drives and psychosexual organization as ourselves, who yet freely regarded the world and analyzed themselves with values and concepts radically different from our own. The deep and subtly calibrated balance Brown finds between an unstated psychological premise of human universality and an explicit historical sense acutely sensitive to local cultural pressures accounts for his ability to make the most austerely removed desert ascetic seem to turn and show us a human face. The presence of a successful "double discourse" (whether or not the author worked it out with conscious intent) is signaled by the reader's sense of richly expanded insights: the sense of recognizable human lives adapted to, yet in tension with, the requirements of the social world. Brown's work is offered in the pre-postmodern (alias, traditional) theory-free manner, and in an entirely personal style of evocative, almost painterly metaphor. A generational audience who no longer read Freud or any of his successors might easily not even recognize that this is psychoanalytically informed history.[34]

The structure of human *experience* of the body and desire from the second century CE to the death of Augustine traced so sensitively throughout this study is "an encounter of mind with world, neither of these ever simple or wholly perspicuous," in Peter Gay's elegantly plain-language psychoanalytic definition.[35] Every human being brings an innate endowment of psychological organization, mind, to encounter the social structures and belief systems of the surrounding society, world. Human experience emerges from the ensuing negotiations, frustrations, and re-conciliations of this endless traffic. Culture and social pressures are one great dimension, but only one dimension, of human experience. We never seem to encounter any people in constructivist studies, just bundles of behaviors or collective thought patterns linked to names. In Peter Brown's writing, the most attenuated sun-dried hermit is a man:

> Sexual fantasies highlighted the areas of intractability in the human person. But this intractability was not simply physical. It pointed into the very depths of the soul. Sexual desire revealed the knot of unsurrendered privacy that lay at the very heart of fallen man. Thus, in the new language of the desert, sexuality became, as it were, an ideogram of the unopened heart.[36]

Explicitly realized intuitions into sexuality as the unified connector of body and mind were fully developed by the time of Augustine, and Brown notes that this insight was established "from now onwards." Medievalists should accept this conclusion at its full weight. There are endless consequences for the discipline of history in its entirety of a choice between the social constructionist vision of human life and a history based on humans with complex psychosexual organization. The specific consequences for the history of women are crucial. The question for feminist scholars should *not* be whether everything psychoanalysis has to say about women is perfectly flattering, but which body of assumptions helps us to the richest, most complex and generous understanding of women – especially the women of frankly misogynist societies. Which set of assumptions offers them humanity, and which reduces them to passive anthropological exhibits?

3 Ambitions of the Self: Heloise at Argenteuil

No one having skill in medicine judges an inward disease by inspection of the outward appearance.

Heloise to Peter Abelard[37]

Heloise, more than any other female voice, can tell us something important about what it was to be a woman in the twelfth century. She does us the great service of candidly anatomizing the full resources available to the conscious mind: rational argument, acquired knowl-edge, wishes, fears, memories, self-conscious reflections, waking fantasies, dreams. Her logic is Augustinian (the mind is self-divided, and the will is incorrigibly willful), her style a classical/patristic pastiche, but her voice is her own. If we ask unprejudiced questions about her life, and are willing to remember Devereux's principle that "a given human act can be made to seem inevitable in terms of either sociocultural or psychological–psychoanalytic explanations of it,"[38] she offers us generous and candid answers which are both culturally patterned and specific to her alone. This is a point that can too easily be lost. Because Heloise was not ordinary and did not live an ordinary life, we should never lapse into regarding her as a sport or marginal deviant of her society. For all her striking talent and education, and through all the dramatic plot of her life, she was fully intelligible to those who knew her; she attracted sympathy, trust, and respect from very discerning friends. And she was profoundly known to herself.

Her bizarre postmortem career as an honorary man in literary drag has been recently analyzed by Barbara Newman in an extraordinarily fine essay, "Authority, Authenticity, and the Repression of Heloise,"[39] whose frank title tells us its plot. One hopes that after this meticulously argued exposé, Heloise's literary gender will be permanently attached to her literal sex, and that both, reunited in her historical self, will finally be allowed undisputed ownership of her letters.[40] Newman's own analysis of Heloise, grounded in the idea that complex personalities must incorporate conflicts and self-contradictions, is sensitive, generous, and real. This view of Heloise takes her seriously. It makes her intensely developed intellectual life the central source of the multiplied feminine (and often misogynist) paradigms Heloise enacted for and to her one love: "she enacted each of these roles vis-à-vis a single beloved other who became in turn her Ovidian seducer, her Pompey, her Aeneas, her Jerome; she could be his Corinna or Cornelia, his Dido, or his Paula."[41] All I wish to add here are a few emphases in tone and nuance to point up the advantages of a psychologically grounded approach in dealing with the Heloise themes of feminine abjection and sublimation.

The historically specific, culturally constructed nature of Heloise's experiences, from her classical/patristic Latin education to her office as abbess, is apparent to us. What has to be thought about through another optic is exactly *who* was having those experiences. Peter Gay's explication of mind and world is acute and sympathetic: "The human mind hungers for reality; except for the largely encapsulated id, which is the depository of the raw drives and of deeply repressed material, the other institutions of the mind, the ego and the superego, draw continuously and liberally on the culture in which they subsist, develop, succeed, and fail. While the mind presents the world with its needs, the world gives the mind its grammar, wishes their vocabulary, anxieties their object."[42] The openness of the mind to its world, its conformity and its ability to push back – the reality principle, so central to psychoanalytic thought

– is the bridge between the double discourses of mind and culture. My remarks about Heloise are my own attempt at an interpretation built on complementary frames of reference.

Heloise's letters do not sustain a psychohistorical inquiry because she was neurotic; quite the contrary. Heloise displays what a strong and well-adapted female personality looks like in the cultural world she shared with everyone else of her time, in the personal crisis she faced alone, and under the most poignant and unremitting disappointments. She was not happy, admittedly, but consistent good luck has never been a necessary condition for any serious conception of psychic health. The keynote of the letters is her refusal to sacrifice her personality and history to embittered shame disguised as religious compunction (Abelard's strategy). She never cultivated emotional numbness as an antidote to reality:

> For what repentance of sins is that, however great the mortification of the body, when the mind still retains the same will to sin, and burns with its old desire? Easy is it indeed for anyone by confessing his sins to accuse himself, or even in outward satisfaction to mortify his body. But it is most difficult to tear away the heart from the desire of the greatest pleasures. . . .[43]

The mind seeks its pleasures – and so it follows perfectly from the logic of this vigorous mind, open to experience and strongly reality-principled, that Heloise *would* naturally have sought the alternative gratifications offered to her in the religious life she perforce led: the respect, honors, and daily sense of achievement earned by her work as abbess of Argenteuil. There is no contradiction here between her frank longings for past delights and her exemplary life in the convent: just as she refused to suppress memory and desire, so she also acknowledged the claims of external reality in the present. With all her longings and frustrations, her anger and regrets, Heloise never fails to meet a psychoanalytic standard of psychic health: strong reality principle, the capacity to adjust and readjust to changing circumstance without self-destroying conformity, a correct appreciation of the difference between her own wishes and the external pressures imposed by her society.

Heloise had arrived at a deep understanding of the divide between inner and outer lives, between the pressure of wishes and the frustrations of reality. Every configuration of her life had accentuated that division between what she would demand of reality and what reality instead demanded of her. She rebuked Abelard for his slack and convenient willingness to accept her outward role, The Abbess, as the totality of her identity: "No one having skill in medicine judges an inward disease by inspection of the outward appearance." She was not speaking here literally about disease or herself as a diseased person. The metaphor of medical examination expresses her scorn of superficiality and literalness, with Abelard cast as the stupid doctor unable to diagnose an affliction of the heart. Provoked beyond the self-suppressing decorums of medieval literary convention by Abelard's dismissive and banal reply to her first letter, Heloise let herself speak from her self.

Her second letter is an insistent, multiply argued demonstration of the truth that she had not become merely the sum total of her manifest daily behavior. "They preach that I am chaste who have not discovered the hypocrite in me. They make the purity of the flesh into a virtue, when it is a virtue not of the body but of the mind."[44] The "outward appearance" is not all. Although she had conformed her speech and her actions to the demands of her office, she had not surrendered her mind. Her deepest and most intransigent assertion is *not* of a continuing sexual urge (that is the fiercely defiant evidence: fantasies during mass, dreams at night, unsuppressed memories), but of her continuing *identity*: "I *am*." I desire and thus prove that I persist as my self, not as my role as The Abbess, or The Penitent, or even The Victim. If there is any shock value in Heloise's second letter, it is not found in a shocking eroticism, but in the shock of recognition we feel at being addressed so directly by a mind that speaks to us from the interior of the self.

The first and overwhelming fact about Heloise is that she never attempted to obliterate or neutralize the reality and force of her original and enduring desires. She seemed to locate and ground her identity in precisely those desires, body and mind "mysteriously interconnected through sexuality," as Peter Brown put it. This is crucial to any assessment of Heloise and encourages us to think about the permanent qualities of human life over time. In the first place, no epistemic system or discursive pressures we can discern in medieval culture seem to suggest, much less support and justify, the strategy of mind and will Heloise allows us to witness. Secondly, her revealed personality points directly to developed interiority, to unusual possibilities of autonomous maneuver under great pressure to conform, to an astute understanding of social forces as distinct from the self, to an emotional decision to support the unique "I" even at the cost of great pain and inner turmoil.[45] In short, Heloise is only understandable as a self, a psyche compounded of the drives we all share, developed in a particular time, place, and culture – a person negotiating her life between wishes and denials, internal pressures and external stresses.

She never acceded to the massively overdetermined pressures of religious and social authority, even when Abelard added his personal influence to them, to attempt the desire-erasing process of repentance and atonement. By her own account, she recognized that her thoughts were sinful, but she never repented and never atoned. She never turned herself against herself; she preferred the inner triumph of the intact "I" of her *own* history, her own desires, her own identity. All her words and reported behavior point to a recognition on her part that the obliteration of her deepest wishes would be a disorganizing assault on her identity.

Her love for Abelard had focused and condensed all her powerful intellect and heroic emotions onto one object. This complicated love carried her ambitions (highly developed with very little outlet), her full ego ideal, her powers of sublimation, and her defiance/compliance with the society that constrained her, as a woman, to channel all her wishes "through him," through some Him.

Sublimation is easily misunderstood; it does not mean the vaporizing of libido, or an ethereal or ascetic turning away from worldly pursuits, nor does successful sublimation require giving up all sexual pleasures. In a classically simple statement: "This capacity to exchange its originally sexual aim for another one, which is no longer sexual but which is psychically related to the first aim, is called the capacity for sublimation."[46] Sublimation is the routine work of civilization, and its projects are found in and suggested by the world. Chief among these is the pursuit of knowledge. Heloise is a perfect instance of the close and energizing connection between well-developed sexual curiosities arising in early childhood and the intense intellectual interests of adulthood; Freud noted that sexual excitement is often aroused by concentration on intellectual work.[47] Heloise and Abelard (like Paolo and Francesca) knew the erotic power of books. Freud also acutely remarked that the systematic punishment and suppression of sexual curiosity in small girls undoubtedly inhibited and depressed their intellectual development: "In this way they are scared away from *any* form of thinking, and knowledge loses its value for them." This "special application of [the] proposition that sexual life lays down the pattern for the exercise of other functions"[48] is shown at its exuberant opposite by Heloise's passionate learning and learned passion. These mirrored and mutually reinforcing sexual and intellectual drives *were* her achieved sublimation, not the enforced discipline of monastic life.

She did not learn from Abelard her ideal of "the philosopher" – pinnacle of human achievement and object of reverence and renown; that was her own fantasy/ideal, one wholly denied to her by every convention and institution she knew. Heloise's interior style was to turn exterior suppression inside out: she internalized the self-suppression and social limitations imposed on her and remained so heroically resolute in this discipline that she exasperated and frightened Abelard and her uncle, who were always prepared to compromise much more easily. Since she could not become a famous philosopher herself, she would do nothing *except* what furthered and protected Abelard's career even if it meant refusing to marry after she had a child and Abelard wished to marry her. Once she was coerced into the marriage, she steadfastly refused to acknowledge it, although her uncle had broken his own promise of secrecy, and disaster threatened from the confusion her denials caused. For all of Abelard's notorious ambition and touchy vanity, Heloise was the one who had the clearest and most ambitious conception of what a "philosopher's" life must be, and she *insisted* on sacrificing herself to that ideal. It was her own fierce ambition, suppressed and channeled through Abelard.

Her love for Abelard was masochistically tinged (and unsurprisingly, he describes his for her with sadistic callousness.) She cultivated, rapturously exaggerated, her erotically charged idea of Abelard as father/teacher/lord/autocrat of love. Patriarchy has never been rendered so exciting. Her acknowledgment of sin, her understanding of sin, was, unremarkably, what she had learned from patristic and contemporary Christianity. Yet fervently self-critical as she was, and only too eager to share in the blame for the calamities of Abelard's life, she never apologized for the feelings and acts for which she had no honest regrets:

> I call God to witness, if Augustus, ruling over the whole world, were to deem me worthy of the honour of marriage, and to confirm the whole world to me, to be ruled by me for ever, dearer to me and of greater dignity would it seem to be thy strumpet than his empress.[49]

It does not require any deep commitment to feminism to find this peculiarly energetic self-abasement a little unnerving (although we should also note that her fantasy is of being emperor, not mere consort). "No reward for this [monastic life] may I expect from God, for the love of whom it is well known that I did not anything. . . . I have forbidden myself all pleasures that I might obey thy will. I have reserved nothing for myself, save this, to be now entirely thine."[50] It is hardly surprising that Abelard begins his cautiously distanced reply, "To Heloise his dearly beloved sister *in Christ*, Abelard her brother *in the Same* [my emphasis]," by bringing in a third party as witness and chaperon. Heloise had managed to turn the conventional submissiveness of women into a weapon.

Her style of love is more abject than anyone, man or woman, now admires: she cultivated a passionate abjection, an unreserved insideout aggression of total surrender to one solitary exalted object (who may have been as oppressed by this gift as any modern man would be). This strain of overrefined masochism, with its secret core of control and manipulation never perfectly hidden, was not entirely unfamiliar to her contemporaries. If the chosen lover's name were Jesus, the rhetoric of cultivated pain, languishing, and total erotic submission could be recategorized into respectability.[51] This erotic style fit Heloise's requirements, but it was also culture-specific, endlessly exploited and elaborated in monastic and mystical practice, and in women it seems to build on a deep structure of unresolved lack and sense of need (I am nothing/you are everything), a deep psychic base externalized and given massive cultural endorsement by the near total male dominance in society. In another time and place she might have pursued her vision of intellectual and moral distinction by a less indirect route. In twelfth-century Paris she had little choice but to pursue all her aims, sexual, intellectual, her exalted ego ideal, through *Him*.

Offered Abelard's account of his life with Heloise, and the intimate confidences of Heloise's letters, we should feel no need to apologize or equivocate over ascribing to her a psychic structure of drives, internalized strictures of conscience, and a complex, reality-connected conscious ego. Nor is there any reason to hesitate before our sense that Heloise's sexuality was the living core from which the full expression of her personality radiated; she clearly felt it to be so. She assures us that there is a human mind, intelligible to us in its structure and dynamic, which variously adapts to culture's changing repertory of patterns over time. Heloise's complex sexuality speaks to us intelligibly and powerfully: sexuality speaks to our common humanity. Her femininity, her particular twelfth-century European way of being a woman, living a woman's life, is what disconcerts us: gender speaks of distance and difference. Sexuality may be cruel, but gender can be mean.

4 The Man in the Dress: Once More

When Abelard retreated to the Monastery of St Denis after being castrated, he was doing, in a more sophisticated mode, something analogous to the cross-dressing of the man in the cathedral at Poitiers. He was putting the dress of public and institutional celibacy onto private sexual incapacity: "... with what face would I appear in public, to be pointed out by every finger, scarified by every tongue, doomed to be a monstrous spectacle to all; ... it was the confusion of shame ... that drove me to the retirement of a monastic cloister."[52] There was always something lurking in medieval culture ready to see monks as unmanly. But no one has ever thought that Abelard's gender had slipped loose from his sexual identity; he remained permanently and unproblematically a man in identity, and indeed so conventionally masculine in his feelings that he could not bear the prospect of life in the world where everyone "knew." Without recourse to any special insight or theory, everyone can recognize that Abelard's masculine sensibility, his male pride, was, if anything, intensified by his genital loss. He did not become a social facsimile of a woman in anyone's eyes.

The man at Poitiers, following a simpler logic of desperation and gender calculation, put on the dress of male failure, of effeminated maleness: "might as well be a woman" is not the same as being a woman. Gender is not so easily parted from sex. This is not to deny that gender *roles*, under certain special circumstances, may be available to individuals who do not qualify for them in biological sex but who "earn" them through other attributes of personality and behavior; one of these instances in

Old Norse law which allowed a daughter to substitute for a son is discussed by Carol Clover; another is the "berdache" transvestites of the Plains Indians studied by analyst–anthropologist George Devereux.[53] But these cross-sex gender roles are quite restricted, infrequent, and marginal, very different matters from the allegedly shattering discoveries that social constructivists typically announce when they find evidence that gender and sex are separable in some people's minds some of the time.[54]

A certain kind of hypersophisticated and cavalier talk about the liberating separation of sex from gender has become fashionable in self-consciously "postmodern" scholarship. It is strange how easily subjects like these can become unreal and abstract; we all can benefit from a reality check. For those willing to learn what it is like for an actual human being to experience the total disjuncture of anatomical sex from psychological gender identity, there are the lucid and humane accounts by Robert Stoller, an analyst who worked with transsexuals over many years. Stoller's detailed, candid, and self-critical accounts of his twenty-five years of clinical work are an ideal entry for humanist scholars into the complex configurations that sex and gender can form in real human lives, not textual abstractions. The clinical work was the basis for Stoller's theoretical interest in gender identity: "my ongoing search to understand the origins, development, dynamics, and pathology of gender identity – masculinity and femininity. . . . From the start, my purpose was to find nonbiologic roots of gender behavior. . . ."[55] His clinical work was with people suffering severe identity disorder, but the information leads to an understanding of the normal processes of identity development.

Interestingly, Stoller's psychoanalytic premises (a Freudian model with important modifications) agree entirely with the constructivists in that "sex and gender are by no means related. In most instances in humans, postnatal experiences can modify and sometimes overpower already present biologic tendencies."[56] The psychoanalytic thesis, however, explains the particular circumstances in which this disjuncture can occur in individual lives and offers us a useful way of thinking about sex and gender, about *how* they are related, how the individual works out the terms of mature character in its society. Stoller offers a conceptual model of the earliest stages of infant development, which establish "core gender identity": "a conviction that the assignment of one's sex was anatomically, and ultimately psychologically, correct."[57] This conviction is successfully established in the vast majority of children during the very first year or so of life; it is not easily dislodged by later influences, and forms "the nexus around which masculinity and femininity gradually accrete."[58] In most people (excluding the richly informative but relatively rare cases of those with identity disorders) anatomical sex is the basis for a corresponding core gender identity, which is the central psychic structure for the elaborated, psychologically motivated gender of later life, incorporating sexuality and cultural patterning. This model of gender development offers historians a sensible approach to understanding *both* individual sexuality and culturally patterned gender traits in appropriate balance and tension. Stoller's chapter "A Primer for Gender Identity" is a clear summary of basic information on sex and gender from a medical and psychoanalytic viewpoint, including some widely accepted modifications of Freud's thoughts on female development.[59] Gender as a cultural poetics of power is fascinating, but it needs a human corrective.

The two polar terms of sex and gender (alias: body vs. society; nature vs. culture; biology vs. artifice) offered us in current discussions are just not enough conceptual equipment to address the complex issues of psycho-sexual identity and collective culture. There is no *mind*, the source of variety, the negotiator between private wishes and public requirements, in this too rigid opposition. Asking endless variations on the question of whether fully elaborated, historically variable sets of femininity and mas-culinity are *necessarily* attached to anatomic females and males distorts the discussion. The answer is too obviously no. But if sex is nothing, then gender, the field of social constructs and pressures, is everything, and this concept just cannot bear such forced overelaboration and yield persuasive answers about human behavior. Sex and gender offer an inadequate conceptual framework. A middle or third term is always needed – "self" or "sexuality" will do quite well – to acknowledge the developmental negotiations of mind with world which produce men and women who do tend to be recognizably like others of their same sex (and class, society, etc.) when regarded collectively, but yet are quite distinct and individual seen "close up." Gender, as a concept carrying all the explanatory weight for human behavior, thins out and dehuman-izes the individual while never accounting for the deviance, rebellion, and simple idiosyncrasy which happily fill the historical record. The cur-rently missing middle term of psychosexual development would restore the reality that human beings actively negotiate their way into their worlds; they are not passively processed by them.

The unfortunate cross-dressed man in the church at Poitiers, trapped between the failure of sex and the punishment of gender, was still a man and not a socially constructed woman. If this is the solitary thing we can justifiably say about him, it is at least an important thing. His only offered reason for his behavior – his impotence – points to a core gender identity of maleness, an identity paradoxically strong enough to react with self-punishing exaggeration to its own failure to pass the minimum test of adult masculinity. That his "solution" to his problem (and it was a solution in that it removed him from the threat of hetero-sexual relations) was improvised and idiosyncratic (though simply con-structed from prevailing attitudes) is suggested by the ordinary male life being led by his contemporary, the eunuch servant of the nunnery. The man in the dress gave up even his prima facie claim to a man's social identity. In the absence of a distinct Merovingian social construct to govern the lives of all "unmanly men," only a sexually organized male self in furious revulsion against itself would have arrived at this simple improvisation on gender.

The detailed, anthropological registration of all the varieties of sexual behavior and the minutiae of gender stereotyping in past societies being done by constructivist scholars is obviously important and needs no defense. My objections to the constructivist project are entirely directed to its unbalanced weighting of evidence and its overwrought claims and dehumanizing insistence on the socially constructed, desexualized automaton with which it replaces the self. It is one thing to document exactly how socially generated standards made perfect masculinity and femininity nearly impossible for ordinary males and females to attain. It is quite another to make dogmatic assertions about social construction on the basis of repeatedly "discovering" what everyone knows already: that genital anatomy has never been a sufficent passport to the status and privileges that are routinely monopolized by the elite males (and females to a certain degree) of any society.

It is rewarding to feel that informed, scrupulous, and open-minded attention to the specific preoccupations of past societies can open a kind of secret entry to past life, in its own terms. But the price for carrying this effort too far is a dogmatic cultural relativism, a blinkered perspective in which all behaviors, customs, meanings are exactly what the people most directly involved in them said they were, and nothing else, and nothing more. Writing history can then only be an effort of paraphrase, with no translation or serious interpretation allowed.

The worse limitation that comes packaged with this exteriorized theory of meaning is its devastating consequences for the human being whose image stands at the center of all historical study. The pervasive, inescapable processes of social conditioning impress their lessons *onto* the human object, who is thereby formed, molded, constituted, constructed with inert plastic receptivity. The political implications of such views should not be ignored: with the autonomous self as bearer of inalienable rights removed from the polity, the way is expressly open to utopian projects for constructing ideal citizen-subjects.[60] This theoretical world opens no intelligible space for resistance, refusals to conform, or even skepticism of the limited cultural menu presented in place of human possibility. If men, in this view, are incessantly occupied in playing out their stylized social theater of dominance and submission, women have nothing to do at all, except passively display whatever imprint the patriarchal discourses have directed to their specific class, race, status (e.g. flute dancer or matron). Whatever insults psychoanalysis is accused of inflicting on women, they fade to nothing when compared with complete evisceration of the psychic interior. The young woman in Oxford who spat at her husband and stalked defiantly out of church to return to her lover would have found a more sympathetic confidant in Freud than in Foucault.

Notes

1 Gregory of Tours, *The History of the Franks*, trans. Lewis Thorpe (Middlesex, 1974), p. 570 (10.15). The episode comes from the culmination of the revolt at St Radegund's nunnery at Poitiers, after internal rebellion led by Clotild had caused disorder and finally violence and King Childebert had appointed a commission of bishops, including Gregory, to investigate and reimpose discipline and order to the convent.

    The crucial passage in the original reads as follows: "... eam virum habere in monasterium, qui indutus vestimenta muliebria pro femina haberetur, cum esset vir manifestissime declaratus, atque ipsi abbatissae famularetur assiduae, indicans eum digito: 'En ipsum.' Qui cum in veste, ut diximus, muliebri coram omnibus adstetisset, dixit, se nihil opus posse virile agere ideoque sibi hoc indumentum mutasse," MGH SSrerMerov, 1/1 (new edn 1951), p. 504.

2 Surely no bearded man could remain smooth shaven all the time with sixth-century barbering techniques, unless his self-description as "impotent" imprecisely points to a castration before puberty (in which case he should have looked much more convincingly like a woman at first sight), or this might be a hermaphroditic female with a nonfunctioning penis (in which case the general female appearance would be even stronger). Neither of these speculations strikes me as likely.

3 Walter Goffart, *The Narrators of Barbarian History (A.D. 550–800: Jordanes, Gregory of Tours, Bede and Paul the Deacon* (Princeton, NJ, 1988), offers an empathetic and cunningly argued case for Gregory's conscious intentions in his history; see especially the section "Miracula: A Christian Historian's Answer to Philosophy," pp. 127–53.

4 Cross-dressing itself does not seem to concern Gregory, perhaps because it was not done to assist an otherwise sinful purpose. According to James Brundage, in *Law, Sex, and Christian Society in Medieval Europe* (Chicago, 1987), cross-dressing, although certainly forbidden by canonists of every period in accord with the prohibition in Deut. 22.5, was always treated perfunctorily and without comment or specified penalty; see pp. 57, 213, 251, 314, 473, 537, 571.

5 The work of the psychoanalytic anthropologist George Devereux is of interest on this subject; see notes 26 and 53 below for references.

6 Gregory of Tours, *History*, pp. 570–1 (10.15).

7 The "servants" employed by the convent, or by individual nuns, are usually referred to as men and have no religious functions, as: "While the servants of the Abbess were trying to put down an affray organized by Clotild's gang, they struck one of Basina's servants and the man fell down dead," *History*, p. 569.

8 Even if Abbess Leubovera had been guilty of Byzantine grandiosity and had wanted a retinue of eunuchs, the eunuchs associated with the imperial court of Constantinople did not dress as women; they were men whose known impairment constituted a legal impediment to the imperial office (thus making them safe in the imperial household, always nervous about coups d'état).

9 I find it difficult to settle on an appropriate term for "social constructivism"; I resist calling it a theory because I think constructivism has far too many logical gaps, inconsistencies, and contradictions to qualify for the term even in the loose usage of the humanities, but "view," "project," "idea," "school," etc., are not entirely right either. I follow writers of this persuasion in using the terms "constructivist" and "constructionist" interchangeably.

10 David Halperin, *One Hundred Years of Homosexuality* (New York and London, 1990), pp. 113–51 for the Diotima essay. The provocative title of the book is a reminder of the central argument: that "sexuality" as an interior psychic organization of the unconscious and conscious mind is an invention dating only from the nineteenth century, and homosexuality as a particular kind of psychic organization is also an invention of recent provenance. Another introduction to the subject could be the anthology *Forms of Desire: Sexual Orientation and the Social Constructionist Controversy*, ed. Edward Stein (New York and London, 1990). This book is entirely focused on the meanings and causes of homosexuality conceived as a rather abstract category term, and the essays are all relentlessly theoretical, but Stein has thoughtfully included a crucial essay by Michel Foucault, several points of view, a bibliography, and a valiant attempt to summarize the controversy, in ch. 12: "Conclusion: The Essentials of Constructionism and the Construction of Essentialism," pp. 325–53. Readers who wonder at these citations to an essay which is not particularly about homosexuality are asked to be patient and remember that theories of sexuality must be adequate for all object choices and erotic modes, for men and women both, or fail a serious test of adequacy.

11 Halperin, *One Hundred Years*, pp. 150, 151. The essay is subtle and beautifully argued, and quite convincing because it deals solely with a literary text deeply embedded in an exclusive male pursuit of philosophy. The general course of argument, however, and the general tone of the conclusions are never confined to masculine literature alone but are assumed to apply to humans generally in actual social and sexual life.

12 The excerpt from the introduction to Michel Foucault's *History of Sexuality*, 1, selected by Stein as a locus classicus for constructionist theory, is very explicit on the subject of power and excitement; "The Perverse Implantation," in Stein, *Forms of Desire*, pp. 11–23.

13 *Before Sexuality: The Construction of Erotic Experience in the Ancient Greek World*, ed. David M. Halperin, John J. Winkler, and Froma Zeitlin (Princeton, NJ, 1990). A collection of essays of very high quality, not all of the authors are equally committed to the strongest version of the argument that "sexuality . . . is a specifically modern production," p. 5. In particular, the last essay in the collection, "Bodies and Minds: Sexuality and Renunciation in Early Christianity," by Peter Brown (pp. 479–93), so effectively contradicts Halperin's theory that it sets up a very interesting argument with the entire book, a point I discuss further below.

Another work of great finesse in cultural explication based on dubious large-scale premises about human life is John Winkler's *Constraints of Desire: The Anthropology of Sex and Gender in Ancient Greece* (New York and London, 1990). From the introduction: "The key Foucauldian thesis is that 'sexuality' is a distinctively modern construction, a new nineteenth- and twentieth-century way of speaking about the self as organized around well-defined (and therefore catalogable) sexual characters and desires," p. 4. The trap of cultural relativism (things are only what contemporaries say they are, and any other frame of reference is anachronistic and therefore unsuitable) is strongly present in constructivist thought.

14 "The medical examination, the psychiatric investigation, the pedagogical report, and family controls . . . function as mechanisms with a double impetus: pleasure and power, the pleasure that comes of exercising a power that questions, monitors, watches, spies, searches out, palpates, brings to light; . . .

capture and seduction, confrontation and mutual reinforcement: . . . *perpetual spirals of power and pleasure.*" It is a shame to truncate the wonderful spiraling quality of the longer passage; Foucault in Stein, *Forms of Desire*, p. 19.

15 Winkler, *Constraints of Desire*, p. 117.

16 Halperin, *One Hundred Years*, p. 38.

17 *Before Sexuality*; see particularly good examples in the essays by Nicole Loraux, "Herakles: The Super-Male and the Feminine"; Anne Carson, "Putting Her in Her Place: Woman, Dirt, and Desire"; John Winkler, "Laying Down the Law: The Oversight of Men's Sexual Behavior in Classical Athens."

18 Winkler, "Laying Down the Law," p. 193.

19 Halperin, *Before Sexuality*, p. 4.

20 Halperin, *One Hundred Years*, p. 44. See also above, n. 9.

21 Halperin, *Before Sexuality*, p. 6.

22 Halperin, *One Hundred Years*, pp. 44–5 for the quotations; the hard questions are attempted in the interview section with Richard Schneider. One of the more annoying characteristics of constructionist polemics is a marked tendency to create unusually stupid straw men as opponents: thus, Halperin proposes that nonconstructionists believe in "such a thing as a 'natural' sexuality, something we are simply born into" (p. 44), when he has to know that sexuality is a complex organization of drives, desires, and sublimations developed over a period of many years. No one, at least no one among the audience for his book, believes that we are "simply born into" our mature sexual identities. The concept of "nature" also comes in for straw-man treatment, with nonconstructionist opinion defined as belief in some very simple, untenable ideas about "natural" behavior, which are then shot down with declarations like the following: "'Nature' is not exhausted by these two possibilities of sexual object-choice" (i.e. same or opposite sex). Did anyone ever think it was? Similarly, Halperin's definition of modern heterosexuality is found in no psychological theory (nor is it held by any person I know): "a population of human males who are (supposedly) incapable of being sexually excited by a person of their own sex *under any circumstances* [his emphasis]." Since nobody thinks this is what a heterosexual person is (most emphatically not Freud), and no one argues for it, it does make the work of constructionist argument rather easier.

23 Stein, *Forms of Desire*, p. 338.

24 John Boswell's essay is cogent and generous-minded, "Categories, Experience and Sexuality," in Stein's *Forms of Desire*, pp. 133–73.

25 Louis O. Mink, *Historical Understanding*, ed. Brian Fay, Eugene Golob, and Richard Vann (Ithaca, NY, 1987), p. 40. It is important to note that Mink does not envision endless modes of comprehension. He identifies three fundamentally different irreducible modes: theoretical or law-forming, configurational, categoreal. Each generates its own form of discourse and appropriate concepts.

26 George Devereux, *Ethnopsychoanalysis: Psychoanalysis and Anthropology as Complementary Frames of Reference* (Berkeley, Calif., 1978), p. 1. Over his long career Devereux published clinical/theoretical studies in psychoanalysis as well as studies based on his fieldwork in anthropology; he is often cited for his work among American Plains Indians. Devereux's writing is fastidious and terse, and his thought is crystalline sharp and unforgiving of muddle and confusion. He is especially noted for his development of the concept of "ethnic disorder," an explanation of the way mental illness follows cultural

patterns while retaining a core of structural similarity across cultures. Devereux was emphatic about refusing to combine or elide psychological and anthropological forms of explanation since each proceeds from its own frame of reference. His methodological principle was complementarity, in which two kinds of explanation, each appropriate and complete in its own terms, could construct a double discourse about human experience in specific societies. His work is not always easy or perfectly inviting (and, of course, it uses politically unreconstructed terms like "normal," "abnormal," "high" and "low" culture), but it offers the strongest directives I have yet found for acknowledging both the inner and outer, the universal and contingent aspects of historical experience. Many of his essays are readily available: in addition to the collection of basic theoretical studies cited above, special studies are collected in *Basic Problems of Ethnopsychiatry*, trans. Basia Miller Gulati and George Devereux (Chicago and London, 1980), with full bibliography of his work.

27 Devereux, *Basic Problems*, p. 157.

28 Although convinced constructionists like Halperin and Winkler profess to believe that no one who lived before the past two centuries is correctly approached via concepts of self or sexuality, they poach in analytic territory for ideas whose force they find irresistible, like projection. Most of the studies dealing with gender, especially male attitudes toward females, rest heavily on the conceptual ground of projection, as in Halperin's "Diotima" essay: "That Diotima's 'femininity' is illusory – a projection of male fantasy, a symbolic language employed by men in order to explain themselves and their desires to one another . . . ," *One Hundred Years*, p. 147 (also reprinted in *Before Sexuality*). Concepts of stereotyping, displacement, and denial also figure largely, if not always by name, in gender studies. The point to note is that although these ideas are widely popularized and superficially used in all kinds of cultural analysis, these are psychoanalytic concepts which do not "work" except in the context of a psychoanalytic structure of mind, and of the pressing interchanges between unconscious and conscious mind. Projection is a psychic maneuver involving ego ideal, repression, reaction formation, strategies of paranoia and displacement; in the bluntest terms, projection requires a psyche – the interior self with its sexuality. For a detailed explanation of the psychic dynamics underlying projection, a good source is the introductory section of Sander Gilman's *Difference and Pathology: Stereotypes of Sexuality, Race, and Madness* (Ithaca, NY, 1985).

29 Halperin, *One Hundred Years*, p. 44.

30 Adam of Eynsham, *The Life of St Hugh of Lincoln*, ed. Decima L. Douie and Hugh Farmer, 2 (London, 1962), pp. 31–2. To finish the story, the bishop excommunicated the girl, who remained defiant even after thinking it over for several days; Adam, among the most censorious of the "shocked," insists rather vaguely that she was soon strangled by the devil.

31 Peter Brown's essay in *Before Sexuality*, pp. 479–93, summarizes central aspects of his *Body and Society: Men, Women, and Sexual Renunciation in Early Christianity* (New York, 1988).

32 Halperin, introduction to *Before Sexuality*, p. 6.

33 Brown, "Bodies and Minds," in *Before Sexuality*, pp. 481, 492.

34 And, of course, the author may not even agree with me, but just as men and women have unavowed stratagems, so can books. Peter Brown is exceptionally concerned that we not impose inappropriate modern preconceptions on

the conscious and almost-conscious preoccupations of people in ancient
societies; for example, he warns us not to be misled by the medical metaphors used by Cassian "to express his sense of psychic powers that burned
like subcutaneous fevers within the unconscious self. . . . Cassian, however,
was a loyal follower of the Desert Fathers on this issue. Sexuality, for him,
was not what it has become in the lay imagination of a post-Freudian age,"
Body and Society, p. 421. The reader should note that we are being offered
meticulous distinctions between what *Cassian* did not intend or mean and
the author's firm and clear use of terms like "psychic powers" and "unconscious self" to describe persons of the fourth century.

35 Peter Gay, *The Bourgois Experience, 1: Education of the Senses* (New York
and Oxford, 1984), p. 11; the general introduction, pp. 3–16, offers the
author's historically sensitive project for bringing the insights of psychoanalysis to history and should allay any fears about often-alleged reductionist
or "essentialist" tendencies as inevitable to psychohistory. "For all the intricate and energetic activity of the unconscious, the historical interpretation of
experience must be sensitive to its conscious no less than to its unconscious
dimensions, to the work of culture on mind – the world, in a word, in which
the historian is most at home," p. 13. "For the psychoanalyst's individual is
a social individual," p. 16.

36 Brown, *Body and Society*, p. 230.

37 Heloise, second letter to Peter Abelard, in *The Letters of Abelard and Heloise*,
trans. C. K. Scott Moncrieff (New York, 1942), p. 83; Latin text in J. T.
Muckle, "The Personal Letters between Abelard and Heloise," *Mediaeval
Studies* 15 (1953), 82.

38 Devereux, *Basic Problems*, p. 157. This is a restatement of his basic principle of complementarity, or multiple explanation through different frames
of reference.

39 Barbara Newman, "Authority, Authenticity, and the Repression of Heloise,"
Journal of Medieval and Renaissance Studies 22 (1992), 121–57.

40 Barbara Newman actually undertakes to read Heloise's first two letters *as if*
they were written by Abelard; the reading which follows this premise self-
destructs, of course, on every ground, which is exactly her argument; see
"Authority, Authenticity," pp. 123–44.

41 Newman, "Authority, Authenticity," p. 151.

42 Peter Gay, *Bourgeois Experience*, pp. 13–14.

43 Heloise, second letter, in Moncrieff, trans., p. 80; Muckle, ed., p. 80.

44 Heloise, second letter, in Moncrieff, trans., pp. 81–2; Muckle, ed., p. 81.

45 In speculative answer to Newman's speculation: "We do not know, of course,
whether or how far Heloise succeeded in this second repression [Abelard's
demand that she obey him and give up her inner loyalty to her original love
for him]" (p. 155), I want to argue that she declined even to attempt it. As
I read the assertive passion of the first two letters, too much of her identity, her sense of existence as a coherent individual, was defined through her
passion for her to undertake this self-obliteration; she was never really self-
destructive. Her "silence" or acquiescence in a proper religious discourse may
be read according to her own dictum about judging "an inward disease by
inspection of the outward appearance."

46 Sigmund Freud, " 'Civilized' Sexual Morality and Modern Nervous Illness,"
Standard Edition . . . , ed. and trans. James Strachey et al., 24 vols (London,
1953–74), 9:187. He goes on to note that extending the displacement of

sexual aims indefinitely seems impossible for nearly all people (acknowledging that intercourse with another person is only one of a multitude of possible sexual activities).

47 Freud's explanation of the deep connection between earliest sexual interests and the full development of the intellect in children is found in *Three Essays on Infantile Sexuality* (1905), specifically part 5, "The Sexual Researches of Childhood," of the second essay, in vol. 7 of *Standard Edition*. These essays admittedly contain some of the theories of female development that feminists find offensive, and which have been largely amended by later psychoanalysts; but it is a serious loss if readers ostracize these indispensable classics.

48 This passage from the essay " 'Civilized' Sexual Morality" (passages quoted from pp. 198–9) deserves fuller quotation: "A special application of this proposition that sexual life lays down the pattern for the exercise of other functions can easily be recognized in the female sex as a whole. Their upbringing forbids their concerning themselves intellectually with sexual problems though they nevertheless feel extremely curious about them, and frightens them by condemning such curiosity as unwomanly and a sign of a sinful disposition. In this way they are scared away from *any* form of thinking, and knowledge loses its value for them. The prohibition of thought extends beyond the sexual field. . . . I do not believe that women's 'physiological feeble-mindedness' [quoting P. J. Moebius's book on female physiology] is to be explained by a biological opposition between intellectual work and sexual activity. . . . I think that the undoubted intellectual inferiority of so many women can rather be traced back to the inhibition of thought necessitated by sexual suppression." Please note that the inferiority Freud mentions is specifically *not* innate, but socially enforced.

49 Heloise, first letter, in Moncrieff, trans., p. 57; Muckle, ed., p. 71.

50 Heloise, first letter, in Moncrieff, trans., p. 60; Muckle, ed., p. 73.

51 Again, Barbara Newman's comparison of Heloise's erotic style with that of later female mystics is very nicely drawn; "Authority, Authenticity," pp. 152–3.

52 Abelard, *Calamities*, in Moncrieff, trans., p. 21.

53 Devereux's main work on this subject is *Reality and Dream: The Psychotherapy of a Plains Indian*, 2nd revd edn (New York, 1969).

54 As, for example, David Halperin's use of a letter from prisoner Jack Abbott to Norman Mailer (*One Hundred Years*, pp. 38–9), explaining the gender system in prison where some men counted as "women" and others as "men" in the sexual transactions of a single-sex institution. Halperin quotes Abbott's letter at length ("it was years before I realized that they were not women, but men . . ."), compares prison society with classical Athens, interprets it all into appropriate "discourse" discourse ("desire is sparked only when it arcs across the political divide, when it traverses the boundary that marks out the limits of intramural competition among the elite and that thereby distinguishes subjects from objects of sexual desire"), and proclaims Abbott an excellent illustration of poststructuralist doctrine "that when meaning is not fixed by reference but is determined solely by the play of differences within a system of signification . . ." etc., etc.

Abbott's sexual attitudes are accepted at face value and given so much respectful attention because they seem to Halperin to support his larger contention that "we need to de-center *sexuality* from the focus of the interpretation of sexual experience – and not only ancient varieties of sexual

experience. Just because modern bourgeois Westerners are so obsessed with
sexuality, . . . we ought not therefore to conclude that everyone has always
considered sexuality a basic and irreducible element in, or a central feature
of, human life." It seems impolite but necessary to bring into the discussion
the fact (ignored by Halperin) that on his parole Jack Abbott killed a man
he had met minutes before, in an act of almost wholly unmotivated macho
rage, following a slight encounter with women in a restaurant. His ideas
about sexuality, sexual identity, and the meaning of gender are the thoughts
of a mind most deeply disordered, self-ignorant and self-deceiving precisely
on these issues of sexuality.

55 The passage quoted is from Robert J. Stoller, *Presentations of Gender* (New
Haven, Conn., and London, 1985), p. vii. His work, both clinical and theoretical, has been published as it proceeded: *Sex and Gender*, 1 (New York,
1968); *Sex and Gender*, 2 (London, 1975); *Splitting* (New York, 1973); *Perversion: The Erotic Form of Hatred* (New York, 1975); *Sexual Excitement:
Dynamics of Erotic Life* (New York, 1979); *Observing the Erotic Imagination* (New Haven, Conn., 1985). Readers interested in sex/gender issues
should note that Stoller's ideas changed as his experience with patients
accumulated, and therefore the later book, *Presentations*, must be read with
the earliest works.

56 Stoller, *Presentations*, p. 6 and n. 3.

57 Stoller, *Presentations*, p. 11.

58 Stoller, *Presentations*, p. 11; it should be noted that core gender identity
does not, by itself, determine later sexual behavior with respect to object
choice or gender roles: "That later gender identity is not so uncomplicated
has been more than amply demonstrated in innumerable psychoanalytic
studies. . . . But it may not be recognized that the earliest and, as it turns out,
unalterable, part of gender identity – the core gender identity – does develop
smoothly, silently, and without conflict," *Sex and Gender*, 2:33.

59 Stoller, *Presentations*, ch. 2 (pp. 10–24); this exceptionally lucid explanation
of how biology, psychology, and social beliefs act and react in the formation
of human character can be very usefully read by historians.

60 Men as different as psychoanalytic anthropologist George Devereux and
linguist Noam Chomsky have seen the political consequences quite clearly.
Devereux: "The *total* disorganization that some advocate as the very essence
of freedom is also a technique of enslavement, for the technique that deprives
man of all organization is the first condition of his slavehood," *Basic Problems*, p. 320. Chomsky: "A vision of a future social order is in turn based
on a concept of human nature. If in fact man is an indefinitely malleable,
completely plastic being, with no innate structures of mind . . . then he is a
fit subject for the 'shaping of behavior' by the state authority . . . ," quoted
in Philip Pomper, *The Structure of Mind in History: Five Major Figures in
Psychohistory* (New York, 1985), p. 8. It remains true that constructivist
scholars are almost invariably political progressives, often activists on behalf
of gay rights, feminism, etc., and do not see the political implications of
their theory as I do.

Part VII

Objectivity

16
Objectivity Is Not Neutrality: Rhetoric versus Practice in Peter Novick's *That Noble Dream*

Thomas Haskell

When it comes to debates over objectivity and relativism, appearances can be deceiving, not just in the world the debaters strive to comprehend, but also in the relation between a debater's position and the rhetoric he or she employs to defend it. For example, as I sift through my reactions to Peter Novick's important and provocative book, *That Noble Dream: The "Objectivity Question" and the American Historical Profession* (Cambridge: Cambridge University Press, 1988), I find it necessary to distinguish the moderate position he actually seems to occupy on the objectivity question from the rather more radical rhetorical posture he adopts in defense of that position. All things considered – that is, taking into account not only what he *says* about the ideal of objectivity, but also what he *does* as a practicing historian, writing about historians' quarrels over that ideal – I conclude that he and I occupy pretty much the same, moderate, position. We admire the same sorts of historical judgments and feel about the same degree of confidence in the end product of the historian's labors. We agree that representing the past is a far more problematical enterprise than most historians realize, and that there are more ways to represent it than the guild currently acknowledges. Certainly I do not believe any more than he does that facts speak for themselves, that political neutrality is a virtue in itself, that scholarship is a wall-building exercise in which each scholar contributes his brick to a steadily accumulating edifice of unchallengeable knowledge, or that the best history is that which provokes no controversy. Nor am I any more sanguine than he about the likelihood that disagreements over historical interpretation will one day fade away in some grand convergence.

Yet I regard objectivity, properly understood, as a worthy goal for historians. Novick, on the contrary, says the ideal is "essentially confused" (6), and the text he has written – which, ironically, passes all my tests for objectivity with flying colors – is in the main designed to persuade readers that the ideal of objectivity is all washed up. We seem not to differ greatly in what we admire and wish to defend in terms of historical practice, but our rhetorical postures *vis-à-vis* the ideal of objectivity are decidedly at odds.

That two people sharing the same position should say different things about it need not be surprising. One obvious reason is the difficulty of forecasting audience response. We all occasionally polemicize on behalf of our own version of the good, the true, and the beautiful, and the posture we assume in public is shaped by our estimate of where our audience already stands on these issues and which way it needs to be moved in order to strengthen the position we admire. Two authors may say very different, even opposite, things in defense of the same position, simply because they have different estimates of where their audience currently stands, or what its members need to hear in order to be moved in the desired direction. For the same reason a single person may, without any inconsistency, adopt different rhetorical postures on different occasions. If, for example, a proponent of the welfare state were to deliver exactly the same speech to the National Association of Manufacturers and the Young Socialist League, we would not applaud the speaker's consistency, but lament the insensitivity of the performance, the failure to anticipate objections coming from different directions. Estimating the composition and likely reaction of the audience for a book is notoriously difficult, so it is easy to see how Novick and I might share much the same position on substantive issues, and yet adopt opposing postures and appear for all the world as if we were completely at loggerheads.

Two further reasons help explain why I want to endorse much of Novick's analysis of objectivity even as I draw what may seem opposite conclusions from it. The first is a matter of strategy. He and I agree that objectivity was the charter under which professional history was inaugurated, in his words, "the rock on which the venture was constituted, its continuing raison d'être" (1). We also agree that the ideal is currently viewed with considerable skepticism, especially by scholars impressed by recent developments in literary criticism; that historians eager to counter that skepticism have sometimes done so naively and ineffectively; and that although attacks in the past have come and gone cyclically, the overall trend has been one of declension. The ideal of objectivity just does not grip us as powerfully as it did the founding generation of the 1880s. Given this state of affairs, Novick's advice to the profession evidently is to cut loose from the ideal, declaring it obsolete – even while silently perpetuating many of the practices associated with it. In contrast, my inclination is to protect those practices by continuing to honor the ideal, meanwhile ridding it of unwanted connotations. Fatefully dissimilar though the two strategies may be, they do not aim at very different outcomes in terms of historical practice.

That difference of strategy immediately points to crucial differences in the way Novick and I use the term "objectivity." My impression, unlike Novick's, is that among the influential members of the historical profession the term has long since lost whatever connection it may once have had with passionlessness, indifference, and neutrality. Eugene Genovese, a much-honored member of the profession and a self-proclaimed Marxist whom no one will think dispassionate or politically neutral, passes my test of objectivity with plenty of room to spare, just as Novick himself does.[1] In my view, what sophisticated historians mean by the term today has precious little to do with neutrality, but a great deal to do with a cultural orientation in which neutrality, disinterestedness, and like qualities did indeed figure prominently in the nineteenth century: that complex of values and practices which Nietzsche contemptuously called "asceticism."[2] If objectivity could be reduced simply to neutrality, I would not bother to defend it; but insofar as it is the expression in intellectual affairs of the ascetic dimension of life, it deserves a defense, for asceticism is not only "common to all culture," it is "the 'cultural' element in culture. . . . Where there is culture there is asceticism."[3]

I regard Nietzsche's attack on asceticism as a cultural calamity, all the more regrettable because of his high seriousness and the brilliance of the assault. Had he directed his wrath merely against Victorian passionlessness there would be no room for complaint, but his ridicule of ascetic values and practices became reckless and indiscriminate, reaching far beyond the foibles of a generation to renunciation itself. Morality is what suffers most from the devaluation of ascetic practices, but such practices are also indispensable to the pursuit of truth. The very possibility of historical scholarship as an enterprise distinct from propaganda requires of its practitioners that vital minimum of ascetic self-discipline that enables a person to do such things as abandon wishful thinking, assimilate bad news, discard pleasing interpretations that cannot pass elementary tests of evidence and logic, and, most important of all, suspend or bracket one's own perceptions long enough to enter sympathetically into the alien and possibly repugnant perspectives of rival thinkers. All of these mental acts – especially coming to grips with a rival's perspective – require *detachment*, an undeniably ascetic capacity to achieve some distance from one's own spontaneous perceptions and convictions, to imagine how the world appears in another's eyes, to experimentally adopt perspectives that do not come naturally – in the last analysis, to develop, as Thomas Nagel would say, a view of the world in which one's own self stands not at the center, but appears merely as one object among many.[4] To be dissatisfied with the view of the world as it initially appears to us, and to struggle to formulate a superior, more inclusive, less self-centered alternative, is to strive for detachment and aim at objectivity. And to turn thus against one's most natural self – to engage in "this uncanny, dreadfully joyous labor of a soul voluntarily at odds with itself" – is to commit that very sin against the will to power that Nietzsche so irresponsibly condemned.[5]

Detachment does not promise access to any transcendental realm and always remains, as Nagel says, "under the shadow" of skepticism.[6] Although it is an ideal and holds out a standard higher than any of us routinely achieve, acceptable performance under its regulative influence does not require superhuman effort. It is that frail and limited but perfectly real power that, for example, permits conscientious scholars to referee one another's work fairly, to acknowledge merit even in the writings of one's critics, and successfully to bend over backwards when grading students so as not to penalize those holding antagonistic political convictions. We try to exercise this capacity every day; sometimes we succeed, sometimes we fail, and we assign praise and blame to ourselves and others accordingly. It is of course true that we sometimes delude ourselves, developing a pseudo-objective standpoint that functions mainly to obscure choice, so responsibility for what we want to do shifts to a seemingly impersonal state of affairs. But to shrug off the capacity for detachment as entirely illusory – to claim that since none of the standpoints the self is capable of imagining are *really* that of "the other," but are self-produced (as is certainly the case), and to argue that all viewpoints therefore are *indistinguishably* contaminated by selfishness or group interest or the omnipresent Nietzschean will – is to turn a blind eye to distinctions that all of us routinely make and confidently act upon, and thereby to blur all that distinguishes villainy from decency in everyday affairs. Not to mince words, it is to defame the species. Fairness and honesty are qualities we can rightfully demand of human beings, and those qualities require a very substantial measure of self-overcoming – more than could exist if Nietzsche's hyperbolic and indiscriminate war on asceticism were permitted to triumph. Objectivity is not something entirely distinct from detachment, fairness, and honesty, but is the product of extending and elaborating these priceless and fundamentally ascetic virtues.[7]

If I am correct in thinking that these virtues of self-overcoming already rank high in historians' practice, that should suffice to show that my strategy of keeping alive the term "objectivity" while ridding it of unwanted connotations is not a matter of appropriating a traditional name as a dignified cover for new practices. The tendency of past generations to associate objectivity with "selflessness," and to think of truth seeking as a matter of emptying oneself of passion and preconception, so as to become a perfectly passive and receptive mirror of external reality, has, for good reason, become notorious.[8] But in valuing (as even Nietzsche did, in his calmer moments) the elementary capacity for self-overcoming, we need not aspire to the unrealistic and undesirable extreme of extinguishing the self or denying that its situation in time and space limits the perspectives available to it.[9] Likewise, in making detachment a vital criterion of objective thinking, we need not make the still greater error of confusing objectivity with neutrality.

I see nothing to admire in neutrality. My conception of objectivity (which I believe is widely, if tacitly, shared by historians today) is compatible with strong political commitment. It pays no premium for standing in the middle of the road, and it recognizes that scholars are as passionate and as likely to be driven by interest as those they write about. It does not value even detachment as an end in itself, but only as an indispensable prelude or preparation for the achievement of higher levels of understanding – higher not in the sense of ascending to a more spiritual plane, where the concerns of the soul displace those of the body, as an earlier generation might have understood it, but higher in Nagel's sense of being more complete, more cognizant of life's most seductive illusion, which is that the world centers on me (or those with whom I choose to identify) and that what matters to me (or us) is paramount.

Detachment functions in this manner not by draining us of passion, but by helping to channel our intellectual passions in such a way as to ensure collision with rival perspectives. In that collision, if anywhere, our thinking transcends both the idiosyncratic and the conventional. Detachment both socializes and de-parochializes the work of intellect; it is the quality that fits an individual to participate fruitfully in what is essentially a communal enterprise. Objectivity is so much a product of social arrangements that individuals and particular opinions scarcely deserve to be called objective, yet the social arrangements that foster objectivity have no basis for existence apart from individual striving for detachment. Only insofar as the members of the community are disposed to set aside the perspective that comes most spontaneously to them, and strive to see things in a detached light, is there any likelihood that they will engage with one another mentally and provoke one another through mutual criticism to the most complete, least idiosyncratic, view that humans are capable of. When the ascetic effort at detachment fails, as it often does, we talk past one another, producing nothing but discordant soliloquies, each fancying itself the voice of reason. The kind of thinking I would call objective leads only a fugitive existence outside of communities that enjoy a high degree of independence from the state and other external powers, and that are dedicated internally not only to detachment but also to intense mutual criticism and to the protection of dissenting positions against the perpetual threat of majority tyranny.

Some hypothetical examples may clarify what I mean by objective thinking and show how remote it is from neutrality. Consider an extreme case: a person who, although capable of detachment, suspends his or her own perceptions of the world not in the expectation of gaining a broader perspective, but only in order to learn how opponents think so as to demolish their arguments more effectively – who is, in short, a polemicist, deeply and fixedly committed as a lifelong project to a particular political or cultural or moral program. Anyone choosing such a life obviously risks being thought boorish or provincial, but insofar as such a person successfully enters into the thinking of his or her rivals and produces arguments potentially compelling, not only to those who already share the same views, but to outsiders as well, I see no reason to withhold the laurel of objectivity.[10] There is nothing objective about hurling imprecations at apostates or catechizing the faithful. But as long as the polemicist truly engages the thinking of the enemy, he or she is being as objective as anyone. In contrast, the person too enamored of his or her own interpretation of things seriously and sympathetically to entertain alternatives, even for the sake of learning how best to defeat them, fails my test of objectivity, no matter how serene and even-tempered.

The most common failure of objectivity is preaching to the converted, complacently presupposing the pieties of one's own coterie and making no effort to appreciate or appeal to the perspectives of outsiders. In contrast, the most commonly observed fulfillment of the ideal of objectivity in the historical profession is simply the *powerful argument* – the text that reveals by its every twist and turn its respectful appreciation of the alternatives it rejects. Such a text attains power precisely because its author has managed to suspend momentarily his or her own perceptions so as to anticipate and take account of objections and alternative constructions – not those of some straw man, but those that truly issue from the rival's position, understood as sensitively and stated as eloquently as the rival could desire. Nothing is rhetorically more powerful than this, and nothing, not even capitulation to the rival, could acknowledge any more vividly the force and respectability of the rival's perspective. To mount a telling attack on a position, one must first inhabit it. Those so habituated to their customary intellectual abode that they cannot even explore others can never be persuasive to anyone but fellow habitués.

That is why powerful arguments are often more faithful to the complexity and fragility of historical interpretation – more faithful even to the irreducible plurality of human perspectives, when that is, in fact, the case – than texts that abjure position-taking altogether and ostentatiously wallow in displays of "reflexivity" and "undecidability." The powerful argument is the highest fruit of the kind of thinking I would call objective, and in it neutrality plays no part. Authentic objectivity has simply nothing to do with the television newscaster's mechanical gesture of allocating the same number of seconds to both sides of a question, or editorially splitting the difference between them, irrespective of their perceived merits.

This conception of the ideal of objectivity, stripped as it is of any association with neutrality and offering no metaphysical guarantees of truth, is not terribly different from that "future 'objectivity'" that even

Nietzsche grudgingly acknowledged in the midst of his slashing attack on asceticism. He spoke without malice of an objectivity "understood not as 'contemplation without interest' (which is a nonsensical absurdity), but as the ability *to control* one's Pro and Con and to dispose of them, so that one knows how to employ a variety of perspectives and affective interpretations in the service of knowledge."[11] Even in one of his fits of hyperbole, as Nietzsche gathered up the last hope of objective knowledge and threw it out the window along with the bathwater of a literal-minded notion of disinterestedness, he let slip a crucial concession. This often-quoted passage proclaims the impossibility of disinterestedness so stridently that it is easy to ignore the second half of the lead sentence and the important qualification that Nietzsche there inserted against the grain of his own thought:

> There is *only* a perspective seeing, *only* a perspective "knowing"; and the *more* affects we are allowed to speak about one thing, the *more* eyes, different eyes, we can use to observe one thing, the more complete will our "concept" of this thing be. But to eliminate the will altogether, to suspend each and every affect, supposing we were capable of this – what would that mean but to *castrate* the intellect?[12]

What needs rescuing here is the thought that some conceptions are more "complete" than others and that by doing what we can to multiply the perspectives brought to bear on a problem, we can achieve higher levels of completeness. Once it is acknowledged that conceptions differ in this way, it is but a small additional step to say that the more complete a conception is, the greater its claim upon us – opening the possibility that we are sometimes *obliged* to give up incomplete conceptions for more complete ones. The ideal of objectivity requires no more of a foothold than this.

The possibility of distinguishing baby from bathwater is lost the moment we confuse objectivity with neutrality. And my most serious reservation about Novick's uncommonly intelligent and wide-ranging history of the objectivity question – the most complete history of the American historical profession ever written for any purpose – is that he virtually equates objectivity with neutrality. Subtle and perceptive though his analysis is, much of his text reads like an exposé. His aim is to show, often through passages selected from personal correspondence, that in spite of all their high-minded public rhetoric about the importance of "being objective," historians have bristled with likes and dislikes and have often conceived of their work as a means of striking a blow for what they liked, be it reunification of North and South in the founding generation, or racial integration in a later one.[13] All this is presented to the reader in a tone of bemused shock and wide-eyed dismay, as if by discovering connections between their scholarship and their likes and dislikes, we were catching the mighty with their pants down. That tone is justifiable in a few sad and striking cases in which prominent historians' dislikes turn out to have been ethnic and ugly. But on the whole, who will be either surprised or disappointed to discover that historians who praised objectivity and thought of themselves as objective had strong preferences about mobilization for World War I, isolationism, responsibility for the cold war, Vietnam, racial segregation, and the like, and wrote books and articles meant in part to advance their side of these major public debates? These commitments betray a lack of objectivity only if we define objectivity as neutrality, and to do that would be to trivialize both the ideal and those who have striven to realize it.

Novick generally construes active political commitment by historians who subscribe to the ideal of objectivity as evidence of either personal insincerity or, more often, the incoherence and emptiness of the ideal. I wonder. Perhaps Novick has defined objectivity too narrowly. Perhaps historians who advocated objectivity and worried, say, about the relativism of Charles Beard and Carl Becker meant neither to claim neutrality for themselves nor to impose it on others. Perhaps instead, by defending what they called "objectivity," they meant, as I do, to sustain that minimal respect for self-overcoming, for detachment, honesty, and fairness, that makes intellectual community possible. Perhaps they were not naive to sense in snappy slogans like "Everyman his own historian," not only the useful corrective to scientism that Novick appropriately sees there, but also the harbinger of a remissive cultural movement corrosive of all constraints upon the will, a movement that over the course of the twentieth century has in fact succeeded in putting on the defensive the very idea of obligation, whether moral ("You ethically *ought* to do *x*") or epistemological ("You rationally/logically *ought* to believe *y*").[14] The upshot, as a new century looms, is that many wonder if "ought" statements capture anything important about human beings and the world they live in, or are merely grandiose masks for preferences that are ultimately personal and self-serving ("I *want* you to do *x* or believe *y*").[15] Some will see in this cultural shift a welcome retreat of authoritarianism; others, a tragic breakdown of authority. Those who lament it as a breakdown will by no means be found only on the political right, for insofar as the left trades on ideas of moral obligation (for example, to the poor, to minorities), or distinguishes between policies that are well or ill suited to the "realities" of our situation, it too has a vested interest in objectivity. Without entering into the debate here, we can simply observe that the stakes in this cultural contest are extremely high, and while the possibility of objective knowledge is a central point at issue, neutrality is not.

Yet in Novick's definition of objectivity, neutrality looms very large indeed. In two key definitional paragraphs near the beginning of his text, Novick spells out in abbreviated form the principal tenets of the ideal of objectivity to which he believes historians have subscribed with little change for the past hundred years.[16] I place the second of the sequential paragraphs first because it strains hardest to identify objectivity with neutrality.

> The objective historian's role is that of a neutral, or disinterested, judge; it must never degenerate into that of an advocate or, even worse, propagandist. The historian's conclusions are expected to display the standard judicial qualities of balance and evenhandedness. As with the judiciary, these qualities are guarded by the insulation of the historical profession from social pressures or political influence, and by the individual historian avoiding partisanship or bias – not having any investment in arriving at one conclusion rather than another. Objectivity is held to be at grave risk when history is written for utilitarian purposes. One corollary of all this is that historians, as historians, must purge themselves of external loyalties: the historian's primary allegiance is to "the objective historical truth," and to professional colleagues who share a commitment to cooperative, cumulative efforts to advance toward that goal. (2)

Although there is much in this sketch that strikes me as accurate, on the whole I find it impossible to reconcile with my impression that most historians, certainly the abler and more influential ones, recognize full well that fine history can be and routinely is written by politically committed scholars. Most historians just do not assign to "neutrality" and "disinterestedness" the inflated value that Novick suggests. Most, I think, would be aghast at the thought that historians must "purge themselves of external loyalties" in order to do their job well. Seeing an analogy between the role of the judge and that of the historian does not imply any overestimation of the value of neutrality: judges, like historians, are expected to be open to rational persuasion, not to be indifferent about the great issues of their day or – bizarre thought – to abstain from judgment. What we demand of them is self-control, not self-immolation. Bias and conflict of interest do indeed arouse our suspicion, not only of judges and historians, but of whomever we depend upon to be fair. The demand is for detachment and fairness, not disengagement from life. Most historians would indeed say that the historian's primary commitment is to the truth, and that when truth and "the cause," however defined, come into conflict, the truth must prevail. But to say that is not to prohibit political advocacy; it is only to set intellectually responsible limits to it – limits without which advocates would discredit not only scholarship but their own cause. Who will trust a scholar-advocate who claims the privilege of lying or obscuring the truth for good causes?

By the same token, Novick is no doubt right that historians see a world of difference between politically committed scholarship, which I think they accept, and propaganda dressed up as history, which they certainly do not, and should not, accept. Historians do indeed become wary, but not necessarily dismissive, when scholarship is performed as a means to exogenous, "utilitarian" ends; they do regard scholarship as a collaborative effort, requiring a great deal of mutual trust, and most no doubt regard a degree of insulation from external influence as indispensable. (The latter point seems impossible to doubt as I write these lines in the summer of 1989, just as the Chinese government rewrites the history of the Tiananmen Square killings and as intellectuals in the USSR and central Europe put their lives on the line by publicly challenging state-sponsored orthodoxies in historical interpretation.) None of these beliefs require historians to "purge themselves of external loyalties," or to be "neutral," or to be "disinterested" in any extravagant sense. What is required is at most a modicum of ascetic detachment.

Does Novick think that even this modicum is too much to ask? It is not easy to tell, either from his two definitional paragraphs or from the 600-plus pages that follow, how much of the ideal of objectivity he actually means to reject. Consider both the passage quoted above and the more general of his two definitional paragraphs (which in his text appears first):

> The principal elements of the ideal of [objectivity] are well known and can be briefly recapitulated. The assumptions on which it rests include a commitment to the reality of the past, and to the truth as correspondence to that reality; a sharp separation between knower and known, between fact and value, and above all, between history and fiction. Historical facts are seen as prior to and independent of interpretation: the value of an interpretation is judged by how well it accounts for the facts; if contradicted by the facts, it must be abandoned. Truth is one, not perspectival. Whatever patterns exist in history are "found," not "made." Though successive generations of historians might, as their perspectives shifted, attribute different significance to events in the past, the meaning of those events was unchanging. (1–2)

Since Novick is evidently out to show that the ideal of objectivity is "essentially confused," one might think that he is prepared to abandon each of the "elements" of the ideal he lists in these two paragraphs. But considering the text in its entirety, and, again, taking into account both his statements about objectivity and his practices as the author of this particular historical narrative about historians' debates, I conclude that his rejection of the ideal is far from total.

Let us examine the elements he lists. What precisely it would mean for a historian or anyone else to doubt the "reality of the past" is not obvious, but surely anyone whose doubt was more than a rhetorical gambit would think twice before writing a 600-page book about it. "Correspondence" as a metaphor for the hoped-for relation between thought and reality has notoriously fallen on hard times, and mention of dualisms such as "knower and known," "fact and value," "history and fiction," will call up important debates familiar to the readers of the journal *History and Theory*. Without slighting in the least either Novick's performance as a historian, or the significance of those debates,

I find it difficult to see how the debates influence the performance. Rhetorically his epistemological anxiety is acute, but it has little effect on the way he writes history. The fault is not Novick's. Knowing that correspondence is an inadequate metaphor, how are historians to conduct themselves differently? Novick gives no answer, either explicitly or implicitly, and was probably wise not to try. As for the ostensible benefits of recognizing the kinship of history and fiction, Novick seems at best half-persuaded. His treatment of Hayden White, the scholar most closely identified with those benefits, is respectful (he calls him our "philosopher of freedom" and laments his scapegoating by objectivists looking for an embodiment of "nihilistic relativism" [601, 599]), but decidedly guarded: White's "trivializing of questions of evidence was in the service . . . above all of his existentialist quasi obsession with the historian's liberty of choice," says Novick, and it requires only a "moderately careless reading," he continues, to conclude that White's relativism is that of the proverbial freshman "for whom any view was as good as any other" (601). These are not the attitudes one expects of a radical on the objectivity question.

"Fact" is another word that has fallen on hard times. Just as there are many historians out there who need to be reminded that, for all their differences, the writing of history and the writing of fiction are kindred activities, so there are also historians who still need to learn that facts only take shape under the aegis of paradigms, presuppositions, theories, and the like. There are even historians who might benefit from writing on the blackboard twenty times, "facts are just low-level interpretative entities unlikely for the moment to be contested." That said, it must also be observed that one of the virtues of Novick's book is that it is jam-packed with such low-level entities. I would be very surprised if he really thought that the value of his higher-level interpretations was independent of their ability "to account for" the lower ones, and I would be still more surprised if he retained in his book any higher-level interpretations that he really thought were flatly "contradicted" by the lower ones. He is much too good a historian for that.

As for Novick's questions about the oneness of truth and the origin of the patterns historians "find" in history, his subsequent discussions make perfectly clear his sensible refusal to grasp either horn of such either-or dilemmas. He appears in practice to believe, as I do, that some truth claims are irreducibly perspectival, while others lend themselves to rational resolution. His practice seems compatible with my view (not at all unusual among historians) that historical patterns are "found," but not without a process of imaginative construction that goes far enough beyond the intrinsic properties of the raw materials employed that one can speak of their being "made" – though certainly not out of whole cloth. Once again, sweeping though Novick's abandonment of objectivity sometimes sounds, in practice he is usually what I would call a sensible moderate.

Although the most conspicuous struggle under way in this text is between the author's practice and his rhetorical posture, the rhetorical posture itself is also conflicted. Novick claims, interestingly, that he is more concerned to report the debate over objectivity than to take a position: "What I can't do," he says, "is hope to satisfy those who exigently demand to know if I am 'for' or 'against' objectivity." Having said this, he then proceeds in the next two paragraphs to speak of the ideal and the distinctions it gives rise to as "confused," "dubious," "naive," "unreal," "empty," and "incoherent" (6). Summing up this uniformly critical commentary, he says, "Another way of describing my stance is to say that, in general and on the whole, I have been persuaded by the arguments of the critics of the concept; unimpressed by the arguments of its defenders" (6). Clear though his rejection of objectivity seems at this point, he reasserts two paragraphs later his role as nonjudgmental reporter: "Above all, the reason why I cannot take a position for or against objectivity is my historicism, which here means simply that my way of thinking about anything in the past is primarily shaped by my understanding of its role within a particular historical context, and in the stream of history" (7).

Novick's characterization of his own views seems most promising to me when he likens objectivity to a myth that, while resisting classification as either "true" or "false," indubitably sustains valued practices and thus comes to possess many of the qualities of tenacity and inescapability that we associate with truth. In the same vein he likens objectivity to the inalienable and self-evident rights of the Declaration of Independence; hopelessly ambiguous, philosophically indefensible, even "nonsense," perhaps, but, in Novick's words, *"salutary nonsense"* (7), in view of the form of life they have fostered.[17] On balance, however, Novick is not content to regard the ideal of objectivity as salutary: "it promotes an unreal and misleading invidious distinction between, on the one hand, historical accounts 'distorted' by ideological assumptions and purposes; on the other, history free of these taints" (6). Nor does the idea of myth provide much shelter, for in Novick's eyes the valued practices sustained by the myth of objectivity are strictly those of historians striving to professionalize their discipline, enhance their dignity, and maximize their incomes. He would evidently give little credence to my own view, which is that although the ideal of objectivity has been most fully and formally developed by scholars and serves importantly to legitimize their work, it was not invented by them and in fact pervades the world of everyday affairs. As I see it, the ideal is tacitly invoked (sometimes as a test, sometimes in a gesture of blind faith) every time anyone opens a letter, picks up a newspaper, walks into a courtroom, or decides which of two squabbling children to believe. All of us, professional or not, invoke the ideal every time we choose between conflicting interpretations with confidence that they are not simply different, but that one is *superior* to the others, superior as a representation of the way things are. No wonder Novick is less concerned than I about the fate of the ideal: for him the consequences of abandoning it are confined to the academic professions; for me the cultural ramifications are incalculably wide.

Although I disagree with many of Novick's judgments, I have high confidence in his objectivity as a historian. He sees little connection between the scholar's ideal and the humble virtues of fairness, honesty, and detachment, and therefore assumes a posture *vis-à-vis* objectivity that seems to give those virtues short shrift. In practice, however, he takes them seriously enough. It would be tedious to recite many examples, but even his introductory comments about the near-fatal inadequacy of the ideal of objectivity are interspersed with declarations of respect for the homier virtues that constitute the very taproots of that ideal as I would define it. Thus, having declared himself persuaded by the critics of objectivity, he expresses the hope, in the very next sentence, that he has succeeded in setting forth "fairly" (12) both sides of the argument. I wonder how he could explain the high value we place on fairness – or even explain what fairness means in this context – without resorting eventually to the language of objectivity. Similarly, in defense of his self-conscious tendency to give rather more explanatory weight to extra-rational factors than most historians do, Novick hastens to assure the reader that he has done his best "to extend such treatment evenhandedly: as much to the thought of those with whom I am in sympathy as to those whose views I dislike" (15). Again the practice he promises is not something other than objectivity, but a facet of it.

He even aspires to detachment. Noting that most historians write about their profession "the way Arthur Schlesinger, Jr., writes about the Kennedys," he fears that "what I think of as my attempt at detachment may be read as hostility" (13). In the narrative account that follows, he seems to me generally to live up to the promise of these declarations. If we could be sure that abandoning the ideal of objectivity meant that all the profession's members would continue (or begin) to go about their work as scrupulously as Novick, we could rest easy. But we cannot. . . .

The academic air is thick nowadays with sensational pronouncements about the failures of reason. Given Novick's silent loyalty, in practice, to the ascetic values that I associate with objectivity, I do not think that he can be counted among those who imagine that we stand at the threshold of a new epoch of endless interpretative play, in which words like reason, logic, rationality, truth, and evidence can be merrily and painlessly dispensed with. The tone of his concluding chapters is more suggestive of the breaking of the seventh seal than the dawning of a brave new world, and like all authentic skeptics he extends his skepticism at least intermittently to the claims of skepticism itself. He understands that relativism predicts its own relativity; he knows that if one supposes historicism to be "right," one must suppose it to be so only during a passing phase of history – observations that have, of course, never been enough to silence doubt about reason.

Tempered though his skepticism is, he does believe that the ideal of objectivity, the "founding myth" of the profession, is more or less defunct, presumably leaving the practice of historical representation foundationless, adrift in the cosmos. Toward the end of the book, in a discussion that slides back and forth between talk of cognitive crisis and concrete institutional conundrums such as the growth of specialization, decay of the academic job market in the 1970s, the exponential growth of the literature each of us tries to stay abreast of, and the inherently dispersive character of a discipline that, unlike English and Philosophy, lacks even the possibility of defining a single canon familiar to all practitioners, Novick repeatedly suggests that history is today so fragmented – politically, institutionally, and intellectually – that it "no longer constitute[s] a coherent discipline" (577, also 592). He even concludes that a sense of "dismay," "disarray," and "discouragement" is more prevalent among historians than among the members of any other discipline (578) – hardly likely in view of the state of numb exhaustion that prevails in the literary disciplines after a decade of theory wars that make historians' quarrels look like family reunions.[18] Whether he intends it or not, all this gloom and doom might well lead the reader to conclude that writing a history of anything – even a history of historians' quarrels about objectivity – is a preposterous undertaking that only a fool would attempt. As if to encourage that reading, Novick closes the book with a rather portentous passage from Sartre: "In the domain of expression . . . success is necessarily failure. It is impossible to succeed, since at the outset you set yourself the goal of failure (to capture movement in immobile objects, for instance). . . . So there it is. You never quite grasp what you set out to achieve. And then suddenly it's a statue or a book. The opposite of what you wanted" (629).

Coming from an author who is (at least in practice) as securely wedded to conventional modes of representation as Novick, this display of epistemological angst is harmless enough. It is, however, strongly reminiscent of the distinctively "postmodern" syndrome a literary critic had in mind when he observed that many scholars influenced by deconstructionist doctrines seem to feel that they "live upon inevitable but somehow invigorating failure."[19] This characteristically postmodern authorial stance in which the author cheerfully acknowledges that what he or she is saying is unsubstantiable or worse, and then goes on to assert it exactly as if it were "true" – always ready, if challenged, to fall back on the initial disclaimer – has the undeniable advantage of allowing an author to indulge in quite ordinary forms of communication and common sense while preserving a reputation for sophistication and undeceivability.[20] The benefits are obvious at a time when strife over epistemological questions is so intense that only the debater with no recognizable position is unassailable. In an age of guerrilla scholarship, the thing to do is stay always on the offense and unburden oneself of any convictions, lest they require a defense. The ancient military advice of Sun Tzu applies: "Subtle and insubstantial, the expert [warrior] leaves no trace; divinely mysterious, he is inaudible. Thus he is master of his enemy's fate."[21]

The most striking example of what might be called "the undeceivability ploy," and one that by its very extremity sheds light on the much more modest gap between Novick's rhetoric and his practice, comes straight from the author of *The Postmodern Condition*, Jean-François Lyotard himself. In his latest book, Lyotard fondly recalls an old friend, Pierre Souyri, a comrade-in-arms with whom he served for many years on the barricades of the Parisian left. Together they helped publish radical Marxist organs with titles such as *Socialisme ou Barbarie* and *Pouvoir Ouvrier*. What is immediately noteworthy about this reminiscence, or "memorial," as Lyotard calls it, is not so much its deceased subject as the display of epistemological anxiety and contrition with which it begins. The author's first words announce the unworthiness of his efforts. "The only testimony worthy of the author of *Révolution et Contre-révolution en Chine*," worries Lyotard, "is the one I cannot give him: it would be to write the history, in Marxist terms, of the radical Marxist current to which he belonged." But this is impossible, says Lyotard, for "I am not a historian."[22]

Lyotard hesitates to take up the historian's pen not because he feels untrained or insufficiently talented. Nor is it simply that, having lost faith in Marxism, he fears that even his best efforts to represent his friend's life will embody terms and assumptions that Souyri himself, whose own devotion to the cause never faltered, would find unacceptable. Rather, Lyotard explains, what makes it impossible for him to write the history his friend deserves is that he lacks faith of another sort, shared by Marxist and non-Marxist historians alike: faith in the reality of the past and the possibility of representing that reality in words:

> Obviously, I lack the expertise, the knowledge, the fine tuning of the mind to the methodology; but above all I lack a certain way of interrogating and situating what is spoken of in relation to what one is saying. To be brief, let us call this the postulate of realism. That which the historian recounts and explains had [*sic*] to be real; otherwise what he is doing is not history. As in legal rhetoric, everything is organized in order to explore the clues, produce proofs, and induce the belief that the object, the event, or the man now absent were indeed there just as they are being depicted. The opposing party against whom the historian argues with all his force is not easy to beat; it is the forgetting which is the death of death itself.

He cannot subscribe to such hubris and naiveté:

> However, I cannot manage to make this pious activity my own, to share the historian's confidence in its ends, to believe in the fidelity or the plausibility

of that which is, in any case, only a representation. I cannot manage to forget that it is I, the historian, who makes my man speak, and speak to men he did not know and to whom he would not necessarily have chosen to speak.[23]

Once an author has carried skepticism to this extreme, one might expect him or her simply to fall silent: better to say nothing than to soil one's hands in the shabby illusions of historical representation. Or alternatively one might expect these words to introduce an experimental form of communication, a text designed to overcome the conventional limits of representation, or at least to acknowledge those limits with greater candor and precision. But none of these expectations is borne out.

Having warned his readers of the inescapable futility of all efforts to represent the past "as it was," Lyotard then embarks upon the very course he has just declared to be impossibly naive. Having shown that the historian's pious, death-defying claim to know "how things really were" does not deceive him in the least, Lyotard proceeds to tell us ... well, how it really was with his friend Souyri. In spite of himself, Lyotard commits a historical representation. He makes Souyri speak. And, by all appearances, he puts his representational pants on pretty much the same way the rest of us do. He informs us that he sent his friend a letter announcing his resignation from the *Pouvoir Ouvrier* group in 1966. Souyri answered him in October. "He affirmed that our divergences dated from long before . . . he considered it pointless to try to resolve them. . . . He attributed to me the project of. . . . He added. . . . He knew himself to be bound to Marxist thought. . . . He prepared himself. . . . We saw each other again. . . . I felt myself scorned. . . . He knew that I felt this. . . . He liked to provoke his interlocutor. . . . [He was] a sensitive and absent-minded man in daily life."[24] And so on. The representation is unexceptional. It is successful enough as representations go – we feel that we have learned something of Souyri and of the relation between the two men – but there is nothing to distinguish it from representations each of us hear, read, and produce dozens of times every day, not just in writing history but in the conduct of the most mundane affairs of life. Nor, in spite of all the cautions Lyotard has urged upon us, do we know any better how to assess the trustworthiness of this portrait of Souyri than we would if its author had simply set it forth as a "true account."

Does Lyotard believe in the "postulate of realism"? Certainly not, if we judge from what he says on the subject. But if we take into account what he *does* as well as what he says, he seems in the end, in practice, unable to escape it. Notwithstanding all his skeptical rhetoric, in telling us about his deceased friend he acts as if the past is real, as if some representations of it are preferable to others, and as if the criteria of preference are far from idiosyncratic. We are reminded of Thomas Nagel's suggestion that objectivity and skepticism are not opposites but complementary ideas; that every effort to get beyond appearances postulates the real. The gap between Lyotard's hyperskeptical rhetorical posture and run-of-the-mill realist practice is immense and evidently unbridgeable. What is to be gained from it? Nothing that I can see, except a reputation for undeceivability and possibly (as Denis Donoghue said of deconstruction) a "Pyrrhic victory of angst over bourgeois liberalism."[25]

What, then, are we to think when able people like Novick tell us that the effort to represent the past, and "get it right," is bound to fail – and then do a rather good job of getting it right? The obvious answer is to do as they do, and not as they say. But in closing allow me to suggest, in the compact form of a parable, the outlines, at least, of a more expansive answer. It is as if we are lost in the French countryside, trying to find our way to Paris with maps that do not agree. We happen upon a native philosopher, Jean, whom we ask for help in deciding which map to believe. He examines the maps and frowns, saying, "None of these documents will do. They give only a two-dimensional representation of a path that is at least three dimensional, even disregarding what Einstein says . . . no, they won't do at all. These are mere pieces of paper, and they fail utterly to convey any sensation of movement, of passage from one town to another, of what the scenery along the route looks like, the feel of the road beneath one's feet, the aromas, the sounds of the birds as you pass by! And look at this! Why, these pieces of paper rely on mere round black dots to represent whole cities of people: families, complex souls, individuals full of life and variety and mystery, all absurdly compressed into a dot!" Stretching himself to his full height, Jean, exasperated, hands the maps back to us, and asks, incredulously, "How can anyone ever have thought that anything so sublime as getting to Paris could be represented by a few marks on a sheet of paper?"

Confronted with such radically misplaced expectations, we can only walk on, in hopes of finding a more discriminating philosopher. What Jean wants, maps cannot supply.[26] But we want to go to Paris, we know perfectly well that maps can help us get there, and we also know that some maps are better suited to the purpose than others. (Why that should be so is the really interesting question, though it seems not to arouse much curiosity nowadays in Paris.) Take with a grain of salt Novick's distress over the supposedly insuperable difficulties of mapmaking; be glad that, in spite of them, he has helped us find our way into this past so effectively.

Notes

I am indebted to Peter Novick for several very open and informative letters sent in response to my initial reactions to his book. Although the essay was materially improved by the advice of Sandy Levinson, its tone and conclusions are my responsibility alone. Subsequent page references to *That Noble Dream* appear in parentheses.

First published in *History and Theory* 29 (1990): 129–57. Copyright ©
Wesleyan University.

  1 Eugene Genovese and Elizabeth Fox-Genovese do not hesitate, for example,
    to speak of "Braudel's great and anti-Marxist work" – and then follow
    through on what might otherwise be an empty gesture with a close and crit-
    ical analysis of that work. I look forward to the day when spokespersons for
    other movements can treat their opponents with similar detachment. Elizabeth
    Fox-Genovese and Eugene D. Genovese, *Fruits of Merchant Capital: Slavery
    and Bourgeois Property in the Rise and Expansion of Capitalism* (New
    York: Oxford University Press, 1983), 188.
  2 Friedrich Nietzsche, *On the Genealogy of Morals and Ecce Homo*, trans.
    Walter Kaufmann and R. J. Hollingdale (New York: Random House, 1969).
    See especially the third essay of *On the Genealogy of Morals*, titled "What
    is the Meaning of Ascetic Ideals?"
  3 Geoffrey Galt Harpham, *The Ascetic Imperative in Culture and Criticism*
    (Chicago: University of Chicago Press, 1987), xi, xii.
  4 Thomas Nagel, *The View from Nowhere* (New York: Oxford University
    Press, 1986), 4–6, 68.
  5 Nietzsche, *On the Genealogy of Morals*, 87.
  6 Nagel, *View from Nowhere*, 71.
  7 Although in other respects people attracted to "postmodernism" are often
    especially eager to give the subjective element its due, they tend not to take
    seriously detachment, self-restraint, self-denial, or any of the other subjec-
    tive experiences of *self versus self* upon which asceticism builds. No wonder:
    postmodernism typically presupposes a self too vaporous to resist anything,
    least of all its own all-consuming desires. From the postmodernist stand-
    point, the self is not a discrete agent that takes *cognizance* of circumstances,
    and selects a course of action *in light* of them; instead its "situatedness" is
    so thoroughgoing that, like the electrified gas inside a neon tube, it can
    only conform to the shape of its circumstantial container and respond on
    cue as environing forces surge irresistibly through it. Thus Stanley Fish, in a
    candid, if characteristically reckless, essay titled "Critical Self-Consciousness,
    or Can We Know What We're Doing?" derides the idea that there is any
    emancipatory potential in striving to become more self-aware: "To be in a
    situation (as one always is)," says Fish, "is already to be equipped with an
    awareness of possible goals, obstacles, dangers, rewards, alternatives, etc.,
    and nothing is or could be aided by something called 'self-consciousness.'"
    Consciousness is exhaustively determined by situation: the first lesson of anti-
    foundationalism, Fish says, is precisely that "being situated means that one
    cannot achieve a distance on one's beliefs." His root assumption is straight-
    forwardly fatalistic: our subjective experience of freedom to choose between
    options is simply an illusion. "Freedom, in whatever shape it appears, is
    another name for constraint" (*Doing What Comes Naturally: Change, Rhet-
    oric, and the Practice of Theory in Literary and Legal Studies* [Durham, NC:
    Duke University Press, 1989], 466, 467, 459). It is ironic that although Fish
    has little use for the idea of objectivity and Nagel defends it, Fish's error, as
    seen from Nagel's standpoint, is precisely that Fish is trying too hard to "be
    objective." Fish, that is, gives no credence at all to the "internal" (subjec-
    tive) view, according to which our own power to bring one event rather
    than another into existence seems quite indisputable, and instead he tries
    once and for all to substitute for that view the "external" (objective) one,

according to which the real causes of our acts may well lie outside our deceptively vivid experience of conscious choice. Nagel, in contrast, accords to some subjective experience a status no less real than that derived from the "view from nowhere." In his words, "the seductive appeal of objective reality depends on a mistake. It is not the given. Reality is not just objective reality. Sometimes, in the philosophy of mind but also elsewhere, the truth is not to be found by traveling as far away from one's personal perspective as possible" (Nagel, *View from Nowhere*, 27. See also 114–15).

8 Throughout this essay I have, for purposes of argument, accepted the conventional wisdom that our Victorian forebears really expected through self-annihilation to be transported into the realm of truth. In fact, my guess is that a more sensitive contextual reading would show that they were less naive than we like to think. The important book that has come to epitomize conventional wisdom on this point is Richard Rorty, *Philosophy and the Mirror of Nature* (Princeton: Princeton University Press, 1979).

9 For Nietzsche's sincere admiration for the human capacity for promise keeping and other basic renunciatory traits, see the second essay of *On the Genealogy of Morals*, especially 57–61 and 84–5. Walter A. Kaufmann's *Nietzsche: Philosopher, Psychologist, Antichrist*, 3rd edn (Princeton: Princeton University Press, 1968), develops the theme of self-overcoming at length.

10 I find it difficult to imagine that a person so narrowly committed would, as a matter of fact, succeed in entering sympathetically into the thought of another, even for polemical purposes, but the assertion still holds – if he or she *did* succeed, there would be no other reason to deny the objectivity of the performance.

11 Nietzsche, *On the Genealogy of Morals*, 119.

12 Ibid.

13 Novick is insistent about the virtual identity of objectivity and neutrality. Thus when one of the profession's founders, Hermann Eduard von Holst, the prominent German historian who established the department at the University of Chicago, tried to disentangle the idea of objectivity from that of neutrality, Novick complains of the "elusiveness" and "ambiguity" of his language: "Von Holst, with no apparent sense of inconsistency, could profess 'the objectivity of the historian,' of the 'cool, unbiased student' aiming at the 'stern historical truth,' and yet praise Woodrow Wilson for being 'no votary of that exaggerated, nay, impossible *objektivität*, which virtually amounts to a denial of his right to hold any political or moral opinion as to the events and men he is treating of. But he has no thesis to prove. With unimpeachable honesty and undeviating singleness of purpose he strives – as Ranke puts it – "simply to say how it was." ' The elusiveness and ambiguity in von Holst's usage was characteristic" (25–6). Von Holst's statement is no model of clarity about the relationship between objectivity and neutrality, but it does make it clear that, even among the founding generation, the necessity of distinguishing between the two was recognized. That is a fact with which Novick never comes to terms.

14 For three quite different, though related, accounts of the movement I have in mind, each assigning it different causes and chronologies, see Alasdair MacIntyre, *After Virtue: A Study in Moral Theory*, 2nd edn (Notre Dame, Ind.: University of Notre Dame Press, 1984); Philip Rieff, *The Triumph of the Therapeutic: Uses of Faith after Freud*, with a new preface (Chicago: University of Chicago Press, 1987); and T. J. Jackson Lears, *No Place of*

318   *Thomas Haskell*

Grace: Antimodernism and the Transformation of American Culture, 1880–1920 (New York: Pantheon, 1981).

15 A culture that acknowledges no significant difference between "You *ought* to do/believe *x*" and "I *want* you to do/believe *x*" – the former an invocation of objective obligation, the latter a report of merely subjective desires – is, I believe, in serious trouble. But there is, in my view, no help to be had outside the sphere of history and convention. After three centuries of inquiry into the basis of moral judgment it appears that no ultimate, metaphysical foundations are to be found – in nature, divine will, or anywhere else. Admitting that moral judgment cannot be based on timeless absolutes, universally applicable and utterly independent of human consciousness and practice, does not mean, however, that we must set morality adrift and leave it at the mercy of whimsy and fashion. Thomas Kuhn has shown how authoritative science remains even when we admit the social, conventional quality of scientific understanding and give up the claim that scientists aim at correspondence with eternal verities: *The Structure of Scientific Revolutions*, 2nd edn (Chicago: University of Chicago Press, 1970). Similarly, the most sophisticated proponents of moral realism today do not try to rally faith in supposedly self-evident absolutes or claim that moral rules are independent of cultural conditioning; they admit the historicity and even the conventionality of our ethical thinking and seek to re-establish grounds for obligation on that more modest base. Moral realists have been fighting an uphill battle for a long time, but there is no lack of able voices: see, in addition to MacIntyre's *After Virtue*, Peter Railton, "Moral Realism," *Philosophical Review* 95 (1986): 163–207; the essays by Simon Blackburn and John McDowell in *Morality and Objectivity: A Tribute to J. L. Mackie*, ed. Ted Honderich (Boston: Routledge and Kegan Paul, 1985); and Derek Parfit, *Reasons and Persons* (New York: Oxford University Press, 1984). I have discussed these issues at greater length in "The Curious Persistence of Rights Talk in the 'Age of Interpretation,'" *Journal of American History* 74 (1987): 984–1012 and "Convention and Hegemonic Interest in the Debate over Antislavery: A Reply to Davis and Ashworth," *American Historical Review* 92 (Oct. 1987): 829–78.

16 Of the two paragraphs he says: "Although radically compressed, this is, I think, a fair summary of the original and continuing objectivist creed – an ideal to be pursued by individuals, policed by the collectivity." He concedes that over the past century the concept has been modified – objectivists are less confident that they can purge themselves of values and preconceptions; more likely to ground objectivity in social mechanisms, as opposed to individual qualities; more tolerant of hypotheses; more willing to think of truth seeking as a matter of "tacking" toward reality, or proceeding dialectically, as opposed to brick making and wall building. "But," he concludes, "despite these recent modifications, older usages remain powerful, and perhaps even dominant" (2).

17 Novick also likens objectivity to the Christian myth of the redemptive death of Christ and the Marxist myth of the emancipatory potential of the proletariat. In a footnote apologizing for his use of the neologisms "objectivism" and "objectivist," he observes that "it would be very difficult to write several hundred pages on the belief in the divinity of Christ, and on believers, without 'Christianity' and 'Christians'" (3n).

18 For a sample of the conflict in literary circles, see Frederick Crews, "The Parting of the Twins," *New York Review of Books*, July 20, 1989, 39–44,

and subsequent letters to the editor, ibid., Sept. 28, 1989, or any issue of the journal *Critical Inquiry*.

19 Denis Donoghue, "The Strange Case of Paul de Man," *New York Review of Books*, June 29, 1989, 37.

20 "I, too, aspire to see clearly, like a rifleman, with one eye shut; I, too, aspire to think without assent. This is the ultimate violence to which the modern intellectual is committed. Since things have become as they are, I, too, share the modern desire not to be deceived. . . . This is the unreligion of the age, and its master science. . . . The systematic hunting down of all settled convictions represents the anti-cultural predicate upon which the modern personality is being reorganized" (Rieff, *Triumph of the Therapeutic*, 13).

21 Sun Tzu, *The Art of War*, trans. and intro. by Samuel B. Griffith, foreword by B. H. Liddell Hart (New York: Oxford University Press, 1963), 96–7.

22 Jean-François Lyotard, *Peregrinations: Law, Form, Event* [The Wellek Library Lectures at the University of California, Irvine] (New York: Columbia University Press, 1988), 45–6.

23 Ibid., 46.

24 Ibid., 47–8, 51.

25 Donoghue, "The Strange Case of Paul de Man," 37. Is it wrong of me to expect an author's rhetoric about "theoretical" matters to have a bearing on his or her practice? Stanley Fish would say it is. Fish (a Milton scholar who is no doubt conversant with the rhetorical strategies employed by Puritan divines to ward off the seemingly fatalistic implications of predestination) has repeatedly argued that theory neither has nor needs to have any consequences for everyday practice. For Fish the inconsequentiality of antifoundationalist theory (the "truth" of which he does not doubt) is a corollary of the self's radical situatedness and its consequent inability to achieve detachment. His often repeated thesis is that "being situated not only means that one cannot achieve a distance on one's beliefs, but that one's beliefs do not relax their hold because one 'knows' that they are local and not universal. This in turn means that even someone . . . who is firmly convinced of the circumstantiality of his convictions will nevertheless experience those convictions as universally, not locally, true. It is therefore not surprising but inevitable that at the end of every argument, even of an argument that says there can be no end, the universalist perspective will reemerge as strongly as ever" (*Doing What Comes Naturally*, 467). There is an important kernel of truth in what Fish says, yet we are left wondering why, if antifoundationalism is without consequences, anyone finds it illuminating or worth arguing about. One also wonders if it is wise to engage in conversations with people who feel entitled, for all practical purposes, to regard their own beliefs as universally valid, while regarding everyone else's as unfounded and parochial. For parallel Puritan arguments, see Perry Miller's classic essay, "The Marrow of Puritan Divinity," in his *Errand into the Wilderness* (New York: Harper and Row, 1956), 48–98.

26 As John Dunn put it in a context that is similar, though not identical, "maps are maps, not regrettably ineffectual surrogates for physical environments" (*Political Obligation in Its Historical Context: Essays in Political Theory* [Cambridge: Cambridge University Press, 1980], 14).

17
Objectivity and Truth in History

J. L. Gorman

It is widely held that "objective," when we have sorted out its vague everyday uses, is a concept which is to be applied, most naturally, to *statements* or to *methods* or to *disciplines*. Indeed, even its application to methods or to disciplines would seem to be an extension of its application to statements, for we may describe a method or a discipline as "objective" only insofar as it leads us to knowledge of objective statements. This concept of "objective" is, then, to be used fundamentally as a predicate of statements; as such, "objective" means little more than "true." R. S. Rudner, for example, in his book *Philosophy of Social Science*,[1] gives an analysis along these lines, and he says "when we speak of someone as giving 'a factual, or objective, account' of something, we appear to be saying little more than that it is a true account." He holds also, in a footnote, that to say that an account is objective is to say that it does not dispose us to believe certain other statements which are false. Thus, on this sort of analysis, objectivity has to do with the truth or falsity of statements. Such an understanding of objectivity is commonly used by philosophers, particularly in the philosophy of science. For example, K. R. Popper's notion of "falsifiability" presupposes such an analysis.

History is the most rational form of our understanding of the past. Historical writing deserves closer attention than has been given it by analytical philosophers. For historical writing, I hold the usual analyses of "objective," outlined above, to be inappropriate and implausible. I propose in this essay to show this, to suggest a more suitable analysis of "objective," and in passing to give a different perspective to philosophical problems of history from that involved in studying the nature of historical explanation, which is so often unfruitful.

I

I begin with an example of historical writing, a rather longer example than is usually considered by philosophers when they look at history. It is taken from *English History 1914–45* by A. J. P. Taylor.[2] The statements in it I have numbered in order to simplify the analysis and make it easier to follow.

"(1) Joyce was born in New York. (2) His father was a naturalised American citizen. (3) Joyce never acquired British nationality, though he spent most of his life in England and was a rabid patriot. (4) He became a Fascist, for whom Sir Oswald Mosley, the 'Bleeder', was too moderate. (5) In 1938 Joyce applied for, and obtained, a British passport, stating falsely that he was a British subject. (6) In August 1939 he renewed his passport for one year and went to Germany. (7) In September 1940 he became a naturalised German. (8) As Joyce had never been a British subject, it seemed that he was secure from a charge of high treason. (9) It was, however, argued that Joyce had sought the protection of the Crown by acquiring a British passport and therefore owed allegiance while he retained it. (10) Even on this tawdry basis, the charge against Joyce was not proved. (11) It was not shown that he had retained his passport once he was in Germany, though he probably did; nor was any satisfactory evidence produced that he had broadcast for the Germans during the period of the passport's validity. (12) Technically, Joyce was hanged for making a false statement when applying for a passport, the usual penalty for which is a small fine. (13) His real offence was to have attracted to himself the mythical repute of Lord Haw-Haw. (14) Most of the broadcasts attributed to Joyce were not in fact made, either by him or by anyone else. (15) No German broadcaster, for instance, ever gave the names of British towns which the *Luftwaffe* would bomb the next night nor state that the clock at Banstead was ten minutes slow. (16) These legends were the manufacture of war-nerves."

This section supports the following account of Joyce in the main narrative:

"(17) The Germans waged political war with equally little success. (18) William Joyce, their principal English broadcaster, (known as 'Lord Haw-Haw' from his supposed way of speaking) excited amusement, not alarm, though this did not prevent his being executed on a trumped-up charge at the end of the war."

I suggest that this account is unacceptable; many of those who heard Joyce speak during the last war would, I think, regard it as too pro-Joyce. I postulate a hypothetical objector who will speak on behalf of those who do not accept the account, and I propose to characterize the kinds of objections to the account which might be made.

First, I take it that it is uncontroversial to hold that if any statement in the account is *false* then that statement should be modified so as to make it true, or removed altogether. But we at once have the philo-sophical problem: how do we *know* when a particular statement is true or false? Perhaps the evidence we might use to verify some statement might be consistent with a contrary statement. There are a great many issues in the philosophy of knowledge and science which involve problems of the validity of our claims to know the truth or falsity of some state-ments. But I am going to ignore these problems here, as they are com-mon to all knowledge, and I will thus be able to concentrate on those problems which are more peculiar to *historical* knowledge. I take here the commonsense attitude that we can and do know the truth or falsity of some historical statements – there is no practical doubt that "the Battle of Hastings occurred in 1066" is true. So I accept that we can, in principle, assess an historical statement for truth or falsity, and I hold that false statements in historical accounts can and should be removed.

Secondly, I take it that it is uncontroversial to hold that an historical account should not contain emotive or subjective statements. Now it is difficult to agree about what is and is not an emotive statement – there are a great many borderline cases. A philosophical problem arises here, also: perhaps *all* the statements which we can make presuppose some evaluation on some subjective basis. But here, too, I am going to adopt a commonsense approach and ignore such philosophical problems. We still have the practical problem of when a particular statement is emo-tive; where there is any difficulty about this, I shall assume that the state-ment *is* emotive, and consequently recommend that it be re-expressed in non-emotive language. (Note that an emotive expression occurring in a statement is not sufficient to make the statement itself emotive; thus to describe Sir Oswald Mosley as *having been called* a "Bleeder" is not the same as describing him *as* a "Bleeder"; both statements use the same emotive term, but I take it that the former is not emotive although the latter is.) So I hold that we can and should remove or modify statements which display emotive bias.

So far I have suggested two grounds of objection to an account which might be made: that it contains false statements, and that it contains emotive statements. I have ignored the philosophical problems which might be raised about this, and on the usual analyses of objectivity I have thereby virtually defined away the whole issue. But for history the most important part is to come, and I shall next modify Taylor's example in order to show this, by removing the false and emotive statements.

Thus,

(1)   is true.
(2)   is true.
(3)   is complex. It may be analysed as three separate statements:
(3a) "Joyce never acquired British nationality." This is just what, in effect, he *did* do, if the court's decision was correct. My hypothetical

objector can hold (3a) to be false. I paraphrase what I take it Taylor "really" means here: Joyce did not become naturalized through the normal channels; he never formally applied for naturalization. Our objector might hold that Joyce was "morally" British while agreeing with this true statement.

(3b) "Joyce spent most of his life in England" is true.

(3c) "Joyce was a rabid patriot." This is, or could be, an emotive statement. But, this apart, is it *true*? How could Joyce have been a patriot, our objector might ask, bearing in mind what he subsequently did? We need to modify this statement so as to make it true, and to make Taylor's point clearer. We cannot substitute "Joyce passed himself off as a patriot," for although this might be true, it suggests that he wasn't one. This was not Taylor's point. Such a description is biassed the other way. The argument here is analogous to J. L. Austin's argument against those who assert that all we are justified in claiming is the truth of such statements as "there appears to me to be a table there." This may make a philosophical point well, but it implies *doubt* (which is, of course, what the philosophical point is), and hence an "appearance" statement is not equivalent to what we "really" mean when we say that we see a table there. We need, with respect to Joyce, a statement which says no more than that Joyce behaved as a patriot (for that is all that the evidence entitles Taylor to say) without implying that he wasn't one. Although "patriot" can be an emotive word, this is not the reason for the difficulty here. We may say that Joyce was regarded as patriotic. This is true and does not fall into the above dilemma.

(4) is true.

(5) is true.

(6) is true.

(7) is true.

(8) is subject to the same doubt as (3a). It needs to be modified in the same way.

(9) is true.

(10) is probably false. It would be best simply to point out that the argument in (9) was accepted.

(11) is true, but this would not necessarily imply that (10) were true.

(12) is false. "Technically," Joyce was hanged for what he was charged with, i.e. high treason. But substantially the same point can be made in a true fashion: "If Joyce had not made a false statement and been granted a British passport he might not have been hanged." As a counter-factual conditional statement the truth of this cannot be guaranteed, but it seems probable, and our objector has no reason to doubt it. Taylor's statement about the usual punishment for this offence is true.

(13) is false, but for a rather trivial reason. Joyce's "real" offence, again, was what he was convicted for. "Offence" is a technical term. However, it is true that Joyce attracted to himself the mythical repute of Lord Haw-Haw. (He also attracted to himself the justified repute of Lord Haw-Haw. This was because he *was* Lord Haw-Haw. Taylor has left this out.)

(14) Until we know how many broadcasts were attributed to Joyce, we cannot decide whether this is true or not. In all probability it is true, because of the effect of war-nerves. My hypothetical objector will take it as true.

(15) is true.

(16) is true.

(17) is true.

(18) is complex. It may be analysed as five separate assertions:

(18a) "Joyce was their principal English broadcaster" is true.

(18b) "Joyce was known as 'Lord Haw-Haw' from his supposed way of speaking" is true, except that "manner" would be better than "supposed way," as the latter might suggest that there was no speaking.

(18c) "Joyce excited amusement" is true.

(18d) "Joyce did not excite alarm" is false.

(18e) "Joyce was executed on a trumped-up charge at the end of the war" is false.

In the light of the modifications suggested above, I now put together all those statements which my hypothetical objector has agreed to accept.

I suggest that the following account contains only true and emotive-free statements:

"Joyce was born in New York. His father was a naturalized American citizen. Joyce never made a formal request for British nationality, though he spent most of his life in England and was regarded as patriotic. He became a Fascist, for whom Sir Oswald Mosley, the 'Bleeder,' was too moderate. In 1938 Joyce applied for, and obtained, a British passport, stating falsely that he was a British subject. In August 1939 he renewed his passport for one year and went to Germany. In September 1940 he became a naturalized German. As Joyce felt that he had never been a British subject, it seemed to him that he was secure from a charge of high treason. It was however argued that Joyce had sought the protection of the Crown by acquiring a British passport and therefore owed allegiance while he retained it, and this argument was accepted. It was not shown that he had retained his passport while he was in Germany, though he probably did; nor was any conclusive evidence produced that he had broadcast for the Germans during the period of the passport's validity. If Joyce had not made a false statement and been granted a British passport he might not have been hanged. The usual penalty for making such a false statement is a small fine. Joyce attracted to himself the mythical repute of Lord Haw-Haw. Most of the broadcasts attributed to Joyce were not in fact made, either by him or by anyone else. No German broadcaster, for instance, ever gave the names of British towns which the *Luftwaffe* would bomb the next night nor state that the clock at Banstead was ten minutes slow. These legends were the manufacture of war-nerves. . . . The Germans waged political war with equally little success. William Joyce, their principal English broadcaster (known as 'Lord Haw-Haw' from his manner of speaking), excited amusement, though this did not prevent his being executed at the end of the war."

It seem to me that this account is still very nearly as unacceptable as the original – indeed, unless one concentrates upon them it is very difficult to tell them apart. But now that the false and emotive statements have been removed, what else is it that we find unacceptable about the account? Or are we wrong to find it unacceptable?

Consider the following extract from the entry on Joyce in *Chambers's Encyclopaedia*:

Joyce, William (1906–46), traitor, was born in Ireland, according to the application for a British passport made by him in 1933. Subsequently, during his trial for treason, he claimed to have been born in the United States. . . . In August, 1939, a few days before the outbreak of hostilities, he went to Germany and offered his services to the German ministry of propaganda. . . .

I have no reason to think that this account is not literally true, in the sense of containing nothing but true statements. It is therefore logically compatible with Taylor's account, as modified above. It seems to contain no emotive statements. Are we therefore to take this account to be acceptable?

It does seem to me that Taylor's account as modified and the Chambers account are each biassed, the former for and the latter against Joyce. Now it may be that you do not agree with this; you may feel, for example, that Taylor's is not a pro-Joyce line. But I do not, in order to develop my argument, *need* to characterize correctly whatever bias there may be. It seems to me – and this *is* an important part of my argument – that Taylor's and Chambers's accounts are in some significant sense *incompatible*, and therefore not both acceptable (in spite of the fact that they are *logically* compatible as each contains only true statements).

I have produced two accounts which are about the same thing (this is only a manner of speaking – I am not sure that we could ever correctly characterize what an historical account was *about*, exactly), and which each contain only true statements, and no emotive statements. I hold that they are incompatible, and given this, at least one of them must be unacceptable for reasons which are something other than falsity or emotive statements. If one were to hold that one account were acceptable, then one would hold that the other was unacceptable. (As it happens, I do not think that *either* is acceptable, but they are, one might say, unacceptable in opposite ways.)

An objection might be raised here, that once I have shown that Taylor's and Chambers's accounts each contain only true and value-free statements, then they *must* be acceptable, and consequently they must also be compatible. Now it may be, perhaps, that the examples which I have used do not make their incompatibility as obvious as they might, and perhaps there is room for disagreement about this (although they do have the advantage of being real examples).

But, given that all the statements in each of these accounts are true and value-free, it is possible to select them in such a way that they reappear in other different accounts – accounts which are *so* incompatible that it is highly implausible to deny it. All that is required is that the truth-value of each statement remain constant, regardless of which account the statement appears in. Philosophers brought up on truth-functional analysis will have no difficulty in accepting this requirement. Two such accounts follow:

(A) "Joyce was born in Ireland, according to the application for a British passport made by him in 1933. He became a Fascist, for whom Sir Oswald Mosley, the 'Bleeder,' was too moderate. In August 1939, a few days before the outbreak of hostilities, he went to Germany and offered his services to the German ministry of propaganda. He was the Germans' principal English broadcaster (known as 'Lord Haw-Haw' from his manner of speaking). He was executed as a traitor."

(B) "Joyce was born in New York. His father was a naturalized American citizen. Joyce never made a formal request for British nationality, though he spent most of his life in England and was regarded as patriotic. In September 1940 he became a naturalized German. Joyce attracted to himself the mythical repute of Lord Haw-Haw. These legends were the manufacture of war-nerves. He was executed as a traitor."

I take it as clear that these accounts are in some significant sense incompatible, and that at least one, and very likely both, of them is unacceptable.

I have some interim conclusions: that the truth and value-freedom of the statements in an account is not a sufficient condition of the acceptability of the account; that the value-freedom of the statements in an account is not a sufficient condition of the acceptability of the account; and that the truth of the constituent statements in an account is not a sufficient condition of the acceptability of the account. The first conclusion implies the second two, but I have separated out its implications in order to present the last conclusion in as clear a manner as possible. We have thus begun to loosen the apparent ties between acceptability and truth.

I shall now put forward an account which is, I suggest, not as unacceptable as either the anti-Joyce (A) account or the pro-Joyce (B) account. It will be a "middle-of-the-road" account; not wholly acceptable, perhaps, but more acceptable than the examples put forward so far.

"Joyce was born in New England, the son of an American citizen. In 1934 he came to England, when he applied for a British passport, stating that he was born in Britain. He spent most of his life in Hampshire, and until 1940 was regarded as patriotic. He later became a Fascist, and was as extreme as Sir Oswald Mosley. In September 1939 he went to Germany and offered his services to the German ministry of defence. He was the Germans' principal British broadcaster. In August 1940 he became a naturalized German. He was known as 'Lord Haw-Haw' from the peculiar cough which he had, which he used to great effect over the air. He was known to have announced the towns which the *Luftwaffe* would bomb the next night, and was thought to have announced that the clock at Wanstead was ten minutes slow, but this idea was the manufacture of war-nerves. He was tried in 1945, when it was held that his application for a British passport which stated that he was born in Britain meant that he always owed allegiance to the Crown. For his treasonable broadcasts he was executed in 1945."

I take it that every statement, and where the statement is a conjunction, every part of a statement, in this account is false. Nevertheless it is, I hold, a more acceptable account than at least some accounts which contain only true statements. I have then a further conclusion: that, at least for the relative acceptability of two accounts, truth is not a *necessary* condition, in addition to not being a *sufficient* condition. I do not, however, deny that when we assess the acceptability of one account by itself (that is, not in comparison with another) it might be preferable that, other things being equal, its constituent statements should be true rather than false. Thus, for what might be termed "absolute" rather than "relative" acceptability, truth may be a necessary condition; but it is nevertheless a fairly insignificant part of our assessment of acceptability – other matters are more important.

II

So far I have shown that truth is neither a necessary nor a sufficient condition for the relative acceptability of historical accounts, and is insignificantly necessary and not sufficient for the absolute acceptability of historical accounts.[3]

We come, then, to the problem: what *is* necessary and sufficient for the relative or the absolute acceptability of historical accounts? What is it, other than falsity or emotive statements, which we can find unacceptable in historical accounts?

Rudner suggested that an account should not dispose us to believe in certain false statements. He did not say *which* false statements; I assume he means *any* false statements. He does not use the strong term "imply" rather than the weak term "dispose" – perhaps because he recognizes that a requirement that an account should not *imply* false statements is too easily complied with, while leaving open the possibility of bias. Certainly the accounts which I have produced, given the truth of the constituent statements, do not *imply* any false statements. But do they *dispose* us to believe in any false statements? No doubt they do: some people will believe all manner of true and false statements on the strength of some simple assertion. Rudner's criterion here, depending as it does on what may be purely personal dispositions to respond to an account, is quite unworkable.

But suppose there were some way of making clear what it is reasonable to believe on the basis of some assertion? Perhaps some rational ground for a false belief may be found which falls short of implication. Given this assumption, we might then find a statement to be unacceptable on grounds other than falsity or emotivity of expression – because it "rationally disposes" us to believe in some false statement. Given the unacceptability of a statement, the unacceptability of the account in which it appears would then follow. But even if there were some way of deciding some belief which we are reasonably entitled to hold on the basis of some assertion, this would not help. For we saw in the preparation of accounts (A) and (B) that the *same* statements which had appeared in Taylor's and Chambers's accounts (with the same implications and dispositions caused thereby) could be selected to reappear in different accounts, and the acceptability of the resulting accounts varied with the selection. Thus the problem of the acceptability of accounts is one which arises *over and above* the problem of the acceptability of statements. My examples in the first section of this essay show that the acceptability of statements (on *whatever* ground such acceptability is decided) is not a sufficient condition for the absolute acceptability of historical accounts, and neither a sufficient nor a necessary condition for the relative acceptability of historical accounts.

What, then, is involved in the acceptability of an account, other than the acceptability of the constituent statements? If we consider the example which consisted of only false statements, and we compare it with either Taylor's account or account (B), we can see that what makes it more acceptable is its mentioning a supposed example of what Joyce actually said: "He was known to have announced the towns which the *Luftwaffe* would bomb the next night . . ." This assertion implies (a) that Joyce actually said something (which is true), and (b) that Joyce made the particular announcement mentioned (which is false). What is important for the acceptability of the account is that it should mention that Joyce said something apparently treasonable in a broadcast, rather than that it should mention correctly the actual details of what he said. What seems to be central to the problem of the acceptability of historical accounts, in the light of this example, is that certain statements ought to be included or left out in certain circumstances, regardless of their truth or falsity. It seems, then, that it is the acceptability of the *selection* of statements which is the central and significant feature of the acceptability of historical accounts.[4] I suggest that the acceptability of the selection of statements is a significantly necessary condition for, and (with the acceptability of statements) jointly sufficient for the absolute acceptability of historical accounts, and a necessary and sufficient condition for the acceptability of one account rather than another.

The latter suggestion, that acceptability of selection is a necessary and sufficient condition for the relative acceptability of historical accounts, is a strong one. It follows that if we compare two accounts for relative acceptability, one of which contains an acceptable selection with an unacceptable statement, while the other involves an unacceptable selection, then the account with the unacceptable statement is the more acceptable. But, it may be objected, is it never the case that a "whopping falsehood" is more unacceptable than some minor though relevant detail? I suggest, never; I cannot see that a "whopping falsehood" would ever be fit for selection, while no statement which ought to be selected could ever be trivial, at least from the point of view of the account into which it entered.

Another objection may be made to my conclusion that the acceptability of the *selection* of statements is necessary and jointly sufficient (with acceptability of statements) for the absolute acceptability of accounts. I have not specified any kind of *ordering* of statements, and it might be felt that this was likely to be a necessary condition, following the discussion in the last ten years on the place of *narrative* in historical writing. It might be felt that just to *select* statements was not enough – one might have an over-all distortion through putting true statements in the wrong order, or at least in different orders so as to give different levels of acceptability. Haskell Fain, in *Between Philosophy and History*,[5] quotes an example from a school textbook, which requires that the pupil put the following statements in the right order:

1 He started up the engine.
2 Mr Smith opened the garage doors.
3 He got out and closed the doors behind him.
4 He drove out of the garage.

Fain (who does not have our problem in mind here) suggests that we have certain intuitions as to what he calls "narrative coherence," and these enable us to put these statements in the right order, which is presumably: 2, 1, 4, 3. However, I suggest that if there is more than one way into the garage then the order might be: 1, 2, 4, 3. Depending upon whether there is more than one way into the garage, we can have two possible orders of apparently true statements, one of which might be "false" as a whole and the other "true," although only one *selection* of statements is involved here.

However, the textbook also requires the pupil to preface each statement, when in the right order, with "first," "next," "then," and "finally." We assume, when we read a narrative sequence which is like the simple example which Fain quotes, that the order in which the statements appear on the page is the order in which the events described by those statements actually occurred. Hence the narrative order of statements is equivalent to those statements without an order but with such temporal adverbs as "first," "next," etc., made explicit. Hence for a selection of such statements to be in the wrong order implies that one or more of the statements is false, since its implicit temporal adverb is incorrect. To put statements in the wrong order is to falsify one or more of them. To use ordering rather than explicit temporal adverbs is simply a heuristic device for easy reading. The objection based on Fain's example thus reduces to a problem of the acceptability of statements, which has been dealt with already. I hold, then, to my conclusion that it is the selection of statements which has to be acceptable for the account as a whole to be acceptable in the way already described.

What, then, makes the selection of statements itself acceptable? If we consider again the examples (A) and (B), we may note that although each of them is biassed in roughly the opposite way to the other, the failure of each selection is not just that it leaves out statements which the other includes. We can see this if we add the two accounts together in the most intuitively acceptable way possible:

"Joyce was born in New York. His father was a naturalized American citizen. He was born in Ireland according to the application for a British passport made by him in 1933. Joyce never made a formal request for British nationality, though he spent most of his life in England and was regarded as patriotic. He became a Fascist, for whom Sir Oswald Mosley, the 'Bleeder,' was too moderate. In August 1939, a few days before the outbreak of hostilities, he went to Germany and offered his services to the German ministry of propaganda. In September 1940 he became a naturalized German. He was the Germans' principal English broadcaster (known as 'Lord Haw-Haw' from his manner of speaking). Joyce attracted to himself the mythical repute of Lord Haw-Haw. These legends were the manufacture of war-nerves. He was executed as a traitor."

This account still seems unacceptable, and seems to be inclined in favour of Joyce although less so than account (B). The reason is that it leaves out the statement about the justified, as opposed to the mythical,

repute of Lord Haw-Haw. This bears out Sir Herbert Butterfield's assertion that we do not gain true history by merely adding the speech of the
prosecution to the speech for the defence.[6] Obviously selection is not a
simple matter, and we need some criterion of which statements ought to
be included in an account.

I propose to describe a statement which ought to be selected for inclusion in an account (for the account to be acceptable) as "relevant," and
one which ought not to be so included as "irrelevant." However, such
terms should not be regarded as simply predicates of statements, rather
as "true" and "false" are: we should always remember a tacit "to" –
statements are relevant *to* some account. Thus a decision about the
relevance of a statement is not a decision about the acceptability of
the *statement*, but a decision about the acceptability of the *account*
into which it enters. Statements do not carry a "relevance-value" with
them just as they carry a truth-value, regardless of where they appear.
A statement is relevant if and only if it ought to be selected for inclusion in an account.

It is thus possible for a selection to fail to be acceptable through including irrelevant statements or omitting relevant statements. In account (B),
it is relevant that Joyce attracted to himself the mythical repute of Lord
Haw-Haw, but it is also relevant that Joyce attracted to himself the
justified repute of Lord Haw-Haw. The relevance of the former statement depends on the inclusion of the latter statement, so that if the
latter is selected then so should the former be; if the latter is not selected
then the former is not relevant to the account, and if we include the
former and omit the latter the account will be unacceptable, probably
more unacceptable than it would have been if both statements had been
left out. We cannot therefore assess one statement by itself for relevance
and expect by including it to add to the acceptability of the account in
which it appears. One cannot say *a priori* what proportion of statements
in an account should be relevant for the account to be more acceptable
than another, nor how far the inclusion of some irrelevant statements
will render the account more unacceptable than another. The relevance
of any one statement would seem to have a lot to do with the relevance
of all the other statements included or available for inclusion – yet we
must avoid what D. H. Fischer calls the "Holist fallacy," where an historian selects "significant details from a sense of the whole thing."[7] We
need a criterion of relevance.

One of the reasons why philosophers have not studied problems
concerned with the nature of relevance is that they usually believe that
selection is made on the basis of personal evaluation of importance,
or a subjective sense of significance. There is a general line of argument
which goes like this: "Historians do not and cannot describe everything
that happened – it is not their job to describe and record every trivial
event. They have to make use of a principle of selection – they have to

distinguish the important from the trivial. But what are their standards of importance and triviality? What is their criterion of significance?"[8] But we then begin on problems which are really getting away from the point: are events "intrinsically" important? Is their importance a function of the interests of the historian? But there is confusion here. E. H. Carr, for example, holds that whatever is significant in the past is relevant to the historian.[9]

The words "significance" and "relevance" are often used interchangeably in some contexts, but it is necessary here to distinguish them. "Relevance," I have already explained, is a predicate of *statements*, when they are considered with respect to *accounts*. "Significance," on the other hand, tends to imply "importance," and is usually regarded as a subjective matter; it is typically a predicate of *events*, *episodes*, or *problems*. We would not normally say that a *statement* was significant, although we might say that the event it was about was significant. But statements are not relevant only insofar as the events they are about are significant: thus the statement about where Joyce was born is, to our account, relevant; the event it describes, however, is not of great historical significance. On the other had, our winning the last war was a significant historical event, but a statement about it is of no relevance to the account we are concerned with. If we confuse significance with relevance we are too easily led to think that the central problem of relevance is one about the personal evaluations of events by the historian. This need not be the case.

In distinguishing relevance from significance I have also distinguished events, episodes, or problems, from statements; these are further distinguished from accounts, and from evidence. Now it is not unusual to find a problem of selection to be central to the problem of objectivity in history, but the problem usually discovered is that of the selection of *evidence*, or that of the selection of *events*. These are not the problems which I am concerned with. I do not think that they raise important philosophical problems at all, other than what they have in common with the problem of the selection of statements. Certainly historians select *evidence*; so do scientists. If one wished to know whether it was true that the Battle of Hastings occurred in 1066, one would leave out whole areas of evidence in one's research, because it would not be pertinent to the problem (or, on a slightly different reading of the word, it would not be "evidence" at all). One might, of course, make mistakes in doing this, and this suggests that there is some methodological principle which one would be transgressing in making such a mistake. It cannot reasonably be claimed that one is failing to be objective in selecting evidence in this way.

The problem of selecting events in the past has two parts. First, I do not think that it can reasonably be claimed that an historian is failing to be objective because he selects some problem of the past as more worthy of study than another – he is no different from the scientist here, who also may select (no doubt on subjective grounds) some problem for study. The philosophical issue is surely whether or not he can give an objective *answer* to such a problem – and here, as far as history is concerned, it is the problem of the selection of statements which is the fundamental one. Secondly, some events are selected, not as *setting* the problem, but as entering into the *solution* of the problem; but here they are selected, not necessarily on a subjective basis, but because statements describing them are relevant to the account one is seeking to give in answer to some problem. The central philosophical issue which arises is that of the relationship of statements to accounts, and my argument has shown that, for an historical account to be acceptable, we need an acceptable criterion of relevance.

III

Can history be objective? It is common to reply to this question, "It all depends on what you mean by 'objective.'" But it does not all depend on that; it depends, also, on the meaning of "history."

The word "history" is ambiguous: it can mean either the course of past events, or the study of past events. When I ask if history can be objective I am asking if the study of past events can be objective. But "the study of past events" is also vague: it involves historians themselves, their methods, and also their writings about the past. I do not intend, in my use of the word "objective," to reflect adequately all normal uses of the word, and I propose to restrict the applicability of "objective" to historical *writing*. I think that it is likely that an historian's method is objective just insofar as the writings which he produces on the basis of that method are objective, and so I am not, in ignoring the applicability of "objective" to method, leaving out anything of great importance. On the other hand, I am ignoring one natural and common use of the word. It is often predicated of historians rather than their writings, and when one historian questions the objectivity of another he is often questioning the other's reasons for writing some account, rather than the objectivity of the account itself. A philosopher may wish to say that an historian is objective if and only if his writings are objective, but I do not think that such an equivalence holds for normal speech. In any event, such problems of descriptive linguistic analysis are not here relevant, beyond a simple delineation of my meaning. When I ask if history can be objective, I am asking if historical writing can be objective.

By "objective" I mean "rationally acceptable." This is, I suggest, the fundamental meaning behind most, if not all, of our philosophical uses of the word. I have, in the second section of this essay, made use of the notion of acceptability already, and I do not think that this notion is in need here of explication; the concept of rationality involved does, however, need explicating. Christopher Blake, in his article "Can History be Objective?," gives us a descriptive analysis of objectivity which suggests that history is objective insofar as it can be written so as to be acceptable to all reasonable people.[10] But "rationally acceptable" does *not* mean "acceptable to all rational people." A Beethoven symphony may, in fact, be acceptable to all rational people, but that would not make it objective. Rational people may just happen to accept something for which no rational acceptance procedure, standard, or criterion was appropriate, and it is conceivable that historical writing is something for which no such standard is appropriate. A given historical account may fail to be objective in two ways: it may be *unacceptable* on the basis of a rational standard, or it may be *acceptable*, but not on the basis of a rational standard. It is not enough for objectivity, then, that rational people find something to be acceptable; there has to be an element of rationality about their finding it so. *Given* a rational acceptance standard, only then could we say that an account was objective just insofar as it was acceptable to all rational people, and only then could we say that a rational person was required to accept an account when it was rational to do so, and to reject an account when it was not rational to accept it. The rational man's compliance with such a rational requirement would be what made him rational, as a matter of definition. Such a requirement would be a rational demand, although a demand which it would be logically possible to disobey, on pain of being described as irrational. People are rational if and only if they have and use rational standards. Thus, when I ask if history can be objective, I am asking if historical writing can be rationally acceptable, and I hold that historical writing is rationally acceptable if and only if it is acceptable according to a rational standard. The question becomes: can there be a rational standard for accepting historical writing?

I have now to explain what makes some standard a *rational* standard. The best way of considering the general conditions of the rationality of standards is to examine an example of a rational standard. Science is widely regarded as the paradigm of rational claims to knowledge, and our standards of acceptability of scientific theories are likewise regarded as the most rational we have for what we can say about the world. I shall, therefore, briefly consider some general issues of rationality in the philosophy of science.

Rudner, quoted above, suggested that "objective" means little more than "true," but even in science it means more than this. Truth is nevertheless an important requirement. A science is well on the way to objectivity if it makes true statements about the world, but the philosophical problem arises, *can* science make true statements about the world? And even if it can, can we know about it? In the logic of science we distinguish two sorts of statements of particular interest: general statements, and singular statements. A scientific theory is widely regarded as consisting of a set of general statements about the world, which we claim to know to be true. But is our claim justified? The evidence we put forward in justification consists of singular statements descriptive of observation, but it is apparent that we cannot derive with any certainty a general statement from a limited number of singular statements – our observations do not wholly confirm our theories. But if theories go beyond our evidence, perhaps we have no rational ground for holding them – perhaps they are no better than flights of fancy. The search for a rational guarantee of the truth of the general statements we claim to know to be true is called "the problem of induction." It is enough to say that no solution to the problem has been found.

If the only rational ground for accepting a general statement is that it has been shown to be derived from singular statements descriptive of observation, then, since such derivation is impossible, it follows that we do not accept our general statements on rational grounds at all. But such a view of science is too implausible to hold, and there is a simple way of avoiding the conclusion: perhaps the requirement of derivation is too strong as a ground of rational acceptance of general statements.

The work of Sir Karl Popper has provided us with a new standard for the rational acceptability of scientific statements of this sort.[11] Popper noted that general statements, although they could not, as a matter of logic, be conclusively *verified* by singular statements descriptive of observation, could be conclusively *falsified* by such statements. It is, on his view, rational to accept a statement so long as it is consistent with all our observations – as long as it has not yet been falsified. We should, for a sound method in science, try to falsify our general statements by testing them; they are so much the stronger insofar as they resist actual falsification. But of course such strength is only arrived at where falsification is conceivable: a general statement is of no value if it is consistent with all conceivable singular statements. It is not enough that a general statement be unfalsified in order to be accepted; it must be possible to falsify it in principle – that is, it must be falsifiable. A statement is rationally acceptable if it is falsifiable. Falsifiability is our rational standard.

What, however, makes Popper's criterion of falsifiability qualify as a rational standard? It is not just that, in actual scientific practice, this is the standard of rationality used. This *is* the case, but for a trivial reason: nothing else is to count as scientific activity, for the falsifiability criterion is used by Popper as a way of demarcating science from non-science. But, fortunately, those activities which have traditionally been accepted as scientific seem, by and large, to remain scientific when tested against the criterion; our history of science has much the same content as it has always had. The criterion of scientific rationality is not, then, wholly descriptive in its application, and some practices which made doubtful claims to be scientific fail the standard and are regarded as pseudo-scientific, such as psychoanalysis or astrology. One can only be scientific, or rational, if one operates on the basis of the falsifiability criterion:

the criterion is prescriptive. Popper puts his criterion forward simply as a proposal for agreement,[12] although he has a general theory of experience which underlies his position.

But presumably we cannot agree that just *anything* will do for us as a rational standard. I suggest that the reason the falsifiability criterion qualifies as a rational standard of acceptability is that it derives from the purposes of the community of scientists. The purposes – to describe and explain natural phenomena – are a matter of agreement among the community, as are the methods to be used. It is, ultimately, simply a matter of agreement that scientists seek to make true statements about the world, and simply a matter of agreement that the falsity of a statement should be a good reason for rejecting it. This latter agreement by the community is not necessarily an obvious one to reach; for example, Nietzsche held that falsification is not a good reason for rejecting a statement. The falsifiability criterion is rational insofar as it enables us best to attain our purposes; judgment as to which criterion is best is, again, a matter for agreement, but this need not be difficult to reach, for, given the purposes, the restrictions on potential criteria will be tight. Our purposes, however, are always questionable.

Although scientists agree that falsification is a ground for the rejection of a statement, and although they might agree to use the falsifiability criterion as their rational standard, this would not define away the case of those who deny objectivity. For although *which* standard used is ultimately a matter of choice, it must *be* a standard – that is, it must work. Does Popper's work? His theory requires, among other things, that the concepts used in statements have consistently definite meanings, for one cannot falsify "All *A*s are *B*s" with the statement "*A* is not *B*" unless the "*A*" and "*B*" which appear in both statements mean, respectively, the same. But (some recent objectors to Popper's theory suggest) they may not do so; and, anyway, the meanings which are used may be those which presuppose the acceptability of the general statements. The possibility of falsifiability being used as a rational standard would be illusory under such conditions, and if such a standard was used the acceptability of scientific theories would not be rationally based. The problem for philosophy of science is not so much finding which of several standards is the most rational, but of finding any one at all which actually works. To deny objectivity is to deny that one can be found, and discussion for and against objectivity in science therefore takes place on further issues in the philosophy of experience. Perhaps, then, Popper's criterion does not work, but this has yet to be conclusively shown.

I suggest that, at the level of agreement about rational standards of acceptability, the agreement among a community must be total, for the person who did not accept the standard would not be regarded as a member of the community at all, for he could not share the common purposes (for example, to truly describe the world) from which the standard was derived. A standard is rational, then, if it is derived from the purposes of a community, universally agreed upon by them, and actually workable. For the present, I assume that Popper's criterion of falsifiability does meet these requirements, and is therefore suitable as a standard for the rational acceptability of scientific statements.

Let us now consider how far Popper's criterion of rational acceptability is applicable to history. It seems at first sight that it may be applicable: historical statements may, perhaps, be regarded as being held true on the strength of evidence which is not sufficient to guarantee their truth, but which is suitable for testing it. It may be, therefore, that just as "there can be no ultimate statements in science"[13] there can be no ultimate statements in history, either. However, many historical statements have a singular rather than a general form, and, given the evidence, there seems to be no reason why their truth should not be guaranteed. On the other hand, we may recall the objections to Popper's criterion based on problems of meaning; it is certainly the case that historical concepts are very much more open to misunderstanding and loose usage than those of scientists – perhaps necessarily so.[14] There is not, at present, any agreed standard for the acceptability of the statements in an historical account on the basis of the concepts used in them. Thus Popper's criterion would seem to be inapplicable here, and an effective standard needs to be sought, both for science and for history.

Regardless, however, of the doubt we may entertain about the applicability of Popper's criterion to historical *statements*, a more serious objection to his position may be made. In the first two sections of this essay I showed that the acceptability of historical statements was neither necessary nor sufficient for the relative acceptability of historical accounts, and insignificantly necessary and not sufficient for the absolute acceptability of historical accounts. I showed that it was the *selection* of statements which had to be acceptable for the account as a whole to be acceptable: the acceptability of selection was significantly necessary for the absolute acceptability of historical accounts, and both necessary and sufficient for the relative acceptability of historical accounts. Regardless, therefore, of whether or not Popper's falsifiability criterion is applicable to historical *statements*, the only significant issue is whether or not it is applicable to historical *selections* of statements.

What sort of criticisms of selection were raised in the consideration of the examples which I presented in the first section of this essay? I did not rely on the reader "intuiting" the unacceptability of the accounts which I put forward. The reasons for their unacceptability could be made explicit – that the accounts contained irrelevant statements, or excluded relevant statements. The reader had to know what else might have been said before he could adequately judge a selection. It was important to the presentation of accounts (A) and (B) that a "pool" of statements in Taylor's and Chambers's accounts had already been shown. It was, then, a criticism of an account that it did not contain all and only relevant statements. Now such a criticism could only be made on a rational basis if a standard of relevance was available which met the conditions of rationality described above: that it was derived from the purposes of the community of historians, universally agreed upon by them, and actually workable. I do not think that there is any doubt that historians would agree that it follows from the purposes of their community, to write accounts about the past, that all and only relevant statements should be included in such accounts. The only problem is whether the third condition can be met – whether we can have a workable criterion of relevance.

I think it is plain that falsifiability is simply unworkable as such a criterion of relevance; neither falsifiability nor verifiability, nor any derivative from them, can be used; in general, rational standards for the acceptability of statements are simply not applicable to the acceptability of selections of statements. Falsifiability, even if adequate for the physical sciences, and even if adequate for historical statements, is clearly not adequate for historical accounts.

Virtually all of the traditional problems of objectivity in either science or history may be regarded as a subgroup of problems about the acceptability of statements. It does not seem, then, that we can draw on work in the philosophy of science to help us in the search for a criterion of rational acceptability of historical accounts. Indeed, philosophers can be curiously blinkered: Ernest Nagel, for example, in *The Structure of Science*, says that

> it is not inconceivable that each of two historical accounts of the same period could contain only indisputably correct statements about matters of particular (or "simple") fact but that each would nevertheless be marked by a distinctive bias.

However, he says, "the argument hardly warrants a wholesale skepticism toward the possibility of historical objectivity."[15] This, I hold, is just what it *does* do.[16]

We must seek, then, for a workable criterion of relevance, and only if we find one can we conclude that historical writing could be rationally acceptable, or objective. I hope that my examples in the first section show that it is highly implausible that such a criterion should *not* be available – are we really to hold that no brilliant account of Joyce, no matter how good, can be rationally shown to be an improvement on either of my accounts (A) or (B)? My argument in the first two sections of this essay shows that the rationality of selection is highly plausible.

But although the falsifiability criterion fails to apply to historical writing, this does not rule out Popper's position entirely. For the notion of falsifiability is a special case of a wider notion of *testability*, or "rational criticizability," which is also a central feature of Popper's philosophy.

There are two possibilities for objectivity in general: the possibility of ultimacy – rational irrevisability – of what we say about the world; and the possibility of rational criticism of what we say about the world. Popper has called these two positions "justificationist" and "fallibilist" respectively.[17] Popper himself is a fallibilist. When we carry these two positions over into history, we may say, either, that history is objective insofar as ultimate accounts (based on correct selection) are possible (this was the history for which Lord Acton sought); or, we may say that history is objective insofar as we can have a rational criticism of historical accounts. The latter view, following Popper, is the weaker one. There is, in the philosophy of science, a (no doubt correct) defeatism about the solution to the problem of induction. This has carried over into a general view that we should not claim any ultimacy for what we say about the world. We can have no rational basis for the determination of truth, and it is enough that we should have a rational basis for the criticism of alleged truth.

But the denial of justificationism in science depends only upon a technicality in logic: it is a logical failing of general statements that they cannot be verified by a finite number of singular statements. But there is no analogue for this logical failing in history; there seems to be no logical reason why we should not seek for a *justification* of selection rather than just a basis for criticism of selection. There is no analogue for the problem of induction in history. We have, then, a choice in the philosophy of history: we may seek for guarantees of selection, or for grounds for criticism of selection.

However, I think that many historians would be against a justificationist approach. The accounts (A) and (B) were introduced as being incompatible and not both acceptable (and I do not doubt that this is correct), but there are historians who would wish to accept both of what they thought to be incompatible accounts. Thus two different biographies of the same man may have contrary approaches, and yet both be acceptable; we could not, then, determine which involved *the* correct selection. At best we could only have a fallibilist approach, which would be sufficient to rule out (A) and (B), but not sufficient to determine the one correct biography. But the notion of a "contrary approach to the same man" is a very unclear one; it may still be the case that we could hope to determine all and only those statements relevant to one *approach* rather than the other, and thus keep a justificationist view. Clearly the choice between fallibilism and justificationism is still an open problem in history.

When philosophers in the past have asked whether history could be objective, they have usually reduced their question to the question of whether history was a science. In doing so they ignored the question, now current, of whether science itself is objective, and they also ignored the point that history might well be objective even if it was not a science. The assumption which underlay their approach was their view that science was the paradigm of rational activity, but it is clear that science has its limitations as such a paradigm. Indeed, from a logical point of view, scientific method would seem to be a small part, a special case, of historical method. Certainly we claim some facts of history to be true with greater certainty than any facts in science. Perhaps we would have done better to have chosen *history* as our paradigm of rational activity.

The argument in this essay has some implications for the "unity of science," by which is meant that undiscovered rational basis common to all branches of knowledge. Popper, after Hume, has shown that justificationism is impossible in science. But, if it is possible in history, then the unity of science is denied. On the other hand, perhaps we may hope for no more than fallibilism for both science and history, but it will be a vague standard, for the only accurate form of it – falsifiability – is inapplicable to history. But falsifiability does not only fail for history: it fails, also, for any activity which involves any form of selection whatever, and problems of significance and relevance extend throughout all our social and political life and understanding. Falsifiability cannot be used to assess such things. Popper has argued in many fields, on the basis of falsifiability and fallibilism, without any proper theory of relevance, in particular in his work *The Open Society and its Enemies*.[18] I do not wish to be taken to be an enemy, but we can only decide such things when we have sought for (and failed to find, if it so happens) a criterion for the rationality of selection. And we begin that search in the search for a criterion of historical relevance.[19]

Notes

1 R. S. Rudner, *Philosophy of Social Science*, Prentice-Hall, Englewood Cliffs, NJ 1966, pp. 73ff., esp. p. 76.

2 A. J. P. Taylor, *English History 1914–45* (1965), Pelican, London 1970, p. 647 note B, p. 628.

3 I have ruled out truth as sufficient, but perhaps I should further explain here what I mean by "truth." I mean only truth as applied to statements, in the way familiarly used in post-idealist philosophy. But one *might* want to say that some accounts which contain only true statements are *so* distorted as to be, as a whole, "false," and that the use of "truth" and "falsity" as applied to accounts as a whole in this way is the more significant use. It may be noticed how idealist metaphysicians (Hegel and Bradley are examples) were frequently interested in the philosophy of history, and used "truth" in a way which seems to reflect this "whole account" use which I have mentioned. If we use "truth" in this way, as appropriate only for whole historical accounts, we may firstly understand the notion of "degrees of truth" (always a puzzling one) rather better, secondly we may note that such a use reflects significant problems of historical objectivity rather better than statement-truth, and thirdly we are not obliged to disregard twentieth-century advances in philosophical logic, which are complementary to such a notion. However, I repeat that such a notion is not mine.

4 We might regard an historical account which consists of many statements as being a conjunction of statements, and therefore equivalent itself to one long statement. But to allow this equivalence is to obscure the problem of selection of statements. I wish to make clear that I mean by a "statement" no more than was meant by Russell's "atomic" statements – "a single sentence, for our purposes, must be one which says something that cannot be said in two separate simpler sentences" (*An Inquiry into Meaning and Truth* [1940], Pelican, London 1967, p. 28).

5 Haskell Fain, *Between Philosophy and History: The Resurrection of Speculative Philosophy of History within the Analytic Tradition*, Princeton University Press, Princeton, NJ 1970, p. 283.

6 H. Butterfield, *The Whig Interpretation of History* (1931), Bell, London 1968, p. 7.

7 David Hackett Fischer, *Historians' Fallacies*, Routledge & Kegan Paul, London 1971, p. 65.

8 Based on H. B. Acton's view in *The Philosophy of History*, Vol. XL (1939–40) of the *Proceedings of the Aristotelian Society*, pp. 80–1.

9 E. H. Carr, *What is History?* (1961), Penguin, London 1970.

10 Christopher Blake, "Can History be Objective?," *Mind*, Vol. 64 (1955), p. 61; reprinted in Gardiner (ed.), *Theories of History*, The Free Press, New York: Collier-Macmillan, London 1959, p. 329.

11 Particularly in *The Logic of Scientific Discovery* (1959) (a translation of *Logik der Forschung*, 1934), Hutchinson, London 1968.

12 Popper, *The Logic of Scientific Discovery*, p. 37.

13 Popper, ibid., p. 47.

14 As W. B. Gallie suggests in *Philosophy and the Historical Understanding*, Chatto & Windus, London 1964, ch. 8.

15 Ernest Nagel, *The Structure of Science: Problems in the Logic of Scientific Explanation*, Routledge & Kegan Paul, London 1961, pp. 580–1, and note 25.

16 I have not discussed "bias" in this essay. I mean by it "unacceptability," so that we find an account to be acceptable just insofar as it is unbiassed, and unacceptable just insofar as it is biassed. Like the word "objective," there is a common use of it where we ascribe it to historians rather than to what they write. I distinguish this use from the one which I am concerned with.

17 K. R. Popper, *Conjectures and Refutations* (1963), Routledge & Kegan Paul, London 1969, p. 228.

18 K. R. Popper, *The Open Society and its Enemies* (1945), Routledge & Kegan Paul, London 1966.

19 The present article is derived from part of my Cambridge Ph.D. dissertation entitled *The Possibility of Objectivity in History*; the research was supervised by Professor W. B. Gallie, whom I cannot thank enough.

18

Historical Knowledge and Historical Reality: A Plea for "Internal Realism"

Chris Lorenz

Once there was a farmer who got hold of a copy of Kant's *Critique of Pure Reason*. He opened the book and started to read, but he did not get very far. After a short while, he closed the book and sighed: "I wish I had his worries."[1]

This anecdote was used by the German historian Christian Meier twenty years ago to sketch the troublesome relationship between historians and philosophers, comparing the historians to the farmer. I will take Meier's sketch as a starting point for my analysis of the relationship between history and philosophy of history. I will argue that doing history is a more philosophical activity than most historians realize and that recognition of this fact can improve the scope and quality of historical discussion. Contrary to philosophers of history like Atkinson, I will defend the view that historians can profit from philosophy because "doing history" can be improved by philosophical insights.[2] At the same time, however, I will argue that this will only be the case as long as philosophers of history take the concerns of professional historians seriously – and this means that debates of historians should always form the raw material of philosophical analysis as philosophers like Dray and Martin have emphasized.[3]

To state my point, I will analyze a recent discussion among German historians – the famous *Historikerstreit*. In doing so I will elucidate the relationship between history and philosophy of history by defending three theses. First, I will maintain – contrary to the widespread postmodern fashion – that historians always claim knowledge of a real past; and as all claims of knowledge embody truth claims the justification of truth claims must remain equally central to history as to philosophy of history – *pace* Rorty, Ankersmit, and postmodernism.[4] Second, I will maintain that this plea for a return to justificationism in philosophy of history presupposes realism with regard to the past among historians as well as among philosophers of history. The unmasking of naive realism – or objectivism, as it is often called – thus does not imply the rejection of realism altogether nor the need to embrace idealism (as some Collingwoodians think) or estheticism – or other brands of relativism.[5] Third, I will argue that the brand of realism I shall elaborate – so-called "internal realism" – makes it possible to elucidate anew the classical problem of facts and values that has haunted historians as well as philosophers of history for so long. This analysis will lead to the conclusion – already drawn by Jürgen Habermas, Jürgen Kocka, and Jörn Rüsen – that the normative dimension of history cannot be eliminated and therefore is in need of rational justification.[6]

1 The *Historikerstreit*

The *Historikerstreit* reached its apex in 1986 and 1987.[7] Its central subject was the place of the "Third Reich" in German history – a subject widely debated among German historians since the late 1960s. I have chosen this discussion as an example because of its eruptive quality. The *Historikerstreit* therefore can be analyzed as a kind of collective "Freudian slip" of the historical profession: it uncovered aspects usually left hidden in "normal" debates. I will focus my attention on the main proponents and schematize the debate deliberately as an argument between two groups. One group is centered around Ernst Nolte and Andreas Hillgruber. The other group consists of their critics, led by Jürgen Habermas, Hans Mommsen, and Martin Broszat. It will be shown that these historians justified their claims to knowledge by an appeal to "facts," "reality," and "truth"; at the same time it appears that they try to undermine competing claims to knowledge by denouncing them as "value-judgments."

The *Historikerstreit* commenced with an article by the philosopher and sociologist Habermas in *Die Zeit*.[8] Habermas criticized the apologetic tendencies in recent interpretations of National Socialism by West German historians. Nolte and Hillgruber – both well-known specialists – were his most important targets. In his most recent writings Nolte had proposed to put the history of the Third Reich in a new perspective.[9] In his view this was necessary because the old picture of the "Third Reich" as the empire of pure evil was outdated. Historians supporting this picture, according to Nolte, used a figure of speech introduced by the Nazis: the ascription of a collective guilt. The only difference involved was the fact that the collective guilt was imputed to the Germans instead of the Jews. In Nolte's eyes the negative image of the "Third Reich" not only induced thinking in black and white contrasts, but also produced a "negative nationalism." This was an obstacle to scientific history because historical understanding depended on the recognition of the various shades of gray.

Nolte gave two examples of his new perspective of the context in which Nazi Germany should be interpreted. National Socialism in general and the Nazis' crimes towards the Jews in particular should not be interpreted within the framework of a German history; instead of a national perspective a comparative European or even global perspective was mandatory. This was the case because the history of the twentieth century had become global history in the most literal sense; a national history of this period therefore would be a pure anachronism. The supranational character of twentieth-century historical reality simply demanded a supranational perspective from the historian. Consequently Hitler could no longer be treated by historians as an unsuccessful imitation of the German Bismarck, but should be seen as the European "Anti-Lenin." Historians who failed to recognize this elementary fact were the pitiful victims of delusion.

On the basis of this argument Nolte insisted that the crimes of the Nazis towards the Jews should be put in the perspective of the other mass murders in the twentieth century, beginning with the Turkish genocide of the Armenians, the Russian mass murders during and after the Russian revolution, and most recently slaughters in Vietnam, Cambodia, and Afghanistan. According to Nolte, these massacres must be understood in the context of social and cultural processes of uprooting and of the ideologies formulated to cope with these processes. This process of uprooting is seen by Nolte as a consequence of the modernization process beginning with the Industrial Revolution.

Central to the ideologies in question is the idea that the physical liquidation of a specific social group constitutes the solution to the problems of "modern times" because this liquidation is a necessary condition for a utopia. The most influential of these "utopian fantasies of annihilation" have been Marxism and National Socialism, says Nolte. This influence was due to the fact that these ideologies have been adopted by successful political movements and were transformed into state ideologies in Russia after 1917, and in Italy and Germany after 1922 and 1933 respectively. In Russia and Germany these "fantasies of annihilation" were later put into practice.

According to Nolte, these developments were connected to each other because the German practice of annihilation had been "caused" by the Russian example. It is evident that this thesis is the most controversial ingredient of Nolte's new perspective on German history. This causal relationship, which he interprets as a necessary and not as a sufficient condition, is localized by Nolte to the mind of Hitler and his companions. It was the threat of the Russian revolution and the fear of being annihilated just as the Russian bourgeoisie had been by Bolshevism that induced Hitler to the practice of Auschwitz, says Nolte. In the National

Socialist mind, Bolshevism was a Jewish invention and the Soviet Union a state dominated by the Jews. Therefore Hitler identified the struggle against Bolshevism with the struggle against the Jews – with fatal consequences for the latter. In Nolte's view, the anti-Semitism of the Nazis should thus be seen as a historically comprehensible transformation of their "legitimate" fear of Bolshevism. Traditional anti-Semitism played no role whatsoever in this process.

Quite independently, Andreas Hillgruber had also developed a new perspective on the history of Nazi Germany.[10] Like Nolte, he proposed to approach this episode from the East, and like Nolte he criticized others for their lack of scope. This "lack" referred to their blindness to the *two* national catastrophes of World War II and their interrelationship – the catastrophe of European Jewry and the German catastrophe. The latter consisted in the expulsion of twelve million Germans from Eastern and Central Europe in 1944–5, the annexation of their former homelands by Russia and Poland and the German partition. According to Hillgruber, historians up till now had not interpreted the relationship between these two catastrophes in the right European perspective. They presupposed a direct relation between the German and the Jewish catastrophe in interpreting the former as an Allied punishment for the latter. This point of view was not correct because the Jewish catastrophe was not yet known at the time the Allies made their plans for Germany after its defeat. Therefore the Allied policy towards postwar Germany cannot be connected with the German crimes towards the Jews and should be related to the so-called "Prussia-stereotype." This stereotype consists of the idea that there was a "German danger" in Europe and that this danger would only disappear together with the militaristic state of Prussia (with its heartlands east of the Elbe). Thus, the Jewish and the German catastrophe were causally unconnected.

Still there was a connection between both catastrophes, according to Hillgruber, because a hidden factor could explain *both*. This hidden cause consisted in the practice of deporting and liquidating total populations emanating from the idea of "ethnic cleansing," developed in the twentieth century. Stalin and Hitler could only be distinguished from other mass murderers by the radicalness with which they put this idea into practice. The Jewish catastrophe has been the most visible result such that the German catastrophe – as a consequence thereof – receded into the background. Yet they belonged to the same historical context.

Like Nolte's, Hillgruber's new perspective suggests a direct connection between the *German* practice of annihilation and general *European* history. This does not imply that Hillgruber totally ignores the argument that without Nazi Germany Auschwitz would have been impossible and therefore Germany's defeat was most desirable. This problem is presented as a tragic dilemma for the German army, a dilemma without any hope of a solution. By protecting the German population against the advancing Red Army, the Wehrmacht unconsciously and unwillingly enabled the Nazis to continue their murderous practices in the concentration camps behind the front line. The only avenue open to German historians to make this tragedy comprehensible was to transport themselves mentally into this situation. The key to historical understanding, according to Hillgruber, was seeing the situation through the eyes of the German army and describing it through this perspective because this is what the German population did. Therefore only the perspective of the Wehrmacht was "realistic" for the historian of the Eastern front. Like Nolte, Hillgruber thus tries to legitimize his perspective by appealing to historical reality.

The two perspectives just summarized generated the *Historikerstreit*. During this controversy German historians split into two camps. Historians with leftist sympathies of one kind or another tended to support Habermas's critique. Their contributions were published mainly by the left-wing liberal weekly newspaper *Die Zeit*. Historians with a more conservative frame of mind tended to support Nolte and Hillgruber and tried to protect them against the criticism of Habermas and others. Their contributions appeared mainly in the conservative daily newspaper *Frankfurter Allgemeine Zeitung*.

This controversy is really a postmodern spectacle. Almost all the firm ground historians usually stand on turned into a swamp of relativism and subjectivity. All of the pillars of "normal" historical science – such as sources, facts, and historical method – sank in this swamp without any trace. Even the question whether there has been any genuine discussion between the two camps appears to be debatable: the defenders of Nolte and Hillgruber simply deny the existence of a historical debate and refer to the "so-called *Historikerstreit*" or to an ignoble "political and moral campaign" directed against them, or to "the Habermas controversy."[11] The sentence "your reality is not the same as mine" probably can be labeled as the only *non*-debatable statement in this whole controversy.

Testimony to this is that factual statements of one party in this debate are not recognized as such by the other and often are denounced as political "value judgments." An example of this is the way in which the annihilation of the Jews by Nazi Germany if characterized. The critics of Nolte and Hillgruber regard the quasi-industrial character of the destruction of European Jewry by the Nazis as a unique historical fact which distinguishes this event from other mass murders in world history. This view is founded on the consideration that the Nazis deliberately used the apparatus of a "civilized" state to reach their murderous goal while other mass murders took place in the chaotic context of war or civil war. Placing Auschwitz in a comparative perspective of European or world history – as Nolte and Hillgruber do – therefore obliterates the most important factual feature of National Socialism: its uniquely destructive quality. If historians rewrite German history as European history they are not looking for new scientific insights but only misusing the comparative perspective with the political intent to repress this traumatic historical fact.[12]

People who defend Nolte – like Joachim Fest and Klaus Hildebrand – do not regard this unique quality of the destruction wrought by National Socialism as a historical fact at all; instead they attribute it to a belated manifestation of the German "Herrenvolkgesinnung" because it boils down to the statement that German people are superior to others, even when it comes to killing civilians.[13]

Another crucial fact for critical historians like Hans Mommsen and Martin Broszat is the observation that Germany was not a monolithic one-man dictatorship; this state could not have functioned without the active cooperation of the conservative commercial and industrial élites, the army, and the bureaucracy. From their perspective, the crucial fact about the Third Reich was not the presence of an ideological muddle-head, but this muddle-head becoming the head of state and gaining the enthusiastic support of the élites and the state apparatuses for a criminal policy over a twelve-year period. They regard the causal reduction of the Nazi crimes to Hitler's frame of mind and his fear of Bolshevism as a politically motivated effort to obscure the crucial role of this conservative "Funktionseliten" in the Third Reich – and by the same move shifting the responsibility for the Third Reich to Communism.[14]

Nolte, as is to be expected, adopts a different perspective. He does not recognize the collaboration of the conservative élites with Hitler as a historical fact because (almost) all Germans cooperated during the war – and this was as true for the former leftist workers as for the traditionally rightist élites. Ascribing a special responsibility to these élites boils down to putting the blame exclusively on these groups and creating a contrast in black and white. In fact, these historians, argues Nolte, are misusing the Third Reich as an instrument for their leftist critique of today's society.[15]

In their turn, the critics of Nolte and Hillgruber deny that their crucial facts are indeed facts. Because facts are states of affairs that can be stated in true statements, factual claims pertain to both the descriptive and the explanatory level of narratives.[16] Nolte's factual claim that National Socialism can be causally reduced to Bolshevism is dismissed as political humbug. Hillgruber's factual claim that the Jewish catastrophe is causally related to a "hidden factor" in general European history and not specially to Nazi Germany meets the same harsh fate. Their critics underline the direct connection between Nolte's and Hillgruber's urge for "scientific renovation" and the conservative political urge in the Federal Republic of the 1980s "to step out of Hitler's shadow – at last."[17] The creation of a self-image as a "normal" nation is seen as the political aim of these "new perspectives" on German history.

Of course, Nolte and Hillgruber are a bit distressed by all these "mis-understandings" of what they see as their noble and purely scientific intentions. To confound these with apologetic intentions in their eyes surely proves their opponents have been blinded by their leftist ideological blinkers. They impede the registration of unpleasant truths, the more so when these truths are revealed by a person with "wrong" – that is, rightist – political persuasions. Science, however, demands an "unpolitical" stance and a recognition of the truth without any consideration of the political color of the person who states it. For it is impossible for a true science to exist if there are "forbidden" questions.[18]

In sum the disagreements between the two camps in this discussion could not possibly have been more fundamental since both descriptive statements about facts and explanatory statements about relationships between facts were involved. The distinction between factual statements and value judgments regularly became a topic of debate, a debate which became contentious to an unusual degree.

2 Internal Realism

A philosopher of history may react in different ways to agitated discussions like the *Historikerstreit*. The first way is to react as Nolte and Hillgruber did: in this case one draws the conclusion this debate has not been scientific but political. This conclusion presupposes that science – contrary to politics – is a factual debate about truth claims and this type of debate ends – at least in the long run – because consensus has been reached. This consensus on facts constitutes the foundation of scientific knowledge. One could label this type of reaction and this view of scientific knowledge as objectivistic, because it is based on the classical ideal of objective historical knowledge.[19] In this view, the historical method is regarded as a filter between truth and untruth and therefore as the foundation of consensus within the scientific community. The frequent appeals by Nolte and Hillgruber to "the facts," "the sources," "the truth," and "science" are testimony to their objectivism.[20] Within this frame of reference, however, it is impossible to understand the fact that historians frequently *keep* disagreeing on facts and relationships between facts; nor is it possible to understand why rational, scientific discussions about facts often resemble irrational, political discussions about values.

The second way for the philosopher of history to react to discussions like the *Historikerstreit* is to conclude that history is not a scientific discipline at all and does not constitute knowledge. History then can be labeled (wholly or in part) as an individual "form of art," "act of faith," or "expression of culture" which cannot be rationally justified in terms of (the truth of) factual arguments. Such a reaction has traditionally been produced by relativists and can be interpreted as the philosophical mirror image of the objectivistic reaction.[21] Just like objectivists, relativists presuppose that there is a consensus in real science on facts and their explanatory relationships; because such a consensus is lacking in history, they conclude that history is not scientific (wholly or in part) and classify it as an "expression of culture" without a claim to truth. This conclusion is inevitable since every claim of knowledge is *ipso facto* a truth claim, as Hamlyn has demonstrated.[22] Within this frame of reference, however, it is completely incomprehensible why historians cling to the custom of justifying their claims to knowledge by appealing to the facts. If the relativistic view of history is right, they might as well save their energy for other purposes; the truthful reproduction of the facts by the historian would contribute as little to the quality of the product of the historian as would be the case with painters and their products. In both cases, it would be neither a necessary nor a sufficient condition for quality.[23]

Neither traditional objectivism nor traditional relativism thus seem capable of explaining why historians do engage in discussions like the *Historikerstreit* and appeal to facts if their perspectives are challenged by opponents. If we want to consider history as a scientific enterprise and discount the phenomenon of science *without* consensus, we therefore have to look for a frame of reference in philosophy of history beyond objectivism and relativism. This is possible, in my opinion, by linking philosophy of history with modern epistemology and philosophy of science – *pace* postmodernism and its allergy to the problem of truth. This allergy stems from the traditional but mistaken identification of the search for knowledge and the search for certainty.[24] Epistemology is called for because this branch of philosophy elucidates the possibility of knowledge and therefore constitutes a bulwark against all brands of skepticism – old and new. Skeptics, who often regarded history as one of their favorite playgrounds, cast doubt on the possibility of reliable knowledge altogether.[25] The struggle against skepticism therefore is the logical point of departure of any philosophy of history worthy of the name. Philosophy of science – including social science – is needed because the characteristics of history as a discipline can only be elucidated in comparison with other sciences. As these, in turn, are elucidated by their philosophers, philosophers of history cannot afford to fall victim to outdated versions, the more so because they traditionally "lend" the *concept* of science to other disciplines. Since the philosophical identity of history is often formulated in contrast with images of other sciences the risk of errors and empty contrasts is a serious one.

As for epistemology and the struggle against skepticism, philosophy of history in the 1990s must come to terms with the postmodern versions of narrativism.[26] As for philosophy of science, philosophy of history must incorporate the post-positivistic view of scientific knowledge.[27] The terminus of relativism then functions as the point of departure: the recognition of the fact that historical knowledge does not have a certain and uniform foundation in facts or logic and therefore does not *per se* presuppose a consensus. In modern epistemology – since Wittgenstein's *Philosophical Investigations* – and modern philosophy of science – since Popper's *Logic of Scientific Discovery* – this insight did not lead to the epistemological skepticism of the relativists, but to fallibilism and contextualism.[28] Contextualists recognize that all knowledge is relative to specific epistemic contexts. And fallibilists recognize that *all* claims to knowledge are corrigible, and assume a hypothetical character, because there are no firm foundations of knowledge – either in the senses or in human reason. The demise of "foundationalism" thus does *not* lead necessarily to epistemological skepticism – as many postmodernists seem to think – but to quite a different and more constructive philosophical position.[29] This position might "save" historians from the skeptical consequences of postmodernism, such as relativism and subjectivism with respect to epistemology and ethics. As long as historians claim to produce *knowledge*, philosophers of history cannot permit themselves an allergy to the problem of truth and to the justification of truth claims because this would amount to philosophical suicide.

The problem of the justification of knowledge therefore does not disappear. The – insoluble – problem of the *foundation* of certain knowledge is merely transformed into the – soluble – problem of *argumentation* of claims to fallible knowledge. The problem of justification in philosophy of history boils down to the question of what kinds of argumentation historians use to argue their claims to knowledge – or to refute competing ones – and which arguments can be reconstructed *ex post facto*. So "anti-foundationalism" does not of necessity force philosophers and historians to say goodbye to epistemology and embark on a "narrativistic" course, as Ankersmit suggested.[30] I hope to show that there is an alternative, more fruitful route in philosophy along which the problem of justification is not *eliminated*, but *expanded* so as to include normative discourse. This route is the more attractive since the "factual–normative" dual character of historical discourse has so long troubled historians as well as philosophers of history. This route can be elucidated by an analysis of the communicative role of language.

If philosophers of history take this road they leave behind two fundamental presuppositions with regard to the character of scientific knowledge shared by objectivism and relativism. First, the presupposition that rational consensus constitutes the hallmark of scientificity; and second, the presupposition that the rationality of science can be explicated in a formal method (that is, an algorithm), or in an explicit set of formal rules. Beyond objectivism and relativism one recognizes the presence of rational *dis*agreement in science and the existence of a fundamental and non-reducible plurality of points of view.[31] This "third way" in philosophy of history beyond objectivism and relativism – a path we could label, following Hilary Putnam, "internal realism"[32] – makes it possible to analyze the practice of history eschewing the false dilemmas produced by traditional but outdated ideas about the nature of rationality and science. Along this path philosophy of history can elucidate the fact that historians "still want to call historical knowledge a *reconstruction*, not a construction *simpliciter.*"[33]

Like all brands of realism "internal realism" rests on basic presuppositions: first, that reality exists independently of our knowledge thereof; and second, that our scientific statements – including our theories – refer to this independently existing reality.[34] This realist interpretation of scientific knowledge, which at least explains the success of natural science,[35] must face two problems that are generated by the confrontation of this interpretation with the history of science. First, the correspondence theory of truth becomes a problem because the history of science is characterized by a radical conceptual discontinuity – as Thomas Kuhn and others have argued. Because of this conceptual discontinuity it is no longer possible to suppose direct correspondence between scientific statements and reality. Second, the reference of scientific concepts becomes a problem: the historical fact that scientific concepts do change in time in a discontinuous manner – as exemplified in Kuhn's famous "paradigm shifts" – generates the problem to what entities in reality scientific concepts refer. Though linguistic entities may change, according to realism – in contrast with idealism – real entities are supposed to be invariant. Ankersmit's narrative idealism or White's linguistic idealism, for instance, posit that the object of history is constituted by the historian and lacks a referential relationship to a real object.[36] Paradoxically the history of science thus can be used as an extra argument to interpret historical knowledge in an "internal-realist" way because it confronts us with the lack of fixity and lack of "transparency" of scientific concepts *vis-à-vis* the reality they describe. Traditionally this lack of fixity was regarded as a characteristic of *historical* concepts only and therefore was used as an argument by idealists to set history apart from science.[37]

The two problems of correspondence and referentiality must be addressed because realists suppose that the possibility of knowledge is founded in the capacity of – true – statements to correspond to reality and in the capacity of – adequate – concepts to refer to real entities. Following Putnam we can elucidate these two problems by interpreting correspondence and reference as notions that *derive their meaning from and therefore are relative to specific conceptual frameworks.* Therefore the question "what is factual?" alias "what is true or real?" is always dependent on and *internal* to the specific linguistic framework in which reality is described. Putnam argues for "internal realism" as follows:

The perspective I shall defend has no unambiguous name. It is a late arrival in the history of philosophy. . . . I shall refer to it as the *internalist* perspective, because it is characteristic of this view to hold that *what objects does the world consist of?* is a question that only makes sense to ask *within* a theory of description. Many "internalist" philosophers, though not all, hold further that there is more than one "true" theory or description of the world. "Truth," in an internalist view, is some sort of (idealized) rational acceptability – some sort of ideal coherence of our beliefs with each other and with our experiences *as those experiences are represented in our belief system* and not correspondence with mind-independent or discourse-independent "states of affairs." There is no God's Eye point of view that we can know or usefully imagine; there are only various points of view of actual persons reflecting various interests and purposes that their descriptions and theories subserve.[38]

The acknowledgment that the relationship between language and reality is not "transparent" therefore does not lead to the favorite conclusion of postmodernists that language is "opaque" and not capable of corresponding to and referring to reality, but to the much more "realistic" conclusion that reference and correspondence must be interpreted as relative and internal to specific conceptual frameworks[39] – as Carlo Ginzburg hinted in his critique of postmodernism in history.[40] The fact that reference and correspondence must be interpreted relative to discourses cannot be used as an argument against the applicability of these notions, as often is suggested. Although the critics of the correspondence theory of truth have convincingly established that correspondence cannot be conceived of as a criterion of *verification*, that is for the *control* of truth, correspondence remains the criterion of *meaning* for the truth of statements. This is so because – as Wittgenstein showed – knowledge of the meaning of a concept presupposes the ability to apply the concept; and this in turn presupposes knowledge of the type of things the concept refers to and knowledge of the ways in which this concept is *correctly* used in statements. And one can only be said to understand the meaning of statements *correctly* if one knows under what conditions they can be said to be *true*, that is, when they correspond to fact. If this was not the case, that is, if the meaning of a concept did *not* presuppose knowledge of its *truth-conditions*, a competent language-user would not be able to tell the difference between, for instance, someone who actually suffers pain and someone who fakes pain, that is, the difference between the correct and incorrect application of these concepts. Since competent language users normally *do* know the difference between concepts they normally do know their truth-conditions. The mistakes that are sometimes made in this respect do not contradict this fact; to the contrary, the notion of mistake only makes sense in a context of rules and one can only speak of rules if they are *normally*

followed in a *correct* manner. So the fact that the relationship of correspondence between a true statement and the world it refers to is a conventional relationship within a conceptual framework does *not* invalidate
the notions of reference and of truth as correspondence. Without these
notions it is, as a matter of fact, impossible to understand *what we are
talking about* when we talk.[41]

From the viewpoint of "internal realism" we can understand where
the strong pull towards idealism in the philosophy of history – from
Dilthey and Collingwood to H. White and Ankersmit – comes from
and why it is misguided. The "idealistic temptation" has always been
based on the argument that history as a discipline – in contrast with the
natural sciences – does not deal with a material object and therefore this
object must first be constituted in a mental (Collingwood) or a linguistic
(White, Ankersmit) manner and universe. Because history lacks a material object historians – in contrast with natural scientists – miss a *direct*
sensorial entry to their objects;[42] therefore historical knowledge – in contrast with scientific knowledge – cannot be founded on empirical statements and cannot be interpreted as knowledge of "the real" and thus is
"imaginary," "mythical," and so on. According to this traditional idealistic argument, history cannot be(come) a science, but is a form of art,
a form of ideology, a branch of literature, and so on.

From the viewpoint of "internal realism" this argument is based on
two, internally related, conflations: first, the conflation of materialism and
realism;[43] and second, the conflation of empiricism (that is, the empiricist brand of foundationalism) with scientific knowledge per se. The first
conflation manifests itself in the tendency to deny non-material objects
reality in some sense and the resulting tendency to grant this class of
objects a purely mental or linguistic status.[44] Because of this "unreality"
it is supposedly impossible for statements to refer to or correspond to
these objects and therefore they cannot be true or false. As the objects
of historical narratives – such as feudalism, absolutism, the Renaissance, and so on – are categorized as members of this (non-material)
class, historical narratives (that consist of conjunctions of singular existential statements) cannot be true or false.[45] Historical narratives that
present "interpretations" contrast with the individual singular existential statements that present "factual" information; only the latter can be
true or false. At the level of interpretation, therefore, the problem of
truth is supposedly of no importance in philosophy of history and consequently (post)modern philosophers dedicate their energy to an ideological, political, linguistic, or aesthetic analysis of historical narratives.[46]

The second conflation is another legacy of crude empiricism. As the
first conflation sprang from the idea that "what cannot be confronted
directly cannot be real," the second conflation springs from the idea that
"what cannot be observed directly cannot be known" and therefore

cannot be counted as knowledge. Though this argument has long been discredited in epistemology and philosophy of science it has been surprisingly tenacious in philosophy of history – from the German idealists via the relativism of Becker and Beard to the narrativism of H. White and Ankersmit.[47] If one realizes that this whole train of thought is based on a mistaken identification of realism and materialism and on an outdated epistemology, the whole idealistic line of argument begins to crumble. It is not necessary for (conjunctions of) singular existential statements to refer to material objects in order to be true or false, nor is it necessary for these (conjunctions of) factual statements to refer to concrete objects in order to be true or false.[48] And neither are (conjunctions of) these statements necessarily "imaginary," "mythical," or arbitrary because they cannot be "founded" in sensory experience.[49] If that were the case theoretical physics should as well be labeled "mythical" given the fact that entities like quarks and quasars have as little "foundation" in sensory experience as renaissances and revolutions. Because historians often borrow ideas from philosophers when they reflect on their discipline, philosophical mistakes are not as innocent relative to the practice of history as is usually taken for granted.

3 Internal Realism and the Interpretation of Historical Debates

To show the fruitfulness of "internal realism" for philosophy of history I will now clarify some aspects of the *Historikerstreit* from this perspective that could not be clarified by either objectivism or relativism. The point of departure of "internal realism" is the insight that all our knowledge of reality is mediated through language; this means reality for us is always reality within the framework of a certain description. The "Third Reich," for instance, is not known in a direct, unmediated way but only through descriptions of historians that are based on specific central concepts. Some historians of the "Third Reich" use the conceptual framework of the *Führerdiktatur* – the German state is then described as a unique one-man dictatorship; others use the conceptual framework of theories of fascism or totalitarianism – the Nazi state is then described as one form of fascism or as one brand of totalitarian dictatorship.[50] *Mutatis mutandis* the same goes for nature since our knowledge thereof is mediated through descriptions of physical scientists. The descriptions embody *points of view* or *perspectives* from which reality is observed. As such, the perspectives belong to the frame of description and not to reality itself. This observation is not contradicted by the fact that in sociohistorical reality we *also* confront perspectives at the object-level, as is illustrated so explicitly by Hillgruber's contributions to the *Historikerstreit*. So in quite a literal sense historians construct a perspective on perspectives, so to speak. This fact does, however, explain why the choice of perspective in sociohistorical sciences generates the problem of "partisanship," as is also illustrated by Hillgruber (see below).

When we talk about facts and reality, we therefore *always* refer to reality *within a specific frame of description* (this is why we refer to this view as *internal* realism). This explains how it is possible that with regard to an individual subject – National Socialism, for instance – different historians *keep* referring to different states of affairs as facts and *keep* referring to different statements as true, and thus how it is possible that there is no guarantee of consensus in history. This fact is explained by the circumstance that factual statements and their truth vary with their frames of description. The possibility of plural and even incompatible true statements about the "same" subject is thus elucidated; historians who are baffled by this state of affairs can now be saved from epistemological confusion and despair.[51] An example can be borrowed from Nelson Goodman: he pointed to the fact that both the statement "the sun always moves" and the statement "the sun never moves" are both true depending on the frame of reference.[52] In the same vein, the statement "Auschwitz was a unique historical phenomenon" and the statement "Auschwitz was not a unique historical phenomenon" may both be true depending on the (aspects of the) phenomena under comparison. So the mere fact that truth in science is not uniform and undivided does not have to worry historians or force them towards skeptical and relativistic conclusions about the scientific status of history. Of course, this does not imply any statement about *particular* truth claims because only the *possibility* of different statements about the same object is elucidated. The merits of every particular truth claim in history are not to be judged by philosophers of history but by the historians themselves.[53]

Because all statements of fact are dependent on frames of description, the claim that such and such is a fact can only mean that the description under consideration is adequate. So, considered more closely, a factual statement is just a *claim to truth*. This is so because the notion of truth and fact are conceptually interdependent;[54] therefore, as long as historians are referring to facts, they are referring to truth. And as long as they back their claims with regard to the adequacy of "interpretations" with an appeal to facts – as they *in fact* do, as is demonstrated even by a quasi-postmodern debate like the *Historikerstreit* – the problem of truth cannot be deleted from the agenda by any philosopher of history.[55] Factual claims, however, can never be "proved" or "founded" in reality but only argued for. What "reality" looks like, or what "the facts" are, always remains debatable for exactly this reason. On a closer view, the uttering of factual statements always means presenting a specific frame of description and a specific perspective on reality. I will now go back to the *Historikerstreit* and see what further insights can be gained from this philosophical angle.

Both Nolte and Hillgruber claimed that their perspectives on the Third Reich – that is, their frames of description – were in accordance with the "true nature" of National Socialism. Nolte argued for his perspective with an appeal to the European if not global nature of twentieth-century history while Hillgruber argued for his "Wehrmacht-perspective" with an appeal to the Eastern front itself (or at least to the German side thereof). Considered from the viewpoint of "internal realism," it is easy to see why Nolte and Hillgruber did not convince their critics. If one realizes what "reality" looks like always depends on a frame of description – and therefore a perspective – it comes as no surprise that reality cannot be used as an argument in favor of, or even for the "necessity" of, a particular perspective. This presupposes a direct fit between reality and a specific linguistic framework – a presupposition linked up with naive realism and discarded with empiricism in epistemology. It is rather the other way around: it is the historian who tries to determine what the past "really" looked like by arguing for his or her perspective. Thus it is the historian, not the past, who does the "dictating" in history.

This does not imply that the past does not "really" exist or that individual historians are free to "dictate" any picture of the past they like – as some postmodern thinkers seem to suggest. Narrativists like White and Ankersmit inspired by literary theory take this suggestion very far in emphasizing the autonomy of the historical text in relation to the past. Their view, however, cannot explicate how it is possible that historians often reject texts as historically inadequate. This *fact* of historical practice can only be made comprehensible if one presupposes a referential relationship between the texts of historians and the real past – because without this relationship the notion of adequacy makes no sense – and thus if one resists the temptation to grant historical texts a status independent of the past they are supposed to describe. Anyone who applies Derrida's *"il n'y a pas de hors texte"* to the writing of history ceases to be of interest to the historian *qua* historian.

The separation of the referential relationship between the historian's narrative and the past itself is argued for by removing the link between the historical narrative and its factual foundation. White, for instance, recently argued that events like the assassination of John F. Kennedy, the explosion of the Challenger, or the Holocaust (*bien étonnés de se trouver ensembles*) should be regarded as the paradigm cases of the (modern) historical event.[56] What distinguishes this type of event according to White is that factual statements relating to them cannot be founded and that further research does not *reduce* but *enhances* the puzzlement about "what really happened." White calls this the "evaporation of reality" or the " 'derealization' of the event itself, which means, among other things, either the impossibility of telling any single authoritative story about these events or the possibility of telling any number of different stories about each of them."[57] So White concludes – according to the familiar either-or scheme – that when the God of the "single authoritative story" of history is dead the historian is engulfed by chaos and arbitrariness: "*any* number of different stories" about the past can be told, apparently without *any* constraint of the evidence. So the "underdetermination" of the historical narrative by the evidence receives with White a very radical interpretation. The "evaporation" of the borderline between fact and fiction and between history and literature is the logical consequence of this remarkable line of reasoning.[58]

In Ankersmit's recent writings we confront a similar line of argument. Like White he tries to undermine the relationship between historical narratives and their factual grounding. In his view this separation of the historical narrative from the evidence is best exemplified by so-called "postmodern" or "new" historiography: "For the modernist, the evidence is a tile which he picks up to see what is underneath it; for the postmodernist, on the other hand, it is a tile which he steps on in order to move on to other tiles: horizontality instead of verticality."[59] "For the new historiography the text must be central – it is no longer a layer which one looks *through* (either at a past reality or at the historian's authorial intention) but something which the historiographer must look *at*."[60]

Like White, Ankersmit does not seem to be disturbed by the fact that most historians keep subscribing to the "vertical view" on historical evidence and do not embrace their "postulate of the *non*-transparency of the historical text" in their radical manner. And historians do so with good reason because if they did take these philosophical views seriously, it would be completely incomprehensible why they would actually leave their armchairs to do *research*. The "underdetermination" of historical narratives by the evidence by no means justifies their separation. The "lack of transparency" merely implies that historians cannot appeal directly to reality to back up their narratives and therefore have to *argue* in favor of a reconstruction of past reality – just as is the case with the paleontologist or the geologist. In this process of argumentation the factual evidence plays a crucial role.

Still there is an important difference between history on the one hand and paleontology and geology on the other, because the object of history consists of the *human* past.[61] Because humans tend to be interested in the way in which their past is presented in histories (as this is the way individual and collective identities are constructed) they tend to value the perspectives involved. As a consequence histories may be *true* but not *acceptable* because they conflict with the conception of identity of the audience addressed. This practical "interest" of history, which has been analyzed by Jürgen Habermas, Emil Angehrn, Jörn Rüsen, and Herta Nagl-Docekal, is lacking in the sciences that deal with a nonhuman object.[62] Because Putnam develops his "internal realism" only in relationship to natural science we have to link this idea of practical interest to "internal realism" when we become "realistic" in philosophy of history. Combined with linguistic analysis this version of "internal realism" is capable of pushing the analysis of the problem of values beyond objectivism and relativism, as I hope to show now.

4 "Internal Realism," the Problem of Values, and the *Historikerstreit*

Before proposing a frame of analysis I will first comment on the problem. The problem of values is traditionally interpreted in the spirit of Max Weber and his "postulate of ethical neutrality" (*Wertfreiheit*), although many historians prefer to cite Ranke's famous lines on the task of the historian in this context.[63] By this postulate Weber meant a methodological rule for scientists (as scientists) not to pronounce any judgment of value related to an object under investigation and to restrict oneself in science to statements of fact. With objectivism and relativism Weber was convinced of the "absolute heterogeneity" of statements of fact and statements of value; therefore science, as the realm of facts, should be strictly separated from the realm of values, that is ethics, esthetics, and politics.[64] The problem of values thus was localized by Weber on the level of singular existential statements and singular value-judgments and not on the level of frames of description or conceptual frameworks, that is, the level of the historical narrative *in toto*. As a consequence the most important value-problem in historiography, related to the choice of perspective, falls outside the traditional frame of analysis, as I shall demonstrate in the case of the *Historikerstreit*.

The normative aspects related to the choice of perspective are most important in historiography because they are most debated by historians.[65] This does not, of course, mean that there is no "problem of values" at the level of individual statements – there surely is – only that this level is *relatively* unimportant. As in the domain of epistemology a "holistic" and a "linguistic turn" is needed in the domain of normative analysis and for exactly the same reason: like descriptive statements in historical narratives, normative statements do not parade individually and present themselves one by one, because they are interconnected at the conceptual level.[66] As descriptive statements presuppose theories of observation, normative statements always presuppose theories of morality (that function as unproblematic background knowledge).[67]

When we analyze the *Historikerstreit* from this point of view the first fact to be noted is the persistent attempt of Nolte and Hillgruber to keep the problem of values out of the discussion by appealing to Weber's "postulate of ethical neutrality." They deny any relationship between their perspectives, as embodied by their explanatory schemes, and the ascription of moral responsibility to one party; they thereby emphasize the fundamental gap between scientific history and politics or ethics. This line of argumentation is rather awkward when one brings the main issue to mind: after all, the *Historikerstreit* revolves around the place of the Federal Republic in German history – that is the historical identity of the *Bundesrepublik* – and this is as much a political as a scientific problem. In spite of this fundamental fact Nolte and Hillgruber keep appealing to the unbridgeable gap dividing their pure scientific inquiries from politics. In their objectivistic frame it appears to be impossible to incorporate the idea of practical interest.

Hillgruber thereby flatly denies that his choice in favor of the perspective of the "*Wehrmacht*" conceals a normative choice. He presents this choice as one dictated by historical reality itself. The historian of the Eastern front, according to him, is confronted with the following alternatives: to choose to write history from the perspective of Hitler, or from the perspective of the Russians, or from the perspective of the inmates of the concentration camps, or from the perspective of the German civilian population and the German army protecting it. The first three perspectives do not match reality, according to Hillgruber, because the German population did not identify itself with one of these parties. Therefore the perspective of the German army remains as the only "realistic" point of view for the historian.[68]

To uncover the normative choices hidden behind Hillgruber's quasi-factual argumentation is not a very difficult task since his attempts to clear the German army and civilian population from responsibility for the Nazi crimes are rather clumsy. *His* formulation of the *factual* historical problem evidently hinges on the separation in his frame of description between (1) Hitler on the one side and the German army and civilian population on the other, and (2) the German army and population on the one side and the inmates of the concentration camps on the other. Apparently the latter – mainly Jews, gypsies, Communists, and socialists – are not "real" Germans in Hillgruber's view, because they are not identified as such by either the majority of the German population then – this is an undisputed historical fact – or the (present-day) German historian in the 1980s – this is his normative choice. The factual description of the Third Reich by the historian then simply boils down to the uncritical reproduction of the *Wehrmacht*-perspective on reality, including its *normative* definition of the "real" Germans and the "real" Germany.[69] This remarkable point of view stems from Hillgruber's apparent identification of the (German) past with what was supposedly directly "observable," the (German) sources – a well-known empiricist fallacy, that has not gone unnoticed in the debate.

The descriptive separation of Hitler and the German army makes it possible for Hillgruber to typify the struggle on the Eastern front as a "tragedy." This typification carries a hidden normative load since tragedies presuppose that *both* parties to a conflict are able to justify their actions by an appeal to an ethical principle; moreover, the conflict between these principles is as comprehensible as it is inevitable. In this way the role of the *Wehrmacht* in continuing "Hitler's war" even after it became apparent during the winter of 1942–3 that it had already been lost is legitimized by Hillgruber forty-five years after the fact. He is consistent in describing the few members of the German military who actually rose against Hitler in July 1944 as "irresponsible" and "unrealistic."[70] Surprisingly for Hillgruber the historical reality of July 1944 thus is exactly what the Hitler-supporting majority of the *Wehrmacht* took it for (and made of it) with the exclusion of all other perspectives – such as the perspective of the military resistance, of the camp-inmates, or of the Russians.

Nolte's normative choices are better hidden than Hillgruber's in a quasi-factual guise in his frame of description. Most important in this respect is his "factual" statement that the historiography of the "Third Reich" up till now has been based on "ascriptions of collective guilt"; therefore this historiography is labeled as "moralistic" and "factually inadequate" and is in dire need of "scientific revision." Nolte repudiates any "ascription of collective guilt" because this figure of argumentation sprang from the Nazis. In spite of its intentionally "innovative" and "scientific" character Nolte's own argumentation at this point suffers from a serious inconsistency that leaps to the eye: he repeatedly criticizes his opponents for denouncing his arguments because of their (rightist) political origins instead of judging their factual adequacy. According to Nolte, in *his* case this constituted a serious breach of the ethics of science. This at least was his argument for using radical rightist pamphlets as historical sources (neglected by other historians) in order to document the Nazis' "fear of Bolshevism."[71] The question of the historical German guilt and responsibility for Auschwitz – *the* central problem defined by the perspectives of his critics – was in this way eschewed as a factual problem for history and dismissed as "moralistic."[72]

The distinction between science as the realm of facts and politics as the domain of values thus may cause serious trouble and controversy in historical debates, as is clearly demonstrated in the *Historikerstreit*. This direct link between factual and normative judgments is rooted in the practical interest of history, even when this is explicitly denied – as is the case with Nolte and Hillgruber. Both historians were attempting to restore an *acceptable* past for the Germans through the construction of a less painful historical identity by relativizing the German responsibility for the catastrophes brought about by the Germans between 1939 and 1945. This direct linkage between history and identity can explain why it is no use trying to expel ethical discussion from the territory of historians and why "the problem of ethical neutrality" of the historian is as old as historiography itself.[73] As long and as far as collectivities derive their identity from history, the writing of history preserves this practical and normative character.[74] Therefore the normative points of view of historians are better argued out in the open, as the *Historikerstreit* clearly shows, the more so since in many historical controversies the explicit, conflicting factual judgments appear to be rooted in implicit, conflicting normative judgments. The rationality of historical discussions could be enhanced in this way. In the Jewish contributions to this debate – for instance those of Saul Friedländer and Dan Diner – this argument is explicitly stated. They, for instance, argue that the history of the Third Reich should not be written from the perspective of the German contemporaries – as Hillgruber proposed – because this would imply a duplication in historiography of their moral indifference towards its victims. The violence that the Nazis used to silence their victims would thus be reproduced by the historian.[75] The same explicit appeal to the normative principles involved is found in Habermas's contributions; according to him the Nolte–Hillgruber group accepts the German nation as the ultimate value while their critics give primacy to democracy. This normative primacy of democracy is the foundation of their critical attitude towards the undemocratic traditions in the German national past.[76]

Within the framework of "internal realism" – in its amended form – this source of trouble can be faced in the open and be made comprehensible in three steps. The first step demonstrates the relativity of the "gap" between the domain of facts and values. The second step is revealing the multiplicity of the functions of language on the basis of general linguistics. The third and last step is introducing the notion of a "horizon of expectation" as a link between factual and normative discourse.

With regard to the first step all the arguments have already been brought forward. For the idea of an "absolute heterogeneity" of facts and values and the plea for a "value-free" science of history are ultimately founded on the presupposition that factual judgments can be founded in reality in contrast to value judgments and the related presupposition that language in science exclusively fulfills a representative function. Therefore facts and values were supposed to be separated by an unbridgeable abyss, with factual discussions decidable by rational means while debates regarding judgments are inherently irrational. All this is derived from "foundational" imagery. The same applies for the representation of factual discussions as leading to a consensus and the debates about values as the opposite of their factual counterparts. The possibility of a foundation of statements therefore was regarded as the ultimate basis of rationality. These presuppositions were shared by both objectivists and relativists.[77]

From the point of view of "internal realism," all the "foundational" ground for these dichotomies has disappeared. As one recognizes that factual claims too cannot be founded in reality but can only be argued for, one loses all *a priori* "philosophical guarantees" – so desired even in the recent past – that argumentation will compel any rational audience so addressed to come to a rational consensus. After this presupposition is dropped the "unbridgeable gap" between factual and normative discourse changes from a solution into a problem that can be discussed in the open.[78] At the same time, the apparent fact that in historical discourse it may be very difficult to separate the factual from the normative controversies – as was so obvious in the *Historikerstreit* and in contemporary German history in gereral[79] – is rendered comprehensible.

Beyond objectivism and relativism, thus, there is no longer a self-evident "foundational" gap between facts and values; therefore this gap cannot be used as an argument to keep the normative dimensions of historiography out of discussion. If historians would take notice of "internal realism" in philosophy of history the temptation to disguise normative judgments as factual statements – as exemplified by Nolte's and Hillgruber's essays – might even disappear. This is to say that the supposedly "stronger" (foundational) character of the latter turns out to be illusory because *both* types of statements are in need of justification through argumentation. Nolte's and Hillgruber's critics seem to be aware of this fact since they overtly use normative arguments against their opponents. For instance, they argue that a German national perspective is undesirable given the disastrous historical record of the consequences of German nationalism for the other nations of Europe. Hillgruber's proposal to rewrite the history of the Eastern front is rejected on this score. Another example is their rejection of "scientific" attempts like Nolte's and Hillgruber's to deny Germany's responsibility for Auschwitz through a quasi-factual "Europeanization" of the German mass murders in contemporary history. Philosophy of history thus is capable of elucidating the connections between implicit philosophical presuppositions of historians – as the distinction of facts and values in this debate – and their delimitation of the scope of legitimate scientific discussion. In doing this it can contribute to the widening of this scope and thus to the heightening of the level of rationality.[80]

The second argument for pushing the analysis of the problem of values beyond objectivism and relativism can be derived from modern linguistics. Connected with "internal realism" – as I proposed earlier – it may shed new light on the normative aspects of historiography.

Essential for this line of argument is the acknowledgment that language functions not only as a medium of representation of reality but also as a pragmatic medium of communication.[81] All linguistic utterances can also be analyzed as "speech acts," as Austin and Searle have shown: all use of language is a form of social interaction. Therefore, the use of language is not only the subject of syntactic and semantic analysis, but also of linguistic pragmatics. All social interaction takes place in a context that presupposes a speaker – who performs the "speech act" – and a hearer. In history, the historians are the speakers, their texts a collection of speech acts, and their audiences the hearers. The main functions of speech acts are the bringing about of contacts and relationships, giving information, expressing emotions, evaluating, entering an engagement, and playing an esthetic role. Traditionally, philosophers of history have almost completely been preoccupied with the information function of historical language, because the agenda of critical philosophy of history was dictated by analytical philosophy of science with its focus on the formal structure of scientific explanations. Though since the demise of analytical philosophy of science in the 1960s philosophy of history has also rediscovered the evaluating and esthetic dimensions of historical discourse, the analysis of the normative functions of the language of the historian has remained somewhat rudimentary.[82] This neglect is rooted in objectivism and relativism, since both presuppose that the normative function of language excludes the representative function as a consequence of the supposedly "unbridgeable gap" between judgments of fact and judgments of value. The normative dimension in historical discourse therefore was usually identified in historical discourse as "the problem of ethical neutrality." The solution of this problem was essentially conceived along empiricist lines, that is the "emptying of the mind" of all factors disturbing the acquirement of true knowledge. This boils down to eliminating all Baconian *idola*, that is all ideological – evaluational – influences. Although most historians have their doubts as to whether this process can be completed, this is conceived as a practical and not as a fundamental problem. The normative functions of the language of the historian thus are conceptualized as a threat to the representative function.

This "repression" of the normative function of language has roots in empiricism with its strict separation of facts and values and its foundational paradigm of scientific knowledge. Paradoxically empiricism even still bedevils philosophies of history that explicitly aim to "overcome" empiricism – like Hayden White's brand of narrativism – because the labeling of all forms of historiography as "ideological" is a simple inversion of empiricism on this score. The version of "internal realism" I advocate is capable of avoiding the sterile dilemma of "science versus ideology" because it recognizes that the language of the historian is capable of fulfilling both representative and normative functions *at the same time* (and that is exactly what is happening when one constructs an identity).[83] Because of its "holistic" character "internal realism" has no problems in acknowledging that the *same* statement can fulfill *different* functions at the *same time*.[84] Presumably descriptive statements, for instance, "Von Staufenberg was a real German officer," "Adolf Hitler was an Austrian bastard," or "The struggle at the Eastern Front was a tragedy" can also be interpreted as normative statements.[85] Therefore the "fundamental difference" between judgments of fact and judgments of value can no longer be taken for granted and can no longer be used as an argument to narrow the scope of historical discussion. The "value-ladenness" and the "essentially contested character" of sociohistorical concepts[86] – aspects of historiography that have more often been observed than analyzed – can be elucidated in this way, avoiding the Scylla of "value-free" objectivism and the Charybdis of "ideological" relativism.

The third and last step in order to push the analysis of the problem of values in historiography beyond objectivism and relativism can be set by introducing the notion of "horizon of expectation" (*Erwartungshorizont*) in the analysis of historical debate.[87] This concept helps to clarify how different normative conceptions relate to different descriptions of historical reality because it can function as a bridge between the "domain assumptions"[88] of the historians and their audiences. These domain assumptions, that have their origins in social ontologies,[89] are shared with political ideologies; therefore it makes sense to talk about "liberal," "conservative," and "Marxist" traditions in historiography and to link historiographical controversies to the politico-ideological competition of "world views."

To elucidate the "horizon of expectation" we first have to take a closer look at the ways in which historians argue their claims to knowledge in order to locate its effects. The argumentative process of historians is traditionally divided into the phase of factual research and the phase of interpretation and explanation. Facts are normally judged on the basis of inferential arguments relating to the relative measure of backing by the sources; interpretive and explanatory claims are normally judged on the basis of comparative arguments on the interpretive and explanatory capacity of central concepts.[90] Elimination of rival arguments is a basic strategy in this phase.[91]

As can be observed in a paradigmatic manner in debates like the *Historikerstreit* the arguments in both phases are not automatically "rationally compelling" and do not automatically lead to a consensus.[92] No appeal to "*the* historical method" can hide this fact.[93] The notion of "horizon of expectation" helps to elucidate one aspect of this absence of consensus – and thus of pluralism – in historiography because it makes us aware that historians do not reconstruct the past *in vacuo*, but with particular audiences in mind; therefore the multiplicity of perspectives in historiography can also be elucidated from the consumer side of historiography – professional and lay. Thus, although all "scientific" historians are bound by the "reality rule," they are *at the same time* bound by what can be labeled as the "audience rule." The latter rule can help us to explain the ways in which the "narrative space" is used by historians: it helps to elucidate which of all possible true histories are also *accepted* as such. This is no triviality since historians, just like natural scientists, are not after truth *per se* nor after the *whole* truth but only after the *relevant* truth.[94] Because the primary sources do not directly "dictate" the mode of reconstructing the past, they always offer a narrative space for several explanatory accounts (this remains the rational kernel of White's *Metahistory*). Which of these accounts possess *a priori* plausibility varies not only with the cognitive expectations but also with the normative expectations of the audiences addressed. The latter characteristic is well documented in the history of historiography, especially in the "hot" controversies such the *Historikerstreit* or the "Fischer-controversy."[95]

The cognitive expectations pose a limit to the *kind* of factors which can be presented as causal agents – as, for instance, individual states of mind (cf. Nolte) versus supra-individual, collective factors (cf. Mommsen).[96] The normative expectations limit the *particular choice* of factors – for example individuals and collectivities – which can be selected as causal agents. This normative choice is, as Dray has shown, directly linked to the attribution of responsibility and blame.[97] In national histories, the nationality of the "heroes and villains" offers a concrete example (even when these national histories are dressed up as comparative, international histories). So it is by no means accidental that according to the conservative Nolte–Hillgruber group the Soviet dictator Stalin was ultimately responsible for the crimes of his German "twin brother" in politics, Adolf Hitler. This train of thought – including the idea that in 1941 Hitler launched the war in the East only to prevent the war Stalin planned for 1942 – was already well entrenched in conservative circles in the Federal Republic of Germany.[98] Nor is it accidental that their critics vehemently rejected this historiographical "export" of German historical responsibility since in the liberal and leftist circles of the Federal Republic the conviction was widely held that it was necessary for the Germans to "rework" *their* Nazi past (*Aufarbeitung der Vergangenheit*). Historians take these "horizons of expectation" into account because they vary widely and to an extent determine the reception of historical studies. That the two camps in the *Historikerstreit* published their contributions in publications of widely differing political complexions, and so addressed very different audiences, illustrates this fact. The main peculiarity of the *Historikerstreit*, in comparison with other historical debates, was only that these horizons of expectation were far more visible than usual.

5 Conclusion

In this essay I have argued that it is the task of philosophy of history to elucidate the practice of history; therefore philosophy of history must

stick to the analysis of the products and the debates of historians –
including their presuppositions. It must elucidate the fact that historians
present reconstructions of a past reality on the basis of factual research
and discuss the adequacy of these reconstructions; at the same time it
must elucidate the fact that these discussions seldom lead to a consensus and that therefore pluralism is a basic characteristic of history as
a discipline.

An analysis of the *Historikerstreit* shows that traditional objectivism
and relativism cannot account for the fact that historians do debate; it
also reveals that a fuzzy distinction between judgments of fact and judgments of value plays a crucial role in this debate because judgments of
value are supposed to fall outside the scope of rational debate. This distinction can be traced back to outdated presuppositions with regard to
the rationality of science shared by objectivism and relativism. Internal
realism goes beyond objectivism and relativism in historiography, though
in order to transfer "internal realism" from the realm of the philosophy
of natural science – where it was formulated by Hilary Putnam – to
history, the notion of the practical interest of history was introduced.
With the help of this notion and the implied notion of identity, the
normative roots of pluralism in historiography can be brought to the
surface. Second, an analysis of the fact–value distinction uncovers its
roots in objectivism and relativism; it must therefore be re-analyzed
within the frame of "internal realism." This analysis, put to work in the
Historikerstreit, shows the relativity of this distinction and the unsatis-
factory character of the attempts to clarify the normative dimensions of
history: the arguments for the expulsion of the normative discussion
outside the domain of legitimate scientific debate are unfounded and
outdated. Third, the theory of "speech acts" and the notion of "horizon
of expectation" can be connected to "internal realism" in order to give
a more adequate elucidation of the normative aspects of historiography.
Fourth, historians can profit from "internal realism" because the scope
of their discussion would be widened to include the traditionally implicit normative issues involved. Thus, although philosophers of history
take the products and the debates of historians as points of departure
and as the raw material to analyze, philosophy of history does not simply
reproduce the convictions of historians about their trade.

This interpretation of the task of philosophy is necessary in my view
to keep philosophy of history and history connected and to prevent
a degeneration of philosophic analyses into "formalistic tumors which
grow incessantly by feeding on their own juices."[99] "Internal realism" in
its amended form offers both historians and philosophers of history a
"realistic" way to get beyond objectivism and relativism while avoiding
the mistakes of narrativism, a move from the swamps of positivism to
the quicksands of postmodernism. Historians themselves claim to represent the past and thus subscribe to the "reality-rule"; the mere fact that

the past is only known by us through a frame of description therefore does not entail the conclusion that the past *is* a description or can be regarded as such.[100]

Notes

1 C. Meier, "Narrativität, Geschichte und die Sorgen des Historikers," in *Geschichte: Ereignis und Erzählung*, ed. R. Koselleck and W. Stempel (Munich, 1973), 571–85.

2 R. F. Atkinson, "Methodology: History and its Philosophy," in *Objectivity, Method and Point of View: Essays in the Philosophy of History*, ed. W. J. van der Dussen and L. Rubinoff (Leiden, 1991), 12–22.

3 L. Rubinoff, "W. Dray and the Critique of Historical Thinking," in Van der Dussen and Rubinoff, eds, *Objectivity*, 1–11; R. Martin, *The Past Within Us: An Empirical Approach to Philosophy of History* (Princeton, 1989), 3–16.

4 R. Rorty, *Philosophy and the Mirror of Nature* (Oxford, 1980); F. R. Ankersmit, "Historiography and Postmodernism," *History and Theory* 28 (1989), 137–53 [ch. 9, this volume]; P. Zagorin, "Historiography and Postmodernism: Reconsiderations," *History and Theory* 29 (1990), 263–74 [ch. 10, this volume]; F. R. Ankersmit, "Reply to Professor Zagorin," *History and Theory* 29 (1990), 275–96 [ch. 11, this volume]. For further literature on the relationship of history and postmodernism: "Herausforderungen durch die Postmoderne" in *Grundlagen und Methoden der Historiographiegeschichte*, ed. W. Küttler et al. (Frankfurt, 1993), 17–97; L. Stone, "History and Post-modernism," *Past and Present* 131 (1991), 217–18; P. Joyce and C. Kelly, "History and Post-modernism," *Past and Present* 133 (1991), 204–13; G. Spiegel, "History and Post-modernism," *Past and Present* 135 (1992), 189–208; J. Caplan, "Post-modernism, Poststructuralism and Deconstruction: Notes for Historians," *Central European History* 22 (1989), 260–78.

5 For an example of the Collingwoodian train of thought see W. J. van der Dussen, *Filosofie van de geschiedenis: Een inleiding* [Philosophy of History: An Introduction] (Muiderberg, 1986), 144–79; for the problem of relativism see R. Bernstein, *Beyond Objectivism and Relativism* (Oxford, 1983), 1–16.

6 For references see C. Lorenz, *De constructie van het verleden* [The Construction of the Past] (Meppel/Amsterdam, 1990), 255–82. For "internal realism" see H. Putnam, *Reason, Truth and History* (Cambridge, 1981), 49.

7 The literature on this debate is immense. For overviews and analyses see R. Evans, *In Hitler's Shadow: West German Historians and the Attempt to Escape from the Nazi Past* (London, 1989) and C. Maier, *The Unmasterable Past: History, Holocaust and German National Identity* (Cambridge, Mass., 1988). The original contributions to the debate are collected in *"Historikerstreit." Die Dokumentation der Kontroverse um die Einzigfartigkeit der nationalsozialistischen Judenvernichtung* (Munich, 1987), to be cited henceforth as *Historikerstreit*.

8 J. Habermas, "Eine Art Schadensabwicklung: Die apologitische Tendenzen in der deutschen Zeitgeschichtsschreibung," in *Historikerstreit*, 62–77.

9 E. Nolte, "Zwischen Geschichtslegende und Revisionismus? Das Dritte Reich im Blickwinkel des Jahres 1980" and "Vergangenheit die nicht vergehen will," in *Historikerstreit*, 13–36 and 39–48. For his self-defense and commentary on the discussion see E. Nolte, *Das Vergehen der Vergangenheit: Antwort auf meine Kritiker im sogenannten Historikerstreit* (Berlin, 1987).

10 A. Hillgruber, *Zweierlei Untergang: Die Zerschlagung des Deutschen Reiches und das Ende des europäischen Judentums* (Berlin, 1986).

11 Nolte, *Vergehen der Vergangenheit*, 13–68; A Hillgruber, "Jürgen Habermas, Karl-Heinz Janssen und die Aufklärung Anno 1986," in *Historikerstreit*, 331–52; I. Geiss, *Die Habermas-Kontroverse: Ein deutscher Striet* (Berlin, 1988).

12 H.-U. Wehler, *Entsorgung der deutschen Vergangenheit? Ein polemischer Essay zum Historikerstreit* (Munich, 1988), 16–17; Maier, *The Unmasterable Past*, 83–4; Evans, *Hitler's Shadow*, 175.

13 J. Fest, "Die geschuldete Erinnerung: Zur Kontroverse über die Unvergleichbarkeit der nationalsozialistischen Massenverbrechen," in *Historikerstreit*, 104–13; K. Hildebrand, "Das Zeitalter der Tyrannen," in *Historikerstreit*, 91.

14 H. Mommsen, "Suche nach der 'verlorenen Geschichte'? Bemerkungen zum historischen Selbstverständnis der Bundesrepublik" and "Neues Geschichtsbewusstsein und Relativierung des Nationalsozialismus," in *Historikerstreit*, 156–74 and 174–89; M. Broszat, "Wo sich die Geister scheiden: Die Beschwörung der Geschichte taugt nicht als Religionsersatz," in *Historikerstreit*, 189–96; H.-A. Winkler, "Auf ewig in Hitlers Schatten? Zum Streit über das Geschichtsbild der Deutschen," in *Historikerstreit*, 256–64; W. J. Mommsen, "Weder Leugnen noch Vergessen befreit von der Vergangenheit: Die Harmonisierung des Geschichtsbildes gefährdet die Freiheit," in *Historikerstreit*, 300–32.

15 Nolte, *Vergehen der Vergangenheit*, 57, 88–9; Nolte, "Geschichtslegende," 23; Nolte, "Vergangenheit," 41.

16 See D. W. Hamlyn, *The Theory of Knowledge* (London, 1970), 136–42 for the relationship between facts and truth, and especially 137: "It is true that a fact is what is stated by a true statement, but it does not follow from this that this is the same as the latter; nor would it be true to say that a fact is *just* what is stated by a true statement. This might suggest that facts do not exist until a statement is made that happens to be true, whereas it would appear that on the contrary there are countless facts that have never been stated and never will be."

17 This famous phrase was formulated by the late conservative CSU politician Franz-Joseph Strauss. For the political context of the debate see *Ist der Nationalsozialismus Geschichte? Zu Historisierung und Historikerstreit*, ed. D. Diner (Frankfurt am Main, 1987) and *Streit ums Geschichtsbild: Die "Historikerdebatte." Dokumentation, Darstellung und Kritik*, ed. R. Kühnl (Cologne, 1987), especially 200–92.

18 Nolte, "Vergangenheit," 45 and *Vergehen der Vergangenheit*, 91; Hillgruber, "Frageverbot," 232–8.

19 For a definition of traditional objectivism in history see P. Novick, *That Noble Dream: The "Objectivity Question" and the American Historical Profession* (Cambridge, 1988), 1–2. For the philosophical presuppositions of objectivism see Bernstein, *Beyond Objectivism and Relativism*, 8–9, 19.

20 Nolte, for instance, presents his thesis that Auschwitz constitutes a "reaction" and a "distorted copy" of the Bolshevistic murder of the Russian bourgeoisie as a pure "fact" ("Tatsache"); Nolte, "Revisionismus," 23 and *Vergehen der Vergangenheit*, 73.

21 Cf, Novick, *Noble Dream*, 3 and Bernstein, *Beyond Objectivism and Relativism*, 18 on "the Cartesian anxiety." William McNeill's proposal to label all historiography "mythistory" – because nothing is absolutely certain in history – is an example of this procedure of inversion; see his *Mythistory and Other Essays* (Chicago, 1986), 6–7, 19.

22 Hamlyn, *Theory of Knowledge*, 95–103.

23 This paradoxical problem is faced by all brands of narrativism – as developed by Hayden White or Frank Ankersmit – that regard the past as it is presented by the historian as a text without a referential relationship to a real past. For an excellent analysis and criticism of H. White's *Metahistory* (Baltimore, 1973), and his later developments cf. W. Kansteiner, "Hayden White's Critique of the Writing of History," *History and Theory* 32 (1993), 273–96. Kansteiner, 286, also indicates that White's position is inconsistent with regard to the problem of referentiality.

24 Hamlyn, *Theory of Knowledge*, 10–16.

25 Cf. for skepticism in general: Hamlyn, *Theory of Knowledge*, 23–53; for skepticism in history: *Versions of History from Antiquity to the Enlightenment*, ed. D. Kelley (New Haven, 1991), 12–13, 264–7, 502.

26 Rex Martin also recently called for a return to epistemology in philosophy of history in "Objectivity and Meaning in Historical Studies: Towards a Post-analytic View," *History and Theory* 32 (1993), 25–50.

27 Cf. W. Callebaut, "Post-positivistic Views on Scientific Explanation," in *L'Explication en sciences sociales: la recherche des causes en démographie*, ed. J. Duchène and G. Wunsch (Brussels, 1989), 141–96; W. Salmon, *Four Decades of Scientific Explanation* (Minneapolis, 1989).

28 For the history of this debate see Bernstein, *Beyond Objectivism and Relativism*.

29 The same holds for philosophy of social science. Cf. Bohman's analysis of skepticism in postmodern anthropology in J. Bohman, *New Philosophy of Social Science: Problems of Indeterminacy* (Cambridge, Mass., 1991), 103–39.

30 F. R. Ankersmit, "The Dilemma of Contemporary Anglo-Saxon Philosophy or History," *History and Theory, Beiheft 25, Knowing and Telling History: The Anglo-Saxon Debate* (1986), 27. A. Fell, " 'Epistemological' and 'Narrativist' Philosophies of History," in Van der Dussen and Rubinoff, eds, *Objectivity*, 82–3, criticizes Ankersmit on the same score.

31 In modern philosophy of science this position has been stated most radically and eloquently by P. K. Feyerabend in *Against Method: Outline of an Anarchistic Theory of Knowledge* (London, 1975).

32 Putnam, *Reason, Truth and History*, 49–50.

33 L. O. Mink, "On the Writing and Rewriting of History," in Mink, *Historical Understanding*, ed. Brian Fay, Eugene O. Golob, and Richard T. Vann (Ithaca, NY, 1987), 94.

34 J. Leplin, "Introduction," in *Scientific Realism*, ed. J. Leplin (Berkeley, 1984), 2; H. Radder, "Het probleem van het wetenschappelijk realisme," in *Wetenschapsleer*, ed. M. Korthals (Meppel/Amsterdam, 1989), 72–3.

35 Cf. H. Putnam, "What is Realism?," in Leplin, ed., *Scientific Realism*, 140: "[And] the typical realist argument against idealism is that it makes the success of science a miracle."

36 I criticized Ankersmit's "narrative idealism" and its idea of the self-referentiality of historical texts – as propounded in his *Narrative Logic: A Semantic Analysis of the Historian's Language* (The Hague, 1983) – in "Het masker zonder gazicht: F. R. Ankesmits filosofie van de geschiedschrijving,"

Tijdschrift voor Geschiedenis 97 (1984), 169–95. I deal with his later developments in my "Ankersmit en het postmoderne denken over de maatschappe-
lijke functies van de geschiedenis," in *Feiten en waarden: De constructie van
een onderscheid*, ed. D. Pels et al. (Amsterdam, 1990), 139–48. Although
Ankersmit dropped the term "narrative idealism" later in the 1980s, he has
not changed his position regarding the issue of referentiality; cf. his *The
Reality Effect in the Writing of History: The Dynamics of Historiographical
Topology* (Amsterdam, 1989).

Similar criticism has been formulated by W. Walsh, "Fact and Value in
History," in *Facts and Values: Philosophical Reflections from Western and
Non-western Perspectives*, ed. M. C. Doeser et al. (The Hague, 1986), 57:
"If an historian writes 'What followed was a veritable renaissance' there
is no observable state of affairs against which a contemporary could have
checked the truth of the claim. By contrast 'Jane Austen wrote Emma' and
'Napoleon died on St. Helena' might conceivably be accepted on the testimony of eye-witnesses. But though this is an important difference, it does
not follow that something like a renaissance exists only in the mind of the
person who judges it to have occurred."

For criticism of White on this score see for instance W. H. Dray's review
of White's *The Content of the Form* in *History and Theory* 28 (1988),
284: "Are events rendered 'imaginary' (again White's own term) by being
brought under colligatory concepts?"

37 This is also the case with White and Ankersmit.
38 Putnam, *Reason, Truth and History*, 49–50; cf. N. Goodman, *Ways of
Worldmaking* (Indianapolis, 1978), 17–20.
39 Putnam, *Reason, Truth and History*, 72–3: "The trouble . . . is not that
correspondences between words or concepts and other entities don't exist,
but that too many correspondences exist. To pick out just one correspondence between words or mental signs and mind-independent things we would
already have to have referential access to mind-independent things." Cf.
Hamlyn, *Theory of Knowledge*, 140: "[Thus] talk of facts and talk of correspondence with fact implies a form of realism, not in the sense that facts are
identical with concrete states of affairs, but in the sense that a necessary
condition of there being objective truth is that there should be an independently existing world. To say that a statement corresponds to the facts is to
say that the statement conforms to whatever standard of objective truth is
applicable."
40 C. Ginzburg, "Checking the Evidence: The Judge and the Historian," *Critical Inquiry* 18 (1991), 79–98. Ginzburg also criticizes the postmodernist
position as "inverted positivism." He proposes to regard historical sources
as lenses instead of the false dilemma to regard them as transparent pieces
of glass – as is the case in "positivism," or as a blind wall – as is done in
postmodernism.
41 Hamlyn, *Theory of Knowledge*, 53–78, 132–45, especially 67: "the use of
language *presupposes* the idea that linguistic expressions have meaning and
that meaning cannot be fully elucidated by or reduced to use."
42 Cf. B. van Fraassen, *The Scientific Image* (Oxford, 1980), 13–19, for a
recent and effective demolition of the idea of a "direct" observation in
natural science.
43 According to realism – that is, an epistemological position – objects of
human knowledge exist independently of knowing subjects. According to

materialism – that is, a metaphysical position – all reality consists of matter and therefore only material things exist.

44 Cf. K.-G. Faber, *Theorie der Geschichtswissenschaft* (Munich, 1974), 24–5.

45 It is not without significance that Johan Huizinga, who is often cited as one of the intellectual fathers of narrativism, held a different opinion. In his essay on the "esthetical character" of historical narratives (1905) he explicitly referred to the danger of projecting images on the past because this would lead to "*pictures*, that are *untrue*" (my italics). Cf. J. Huizinga, "Het aesthetische bestanddeel van geschiedkundige voorstellingen," in *Verzamelde Werken VII* (The Hague, 1950), 25.

46 Both Ankersmit and White hold that *singular* existential statements by historians do refer to the past and can be true or false while denying that this is the case with *conjunctions* of these statements, that is the level of historical interpretation or narrative. The same position was held by well-known relativists such as Becker and Beard. This distinction sets relativism apart from outright skepticism that denies the possibility of true knowledge in all forms.

47 White and Ankersmit both argue that because historical narratives do not represent the past reality *directly*, they do not refer to reality *at all*; therefore they are self-referential and can be analyzed as a purely linguistic universe in which the problem of truth has disappeared. This train of thought is the linguistic variant of the arguments used by Becker and Beard half a century ago. They too argued that because historical narratives – or "interpretations" – cannot be founded in historical reality, they cannot be "objective" and therefore are "imagined," based on "an act of faith" and strictly "personal." Then as now arbitrariness and indifference to the problem of truth is presented as the only alternative for a rock-bottom epistemological foundation and a universal cognitive consensus. Cf. C. Becker, "What Are Historical Facts," in *The Philosophy of History in Our Time*, ed. H. Meyerhoff (New York, 1959), 132: "Thus into the imagined facts and their meaning enters a personal equation. The history of any event is never the same thing to two different persons," and C. Beard, "Written History as an Act of Faith," in Meyerhoff, ed., *The Philosophy of History in Our Time*, 148–9: "His faith is at the bottom a conviction about the movement of history and his conviction is a subjective decision, not a purely objective discovery." Both relativistic and narrativistic arguments reflect the Cartesian train of thought that everything that does not exist objectively in an external world must be interpreted as a subjective creation of the human mind. Cf. Rorty, *Mirror of Nature*, 342. The fundamental distinction between facts (external) and values (internal) also stems from this "Cartesian Anxiety" (Bernstein).

For a fundamental analysis and criticism of narrativism in philosophy of history and its links to literary criticism see J. Zammito, "Are We Being Theoretical Yet? The New Historicism, the New Philosophy of History and 'Practicing Historians,'" *Journal of Modern History* 65 (1993), 783–814. Also illuminating is A. P. Norman, "Telling It Like It Was: Historical Narratives on Their Own Terms," *History and Theory* 30 (1991), 119–35 [ch. 8, this volume].

48 Hamlyn, *Theory of Knowledge*, 139: "It is possible to refer to a thing, without that thing being a concrete physical object (e.g. abstract entities, like justice); similarly for facts."

49 Kansteiner, "Hayden White's Critique of the Writing of History," 286, convincingly shows that White is inconsistent on this score: "[Thus] the problem of representational transparency, shown out the front door, returns at the back."

50 Cf. I. Kershaw, *The Nazi Dictatorship: Problems of Perspectives and Interpretation* (London, 1989), 1–42.

51 The Dutch historian L. de Jong could serve as an example – see his "Zelfkritiek," *Bijdragen en Mededelingen tot de Geschiedenis der Nederlanden* 105 (1990), 2, 179, 182–3 or the American historian William McNeill – see his *Mythistory* (note 21).

52 Goodman, *Ways of Worldmaking*, 2–3.

53 According to most commentaries Nolte and Hillgruber should be regarded as the losers of the "Historikerstreit": D. Peukert, "Wer gewann den Historikerstreit? Keine Bilanz," in *Vernunft riskieren: Klaus Dohanyi zum 60. Geburtstag*, ed. P. Glotz et al. (Hamburg, 1988), 38–50; I. Kershaw, "Neue deutsche Unruhe? Der Ausland und der Streit um die deutsche National- und Zeitgeschichte," in *Streitfall Deutsche Geschichte*, ed. Landeszentrale für politische Bildung NRW (Düsseldorf, 1988), 111–31.

54 Hamlyn, *Theory of Knowledge*, 135–42, especially 135: "indeed, if one considers what could be the general necessary and sufficient condition of any statement being true, it will appear that the only thing that could be would be that the statement should correspond to fact."

55 Cf. Zammito, "Are We Being Theoretical Yet?," 812: "Veridicality and coherence are indispensable to the practice of history, but the standards of appraisal are disciplinary, not abstract."

56 H. White, "The Fact of Modernism: The Fading of the Historical Event" (1993 ms.). For White's development and inconsistencies see Kansteiner, "Hayden White's Critique."

57 White, "Fact of Modernism," 8.

58 Ibid., 23. This line of reasoning is even more remarkable because it is inconsistent. While denying that there is reliable knowledge about the (recent) past – cf. JFK and the Holocaust – White presents a full-blown characterization of just this (recent) past: while undermining the notion of fact he tries to convince his readers of a fact, his "fact of modernism." One can't have one's cake and eat it too.

59 F. R. Ankersmit, "Historiography and Postmodernism," *History and Theory* 28 (1989), 137–53 [ch. 9, this volume]. Remarkably enough Ankersmit presents Ginzburg's *The Cheese and the Worms: The Cosmos of a Sixteenth-Century Miller*, trans. John and Anne Tedeschi (New York, 1982) as a prime example of postmodern historiography, while Ginzburg himself is clearly hostile to this interpretation. See his "Checking the Evidence."

60 F. R. Ankersmit, *The Reality Effect in the Writing of History: The Dynamics of Historiographical Topology* (Amsterdam, 1989), 8. It is paradoxical that Ankersmit recently has left his "textual trail" and has presented an analysis of "the historical experience" – independent of its linguistic expressions. See his *De historische ervaring* [The Historical Experience] (Groningen, 1993). Now that White is philosophizing about *the* historical event and Ankersmit about *the* historical experience one wonders where narrativism will bring us next.

61 Although the concept of history is ontologically neutral – since there is, for instance, a history of the earth and a history of extinct animal species

alongside human history – I reserve this concept in this context for the history of humans.

62 E. Angehrn, *Geschichte und Identität* (Berlin, 1985); J. Rüsen, *Historische Vernunft: Grundzüge einer Historik I: Die Grundlagen der Geschichtswissenschaft* (Göttingen, 1983); H. Nagl-Docekal, *Die Objektivität der Geschichtswissenschaft* (Munich, 1982); J. Habermas, "'Geschichtsbewusstsein und post-traditionelle Identität," in *Eine Art Schadensabwicklung* (Frankfurt, 1987), 159–80. For a summary of Habermas's theory see Bohman, *New Philosophy of Social Science, passim*; for a summary of Rüsen's theory cf. A. Megill, "Jörn Rüsen's Theory of Historiography between Modernism and Rhetoric of Inquiry," *History and Theory* 33 (1994), 39–61.

63 For references cf. R. Vierhaus, "Rankes Begriff der historischen Objektivität," in *Objektivität und Parteilichkeit*, ed. R. Koselleck et al. (Munich, 1977), 63–77.

64 This problem cannot be dealt with here in all its aspects; for a further treatment see W. Schluchter, *Wertfreiheit und Verantwortungsethik* (Tübingen, 1971).

65 For recent analyses of this old problem cf. J. Scott, "History in Crisis? The Other Side in History," *American Historical Review* 94 (1989), 680–92, and A. Megill, "Fragmentation and the Future of Historiography," in *American Historical Review* 96 (1991), 693–8.

66 The "holistic" and "practical" aspects of historiography are also stressed by Allan Megill, "Recounting the Past: Description, Explanation and Narrative in Historiography," *American Historical Review* 94 (1989), 3, 627–54, especially 647: "Finally, the historian interprets the past – that is, necessarily, views the past from some present perspective. The perspective permeates all that the historian writes." He also stresses the normative aspect connected with the choice of perspective: "Since the historical account is necessarily written from a present perspective, it is always concerned with the meaning of historical reality for us, now – even if, on an explicit level, it seeks to deny that it has any such concern. To the extent that the concern with present meaning is dominant, the historian becomes not simply a historian but a social or intellectual critic as well" (647).

The same points are made by T. Ashplant and A. Wilson in "Present-centred History and the Problem of Historical Knowledge," *Historical Journal* 31 (1988), 2, 253–74.

67 Cf. A. MacIntyre, *After Virtue* (Notre Dame, Ind., 1984) and B. Rundle, *Facts* (London, 1993), 82–3: "The root of the problem is not a gulf between fact and value; rather, the difficulties divide between the factual and the conceptual: it is often practically impossible to reconcile conflicting interests. . . ." For an apt formulation of the relationship between theory and observation see Goodman, *Ways of Worldmaking*, 97: "Facts are small theories and true theories are big facts."

68 Hillgruber, *Zweierlei Untergang*, 20–5.

69 Since the *Wehrmacht* actually defined Nazi-Germany *in practice* by physically eliminating its opponents Hillgruber's stance implies a total indifference to its victims.

70 Hillgruber, *Zweierlei Untergang*, 20–1.

71 Nolte, *Vergehen der Vergangenheit*, 25, 137. Nolte, However, misinterprets his critics. They did not object to the use of right-wing propaganda in order to document the Nazi-state of mind – *in casu* their fear of Bolshevism

– but to the uncritical identification by Nolte of this propaganda with historical reality and the elevation of this presumed historical reality to *the* cause of the Nazi mass murders. For a devastating critique of Nolte's use of these sources see Wehler, *Entsorgung der deutschen Vergangenheit?*, 147–54 and Evans, *Hitler's Shadow*, 84–5.

72 Nolte thus ignores the fundamental fact that when a historian *de*scribes the actions of an individual or collective as *its* or *their* actions, he or she at the same time *a*scribes moral responsibility and constructs an identity. This identity is not only constituted by intentional actions, but also by unintended consequences of action. The way the intentions are reconstructed and the way unintended consequences are ascribed depends both on descriptive and normative considerations; therefore identity is both a factual and a normative notion at the same time. For this important characteristic of historiography cf. Angehrn, *Geschichte und Identität*, especially 60–2.

73 Cf. Kelley, *Versions of History*, 5–7.

74 This stems from the fact, as Rüsen and Angehrn have showed, that the concept of identity is normative and factual at the same time; see also Lorenz, *De constructie*, 255–62. Ann Rigney has also stressed the interweaving of the "factual" and normative discourses in the representation of history: A. Rigney, *The Rhetoric of Historical Representation: Three Narrative Histories of the French Revolution* (Cambridge, 1990) and her review of Lionel Gossman's *Between History and Literature* in *History and Theory* 31 (1992), 208–22.

75 As is stated in Diner's and Friedländer's contributions to *Ist der Nationalsozialismus Geschichte? Zur Historisierung und Historikerstreit*, ed. D. Diner (Frankfurt, 1987). Cf. Friedländer's discussion with Martin Broszat: M. Broszat and S. Friedländer, "Um die 'Historisierung des Nationalsozialismus.' Eine Briefwechsel," *Vierteljahrshefte zur Zeitgeschichte* 36 (1988), 339–73.

76 Habermas, "Geschichtsbewusstsein und post-traditionelle Identität," 159–80.

77 Rorty, *Mirror of Nature*, 341–2, 363–4; Putnam, *Reason, Truth and History*, 143; Goodman, *Ways of Worldmaking*, 139–40.

78 Bundle, "Facts and Values," in *Facts*, 55–85; D. Pels, "De 'natuurlijke saamhorigheid' van feiten en waarden," in Pels and De Vries, *Feiten en waarden*, 14–44; M. Doeser, "Can the Dichotomy of Facts and Values Be Maintained?," in Doeser et al., eds, *Facts and Values*, 1–19; J. Mooij, "Feiten en waarden," in *De wereld der waarden* [The World of Values] (Amsterdam, 1987), 28–45; A. MacIntyre, *After Virtue*, 1–36; Rorty, *Mirror of Nature*, 341–2, 363–4; Putnam, *Reason, Truth and History*, 143; Goodman, *Ways of Worldmaking*, 139–40.

79 I have analyzed this interweaving of political and factual discourse in German historiography recently in "De *Sonderweg* in de Duitse historiografie: Posities, problemen en discussies," ["The *Sonderweg* in German Historiography: Positions, Problems and Discussions"] in *Geschiedschrijving in de twintigste eeuw*, ed. H. Beliën and G.-J. van Setten (Amsterdam, 1991), 141–81.

80 This is also the aim of Rüsen's project; cf. his *Historische Vernunft*.

81 S. Dik and J. Kooij, *Algemene Taalwetenschap* [General Linguistics] (Utrecht, 1991), 20–39.

82 For an overview of the demise of analytical philosophy of science see Salmon, *Four Decades of Scientific Explanation*. For an overview of the

demise of analytical philosophy of history see F. R. Ankersmit, *De navel van de geschiedenis: Over interpretatie, representatie en historische realiteit* [The Navel of History: On Interpretation, Representation and Historical Reality] (Groningen, 1990), 23–43.

83 Rüsen, *Historische Vernunft*, 78: "Identität, die im Erzählen von Geschichten zur Sprache kommt, ist kein fixer Tatbestand. Wer man ist, hängt auch davon ab, was andere einen sein lassen and was man im Verhältnis zu den anderen selber sein will."

84 Mooij, "Feiten en waarden," 28–44.

85 Cf. Bundle, *Facts*, 66–7.

86 W. Gallie, "Essentially Contested Concepts," in *Proceedings of the Aristotelian Society 1955–1956* (London, 1957), 167–98.

87 For further analysis of this notion see M. Thompson, "Reception Theory and the Interpretation of Historical Meaning," in *History and Theory* 32 (1993), 248–73.

88 See A. Gouldner, *The Coming Crisis of Western Sociology* (London, 1970), 30–1.

89 S. James, *The Content of Social Explanation* (Cambridge, 1984). Involved are, for instance, different concepts of social causation.

90 In this phase it is useful to distinguish between a problem-oriented type of history (*histoire problème*), which seeks explanations for specific and explicitly stated hypotheses, and an interpretive type of history, which seeks to present global and descriptive interpretations (*histoire total*). In the former type the elimination of rival explanations is the basic strategy, in the latter type the demonstration that certain concepts possess the capacity to integrate disparate facts into a meaningful whole. In already densely populated niches of historiography this is usually done by elimination of rivals. On the use of evidence by historians see P. Kosso, "Historical Evidence and Epistemic Justification: Thucydides as a Case Study," *History and Theory* 32 (1993), 1–14.

91 Cf. Martin, *The Past Within Us*, 30–85.

92 Although factual arguments are judged by other historians on the basis of the criterion of consistency – consistency with the information adduced from and supported by the sources – this criterion does not in itself guarantee a consensus. This lack of consensus has two roots at the level of the sources: not only is it possible for different historians investigating the "same" object – like the Third Reich or the Holocaust – to use different sources but it is also possible for different historians to interpret the same sources differently – as was the case with Nolte's right-wing pamphlets.

93 For analyses and the history of the conception of "historical method" see *Historische Methode*, ed. C. Meier and J. Rüsen (Munich, 1988), especially the contributions of J. Rüsen, J. Topolski, and J. Meran.

94 Cf. Goodman, *Ways of Worldmaking*, 18.

95 For the "Fischer-controversy" cf. A. Sywottek, "Die Fischer-Kontroverse: Ein Beitrag zur Entwicklung des politisch-historischen Bewusstseins in der Bundesrepublik," in *Deutschland in der Weltpolitik des 19. und 20. Jahrhunderts*, ed. I. Geiss and B. J. Wendt (Düsseldorf, 1974), 19–46.

96 Of course the descriptive and the explanatory level are conceptually intertwined, but nevertheless it is useful to make an analytical separation because the answer to the "what"-question does not determine the answer to the "why"-question; cf. R. Martin, "On Dray's 'Conflicting Interpretations,' "

in *Hermeneutics: Questions and Prospects*, ed. G. Shapiro et al. (Amherst, 1984), 262: "the characterization of the event to be explained suggests the level, and sets constraints, for what is going to count as the explanation." For the philosophical arguments cf. James, *Social Explanation, passim*; for the historical arguments see for instance the discussion about Hitler's role in German history: M. Broszat, *Nach Hitler: Der schwierige Umgang mit unserer geschichte* (Munich, 1988), especially 11–33, 119–31 and 227–34; H. Mommsen, *Der Nationalsozialismus und die deutsche Gesellschaft* (Hamburg, 1991), especially 67–102 and 184–233. For a discussion about the explanatory role of the individual in history see C. Lorenz et al., *Het historisch atelier: Controversen over causaliteit en contingentie in de geschiedenis* [The workshop of the historian: Controversies on causality and contingency in history] (Amsterdam/Meppel, 1990).

97 W. H. Dray, *Philosophy of History* (Englewood Cliffs, NJ, 1964), 21–41. Cf. L. Pompa, "Value and History," in van der Dussen and Rubinoff, eds, *Objectivity*, 112–32 for further references and discussion.

98 Cf. Evans, *Hitler's Shadow*, 138: "How people regard the Third Reich and its crimes provides an important key to how they would use political power in the present and in the future. That is why the neoconservatives' reinterpretation of the German past is so disturbing. For many if not most of the arguments are derived, consciously or unconsciously, from the propaganda of the Nazis themselves"; Maier, *Unmasterable Past*, 64: "The Nolte-Fest position has given academic credentials to what hitherto was the underground discourse of the *Soldatenzeitung* or SS-reunions."

For a recent overview see A. Lüdtke, "'Coming to Terms with the Past': Illusions of Remembering, Ways of Forgetting Nazism in West Germany," *Journal of Modern History* 65 (1993), 542–72.

99 Feyerabend used this phrase to characterize the development of philosophy of science; see P. Feyerabend, "Philosophy of Science: A Subject with a Great Past," in *Minnesota Studies in the Philosophy of Science*, ed. R. Stuewer (Minneapolis, 1970), V, 183.

100 Compare Zammito's critique of the "pan-textualism" and the "intra-textual narcissism" of the "new" philosophy of history and its dissolution of all referentiality of historical narratives in "Are We Being Theoretical Yet?"

19

Progress in Historical Studies

Raymond Martin

It would be difficult to dispute that in the physical sciences there has been progress. One can debate the niceties. The hard rock is that our ability to predict and control natural events and processes is greater now than it has ever been. And there has been astonishing technological fallout.

What about historical studies? Has there been progress there? Surely in one way: we're continually learning more about the past. But more knowledge does not necessarily mean more understanding. And without more understanding it is hard to see how one could claim justifiably that meaningful progress has occurred.

What would it take for us now to have more understanding of the past? Not necessarily that some later interpretations are better overall than all earlier ones. Rather, just this: that on the basis of *a* set of interpretations that *includes some later* ones, we can understand the past better than on the basis of *any* set of interpretations that includes *only earlier* ones. So much for the "more" in "more understanding." What would it take for there to be more *understanding*? Answering this question is one of my two main objectives in the present essay. The other is determining, in the case of one interpretational controversy, whether there has been progress in historical studies. So, what would it take for there to be progress in historical studies? Just this: that we now understand the past better.

Historical studies are not in the prediction and control business, and they have no technological fallout. So, what many have looked for as evidence of progress is interpretational convergence. Failing to find that, and finding instead what can look like fragmentation that has spun out of control, some have despaired. Peter Novick is a case in point. He said that as of the 1980s it was "impossible" in historical studies to locate "scholarly consensus" and that "convergence on anything" was "out of the question." What one found instead, he said, was "either factional polarization or fragmented chaos which made factionalism seem, by comparison, like a kind of order." "As a broad community of discourse, as a community of scholars united by common aims, common standards, and common purposes," he continued, "the discipline of history had ceased to exist." The situation, he concluded darkly, was "as described in the last verse of the Book of Judges: 'In those days there was no king in Israel; every man did that which was right in his own eyes'."[1]

I take a much more optimistic view. In my opinion, in virtually every major, long-standing, interpretational controversy in historical studies there has been significant progress: we not only know more now, we understand better. Obviously I cannot here defend such a global claim. Instead, I will defend it in the case of just one interpretational controversy – that over the American Revolution.

1 The American Revolution

Whig interpretations came first; then Imperialist interpretations; then Progressive interpretations; then Neo-Whig interpretations; finally, the current mélange of contemporary perspectives, so mixed that the old Whig–Progressive dichotomy, so long a staple of American historiography, may now be obsolete. Since there is so much ground to cover I shall have to be ruthlessly schematic.

David Ramsay, a participant–observer, and then, later, George Bancroft, are the quintessential Whig historians. For present purposes, five things about their interpretations are important: they told the story of the Revolution only from one point of view, that of the revolutionary élite; they accepted as the reasons for the Revolution the reasons this élite gave for revolting (hence, they accepted that the Revolution was fought primarily over principles); they structured their accounts to justify the colonists' break with Britain; they wrote about the past as if it were an anticipation of the present; and, finally, they embedded all of colonial history, including the break with Britain, into a grand story of human progress, thereby providing Americans with a national identity they could embrace with pride.

In Ramsay's view, the colonists revolted so that they could be free to determine their own destinies.[2] His focus was on explaining, first, how they came to want their freedom and, second, how a succession of events allowed them to get it. In his view, the colonists were disposed to want their freedom from the beginning, and primarily for two reasons; Puritanism in particular, and Protestantism in general, encouraged them to oppose authority and "nurtured a love for liberty"; and the prerogatives "of royalty and dependence on the Mother Country were but feebly impressed" on the colonists, who "grew up in a belief, that their local assemblies stood in the same relation to them, as the Parliament of Great Britain to the inhabitants of that island." Why "but feebly impressed"? Because prior to the 1760s England had given the colonists "full liberty to govern themselves by such laws as the local legislatures thought necessary and left their trade open to every individual in her dominions." Nevertheless, according to Ramsay, in the pre-Revolutionary period the benefits to the colonists of imperial rule outweighed its disadvantages, and problems between England and the colonies were minor. The Stamp Act, he said, changed this happy state of affairs; and the subsequent publication of *Common Sense* solidified the change.

The Stamp Act led the colonists to view England as more dependent on them "for purchasing her manufactures" than they were on England "for protection and the administration of civil government." It also inspired the colonial ideal of no taxation without representation. This new view and ideal, he said, are what got the colonists to consider independence in the first place. Still, in his opinion, as late as the Battle of Lexington revolution was not inevitable. It became inevitable, he said, when Thomas Paine gave coherent expression to so many of "the feelings and sentiments of the people," convincing thousands "to approve and long for a separation from the Mother Country" even though just a few months before they would have viewed that prospect with horror. Subsequently one English provocation after another called forth an understandable and appropriate colonial response. The result was the Revolution.

Bancroft, undoubtedly the most authoritative of the second generation of Whig historians, gave a similar account.[3] He stressed even more strongly the continuous presence and importance of the colonists' desire for freedom. This desire, he said, was evident as early as 1607 in Jamestown, and then expressed itself regularly throughout the troubled period of the 1760s and 1770s. Bancroft was especially blatant about writing as if the past were an anticipation of the present. For instance, he not only said he "dwelt at considerable length" on the seventeenth century "because it contains the germ of our institutions" but even "titled the chapter describing the early English voyages to North America, including the Roanoke settlement in the 1580s, 'England Takes Possession of the United States'."[4] Moreover, in his view, it was not fundamentally that events over time gave birth to the revolutionary ideology as it was that a cosmic plan found a way to express itself in events. He claimed that God caused the colonists to desire freedom and that the "tyrannical George III," by impeding satisfaction of this desire, forced them to revolt. In his view, the whole scenario was somehow written in the stars: the Revolution was part of "the grand design of Providence" and the colonists were God's chosen people; in framing the Constitution the founding fathers achieved an important milestone in humanity's march toward freedom and justice.

As these brief sketches indicate, Whig historians interpreted the Revolution in ways that were monolithic, partisan, and elitist. They not only explained the Revolution from a single point of view but from the very one the Revolutionary leaders themselves adopted to justify it. They ignored how unfolding events were viewed and experienced by the British; and when they did consider this they considered it only from the perspective of the rebellious colonists. They also minimized differences among the revolutionaries. Ramsay, for instance, conceded that colonists who were in different socioeconomic circumstances or lived in different regions had different motives to revolt – only the merchants were driven by fear of losing markets – but he dismissed these differences as but "dust in the balance."[5] He and Bancroft ignored how loyalists viewed and experienced the Revolution and, of course, how the dispossessed (women, the lower classes, natives, slaves) viewed and experienced anything. They not only focused almost exclusively on the reasons the revolutionaries gave for revolting but took these at face value, ignoring the possibility that underlying socioeconomic factors gave rise to these reasons or otherwise played an important role in bringing about the Revolution. Finally, they provided an identity-nourishing framework for narrating the Revolution, as well as subsequent American history, that masked discrimination and marginalization of various sorts. As a consequence, their interpretations were, in essence, thinly veiled attempts to justify the Revolution and, thus, glorify America, sometimes even to the extreme of identifying the Revolutionaries as God's chosen people. Americans craved (and still crave) a national identity of which they could (can) be proud. For many Americans, then and now, Whig historians delivered just such an identity.

Enter the Imperialists. In the half-century since Bancroft had published, the discipline of history had become the province of professionals. Led by Charles Andrews, Herbert Osgood, and George Beer, and spurred on by improved Anglo-American relations, Imperialist interpretations of the Revolution came into vogue early in the twentieth century. As the irascible Andrews put it, self-servingly but nevertheless correctly, in the previous fifty years historians had developed "higher canons of criticism and interpretation, better balanced judgments, and more rational methods of presentation."[6] That assessment led Andrews, whose higher canons could still fire low, to characterize Bancroft's work as "nothing less than a crime against historical truth."[7]

Somewhat ironically, in view of such attitudes, one of the Imperialists' important innovations was to introduce a new ideal of objectivity-as-impartiality. In contrast to the Whigs, they told the story of the Revolution as much or more from the point of view of British administrators as from that of the colonists. They put primary explanatory importance not on issues of principle and ideology but rather on acquisitiveness or on impersonal underlying sources of conflict. And they tended either to distribute blame for the Revolution evenly or to absolve everyone from blame.

Andrews, for instance, was heavily influenced by his view that revolutions in general never come about suddenly but instead were the result of underlying and "almost invisible factors and forces" which influence and often determine human action.[8] In the case of the American Revolution, he said, these underlying factors made British officials inflexibly committed to keeping the colonies dependent and the colonists unyielding in their demands for more self-government, thereby making conflict inevitable. In his view, in the seventeenth and early eighteenth centuries, British officials saw the colonies mainly as a source of raw materials; later, and increasingly, they saw them as a market for British goods. Throughout this initial period, he said, England's greatest need in relation to the colonies was to preserve a mercantilist system. But England's ability to control the colonies was undermined by developments at home, most notably by the Glorious Revolution of 1688. These decreased the power of the crown and created instability and confusion in administrative agencies, particularly in the Board of Trade, which were responsible for overseeing the colonies.

In Andrews's view, until the mid-eighteenth century, the colonists, rather than waiting for the right time to break away from the mother country, had adapted themselves comfortably to the requirements and advantages of the British system and were relatively happy with their subordinate status. However, in 1763 things changed. In fighting the Seven Years War, England had incurred a huge debt and acquired vast new territory that would cost large sums of money to administer. England thus wanted a new relationship with the colonies, which included having them pay the war debt. So England replaced the earlier "mercantilist" framework concerned primarily with the maintenance of commerce, with an "imperialist" one concerned with the control of territory. As part of this change, England moved beyond imposing commercial regulations to imposing direct taxation, initially in the 1760s through the Stamp and Townsend Acts which, Andrews said, were "the first cause of the eventual rupture" between England and the colonies. The subsequent Tea Act, he claimed, was the point of no return. In opposing it, colonial moderates joined with radicals in one unified grievance against the crown.

Did the advent of Imperialist interpretations spell progress for historical understanding? Clearly it did, though not necessarily because Imperialist interpretations of the Revolution were better overall than Whig interpretations. It was enough to spell progress that Imperialist interpretations brought with them other advances: they were based on a more sophisticated evaluation of evidence; they counterbalanced Whig overemphasis on ideology and diplomatic developments by calling attention to underlying social and economic realities; they were less metaphysically speculative; they were more impartial; and – the clincher – they afforded students of the Revolution an opportunity to view it not only from the perspective of the Revolutionaries but also from that of British administrators. As one historian later remarked, "By the late 1920s no serious student of Early American history could doubt that the British had, or at least thought they had, good reasons for undertaking the measures they did."[9] In addition, on the matter of writing about the past as if it were an anticipation of the present, Imperialists did some-what better than Whigs had done. Andrews, for instance, cautioned that colonial American history "should be interpreted in the light, not of the democracy that was to come years later, but of the ideas and practices regarding colonization that were in vogue in Great Britain at the time."[10] On balance, Imperialist historians not only offered an illuminating alter-native interpretation of the Revolution but, in effect, irreversibly changed the rules of the game. Subsequently Neo-Whig historians might still praise the original Whig view.[11] But the Imperialists had expanded irreversibly the range of causal influences and perspectives on the Revolution that henceforth historians of every persuasion (including Neo-Whigs) would have to consider. However, before historians would retrieve what was valuable in Whig interpretations they had to depart from them even fur-ther, in large part because both Whigs and Imperialists shared a common assumption that cried out to be questioned. Both assumed that there was such a thing as *the* American point of view.

Enter the Progressives. In the view of historians such as Carl Becker, Charles Beard, and Arthur Schlesinger, Sr., the Revolution was a struggle not only against England but also for power within America; as Becker famously put it, it was a struggle "not only about home rule but also about who should rule at home."[12] In explaining this struggle, Progressives highlighted the importance of competition among socioeconomic classes in the colonies, in the process assuming (and sometimes arguing) that ideology and appeals to principle should not be taken at face value but rather as expressive of something deeper. They tended to claim that this deeper thing was economic self-interest.

Beard's influence, even though he did not focus on the Revolution *per se*, was enormous. He tried to show that the Constitutional Convention of 1787 was designed to protect the economic interests of the delegates to it, most of whom were lawyers with an economic stake in the out-come of their work in Philadelphia. He wrote that these delegates "knew through their personal experiences in economic affairs the precise results which the new government that they were setting up was destined to attain" and, thus, built it on "the only foundation which could be stable: [the] fundamental economic interests [of themselves and their classes]."[13] Beard later quipped that the essence of his view was that "economics ex-plained the mostest."[14] Actually it was that "greed explained the mostest."

In contrast to Beard, Arthur Schlesinger, Sr., did focus on the Revolu-tion. His account emphasized distinctions among the life-styles, attitudes, and interests of the colonists in three regions: the coastal area from New Hampshire to Pennsylvania, the tidewater region from Maryland to Georgia, and the western settlements.[15] The history of the Revolution, he said, "is the story of the reaction of these three geographical sections to the successive acts of the British government and of their interaction upon each other." For instance, he claimed that merchants in the north-eastern corridor were the most economically active of any group in the three regions and that the new Imperial program seriously interfered with their customary trading operations. From 1764 to 1774, he said, merchants fought the program not to achieve independence, which they thought would hurt them economically, but to restore the old system of trade and commerce. In the southern coastal area, on the other hand, the economy was centered on farming. Plantation owners there had a long tradition of relative self-rule but had been frustrated by their fail-ure to overcome Royal vetoes in passing certain bankruptcy acts, and so were disposed to counter intrusive Imperial laws. Finally, the back-country settlers, who had not only been left out of the political process altogether but had experienced unjust taxation, "brought to the contro-versy a moral conviction and bold philosophy which gave great impetus to the agitation for independence." Thus, central to Schlesinger's inter-pretation was his rejection of the assumption that there was "an Amer-ican point of view." "How," he asked, "could a people who for ten years were not in agreement among themselves as to their aims and aspira-tions, be said to possess a common political philosophy?" To understand a colonist's views, he said, one needs to know to which class and geo-graphical area he belonged.

According to Schlesinger it was the passing of the Stamp Act that first rallied the merchants and planters against Britain, and it was the plan to station troops in the colonies that convinced colonists in general that England was out to subdue them. He said the colonists' responses of non-importation and mostly lower-class mob activity benefited only the merchants. However, by 1766 the merchants, still viewing themselves as the class whose interests were "chiefly imperiled," were beginning to see that inciting mob activity had brought "disruptive forces" to the surface. They began to channel their protests through peaceful means, such as petitions and a campaign for corrective legislation. Subsequently control of the situation got away from the merchants. After 1770 they tended to give up politics for business and, by 1773, when Britain tried to enforce the Tea Act, they were left out of the organized resistance altogether. In Schlesinger's view, "the Boston Tea Party marked a turn-ing point in the course of events"; it was regarded by merchants and moderates in both countries as lawless destruction of private property and an act of wanton defiance which no self-respecting government could wisely ignore." He claimed that after the imposition of severe disciplinary measures against the colonists, moderates, who wanted the colonies to pay for the tea in the hopes of reuniting with the British, and radicals, who opposed compromise and demanded that England recognize the right of the colonies to home rule, vied with each other to control the colonial response. In 1774, when the First Continental Congress convened, moderates were outnumbered; radicals and farmers, after years of being left out of representative government, finally prevailed. The merchants either joined in the cause of the lower classes or became Tories.

Schlesinger claimed that, in defending their actions, the colonists tended "to retreat from one strategic principle to another." For instance, when they abandoned basing "their liberties on charter grants, they appealed to their constitutional rights as Englishmen; and when that position became untenable, they invoked the doctrine of the rights of man." Such strategically motivated vacillation, he said, justified his claim that the colonists' declarations of political principle and abstract rights were insincere. In his view, the Revolution, rather than being about principles and rights, was simply "the refusal of a self-reliant people to permit their natural and normal energies to be confined against their will, whether by an irresponsible imperial government or by the ruling minorities in their midst."

Did Progressive interpretations contribute to progress? Surely they did, for at least three reasons: first, in important respects the Progressives took a more discriminating view of colonial life than had earlier historians and thus corrected for a number of imbalances and oversights; second, they highlighted the importance of considering self-interest as a motivating force; and, third, they introduced the illuminating idea that even apart from considerations of self-interest, reasons should not simply be taken at face value since they may express a more explanatory underlying reality. Yet the Progressives went astray by modeling their interpretations of the American Revolution too closely on then extant interpretations of the French Revolution, thereby overestimating both poverty in the colonies and also the existence and rigidity of class structure. And, in dismissing out of hand virtually all appeals to ideology and principle as mere rationalization, they made a big, insufficiently justified assumption.

Enter the Neo-Whigs, but not just them. Prior to the early 1960s one school of interpretation at a time was at the forefront of interpretational and methodological progress. Since the 1960s progress has occurred simultaneously on several interrelated fronts, including the development of Neo-Whig interpretations, the enormously influential rise of social history, the closely related development of Neo-Progressive interpretations, and, more recently, the rise of the history of culture (*or mentalités*). Nevertheless, by the mid-1950s an emerging group of Neo-Whigs, including Robert Brown, Forrest McDonald, and Daniel Boorstin, had become dissatisfied with the "deterministic interpretations" of the Progressives, claiming that the Progressives had exaggerated the rigidity of class divisions in colonial America and also the oppression and exclusion from politics of the lower classes.[16] To these historians, and eventually to most, the Progressive framework was no longer credible. Partly as a consequence, they again interpreted the Revolution primarily as a dispute over constitutional liberties, in the process returning the focus of attention onto individual actions and events and retreating from the view that colonial aristocrats were merely attempting to secure their own selfish economic interests and thereby to thwart democracy. These Neo-Whigs thus reiterated something like the original Whig view – and in the case of a historian like Oliver Dickerson, something very much like it.[17] They claimed that the founding fathers were moved to action importantly by ideology, and even more basically, as Bernard Bailyn would later put it, by "fear of a comprehensive conspiracy against liberty throughout the English-speaking world – a conspiracy believed to be nourished in corruption, and of which, it was felt, oppression in America was only the most immediately visible part."[18]

However, most Neo-Whigs also made important concessions to the Progressives, especially by looking more closely at ways in which the colonists' ideology and behavior was an expression of evolving social conditions. As Joyce Appleby recently put it, "Freed from the Progressives' preoccupation with conflict," these historians "probed for the footings of social stability in general and asked how American conditions had promoted cooperation, coherence, and consensus." By investigating agricultural practices, inheritance patterns, and the like, they, in the first instance, "took advantage of the wealth of records in New England towns" and thereby "drew a picture of the social dynamics of consensus," documenting "as never before the efforts of settlers to knit themselves into tight little communitarian worlds" and the "pivotal importance of the family." More importantly, they "demonstrated the appeal of the colonial era in its own right, disconnected from the story of the American nation that was to come."[19]

But the core of the old story line persisted, often in a remarkably traditional form, even as it was modified to accommodate the emerging new concern with society and culture. For instance, according to Edmund Morgan's Neo-Whig interpretation, until 1764 the colonists were content with their role in the British empire and tended even to admire and identify with the British.[20] The trouble, he said, began in 1764. The war against the French in North America, which had just been successfully concluded, cost Britain huge sums and left it with vast new territories to administer. To produce revenue, Parliament passed various taxes which provoked the oft-noted colonial responses. Such protests, Morgan said, "inaugurated the Americans' search for principles." In his view, colonial leaders then "found it easy to state the one thing they were certain Parliament could not do: tax people who were not represented in it." The colonists denied that they were "virtually represented" and rejected the prospect of actual representation in Parliament on the grounds that their distance from it made that impractical. The authority to tax them, they said, "was reserved exclusively to assemblies of their own elected representatives."

In Morgan's view, in 1766, when the Stamp Act was repealed, it looked as though things would return to normal. However, a series of new Parliamentary acts and colonial responses led, in 1768, to the arrival of British troops in the colonies, followed two years later by the Boston Massacre and subsequently, in spite of Parliamentary concessions, by the Boston Tea Party. Parliament then quickly passed the Coercive Acts, in response to which in 1774 the First Continental Congress met at Philadelphia. In Morgan's view, in such a step-by-step progression, the demand for complete independence was continually strengthened, nourished by the changing circumstances of life in the colonies, by the provocation of events, and by the continual and relatively consistent development of Constitutional ideals.

In making this case, Morgan cast his evidential nets more widely than had the traditional Whigs. He also read at least the ideological evidence more carefully than either Whigs or Progressives had read it, in the process helping to create a new and higher standard for assessing ideological evidence. For instance, he pointed out that Beard, in support of his view that Roger Sherman "believed in reducing the popular influence in the new government to the minimum," had cited as evidence various remarks Sherman had made, such as that he was "opposed to the election [of members of the national legislature] by the people," insisting that it ought to be by the state legislatures, and that the people "immediately should have as little to do as may be about the government." But Morgan then faulted Beard for ignoring other things Sherman said and did. For instance, "on June 4, four days after the speech Beard quoted, Sherman was against giving the President a veto power, thus thwarting 'the will of the whole,' since no one man could be found so far above all the rest in wisdom." And, on June 21, Sherman "argued again for election of the House of Representatives by the state legislatures, but after election by the people had been decided upon, spoke for annual elections as against triennial, because he thought 'the representatives ought to return home and mix with the people'."[21]

Bernard Bailyn also emphasized the colonists' devotion to constitutional principles, claiming that their ideology was formulated in pamphlets a decade before independence. In these Bailyn detected the influence on colonial thought of a group of eighteenth-century "radical publicists and opposition politicians in England" who carried forward into the eighteenth century "the peculiar strain of anti-authoritarianism bred in the upheaval of the English Civil War." These radicals, he said, spoke of excessive corruption in English government, which showed itself "in the adroit manipulation of Parliament by a power-hungry ministry, and more generally in the self-indulgence, effeminizing luxury, and gluttonous pursuit of gain of a generation sunk in new and unaccustomed wealth."[22]

In Bailyn's view, colonial writers identified with these radicals and, after 1763, drew heavily upon their ready-made arguments to formulate their own indictment of British rule. He said, for instance, that because of their commitment to the ideology of these radicals "it was not so much the physical threat of the [arrival in October, 1768, of British] troops [in Boston] that affected the attitudes of the Bostonians" but, rather, what they took to be "the bearing their arrival had on the likely tendency of events." He said that the colonists interpreted these actual events from "the perspective of Trenchard's famous tracts on standing armies" and "the vast derivative literature on the subject that flowed from the English debates of the 1690s." From this perspective, he said, the British troops "were not simply soldiers assembled for police duties; they were precisely what history had proved over and over again to be prime movers of the process by which unwary nations lose 'that precious jewel, liberty'." Bailyn, thus, argued that more important for the Revolution than social change in the colonies were changes in the colonists' perception of government and its function. The Revolution, he claimed, was primarily the result of the colonists' "thinking through" certain fundamental concepts and, then, of their acting on their reflections.

However, in later writings, Bailyn would downplay the suggested implication of his earlier work that there was a causal progression from "formal discourse" to "articulated belief" to political action. Now he claimed that formal discourse, such as is found in the pamphlets, was merely implicit "in the responses of the colonists" and could neither "form the immediate instrumental grasp of their minds" nor "explain the triggering of the insurrection."[23] Thus, rather than a direct link between the formal discourse of the pamphleteers and the political action of the colonists, the link was now said to be primarily between the previously unarticulated attitudes and values to which the British pamphleteers had given expression and the "shifting patterns of values, attitudes, hopes, fears, and opinions" of the colonial Americans. "It is in these terms," Bailyn concluded, "that ideas – not disembodied abstractions . . . but the integrated set of values, beliefs, attitudes, and responses that had evolved through a century and a half of Anglo-American history – may be understood to have lain at the heart of the Revolutionary outbreak and to have shaped its outcome and consequences."

A second major arena of development has been the spectacular rise of social history, which since the 1960s has been the major growth area in historical studies of early America. Not a school of interpretation but a social science-oriented approach to previously ignored data, social history has dislocated much of what historians of all persuasions had earlier thought about the Revolution, due in large part to the sheer quantity of new knowledge social historians have produced, much of it about people – the poor, women, slaves, and natives – whom historians previously had neglected. For decades this new information was simply more than historians could integrate into their larger interpretive schemes.[24]

In addition, by comparison with other approaches to early American history, social historians often addressed the past less as an anticipation of the present and more on its own terms. And they developed and exploited social science-oriented methodologies far more than most other historians did. For instance, by examining public records, say, of births, marriages, deaths, wills, taxes, and land transfers they reconstructed the immediate personal frameworks within which ordinary people lived. Similarly, by using ethnological methods, historians of culture, who followed quickly on the heels of social historians, attempted to reveal the inner perspectives of North American natives as well as of those Africans who exported their traditions to North America with the slaves.[25] Moreover, in the view of some historians, in its totality the new information collected by social and cultural historians is virtually "inassimilable into any account written to celebrate the nation's accomplishments," perhaps even into any sort of "narrative governed by optimism and progress."[26]

The work of social historians has been corrosive of earlier interpretations in other ways as well. By attending to culture as a source of meaning; by substituting for the older focus on exceptional events, ideas, and men a new one on social mechanisms for distributing such things as power, authority, and respect; and by freeing historians of early America from interpretations that took the project of nation-building as their focus and, thus, allowing them to reconfigure the colonies as part of Western Europe, social historians tended to see colonial America as composed of "early modern communities." Colonial America thus became a testing ground "for a battery of intriguing hypotheses about social change." Previously, when "ordinary people had been studied" it had been "without social scientific models that linked their lives to the emergence of capitalism and the transformation of society"; now the new techniques offered historians "a way to move beyond anecdote to the structural features of society."[27] But not *just* beyond anecdote. By using modern statistical and quantitative techniques social historians have been able to address previously neglected developments "that took place, so to speak, over the heads of the historical participants" and were "unknown to contemporaries" and thereby to develop "the social viewpoint," that is, "a conception of society itself as the organizing theme of their history."[28]

It is hard to say how much of the new social history deserves to be called "Neo-Progressive." E. P. Thompson's Marxist-oriented *The Making of the English Working Class*, with its focus on the "lived experience" and agency of those at the bottom of society, has been a potent source of inspiration; in Novick's view, "no work in European history ever so profoundly and so rapidly influenced so many American historians."[29] In any case, in the United States several historians who might, perhaps misleadingly, be labeled Neo-Progressives have emerged. Rather than trying to replace Neo-Whig interpretations with spruced-up Progressive ones, for the most part these historians have simply highlighted the importance of lower-class perspectives and patterns of living. For instance, whereas Bailyn and Morgan had suggested that among free whites, poverty was unknown in colonial America and hence that "social strains" generated by poverty were not among the causes of the Revolution, Gary Nash claimed to have found in tax, poor relief, and probate records, abundant evidence of poverty in colonial times.[30] According to Nash, the Neo-Whigs need to explain this evidence. In addition, he said, the Neo-Whigs have to attend to a "popular ideology" of the artisans, which "resonated most strongly within the middle and lower strata of society and went far beyond constitutional rights to a discussion of the proper distribution of wealth and power in the social system." Nash claimed that "it was this popular ideology that undergirded the politicization of the artisan and laboring classes in the cities and justified the dynamic role they assumed in the urban political process in the closing decades of the colonial period." Jesse Lemisch has argued similarly.[31] According to him, when Bailyn said that the views of the English opposition influenced American views, we're entitled to know which Americans he had in mind. The answer, Lemisch said, is that Bailyn had in mind "informed Americans," especially certain pamphleteers whose work he collected and analyzed. But what, Lemisch asked, about the rest?

Others have voiced similar concerns, while at the same time calling for a more discriminating view even of élite ideology. Marc Egnal, for instance, conceded that the traditional Progressive view "takes a narrow, deterministic view of human behavior" and that a lower-class struggle against Britain and a conspiratorial role on the part of the merchants and planters is "doubtful."[32] He also conceded that the colonists' ideas are important in explaining their behavior. However, like other Neo-Progressives, Egnal claimed that Neo-Whigs, by fashioning "a model in which motivating ideas are divorced from day-to-day concerns," have overreacted to "the economic determinism that often underlay the work" of Progressive historians. In the case of élite ideology, Egnal said, motivating ideas cannot be linked to any distinct groups, and so "cannot explain the deep, sustained divisions within the ruling class of each colony," particularly since many future loyalists expressed the same ideology as some of the most radical revolutionaries. Also, he claimed, because the Neo-Whigs were blinded by what they took to be "the resolute stand" the colonists took against British taxation, they have neglected the sharp contradiction between the colonists' rhetoric of protest and their actual deeds; for instance, even though the Sugar Act "was unmistakably designed to raise revenue" the colonists "accepted it with little protest, contributing over twenty thousand pounds sterling to the royal coffers every year between 1766 and 1774." Finally, Egnal accused the Neo-Whigs of focusing their attention too narrowly on the political writings of pamphleteers while neglecting the colonists' views about "trade,

defense, mercantile regulation, and more broadly, the political economy of the New World." In sum, in his view, Neo-Whigs have failed to
account for the "specifics" of colonial resistance.

2 Understanding

As my survey illustrates, an impressive array of reasons exists for thinking that there has been progress in our understanding of the Revolution.
For one thing, as time has gone by more – a *lot* more – has become
known about early American history. For another, as more has become
known, interpretations of the main competing kinds have tended to
become more accurate, more comprehensive, better balanced, and better
justified; more accurate because many factual and explanatory mistakes
in previous interpretations have been corrected and the corrections have
tended to be cumulative; more comprehensive and better balanced because
more sorts of causal influences have been taken into account, more sorts
of subjective perspectives of the people whose history is being interpreted have been portrayed, interpretive structures have become more
accommodating and inclusive, and interpretations have tended to become
less partisan; better justified because the sheer quantity of evidence on
which interpretations are based has grown enormously, and more careful
and sophisticated methods for assessing evidence have been introduced.

I claim that, all else being equal, it is reasonable to believe that the
introduction of interpretations that are more accurate, more comprehensive, better balanced, and more justified has enhanced historical understanding. I also claim, in stark contrast to the views of someone like
Novick, that the introduction of such interpretations has encouraged
convergence and consensus – if not overall, then at least within what I
shall call *interpretive polarities*. By *interpretive polarities* I mean traditions of interpretation in which, at any given time, the main competition is between two schools, or traditions, of interpretation that share
the same basic *interpretive focus* yet conflict importantly about why
the common phenomenon they are interpreting occurred and/or what
it means that it occurred (or that it occurred for the reasons it did). By
interpretive focus I mean a leading idea which acts as a kind of lens
through which a school or tradition contextualizes the episode under
investigation.[33] In the debate over the Revolution there has, in my view,
been just one interpretive *polarity*: the tradition of opposition between
Whig- and Progressive-oriented interpretations, both of which share
the *focus* that the Revolution is best understood as a phenomenon of
nation-building.

Recently, interpretations of the Revolution have begun to move away
from this traditional interpretive focus toward a new one in which the
Revolution is viewed not primarily through the lens of nation-building
but rather through that of participation in a transatlantic social and

cultural transformation. Gordon Wood, in *The Radicalism of the American Revolution*, takes this newer focus seriously enough that he is able to devote very few pages to the actual fighting between Britain and the colonies and to dismiss the actual achievement of political independence by the colonists as a mere "clarifying incident."[34] In contrast, the story of this achievement is a centerpiece of virtually every more traditional interpretation of the Revolution.

Another example of a change in interpretive focus can be found in Edward Countryman's recent reconceptualization of interactions among colonists, transplanted Africans, and native populations in colonial America, in terms of the notion of a center of influence. Rather than conceptualizing the various transformations in what is now the eastern half of the United States in terms of the traditional Eurocentric notion of a frontier that moved continually westward, Countryman advocates thinking of these transformations in terms of multiple and multi-dimensional "frontiers" emanating from different centers of cultural and political influence: "Only very recently have historians shown us that other lines were drawn and maintained by other people and that both people and lines were part of the unstable, volatile, colonial social order, not separated from it by some meta-line we call 'the' frontier."[35] Other examples of changes in interpretive focus include recent attempts to conceptualize aspects of the struggle for power both in early America and also in modern Europe in terms of changing *gender* relationships rather than in terms of more traditional categories.[36]

Much more needs to be said about the notion of interpretive focus, My hope is that without saying it here, the notion, though admittedly vague, is nevertheless clear enough that one can understand the competition between Whig-oriented and Progressive-oriented interpretations of the Revolution as an interpretive polarity. Assuming that one can do this, then my survey reveals that within this interpretive polarity there has been more or less continuous movement toward theoretical convergence. That is, Neo-Whigs have tended in important ways (and also overall) to be closer to Progressives than were the Whigs; Neo-Progressives have tended in important ways (and also overall) to be closer to Neo-Whigs than were the Progressives to the Whigs. Allowing for poetic license, one could almost say that a kind of Hegelian dialectic has been at work: Whig interpretations called forth their "opposite," Progressive interpretations, which then called forth their "quasi-opposite," Neo-Whig interpretations, which then called forth their "quasi-opposite," Neo-Progressive ones, and so on. In this zigzag progression, at least by the time one gets to the Neo-Whigs, each new school of interpretation seems to have taken what it could from the interpretations it superseded, both from those in its own and in the opposing tradition. By the time we get to the "Neo-Progressives" the two schools are so intertwined that it is questionable whether there still are two schools.

Yet, Novick might protest, even if we allow that within a Whig–Progressive interpretational polarity there has been movement toward convergence of more or less the same *kind* as often occurs in the physical sciences, it seems clear that there has not been convergence to anything like the same *degree*. Why, then, in historical studies has there not been that same degree of convergence? The issue is a complicated one. To simplify, consider first just historians of the Revolution who have focused on nation-building and offered fully developed interpretations, rather than monographs or so-called micro-histories. Then, in my view, a certain sort of ignorance, coupled with our desire for interpretations that are maximally coherent and meaningful, is mostly responsible for there not being more convergence within interpretive polarities.

The ignorance that has mattered most has been ignorance of the degree to which self-interest motivates human behavior. The reason this ignorance has mattered so much is that in order to arrive at interpretations that are maximally coherent and meaningful, which is required if one is to give a fully developed interpretation, historians of the Revolution have had to take a stand one way or another, but without being able to rule out as equally defensible conflicting stands, on the question of how sincere the colonists were in their declarations of principle. So historians have had to take leaps of faith. Some historians, to their credit, have taken such leaps seemingly in full awareness of what they were doing. Edmund Morgan, for instance, in introducing his interpretation of the Revolution, admitted that "many historians are inclined to doubt the strength of the [colonists'] attachment" to principle and that "it is of course impossible to tell why men act as they do." Even so, he continued, he "has proceeded on the conviction that [the colonists' attachment to principle] was genuine."[37] He did not then try to defend his proceeding on this conviction. However, had he wanted to defend it, could he have done so successfully? I think so. He could have appealed to the fact that when it comes to such questions about human motivation, anyone who seriously aims to provide a maximally coherent and meaningful interpretation of the Revolution has to take a stand, one way or another, on this question of motivation and, hence, has to make some such leap of faith, either the one he took or some other. Of course, that such a defense could be developed adequately is debatable. I am suggesting that it could be. Some of what I say below will be relevant to explaining why.

Even so, it is not only, and perhaps not even primarily, the need to take such leaps of faith that inhibits interpretational convergence in historical studies. Other aspects of the quest for richer and more relevant meaning are also potent inhibitors. Chief among these is that in historical studies the meaning of events that is conveyed by an interpretation is not separate from, but is intimately intertwined with, how events are contextualized within the interpretation. Even within the same interpretive polarity there are different ways to contextualize the same events. For instance, historians may portray the same events from different subjective perspectives; consider, for instance, Bailyn's attempt to view Revolutionary hostilities from the perspective of the loyalist, Thomas Hutchinson.[38] A change in which subjective perspectives are favored may entail a change in the shape of the historian's narration, say, from one of progress and hope to one of failure and disappointment. Or historians may highlight one sort of development – say, economic – at the expense of others – say, political. And, of course, more dramatic recontextualizing occurs when historians choose different interpretive foci, say, by interpreting the Revolution not as an episode in nation-building but rather as an aspect of larger social and cultural transformations. In the physical sciences it is not an objective to convey meaning beyond explaining what and why, and by comparison with historical studies the recontextualizing that occurs in science, during periods of so-called "normal" science, generally takes place within relatively narrow bounds.

Such differences between historical studies and the physical sciences explain why *interpretational* convergence, even within interpretational polarities, does not occur in long-standing major interpretational controversies in historical studies to anything like the degree *theoretical* convergence often occurs in the physical sciences. Such differences are partly why Novick was right – absolutely right – to say that in historical studies interpretational convergence is "out of the question." However, they are also partly why he was wrong – dead wrong – to suggest that in historical studies interpretational *divergence* is symptomatic of lack of progress. To know whether interpretational divergence contributes to progress, inhibits progress, or is neutral with respect to progress, one has to know its effect on historical understanding. And there is no reason why interpretational divergence may not *enhance* historical understanding. After all, within the context of controversy among interpretations with the same interpretational focus, there can be progress in historical understanding when we achieve greater representation and more balance in our understanding of different, yet relevant, *subjective* perspectives and agencies, even when this fosters interpretational divergence. So why, in the larger scheme of things, might there not also be progress in historical understanding when we achieve greater representation and more balance in our understanding of different, yet illuminating, *interpretational* perspectives?

I do not say that the introduction of new subjective or interpretational perspectives necessarily enhances historical understanding, but only that it is plausible to suppose that it sometimes does. When does it? Why, of course, when it is genuinely illuminating. And how do you tell, in general, whether the introduction of a new subjective or interpretational perspective has been genuinely illuminating? By surveying the evolutions of several major interpretational controversies that involve the introduction of such new perspectives and then noting how those that promote historical understanding differ from those that do not. The task is not in principle any different from the one undertaken in the survey part of the present essay. The main difference is that in the controversy over the Revolution the introduction of new interpretive foci, unlike the introduction of new competing interpretations within the same interpretive polarity, has been too recent to track its consequences. But it is, I think, prima facie obvious that the introduction of new interpretational foci can be genuinely illuminating, and that is all we need to know for present purposes. On the plausible assumption that when the introduction of new interpretational foci is genuinely illuminating, it contributes *both* to interpretational *progress and* to interpretational *divergence*, it follows that it is wrong to suggest, as Novick did, that interpretational divergence necessarily means lack of progress.

I have argued elsewhere that the use of interpretational convergence as a criterion of progress in historical studies rests on a profound and widespread misunderstanding of the differences between historical studies – at least humanistic historical studies – and the physical sciences.[39] Suffice it to say here that while theoretical convergence in the physical sciences may be a noble dream – witness, for instance, the benign enthusiasm generated by the quest for a unified field theory – the analogous dream of interpretational convergence in historical studies is – or, at least should be – a nightmare. One can get a feel for the problem that would be posed by interpretational convergence in historical studies on one grand, synthetic account by reflecting on the fact that such a convergence would be analogous to there being all but universal agreement on just one *philosophical* view. Some have dreamed of that as well, most notably the Catholic Church and the Communist Party. Fortunately, they have not been able to translate their dreams into reality. Fortunately also, historians who have dreamed of establishing the hegemony either of their own interpretational perspectives or, more neutrally, just of some interpretational perspective or other, have not, at least in any open society, been able to translate their dreams into reality. We need to be more careful about what we want.

The moral is that if our goal in historical studies is, as presumably it should be, progress in the sense of growth in historical understanding, then there may well be limits to how much interpretational convergence we want in our accounts of the past. In my view, in the case of the interpretational controversy over the Revolution, we should want at least as much interpretational *divergence* as we have gotten so far. In fact, we should want even more, provided it is of the right kind. The seeming-descensus that results, far from being an embarrassment to historical studies, should be regarded as one of its best features. However, typically it has not been so regarded, at least not by American historians. Throughout *That Noble Dream* Novick has documented impressively that to a remarkable degree the founding members of the American historical profession, and many of their professional descendants, have thought they were fashioning bricks of incontrovertible historical fact that would one day be used to build a mighty edifice of historical knowledge – a single mansion, however many rooms it might contain. It did not work out that way. In my view, the reason it did not work out that way is not that historians failed to do their work well enough; and it is not that the time is not yet ripe for that sort of interpretational convergence; and it is certainly not, as Novick ultimately suggests, that historical studies are somehow inherently deficient. Rather, the reason it did not work out that way is that historical studies do not lend themselves to interpretational convergence on just one grand synthetic account. And the primary reason for that is that main-line, fully developed historical interpretations tend to be humanistic, which means that the historians who propose them and the core communities for whom they write have among their objectives not only to make the human world comprehensible but also to make it meaningful, and not all legitimate meanings reduce to just one meaning.

In historical studies, conveying meaning typically involves portraying the events under discussion so that we – the historian's intended audience – can grasp them whole, that is, so that we can get an accurate overview of what happened in a way that facilitates our appreciating its human significance. This is accomplished at least as much by showing as by telling. It is shown primarily by the ways in which historians structure their interpretations, which largely determines how what happened is portrayed. At the deepest level, such structuring has to do with the interpretational perspective adopted – for example, nation-building or transatlantic social and cultural transformation. At shallower levels, it has to do with various ways in which historians, like political managers, "spin" their presentations of events. In fully developed interpretations, historians try to relate what they take to have happened with the shared concerns and values of their intended audience, so as to convey at least an important aspect of what they consider to be the human significance of whatever they are discussing. Since there is no limit to the ways in which something can be humanly significant there is no limit to what events can mean and, hence, no such thing as *the* meaning of events. This is largely why understanding is best achieved differently in humanistic historical studies and the physical sciences. Typically, for instance, if one wants to understand some phenomenon of fluid mechanics, one does so from the perspective of the best extant theory of fluid mechanics, and that is all there is to it. There is no need to consult alternative and especially competing theories in order to augment one's understanding of the phenomenon in question. By contrast, in humanistic historical studies there is always such a need.

In sum, what I have been suggesting is that to understand the relationship between interpretational convergence and growth in historical understanding, we need to distinguish between how things have gone within interpretational polarities and how they have gone overall. *Within* interpretational polarities, it is reasonable to expect that over time there will be significant movement toward convergence and consensus. In the case of the controversy over the Revolution that is what we find. However, even within interpretational polarities, ignorance coupled with our entirely reasonable desire to arrive at interpretations that are maximally coherent and meaningful virtually insures that there will not be nearly as much convergence as often occurs in the physical sciences. In addition, in humanistic historical studies the desire for enriched meaning creates added pressure for representing previously neglected yet relevant subjective perspectives and for introducing new and illuminating basic interpretational foci. These then become an additional source of divergence. However, if the introduction of such new perspectives and foci is genuinely illuminating, the divergence and seeming-descensus they generate, rather than thwarting growth in historical understanding, actually contribute mightily to it. But to understand why these contribute to growth in historical understanding one has to free oneself from the assumption that growth in historical understanding is just like growth in understanding in the physical sciences. It is not. Humanistic historical studies and the physical sciences have different objectives. Physical scientists *qua* scientists are concerned only with making the world comprehensible, and not otherwise concerned with making it meaningful. Because of that, in the physical sciences, at least during periods of so-called normal science, understanding tends best to be achieved from a perspective that is situated squarely within the framework of the best extant theory. However, in humanistic historical studies – for the reasons explained, which include that they are concerned not only with making the world comprehensible but also with making it meaningful – understanding tends best to be achieved not from a perspective that is situated squarely within the framework of whatever one regards as the best extant interpretation but, rather, from that of sympathetic appreciation of the tensions among competing interpretations.

3 Relativism and Skepticism

I have been arguing that there has been progress in historical studies, at least in the case of the interpretational controversy over the American Revolution. I want now to consider briefly two objections to my argument that are sure to occur to many readers.

What I shall call the *objection based on relativism* might be put by a critic as follows: in arguing that progress has occurred, you have privileged certain criteria of interpretational adequacy on the basis of which, you have assumed, historians *currently* assess the relative merits of competing interpretations. Even if that assumption is correct, there are other criteria of interpretational adequacy. For instance, at various times in the past a majority of historians may have assessed the relative merits of competing interpretations on the basis of different criteria. Or, in the past and also currently, there might be criteria on the basis of which various minorities of historians have tended, or do now tend, to assess interpretations. Finally, there are possible criteria of interpretational adequacy, which though they have never actually been adopted, might be adopted. You've assumed without argument that you have a right to privilege certain criteria over others. But you have not shown, and cannot show, that objectively you have any such right. And if your choice of criteria of interpretational adequacy is merely subjective, then it is arbitrary, in which case your argument that there has been progress in historical studies fails.

In response, I would only point out that if we are going to investigate whether there has been progress in historical studies (and not just have a meta-investigation of what, if anything, we should mean by *progress*), then we are going to have to assume some criterion of progress or other. Of course, as suggested in the objection, we should have good reasons for assuming the criterion of progress we employ. However, contrary to what is suggested, we can have good reasons for employing some particular criterion of progress other than the reason that that criterion is *objectively right*, whatever exactly that might mean. For instance, all else being equal, a good reason for employing a particular criterion of progress is that among the sorts of progress that are feasible as objectives in historical studies, we care maximally about promoting progress of that sort (that is, there is no other kind of feasible progress we care more about promoting). Prima facie, a notion of progress that embodies those criteria, on the basis of which historians currently assess the relative merits of competing interpretations, is progress of a sort that historians care maximally about promoting. If it were not, then historians would modify the criteria on the basis of which they assess interpretations. Assuming that the rest of us share the interpretational concerns of most historians, then a notion of progress that embodies those criteria on the basis of which historians currently assess the relative merits of competing interpretations is progress of a sort that we also care maximally about promoting.

A good argument to the effect that historians – or we – ought to be assessing the relative merits of competing interpretations on some basis other than those on which historians currently assess them would require an extended reply. But the objection under discussion contains no such argument, and it is not easy to imagine a good reason for deleting any of the criteria of interpretational adequacy I have been employing. Should we, say, prefer to interpretations that are more accurate, more comprehensive, better balanced, better justified, and so on, interpretations that are less so? Or is the suggestion that we should prefer interpretations

that have not only these characteristics but also some additional characteristic? But if this is the suggestion, then we need to be told which
additional characteristic. And since to be relevant to the current discussion this additional characteristic must be something feasible for historians to adopt as an objective, then it seems likely that over time there
would also have been movement toward satisfaction of the fuller criterion
of progress that results from taking this additional characteristic into
account. But without being told what the additional characteristic is, it
is idle to speculate how our being told what it is would affect my argument for progress. In any case, we are now discussing a different objection
that the one I have called the objection based on relativism. For instead
of proposing a plausible competing criterion of interpretational assessment, what the objection based on relativism actually does is merely
point out that because no criteria of assessment are objectively right,
then the criterion we, or historians, employ must be arbitrary. But, as
we have seen, this conclusion does not follow; and, prima facie at least,
it is unfounded.

Second, what I shall call the *objection based on skepticism* might be
put by a critic as follows: your notion of progress is underdeveloped.
Were it properly developed it would commit you to progress of a sort
that you could never have good reason to believe has actually occurred.
In particular, while you have said that progress is growth in historical
understanding of the past, you've neglected to say whether that understanding is of the past as it really was, and, if it is, how one gets access
to that past. In short, if the past you have in mind is the past as it really
was, then you've made a big objectivist assumption that is going to be
difficult, if not impossible, to support without begging the question against
a certain sort of (perhaps, postmodernist) skeptic. To support this assumption you are going to need to show that assessing historical interpretations on the basis of the criteria you've claimed most historians currently
employ implies some sort of external (interpretation-independent) constraint on interpretations. And it is going to be hard to show that. On
the other hand, if you are not claiming that the growth in understanding that you say has occurred is of the past as it really was, then you not
only need to explain which past it is of, but also why a kind of progress
that might result from growth in understanding of *that* past is progress
worth caring about.

In response, I want to claim that there are in historical studies, if not
external checks on the adequacy of interpretations, then something that
is close enough to them to promote a kind of growth in historical understanding that is progress worth caring about. The external checks are
"facts," or, more precisely, they are what are mutually accepted as facts
by all historians who are engaged, at a given time, in an interpretational
debate – so, call them *agreed-upon facts*. I claim that, at any given time,
historians who are engaged in an interpretational debate always accept

a large body of agreed-upon facts and that, at *that* particular time, in *that* particular context of debate, such agreed-upon facts serve *as if* they were external checks on interpretations. Over time the status of many of these putative facts may change from agreed-upon to highly questionable. However, in a relatively advanced stage of any major, long-standing, interpretational controversy, changes in the status of agreed-upon facts are slow and piecemeal. It is never the case that most such "facts" change from agreed-upon to highly questionable at the same time.

If I am right about this, then there are two possibilities worth discussing. First, assume that at any given time we *have good reason* to believe that the vast majority of agreed-upon facts are actual *objective* facts (leaving it open, for now, exactly what it might mean for facts to be *objective*). In that case, then insofar as our interpretations adequately account for these facts, they are tracking "the real world" and growth in historical understanding is growth in understanding of "the past as it really was." Since truth is widely acknowledged to be a worthwhile objective, if growth in historical understanding is growth in understanding of the past as it really was, then it would be fairly noncontroversial that the progress I've argued has occurred in historical studies is progress worth caring about.

Second, assume that at any given time we *do not have good reason* to believe that the vast majority of agreed-upon facts are actual objective facts. Still, generally speaking, facts become agreed-upon by historians because they are backed by the kind and degree of evidential support that we commonly assume provides us with good reasons to believe that a putative fact is an actual fact. So, if at any given time we *do not* have good reason to believe that the vast majority of the agreed-upon facts are actual objective facts, then it has to be *either* because we have good reason to believe that some *competing* facts are actual facts *or else* because we do not have good reason to believe that any facts are actual objective facts. The first of these two options is unrealistic. As already noted, in mature historical controversies changes in the status of putative facts from agreed-upon to highly questionable tends to be gradual and piecemeal. So, if we *do not* have good reason to believe that the vast majority of agreed-upon facts are actual objective facts, then it has to be because we do not have good reason to believe that *any* facts are actual objective facts. In other words, it has to be on the basis of an argument for universal skepticism.

This might seem to be the place for me to argue for objectivism and against such skepticism. But if one knows anything at all about philosophy, one knows that any such argument that is going to have any semblance whatsoever of success is going to be long and involved; and one also knows that probably it will end up by begging the question. Skeptics are wily. They have been around for a long, long time, and are not easily refuted.[40] The main reason they are not easily refuted is that they call

into question the very rules on the basis of which ordinarily we determine what is factual and what not. And if, in arguing with the skeptic,
somehow we manage to give a plausible, second-order justification for
the rules we employed in our first-order determinations of what is factual,
then the skeptic will call into question the rules we employed in our
second-order justification of our first-order rules, and so on, *ad infinitum*
(or at the very least, *ad nauseam*). It is not difficult to see that while
skeptics may not win this game, they are not likely to lose it either. I
want to sidestep this whole debate.

In my view, for the purpose of determining whether there has been
progress in historical studies, we can bracket the question of whether
over time interpretations have more closely approximated "*objective*"
truth and, thus, bracket perhaps the main issue that divides objectivists
and skeptics. Yet we can still determine that the evolution of interpretations in long-standing major historical controversies has been progressive,
where the progress in question is a kind worth caring about. We can do
this without getting sidetracked into abstract epistemological and metaphysical investigations, so long as we remember that the progress in question can be a kind worth caring about if, over time, as our understanding
of some historical phenomenon grows, the truth that we more closely
approximate, *whether or not* it is also objective truth, is at least what
I shall call *methodological truth*. This can happen provided that over
time our continually evolving understandings more adequately account
for agreed-upon facts, even though there are continual (but relatively slow
and piecemeal) changes in which facts are accepted as agreed-upon. In
other words, in my view, progress worth caring about takes place provided that, at any given time, at least *one* collection of interpretations that
includes a later one better accounts for whatever facts are agreed-upon
at that time than does *any* collection of interpretations that includes
only earlier ones.

What does it mean for an interpretation to better account for some
collection of agreed-upon facts? That should be a central question in
philosophy of history. Sadly, it has been neglected. In my view, part of
what it means is this: that all else being equal, over time, as more has
become known, our interpretations of the past have tended to become
more accurate, more comprehensive, and better balanced. To find out
what else it may mean, or in more detail what each of the characteristics
mentioned – accuracy, balance, and so on – involves, there is no better
approach than one which begins by descriptively characterizing actual
interpretational controversy in historical studies. That is the approach I
have tried to follow. Yet, in the philosophy of history literature, there
are very few such descriptive characterizations.

Is the continual development of interpretations that, together perhaps
with some earlier ones, better account for the continually evolving collection of agreed-upon facts progress enough to sustain our faith in the

value of historical studies? In my view it is. Judging from the energy historians devote to doing history, in the views of many of them also it is. For without the objectivists among them begging the question against the skeptic, it may be the only kind of progress they can *show* they have made. And even skeptics and relativists can afford to concede that the ongoing development of interpretations that, together perhaps with some earlier ones, better account for the continually evolving collection of agreed-upon facts is progress enough to sustain our faith in the value of historical studies. For in their practical work as historians, not to mention in their daily lives, even they tend to ignore their skepticism and relativism and hence to acknowledge the legitimacy of a perspective from which at least this much progress can be shown to occur.

An anecdote nicely illustrates the point. Novick relates that in the late 1920s Harry Barnes was embroiled in an increasingly personal and acrimonious public debate with Bernadotte Schmitt over the question of German responsibility for the World War.[41] Carl Becker (a self-identified relativist), he says, was sympathetic to Barnes's revisionist views but was put off by the personal tone of Barnes's arguments. Becker wrote to Barnes that "if we indulge in personalities it will not only create an unpleasant atmosphere but will damage cool and scientific research." Becker continued, "Prove the truth of your assertions objectively without going into the problem of what warps Schmitt's judgment of the facts." Becker then cautioned Barnes that the "truth or falsity of a historical thesis can be and should be settled by appeal to evidence alone." Surely Becker was right, and in his own historical work he practiced what he preached to Barnes. But then, in the last analysis, old-fashioned appeals to and use of evidence are the way to settle historical disputes, even according to an arch-relativist like Becker.

Moreover, historians having made progress in the limited sense that they develop interpretations that more closely approximate methodological truth does not preclude their having also made progress in some stronger, objectivist sense of progress. In particular, it does not preclude their having developed interpretations that (together with some earlier ones) better account for the past *as it really was*. If it is the case, as such historians (and, most of the time, most of the rest of us as well) *assume*, that the evolution of interpretations *is* also progressive in this stronger, objectivist way, then that, so to speak, is just metaphysical icing on what is already a nourishing and tasty interpretational cake. To most of the historians who founded the American historical profession and to many of their objectivist descendants right down to the present day, it would have been unthinkable to serve up the cake without that metaphysical, objectivist icing. But times have changed. Today, thanks to postmodernists, it is no longer unthinkable. What I have been suggesting is that by practicing thinking it, and then proceeding accordingly, we can all arrive at a more refined understanding of progress in historical studies.

Notes

1 P. Novick, *That Noble Dream: The "Objectivity Question" and the American Historical Profession* (Cambridge, 1988), 572, 628.

2 D. Ramsay, *History of the American Revolution* (Philadelphia, 1789). Thanks to Kevin Levin for help with my characterizations of the interpretations of historians of the Revolution.

3 G. Bancroft, *The History of the United States of America from the Discovery of the American Continent*, 10 vols (Boston, 1842–54).

4 I owe this observation to Gordon Wood, "A Century of Writing Early American History: Then and Now Compared; Or How Henry Adams Got It Wrong," *American Historical Review* 100 (1995), 680.

5 Ramsay, *History of the American Revolution*, 310.

6 H. Ausubel, *Historians and Their Craft: A Study of the Presidential Addresses of the American Historical Association, 1884–1945* (New York, 1950), 77.

7 A. S. Eisenstadt, *Charles McLean Andrews: A Study in American Historical Writing* (New York, 1956), 165.

8 C. Andrews, *The Colonial Background of the American Revolution* (New Haven, 1924).

9 J. Greene, *The Reinterpretation of the American Revolution* (New York, 1968), 6–7.

10 Andrews, *The Colonial Background of the American Revolution*, 121.

11 See, for example, E. Morgan, *The Birth of the Republic: 1763–89* [1956] 3rd edn (Chicago, 1992), 185.

12 C. Becker, *The History of Political Parties in the Province of New York* [1909] (Madison, 1968), 22.

13 C. Beard, *An Economic Interpretation of the Constitution of the United States* [1913] (New York, 1986), 7–8.

14 Novick, *That Noble Dream*, 167.

15 A. Schlesinger, Sr., "The American Revolution Reconsidered," *Political Science Quarterly* 34 (1919), 61–78.

16 R. Brown, *Middle-Class Democracy and the Revolution in Massachusetts, 1691–1780* (Ithaca, 1955); F. McDonald, *We the People: The Economic Origin of the Constitution* (Chicago, 1958); D. Boorstin, *The Americans: The Colonial Experience* (New York, 1958). See G. Wood, "Rhetoric and Reality in the American Revolution," *William and Mary Quarterly*, 3rd ser., 23 (1966), 3–31; J. Greene, "The Flight from Determinism: A Review of Recent Literature on the Coming of the American Revolution," *South Atlantic Quarterly* 61 (1962), 235–59.

17 O. Dickerson, *The Navigation Acts and the American Revolution* (Philadelphia, 1951).

18 B. Bailyn, "The Transforming Radicalism of the American Revolution," Introduction, *Pamphlets of the American Revolution, 1750–1776*, ed. B. Bailyn and J. Garrett (Cambridge, Mass., 1965), I, x.

19 J. Appleby, "A Different Kind of Independence: The Postwar Restructuring of the Historical Study of Early America," *William and Mary Quarterly*, 3rd ser., 50 (1993), 2252–3.

20 Morgan, *The Birth of the Republic*, 13.

21 Ibid., 24–9.

22 B. Bailyn, *The Ideological Origins of the American Revolution* (Cambridge, Mass., 1967).

23 B. Bailyn, "The Central Themes of the American Revolution: An Interpretation," in *Essays on the American Revolution*, ed. S. G. Kurtz and J. H. Hutson (Chapel Hill, 1973); reprinted in B. Bailyn, *Faces of Revolution: Personalities and Themes in the Struggle for American Independence* (New York, 1990), 205–7.

24 J. Appleby, L. Hunt, and M. Jacob called this new information "more history than the nation can digest," *Telling the Truth About History* (New York, 1994), 158; G. Wood called it "an embarrassment of riches," "A Century of Writing Early American History," 687.

25 Appleby, "A Different Kind of Independence," 250, 260.

26 Appleby, Hunt, and Jacob, *Telling the Truth*, 189, 217.

27 Appleby, "A Different Kind of Independence," 247–9, 250–2.

28 Wood, "A Century of Writing Early American History," 690.

29 E. P. Thompson, *The Making of the English Working Class* (London, 1963); Novick, *That Noble Dream*, 440–1.

30 G. Nash, *The Urban Crucible: The Northern Seaports and the Origins of the American Revolution* (Cambridge, Mass., 1992).

31 J. Lemisch, "Jack Tar in the Streets: Merchant Seamen in the Politics of Revolutionary America," *William and Mary Quarterly*, 3rd ser., 25 (1968); reprinted as "The Radicalism of the Inarticulate: Merchant Seamen in the Politics of Revolutionary America," in *Dissent: Explorations in the History of American Radicalism*, ed. Alfred Young (De Kalb, Ill., 1968), 39–55.

32 M. Egnal, *A Mighty Empire: The Origins of the American Revolution* (Ithaca, 1988).

33 Each of these ideas needs to be clarified. I have done so in *Philosophy of History from the Bottom Up: An American Revolution*, forthcoming.

34 G. Wood, *The Radicalism of the American Revolution* (New York, 1992), 125.

35 E. Countryman, "Indians, the Colonial Order, and the Social Significance of the American Revolution," *William and Mary Quarterly*, 3rd ser., 53 (1996), 342–66.

36 L. Kerber et al., "Beyond Roles, Beyond Spheres: Thinking about Gender in the Early Republic," *William and Mary Quarterly*, 3rd ser., 46 (1989), 565–85.

37 Morgan, *The Birth of the Republic*, 51.

38 B. Bailyn, *The Ordeal of Thomas Hutchinson* (Cambridge, Mass., 1974).

39 R. Martin, "The Essential Difference between History and Science," *History and Theory* 36 (1997), 1–14.

40 See, for example, R. Fogelin, *Pyrrhonian Reflections on Knowledge and Justification* (New York, 1994).

41 Novick, *That Noble Dream*, 218.

Name Index

Abbott, Jack, 260–2
Abelard, Peter, 280, 282–6
Adams, Henry, 90–2
Adorno, Theodor, 239
Andrews, Charles, 380–2
Angehrn, Emil, 357
Ankersmit, F. R., 193–203, 238, 342, 350, 351, 353–4, 356–7
Appleby, Joyce, 385
Arendt, Hannah, 228–9
Aristotle, 10, 121, 139, 146
Artemidorus, 257–8
Atkinson, R. F., 342
Auden, W. H., 262
Auerbach, Erich, 233
Augustine, 26, 86, 139
Austin, J. L., 163, 178, 323, 362

Bailyn, Bernard, 386–7, 389, 393
Bakhtin, Mikhail, 107–8, 110
Balzac, Honoré de, 102
Bancroft, George, 30, 378–80
Barnes, Harry, 401
Barthes, Roland, 34, 102, 139, 140, 142, 154, 162, 227, 231
Bataille, Georges, 105
Beard, Charles, 92, 306, 382, 386
Becker, Carl, 92, 306, 382, 401
Beckett, Samuel, 98
Beer, Samuel, 380
Bertels, C. P., 182
Bertens, Hans, 181
Blake, Christopher, 334
Blanchot, Maurice, 105
Boethius, 130
Boorstin, Daniel, 384
Boswell, John, 276
Bourdieu, Pierre, 213
Braudel, Fernand, 179, 216
Braun, Robert, 245–50
Broszat, Martin, 343, 347
Brown, Peter, 278–80, 283
Brown, Robert, 384

Burckhardt, Jacob, 30, 179
Burke, Edmund, 29
Burke, Kenneth, 81
Butterfield, Herbert, 74–5, 86, 331

Campion, Edmund, 65–6
Carr, David, 154, 156–60
Carr, E. H., 332
Carrard, Philippe, 233, 235
Carroll, Noël, 11
Chatman, Seymour, 139
Clover, Carol, 287
Collingwood, R. G., 17–19, 123, 177, 203, 353
Comte, Auguste, 206
Condorcet, 206
Copernicus, 214
Countryman, Edward, 391
Cranmer, Thomas, 65–6
Crillon, Edward de, 90–2
Culler, Jonathan, 179, 188, 199

Danto, Arthur, 123, 143, 145, 183, 214
Davis, Natalie Zemon, 187
Deleuze, Gilles, 140
de Man, Paul, 91, 100, 105
Derrida, Jacques, 98, 100–5, 108, 112, 182, 188, 356
Descartes, René, 121, 154
Devereux, George, 227, 281, 287
Dewey, John, 10
Dickerson, Oliver, 385
Dilthey, Wilhelm, 106, 353
Diner, Dan, 361
Dodds, E. R., 278
Donoghue, Denis, 315
Douglas, David, 76–7
Dray, W. H., 342, 365
Droysen, J. G., 207
Duby, Georges, 184–5, 187, 189

Egnal, Marc, 389–90
Elton, Geoffrey, 132
Erasmus, 63–4

Fain, Haskell, 329–30
Fest, Joachim, 347
Fielding, Henry, 77–8
Fischer, D. H., 331
Fish, Stanley, 7, 9–11
Foucault, Michel, 103, 108, 140, 184–5,
  190, 193, 194, 216, 253–4, 262, 274,
  289
Freud, Sigmund, 26, 93, 102, 109, 113, 185,
  190, 235, 284, 289
Friedländer, Saul, 361
Frye, Northrop, 16–17, 19, 21–3

Gadamer, Hans-Georg, 82–3, 198
Gallie, W. B., 124–5, 132–3
Gauthier, David, 197
Gay, Peter, 182, 216, 280–1
Geertz, Clifford, 106
Genovese, Eugene, 301
Gibbon, Edward, 16, 30, 78, 86, 201, 216
Ginzburg, Carlo, 187–8, 237, 239, 352
Godelier, Maurice, 257
Goffart, Walter, 269–70
Goldstein, L., 212
Gombrich, E. H., 182
Goodman, N., 182, 355
Gossman, Lionel, 216
Gregory of Tours, 268–71

Habermas, Jürgen, 163, 343, 357
Haeckel, Ernst, 189
Halperin, David, 273–6
Hamlyn, D. W., 349
Harbison, E. H., 63
Hardy, Barbara, 135, 140
Hartman, Geoffrey, 27
Haskell, Thomas, 11
Hegel, G. W. F., 16, 26, 28, 37, 39, 48–9,
  107–8, 121, 149–50, 184, 190, 206
Heidegger, Martin, 105, 144
Heloise, 280–6
Hempel, Carl, 138, 154, 193–4
Herodotus, 75, 86, 190
Hesiod, 206
Hesse, Mary, 183
Hexter, J. H., 196
Hilberg, Raul, 227–9, 234–5, 239
Hildebrand, Klaus, 347
Hillgruber, Andreas, 234, 343, 345–8, 354–6,
  358–62, 365
Hilter, Adolf, 229, 344–5, 347, 359–60, 365
Hobbes, Thomas, 175–6, 196–8, 216, 218–19
Huizinga, Johan, 179, 203, 217
Hume, David, 340
Husserl, Edmund, 141
Hutchinson, Thomas, 393
Huxley, Thomas, 77

Jakobson, Roman, 28–9, 81, 200
James, Henry, 73
Jameson, Fredric, 195

Jaspers, Karl, 228–9
Jay, Martin, 236–7, 239
John of Leiden, 65–6
Johnson, Samuel, 70, 74
Joyce, James, 98
Joyce, William, 321–32

Kansteiner, Wulf, 245–50
Kant, Immanuel, 10, 18, 46, 206, 342
Katz, Steven, 246
Kellner, Hans, 208, 216, 245–50
Kellogg, Robert, 121, 143
Kermode, Frank, 71, 139, 141
Kimball, Bruce, 7
Klüger, Ruth, 227
Kocka, Jürgen, 343
Kuhn, Thomas, 2, 11, 351

LaCapra, Dominick, 208
Ladurie, Emmanuel Le Roy, 187–8
Lang, Berel, 11, 229–30, 233–6, 239
Lange, John, 235
Lanham, Thomas, 3
Lanzmann, Claude, 227
LaPlace, Pierre, 128–9
Lardreau, Guy, 184–5
Latour, Bruno, 218
Le Goff, Jacques, 226
Lemisch, Jesse, 389
Lévi-Strauss, Claude, 24, 35
Lorenz, Chris, 11
Loyola, Ignatius, 65–6
Luther, Martin, 65–6
Lyotard, J. F., 162–3, 178, 186, 239, 313–15

McCloskey, Donald, 228–9
McCumber, John, 162, 164
McDonald, Forrest, 384
MacIntyre, Alasdair, 140, 142, 146, 154,
  156–60, 164, 166
Macpherson, C. B., 197–8
Madison, James, 91–2
Mailer, Norman, 260
Mandelbaum, Maurice, 154
Margolis, Joseph, 36, 50
Martin, Raymond, 11, 342
Marx, Karl, 16, 18, 26, 35, 39, 179, 181,
  188
Mattingly, Garrett, 125
Megill, Allan, 182
Meier, Christian, 342
Meinecke, Friedrich, 207
Merleau-Ponty, Maurice, 141
Michelet, Jules, 19, 28, 29, 30
Milton, John, 69–70
Mink, Louis, O., 6, 34, 37, 138–40, 143,
  145–6, 153, 154, 162–3, 211, 277
Mommsen, Hans, 343, 347, 365
Morgan, Edmund, 385–6, 389, 392
Mosley, Oswald, 321–2, 324, 326–7, 330
Munz, Peter, 140

Nagel, Ernest, 338
Nagel, Thomas, 301, 314
Nagl-Docekal, Herta, 357
Nash, Gary, 389
Newman, Barbara, 281
Nietzsche, Friedrich, 16, 34, 175, 180, 182, 190, 301–2, 305, 336
Nolte, Ernst, 343–8, 356, 358–62, 365
Norman, Andrew P., 11
Novick, Peter, 92, 238, 299–301, 305–13, 377, 388, 390, 392–5, 401

Oakeshott, Michael, 197, 212
O'Connor, Sandra Day, 41–2, 50
Olafson, Frederick, 140, 156
Orr, Linda, 232–3
Osgood, Herbert, 380

Padgug, Robert, 255, 258
Paine, Thomas, 379
Partner, Nancy F., 11
Pascal, Blaise, 130
Paul IV (Pope), 65–6
Peirce, C. S., 22
Plato, 128, 149, 259
Popper, K. R., 320, 335–40, 350
Portman, John, 195
Putnam, Hilary, 351–2, 357

Quine, W. V. O., 182

Ramsay, David, 378–80
Ranke, Leopold von, 5, 30, 61, 207, 358
Reagan, Ronald, 41–2
Rich, Adrienne, 262
Richardson, Samuel, 77–8
Ricoeur, Paul, 35, 139–40, 151, 181, 198
Romein, J., 176, 188
Rorty, Richard, 185, 188, 208, 342
Rosenstone, Robert, 232
Rousseau, Jean-Jacques, 26, 189
Rudner, R. S., 320, 334
Rüsen, Jörn, 186, 343, 357
Russell, Bertrand, 181
Ryle, Gilbert, 177

Sartre, Jean-Paul, 16, 149, 154
Saussure, Ferdinand de, 107, 213
Scalia, Antonin, 41–3
Schlesinger, Arthur, Jr., 311
Schlesinger, Arthur, Sr., 382–4
Schmitt, Bernadotte, 401

Scholes, Robert, 121, 143
Schutz, Alfred, 144
Searle, John, 362
Servetus, Michael, 65–6
Sherman, Roger, 386
Skinner, Quentin, 197
Skocpol, Theda, 215
Sloane, William M., 90–1
Souyri, Pierre, 313–14
Spengler, Oswald, 16
Spiegelman, Art, 232
Stalin, Josef, 345
Stanford, M., 212
Stoller, Robert, 287–8
Strauss, Leo, 197

Tacitus, 85–6
Taine, Hippolyte, 28
Taylor, A. E., 197
Taylor, A. J. P., 321, 323, 325–6, 328, 337
Taylor, Charles, 106, 109
Thompson, E. P., 388
Thucydides, 30, 75, 191
Tocqueville, Alexis de, 19, 28, 29, 179
Toews, John, 92, 107–8, 110
Toynbee, Arnold, 16

Vernant, Jean-Pierre, 231
Vico, Giambattista, 27

Wallerstein, Immanuel, 215
Walsh, W. H., 211
Warrender, Howard, 175, 197–8
Watkins, John, 175, 197
Weber, Max, 179, 358
White, Hayden, 2, 34–40, 42–52, 80, 84, 99, 138–41, 143, 154–5, 181, 193–4, 208, 216, 229–33, 235–6, 239, 247, 309, 351, 353–4, 356–7, 363, 365
White, Morton, 133
Wilamowitz, E., 190
William, Duke of Normandy, 76–7
Winkler, John, 274–5
Wittgenstein, Ludwig, 163, 180, 212, 350, 352
Wood, Gordon, 391
Woolf, Virginia, 98

Young, James, 248

Zagorin, Perez, 206–11, 213–20
Zeitlin, Froma, 274